The Past is Present

CANADIANA

Literaturen/Kulturen – Literatures/Cultures – Littératures/Cultures

Herausgegeben von Klaus-Dieter Ertler und Wolfgang Klooß

Band 11

PETER LANG

Frankfurt am Main · Berlin · Bern · Bruxelles · New York · Oxford · Wien

Christian J. Krampe

The Past is Present

The African-Canadian Experience
in Lawrence Hill's Fiction

PETER LANG
Internationaler Verlag der Wissenschaften

Bibliographic Information published by the Deutsche Nationalbibliothek
The Deutsche Nationalbibliothek lists this publication in the Deutsche Nationalbibliografie; detailed bibliographic data is available in the internet at http://dnb.d-nb.de.

Zugl.: Trier, Univ., Diss., 2012

D 385
ISSN 1613-804X
ISBN 978-3-631-62556-9

© Peter Lang GmbH
Internationaler Verlag der Wissenschaften
Frankfurt am Main 2012
All rights reserved.

www.peterlang.de

Acknowledgements

I would like to thank a number of institutions and individuals without whose assistance I would never have been able to complete this study.

I begin at the beginning: my heartfelt thanks to Lawrence Hill and George Elliott Clarke, both of whom have spent hours with me on interviews and discussions. I have always greatly enjoyed your company.

Several institutions have been generous enough to provide assistance: The GKS (German Association for Canadian Studies) provided a travel grant (*Förderpreis*), the University of Trier a Ph.D. grant (*Landesgraduiertenförderung*). I would like to thank the staff at the Institute of Canadian Studies, University of Ottawa, and at Dalhousie University's Special Collections.

For years, the Canadian Studies Centre at the University of Trier has been both a workplace and a home away from home. Annekatrin Metz, Wolfgang Klooß, Markus M. Müller, and Lutz Schowalter: hard work has never been so much fun. Norbert Platz got me on track in the first place, Klaus-Dieter Ertler helped to get this volume published in the *Canadiana* series. Thanks to all of you.

Prof. Klooß and Prof. Staines have shown more patience than anyone could ask for.

I am greatly indebted to Dorothea Buschmann and Bryan Ebel for their diligent proofreading and motivating remarks.

My deepest gratitude of course goes out to my family. My parents have supported me unflinchingly throughout the years. All your dedication, commitment and love are greatly appreciated. My wife Tina has always been there for me, and I sometimes wonder why. You are amazing, and this one is for you, with all my love. Our little daughter Johanna has had to put up with a father often doing several jobs at a time. I will never forget the brave smile on her face when she would point at my desk, saying, "Papa arbeiten" – "Daddy work." Noah, you're lucky – work on this book has come to an end.

> *"Begin at the beginning,"* the King said,
> *very gravely, "and go on till you come to*
> *the end: then stop."*
>
> *(Lewis Carroll,* Alice in Wonderland*)*

Contents

Abbreviations used for Lawrence Hill's primary works:

SGT: *Some Great Thing.* Winnipeg: Turnstone Press, 1992.

AKB: *Any Known Blood.* Toronto: HarperCollins, 1997.

BBSJ: *Black Berry, Sweet Juice. On Being Black and White in Canada.* Toronto: HarperCollins, 2001.

BN: *The Book of Negroes.* Toronto: HarperCollins, 2007.

1. Introduction

It is difficult enough to figure out what it means to be Canadian, let alone African Canadian. (Clarke 1998, 98)

In his article on Lawrence Hill's second novel, *Any Known Blood* (1997), Winfried Siemerling asserts: "Our most post-identitarian moments and movements notwithstanding, identities are hardly a matter of the past." (2004, 30) As I shall argue in this study, issues of identity might well be a matter of the past – yet this past is still vividly present. In exploring the constructions of collective memory in Lawrence Hill's historical fiction, issues of identity are conceptualized as a selection and representation of memories from a contemporary perspective to create what Lois Zamora (1997) has termed a 'usable past'. More precisely, the constructions of collective memory in Hill's writing represent a counter-hegemonic version of a usable past which amends mainstream Canadian constructions. In this endeavor, Hill is in fact emblematic of the vast majority of African-Canadian literature. As the epigraph above suggests, the proverbial preoccupation of Canadian literature with questions of identity – whether they are framed in terms of who/where, here/there, national/regional, or colonial/postcolonial[1] – is mirrored, in fact even intensified, in Black Canadian literature. Evidently,

---

1 Cf. for instance Frye 1965 and 1976 (here: 2003a and 2003b); Atwood 1972; Robertson 1973; Metcalf 1988; Klooß 1992 and 1994; Davey 1993; Gross 1994 and 1995; Staines 1998; Godard 2000; Moss 2003b; Morris 2004; Brydon 2002 and 2007 (incorporating an explicit African-Canadian perspective); Kuester 2008. With the exception of Atwood 1972, Metcalf 1988 and Davey 1993, all of the studies mentioned here are essay-length papers and may thus serve as points of departure. Unsurprisingly, most scholars suggest that the most fruitful approach to identity can (best/only) be found through *their* lens, be that postcolonialism, gender or ethnic studies, a thematic approach or indeed any given conceptual framework; cf. for instance Robertson 1973, 81 (emphasis added): "The discussion of identity is not dead nor will it die until identity can be defined within its *true* context, that of commonwealth literature." In recent scholarship, one of the prevailing views holds that identity has indeed remained one of Canadian literature's key topics and one of literary criticism's favorite subjects, yet both are embedded in more diverse contexts: "By a curious logic of history the Canadian identity question so dear to the cultural nationalists is

definitions of identity do not take place on a *tabula rasa* but are revisions of existing notions. For Black Canadians, the revisionist moment is augmented by the fact that for centuries, African-Canadians have largely *been* defined. On his urge to reclaim the power over identifications, Hill states:

> Identity is fluid and is evidently evolving. Initially other people tried to tell us [Blacks] who we were and tried to brand us with their own views of who we were. We have spent a few centuries trying to climb out from under that and to assert how we see ourselves. [...] Part of it is reclaiming one's identity and rejecting imposed definitions. (Hill 2006, 145)

In this thesis, I set out to provide an analysis of the reasons, the modes and the ways in which Hill is "reclaiming one's identity and rejecting imposed definitions" in his fictions. Hegemonic definitions largely rest, as many Black Canadian writers have consistently claimed,[2] on three faulty assumptions, or rather lopsided perceptions. The first notion is the false supposition that, in contrast to the United States, African slavery never existed in Canada. In a 1995 poll, 83% of Canadians did not know that slavery indeed existed in what was to become their nation (cf. Clarke 1998, 103). On the contrary, it is maintained, Canada has proven to be a safe haven for American slaves, the north star promising freedom under British protection. The second assumption is that those Blacks coming to the True North found there racial equality and socioeconomic prospects. Black Loyalists, for instance, who sided with the British Empire in the American Revolutionary War, were granted not only freedom, but equality and economic opportunity fostered by land grants – at least this is what British officials promised. This allegedly benevolent nature is then extended into the present and underlies the third belief: Canada is, by virtue as much as by proof of its multicultural make-up and policy, a nation virtually free from the malignant racism purportedly dominating race relations south of the border. "In Canada, the party line goes, there are no racists save those who watch too much American television." (Clarke 1998, 101)

Based on historical misperceptions and misrepresentations, a view of Canadian race matters thus prevails which underplays the hardships faced by Black Canadians both past and present, while simultaneously promoting the notion of a Canaanesque nation north of the 49th parallel.

> In Canada, the prevailing view suggests, nobody has doors slammed in their faces because of the colour of their skin, for Canada has the potential to be one big, comfortable home for all people fortunate to live within its boundaries. [...] No, the prevailing view argues, minority groups have no reason to whine or complain. Not in Canada, not in the place that had been

---

still the central question in the new wave of multicultural novels, though questions of identity have become more complicated." (Kröller 2004, 209) Martin Kuester agrees, arguing that even though there has been a widening of foci to include more diverse centers of attention, the "question of Canadian identity and its survival certainly remains one of the central themes of English-Canadian literature until the present." (2008, 311)

2   Cf. for instance Clarke 1998, 101 and 103; 1999, 7; 2006a, 5f.; Compton 2001, 27; Cooper 2004, ii; Foster 1996, 31f.; Hill 2006, 143; Moynagh 2005b, 17; Walker 1982, 6 and 19.

the terminus of the Underground Railroad for American Blacks fleeing slavery.   (Foster
1996, 31f.)

In his historical fictions, Lawrence Hill sets out to correct the flawed constructions professed
by, as Foster phrases it, the "prevailing view". Fiction, in Hill's estimation, has a "major social function" (2006, 132) in this regard. It may serve as a repository of memories repressed in
hegemonic discourse and hence contribute to the ways in which groups define themselves
and/or are defined by others:

> I am interested among other things in exploring fascinating and important elements of the
> Black Canadian experience and exploring them dramatically. [...] I feel that revealing dra-
> matic moments in our lives is one way of showing people who we are.   (Hill 2006, 135)

Questions of the veracity of widely held assumptions and the (self-) definitions based on these
assumptions have long dominated Black Canadian literature. As such, Hill's fiction can be
considered representative of a vast majority of works. African-Canadian authors have regularly pitted their version of the Black experience in Canada against mainstream constructions
(which are, as a matter of fact, often based in part on the writings of Black North Americans
themselves, such as the slave narrative, whose influence will be discussed *in extenso* in the
course of this study). Consider, for instance, Priscilla Stewart's poem "A Voice From the Oppressed to the Friends of Humanity" (1858) which Wayde Compton reprints in *Bluesprint:
Black British Columbian Literature and Orature* (2001):

> [...]
> God bless the Queen's majesty,
> Her scepter and her throne,
> she looked on us with sympathy,
> And offered us a home
>
> Far better breathe Canadian air,
> Where all are free and well,
> Than live in slavery's atmosphere
> And wear the chains of hell.

The contrast between Canada and the US established here in terms of heaven vs. hell has fed
the Canadian imagination. Likewise, the slave narratives corroborate the dichotomy found in
Stewart's poem by structuring the African slaves' escape to (what would later on become)
Canada in terms of one of their key leitmotifs, the biblical Exodus. In Lawrence Hill's fiction
as much as in African-Canadian literature in general, this dichotomy is questioned. In fact,
there is frequently an outright reversal of the common notion that Blacks found – and continue to find – their 'Promised Land' in Canada. Commenting on the 'Exodus' of refugees and
fugitive slaves to Canada, Walter Borden (1992) for instance counters the view held in Stewart's poem:

The Hebrew Children

[...]   Segregated schools,
Ham's descendants   And land titles,
shouted HALLELUYAH,   And housing,
Caught a train   And equal opportunity
And travelled   In general;
To the Warden of the North   And threatened
Who counted heads,   Every kind of social action.
Heaved a sigh,
And told them: Last I heard, God was at
Go, and make potatoes   The Lieutenant Governor's
Out of rocks!   Garden Party
                                          Telling people
Then God stopped   It was nice
Gabbing   To see the coloured population
With the Angels   Represented,
Long enough to promise   And yes, He was preparing
Deep investigation into   A paper on
                                          Discrimination!

                                          Can I hear an AMEN?

In a plain and highly accessible way, Borden summarizes the African-Canadian experience while focusing on its disillusioning quality. When African slaves ("Ham's descendants") left the slave-ridden United States via the Underground Railroad ("caught a train") or as Black Loyalists ("the Warden of the North" indicates Halifax, the capital of Nova Scotia, where most of the Black Loyalists were headed), they expected a Promised Land. What they found instead was disenchanting, to say the least ("Go, and make potatoes / Out of rocks!"). Going through a chronological list of segregation, racial inequality, inadequate living conditions and the like, Borden delineates Black Canadian history, culminating in the complacent, bureaucratic responses of today's multicultural Canada.

Evidently, Hill's approach to African-Canadian history is rather more complex than the rendition offered by Borden in a single poem. Hill does, however, likewise deal with the issues mentioned above: in his three novels published to date, Hill touches on most major aspects of African-Canadian history – from the late 18th to the late 20th century. It is a history which seems to have been largely neglected by mainstream Canadian discourse, a void many African-Canadian writers set out to fill. Hill himself is very explicit about the goal of saving, through fiction, parts of the Canadian history which are on the verge of being forgotten or have already been removed from view:

> We still have probably twenty-five million Canadians who know extraordinarily little about the Black experience in the world and the Black experience here in Canada. The fact of the matter is that it is a fascinating history and I don't care to have it forgotten. The novel is one way to accomplish that." (Hill 2006, 143)

The aim of mending what is perceived as a pitted and unbalanced mainstream understanding of course is didactic in purpose as much as it is sociopolitical in effect. Issues of agenda setting and discourse formation are part of his writing's larger contexts. A theoretical framework to fruitfully approach these contexts can be found in conceptions of collective memory. Originally devised by French sociologist Maurice Halbwachs in the 1920s, collective memory theory has been modified and tailored to serve as a powerful tool in the analysis of the nexus between literature, memory, identity and sociopolitical practice.[3] Taking advantage of the refined corpus of studies and models available by now, I will make use of a slightly adapted version to supplement and guide the following analyses, thus replacing the more pragmatic terminology ('history', 'forgetting', etc.) employed so far.

Obviously, the following chapters will hence provide a significantly more nuanced picture than the one offered by contrasting Stewart's "A Voice from the Oppressed to the Friends of Humanity" with Borden's "The Hebrew Children" – just as Hill himself of course proceeds in considerably more complex ways, yet without losing track of the general argument also illustrated by Borden. Amending what is taken to be an absence due to involuntary ignorance and/or willful neglect, an important part of Canadian constructions of identity, viz. the "Black Tile in the Mosaic" (Winks 1997, 470), has to be (re-) inserted. In order to do so, Hill reveals the supposed misconceptions *and*, importantly, provides an alternative conception. It will be a major concern of this study to delineate the ways in which Hill both reveals/refutes the lopsided model and offers/implements a counter-model.[4]

---

3   As Birgit Neumann rightly observes, Canadian literature has extensively dealt with the connection of memory and identity: "Dass zahlreiche dieser Werke [referring to a list of six novels] mit dem General Governor's Award [sic], Kanadas wichtigstem Literaturpreis, ausgezeichnet worden sind, zeigt, dass die Themen Erinnerung und Identität in Kanada zu einem Kulturthema ersten Ranges avanciert sind: [...]" (Neumann 2005, 10) Incidentally, however, only one (instead of the 'numerous' suggested) out of the six novels she lists has indeed received the Governor General's Award. Yet, in regard to African-Canadian literature, there has in fact been a significant increase in critical acclaim; accordingly, Hill remarks that "it's wonderful to see how African Canadian literature has exploded in recent years. Just look at the awards!" (Hill 2006, 133) In fact, Black Canadian involvement in the Governor General's Award (jury members and/or finalists) has risen from zero before 1990 to 34 until 2007 alone. See the appendix for a diagram of African-Canadian jury members, finalists and winners of the Governor General's Award, the Giller Prize and CBC's Canada Reads between 1990 and 2007. Revealingly, Black Canadian poetry has largely dominated critical reception here as well.

4   It should have become obvious by now that, strictly speaking, qualifiers like "supposed", "alleged" or "perceived" ought to be added to most remarks pertaining to the "perceived" lopsided constructions of identity. This is not only impractical but superfluous. Though I often tend to agree with Hill's assessments as well as with points made by other African-Canadian authors (such as cited above), I strive to *describe* a stance while not necessarily *taking* one. While there is no such thing as a disinterested theory or fully objective scholarship, I am not pursuing a political or even ideological agenda here.

(Con-) Texts

Two out of the three novels Lawrence Hill has published to date will be at the center of interest in the literary analyses provided in chapters four, five and six of this thesis. Hill's first
novel, *Some Great Thing* (1992) will be used comparatively (for instance in section 6.2.1.,
"Authorship"), yet there will be no separate chapter dedicated to Hill's debut as it is largely
concerned with contemporary matters, such as Francophone minority rights in Manitoba,
whereas the two works dealt with in depth here can unanimously be classified as historical
writing – the main interest here. Comments on other fictional works by African-Canadian
authors, e.g. George Elliott Clarke's libretto *Beatrice Chancy* (1999), his novel *George and
Rue* (2005), or Austin Clarke's *The Polished Hoe* (2002)[5] will be interspersed throughout this
study. Moreover, (references to) poems will be used to illustrate certain points on occasion,
thus underlining the pervasiveness of certain issues in African-Canadian literature irrespective
of its concrete genre.[6]

In terms of secondary literature, there is a significant chasm between studies focusing
on social or cultural aspects in general and literature in particular. As for the first category, a
substantial number of works exist.[7] These surveys usually take the form of collections, often
including one or two essays on literature as well, but largely concentrating on other issues. In
terms of studies dedicated to African-Canadian literature specifically, their number is far more
limited (back in 1997, Peter Hudson for instance went so far as proclaiming a "critical waste-
land for African Canadian literature"; 5). The situation has improved, partly by sidestepping

---

5   For some authors and scholars, first names will be used in addition to last names in order to avoid
     confusion (e.g. Austin / George Elliott Clarke, Aleida / Jan Assmann).

6   The research interest leading to the present thesis in fact originated in African-Canadian poetry.
     Based on an annotated bibliography of more than seventy-five poems concerned with the collec-
     tive memory of slavery and/or genealogy, many of the working hypotheses informing this study
     have actually been derived from an exploration of Black Canadian poetry. It should be noted that
     the present study is limited to an Anglophone African-Canadian context alone; the claims made
     here thus apply to Black Canadian literature *in English* exclusively.

7   A provisional and partial (pun intended) list includes early collections such as Dionne Brand's
     Rivers Have Sources (1986; some titles in this list are abbreviated) or *Bread out of Stone* (1994;
     her latest non-fiction collection *A Map to the Door of no Return,* 2002), *We're Rooted Here* by
     Peggy Bristow et al. (1994), Marlene NourbeSe Philip's influential *Frontiers* (1992) as well as
     her (lesser known) *Showing Grit* (1993). Also by Philip: *A Genealogy of Resistance and Other
     Essays* (1997). Cecil Foster's *A Place Called Heaven* (1996) is among the first key collections *not*
     to be authored/edited by African-Canadian *women* writers. Foster, who is also a novelist, followed
     his 1996 essays with *Where Race Doesn't Matter* (2005) and *Blackness and Modernity* (2007).
     Althea Prince's *Being Black* (2001) combines minor elaborations on the literary scene with essays
     of a more general nature. *Talking about Identity* (2001), though not being limited to Black Cana-
     da, offers some useful articles, including "Zebra", by Lawrence Hill. Rinaldo Walcott's *Rude*
     (2000) and *Black Like Who?* (2nd ed., 2003) comprise thoughts on literature to a certain extent,
     but not primarily; the same applies to collections by Charmaine and Camille Nelson (*Racism,
     Eh?,* 2004) or David Divine (*Multiple Lenses,* 2007).

established venues such as mainstream literary magazines, essay collections and monographs (of which there exist next to none).[8] Instead, introductions to several anthologies provide a good source of information, e.g. George Elliott Clarke's various collections (1991, 1992a, 1997, 2008a), Janet Sears's anthology of African-Canadian drama (2000/2003), Donna Bailey Nurse's collection *Revival* (2006b), or Wayde Compton's *Bluesprint* (2001).

While individual papers on Black Canadian literature have slowly begun to make their way into literary magazines as well, special editions still offer the greatest wealth of useful articles (e.g. *Westcoast* 22, 1997 or *Canadian Literature* 182, 2004). H. Nigel Thomas's valuable *Why We Write* (2006) assembles interviews with fifteen African-Canadian writers. Likewise, Donna Bailey Nurse's *What's a Black Critic to do?* (2003) not only offers almost two dozen very brief profiles of African-Canadian writers and an equal number of short reviews but half a dozen interviews with Black Canadian Writers as well. By now, African-Canadian literature has also secured a spot in most literary histories (cf. for a German context e.g. Lutz 2005 or the brief comments in Banita 2008). The one volume still dominating the literary scene, however, is George Elliott Clarke's 2002 *Odysseys Home: Mapping African-Canadian Literature* [2002a]. By reversing the ratio of cultural/social and literary studies found in other collections, Clarke's assemblage of essays published between 1991 and 2001 provides the most comprehensive view on African-Canadian literature to date. Moreover, the "Africana Canadiana" bibliography annexed to Clarke's own extensive writings offers an encompassing list of Black Canadian publications from 1785 onwards; Clarke has thus created an indispensable means for any scholarly research in the field.

Structure

The present study is structured into four main parts: after an introduction to the theoretical framework and a short survey of African-Canadian history, a chapter on the theoretical underpinnings of Lawrence Hill's fiction is provided before the in-depth literary analyses, which constitute the bulk of this thesis, are presented.

In chapter two, "Theoretical Framework", a brief examination of the developments in the field of theorizing collective memory (going from the 1920s models by Maurice Halbwachs through contemporary theories by Aleida and Jan Assmann) is followed by a description of the working model employed in this study. This chapter is largely of a synoptic nature; I will not be concerned with developing new theoretical concepts but with adapting

---

8   One of the reasons for engaging in this study is the existing lack of scholarship in the field. *African-Canadian Theatre*, edited by Maureen Moynagh (2005a), provides a useful, though short, introduction to the genre of drama; G. E. Clarke's writings are wide in scope and substantially cover Africadian literature (poetry in particular). In a majority of further studies, female African-Canadian poets figure most prominently, e.g. Dionne Brand, Marlene NourbeSe Philip, and Claire Harris. As for Hill's *Any Known Blood*, only some short pieces have been published (cf. the respective chapter of this thesis as well as Harris 2004), while for the hugely successful *The Book of Negroes*, no detailed studies are available to date.

existing ones to the given literary field. Consequently, the working model used here comprises modifications and alterations, but no novel conceptions *per se.*

Chapter three, "The Black Presence in Canada", consists of an outline of the history of Blacks in Canada, focusing on two aspects particularly salient for the discussion of Hill's *The Book of Negroes* and *Any Known Blood*: the history of slavery in Canada as well as refugee and fugitive slaves arriving from the US either on the Underground Railroad to Ontario or as Black Loyalists sailing to Nova Scotia. As the primary interest lies in the historical dimension itself, there will be no extensive discussion of the contemporary Black presence in Canada (see on this aspect e.g. the collections listed in footnote 7). A bare minimum of historical background is necessary, however, to assess the historical veracity of the two novels discussed in depth in chapters five and six.

A general introduction to Lawrence Hill's oeuvre is provided in chapter four, supplemented by some very brief remarks on his biography. Since Hill has included extensive autobiographical details in *Black Berry, Sweet Juice,* it is superfluous to comment at length on his life here. Interdependencies between his biography and his fictional writing will be pointed out, however, in the respective analyses. As Hill uses the term 'faction' to describe his own writing, a brief survey of this term in literary criticism is given, followed by an examination of the ways in which Hill conceives of this notion. Hill's writing (in fact, there is a slight focus on *The Book of Negroes* in this section, while both *Any Known Blood* and fictions by other authors are included as well) is subsequently compared to the criteria identifying historiographic metafiction as conceptualized by Linda Hutcheon. The aim of this comparison is to clarify the mode/s in which Hill writes; in how far, for instance, do Hill and other African-Canadian writers share historiographic metafiction's questioning stance regarding the possibility of a 'truthful' rendition of history? The criteria of a further generic category, Barbara Foley's documentary novel, are then applied to Hill's fictions in order to find out whether Foley's model might possibly offer a more fruitful explanation of Hill's mode of writing. In the course of the generic analysis, it will become clear *how* and *why* Hill writes in the mode he calls faction.

The *what*, i.e. the actual content of Hill's fictions, will be examined more closely in chapters five and six. In fact, both chapters are structured in a parallel way, both offering a deductive approach to *The Book of Negroes* and *Any Known Blood,* respectively. After commenting on the (narrative) structure of the novels and briefly summarizing their plots ("Preliminaries"), chapters five and six both proceed with a section on "Narrative, Memory, Authenticity". In these sections, I will look at the way memories are, narratively, presented in the two novels.

For *The Book of Negroes*, the decisive structuring device will be a comparison with the (Neo-) slave narrative. By defining three basic aspects (composition, content, goals), I will examine in how far Hill complies to the mold of the classic fugitive slave narrative, where he diverges and why he does so. For *Any Known Blood*, the section "Narrative, Memory, Authenticity" is mainly concerned with the ways in which Hill provides 'fictional authenticity' for his narrative; questions of the archive, of fictionality, written and (or *versus*?) oral history, reliability and the passing on of memories (over generations as well as in fiction) are addressed here.

The third main section in both chapters deals with "Movements", indicating not only the actual movements of the respective novels' protagonists but the changes in memory constructions Hill's novels promote. In line with the deductive approach of chapters five and six, these sections concretize what has been examined in the preceding chapters: having established the *why* and the *how*, these discussions provide the *what*, i.e. they focus on the concrete (memory) constructions provided by Hill. Close readings of key aspects of both novels reveal the alternative collective memory suggested to amend the perceived misrepresentations. In regard to *The Book of Negroes*, such issues as the (forgotten) history of Canadian slavery and indenture are dealt with; the traumatic Middle Passage is considered, and, serving as a conclusion of sorts, the Canadian perspective is examined: has Canada indeed been the Canaan for 'freed' slaves it is so consistently taken for? For *Any Known Blood*, in turn, the major issues arise out of its dual structure as a Canadian/US-American intergenerational tale. First dealing with its embedded slave narrative, the novel's take on the Cane family's migrations back and forth across the 49th parallel is considered as a construction offering new perspectives on the porous nature of this boundary. Importantly, however, these movements are also read as a stringent and forceful comment on the differences in terms of the two North American nations' approaches towards race both past and present. What emerges from the discussions provided in chapters five and six is thus an account and an explanation of the collective memory construction offered by Hill's novels; a construction, I claim, which may serve as a corrective for lopsided hegemonic memory constructions and as such is representative of a forceful general trend in African-Canadian literature as a whole.

Following a general conclusion (chapter seven) and the list of works cited (chapter eight), the last chapter consists of an appendix comprising two interviews: the first one with Lawrence Hill, conducted shortly after the publication of *The Book of Negroes* in 2007, the second one with George Elliott Clarke, conducted in 2004.[9]

---

9 While the latter conversation indeed took place quite a while ago (seven years prior to the writing of this study) and was in fact conducted while I was pursuing a different trajectory of this project, I believe Clarke's comments are both as topical and as noteworthy today as they were in 2004.

A note on terminology

What's in a Name?

I always thought I was Negro
till I was Coloured,
West Indian, till I was told
that Columbus was wrong
in thinking he was west of India –
that made me Caribbean.
And throughout the '60s, '70s and '80s,
I was sure I was Black.
Now Black is passé,
African de rigeur, [sic]
and me, a chameleon of labels.

(Philip 1994)

Throughout this study, I will categorize people under certain labels, such as 'African-Canadian/s', 'Black Canadian/s', 'Black North American/s', 'Africadian/s', 'Black/s', 'White/s'. These categories will not mean a lot to some readers but will strongly reverberate with others. The latter may agree with my choice of terminology or protest that I am, either intentionally or out of neglect, lumping together a diverse set of people under a common label to which they might not even agree.[10] On a deeper level, this question is an issue of colonial posture or postcolonial endeavor. It is also a comment on essentialism, nationalism, unity and diversity. In the following, I will plead to be *d'accord* with most of the contentions made by George Elliott Clarke in the introductory section of his essay collection *Odysseys Home: Mapping African-Canadian Literature*. He maintains that

> [i]n all of these essays, I assume a modicum of *essentialism*, so that I am enabled – empowered – to discuss 'Africadian' and 'African-Canadian' literature with a fair (or black?) conviction that 'Africadians' and 'African Canadians' have *some* corporeal, 'real' existence. For, if these peoples do not have some coherency in the world, this book is so much nothing. (Clarke 2002a, 15)

Clarke, a noted scholar and seventh-generation Canadian, admits to a "modicum of *essentialism*" in order to be able to speak about a literary field delimited by its authors' race. The term 'race' itself is of course debatable (should it not have been superseded by 'ethnicity' or other more obviously theoretical concepts long ago?), yet to admit to essentialism is akin to sacri-

---

10 Cf. Tettey/Puplampu 2005, 6ff. for a thorough discussion of the matter. They distinguish four approaches toward a definition of 'African-Canadian', dismissing all except one as simplistic and/or misleading. What they arrive at, then, is a slightly unwieldy identification of the group to which they turn their attention: "first generation, Black, continental Africans who have immigrated in the last forty years and who have traceable genealogical links to the continent." (ibid., 12) It should be obvious that such an 'exact' definition is significantly too limiting for a study such as the present one. Nor do I agree with Cuder-Domínguez, who argues that "the term 'African Canadian' is thus an umbrella notion that fails to capture – indeed obscures – black-black difference while simultaneously (over?)emphasizing white-black difference." (2003, 70f.)

lege, particularly for someone "[s]chooled in post-colonial theory" such as Clarke (ibid., 13). After all, postcolonial theory is fundamentally concerned with challenging essentialisms and Manichean distinctions. Clarke indeed "hold[s] that African Canada is a conglomeration of many cultures, a spectrum of ethnicities" (ibid., 14), but admits that he "must be 'essentialist' enough to believe that an entity describable as 'African Canada' exists" (ibid.) in order to be able to depict a literature that is necessarily shaped by the writer's "communal affiliation", of which "no writer ever does *completely*" write independently (ibid.). The writers labeled by Clarke as "African(-)Canadian", several of whom I will deal with *en passant* in this thesis, in fact come from a diverse background. Should not literary criticism take into account this diversity instead of glossing it over with a label such as "African-Canadian"? Or, worse, with a label such as "Black Canadian", indicating an essentialist, racial collective? Yes, the background of writers such as Dionne Brand (who immigrated from Trinidad and Tobago in the 1960s and was raised in Toronto), mixed-race Lawrence Hill, whose parents came from the United States to Canada, and Clarke himself (a seventh-generation Canadian who grew up in the North End of Halifax) do merit differential treatment. But their oeuvres, to the extent that they reflect part of a common experience, allow us to deal with them as a collective.

In postcolonial terms, this approach could be filed under 'strategic essentialism': being aware of the terminology's and the conception's grave flaws, 'race' is accepted temporarily as a stable marker in order to make further theorization (or action) possible at all.[11] This notion does not grow out of any assumptions about the biological determinant of race. The mere coincidence of skin pigmentation of course cannot possibly determine the categorization of a literary syllabus. Race, that much is obvious, is useful as an analytical category only if taken as a socio-cultural concept. This is the reason why I capitalize the term 'Black': to signal its nature of being a construct, a theorem rather than a 'given' category. Consequently, I also capitalize the term 'White' – after all, if race is a social construct, then this certainly applies to all categories involved.[12]

---

11 Cf. Spivak 1996 (she devised the concept in the mid-1980s) and Hall 1996b; also cf. Adams 2001, 242; Barker 2004, 189; Gordon 2006, 19f.; Morton 2007, 126f.

12 I will use the terms 'Black Canadian', 'African-Canadian' or 'Black' interchangeably. This is often due to stylistic or other pragmatic reasons; if I were to describe Aminata Diallo, *The Book of Negroes'* protagonist, other than 'Black', I would continually be facing questions such as, When did she become an 'African American'? After the Middle Passage? How long does she need to have lived in Canada to be called an 'African-Canadian'? A Year? Ten? Does she become simply an 'African' again when she temporarily returns to her native Africa? Or does she stay an African throughout, even though not having spent more than a mere fraction of her life there? Calling Aminata a 'Black' person, however, is indicative of her social position in a slave society while avoiding Gordian elaborations on the questions above. Note that I will use the hyphenated version 'African-Canadian/s' throughout as currently, the hyphen is used more often than not in the respective literature. Besides, I find the optical connective intriguing in terms of the notion's underpinning. In contrast, in my spelling of 'African American' I will not make use of the hyphen, as this variant seems to be more acceptable at the moment. No distinctions of 'mosaic'/'salad bowl' vs. 'melting pot' are implied in this decision. On occasion, I will also use the term 'Africadian', which has been coined by George Elliott Clarke by amalgamating 'African' and 'Acadian', hence basically designating Black Nova Scotians.

Skin color thus does not determine anything *per se*; it does, however, elicit certain social schemata, which have greatly varied over the course of time and have led to different collective experiences, as Clarke argues: "Yet, five centuries of Eurocentric imperialism have made it impossible for those of us descending from Africa [...] to act as if we are pure, raceless beings." (ibid., 17) Clarke defines what Stuart Hall has called the "politically and culturally constructed" nature of race (cf. Clarke 2002a, 16; Hall 1996b, 166) as a set of shared *experiences, histories and cultures* (cf. Clarke's basis: Hall 1996b, 169f.). These "particular experiences" (ibid.) today may consist of minor facets, such as authors being grouped as 'Black Canadian writers' or 'African-Canadian authors' on many bookshelves across Canadian bookstores and libraries. They do, however, also include major chunks, which encompass the experience of slavery,[13] segregation and disillusionment, and which make up the collective memory of a group. "Five centuries of imperialism" have thus neither been forgotten nor superseded. Instead, they have left us with a category such as 'African-Canadian', a category which we might wish to deconstruct ('decolonize') one day – giving prominence to a notion Clarke cites D'Alfonso with: "in the end, it is the individual who will count most" (Clarke 2002a, 14) – but whose existence cannot be 'wished away' or replaced terminologically or analytically by notions of ethnicity or difference.[14]

In the course of this work, I will maintain that, on the contrary, African-Canadian authors insist on a certain amount of unity and on a certain sense of essentialism; again, in terms of the postcolonial project, this essentialism must be viewed as a strategic one, positioning the Black subject, viz. the cultural 'Other' in a predominantly White settler society, as a largely homogenized group involved in active struggle against a whitewashed hegemonic discourse. In an interview, George Elliott Clarke affirms the claim that a distinct level of homogenization or unity has to be established in order to be effective, and that this unity can largely be based on the shared history noted by Hall:

> In Canada, there are so many things that divide us [African-Canadians] that we do have to lay claim to some kind of common history in order to have some grounds for unity. And so that common history does go through slavery, does go through colonialism, and of course the experience of racism today in Canada. So, partly, too, remembering of this trauma is, again, a way of building some intellectual unity among our very disparately originated communities. (Clarke, Appendix 320)

---

13 DuBois holds that "the physical bond [of race] is least and the badge of color relatively unimportant save as a badge; the real essence of this kinship is its social heritage of slavery; the discrimination and insult; [...]" (1984, 117). For a discussion of the term 'slave' as a possible "misnomer" for African-Canadians' ancestors, cf. Prince 2001, 39ff.

14 "The fact is 'black' has never been just there either. It has always been an unstable identity, psychically, culturally, and politically. It, too, is a narrative, a story, a history. Something constructed, told, spoken, not simply found. [...] These are 'imaginary communities' – and not a bit less real because they are also symbolic." (Hall 1996a, 116)

2. Theoretical Framework

> *Just as public or national myth can weigh heavily on private*
> *tradition and experience, it particularly threatens those of*
> *minorities. So the collective memories of minorities need con-*
> *tinual active expression if they are to survive being absorbed*
> *or smothered by the historical traditions of the majority.*
> *(Samuel/Thompson 1990, 18)*

It is not farfetched to claim that the term 'collective memory' – including its variations as 'cultural memory', 'national memory' or 'group memory' – has for several decades gained much prominence and is on the verge of becoming an inflationary ingredient of public discourse, particularly in mass media discourse.[15] At the same time, research on the specific mechanisms, functions and malfunctions of memory, both individual and collective, has thrived. From the perspective of German-speaking academia, but by far not limited to it, the seminal work(s) of Aleida and Jan Assmann have greatly contributed to this surge in scholarly interest. Firmly based on Maurice Halbwachs and going through Aby Warburg, Pierre Nora, and others, Aleida and Jan Assmann have fine-tuned the concept of collective memory and made it available as an analytical tool in literary analysis. The particular merit of the theory of collective memory is its linking of the ever-present but more often than not slippery usage of 'identity' to psychological, socio-psychological, and sociological findings. The study of identity is thus substantiated by theoretical concepts based on science, not mere musing. This interdisciplinary approach enables a multi-faceted and mutually enhancing perspective on phenomena that might otherwise remain elusive. An inflationary term in publicized discourse, collective memory thus proves to be a valuable analytical tool. Accordingly, research on collective memory has become a well-established section of scholarly interest.

---

15 The weekly *TIME Magazine* alone has used the terms 'collective' or 'cultural memory' well over 1,200 times since 1924 – more than half of the instances have appeared within the last twenty years (cf. *TIME Magazine* archives at <http://search.time.com>).

2.1. Basic Principles of Collective Memory Theory: Maurice Halbwachs

2.1.1. Maurice Halbwachs's conception of collective memory

Theories of collective memory generally take their initial starting point in the works of Maurice Halbwachs (1877-1945). A student of Henri Bergson and Émile Durkheim, Halbwachs studied in France and Germany, taught at the Sorbonne, in Strasbourg and Chicago. Under the Nazi reign in Germany, he was deported to the KZ Buchenwald, where he died during the final period of World War II.[16] Halbwachs sketches the ways in which individual memory/memories are affected and, indeed, shaped by their carriers' social surroundings. Still a methodological step away from declaring collective memory an externalized mode of memory, Halbwachs presents this basic assumption at the outset of *La mémoire collective* (which was, though unfinished, posthumously published in 1950) in what has become the quintessential and probably most-quoted metaphor for socially affected memories, the so-called 'walk through London'.[17] In this passage, Halbwachs explains how the individual, when processing new information and new impressions, is guided by his or her friends and acquaintances – even though they are not physically present. Walking through London, Halbwachs tells us, he recalls seeing the architecture as if walking with his architect friend, visiting the museums as if accompanied by an artist friend, engaging in imaginary dialogues.[18]

> Das bedeutet, daß wir in Wirklichkeit niemals allein sind. Es ist nicht notwendig, daß andere Menschen anwesend sind, die sich materiell von uns unterscheiden: denn wir tragen stets eine Anzahl unverwechselbarer Personen mit und in uns. (Halbwachs 1967, 2)

The impressions that Halbwachs collects are influenced by his social surroundings – friends, family, colleagues, what he calls the social milieu[19] – even though one might deem his solitary walk through London an entirely individual experience. Halbwachs thus demonstrates that at a very early stage in the process of re-collection (the earliest possible stage, i.e.: the collection), our perception is influenced by others, causing our apparently individual memories to

---

16 For more extensive biographical information, cf. for example Halbwachs 1966, 11ff., Halbwachs 1967, VI ff., or the introduction to Halbwachs 1992.

17 Cf. J. Assmann 2005, 70ff.; Echterhoff 2005, 254f.; Echterhoff/Saar 2002, 19; Erll 2002; Erll 2004, 7f.; Erll 2005, 259; Hobi 1988, 27f.; Neumann 2005, 124f.; Nießeler 2006, 143f.

18 Halbwachs engages in what has later on been dubbed 'memory talk' in terms of how children in particular learn to structure their memories dialogically (cf. Welzer 2008, 96ff.; Markowitsch/Welzer 2005, 21; Neumann 2005, 57, and the essays in Schacter/Scarry 2001, Parts II and III, particularly Nelson, 266).

19 Halbwachs's expression *milieu* not only denotes social surroundings, but also represents the rough equivalent of later conceptions of 'memory groups' and 'memory cultures'. His *milieux* are astonishingly flexible in size: Though the immediate family is his prime example, he extends the scope of *milieux* up to the level of nation-state (cf. Halbwachs 1967, 35).

be shaped by social factors. Halbwachs thus assumes that there can be no such thing as a completely individual memory (except for dreams, cf. section 2.1.3., p. 31), as individuals will always employ certain modes of perception – selection, interpretation[20] – that are socially given. Encoding is thus a social phenomenon. The same holds true for the decoding process, viz. the actual act of remembering. In recalling events of the past, Halbwachs claims, we can rely on the memories of others; as they have had a hand in encoding the recollections, they are 'present' in the process of re-membering as well:

> So gehören Begebenheiten und Kenntnisse, die wir uns am mühelosesten ins Gedächtnis zurückrufen, dem Gemeingut zumindest eines oder einiger Milieus an. In diesem Maße sind sie also 'aller Welt' zu eigen; und weil wir uns auf das Gedächtnis des anderen stützen können, sind wir jederzeit und wann immer wir wollen fähig, sie zurückzurufen. (Halbwachs 1967, 29)

It is through this social influence on the processes of en- and decoding that collective memory comes into being. The real novelty of Halbwachs's concept, however, lies in the fact that he, in a subsequent step, sees collective memory as an externalized memory, detached from its individual carriers in principle, though not in biological actuality. Memories cannot be physically detached from their carriers; without a neuronal structure to provide a bio-physical storage device, memories are lost. However, collective memory is externalized in that it constitutes a collective, a pool of recollections that encompasses, but not conflates with, the individual memories: "Das kollektive Gedächtnis andererseits umfaßt die individuellen Gedächtnisse, aber verschmilzt nicht mit ihnen." (Halbwachs 1967, 35) In contrast to the individual neurological memory, collective memory is thus conceptualized as an abstraction.[21] Due to its conceptual, though not actual, detachment from individual neurological structures offered by human brains, collective memory – devised as an 'interior dialogue' with a particular social milieu – presents the individual with the possibility to integrate into his own recollection the memory of events he has not in fact witnessed in person: as Jan Assmann phrases it, only individuals 'have' memory, but it is always coined collectively (cf. J. Assmann 1992,

---

20 Halbwachs describes the process of perception/encoding as the use of "Instrumente, die durch die Worte und Vorstellungen gebildet werden, die das Individuum nicht erfunden und die es seinem Milieu entliehen hat" (Halbwachs 1967, 35; 'instruments created by words and conceptions that the individual did not generate but copied from his *milieu*'); the collective framing of individual memory includes particular types of "Denk- und Erfahrungsströme" (Halbwachs 1967, 50), which shape the perception as well as the structure of the encoding and decoding of memories. In *Les cadres sociaux de la mémoire* (*Das Gedächtnis und seine sozialen Bedingungen,* Halbwachs 1966), Halbwachs describes what he later calls milieus as *cadres sociaux*, social framings, first referring to one's social surroundings in terms of people, then slightly shifting focus to include what today is thought of as cognitive schemata. *Cadres sociaux* thus designate the social influences on people's cognitive patterns by socially pre-formed cognitive structures such as modes of perception, of encoding or decoding/interpreting.

21 It must be added that Halbwachs himself did not subscribe to theories of neuronal storage of memories; in *Das Gedächtnis und seine Bedingungen* (1966, French original published in 1925), he explicitly dissociates himself from theories that would describe 'processes in the brain' ("Hirnprozesse") in terms of neurological activity (Halbwachs 1966, 21f.).

36). The ability to participate in 'second-hand experiences' is one of the crucial (and, in terms of the literary analysis presented here, most fruitful) tenets of Halbwachs's theory. In the following passage from *La mémoire collective* (Halbwachs 1967, 35), Halbwachs designates certain collective memories to a nation-state, arguing that he is able to share these memories via media transmission:

> Im Laufe meines Lebens ist die nationale Gruppe, der ich angehöre, der Schauplatz einer bestimmten Anzahl von Ereignissen gewesen, von denen ich behaupte, daß ich mich an sie erinnere, die ich jedoch nur aus Zeitungen kenne oder durch die Zeugnisse jener, die unmittelbar in sie verwickelt gewesen sind. Sie nehmen im Gedächtnis der Nation einen bestimmten Raum ein. Aber ich habe ihnen nicht selbst beigewohnt. Wenn ich sie wiederaufleben lasse, bin ich genötigt, mich völlig auf das Gedächtnis anderer zu verlassen, das hier nicht das meine ergänzt oder verstärkt, sondern das die alleinige Quelle dessen ist, was ich mir von ihm vergegenwärtigen will. (Halbwachs 1967, 35f.)

This particular section is of intense interest because of four elements Halbwachs introduces here: 1) A milieu such as a nation-state accumulates a collective memory that serves as a 'pool' for its individual members.[22] 2) In order to participate in a particular collective memory, one does not need to have had the actual, first-hand factual experience. 3) Collective memory may be transmitted through media. Halbwachs explicitly names the two most significant media resources: oral and written transmission. The usefulness of this conception for literary studies should be obvious, as Halbwachs assigns to written texts the ability to transmit memories and to 'pool' these memories at certain levels of milieus.[23] Literature may thus serve as a reservoir of recollections that are actualized at the level of individual readers in an 'as-if' situation, 'as if' he had experienced these memories himself. 4) The term 'reinvigorate' already hints at a notion that is essential to Halbwachs's entire conception: reconstruction.[24] The act of remembering is an actual re-membering, an assembling anew in a possibly new shape. Memory thus ceases to be a faithful reproduction of neurological inscriptions on a

---

22   It needs to be emphasized, however, that Halbwachs indeed *focuses* on significantly smaller milieus such as the family, the working environment, social classes etc. Specifically, the groups situated at the level *between* person and nation-state are those with the most immediate impact on a person's memory constructions (cf. Halbwachs 1967, 65).

23   It is interesting to note that literature is occasionally neglected as a medium of (collective) memory transmission even by those who use it; Afua Cooper, an African-Canadian scholar and author, for instance writes on the occasion of the 400th anniversary of the Black presence in Canada: "How do we remember this 400-year history? What do we choose to remember? And how do we memorialize it? I would argue that there are at least two ways in which to do so. First, through the vehicle of public history: museums, exhibits, historic sites, and monuments, and websites; and second, through the medium of academic history: research, writing, publishing, and teaching." (Cooper 2007, 11) Apparently, literature is subsumed here under "at least".

24   As early as 1925, Halbwachs claims that memories are not 'retained', but 'reconstructed, starting from the present' rather than from the past itself (Halbwachs 1966, 22); as our perspective changes over time, 'we may not claim that our memories have remained the same, even if they seem familiar' (ibid., 126).

'mental hard-drive'. Instead, the pure mimesis gives way to reconstruction, variation and *imaginatio*:

> Wir haben es oft wiederholt: die Erinnerung ist in sehr weitem Maße eine Rekonstruktion der Vergangenheit mit Hilfe von der Gegenwart entliehenen Gegebenheiten und wird im übrigen durch andere, zu früheren Zeiten unternommene Rekonstruktionen vorbereitet, aus denen das Bild von ehemals schon verändert hervorgegangen ist. (Halbwachs 1967, 55f.)

Of course, the reconstructive, creative and malleable character of memories is taken for granted in current scientific approaches. Halbwachs, however, must be credited with realizing for the first time that in addition to the variability of individual memory (which, through the mere fact of forgetfulness, has been commonplace experience), collective memory is a construct as well, governed by current conditions. The act of remembering is thus shaped to a large degree by recalling an individual's or group's present situation (cf. Halbwachs 1966, 126). In the literary analysis, this notion will play a salient role, as current needs (of political assertion, identity negotiations, agenda setting issues etc.) govern the ways in which the authors devise the memories they present. In addition to the constructiveness and the influence of the present on the construction of the past as we recall it, Halbwachs realized that the act of remembering is a recursive construction. Not only are memories modified in the act of en- and decoding; they are altered in the act of re-encoding as well, which is to say that in the process of re-membering, a recollection is altered once more. Halbwachs thus postulates the influence of past reconstructions on present reconstructions. This reciprocity adds further layers of influences on memories, so that recollections receive what would in software programming be called a version history: an event, person, emotion etc. is added to the (collective) memory, being shaped by the social framework that exerts its influence through the socially conditioned modes of perception and encoding (version 1.0 of that memory). Upon recollection, the memory is altered again – shaped by the social framework as well as the current needs of the recalling person and/or his social surroundings[25] (version 1.1). By 'updating' the memory to version 1.1, the memory is altered and re-encoded in its altered form. Consequently, future recollections will draw on version 1.1 of this memory, reconstructing it anew and again adjust it to the given situation (version 1.2). A memory recalled many times thus undergoes a series of recursive changes, each modification being based upon the previous adaptation.

2.1.2. Collective memory vs. historical memory

> Aus allem Vorausgegangenem geht hervor, daß das kollektive Gedächtnis nicht mit der Geschichte zu verwechseln ist [...]. Das bedeutet, daß die Geschichte im allgemeinen an dem Punkt beginnt, an dem die Tradition aufhört – in einem Augenblick, in dem das soziale Gedächtnis erlischt und sich zersetzt. (Halbwachs 1967, 66)

---

25 "Die Gruppen, denen ich zu den verschiedenen Epochen angehöre, sind nicht dieselben. Ich betrachte indessen die Vergangenheit aus ihrer Sicht." (Halbwachs 1967, 59)

Halbwachs contrasts two modes of memory: Social or collective memory[26] and historical memory (or, in an alternative phrasing, 'living and written history', Halbwachs 1967, 50). While social memory is devised as a 'continuous stream' (ibid., 68) of memories passed down from eyewitnesses and transmitted as long as the group considers them to be of relevance, historical memory consists of 'dead' recollections devoid of a group of carriers (also cf. J. Assmann 1992, 44). Historical memory thus requires different media to be stored in, as it has left the collective memory and the individual neuronal structures offered by its group. Consequently, historical memory necessitates a reification, an objectification most often – but of course not exclusively – provided by written documents. It is self-evident that memories shared by a group do not necessitate reification; after all, these memories are 'alive' within their collective. Equally, social memory does not need to rely on specialists to manage their reservoir of memories, while historical memory has authorities, professionals, chroniclers, managers of its pools: historians, librarians, scholars. Furthermore, historical memory is not limited to a certain group, its thrust and audience are general ones. Collective memory, in contrast, is per Halbwachs's definition restricted to one particular group, as 'every collective memory has as its carrier a group limited in time and space'.[27]

A problem posed by this tenet, however, is the possibility of memory fossilization, i.e. the transformation of collective memory into historical memory whenever memories are deemed irrelevant by a certain group or their personal connection to these memories is broken. The latter case in Halbwachs's conception imposes a temporal limit on the durability of collective memory: collective memories have a validity of well under a century – and often significantly less.[28] Jan Assmann, as will be discussed later on, modifies this tenet to arrive at a concept of 'communicative memory' that requires direct witnessing by at least a number of group members, after which a 'floating gap' severs the group from a memory; Assmann, however, includes the possibility of media transmission of collective memory beyond the existence of direct witnesses. In Halbwachs's model, in contrast, collective memory withers away with the death of the witnesses. This notion contradicts earlier statements that allow for a media transmission of collective memory and thus circumvent the limitations of direct oral transmission by eyewitnesses.[29] Consequently, a modified version of Halbwachs's conception

---

26 Halbwachs employs both terms, though "collective memory" is the prevalent one.

27 "Jedes kollektive Gedächtnis hat eine zeitlich und räumlich begrenzte Gruppe zum Träger." (Halbwachs 1967, 73)

28 "Das kollektive Gedächtnis dagegen sieht die Gruppe von innen und während eines Zeitabschnitts, der die durchschnittliche Dauer des menschlichen Lebens nicht überschreitet, der sogar meist kürzer ist." (Halbwachs 1967, 76)

29 Halbwachs is inconsistent in this regard. Having proclaimed the transformation of collective memory into historical memory after a time period of under a generation (Halbwachs 1967, 76), he acknowledges a 'religious collective memory' that goes back to 'events far removed in time', explicitly referring to Jesus on the biblical Mount of Olives (ibid., 159). In *Das Gedächtnis und seine sozialen Bedingungen* (1966), 'religious memory' is set apart as an exception regarding the longevity and unchangeable nature of its memories (259ff.). *La topographie légendaire des évangiles en Terre Sainte* (1941; Halbwachs 2003) comprises lengthy investigations into myths

must be applied to literary analyses lest it be restricted to the analysis of contemporary works (in its literal sense). It is largely the merit of Aleida and Jan Assmann to have overcome this impasse and to have incorporated the media aspects of collective memory in a way that renders it effective for literary analyses.

In other respects, Halbwachs's theory is applicable as it is – even though Halbwachs himself was surely unaware of some of its merits in regard to literary analyses. Concepts such as plurality of voices and polyphonic memories are compatible with his theory, as he acknowledges the existence of a plurality of memory groups ('memory cultures' in current terminology): "Es gibt in der Tat mehrere kollektive Gedächtnisse." (Halbwachs 1967, 71; also cf. A. Assmann 1999, 131) Halbwachs also unequivocally includes the possibility of sub- or counter-memories; instead of a monolithic national memory,[30] Halbwachs explicitly allows for competitive memory versions to exist within a (national) society. In the early 20th century, Halbwachs certainly did not have today's multicultural ethnic plurality in mind as he drafted his thoughts on competing memory versions, yet this aspect can easily be accommodated by his theoretical postulation that memory groups within a country may either assimilate into other memory groups or retain their distinct character;[31] in the latter case, this subgroup's re-actions will differ from that of other groups, as it has its own bases and modes of interpretation:

> Auch das [erinnerte] Ereignis geschieht im Raum, und es kann sein, daß alle Gruppen es wahrnehmen. Wichtig aber ist *die Art*, in der sie es *interpretieren*, der *Sinn*, den sie ihm *geben*. (Halbwachs 1967, 108; emphases mine)

---

whose origins are removed by thousands of years, thus far exceeding the self-imposed one-lifetime frame. In *La mémoire collective*, however, the inconsistency resurfaces. Also cf. the contradiction (in *La mémoire collective*) between memories transmitted by newspapers but adopted into the personal memory under an 'as-if' situation (Halbwachs 1967, 35) and the contrasting un-ambiguous confrontation of 'written' and 'living' history (ibid., 50).

30 A level on which e.g. Pierre Nora later concentrated, cf. Nora 1997 (introductory); Lenger 2005; P. Schmidt 2004 provides a largely critical perspective.

31 "Ein Volk, das ein anderes besiegt, kann das besiegte sich angleichen; dann aber wird es selbst ein anderes Volk oder tritt zumindest in eine neue Phase seines Daseins ein. Wenn der besiegte dem Sieger nicht angeglichen wird, behält jedes der beiden Völker sein eigenes Nationalbewußtsein und reagiert verschiedenartig auf dieselben Ereignisse. Ebenso ist es aber innerhalb eines und desselben Landes, was die religiöse und politische Gesellschaft anbetrifft." (Halbwachs 1967, 109) There is – one is tempted to say: of course – no ethnic component to the subgroups mentioned by Halbwachs. We can safely assume, however, that ethnic and/or racial criteria may either be subsumed under the label of 'political' (taking into account the social constructedness of ethnicity/race) or added as a third category to the existing cleavages of 'political' and 'religious' groups. What Halbwachs – unwittingly – addresses in this paragraph is thus a controversial debate that centers on the question of immigrant societies being characterized as 'melting pots' (suggesting assimilation, "angleichen"), or 'mosaics' (wherein subgroups supposedly retain their distinct character, "eigenes Nationalbewußtsein behalten").

Memory groups (*milieux* in Halbwachs's original terminology) thus differ in their interpretation of events. This is the basis for conflicting memory versions, hegemonic and minority versions of history, the need for agenda-setting and re-negotiations of identity central to the literary analyses provided in chapters 5 and 6 of this thesis. It is of additional salience for later discussions of narrative modes (linear/coherent vs. divergent/incoherent) and postmodern approaches to the construction of the 'self' as a negotiation of discontinuous elements and fractured, competing versions of memory that it is *historical* memory that takes special notice of shifts and fissures in the fabric of memory – such as revolutions, reforms, wars. *Collective* memory, in contrast, seeks to construct coherent versions of the past and avoids the highlighting of structural breaches (cf. Halbwachs 1967, 99f.; 1966, 135f.).[32]

Constructions of 'self' of course lead us back to the initial discussion of questions of identity. Collective memory – in analogy to individual memory and individual identity – is taken to be the basis for collective identities. There is no need to elaborate on the strong ties between memory and identity here, as they have been thoroughly discussed from various angels (cf. for instance J. Assmann 1988, Weber 2001). To state the obvious: Without memories, neither individuals nor groups may lay claim to a distinct identity. Groups are constructed by a feeling of closeness, likeness, of ties that bind it – and in opposition to 'others'. Regarding the ties that bind a group and bring a memory group into existence in the first place, Halbwachs states:

> In dem Augenblick, in dem die Gruppe auf ihre Vergangenheit zurückblickt, fühlt sie wohl, daß sie dieselbe geblieben ist und wird sich ihrer zu jeder Zeit bewahrten Identität bewußt. (Halbwachs 1967, 74)

A group – strongly personified in this quotation – thus constructs a coherent identity based on the memories its members share.[33]

---

32 "Die 'Geschichte' verfährt nach Halbwachs genau umgekehrt wie das kollektive Gedächtnis. Schaut dieses nur auf Ähnlichkeiten und Kontinuität, so nimmt jene nur Differenzen und Diskontinuitäten wahr." (J. Assmann 1992, 42)

33 The notion of coherence emphasized before and recurring in this quotation is a significant aspect of Halbwachs's conception (cf. for instance Halbwachs 1967, 114, where he speaks of 'continuous milieus that have not changed and today are the same as yesterday'. Also cf. Halbwachs 1966, 382: memories are 'deformed by reconstruction in order to offer greater coherence'). The tendency to 'streamline' the collective memory of a group contrasts with attempts to create counter-memories, divergent accounts of history and collective identity and thus leads us into the issue of agenda-setting: different memory versions – each aiming for cohesion and recognition – compete within a superordinate memory culture (cf. section 2.3., "Collective Memory: The Working Model"). Halbwachs himself did not focus on the possibility of competing memory versions of subgroups, but his theoretical framework does account for these processes.

2.1.3. Difficulties of Halbwachs's conception

While the basic conception of collective memory as presented by Maurice Halbwachs may well serve as the basis of a theoretical framework employed in literary study, some aspects require further elaboration and clarification.

Halbwachs's methodological approach, for instance, might be criticized for professing to be more empirical than it actually is. Scholars have pointed out Halbwachs's rootedness in the social and economic sciences (cf. his 1909 PhD thesis in the field of political economy and his 1913 professorial thesis in sociology) and his claim to empirical methods. Halbwachs himself, however, admits to an armchair philosophy approach in *Das Gedächtnis und seine sozialen Bedingungen* ("indem wir entweder uns selbst prüften oder andere darüber befragten", Halbwachs 1966, 362), yet he qualifies this approach by checking his findings against the experiences made by others ("Möglichkeit der Kontrolle der eigenen durch die Beobachtung der anderen," ibid.). Since the 1925 publication of the French original of *Das Gedächtnis und seine sozialen Bedingungen*, however, the basic assumptions of Halbwachs's theory have been corroborated by research in the fields of psychology, social psychology and sociology. Some qualifications have been made to the original theoretical construct, as Halbwachs tended, for example, to extend the collective dimension of memory into metaphorical depths.[34] Likewise, the offhand equation of personal and collective memory has been criticized by some scholars as lacking a scientific basis.[35] Where this is the case, efforts have been made to distinguish those parts that possess analogous forms from those that do not.

A further difficulty arises from Halbwachs's tendency to not clearly distinguish between *socially formed* memories and *externalized* memories. Later theorists have – the difficulties inherent in this distinction notwithstanding – defined the distinguishing features of socially formed individual memory and genuine collective memory more clearly.[36] Relying on Halbwachs's conception alone, one would run the risk of collectivizing the entire spectrum of memories, as Halbwachs's terminology is imprecise at times: his use of the term 'collective memory' occasionally refers to externalized as well as socially formed memory; the difficulty, of course, being that there is no such thing as a memory uninfluenced by the social environment, as Halbwachs himself repeatedly points out. Without clarification, there would consequently be no memory *except for* collective memory (the sole exemption from this rule

---

34 Cf. J. Assmann 1992, 36. In turn, Assmann demonstrates the difficulties of avoiding metaphorical uses by both criticizing the use of the term "Gruppengedächtnis" (group memory) (ibid.) and simultaneously employing it himself (cf. J. Assmann 1992, 89).

35 This strand of criticism is hardly new; Halbwachs's contemporaries Bergson (his teacher) and Freud perceived memory as an altogether individual process; Marc Bloch (one of Halbwachs's colleagues in Strasbourg) explicitly rejected the collectivization of individual experiences (cf. Erll 2003, 158; J. Assmann 1992, 133).

36 Cf. for example Olick's useful distinction between "collected" and "collective memory" (Olick 1999), which will be employed in my working model as well (also cf. Neumann 2005, 53 and Erll 2005, 250f.).

would be dreams, which Halbwachs defines as the only truly individual memory that we can have, cf. the chapter "Der Traum und die Erinnerungsbilder", Halbwachs 1966, 25ff.; also cf. J. Assmann 2005, 71f. and Hanke 2001, 58f.).

Another striking difficulty is posed by the fossilization of collective memory, viz. 'living memory' (Halbwachs 1967, 50), into historical memory. While Halbwachs is inconsistent on the issue, one line of argument would suggest that collective memory cannot be transmitted by media other than personal contact and oral transmission. Reification by encoding collective memories into other media – writing is Halbwachs's obvious main choice here – will lead to the 'death' of memories, and no subsequent reviving is integrated into his conception. Again, later theorists have dealt with this issue at length, introducing a variety of modifications to straighten out this 'flaw'.[37] The distinction of *Speicher- vs. Funktionsgedächtnis*, for instance (cf. A. Assmann 1999, 134), or Jan Assmann's conception of a "floating gap" (J. Assmann 1992, 51) between communicative and cultural memory (cf. ibid., 56) have been devised to deal with this problem. They facilitate studies of collective memory which are unrestricted by or modify Halbwachs's one-lifetime limit and the polar opposition between historical and collective memory.

2.2. Contemporary Conceptions and Adaptations

2.2.1. Aleida and Jan Assmann

The conception of cultural memory ("kulturelles Gedächtnis") devised, supplemented and refined by Aleida and particularly Jan Assmann is commonly identified as the most influential theoretical approach to collective memory in the German-speaking context (cf. Erll 2003, 171). Developing their conception in the late 1980s and largely basing it on the theories of Maurice Halbwachs, the Assmanns have since then produced a wealth of research on collective memory, both on its theoretical aspects and its application in diverse fields, including historical, archaeological and literary studies. Apart from extending the grounds of interoperability between collective memory theory and established scholarly and scientific disciplines, two main aspects distinguish Assmanns' approach from Halbwachs's, which otherwise largely functions as a template: first, Assmanns' models include additional and/or diverging major divisions (cultural *vs.* communicative memory, *ars vs. vis* memory, functional *vs.* storage memory). Second, Aleida and Jan Assmann centrally stress the interconnectedness of memory and social identity, consequently focusing on the political aspects of collective memory even more explicitly than Halbwachs.

---

37   This, of course, is speaking strictly from a cultural, media and literary studies perspective, which is necessarily interested in the transmission of memories qua different media. Regarding the media transmission of (collective) memories, see in particular the *Media and Cultural Memory* series published by de Gruyter.

2.2.2. *Cultural memory and the nexus between memory, identity, and politics*

The distinction between cultural and communicative memory circumvents the difficulties posed by Halbwachs's partly ambiguous treatment of a conceived time limit for collective memory. In *Das kulturelle Gedächtnis. Schrift, Erinnerung und politische Identität in frühen Hochkulturen* (1992), Jan Assmann explicates this subdivision of collective memory, which he had contoured in an earlier paper (J. Assmann 1988). Roughly speaking, communicative memory includes the contemporary experiences of a group, based on the everyday interaction and communication of its living members. As such, it is highly informal, requires neither specialists as its carriers nor media as its objectification, and is limited to a time span of three to four generations. Assmann links communicative memory and its study to concepts of oral history (cf. J. Assmann 1992, 51). Cultural memory, in contrast, relates to ancient (founding) myths and an absolute, distant past; it is highly formalized and ritualized and relies on rigidly fixed objectifications and as such requires specialists to preserve, reproduce, manage and 'perform' the memories.[38]

> Das *kulturelle* Gedächtnis richtet sich auf Fixpunkte in der Vergangenheit. [...] Vergangenheit gerinnt hier vielmehr zu symbolischen Figuren, an die sich die Erinnerung heftet. Die Vätergeschichten, Exodus, Wüstenwanderung, Landnahme, Exil sind etwa solche Erinnerungsfiguren [...]. Auch Mythen sind Erinnerungsfiguren: Der Unterschied zwischen Mythos und Geschichte wird hier hinfällig. Für das kulturelle Gedächtnis zählt nicht faktische, sondern nur erinnerte Geschichte. (J. Assmann 1992, 52, emphasis in the original)

These *Erinnerungsfiguren*, 'key memories' in lack of a better translation, prove to be a fruitful concept for literary studies. For the study of African-Canadian literature in particular, the existence of certain key memories dating back to the establishing of an African-Canadian community – thus in a sense a 'modern founding myth' – are valuable points of interest. As such, the analysis of key memories such as slavery, displacement, diaspora or disillusionment will play a major role in the analytical chapters of this study.

Jan Assmann's conception of a division of cultural and communicative memory has, however, been devised on the background of ancient history; as Jan Assmann's original academic field is Egyptology, the notion of cultural memory has been influenced by this time scale. Assmann assumes a flexible "floating gap" to separate communicative memory (three to four generations, or eighty to a hundred years) from cultural memory (a distant, mythological past) in terms of temporal distance (J. Assmann 1992, 52; he uses the English term "floating gap"; also cf. Niethammer 1995). In its initial designation, Jan Assmann's floating gap of

---

38 For a thorough discussion of the contents, forms, media, time structures and carriers of communicative and cultural memory, see *Das kulturelle Gedächtnis* (J. Assmann 1992; for a quick overview, see p. 56, where Assmann provides a table illustrating the basic characteristics). A concise treatment of the two modes of collective memory can be found in Erll 2003, 171f. Birgit Neumann provides a good discussion informed by a cultural studies perspective (Neumann 2005, part. 87f.).

course comprises thousands of years. It seems feasible, however, to delimitate the gap and shrink it to time spans drastically shorter than that, as its actual extent is of no particular relevance.[39]

The second major distinction separating Aleida and Jan Assmann's approach from Halbwachs's, the focus on the close connection between collective memory and collective identity, is of particular relevance for an investigation of African-Canadian literature. The study of collective memory and its expression via key memories in Black Canadian literature aims at a discussion of conflicting memory versions and thus at an examination of competing versions of identity construction, particularly in terms of dominant *vs.* minority memories/identities. Therefore, connections between memory and identity as well as the possibility of differential memory versions are salient aspects of the theoretical framework. Jan Assmann accounts for both these features:

> Ebenso wie ein Individuum eine personale Identität nur kraft seines Gedächtnisses ausbilden und über die Folge der Tage und Jahre hinweg aufrechterhalten kann, so vermag auch eine Gruppe ihre Gruppenidentität nur durch Gedächtnis zu reproduzieren. Der Unterschied besteht darin, daß das Gruppengedächtnis keine neuronale Basis hat. An deren Stelle tritt die Kultur [...]. (J. Assmann 1992, 89)

> Gegen-Identitäten werden nicht gegen das kulturlose Chaos, sondern gegen die dominierende Kultur ausgebildet und aufrechterhalten, wie es der typische Fall von Minderheiten ist. (J. Assmann 1992, 154)

2.2.3. Memory as ars and vis, functional and storage memory

While Jan Assmann's focus on identity (politics) and its connection to collective memory is a major contribution towards the usability of collective memory as an analytical tool for literary studies, Aleida Assmann introduces several additional aspects that contribute to a systematic study of collective memory in literature. The first distinction she establishes is based on the difference between (ancient) mnemonic techniques and modern conceptions of memory as modifying, reconstructive processes. Assmann terms the first aspect of memory *ars*, while the second one is called *vis*. Memory as *ars* is closely related to rhetorical and mnemonic techniques and represents a 'topological organization of knowledge' (A. Assmann 1999, 28). These storage-and-retrieval techniques aim at a faithful reproduction of certain contents, such as a speech. In order to foster the availability of an exact replica of the items to be remembered in a speech, memory techniques included, for instance, the linkage of these items to a building through whose rooms the orator paces, finding in each room an item of the speech he memorized (thus A. Assmann's term of the 'topological organization'). Famous for his advice on rhetorical styles and an impressive orator himself, Cicero took the *ars* of memory to its peak.

---

39 In fact, the floating gap itself seems to perform no particular function except to account for the time span between the two modes of memory proposed by Jan Assmann.

The *ars* of memory today is of course closely related to digital renderings of memories, as digital storage enables a bit-by-bit encoding that provides exact reproductions.[40]

In contrast to the exact reproduction of stored contents aimed at by *ars* approaches to memory, the *vis* aspect focuses on the reconstructive nature of memory. *Vis* thus designates the 'process of remembering' instead of the 'method of storage' (A. Assmann 1999, 29). This conception of course relies on Halbwachs's understanding of memory as re-membered from a present situation. As such, memory as *vis* conceives of "Gedächtnis nicht als schützender Behälter [i.e. *ars*], sondern als eine immanente Kraft, als eine Energie mit eigener Gesetzlichkeit." (Ibid.) While *ars* represents the technical aspects of memory – as part of the traditional rhetorical process of "inventio, dispositio, elocutio, *memoria*, actio" (A. Assmann 1999, 30; emphasis added) or modern storage-and-retrieval systems, for instance –, *vis* underlines the psychological aspects. It should be self-evident that the *vis* aspect of memory and its accentuation of creative processes, (re-)constructive qualities and acts of performance is taken as the basis for the literary analyses of this study. The *vis* variety of memory has also clearly been the basis of Halbwachs's theoretical conception, as he states: "Reproduzieren ist aber nicht Wiederfinden, es bedeutet vielmehr Rekonstruieren." (Halbwachs 1966, 136)

Another important distinction put forward by Aleida Assmann aims to resolve the difficulties posed by Halbwachs's polar opposition between historical and collective memory and the ensuing one-lifetime limit of collective memory. It has become a commonplace scholarly position to acknowledge the inevitable subjectivity of historiography and its contribution to a *construction* of history (cf. e.g. A. Assmann 1999, 133f.). Halbwachs's idealized notion of a disinterested, objective historiography which attributes equal importance to all events (cf. Halbwachs 1967, 66ff.) can hardly be upheld. Jan Assmann conceives of cultural and communicative memory – placing a floating gap between the two – and thus restructures collective memory from a temporal, agent and media perspective: cultural memory as based on the distant past, specialists as carriers and a high degree of objectification; communicative memory as based on eyewitness experiences, universal carriers and enshrined not in objectifications but in everyday communication. The distinction made by Aleida Assmann, in contrast, focuses mainly on the aspect of content, its qualitative characteristics and functional implications, separating two modes of perspective: functional and storage memory (*Funktionsgedächtnis* and *Speichergedächtnis*). The distinction between functional and storage memory shares a key element with Halbwachs's division between historical and collective memory, viz. the difference between 'living' and 'dead' memories (cf. Halbwachs 1967, 66ff.) – or, in Assmann's terminology, 'inhabited' vs. 'uninhabited' memory (cf. A. Assmann, 134). Inhabited or functional memory is defined as 'relating to groups; selective; linked to norms; oriented towards the future' (A. Assmann 1999, 134), while uninhabited or storage

---

40 The connection of memory as *ars* and digital storage only establishes the encoding and faithful retrieval as an analogy to the 'ideal' storage of a speech as conceived of by e.g. Cicero. It does not account for the perception of information, which of course involves processes of interpretation highly influenced by cognitive schemata, individual and social conditions. *Ars* thus emphasizes the technical, procedural side of memory (cf. A. Assmann 1999, 27f.).

memory tends towards stasis; the storage memory collects those items that are of no vital importance for a group. The recollections kept in the (mode of) functional memory constitute meaning and orientation, whereas the storage memory contains an incoherent, nebulous mass of mementos.

Elements deposited in the storage memory may, however, be reactivated as they reacquire significance for the group, thus shifting these elements (back) to the functional memory: "Das Speichergedächtnis kann als ein Reservoir zukünftiger Funktionsgedächtnisse gesehen werden." (A. Assmann 1999, 40) Though the terminology employed by Assmann suggests the notion of two distinct vessels from which elements are transported back and forth, she rather defines the two modes of memory as a question of perspective: functional memory accordingly serves as a foreground, while storage memory serves as a background from which elements may be brought to the fore (or vice versa), thus effecting changes in the cultural memory (cf. Erll 2003, 175; Neumann 2005, 89). Assmann thus accounts for a bidirectional change – from inhabited to uninhabited or the other way around – which Halbwachs did not conceptualize. If the collective memory in his conception changes, it is unidirectional: by fossilization or withering away, collective memories are converted into historical memories and as such become neutralized and inaccessible for identity formation. Assmann's theory thus allows for memories to be reactivated for processes of identity construction, which of course is a distinct advantage in terms of usability in connection with conceptions of agenda-setting in identity designs.

As *Table 1: Halbwachs, J. Assmann, A. Assmann in comparison* (p. 37) demonstrates, the conceptions presented so far do not differ in their fundamental assumptions, but do so in various critical aspects. Both Halbwachs's and Jan Assmann's models define the carriers, the degree of objectification, the media, the function, the time frame, and the content of collective memory. Originally devised as a differentiation of Halbwachs's notion of collective memory, Jan Assmann's distinction between communicative and cultural memory, however, does not fully comply with Halbwachs's concept of collective memory. If communicative and cultural memory were to be considered subcategories of collective memory (as originally devised), both subcategories would – according to basic tenets of logic – have to fit the criteria of collective memory. In fact, though, communicative memory tends to fit Halbwachs's standards, while cultural memory (the mode that encapsulates one of collective memory's most decisive characteristics: serving as the basis of identity formation) differs in carrier, objectification, media, and time frame. Communicative memory in fact shares most features with Halbwachs's collective memory, but differs in function and the selectivity of contents. Jan Assmann's conception can thus only be read as an alternative, not a coherently compatible model. Aleida Assmann's division between functional and storage memory, however, is adjustable – or: imprecise – enough to be accommodated by both models, as its main achievement is not an all-encompassing model of collective memory but a change of perspective: to see collective memory from the viewpoint of selectivity and relevance rather than based on more formal criteria such as objectification or time frame. As such, it is an addition rather than a general full-scale model. Therefore, Aleida Assmann is also able to incorporate Jan

Assmann's model into her own conceptions (cf. e.g. A. Assmann 2006, 51ff.). The comparison visualized in *Table 1* should thus not be read as a grid contrasting opposing views; instead, it indicates the origins of the respective notions.

	Halbwachs		Jan Assmann		Aleida Assmann	
	collective memory	historical memory	communicative memory	cultural memory	functional memory	storage memory
carriers	clearly defined group; no specialists	unspecific; potentially specialists (historians)	clearly defined group; no specialists	specialists	clearly defined group	unspecific
objectification	impossible	necessary	unnecessary	necessary; rigid	unspecific	unspecific
media	orality	diverse (mainly writing)	orality	diverse	diverse	diverse
function	identity construction	unspecific	unspecific	identity construction	identity construction	repository, reservoir
time frame	< 80-100 years; bridges past, present, future	> 80-100 years; strictly separates past from present	< 80 years	distant past	unspecific	unspecific
			separated by floating gap			
content	selective: everything 'of interest' for the group; 'living memory'	non-selective; 'dead memory'	everyday history	(founding) myths, key memories (*Erinnerungsfiguren*)	selective: everything of salience for the group; 'inhabited memory'	non-selective; 'uninhabited memory'

Table 1: Halbwachs, J. Assmann, A. Assmann in comparison

2.2.4. Further models for literary studies

Current models of collective memory theory employed in literary analyses have adopted and adapted both the basic assumptions of Halbwachs (such as the social framing of memory, the externalization of memories, the reconstructive character of both the en- and decoding of recollections, and the assumption of collective memory as the basis for processes of identity formation) and the tenets put forward by Aleida and Jan Assmann. Jan Assmann's modifications concerning the media transmission of memories and the inclusion of founding myths into processes of identity construction as well as Aleida Assmann's conceptualization of changes in the collective memory of a group via the permeability of functional and storage memory are particularly salient aspects of modification. Further adjustments have been made to these primary models to accommodate further aspects of literary studies, such as narratology, semiotics, or new approaches to cultural studies.[41]

The field of media studies has provided new insights into the processes of collective memory transmission. In this context, new questions have arisen concerning the nature of literature a) *as,* b) *as vessel of,* or c) *as location of* memory. Is literature a carrier of memories? A reflection? A performance? An origin? As for the approach taken in this study, cf. the next section (p. 39).

One of the most recent models employing collective memory as a tool for literary analyses has been developed by Birgit Neumann. Neumann's approach is characterized by its rootedness in cultural studies as well as a focus on narratology and cultural semiotics. Neumann labels her concept 'integrative model' (Neumann 2005, 93) and assigns three main goals to it: to interlock individual and collective mechanisms of memory, to underline the importance of narration for memory processes, and to emphasize the heterogeneity of identity and memory structures (cf. ibid.). While Neumann is deeply indebted to the theories of Aleida and Jan Assmann, her terminology as well as parts of her model slightly diverge from the established conceptions. Neumann's use of the term 'cultural memory' differs from Jan Assmann's. It is, however, akin to Aleida Assmann's notion of storage memory – though Aleida Assmann's model conceives of storage memory as obsolete knowledge (with a potential to be reactivated into the functional mode of memory), while Neumann's cultural memory is a potential accumulated or overall knowledge (cf. Neumann 2005, 95). The kinship, however, is striking, as neither Neumann's cultural nor Assmann's storage memory is relevant to identity-formation processes – the first one because it stores currently irrelevant memories, the latter one because it only exists as an abstract potential. In Neumann's conception, groups select from the abstract, but medially objectified, repository of cultural memory and reconstruct according to their 'culture-specific schemata'[42] those items that inform their collective memory.[43] A 'memory culture' is thus constituted by the acts performed and the media selected by a specific group. The reconstruction according to the group's current needs of meaning assignation is interpreted as a performative act which, as the equivalent and synonym of collective remembering, is the basis for collective identity constructions (cf. Neumann 2005, 96).

---

41 Cf. for instance Erll 2003, 176f.

42 These derive from the cultural memory itself: "Aus dem kulturellen Gedächtnis leiten sich also spezifische bzw. kulturspezifische Schemata ab…" (ibid.).

43 Although Neumann provides extensive explications, it nevertheless remains unclear how the abstract, potential repository of the cultural memory should generate culture-specific schemata which in turn determine the ways in which a collective selects and reconstructs memories from the cultural memory.

Although Neumann discusses the classics of collective memory theory *in extenso*, the central element of Neumann's study is the conception of a novel genre of Canadian (memory) fiction: "*Fictions of memory*" (cf. ibid., part. 156-237) are characterized by an explicitly metamnemonic approach and distinct narratological strategies. Neumann subdivides the *fictions of memory* into four categories – a fifth class, the 'metamnemonic novel', remains rudimentary as its proponents are not numerous enough to inform a thorough discussion – distinguished by three main criteria which might be simplified as follows: Is memory related to and reflected on from the (position of the) present? Is the narrative voice a personal or a communal/authoritative one? Is there one consistent perspective or are there several? (Cf. Neumann 2005, 208ff.) As can be deduced from this short summary, Neumann's study is largely concerned with the formal narrative aspects of what she calls *fictions of memory*. Yet her modifications to the general conception of collective memory seem to add more uncertainties to the Assmanns' model than they resolve. One of the study's indisputable merits, however, lies in a comprehensive theoretical treatment of the subject area of 'literature as memory' (cf. ibid., part. 119-155).[44]

2.3. Collective Memory: The Working Model

Predictably, the model that will be adopted as an analytical tool in this study is based on the core assumptions of Maurice Halbwachs and includes decisive elements from Aleida and Jan Assmann's conceptions.

The basic suppositions common to most theoretical constructs in the field of collective memory will also underlie the working model presented here: the constructiveness of memory is one of these basic assumptions. Welzer's recursive mode of recollection seems to be the most advanced conceptualization of the reconstructive nature of memories (a memory is shaped by the item that is remembered as well as by the recollection of its recollection; layers of influences are thus added upon each reconstruction like skins of an onion attached to a memory by each decoding and re-encoding; cf. Markowitsch/Welzer 2005, Welzer 2001 and 2008; also cf. Halbwachs 1967, 55f.). In the same vein, I will concentrate on memory as *vis*, not as *ars*, as the *vis* variety allows for an analysis of questions of identity, whereas the *ars* variety is more concerned with the faithful reproduction of recollections, e.g. in rhetoric. The *ars* aspect of memory consequently considers the constructiveness of memory to be an obstacle, while the *vis* aspect relies on the malleable nature of memory: in order to adapt to current needs of meaning assignation and identity formation, memories necessitate modifications based on the current situation of an individual or a group.

---

44   For my own study, it is of course interesting to note that Neumann explicitly deals with *Canadian* fiction (though only marginally with African-Canadian literature: André Alexis' *Childhood* is the only Black Canadian work discussed; cf. 2005, 344-345), also referring to concepts of multiculturalism and competing memory versions (cf. ibid., 104-118).

The working model is also informed by additional assumptions not shared by all theorists. It further includes foci that not all models follow. Collective memory, for instance, will be in the center of attention, as opposed to collected memory (cf. Olick 1999). This might sound trivial at first, yet the implications for the literary analyses are profound. While collected memory describes the socially pre- and postformed memories of an individual, collective memory is concerned with the supra-individual practices of remembrance, the cultural objectifications and social institutionalizations.[45] Consequently, the discussion of collected memory centers around individual autobiographical elements in literature, whereas collective memory deals with group phenomena, elements that Neumann calls 'sociobiographical' in her typology of *fictions of memory* (Neumann 2005, 229ff.). Needless to say, elements of individual memory and identity constructions will be included in the literary analyses offered here, yet the prima-ry focus is indeed on the sociobiographical elements and the construction of *collective* memory and identity. It will be assumed that groups – analogous to individuals – tend toward a construction of a 'usable past' (cf. Zamora 1997). Thus, the processes of selection and mod-ification that underlie the recollection of a group profess a predisposition toward the establish-ing of coherent, meaningful sociobiographies – taking into account, of course, the varying standards of 'coherent' and 'meaningful', which might lead to a constant synchronic and dia-chronic re-negotiation of the currently sanctioned collective memories.

In these processes, the concept of veridicality often prevails over notions of accuracy: groups do not necessarily aim to reconstruct their memories as accurately as possible; instead, they disfigure and reconfigure the items of recollection to fit their current needs, thus re-*creating*, not merely repeating certain memories. In terms of accuracy, these memories might consequently be considered 'false' (cf. the "false memory debate" in the USA; concisely summarized by A. Assmann 1999, 266ff.), yet they do not lack *truth*, as they are *true* for the group which reconstructs them. Thus, contrafactual memories might by standards of accuracy be considered idiosyncratic, yet by standards of (collective) truth they are veridical. This no-tion of course carries particular potential for literary analyses, which might thus forego the assessment of factual accuracy and turn towards the implications of (re-)constructed and (re-)configured memories.[46] As will be discussed in chapter 4.1., "Lawrence Hill's Explora-

---

45   As discussed before, Maurice Halbwachs does not clearly and coherently distinguish these two aspects. The distinction between memories *influenced* by a group (consequently, as Halbwachs himself shows, *all* memories except – as he claims – dreams) and memories *selected and shared* by a group could thus be considered the working model's major deviation from Halbwachs's basic assumptions.

46   There is, however, a (permeable) limit to the concept of veridicality. Pure confabulation could scarcely be considered a modification of an actual, pre-existing memory. Nevertheless, there can hardly be a theoretical, comprehensive definition of the limits of 'truth' as defined by a group. The process of selection might serve as an example here: We have witnessed cases of utter denial – the opposite of inclusion, i.e. the conscious or unconscious act of non-selection – of historical facts in a collective memory (cf. the denial of an involvement in or knowledge of the holocaust by large groups of people in post-war Germany – a memory still consciously disavowed internation-ally by contemporary anti-Semites –, the Spanish accord to condone Franco's reign for the sake of national reconciliation, or the denial of the Turkish genocide in Armenia). Are these processes of

tions in Faction", in detail, the treatment of historical 'facts' has been challenged by literary modes such as historiographic metafiction. If, then, Lawrence Hill's fiction – or, indeed, the majority of African-Canadian literature – opts for a 'truthful' rendition of history which is not only veridical but largely *accurate*, this phenomenon is particularly noteworthy. The issue that arises is not simply a matter of comparing historical writing with the collective memories presented in literary accounts, aiming at a verification or falsification of the accuracy of the narratives ('the literary account is correct or incorrect'). Rather, it is the objective to uncover the reasons *why* Hill – and others – do not take greater liberties with the historical material they represent as well as determining the motives and implications of possible modifications ('how and why does the literary account differ from historical memory and what are the – intended – effects?'). It should be obvious, then, that I will not primarily be dealing with un-inhabited, historical memory in the Halbwachsean sense, yet it will serve as an important backdrop and a foil for comparisons. Without the historical accounts to check the given oeuvre's historical accuracy, much of the (intended) impetus of the literary writing would necessarily remain undisclosed.

Other key aspects of the analytical tool employed here are derived from Aleida and Jan Assmann's theories. I will loosely follow Jan Assmann's general approach, yet I will decisively include aspects explicated by Aleida Assmann; furthermore, my terminology will slightly differ. Two major modifications are necessitated by the literary genre and cultural group that will be focused on in the analytical section: First, a shift in time dimensions must be implemented. As Jan Assmann based his approach on ancient civilizations, I will have to remodel his timeframe. Though African-Canadian founding myths may and do include *ancient* myths (i.e. African ones), they also – and I will argue: primarily – include memories of the founding of an African-*Canadian* presence, thus experiences as recent as two or three hundred years ago, among them most saliently the complex memory of slavery and its aftermath. Thus, the floating gap between cultural and communicative memory must be drastically contracted, up to the point of being collapsed altogether.

Considering the specifics of the temporal setting, the given groups and the literature dealt with, it is in fact almost impossible to distinguish coherently between communicative and cultural memory *à la* Jan Assmann. Consequently, it seems inappropriate to employ the term 'cultural memory' instead of 'collective memory', even though I will draw on a number of characteristics identified by Jan Assmann to describe cultural memory. In Assmann's approach, communicative memory, based on oral transmission and limited to a timeframe of under 80 years, is shared by a clearly defined group but requires no specialists, as it collects, keeps and transmits a group's everyday experiences. Cultural memory, in contrast, requires

---

repression historically inaccurate? Certainly so. But are they untruthful for the group concerned? My inclination here would be to suggest that they are untruthful and thus non-veridical, as they are based on pure imagination ('those genocides did not happen') rather than a modification of an actual experience. Consequently, I will not subscribe to radical constructivist claims here, even though these claims may be theoretically well-founded. It should have become clear, however, that the limits of veridicality are permeable and must by necessity partly remain subject to case and/or individual judgment.

specialists for its storage and transmission; it necessitates rigid objectification but allows for a wide range of media; most importantly, its contents relate to a (distant) past, i.e. (founding) myths and key memories (*Erinnerungsfiguren*). These key memories function as bridges between past, present, and future and are – as collective memories in general – reconstructed in the present according to current needs of meaning assignation and identity formation. Cultural memories are thus the salient element in identity constructions. I will integrate these characteristics into my usage of *collective* memory, but hasten to emphasize that the 'distant' past Assmann conceives of is so close as to border on communicative memory. Accordingly, I will employ large parts of Assmann's conception of cultural memory in my own model of collective memory, stripping, however, the concept of its clear opposition to communicative memory.

This necessitates the second modification, which is of a more general nature: as the distinction between cultural and communicative memory will perforce become a subordinate one, the most decisive categorization will be based on Aleida Assmann's perspective differentiation between functional and storage memory. For the given purposes, Jan Assmann's theory relies too heavily on homogeneous memory cultures and largely disregards the implications of heterogeneous (post-)modern societies and competing versions of collective memory. Aleida Assmann's notions provide a model more apt to capture the dynamics involved in memory negotiations and the pitting of minority memories against hegemonic ones. The constant shifting of (sets of) memories from the storage to the functional memory and back again perfectly lends itself to an analysis of discourses defining – or attempting to define – processes of identity construction. Thus, the conscious efforts to bring certain memories to the foreground are a key element of the following literary analyses. What then arises are differential versions of the functional memory, which can be labeled 'minority memory'[47] on the one hand and 'hegemonic', 'mainstream' or 'dominant' memory on the other.

The storage memory hence includes those items that are of no vital, identity-forming importance for a particular group. Recollections from the storage memory can, however, be reactivated and brought to the foreground, viz. the functional memory. This process is determined by the group's current situation and its current needs. Accordingly, it is a process that is highly selective and – as has been emphasized before – highly constructive. Thus, a group 'assembles' and 'forges' the memories it builds its identity on.[48] Likewise, it can 'deselect'

---

47 The term 'counter-memory' could be employed here (in fact, it is occasionally used in the course of my analysis). It is not based, however, on the Foucaltean conception (cf. Foucault 1980, particularly "Nietzsche, Genealogy, History"; also cf. Misztal 2003, 63f.), though a number of its features, such as the closeness to literature or the opposition to dominant history/ideology are implied here as well.

48 While the group itself appears to be the sole agent in this process, it must be added that we are dealing with mechanisms of interdependence here. As we ask questions of 'do memories constitute a group?' or 'does a group construct its own memories at will?', we are faced with intricate causal relations. Chicken or egg – which was first? This principal question may, for the time being, be circumvented by a leap into the concrete subject matter which is constituted by the two competing strands of memory in question: hegemonic Canadian collective memory and minority

certain memories by either not incorporating them into the functional memory in the first place or by opting to 'forget' them in order to erase their impact. Memories can thus be relegated to the back benches of history books once a group considers them obsolete or obstructive in current identity formation processes. As can be deduced from *Illustration 1: Working model* (p. 45), minority memory and hegemonic or mainstream memory do not represent entirely separated entities. They share a certain amount of memories both groups of carriers employ for their self-identification. Possibly, then, as is the case with African-Canadian writers, a minority group may work towards an extended insertion of memories into the mainstream memory which have until then been deselected in hegemonic constructions. It may thus be an aim of any minority memory group to reconcile minority and dominant memories (the same of course holds true for mainstream constructions, which might be intent on assimilating counter-hegemonic constructions – and often are).

In order to come to terms with competing memory constructions, their antagonisms and the ensuing cultural, social and political agenda-setting the literary negotiations of memory and identity are part of, the working model must necessarily subscribe to Halbwachs's notion of a collective memory that is dynamic and particular in its distribution. It is this conception that allows for conflicts between different memory versions – in contrast to Pierre Nora's theory, for instance, which emphasizes a nationally unified memory aided by its *lieux de mémoire* (cf. Nora 1996): Nora's perceived lack of competing memory versions of course neglects the possibility of group antagonisms over hegemonic definitions of collective memory (cf. e.g. Lenger 2005). As will be demonstrated in the literary analyses, this view cannot be fruitfully employed as an analytical approach to African-Canadian literature. Where Nora's theory disqualifies collective memory as the basis for stable identities of subgroups after a possible withering away of an original, national collective memory, both Halbwachs and recent theorists have convincingly argued that collective memory is indeed a significant element of group cohesion and identity formation processes below the level of the nation-state as well (cf. for instance Halbwachs 1967, 35 and 74; Straub 1998, 100) – a view also implemented in the theoretical working model of this study.

While a number of analyses are almost exclusively concerned with the structural – i.e. narratological or stylistic – aspects of collective memory in literature (cf. e.g. Neumann 2005), this study will also concentrate on key memories as literary *topoi*. In compliance with the accentuation of the storage-*vs.*-functional-memory division, content will play a more prominent role than form: the analysis of certain key memories (among them notably the

African-Canadian collective memory. Both groups are initially not primarily constituted by the selection of memories, but by factors largely political, geographical, or even essentialist, thus external to memory: nation-state and race. If, however, race is conceived of as a construct – and it is –, then race is defined as a set of shared experiences, consequently a set of shared memories. The experiences that constitute the group of African-Canadians, in turn, are based largely on ascription, not on voluntary selection. The processes in question, then, do not primarily center around the *coming into being* of this group but on the group's current (self-) identification and its dealing with the given situation. Consequently, the *status quo*, the existence of partly competing memory versions, is the main area of interest here rather than the genesis of groups per se.

memory of slavery and the accompanying sub- and tributary memories such as the continuing disillusionment of being denied a 'Promised Land') will constitute the core of this study. The contents of the functional memory constituted and conveyed by Lawrence Hill and much of African-Canadian literature, the modes of selection, reconstruction and transmission as well as the social and political processes of memory and identity negotiations will thus be given prevalence over the examination of narrative structures or typological questions alone. Questions of narratology and literary classification, for instance discussions of Lawrence Hill's fiction in relation to the slave narrative or historiographic metafiction, still receive ample space; they are, however, no end in itself but serve to explain why and in what ways certain key memories are employed. As such, the approach taken here mirrors Hill's writing in privileging content over form.

In conclusion, the conception of collective memory employed as an analytical tool in the literary studies presented in this paper relies heavily on the theories of Maurice Halbwachs as well as its modifications and amendments by Aleida and Jan Assmann. It emphasizes (recursive) processes of selection and reconstruction, acknowledges a tendency towards the construction of a 'usable past', distinguishes between collective and collected memory (focusing on the former), centrally employs the perspective distinction between functional and storage memory, subscribes to the influence of collective memory on identity formation, emphasizes the capability of key memories to bridge past, present, and future, accounts for the possibility and implications of media transmission of memories, considers key memories to be the central substantiation of collective memory in literature, places more importance on the *vis* than on the *ars* of memory, and is geared toward a description of competing memory and identity versions.

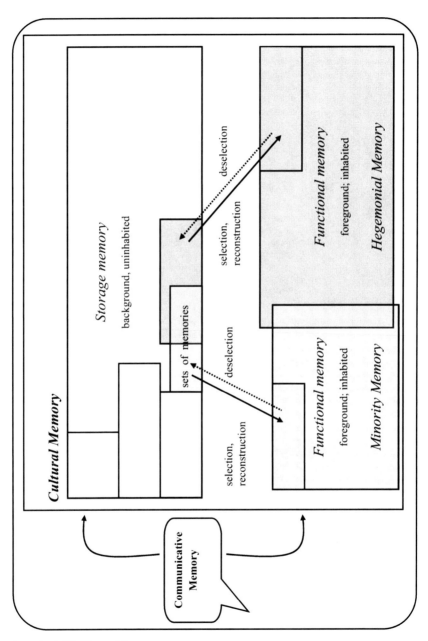

Illustration 1: Working model

3. The Black Presence in Canada

> African Nova Scotians are one of the four charter peoples of Nova Scotia whose presence and contribution range from the seventeenth century to the twenty-first century. Alongside the Aboriginal peoples, the Acadians, and the British, the story of African Nova Scotians is the story of their arrival, settlement, dispersion, adjustment, trials and tribulations, and their contribution to family, community, colony, province, and nation. (Pachai/Bishop 2006, v)

Blacks have played a formative role in the history of Canada and the Maritimes. Particularly in Nova Scotia, and to lesser degrees in New Brunswick and on Prince Edward Island (in this order), they have left their imprint of a legacy of over 400 years. Mathieu da Costa, a member of a French expedition landing in Port Royal, Nova Scotia, in 1604 and possibly a former Portuguese slave, is considered to be the first Black person in the Maritimes.[49] It is an aim of African-Canadian writers to – at last – bring to the fore this longstanding, but often neglected, presence.[50]

Historical research on Black Canada has, on the whole, been comparatively scarce, though some of it dates back to the late 19th and very early 20th century (e.g. T. Watson Smith's "The Slave in Canada", 1899, Allen Jack's "The Loyalists and Slavery in New Brunswick", 1898-9, or W. O. Raymond's "The Negro in New Brunswick", 1903). Nowadays, scholars such as James W. St. Walker, Robin Winks or Bridglal Pachai have extensively researched the history of African-Canadians. While Walker's *A History of Blacks in Canada*

---

49 Cf. the useful work by Whitfield (2006; here: 10ff.); Knutson focuses on George Elliott Clarke but also comments on da Costa (2007a, 33f.); also cf. Clarke 2002a, 18, and Petty 2008, 266, with very brief remarks.

50 As this chapter provides the background for the two novels dealt with *in extenso* in this study, it focuses on three aspects: first, the history of slavery in Canada, as this is one of African-Canadian literature's key memories. Second, it deals with the history of Blacks in the Maritimes, particularly Nova Scotia, and thus primarily with Black Loyalists / refugees (this establishes the historical context for Lawrence Hill's *The Book of Negroes*). The third focus is on the Underground Railroad and fugitive slaves, whose experiences are reflected in Hill's *Any Known Blood*.

and Winks's *The Blacks in Canada* have become the standard reference works of Black Canadian historical research, Pachai concentrates mostly on the local history/ies, i.e. the Black presence in Nova Scotia from 1604 to the present, also incorporating to a large extend the dealings and activities of the Black communities and its leading figures of the last forty years (cf. for instance *Peoples of the Maritimes: Blacks*, 1997, or *Images of Our Past: Historic Black Nova Scotia*, together with Henry Bishop, 2006). Walker's 1976 *The Black Loyalists* has been reprinted in a 1992 edition and serves as the most comprehensive guide to the Black presence in the Maritimes between 1783 and 1870. Since the 1960s, and particularly since the incorporation of the Black Cultural Society in 1977 and the subsequent establishing of the Black Cultural Centre five years later (cf. Pachai/Bishop 2006, 85f.), much effort has been put into the research of a regional or even local Black Maritime history.

On the general difficulties of conducting research on African-Canadian history, Walker noted back in 1982:

> [Research on Black history in scientific publications] was an exercise in futility, for it quickly became apparent that Canadian historical writing almost completely ignores the fact that there is a black community here with a 350-year long history. (Walker 1982, 3)

Of course, in 1982, Winks's *The Blacks in Canada* had already been published in a first edition by Yale University Press (1971), so there was at least *one* standard volume on the history of African-Canadians available at the time. Walker consequently finds high praise for Winks's work, calling it an "indispensable reference" and "the best book" on the subject (Walker 1982, 14). Nonetheless, he also finds fault with Winks's approach, since in his opinion, "black pride and accomplishments receive less attention" (ibid.), a comment that already hints at the emotions and social/political ambitions with which the issue of Black Canadian history is fraught.[51] Winks, on the other hand, in his preface to the 1997 edition, calls Walker the "most formidable critic" (Winks 1997, xvii) of his own utterly detailed 550-page volume.

These two works aside, however, it becomes clear that large-scale research on the subject is less than numerous. Other publications focusing on Black Canadian history, such as Colin A. Thomson's *Blacks in Deep Snow* (1979), or the more recent, student-focused *Towards Freedom* by Ken Alexander and Avis Glaze (1996) have appeared after Winks's seminal work, as have a number of small-scale studies. Yet, the main point of critique remains the lack of a critical and scholarly discussion of Black Canadian issues within *mainstream* history, such as taught in schools. In concurrence with African-Canadian fiction writers, Walker alleges that official historiography perpetuates a lopsided and biased view of the Black Canadian experience: "A student using such [mainstream history] books could not help but believe that Canada's only relationship with slavery was as a haven for American runaways." (Walker 1982, 3) It is a goal not only of (Black) historical research but also of African-Canadian literature to correct this misconception.

---

51 African-Canadian author and scholar George Elliott Clarke repeatedly finds fault with Winks's approach as well; cf. for instance his interview with Herb Wyilie (Clarke 2007, 135f.).

Throughout the relevant literature, four distinct groups of Black newcomers to the Eastern shores of Canada prior to the 20th century are recognized: slaves, Loyalists, Maroons, and fugitives/refugees. The Maroons, a patch of ostracized resistance fighters from Jamaica, spent only half a decade in Canada and have thus left a minor imprint, though their pride and defiance are well-remembered (cf. Pachai 1997, 21f. and 2006, 13f.). Black Loyalists as well as Black refugees and fugitives have to some degree been incorporated into mainstream Canadian historiography – though not as subjects of discrimination and sufferers of unnecessary hardships, but as beneficiaries from the safe haven that Canada ostensibly represented to slaves from the 'immoral' United States during the times of slavery. Yet, even those Blacks who came to the True North to become free men and women (and could thus be implemented into Canadian historiography as emblems of Canadian moral superiority) have, on the whole, been marginalized in historical accounts. *Unfree* Blacks have been virtually eliminated from the history books. Contrary to popular belief, however, slavery officially existed in Canada between at least 1628 and 1834, a two-hundred year stretch of institutionalized oppression that has largely been blanked out (cf. Winks 1997, 471f.).

3.1. Slaves and Loyalists

3.1.1. Slavery in New France

What, then, *is* Canada's relationship with slavery, what *has* been blanked out? It begins with a young Black boy from Madagascar who was brought to New France in 1628 (cf. Walker 1982, 19f.; Winks 1997, 1f.). He was sold to a Québec resident and later on given the name of Olivier Le Jeune. However, he "was neither the first slave nor the first Negro in New France, but he was the first of whom there is any adequate record." (Winks 1997, 1) Native slaves, called *panis*, and other Blacks had been there before, and the First Nations regularly took slaves while raiding enemy tribes – yet, no official records exist of slaves prior to 1628. In the early years of the new colony, slavery existed only to a very limited extent, because the European colonizers, whose main source of income was the fur trade, simply required no slaves at the time. Consequently, there was no formalized legislation concerning the slaves, whether *panis* or Black (cf. Winks 1997, 3). The French *Code Noir* was loosely followed, but mainly, jurisdiction followed the social reality: slaves were the property of their masters, and they were treated by the law as such.

After the 1670s, however, the economy in New France became more diversified, with an increasing demand in unskilled laborers for mining, fishing etc. Still, the majority of Black slaves worked as domestic servants, and occasionally as field hands, in wealthy households. In 1709, the increased number of slaves required explicit legislation. This need arose mainly from the fact that the process of setting slaves free had created confusion; since no regulations existed, masters set their slaves free at will – which of course led to a wave of slaves claiming their freedom without their masters' actual consent. Thus, in 1709, a French *ordonnance* declared Blacks and *panis* who were 'legally purchased' to be the property of their owners. In 1736, another *ordonnance* regulated the paperwork to be completed if a slave was indeed set free (cf. Winks 1997, 6). Still, the number of slaves was comparatively small, with only a fraction working in the fields. In 1759, 1,132 of a total of 3,604 slaves on record were Blacks. Only 192 of these Black slaves worked in the fields; their main occupation was still as domestic servants (cf. Winks 1997, 9f.).

As the Black slaves thus had a close connection to the households they worked for, and as the Roman Catholic church tended to remind slave-owners of their moral obligations,[52] "these slaves of New France, and especially the Negro slaves, seem not to have been treated badly." (ibid., 10) Winks also notes that although slavery in New France might have been a milder form than in the United States (to be), nonetheless people were considered chattel, which of course had both root and effect in a notion of White superiority:

> If slavery in New France was among the most benevolent expressions of the institution in North America, nonetheless it was slavery, with accompanying potentialities toward the dominance of one man, and of one race, over another. (Winks 1997, 17)

Already, the first traces of 'forgetting' slavery appeared both in common people's attitudes and historical writing:

> Soon writers were maintaining that there had been no slavery in New France at all, despite the historical evidence [...], and a new popularly held assumption joined those about climate and cotton to obscure any national memory of French slavery. (Winks 1997, 19)

The assumptions "about climate and cotton" Winks refers to was the belief that slavery could never have existed in Canada because a) Blacks could never have endured the Northern cold, being used to warmer climates, and b) Black slaves, due to their limited skills and intellectual capabilities, could only have performed the task of cotton-picking, and there never was any extensive cotton industry in Canada. Both assumptions of course are absurd, but they very graphically demonstrate the urge to deny that slavery had indeed existed in the upper half of North America. Thus, even though slavery was limited in scope, legal foundation, and economic necessity in New France, notions of Black inferiority closely connected to the institution of slavery can be traced back as far as the earliest settlements north of the 49th parallel.[53]

---

52 Though it rarely spoke out against slavery as an institution, since "slavery was a social reality, and as such, the church accepted it." (Winks 1997, 13)

53 Winks, however, argues that racial prejudice evolved separately from the stigma of slavery; rather, he claims that notions of Black inferiority existed before slavery and not because of slavery (cf. Winks 1997, 20f.). Yet even the assumption of associating Blacks with a limited scope of menial tasks typical of slaves inextricably links an alleged Black inferiority to the institution of slavery, because Blacks were regarded as unfit for any life outside of the state of bondage. Pachai claims: "[...] the legacy of slavery affected race relations in Nova Scotia for centuries, as blacks suffered negative stereotyping and dehumanization in the eyes of whites." (Pachai/Bishop 2006, 8)

3.1.2. Slavery in British North America

Slavery was even less prevalent in the British parts of today's Canada at that time, but in 1767, four years after the French had ceded their mainland colonies in North America to the British in the treaty of Paris, more than 100 out of a total of 3,000 Nova Scotians were slaves[54] (cf. Walker 1982, 19). A 1767 survey indicates that in Nova Scotia, the Black minority was twice as numerous as the Irish (cf. Pachai/Bishop 2006, 2). Between 1763 and 1790, the British formalized slave legislation to guarantee property rights of slave owners, leading to a peak of Black slavery in the Maritimes (cf. Pachai 1997, 9). "In effect, slavery continued under the British as under the French." (Winks 1997, 26). The difference, however, lay in the number of slaves: "It was only with the arrival of the Loyalists, however, that slavery assumed any numerical significance in the province." (Walker 1999, 40) As white slave-owners loyal to the British Crown moved north during and after the American War of Independence, the number of slaves in British North America increased to approximately 2,500 at the close of the 18th century (cf. Walker 1982, 22). The largest contingent arrived in 1883-84, thus in the final phase and the immediate aftermath of the war (cf. Pachai/Bishop 2006, 1).

Within a decade after independence, approximately 2,800 free and 1,200 enslaved Blacks came to Canada in the course of the Loyalist exodus (cf. Pachai 1997, 11), resulting in the spreading of slaves throughout the Maritime provinces,[55] the strengthening of pro-slavery activists (namely the White loyalist slave-owners), the supersession of *panis* slaves by Black slaves, and the diversification of tasks done by Blacks because many of the slave-owners brought better-skilled slaves with them while leaving low-skilled slaves behind (cf. Walker 1982, 20f.; Winks 1997, 28f.). Furthermore, as freed slaves and free Blacks also moved north, greater numbers of free and unfree Blacks now lived side by side in British North America.[56] In 1784, the Black community made up 10 per cent of Nova Scotia's total population, most of them free Black Loyalists who had recently arrived in the Maritimes (cf. Pachai/Bishop 2006, 2).

---

54 Pachai quotes the same number of Blacks based on a return by the British lieutenant-governor, but does not specify the Blacks as slaves; furthermore, he establishes the total population at over 13,000 (cf. Pachai 1997, 7). He also concludes that African-Canadians should consequently be considered one of the "four charter peoples" of Maritime Canada: "These returns [by British officials in Nova Scotia in the 1760s] show that Blacks have lived permanently in most of the Maritimes for some three hundred years. This fact alone qualifies them for inclusion among the first four charter peoples in this region, alongside the Aboriginals, French and English. The return also emphasize that among the first Blacks in the Maritimes, there were both free persons and slaves." (Pachai 1997, 8)

55 "The sale of slaves by public auction was common in Nova Scotia in the eighteenth century. There is evidence also of the existence of slavery in New Brunswick from 1767 and in Prince Edward Island since the 1780s." (Pachai 1997, 11)

56 At times, it has been difficult to distinguish between 'free' and 'unfree' persons as Blacks were often declared "servants" instead of "slaves". In fact, however, their position often equaled the state of slavery, so "[t]hese terms were used interchangeably and the distinction between them was often confusing." (Pachai 1997, 12; also cf. Walker 1999, 40)

3.1.3. *Loyalists*

The British had offered emancipation to all slaves who decided to quit their rebel masters and fight on their side in the War of Independence. This offer was later on extended to all slaves who would run away from their rebel owners, no matter if they joined the British military or not. By order of the Governor General, free grants of land were to be attributed to these runaways in Northern British America. Though some slaves were sold to the West Indies by greedy British officers (cf. Winks 1997, 29), over 3,500 came to Atlantic Canada. Yet, the Loyalists' colonies were ill-prepared for the great influx of Blacks, and "[t]here was no priority for these slaves-without-masters" (Walker 1982, 30). Consequently, they received smaller lots on less fertile ground – if any.[57] Of those Blacks arriving in Nova Scotia in 1783, the first to actually receive land grants did so in 1787; the average size of their lots was 34 acres, while average grants to White newcomers amounted to 74 acres (cf. Pachai 1997, 14).

> All Loyalists, whether white or black, were promised free grants of land in the new country. The problems lay in the amount and quality of the acreage available; in the system adopted for the allocation and distribution of land; in the administrative incompetence […] and in the sheer numbers of people – estimated at nearly 30,000 – clamouring for attention. In such a situation, Blacks stood to lose, and to lose the most. In the social and economic scale, they stood at the end of the line. (Pachai 1997, 13)

As a result, the situation of Canadian Blacks, who were mostly assigned to separate, all-Black communities,[58] was dreary. Some became sharecroppers for white Loyalists, some even entered into contracts of indenture. Indentured Blacks were bound to their 'employers' for a certain number of years. As they worked without payment and could be bought and sold during the time of their indenture, Blacks often found themselves again in a situation very closely resembling slavery (cf. Walker 1982, 31). Moreover, Whites at times took advantage of the Blacks' illiteracy and bound them with indentured servitude contracts for a lifetime. If Blacks could find employment at all, their wages were about a quarter of those paid to Whites (cf. Walker 1982, 32). This, of course, increased the White workers' hatred – if Blacks worked for lower wages, it became harder for them to find employment. Violence was common, as in the case of a mob of White former soldiers who raided the Black settlement of Birchwood in 1784 and pulled down some twenty houses (cf. Winks 1997, 39). Disappointment and disillusionment were prevalent among these Blacks who had come to Maritime Canada:

> The black Loyalists had been attracted to the British by the expectation that they would be accorded completely equal treatment with white Loyalists. […] In the Maritimes their expectations were not fulfilled. In the first place most of them were landless, and so they remained

---

57 Walker estimates that only 30% of Black Loyalists received any land at all (Walker 1982, 30; also cf. Pachai 1997, 14).

58 "In nearly every case the black settlers were segregated." (Winks 1997, 36) The population of large segregated settlements such as Birchtown (a Shelburne suburb) grew to about 2,700 in 1784, making it "perhaps one of the largest urban concentrations of Blacks outside Africa at the time." (Pachai 1997, 12)

> as dependent on whites, economically, as they had been before. Furthermore, they were not allowed to vote or to sit on juries [...]. (Walker 1982, 34)

Pachai arrives at an equally disillusioning conclusion:

> The disappointing experience of the Black Loyalists in their expectation of receiving grants of sufficient land to set them on their way to becoming worthy citizens in the promised land destroyed their morale. Worse followed, in the form of cheap labour, racial riots in which the properties of Blacks were destroyed in Birchtown and Shelburne, and general shortages of food and clothing. (Pachai 1997, 15f.)

For contemporary African-Canadian writers, it is this memory that shapes their works almost as decidedly as the memory of slavery itself; the promise of a Canaan, the dream of a safe haven in freedom and equality had been shattered. In the words of poet Delvina Bernard: "[O]ur home and native land[59] ain't no / land of milk and honey" (Bernard 1992, ll. 17-18) – contrary to what many of the Blacks had been led to believe.

3.1.4. The decline of slavery

Slavery itself was on the demise in the late 18th century. Because of the abundance of cheap Black labor that could be obtained without the quarrels of overseeing, feeding and sometimes recapturing slaves, the market price for slaves decreased rapidly, as did the rewards for runaway slaves. In absence of plantations, "slave labour in Nova Scotia and elsewhere in the Maritimes was not an economic necessity." (Pachai/Bishop 2006, 8) The institution of slavery was under attack from the authorities as well. In 1793, legislation was introduced in Upper Canada making it unlawful to acquire new slaves (even though existing 'property rights' were not infringed); children of slaves born after 1793 were to be free (cf. Winks 1997, 96f.; Walker 1982, 24f.). Nova Scotia legislation had refused to legalize slavery in 1787 and repeated this verdict in 1808 (cf. Pachai/Bishop 2006, 9). Outside Upper Canada, courts effectively abolished slavery by refusing to assist slave-owners in recapturing runaways. Moreover, hardto-obtain proofs of ownership were required to establish property rights. The number of escapees thus increased drastically, while slave owners shied from the risk of buying slaves and then losing them (cf. Walker 1982, 25). Consequently, at the beginning of the 19th century, slavery had virtually ceased to exist in all of Northern British America, even though it continued to be legal until an Act of the Imperial Parliament, effective August 1, 1834, abolished slavery throughout the British colonies. Though compensation was offered for slave-owners for their loss of property, none was claimed in Northern British America, indicating that no slaves were set free as late as the 1830s (cf. Walker 1982, 25f.; Winks 1997, 111f.). "When slavery was finally abolished in the British Empire in 1834, it had long ceased to be of any relevance in the Maritimes, for there were no more slaves to be freed." (Pachai 1997, 17) The fight for equality, however, was far from over:

---

59   An obvious reference to Canada, since this phrase is taken from the Canadian national anthem.

But if slavery had ended in British North America, the Negro was still there, and after 1815 in increasing numbers. [...] And in the coming of Refugee Negroes following the War of 1812 lay the real beginnings of racism in Canada. (Winks 1997, 113)

3.2. Refugees and Fugitives

3.2.1. Exodus to Sierra Leone and new influx

Around 1800, the economic situation of Blacks had slightly improved as terms of indenture ended, slaves had been set free and between a third and almost half the Black population had left to Sierra Leone in 1792,[60] thus diminishing the supply of work force. What could have been a welcome shortage of cheap labour, however, proved to be a mere brain-drain to the Black community, as its elite decided to leave behind the disillusionment and hardships of the promised land that was not to be. In October 1791, Lieutenant John Clarkson of the Sierra Leone Company started to tour Nova Scotia in search of African-Canadians willing to leave the Maritimes for Sierra Leone, where, as Clarkson promised, "[r]acial equality was guaranteed [...] and slavery was absolutely forbidden" (Walker 1999, 117). Three months later, about 1,200 Black Maritimers set sail for Africa, among them many leaders of the Black community (cf. Pachai 1997, 20f.). Joining them was the economic "cream of the crop" (ibid., 21) of Africadians, as only those Blacks without debts and contracts of indenture had been allowed to leave (cf. Walker 1982, 35). The Black communities thus lost almost half of their population – much of its upper half, to be precise. This loss, though it was felt by some communities as a decapitation, was soon partly replenished in quantity – though more often than not in leadership and craftsmanship quality – by a new influx from the United States. Despite the new arrivals, however, the "proportion of blacks in Nova Scotia's population was never the same after 1792" (Pachai/Bishop 2006, 3).

Between 1796 and 1800, around 500 Maroons – 400 of them children, women and elderly men – (were) settled in Nova Scotia. The Trelawny Maroons had been fierce freedom fighters in their native Jamaica and were shipped to Nova Scotia in 1796, where they were expected to participate in the fortification of the Halifax Citadel (cf. Pachai/Bishop 2006, 13f.; Walker 1999, 229f.). "Of all the members of the African diaspora who set foot on Nova Scotian soil, the Maroons were the only ones who did not look to Canada as the land of promise and plenty, of safety and security, of freedom and fortune." (Pachai/Bishop 2006, 3). It came as no surprise that in 1800, the Maroons left for Sierra Leone and joined – in spite of doubts on behalf of the Sierra Leone Company – the Nova Scotians who had left Canada for Africa some eight years before. The Maroon presence thus remained a short interlude in the history of Black Nova Scotia.

---

60 For a thorough discussion of the exodus to Sierra Leone and the subsequent Nova Scotian presence in the new colony, see esp. Walker 1999.

Between 1812 and 1815, a different group of expatriates *did* make Canada their permanent home. During the Anglo-American War of 1812, refugees again were offered British citizenship and freedom if they deserted the Americans. Welcome at first due to the shortage of laborers induced by the trek to Sierra Leone, this new surge of arrivals once more proved too much to handle. Approximately 2,000 Blacks were settled in and around Halifax, often in refugee camps (cf. Walker 1982, 40). One of these depots became the legendary Africville.[61] A post-war depression as well as a new wave of immigration from the United Kingdom made the situation for Blacks even worse. Again, land that had been promised was either not granted or granted in considerably less quantity than anticipated. In 1815, the House of Assembly concluded that Nova Scotian Blacks "competed unfairly with white labourers" and were "unfitted by nature to live in the Canadian climate or to associate with the white colonists" (Pachai/Bishop 2006, 3). Loyalists from the War of Independence and Black refugees from the War of 1812 merged and created a community largely unified in poverty. As a result, Blacks increasingly lost "awareness of the particular origin of [their] ancestors." (Walker 1982, 42) The almost universal adherence to the Baptist faith, which has been assigned a "special place" in the "history of Maritime Blacks" (Pachai 1997, 17) by both historians and writers such as George Elliott Clarke, provided a remedy and a momentum of unity. Consequently, most Africadians repeatedly refused offers to move back to Africa – e.g. to Trinidad in 1807 – or to larger but individually located lots. "The community survived, but the price was continued economic marginality." (Walker 1982, 44)

3.2.2. *Fugitive slaves and the Underground Railroad*

Throughout the late 18th and the first half of the 19th century, another major group of Blacks arrived as fugitive slaves from the United States, where in 1793 (as anti-slavery legislation was passed in Upper Canada) the first Fugitive Slave Act stated that runaway slaves could be reclaimed throughout US territory.

> The fact that it was American slavery [the Blacks ran from] added a political condition to the [abolitionist] campaign [in Canada]. Anti-Americanism, fed by the fact that in slavery existed an absolute example of Canadian superiority, prompted much of the acceptability enjoyed by fugitive American slaves. (Walker 1982, 83)

---

61   The history of Africville and the literary dealing with it warrant a paper of their own, if done properly. For introductory purposes, see the short, but very nicely compiled CBC online summary of the history of the settlement and its destruction by Halifax authorities: <http://www.cbc.ca/news/features/africville.html>, accessed October 1st, 2004. Clairmont/Magill 1999 remains the standard volume on the historical and sociological dimension of Africville's destruction, even though its perspective on Africville's community might be considered overly critical in terms of an alleged cultural underachievement. Perkyns 2003 supplements the historical and sociological perspective, while Nelson 2002 and 2008 focuses on the aspects of space and remembering. Bast 2003, Gerlach 1997 and Moynagh 1998 analyze the literary dealings with the fate of Africville. Also cf. the emblematic poems by Nolan (1992) and Tynes (1990).

By the 1840s, abolitionists' children in the United States were reciting the "Anti-Slavery Alphabet", which included the lines "U is for Upper Canada / where the poor slave has found / rest after all his wanderings, / For it is British ground." (Quoted in Walker 1982, 48) Accordingly, the perception of Canada as a safe haven was again strengthened, and "Canadians came increasingly to congratulate themselves upon their lack of prejudice and to contrast themselves favorably with the immoral and once slave-ridden United States." (Winks 1997, 193)

This feeling was still corroborated by the existence of a network of secret routes from the southern through the northern states of the US which terminated in southern Ontario. Via this network, which has become famous as the Underground Railroad, several thousand Blacks are said to have escaped to Canada. Even though the Underground Railroad has become the most famous of these networks – partially due to the charismatic guide Harriet Tubman, an African-American abolitionist nicknamed *Black Moses* – a number of these routes existed, maintained on an often impromptu basis by abolitionists, Quakers, Wesleyans and freed slaves (cf. Walker 1982, 49f., 59f.; Winks 1997, 233f., Frost 2007).[62] The Underground Railroad thus embodies the ambiguous nature of African-Canadian history: Canada serves as the quasi-mythical destination promising freedom to US-American slaves; it has, however, been exploited as a marker of an ostensibly impeccable history of Canadian race relations.

Since the census did not yet include race/ethnicity, the number of fugitive slaves is hard to determine.[63] Walker estimates the figure to be around 40,000, most of them living in the Ontario area – a situation that put considerable strain on the existing Black community (cf. Walker 1982, 56f.), as the Ontario community basically faced the same problems as the Africadians:

---

62 The Underground Railroad has prompted a number of literary responses by African-Canadian writers. In her novel for adolescents, *Harriet's Daughter* (1988), African-Canadian writer Marlene NourbeSe Philips for instance establishes strong ties between the novel's contemporary setting and the Underground Railroad's famous conductor; in the very first scene, the novel's protagonist and her friends play what they call "the Underground Railroad Game" (ibid., 2) in which the youngsters reenact the escape of slaves by means of the Underground Railroad. Also cf. Barbara Smucker's story for children, *Underground to Canada* (1999; first published 1977), to which Lawrence Hill has added a short introduction. Adrienne Shadd, Afua Cooper and Karolyn Smardz Frost (2005) have compiled a nicely illustrated history of the Underground Railroad likewise aimed at younger audiences.

63 In the 2006 census, more than 780,000 Canadians identified themselves as Black, which amounts to approximately 2.5% of the overall Canadian population. (Statistics Canada. <http://www12.statcan.ca/census-recensement/2006/dp-pd/hlt/97-562/pages/page.cfm?Lang=E& Geo=PR&Code=01&Table=1&Data=Count&StartRec=1&Sort=2&Display=Page> Accessed July 23, 2010.)
Pachai speaks of almost 700,000 "Canadians of African descent" in 2005 (Pachai/Bishop 2006, 1). Cf. Clarke 1998, 98 on the difficulties of identifying as Black / African / colored / African-Canadian in the official census.

> With a few exceptions, such as the areas of Toronto and Hamilton, most post-Civil War black communities in Ontario shared the experience of their counterparts in Nova Scotia. In the rural and semirural areas of southwestern Ontario blacks lived a largely separate life, dependent economically on an indifferent white society but socially and culturally self-sustained. (Walker 1982, 62)

3.3. African-Canadian History: Summary

> [From the end of the 17th century] until the early nineteenth century, throughout the founding of Nova Scotia, New Brunswick and Ontario, there was never a time when blacks were not held as slaves in Canada. Slavery is thus a very real part of our history, yet the fact that slavery ever existed here has been one of our best-kept historical secrets. (Walker 1982, 19)

This is the first important fact of African-Canadian history. Slavery existed in Canada for over 200 years, with many of the slaves customarily being Blacks. The second important fact is that the existence of slavery has never been properly acknowledged. Instead, a stereotype of Canada as a Canaan, a safe haven for Black slaves, has been promoted:

> The exploitation of black labour was an essential element in the foundation of Canada, and by ignoring this fact a false history is perpetuated. The Underground Railroad and Canada's reception of the fugitive slaves can lead to a total misunderstanding unless the racism, separate schools, white Christian exclusivism and employment stereotyping, which were part of the fugitive experience, are also studied. (Walker 1982, 6)

The experience of Black fugitive slaves was seldom one of the mythical 'Free North'. Instead, Blacks faced poverty and hardship. The promises made to Black Loyalists, refugees and fugitives were all too frequently broken, resulting in disillusionment and disappointment among the Black community.

Of course, treatment of slaves was more humane than in the southern part of North America. Of course, there were freedom and prosperity for some Blacks who came to the North. Nonetheless, 'official' history often ignores the realities that lie beneath the stereotype of Canada as the land of freedom and equality; far too often, it is maintained that the fugitive "found in Canada friends, freedom, protection, under the British flag" (official Canadian government marker at an Underground Railroad station; quoted in Winks 1997, x). Official monuments of course enshrine *hegemonic* versions of memory construction (cf. Saar 2001), and in this particular case, the dominant memory construction is one of a safe haven for Blacks in Canada as the terminus of the Underground Railroad. As we will see in detail, it is this kind of ignorance that African-Canadian authors try to write against.

4. Lawrence Hill's Factional Narratives

4.1. Lawrence Hill's Explorations in Faction

The Book of Negroes (2007), which won Lawrence Hill the Commonwealth Writers Prize, is the third novel by Hill, son of social activists and US émigrés to Canada. His earlier novels, *Some Great Thing* (abbreviated SGT, 1992) and *Any Known Blood* (AKB, 1997) will be discussed in chapter six (AKB) and comparatively throughout (SGT) respectively. Hill's bestseller *Black Berry, Sweet Juice: On Being Black and White in Canada* (BBSJ, 2001) serves as a non-fictional background for the analyses of his novels.[64] In his writings, fictional and non-fictional alike,[65] Hill places particular importance on the passing on of memories, on keeping forgotten or suppressed aspects of (Black North American) history alive. Hill's first two novels, *Some Great Thing* and *Any Known Blood*, both feature protagonists who explore their family history, uncover a larger (Black Canadian) history beyond their immediate families' stories and set out to write down what they have learned about their literal and metaphorical ancestors in order to externalize and hand down their newly found knowledge. *The Book of Negroes* also deals – pivotally – with the rescuing and passing on of certain aspects of history that are on the verge, or beyond the verge, of being forgotten. Hill often focuses on the traumatic elements of the Black presence in North America, such as segregation, discrimination,

---

64 The ideas put forward in *Black Berry, Sweet Juice* feature more prominently in Hill's first two novels, as they explicitly deal with the experience of *"Being Black and White in Canada"* (the subtitle of *Black Berry, Sweet Juice*), while *The Book of Negroes'* protagonist, Aminata Diallo, is not of mixed-race descent, nor is the theme of mixed-raced descent as prevalent in this most recent fictional work by Hill.

65 Hill's original vocation as a journalist has contributed to his literary career starting out with non-fictional writing, and his essays continue to receive high acclaim: he won, for instance, the National Magazine Award for the best essay published in Canada in 2005 ("Is Africa's Pain Black America's Burden?"). His stint as a reporter with the prestigious *Globe and Mail* and his position as a parliamentary correspondent for the *Winnipeg Free Press* in the 1980s not only provided him with the skills and experience of non-fictional writing, they also clearly underlie the themes and characters of *Some Great Thing* in particular. Hill has also published an historical account of the Canadian Negro Women's association (1996) and a book of children's history (*Trials and Triumphs: the Story of African-Canadians*, 1993). His works furthermore include a film documentary about the Black Church in Canada (2004) and *The Deserter's Tale: The Story of an Ordinary Soldier Who Walked Away from the War in Iraq* (2007c).

racism, limited upward social mobility for Blacks, stereotyping, violence and racial hatred. In addition, the ideas of belonging, of forging stable and sustainable identities and of contributing to both the Black community and Canadian history, society and culture at large are salient issues. Autobiographical elements are writ large in *Some Great Thing* and, most extensively and with a great deal of family history woven in, in *Any Known Blood*.

Lawrence Hill's paternal grandfather and great-grandfather were ministers of the African Methodist Episcopal church, while his grandparents on his mother's side were White Republicans from Oak Park, Illinois – a highly improbable mix, illustrated by the fact that when Hill's parents met, "even the federal government cafeteria was segregated", as his mother remembers (BBSJ 4). Hill's parents, right after getting married in Washington, D.C., moved to Canada,[66] where Lawrence Hill was born in Newmarket in 1957 – three years after his brother Daniel Hill, a singer/songwriter who continues the family tradition of carrying the name "Daniel Hill" (being Daniel Hill IV[67]), and one year before his sister Karen. Daniel Hill III and his wife Donna both worked as social activists, which greatly influenced their youngest son and his writing. Being the son of a Black father and a White mother, Lawrence Hill grew up in Don Mills, Ontario, which he describes, in *Black Berry, Sweet Juice,* as a place "where race faded (most of the time) into the background" (BBSJ 4). Growing up in an environment that was only faintly racialized, the development of a self-conscious mixed-race identity was a difficult but evidently formative process; Hill therefore traces in detail his childhood and his rising racial awareness ("There's nothing like being called 'nigger' to let you know that you're not white. It didn't happen often. But it happened enough to awaken me." ibid., 5).[68] From treating mixed-race identity in a contemporary setting in *Some Great Thing*, which is interspersed with the history of Black Canadian railway porters, through tracing (a) family history back to a fugitive slave in *Any Known Blood*, Hill in his novels has worked his way backwards in historical terms, setting his latest novel, *The Book of Negroes*, at the end of the 18th century.[69]

66　"They had had enough of racial divisions in their country of birth [the US]." (BBSJ 4)

67　Cf. the male protagonists of *Any Known Blood*, who carry the name of Langston Cane I through V.

68　A number of Black Canadian writers report similar encounters; frequently, these incidents raise, for the first time, a sense of 'racial awareness' in the authors; it is indicative of their overall sense of (in)acceptance by mainstream society that their early encounters with their racial identity is signified by racism (a racism which, due to a lack of preparation owed to a silencing of racial issues, is often not instantly recognized for what it is). Cf. for instance George Elliott Clarke: "... three white boys, only a little older than our four-year-old, three-year-old, and two-year-old selves, had called us 'niggers' and thrown rocks at us. Gracious reader, rest assured that we had promptly returned fire, and I remember clearly shouting the word *niggers* back at our pale opponents." (Clarke 2002a, 3) (Clarke, as an aside, has a mixed-raced heritage just like Lawrence Hill, though his roots includes Mi'kmaq rather than White European ancestry.)

69　This trend, as Hill announces in an interview, will be reversed in his next work, as he is "working on a novel that is entirely contemporary" (Hill, Appendix 302).

Evidently, then, Hill engages in what might be labeled very broadly as 'historical fiction' (prominently so in *Any Known Blood* and entirely so in *The Book of Negroes*, yet to a distinctly lesser degree in *Some Great Thing*). Hill himself employs the term *faction* for (t)his mode of writing.[70] 'Faction', a popular English Studies textbook suggests, "is the term preferred by some writers when seeking to challenge casually extreme notions of fact versus fiction, truth versus falsehood, and reality versus imagination." (Pope 2007, 230) Equally, Pope tells us, Linda "Hutcheon points to the radical and potentially liberating view of history as *faction* rather than fact." (ibid., 133; bold type replaced by italics) It is stating the obvious to correct, or rather concretize, this view by supplying Hutcheon's well-worn phrase 'historiographic metafiction' here instead of 'faction' (cf. Hutcheon 1988, 1993) – faction being a term of which Hutcheon indeed does not take particular notice. *The Penguin Dictionary of Literary Terms* in the respective entry likewise takes a somewhat more dismissive account of the coinage, "which originated *c.* 1970 and denotes fiction which is based on and combined with fact. […] It is a vague term at the best of times and its usefulness has been questioned." (Cuddon 1992, 324) Related terms such as *surfiction* (Raymond Federman 1975), *metafiction* (Patricia Waugh 1984) – more narrowly, *historiographic metafiction* –, *fabulation* (Robert E. Scholes 1979), and others have become more commonly accepted, though each of course signifies slightly different approaches to the complex negotiations of fact as/in/versus fiction.[71]

While not a scholarly well-established or well-defined concept, the portmanteau term faction has the indisputable appeal of patently *visualizing* the merging of fact and fiction and has therefore variously been taken up, typically as indicating "the [porous] fact/fiction distinction in postmodernist 'faction'." (Butler 1997, 39) Dipli Saikia describes faction as "collapsing autobiography, history, social commentary, and fiction [, which] draws our attention to the relationship between cultural representation and self-representation." (Saikia 2008, 111) More pejoratively, the label 'faction' has been used as a marker of an *illegitimate* transgression by those who wish to maintain a strict distinction between fact and fiction, such as Virginius Dabney, who "argues that Chase-Riboud's novel [*Sally Hemings*] is a work of 'faction,' that is, the blending of fiction and fact that became quite popular in the 1960s and 70s." (Pollard 2004, 118) In this view, faction is characterized by being "founded on completely unproven assumptions" (Dabney, qtd. ibid.). One of the foremost scholars of the relationship

---

70 Hill has repeatedly used the term 'faction' in and for his numerous presentations, such as "Faction: Fact And Fiction In Afro-Canadian Literature." (Vrije Universiteit Amsterdam, The Netherlands, 2006), "Faction: the Merging of Fiction and History in the Novel *The Book of Negroes*" (Universities of Greifswald and Trier, Germany, 2007), "Faction: the Merging of History and Fiction" (Black History Month 2008, Kingston), "Faction: Exploring Experience Through Story" (2009 conference of the Canadian Association for the Prevention of Discrimination and Harassment in Higher Education).

71 "It is obvious, however, that most of the terms delineating an area between fictional and factional texts [such as 'transfiction', 'fictual', 'factifiction', and 'faction'] are, in the wake of postmodernism and post-structuralism, attempts at disclosing the fictional quality of reality." (Zander 1999, 404) It will be shown that 'faction' as employed by Hill actually does not underline the *fictionality of reality* but the *factuality of his fiction*.

between historiography (since the mid-19th century considered to represent – double meaning intended here – fact) and fiction, Hayden White, asserts that the abolition of the "taboo against mixing fact with fiction" is the

> aspect of modernism that informs the creation of the new genres of postmodernist parahistorical representation, in both written and visual form, called variously *docudrama, faction, infotainment, the fiction of fact, historical metafiction*, and the like. (White 2000, 67)

The terminological imprecision of 'faction' thus allows Hill to subsume his writing under this notion without the stricter regime imposed by theoretical conceptions such as historiographic metafiction.[72] Whether Hill's 'factional' approach is indeed congruent with the postmodern idea(l) of historiographic metafiction[73] is a question that is worth asking for the simple reason that it reflects the impetus of Hill's novel: Does Hill foreground critical questions of historiographic and literary modes and the unreliable methods of approaching the past (as would be, in the most simplified description possible, suggested by historiographic metafiction), or does he – as I will argue – deliberately forego this aspect and deliver instead an historiographic fiction that indeed *deals* with metafictional issues but never foregrounds them to a degree which would lend an air of self-reflexive uncertainty to his works? There is only a fine line between Hill's faction and historiographic metafiction, but one that is worth exploring. It is one of my more general arguments that the literary mode employed in *The Book of Negroes* is representative of the *gros* of African-Canadian literature in its historiographic approach, its metafictional awareness, but also – markedly – in its affirmative, self-confident rather than self-conscious, stance towards the constructions of the collective memory it presents. In fact, collective memory theory (as S. Schmidt, 2004, 217, has pointed out) may provide an alternative approach to the fact/fiction divide. The two approaches – collective memory theory and postmodern historiographic metafiction – cannot be entirely reconciled.[74] We may safely assume, however, that the fact/fiction split disputed in

---

72 At this point, it might be noted that it is a regular fad to claim works of fiction as part of the category of historiographic metafiction – after all, it bestows upon both author and scholar almost limitless possibilities of (disclosing) self-reflexivity and self-referentiality.

73 Pope's usage would seem to infer as much (he equates faction and historiographic metafiction; quoted above). Linda Hutcheon, in turn, equates postmodern writing with historiographic metafiction – more precisely, she deems the mode of historiographic metafiction to be the archetype of postmodern literature (consequently often collapsing the two terms): "I'd like to argue, in a deliberately polemical fashion, that the term postmodernism should be reserved to describe fiction that is at once metafictional and historical in its echoes of both the events and the texts, the contents and the forms, of the past. The label I have (somewhat awkwardly) been using to describe this paradoxical entity is 'historiographic metafiction'..." (Hutcheon 1987, 169).

74 There are a number of difficulties involved here. Historiographic metafiction, for instance (as, in Hutcheon's conceptualization, its sister term 'postmodern') is both a mode of writing *and* a mode of analysis, while collective memory is a frame of analysis but not so much a *mode* of writing as a presentation of certain memories *per se* – although there are some characteristic narrative strategies prompting generic efforts such as 'fictions of memory'. The division, whether upheld or ruptured, between fact and fiction, for instance, is given different accents in and within both ap-

historiographic metafiction could best be described in terms of the division between historical and collective memory (*à la* Halbwachs) or functional vs. storage memory (*à la* Aleida Assmann). Functional memory, which Assmann in a memorable metaphor calls 'inhabited memory' ("bewohntes Gedächtnis", 1995, 172), in this approach signals group specificity, selectivity, and an orientation towards values and towards the future (ibid., 182f.), whereas storage memory is situated on a secondary level and serves as a reservoir of 'uninhabited' memories. The postmodern rupturing of the barrier between fact and fiction[75] thus most closely corresponds to the interchange between functional and storage memory, as these are not contingent entities either: memories and their assemblages may constantly be in flux, being foregrounded to the functional memory or relegated to the background reservoir of the storage memory. Thus, Aleida Assmann's model, while echoing Halbwachs's split between an identity-shaping area of memories and a realm of memories which are 'dysfunctional' for processes of identity formation, allows for a dynamic interchange between the two areas. Consequently, Assmann's approach defies static renderings of recollection just as convincingly as theories of historiographic metafiction, which focus on the dynamic processes involved in converting 'events' into 'facts'.[76]

---

proaches. Whereas Halbwachs distinguished between 'history book' historical memory and lived collective memory (and Nora made a similar distinction, though claiming that we have reached the end of lived memory altogether), Jan Assmann focuses on the divide between communicative (immediately experienced) and cultural memory (removed by a veritable time span from the person who remembers), Aleida Assmann primarily uses a distinction between the functional (foreground) and storage (background) modes of memory – and these examples are just four out of a multitude of approaches. Historiographic metafiction, then, questions the alleged boundary between fact and fiction; without leveling the two, the claim is that both historiography and fiction use similar (literary) modes and processes, thus showing that the traditional distinction is quite artificial. Historiographic metafiction as a mode of analysis, however, does not conventionally distinguish between 'lived' and 'history book' or between 'inhabited' or 'uninhabited' memories. Whether these memories are labeled as 'fact' or 'fiction' is not of primary importance, as collective memory theory assumes that collective memory is indeed a *construction* and thus a fiction; its main criterion is not accuracy.

75 Hutcheon herself notes that this phenomenon is evidently not a postmodern *invention* but rather one of postmodernism's favorite occupations: "History and fiction have always been notoriously porous genres, of course." (Hutcheon 1988, 106)

76 The transition from 'event' to 'fact' is crucial here: While 'events' are taken to be the abstract building blocks of the past ('the things that happened') *without* meaning being bestowed upon them, 'facts' are events imbued with meaning. Past 'events' become 'facts' by being designated as such by either historiography or fiction; i.e. facts are *made* when events are told or connected to certain schemata: they need to be "related to 'conceptual matrices [...] if they are to count as facts.'" (Munz qtd. in Hutcheon 1988, 122). Thus, "documents become signs of events which the historian transmutes into facts" (Williams) (qtd. ibid.). Hutcheon further argues that just as "in historiographic metafiction, the lesson here [in the semiotics of history] is that the past once existed, but that our knowledge of it is semiotically transmitted." (ibid.) Evidently, the semiotic transmission of the past charges events with meaning and thus renders them into facts. It is, as Hutcheon concludes, "this very difference between events (which have no meaning in themselves) and facts (which are given meaning) that postmodernism obsessively foregrounds." (Ibid.)

We can fruitfully use the distinction between events and facts to make an early twofold generalization about a majority of African-Canadian literature, including Hill's *The Book of Negroes*: it protests the exclusion of certain events – such as Canadian slavery or the disillusionment upon not finding a veritable Canaan in the True North – from being instilled with meaning. These memories are thus precluded from attaining the status of historical 'facts'. Moreover, they are hence exempt from processes of identity-construction, as they are plainly not included in mainstream constructions of collective memory. *If* historical events involving Black Canadians are granted meaning, African-Canadian authors claim, they are interpreted in lopsided ways so that they are attributed *distorted* meanings, which in turn results in a distorted historical representation as well as – via collective memory – in a distorted Canadian self-identification.

Collective memory theory is thus also able to account for dynamic literary processes such as the *revitalization* of certain memories, i.e. the attribution of meaning to events through literature (in fact, 'living memory' is a wide-spread synonym for what Aleida Assmann calls functional, 'inhabited' memory). There is, however, no widely accepted *generic* literary typology based on the insights gained from the study of collective memory, though some have been proposed (Neumann's 2005 typology of fictions of memory could be mentioned *pars pro toto*). Quite the contrary is true for Hutcheon's coinage, which has quickly become an indispensable (though of course contested) category of literary analysis. Consequently, while subscribing to the explanatory power of collective memory theory, it is beneficial to work, for the time being, along the established criteria and categories provided by analyses of historical fiction so far. Thus, let me repeat that it is my argument here that *The Book of Negroes,* and with it, significant parts of African-Canadian fiction, operates within reach of models of historiographic metafiction but stops short distinctly before fully meeting its criteria, which is significant for and illustrative of its overall impetus. If we could indeed fully classify *The Book of Negroes* as historiographic metafiction, my argument that this novel, *inter alia* and alongside other works, presents us with a different, opposing, yet self-assured construction or *version* of collective memory, would be superseded and supplanted by the questioning of the very *modes* of this construction. The main question would consequently be, How do we know these past events? Instead, the question is, How come we *don't* know these facts? African-Canadian literature is keenly aware that history is constructed – after all, the experiences of Black Canadians have repeatedly been precluded from these very constructions. In fact, much of what is currently being discussed in terms of the absence of an 'objective' historiography has already been anticipated by Halbwachs's notion of the past being reconstructed starting from a present situation rather than from the events themselves (cf. Halbwachs 1967, 65).

The characteristics of reconstruction, selection, variation, interpretation, *imaginatio* which are inherent to collective memory (theory) have increasingly been applied to – or rather: identified as formative in terms of – historiography as well. Literary theories involving historiographic metafiction have likewise 'appropriated' several aspects from collective memory theory to be incorporated in their approaches. It has to be noted again, though, that both modes, literary studies and the science of history, still have rather different trajectories and (academic) conventions, such as historiography's academic standards of intersubjectivity and evidence-based claims or its focus on the breaches and fissures rather than the unifying and coherent elements, whereas collective memory theory is usually not concerned with issues of 'truth' (which in its context is as irrelevant a criterion as accuracy) and concentrates on the construction of coherent, smooth, usable memory versions. The emphasis on 'key memories' (*Erinnerungsfiguren*) which are privileged by repetition and scope over other memories underlines the processes of collective memory vs. the (idealized) egalitarian distribution of attention by historiology. The way in which African-Canadian literature emphasizes and reiterates certain key memories – slavery, displacement, failed exodus and the like – clearly shows that it evidently does not participate in standard historiography but in the creation of a collective memory, for which the high-frequency usage of *Erinnerungsfiguren* is vital. Nonetheless, in theories of historiographic metafiction, the transmission of history is conceptually closer to the construction of collective memory than Halbwachs et al. assumed for their definition of historical memory, i.e. when noting the absolute opposition between historical and collective memory.

Consequently, instead of bluntly dismissing the valuable discussions which have evolved around notions of historiographic metafiction simply because they are not entirely congruent with the working model of collective memory employed in this study, I would like to treat historiographic metafiction 1) as a conception *related*, not diametrically opposed, to collective memory constructions, and 2) as a mode of writing with which one might fruitfully compare (in this case largely: contrast) the literary mode employed in *The Book of Negroes* and other African-Canadian fictional works. In accordance with Hill's own usage, I will refer to the mode of *The Book of Negroes* as 'faction', taking advantage of the absence of a widely accepted definition of the term.

4.2. Hill's Faction and Historiographic Metafiction

Though historiographic metafiction has, both as an analytical category and a mode of writing, enjoyed great popularity as well as a substantial body of revisions by a number of scholars, it is still Linda Hutcheon's original description that is most commonly consulted for a definition of the term.[77] According to her, "it is part of the postmodernist stand to confront the paradoxes

---

77 Thus, generally cf. Hutcheon 1988 (esp. the chapter "Historiographic Metafiction: 'The Pastime of Past Time'", 105-23, reprinted simply as "Historiographic Metafiction" in McKeon 2000, 830-849). Nünning critically assesses the notion (materially in *Von historischer Fiktion zu historiographischer Metafiktion*, 1995; in the given context, the more theoretical/general approach of vol. 1 would prove more immediately useful than the case studies of vol. 2); more succinctly, he does so in Nünning 2002; introductory contributions can be found as entries on 'historiography and literature' and 'historiographic metafiction' in Nünning 2004a and 2004b. The collection by Engler/Müller (1994) as well as Stanzel 1995 have elaborated on and concretized Hutcheon's notion. Also cf. Jutta Zimmermann's 1996 *Metafiktion im anglokanadischen Roman der Gegenwart*.

of fictive/historical representation, the particular/the general, and the present/the past." (1988, 106) Historiographic metafiction, being the epitome of postmodern writing (cf. Hutcheon 1987, 169), combines an exploration of historical issues with an intense metaliterary and metahistoriographical impulse, particularly discussing in what ways (and within which limitations) we are able to access the past.[78] It thus permeates and questions rigid generic boundaries separating historiography from fiction – after all,

> [literature and historiography] have both been seen to derive their force more from verisimilitude than from any objective truth; they are both identified as linguistic constructs, highly conventionalized in their narrative forms, and not at all transparent either in terms of language or structure; and they appear to be equally intertextual, deploying the texts of the past within their own complex textuality. (Hutcheon 1988, 105)

While this comparison, drawing pivotally on the textuality and narrativity of historiography[79] (i.e. not so much on the historiographic power of fiction), seems applicable to most types of written texts,[80] Hutcheon also admits that the basic assumption of historiographic metafiction, the "generic blurring [between historiography and fiction,] has been a feature of literature since the classical epic and the Bible [...], but the simultaneous and overt assertion and crossing of boundaries is more postmodern." (Ibid., 113) What is new, consequently, is the "intense self-consciousness" (ibid.; also cf. 1987, 169) that pervades historiographic metafiction. It is exactly at this point where Hill's faction – and with it, predominant parts of African-Canadian literature – diverge from the model of historiographic metafiction while closely following it in other respects. African-Canadian literature indeed "confront[s] the paradoxes of fictive/historical representation, the particular/the general, and the present/the past." (Hutcheon 1988, 106) *The Book of Negroes,* for instance, presents the overtly fictionalized version of a slave narrative and thus a fictive representation of both historical events (turning them, if we subscribe to the leveling of historian and novelist, into facts in the process) and the historical accounts for which the slave narratives are generally taken. Hills' novel also, as I will discuss later on, oscillates between the particular and the general. Although *The Book of Negroes* is set entirely in the past, it pertains to the present, challenging current national self-perceptions as it proceeds to undermine hegemonic memory versions. If this ambition should

---

78 It is often assumed that historiographic metafiction a) collapses fact/history and fiction and b) holds that we cannot know the past at all. Both assumptions are mistaken, as historiographic metafiction does not do away with the distinction between fiction and fact, but problematizes it (cf. Hutcheon 1988, 113); similarly, Hutcheon argues that "our confidence in empiricist and positivist epistemologies has been shaken – shaken, but perhaps not yet destroyed." (Ibid., 106) "Historiographic metafiction does not deny that reality is or was; it just questions how we *know* that and how it was." (Hutcheon 1987, 173; original emphasis)

79 Also cf. Fredric Jameson 1984 and Hayden White 1984, to whom this aspect of Hutcheon's approach is strongly indebted (cf. Hutcheon 1987, 170).

80 Pushing the matter (and reading this passage without acknowledging its context), one could of course argue that the criteria of verisimilitude, the usage of language, the adherence to conventions, complexity/opaqueness and intertextuality apply to written texts from instruction manuals to song lyrics.

perchance be lost on a reader, Hill makes sure – qua paratextual additions – that the aspect of the 'forgotten history', consequently the lack of its integration into current hegemonic construction of history (and *in extenso*, collective memory) is acknowledged.

George Elliott Clarke, in *Beatrice Chancy*, uses the exact same mechanism, prefacing his libretto[81] with a note "On Slavery in Nova Scotia", which begins with one of Black Canadian literature's central tenets:

> A mass ignorance exists about the conduct of slavery in the British North American colonies – including ceded Québec – that remained loyal to Britain during and following the great Anglo-American civil war that birthed both the United States and – a few generations later – Canada. (Clarke 1999, 7)

Clarke explicitly "confront[s] the paradoxes of fictive/historical representation" (cf. above) – tellingly so, however, he does this in the preface: "*Beatrice Chancy* is not a work of history but of imagination." (Clarke 1999, 8; also cf. Clarke 2006b, 54f.) 'Tellingly', because the libretto itself is strictly modeled on Clarke's understanding of Black Canadian history, yet its fictionality is underlined in the preface: the libretto itself remains unfazed by these 'doubts' of fictitiousness. *Beatrice Chancy* grapples with Nova Scotian history; it presents an alternative reading of it, as it is part of an effort to remedy "the mass ignorance" about Canadian slavery (cf. above).[82] What it does *not* do is, in turn, to engage in the self-consciousness and insecurity of historiographic metafiction. Like *The Book of Negroes*, *Beatrice Chancy* is *secure* in its rendition of history, which is exactly what sets it apart from historiographic metafiction. Both works address the traditional boundary between historiography and fiction – yet exclusively so in their *paratextual additions*. Hill begins his appendix, entitled "A Word About History", with a statement resembling Clarke's: "*The Book of Negroes* is a work of my imagination, but it does reflect my understanding of the Black Loyalists and their history." (BN 471) Clarke's announcement at first glance seems to be more diffident concerning the historical content of *Beatrice Chancy* ("not a work of history", cf. above), yet even the most cursory reading re-

---

81 It should be obvious from the generic classification (a libretto which originated as a verse drama – and is perceived by critics primarily as such) that *Beatrice Chancy* cannot fully qualify as historiographic metafiction proper.

82 Maureen Moynagh offers a reading of *Beatrice Chancy* (also including Brand's *At the Full and Change of the Moon* and Hill's *Any Known Blood*), stating: "For contemporary African-Canadian writers, the particular burdens that come with the need to create a usable past have to do, at least in part, with a peculiar variant of that New World myth, and that is the myth that Canada is free of the history of slavery by virtue of being the 'north star', the land of freedom for fugitive slaves." (2005b, 15f.) She goes on to critize the Canadian habit of pointing at their own nation as an example of multicultural benevolence and to the US as an example of a racist country, suggesting that this flawed view could indeed be remedied by literary works such as mentioned above: "These texts confront the complacent multiculturalism of the last 30 years with representations of a history of racism and intolerance that the dominant narratives of nation abjure. The vision of Canada as the 'north star' lives on in the insistence that racism is an American problem, and it is against the smug intolerance of this vision that the transnational imaginary of Canadian postslavery fiction and drama offers an effective counter-narrative." (ibid., 17)

veals that the issues Clarke puts forward in his preface on history are fully echoed in the fiction *per se*.[83] Clarke is keenly concerned with the issue of faithful representation, especially in contrast to the perceived "mass ignorance"; the epigraph hidden in the imprint page reveals as much: "Every line is true, or it is a lie: / Honey poured – honest – over lye." The connection between past and present is underscored by the epigraph to Act I, which begins, "The old enslavement was to nature, and the new one is of one individual to another, beginning with chattel slavery and proceeding to the modern kind", including wage dumping ("wage-slavery") and dependence on banks.[84]

It is an interesting anecdotal connection between *Beatrice Chancy* and *The Book of Negroes* that Lydia Jackson, to whom Clarke dedicates his libretto,[85] is supposed to have been enlisted in the historical ledger known as the Book of Negroes; moreover, her fate is recorded by John Clarkson, a prominent abolitionist who doubles as a secondary character in *The Book of Negroes* as well (cf. Nova Scotia Archives & Records Management 2009; also cf. Hamilton 1994, 27f., and Walker 1992, 50). Both *Beatrice Chancy* and *The Book of Negroes*, then, closely adhere to what their respective authors consider the 'facts' of history. Thus, they do deal with issues of fictive/historical representation, the particular/general and past/present, yet what is missing is the metafictional reference to these issues – there is, for instance, no "overt crossing of boundaries" between fact and fiction (Hutcheon 1988, 113) within the texts themselves. Quite the contrary: In line with other works, such as Clarke's *George & Rue* (2005), it is not self-reflexive but *assertive* in its construction of a (counter-hegemonic) version of (Black) Canadian collective memory.[86] The approach taken by African-Canadian authors here is akin to strategic essentialism:[87] though being fully aware of the modes and complexities of historical and memory constructions, these writers *take advantage* of these mechanisms in a

---

83 In Act I, Scene 1, for instance, we learn that the slaves depicted perform the tasks typical of slave work in Canada, which was work in orchards – as opposed to cotton fields –, household chores – as opposed to chain gangs – etc.; this corresponds fully to the preface's contention that in Canada, "slavery was small-scale, a matter of household 'servants' or of a few coerced field hands. Stubbornly, though, slavery is slavery." (Clarke 1999, 7)

84 The epigraph's author, Hardial Bains (1939-1997) was the founder and leader of the "Communist Party of Canada (Marxist-Leninist)".

85 The dedication reads "À Marie-Josèphe Angélique et Lydia Jackson" (Clarke 1999, 5); Clarke has variously referred to Lydia Jackson, e.g. in his 1982 poem "Hammonds Plains African Baptist Church" (Clarke 1992b; reprinted in Clarke 1994, 72; again reprinted in Clarke 2008b, 3). For a thorough depiction of Marie-Josèphe Angélique, the Canadian slave who allegedly burned down sizeable parts of Montréal, cf. Afua Cooper's *The Hanging of Angélique* (2006).

86 Notice, again, the slip from 'history' to 'collective memory', as for the time being, we move in the vicinity of postmodern theory and historiographic metafiction, which shares a number of the attributes and perspectives of collective memory theory yet employs a different critical vocabulary; my usage of 'history' here should not be confused with Halbwachs's usage, which designates 'dead' memories.

87 Cf. the brief discussion in the introduction.

utilitarian, strategic way without, in their texts, questioning their legitimacy. Thus, Clarke, in *George & Rue*, includes a "Disclaimer" whose beginning reads:

> Though based on several actual persons and one actual crime, this novel employs facts not found in mere trial transcripts[88] – the scratchy songs, the mouthed bits from blues. George and Rufus Hamilton always lived outside boundaries (including knowledge, including history, including archives). (Clarke 2005, v)

Clarke acknowledges the questionable existence of boundaries and the difficulties involved in representations of history and fiction, yet he avoids, in the novel proper, the "overt assertion and crossing of [these] boundaries" (Hutcheon 1988, 113).

The same applies to *The Book of Negroes*, which equally acknowledges, paratextually, these boundaries but blanks them out in the fiction proper, where we are presented instead with a self-assured narrative which seems to claim for itself to not merely be *a* representation of history but to be a (more) *truthful* or authentic version of history.[89] Thus, we could define Hill's version of faction (largely shared by Clarke's non-poetic oeuvre;[90] indeed, characteristic for a good deal of African-Canadian literature) as a literary approach that is fully aware of the mechanisms of historiographic constructions and their fickle interdependencies with fictional accounts – the constraints and limitations involved, but also the possibilities of engagement – without letting this knowledge undermine the version of history (also read here: collective memory) they present in their works. There is a strategic component to this *modus operandi*: though being conscious of the theoretical limitations hampering the knowledge of, access to and representation of history, these doubts are deliberately kept out of the fictions themselves in order to avoid a weakening of the subversive, counter-hegemonic portrayal of Canadian history they put forward. African-Canadian literature is largely concerned with the revision of

---

88 Note the "mere" here, which indicates the author's confidence in fiction – an Aristotelean (in this case, as opposed to a structuralist) perspective. As Clarke's reconstruction of the lives of George and Rue is based on *other* sources as well – he mentions music – it is clear that in Jan Assmann's terminology, Clarke relies on *communicative* as much as on *cultural* memory; in terms of the slave narrative, he employs orature as well as written accounts; in the jargon privileged here (as developed by Aleida Assmann), Clarke avails himself of material from both the storage memory ("mere trial transcripts", uninhabited memory) and functional memory (inhabited memory such as "the scratchy songs and mouthed bits of blues", cf. above).

89 On the contended conception of 'truth' within cultural studies, cf. Barker's useful, very short introductions to issues of truth in relation to hegemony (2008, 70f.) and deconstruction (particularly regarding Derrida; ibid., 87ff.). On Foucault's notion of "regimes of truth", which holds that 'truth' is determined by historical and cultural specifics and thus variable, cf. Foucault 2002.

90 There is a distinct difference between Hill's and Clarke's levels of metafictionality in general; while Hill thematizes the writing process as such (his protagonists are invariably narrators-cum-writers), there is no depiction of the writing process in Clarke's only novel, *George & Rue* (the same naturally applies to *Beatrice Chancy*). In his poetry, however (as in his poetry derivate *Whylah Falls*, which Clarke has also converted into a play), Clarke is highly self-reflexive, often incorporating poets, the writing process and the like (he tends to be more self-reflexive on issues of love and relationships than on issues of the rendering of history, which again underlines the urge not to undermine or question the representation of Black Canadian history).

a memory version; it is not, as Ansgar Nünning contends for historiographic metafiction, moving *beyond* revisionism by overtly and self-reflexively reconsidering the entire nature of historiography and its relationship towards literature (cf. 2004b, 261).

Linda Hutcheon delineates several techniques and strategies characteristically employed by historiographic metafiction; a brief comparison reveals in what ways *The Book of Negroes* concretely adheres to its modes and where it – instructively – differs. It has been noted above that *The Book of Negroes* is neither starkly self-conscious nor overtly and expressly crossing boundaries between fact and fiction in order to illuminate their arbitrariness. Its first-person narrator – and fictional autobiographical chronicler –, Aminata Diallo, does indeed reflect the writing process she is involved in, yet she does not question the autobiographical construction she performs, nor does she question the claims she makes in terms of representing others and thus in terms of recording their collective (in this case: also 'collect*ed*') experiences.[91] On the contrary, her story-telling has a decidedly self-assured tone. Moreover, Aminata even overtly argues that the truthful rendering of her (hi)story has, both orally and in the written form of her memoirs, helped her cope with traumatic experiences (cf. section 5.3.2., "Traumatic memory: The Middle Passage").

Even though it is true that *The Book of Negroes* "plays", *à la manière de* historiographic metafiction, "upon the truths and lies of the historical record" (Hutcheon 1988, 114), it does not consciously falsify certain historical details to highlight loopholes in our ability to access the past (cf. ibid.).[92] While historiographic metafiction regularly reverts to the foregrounding of failing or unreliable memory (cf. e.g. Patrick in Ondaatje's *In the Skin of a Lion*), deliberate errors or adulterations (cf. e.g. Doctorow's *The Book of Daniel*), use of footnotes and other paratextual means (cf. e.g. Alexis's *Childhood*),[93] or personal memory that deviates from official historiography (cf. e.g. Kogawa's *Obasan*; for all four aspects, cf. Richler's *Barney's Version*), *The Book of Negroes* indeed takes liberties with its historical models but does not foreground, textually, these liberties in order to avoid emphasizing an act of 'distortion' or 'forgery'. Thus, the "play[ing] upon the truth and lies of the historical record" (cf. above) is not done in a meta*literary* way; it is not even done in a meta*historiographic* way – the novel reveals what it brands as historiographic shortcomings

---

91 Cf. the discussion of representation, authenticity and the creation of a collective voice in section 5.2.3., "Category three: Goals".

92 Aminata's "playing with the truths and lies of the historical record" refers to the level of *content* exclusively; Hill's protagonist questions and reverts what the mainstream historical record entails, not how it encodes its contents.

93 "Historiographic metafiction often points to this fact [the 'charging' of events with meaning in order to turn them into facts] by using the paratextual conventions of historiography (especially footnotes) to both inscribe and undermine the authority and objectivity of historical sources and explanations." (Hutcheon 1988, 123) Both G. E. Clarke and Hill use paratextual means in the form of prefaces and/or afterwords/appendixes, yet these addenda serve to *authenticate* rather than undermine the historical verisimilitude of their texts. In fact, regarding African-Canadian novels, Alexis is the only writer employing footnotes as a device aimed at unsettling the reader's certainty.

on historiography's own turf, though in a clearly fictional manner. It is not the modes of accessing and (re)presenting history which are challenged, but rather the contents of these representations. Moreover, Hill reveals – almost apologetically – some "key examples" of having "knowingly bent facts to suit the purpose of the novel" (though these are, in fact, minor ones such as setting a race riot in 1787 instead of 1783; cf. BN 473).

Insofar, Hill's approach to faction does not fully conform to Hutcheon's notion of historiographic metafiction, even though it certainly shares a number of historiographic metafiction's concerns. In the same vein, historiographic metafictions do not employ historical figures to validate their version(s) of history but, again, to question our knowledge of the past by having these historical figures appear in clearly altered versions;[94] accordingly, historical characters are often elevated to the front where the modification of their historical record can exert the greatest impact (cf. Hutcheon 1988, 114f.). In Hill's novel, historical characters are frequent, yet none plays a decisive role, let alone the role of protagonist.[95] The only historical character that can be said to develop any stature beyond a flat representation is in fact the abolitionist John Clarkson, to whom Aminata develops a closer, trustful relationship.

An assertive rather than questioning usage, which is what we find in terms of characters in Hill's novel, applies to narrative aspects as well. Historiographic metafiction frequently reverts to narrative perspectives which are not mirrored in *The Book of Negroes*:

> First of all, historiographic metafictions appear to privilege two modes of narration, both of which problematize the entire notion of subjectivity: multiple points of view [...] or an overtly controlling narrator [...]. In neither, however, do we find a subject confident of his/her ability to know the past with any certainty. (Hutcheon 1988, 117)

While *The Book of Negroes* is narrated stringently from a first-person ex-post perspective, hence displaying no multiple points of view at all, its narrator is indeed "overtly controlling". Again, however, the crucial distinction between Hill's faction and Hutcheon's conception of historiographic metafiction lies in a fine distinction between confident narration on the one hand and a suspicious or distrustful narrative mode on the other hand. Aminata overtly con-

---

94 "In many historical novels, the real figures of the past are deployed to validate or authenticate the fictional world by their presence, as if to hide the joins between fiction and history in a formal and ontological sleight of hand. The metafictional self-reflexivity of postmodern novels prevents any such subterfuge, and poses that ontological join as a problem: how do we know the past? What do (what can) we know of it now?" (Hutcheon 1988, 115) Clearly, *The Book of Negroes* tends towards the first approach.

95 Hutcheon, however, is slightly ambiguous in this regard. While claiming that historiographic metafiction relegates historical personages to the front, she simultaneously states that "the protagonists of historiographic metafiction are anything but proper types: they are the ex-centrics, the marginalized, the peripheral figures of fictional history" (113f.). Given Hutcheon's general stance and literary examples (such as the generic closeness between historiographic metafiction and postcolonial literature, which habitually re-centers marginalized characters), it must be assumed that Hutcheon means to indicate that the 'ex-centrics' are brought to the fore; it would be illogical, however, to presume that the marginalized are historical personages – the ones shunned by and the ones focused on by historiography – at the same time.

trols her tale without exploring or thematizing "her ability to know the past" in any *critical* or negative way (the section on authentication will discuss in more detail in which ways Aminata instead verifies and validates her account).

The same holds true for Langston Cane V, the narrator-cum-chronicler in *Any Known Blood*. Though Hill even switches the narrative mode to Langston I in chapter 22, thus creating both an embedded slave narrative and a narrative with multiple points of view – in this context usually indicative of historiographic metafiction –, he does not cast doubt on the verisimilitude or even the accuracy of Langston I's narrative. While the narrative setup of *Any Known Blood* is indeed highly suggestive of historiographic metafiction, it does, like *The Book of Negroes,* not *question* the modes of historiography and fiction; it lays bare its mechanisms and avails itself of them, questioning instead the *content* of what is represented. Langston Cane V, in *Any Known Blood*, reconstructs from a diary, letters and other documents the life of his ancestor four times removed (Langston Cane I). Accordingly, the prototypical postmodern assumption of the mediation of history, viz. its inaccessibility except through text (which, in turn, is only a mediation – Derrida's *différance* is writ large here), is highly visible.

> This kind of post-structuralist thinking has obvious implications for historiography and historiographic metafiction. It radically questions the nature of the archive, of the document, and of the concept of evidence. It separates the (meaning-granted) 'facts' of history-writing from the brute 'events' of the past. 'Facts' in historiography are discursive, already interpreted (granted meaning). (Hutcheon 1987, 175f.)

While Hill, however, exposes the means with which historiography constructs meaning (and, even more important in this context, *refuses* to acknowledge events and construct meaning, consequently denying factual status to these events), he does not destabilize or reject but embraces them. The archive in Hill's fiction – as in the case of other writers, such as George Elliott Clarke or Wayde Compton, who have additionally assembled literary anthologies referring specifically to the archival thrust – is celebrated, not contested. In *Any Known Blood*, Langston I's story, reconstructed from the textual remnants that Langston V painstakingly discovers and assembles, is allowed to stand undisputed. If anything, Hill lets fiction stand *pari passu* next to historiography, yet the intrinsic validity of historiography and its bases – the document, the archive, oral history – are not undermined. Hill does not emphasize the fact that Langston V's narrative is a *second* fictionalization, the first having occurred with the drawing up of the documents the chronicler uses. It would of course have been a simple, undemanding narrative undertaking to highlight the possible fallacies within, for instance, Langston I's diary, which in turn serves as a template for Langston V's rendition of it as an embedded (fictionalized) slave narrative. In fact, the slipping into Langston Cane I's first-person narrative perspective would even have suggested as much, were it not for the authentication that Hill employs here much as in *The Book of Negroes*. Hill thus does not forego historiographic metafiction by chance or by virtue of lacking skill; he employs means to ensure that his novels are not misunderstood as being questioningly self-reflexive. One of these means is that Hill has Langston I repeatedly admit to his weaknesses and flaws. It is significant to note that, as in *The Book of Negroes*, the narrator is straight-faced in this regard and the narrative is not projected as satire, while examples such as Barney Panofsky's reveling in his shortcomings in *Barney's Version* is grossly excessive in order to undercut its own very nature of a truthful, wholehearted confession. Hill refrains from ironic refractions of his protagonist when Langston I, in unison with the story of his great-great-grandfather that he discovers, explores his own weaknesses. The portrayal of these two imperfect characters, particularly Langston Cane I, a former slave, has prompted H. Nigel Thomas, in an interview with Hill, to suggest that *Any Known Blood* should be read as a parody of the slave narrative, which Hill vehemently disputed:

> *[THOMAS:] One of the hallmarks of your fiction is the parodying of genres: the slave narrative, for example, in* Any Known Blood. [HILL:] Let's just stop for a second. In what way do you mean that Any Known Blood parodies the slave narrative? *[Thomas explains that* Any Known Blood's *protagonist is not as flawless as the standard slave narrative's.* HILL:] I am not the best judge of these things; I'm not the best person to evaluate my own work, but I don't consider *Any Known Blood* to be a parody of the slave narrative. I accept that it contains elements of the slave narrative, but I very consciously wanted to create a fictional narrative of a slave who did not lead the life of a saint and who led a fallen life. [...] *[THOMAS:] Inadvertently, that's parody.* [HILL:] I don't see it that way.   (Hill 2006, 137f.)

Hill thus clearly uses the representation of what he calls his "attempt to create a layered and thoughtful three-dimensional narrative of a character who has failings as well as strength and courage" (Hill 2006, 138) to *avoid* – in contradistinction to Thomas's assumption – the ironic (self-)reflexivity of parodistic historiographic metafiction. Other means to the same end are the usage of historical quotes (e.g. John Brown in conversation with Frederick Douglass, cf. AKB 476)[96] as well as a short appendix, "A Word About History". Why, then, does Hill eschew historiographic metafiction's "provisionality and uncertainty (and the willful and overt constructing of meaning) too" (Hutcheon 1988, 117)? In analogy to *The Book of Negroes*, there is what is perceived as an historical truth which is left out of hegemonic memory constructions; Hill uses his fiction/faction to remedy this exclusion. Langston I's involvement in John Brown's raid on Harpers Ferry is an emblematic case of the *pari passu* usage of personal recollection and historical account (indeed, the privileging of the former over the latter); his participation is registered in none of the official accounts, yet Hill presents the ex-slave's claim as perfectly believable: while the Harper Ferry museum archivist leaves room for doubt when he holds that Langston I's exclusion from official accounts "doesn't mean he wasn't there" and cautions Langston V that only if the diary's author "*is to be believed,* was [Langston's] great-great-grandfather" (AKB, 429; emphasis added). Langston V, however, does not subscribe to historiographic metafiction's "provisionality and uncertainty" (Hutcheon, cf. above) and quickly resolves he is now undoubtedly "holding a memoir written by my great-great-grandfather in 1877." (AKB, 429) Even though the past is available to the narrator only through his forefather's account, it is taken at face value; the same, in extension, is claimed for Langston I's story, to whose 'factual' aspects *Any Known Blood*'s readership is expected

---

96 Here as well, the original quotes are not employed in a distorted way aimed to conjure up suspicion on behalf of the reader; instead, they are diligently fitted in their original context.

to trustfully subscribe. In unison with other Black Canadian writers, Hill is quite aware of the fact that the past is by necessity a mediated realm, yet he maintains (necessarily so if he wants to sustain the revisionist stance of his stories) that we *can* access this past. Quite the opposite is true for historiographic metafiction (in this quote, once more, collapsed with the term 'postmodern fiction'):

> ...what postmodern novels teach is that [...] we know the past (which really did exist) only through its textualized remains. [...] There is not so much 'a loss of belief in a significant external reality' [Gerald Graff] as there is a loss of faith in our ability to (unproblematically) *know* that reality and therefore to be able to represent it in language. (Hutcheon 1988, 119)

In addition to the manifest belief in the ability to actually access the past through documentation, there is also the aspect of non-textualized history/memory. The extra-textual influence to which Clarke points in his foreword to *Beatrice Chancy* ("this novel employs facts not found in mere trial transcripts – the scratchy songs, the mouthed bits from blues", cf. above), also applies to *Any Known Blood* and thus adds to the refutation of postmodernism's claim – following Hutcheon – of a gateway to history through text exclusively: there is more to the construction of the past than *just* "textualized remains", at least if we take it that 'text' in this context designates written texts *specifically* and is thus not meant to indicate an all-encompassing term for mediation irrespective of the concrete medium.[97] Both in *Any Known Blood*, where Langston V resorts to oral accounts in addition to written documents, and in *The Book of Negroes,* where the importance of story-telling as well as the shift from oral to written mediation of memories are significant aspects, the co-existence, interdependencies and possible supersession of non-material and reified (in this case: written and oral) sources are made explicit. Over and above, Hill incorporates – fictionalized – first-hand experience. Slave narratives in general oscillate between eye-witness accounts and what would traditionally be categorized as fiction proper; Neo-slave narratives like *The Book of Negroes* or *Any Known Blood* (here, most consistently so chapter 22, of course) hark back to these heterogeneric, in-between pre-texts.[98]

---

97 We can assume as much since Hutcheon explicitly states that history is not *per se* 'text', pointing to Fredric Jameson and Hayden White in this regard (1987, 170).

98 In Jan Assmann's terminology, what both Hill and Clarke incorporate is the existence and importance of communicative memory, which in turn is externalized, reified and made available to the cultural memory.

Regarding the characterization of slave narratives as heterogeneric, cf. Olney 1985, 152.

I am using the term 'in-between' here to avoid, somewhat paradoxically, the term 'hybrid' in this context lest it be confused with Bhabha's notion of hybridity (though it seems to have become commonplace to identify virtually all heterogeneous, mixed-mode, mixed-race etc. fiction as 'hybrid', irrespective of its relation to postcolonialism in general or Bhabha's conceptions in particular). I am of course aware of employing another of his terms instead, yet it is the one less exclusively associated with Bhabha, even though he proclaims his equal "taste for in-between states *and* moments of hybridity" (2007, 298; emphasis added). Although a relationship with Bhabha's in-betweenness could indeed be established here, it is not intended – in spite of shared angles such as Bhabha's take on *rasquachismo*, a "hybrid chicano aesthetic", whose artistic productions he

Hill's approach to fiction – the concept I have dubbed faction here, echoing his own term – is thus a straight-forward one, even though it maintains some intricate dissociations from current conceptions of fiction as/and historiography such as historiographic metafiction. Revealing a thorough understanding of historiographic processes, familiar with the limitations of fiction in these processes, but equally determined to correct what is perceived as a lack and/or a misleading representation of the historical account, Hill employs his faction to come to terms with a pitted or lopsided construction of Canadian collective memory. However, he explicitly rejects one of the key aspects of historiographic metafiction, viz. its focus on exposing the constructedness of *both* fiction and history. Hill describes his own approach as being serious-ly[99] indebted to historical research and aimed at bringing forgotten history to the fore,[100] but distinct from the notion of questioning the very boundary between history and fiction, irrespective of the direction of the assumed permeability:

> I don't feel the need to warn readers that they are reading fiction. I am playing with the motivation of a narrator to step into the process of writing, to justify oneself or navigate through trouble, and to find meaning in life. But I don't think what I am doing is remind the reader 'In case you didn't get it, this is fiction, and you shouldn't forget that.' I like to draw the reader into a fictional bubble. My chief impulse is to tell a story that makes sense of life. Having said that, at the end of *Any Known Blood* and *The Book of Negroes*, I did insert an afterword that acknowledged places where the novels had coincided with history, and other places where they had not. As they exit a novel, I think some readers appreciate a chance to view the work in an historical context. (Hill, Appendix 301)

Hutcheon maintains that historiographic metafiction, "while teasing us with the existence of the past as real, also suggests that there is no direct access to that real which would be unmediated by the structures of our various discourses about it." (Hutcheon 1987, 173) Hill, and

---

describes in the following way: "Such art does not merely recall the past as social cause or aesthetic precedent; it renews the past, refiguring it as a contingent 'in-between' space, that innovates and interrupts the performance of the present. The 'past–present' becomes part of the necessity, not the nostalgia, of living." (2007, 10)

99 Double meaning intended here: this is also meant to indicate a usage of his sources and a reliance on historical research *sans* irony or satire; irrespective of what Hutcheon calls the "new postmodern seriousness" (1988, 117), historiographic metafiction frequently takes its sources as the subject of irony and satire, thus laying bare their constructedness through 'inverted' or exaggerated reconfiguration.

100 Hill argues, regarding his interest in exploring neglected historical issues and in telling stories that have rarely been told before: "Yes, part of my work is to excavate and dramatize aspects of Canadian history that are little known, undervalued, misunderstood or forgotten. That does not guarantee that I am writing well. But it adds to the moral heft of the work, and to its historical significance. So whether it has to do with Canadians participating in John Brown's raid in Harpers Ferry, Virginia, or the role of railroad porters in the early 1900s in Winnipeg, Manitoba, or the largely forgotten British military ledger called the 'Book of Negroes', I'm interested in exciting readers about history." (Hill, Appendix 292) Likewise, Hill states in another interview: "I am interested among other things in exploring fascinating and important elements of the Black Canadian experience and exploring them dramatically. [...] I feel that revealing dramatic moments in our lives is one way of showing people who we are." (Hill 2006, 135)

with him, a majority of African-Canadian writers, for the most part conform to these charac-teristics, yet – again – with one subtle but significant deviation: they agree that the past is real and they show that the access to the past is indeed always mediated, but they sustain the belief that historical *truth* can be, if not accessed with absolute certainty, at least approximated with a good level of confidence. It is in fact one of their foremost tasks to discover and promote their own approximations. In *The Book of Negroes*, for instance, Hill suggests that the estab-lished view of Queen Charlotte Sophia is a mediation that distorts – in this case, as in the case of Canadian history: whitewashes – her ancestry. He does not doubt, however, that we can indeed know her real racialized background; what we need is a new approach to what is me-diated, not a new approach to the very nature and method of the mediation. We have to be aware, though, of the discursive formation of the mediation, as the lopsided (historical) main-stream representation of Queen Charlotte underlines. In its entirety, *The Book of Negroes* em-phasizes this point: though the Canadian collective memory has been either virtually purged of the Black experience or assembled in a way to unfaithfully reflect it (viz. in terms of a Ca-naan), the history of African-Canadians *is* available if people care enough to incorporate it. The historical document called the "Book of Negroes", for instance, is not presented as an inaccessible vault, yet its constructedness is explicit; after all, Aminata is, in Hill's novel, im-plicated in the very process of drawing it up, meanwhile laying bare the negotiations and un-derlying discourses involved (cf. section 5.3.4., "The Canadian perspective: Canaan denied"). Yet Hill's usage of faction suggests that we can find meaning and, indeed, truth, underneath the layers of discursive constructions and mediations that reflect privileges and hegemony in power/knowledge (such as identified by Gramsci and Foucault) if we first carefully decon-struct the discourses that have shaped the mediations of history.

Thus, "the buck stops here", as the phrase popularized by US President Truman goes; Hill insists on a core of historical truth that cannot be endlessly deconstructed. In Derrida's terminology, of course, this means to provisionally put a plug in the infinite tube of *différance*, something that Stuart Hall has proposed as an "arbitrary closure" in order to be able to "say anything at all in particular" (Hall 1996a, 117; aptly termed the "temporary clo-sure of meaning" by Barker/Galasiński; 2001, 43). African-Canadian literature, generalizing here to a legitimate extent as I believe, is as a whole aware of discursive constructions of competing memory versions yet maintains that *its own* are more precise – yes, more truthful – versions than the current hegemonic ones, thus opposing the view that history necessarily remains inaccessible in any reliable way. In this view, it might be difficult to construct a fair and balanced account of historical events in order to make these events available for memory constructions (in other words, to make them available for the infusion with meaning, thus turning them from events into facts), but these events are not, as historiographic metafictions suggest, ultimately elusive. They can be recuperated and transformed into veracious, even accurate, accounts, non-fictional as well as fictional.[101] Hill's explorations in faction are an archetypal endeavor in this regard.

---

101 Hence, charging events with meaning is not an arbitrary act and as such does not reflect the "provisionality and uncertainty (and the *willful* and overt constructing of meaning)" that charac-

4.3. Hill's Faction and the Documentary Novel

It has been useful, I believe, to discuss Hill's faction, his last novel in particular, in contrast to Hutcheon's concept of historiographic metafiction in order to investigate the ways in which Hill approaches his fictional writing. Other generic pigeonholes of course have been developed to account for fiction that is, in the widest sense, historical. If, as I have claimed, Hill indeed aims at a markedly 'truthful' representation of the historical aspects he covers, then the documentary novel might be a fitting generic category – more closely so in this regard than historiographic metafiction:

> Unlike the documentary novel as defined by Barbara Foley, what I have been calling post-modern fiction does not 'aspire to tell the truth' (Foley 1986a [*Telling the Truth*] 26) as much as to question *whose* truth gets told. It does not so much associate 'this truth with claims to empirical validation' as contest the ground of any claim to such validation. (Hutcheon 1988, 123)

In fact, however, Foley goes on to argue that if the documentary novel

> increasingly calls into question the possibility of truth-telling, this skepticism is directed more toward the ideological assumptions undergirding empiricism than toward the capacity of fictive discourse to interpret and represent its referent. (Foley 1986, 26)

It is, in consequence, possible for documentary fiction *à la* Foley to incorporate a questioning of certain modes of historiography (and of allegedly objective science in general), while maintaining the possibility of referentiality. What Foley calls 'metahistorical fiction', a sub-genre of the 'modernist documentary novel', illustrates the documentary novel's ability (and, what is more in terms of the border between fact and fiction, its ambition)[102] to 'tell the truth' but also, in contrast to Hutcheon's slightly simplified rendition, to challenge the modes and bases of representation:[103]

---

terize historiographic metafiction (Hutcheon 1988, 117; emphasis added). As we have seen, the overt fictionality of literary memory constructions does not deprive these accounts of either veracity or impact (possibly, quite the contrary), as 'non-fictional' modes of representation equally resort to certain textual/literary strategies. Concerning the potentially greater effect of fiction, Hill agrees with H. Nigel Thomas when Thomas suggests (referring to a comment by Barbara Kingsolver) that writers of fiction are able to reach a much larger audience than writers of scientific texts (cf. Hill 2006, 135).

102 Succinctly, Foley argues concerning the traditional division between fact and fiction that "the documentary novel constitutes a distinct fictional kind. It locates itself near the border between factual discourse and fictive discourse, but it does not propose an eradication of that border." (1986, 25)

103 For Foley, the documentary novel has passed through the stages of 'pseudofactual novel' (beginning with ancient Greek literature but going through Defoe), the historical novel (particularly popular in the 19th century) and the 'modernist documentary novel' of the (early) 20th century, which in turn is subcategorized into the 'metahistorical novel' and fictional autobiography. Foley

> Clearly the metahistorical novel sets out to refute the empiricist illusion of neutral subjectivi-
> ty and the positivist illusion of neutral objectivity […]. It brings in documentary 'facts' only
> to question their ontological status rather than to assume a priori their value as registers to
> truth. (Foley 1986, 200)

Metahistorical fiction thus "continues to invoke a number of the representational conventions
of earlier historical fictions, but it no longer assumes that historical actuality constitutes a self-
evident object of cognition." (Ibid., 195) The second subcategory of the modernist documentary novel, viz. the fictional autobiography, underlines the flexibility of the borders between
fact and fiction (synonymously, of course, history and fiction) *without* its complete dismissal.
Throughout her study of documentary fiction, Foley stresses the novels' assertiveness, while
Hutcheon's historiographic metafiction, in contrast, focuses on the questioning of the accessibility of quote-unquote 'truth'. The use of paratextual elements such as footnotes is a poignant
illustration: in what Foley categorizes as documentary fiction, such as Sir Walter Scott's Waverley novels, the use of footnotes must be considered an *affirmative* reference (cf. Foley
1986, 150 and 155; also cf. Davis 1993), while footnotes in historiographic metafiction also
aim at destabilizing the construction presented in the text (Hutcheon 1988, 123). In this continuum between the explicit ability versus the explicit inability to represent history faithfully
and affirmatively, Hill's faction of course sides with Foley's descriptions. The caveat, however, is a contradiction that Foley herself concedes when she turns to African-American literature:

> In my discussions of pseudofactual, historical, and modernist documentary fiction, I have
> suggested that writers choose modes of documentary corroboration that both articulate and
> confirm existing types of abstraction, both economic and conceptual – that, in short, writers
> reinforce dominant ideology. In my discussion of the Afro-American documentary novel,
> however, I shall argue that specific social and historical circumstances can set writers in op-
> position to dominant ideology. (Foley 1986, 233)

It is the inversion of the historical novel's characteristic nation-*affirming* impetus – Scott and
Cooper are prototypical examples – that African-American literature embodies, thus to a certain degree posing as a counter-model to established documentary subgenres.[104] While I fully
subscribe to this reversal of impetus and to Foley's general skepticism of the explanatory
power of poststructuralist analyses *as far as African-Canadian literature is concerned*,[105] her

---

    also extensively discusses African-American literature ('Afro-American documentary' in her ter-
    minology) as a particular subgenre of the documentary novel (cf. Foley 1986).

104 Within the 'Afro-American documentary', Foley, in analogy to modernist documentary fiction,
    subdivides into fictional autobiography (e.g. Johnson, *The Autobiography of an Ex-Colored Man*)
    and metahistorical novel (e.g. Reed, *Flight to Canada*).

105 I emphasize this point as I am not making general claims here. Foley's refutation of Derrida's
    phobia of binaries (1986, 35f.) is – *pace* her Marxism – as convincing as her uneasiness with
    poststructuralism is compelling ("I encountered various versions of these polemics ['apocalyptic'
    and poststructuralist critics, the former arguing that technological progress, the experience of the
    Holocaust and other factors make referentiality impossible] […] and they struck me as provoca-
    tive but also profoundly unsatisfactory." (Ibid., 14). Still, what I intend to do here is in fact on a

approach lacks, for my purposes, the explanatory power of generic definitions such as the Neo-slave narrative. In particular, it is Foley's overplaying, due to her "distinctly Marxist" bias (1986, 17f.), the economic aspects of slavery and, in consequence, of Black North American literature. A Leninist approach to slavery must by necessity improperly account for racism as a starkly economic issue (cf. ibid., 237ff.); for *Canadian* race matters, these assumptions are of course even more invalid. Slavery in Canada has, after all, been anything but a decisive economic factor (though after the factual abolition of slavery, economic issues became a severe strain on race relations). While to the American "south, Negro slavery was an economic institution, in the provinces [that were to become Canada] it was merely a convenience" (Winks 1997, 113). Thus, while the Marxist perspective in Lukács's work (on which Foley evidently strongly relies) can be largely blanked out in a discussion of historical fiction *in general* – a genre which Lukács of course helped define with his groundbreaking monograph of the same title (1983 [1937]) –, the nonobservance of Foley's Marxist arguments in her analysis of African-American literature is less unproblematic, rendering Foley's conceptions largely inappropriate for an analysis of African-Canadian literature in this regard.[106]

A large set of characteristics developed by Foley for the documentary novel, however, proves suitable for the purposes at hand; the assertiveness and claims to representing (historical) truth in particular, which are so characteristically absent from historiographic metafiction, are defining features of Hill's faction.[107] As Foley, though somewhat tautologically, closes her study: "The documentary novel's insistence that it has a particular truth to tell thus reinforces rather than undermines fiction's distinct status as a means of telling the truth." (Foley 1986, 268) It is thus not surprising that Hill, in an interview with H. Nigel Thomas, impulsively

---

dramatically smaller scale than Foley's ambition. While she asserts that to "investigate the truth-telling claims of the documentary novel is thus to *illuminate the assertive capacities of fiction in general*" (ibid., 26; my emphasis), I intend to make claims concerning *The Book of Negroes* here, extended to Hill's faction and – at the most general – to the body of African-Canadian literature.

106 As an anti-racism activist, Foley would almost certainly disagree with the contention of her overplaying the economic factor in slavery; as for the specific *Canadian* situation, however, the economic aspect simply cannot be foregrounded as to explain Canadian slavery as a bourgeois plan of stabilizing late capitalism. Revolutionary ideologies in general seem strangely foreign to most Canadian contexts; in this, African-Canadian literature once more proves to be characteristically *Canadian*.

107 As for a final attempt at delineating Hill's conception of faction, Smaro Kamboureli's characterization of the term might well be the closest match available, as it focuses on both the empiricism that underlies it as well as its influence on processes of identity formation. It is, however, also too specifically minted for diasporic contexts to be adopted without serious modifications: "Here 'faction' refers to the way much of this [diasporic] writing, because it is a fictional rendering of the author's own immigrant experience, presents that experience as the essential determinant of subjectivity. The empiricism of this literature, even though it signals difference, is given an ironic privileged status as it reifies both the essentialism of ethnic identity and its marginalized position. 'Fiction', in turn, refers to what is deemed irrelevant to diasporic experience; yet the elements that are excised from these narratives, presumably because their presence would signal fabrication, constitute a paradoxical figure speaking truths that are usually unacknowledged." (Kamboureli 2000, 135)

rejects the label of 'documentary' fiction for his work (*The Book of Negroes* had not yet been published at the time of the interview) but agrees with the genre's pivotal tenet of rendering history as factually and as faithfully as possible:

> [THOMAS:] *Both of your novels, but especially* Any Known Blood, *employ what I term an omnivorous form:* Any Known Blood *is documentary, romance, detective novel, family saga, identity quest... Comment.* [HILL:] The only category I am not in agreement with is documentary, but I guess it depends on how one defines documentary. [...] [THOMAS:] *When I say documentary I am referring to the novel's fidelity to history in those places where it adheres closely to history.* [...] [HILL:] Of course! I would be really disturbed if some historian were to read my novel and say, this is preposterous. [...] If that's what you meant by documentary, I agree absolutely. Much Black writing seeks to explore history that has escaped the attention of others. (Hill 2006, 134f.)

Yet in spite of Hill's adherence to documentary fiction's goal of historical accuracy – even if only an intersubjective one –, Foley's classification is, I believe, still not the most useful or appropriate generic framework available for a thorough analysis of *The Book of Negroes*, even though we could easily classify it as a fictional autobiography under Foley's typology. Instead, however, I suggest that studies of the (Neo-) slave narrative, a genre subsumed under 'modernist documentary fiction' by Foley, prove most productive in explaining both the "truth-telling claims" (Foley 1986, 26) of Hill's novel as well as its more complex typological affiliations and socio-political momentum. Therefore, the relationship of *The Book of Negroes* to the (Neo-) slave narrative will be focused on extensively in the next chapter, preceded by a brief introduction to *The Book of Negroes* itself.

5. The Book of Negroes: 1745-1805

There are, of course, many terrific textbooks about history, and they are well worth reading. But drama of the first rank puts a personal stamp on history that allows us, as readers, to feel the pain and the sorrows and victories of the characters caught up by huge world events. More than giving us dates and details, historical fiction – when it's well done – helps us understand and feel what it was to live in a certain time and place. (Hill 1999, 5)

5.1. Preliminaries

I spend a lot of time on plot. I consider it to be central to my own notion of writing. I realize that the value of plot is downplayed by many writers and critics of contemporary fiction, but I'm not among them. [...] I like [my stories] to make sense, resonate, interrelate, hold together, and be tight. (Hill 2006, 140)

5.1.1. Plot synopsis

With *The Book of Negroes* (2007), Lawrence Hill presents the fictional autobiography of Aminata Diallo, who is captured by slave-traders in Africa in 1756, sold to a plantation in the United States, where she escapes and, via New York, joins the exodus of African-Americans to Nova Scotia, Canada. From there, she goes to Sierra Leone to participate in the first free Black colony. Aminata, born around 1745 in the village of Bayo, Mali, begins the account of her life, which she tells from the perspective of a woman almost in her sixties, with these words: "I seem to have trouble dying. By all rights, I should not have lived this long." (BN 1) Indeed, given the atrocities of the slave trade, the terrifying Middle Passage, an almost constant exposure to sickness and hunger, a merciless workload enforced through the whip, and the arbitrariness of incidents of racial violence, she should not. But, as Aminata says, there "must be a reason why I have lived in all these lands, survived all those water crossings, while others fell from bullets or shut their eyes and simply willed their lives to end." (BN 1) The reason of course is the need to have her story – and the stories of those who died – told, to preserve memories and pass them on.

Aminata is captured by African slave-traders in 1756, after her own reckoning at the age of eleven. Her parents are killed by the slave-traders and Aminata is forced into a slave coffle that is marched to the Atlantic coast. One of the Africans collaborating with the slave-traders is a boy named Chekura, who will later on marry Aminata and father her children. After three months, the coffle reaches Bance Island, one of the slave castles that dot the African shore at the time. Aminata is branded as property of Grant, Oswald & Company (though Aminata will only learn decades later what her branding "GO" stands for) and shipped off to St. Helena Island, by then part of the British Colonies which later constituted the United States. During the Middle Passage – the triangular Atlantic slave trade's second leg, the passage between Africa and the Americas – Aminata serves as an interpreter and the ship doctor's pet. After two months of living through hunger, thirst, maltreatment, sickness, and the crushing of a slave rebellion on board the slave ship, the vessel lands at the coast of South Carolina. Aminata is sold to the owner of an indigo plantation. Her life on the indigo plantation is facilitated by two skills Aminata had picked up from her parents and honed under great difficulties: midwifery and literacy, both of which make her a useful addition to the plantation's slave crew. Aminata is secretly visited by Chekura, who is enslaved on a different estate. At the age of fifteen, Aminata gives birth to Mamadu, her first child. Aminata is separated from her infant boy when she is sold to Solomon Lindo, a Jewish indigo inspector from Charles Town (today's Charleston, South Carolina). Mamadu dies shortly thereafter; the adolescent Aminata has thus lost both her parents and her first child to/through slavery.

When Solomon Lindo takes Aminata to New York City in 1775, she decides to run away from her master. She escapes and takes refuge in Canvas Town, an all-Black settlement in New York's proximity. After eight years in Canvas Town, Aminata is recruited to work for the British on the Book of Negroes, a ledger containing names, short physical descriptions, former or current owners and other information about those Blacks who, under a British proclamation by Lord Dunmore, have earned the right of passage to Canada.[108] Chekura – reunited with Aminata as a freed man – sets sail to Nova Scotia first, to be followed by Aminata. Yet, Chekura's ship, unknown to Aminata, sinks and he drowns. Aminata is pregnant again, and after her employment on the Book of Negroes is completed, she embarks on the last ship to sail to Nova Scotia, hoping to meet Chekura there. After settling in Birchtown, the Nova Scotian equivalent of Canvas Town, Aminata gives birth to her daughter May in 1784. May, however, is abducted by a White couple for whom Aminata had worked as a housemaid. Be-

---

108 The 1775 proclamation by Lord Dunmore was extended by the Philipsburg Proclamation, issued by Sir Henry Clinton in 1779. In essence, the British had, prompted by the Revolutionary War, promised freedom and shares of land to all Blacks who would desert their masters and either work or fight for the Crown. Cf. James W. St. Walker's extensive *The Black Loyalists. The Search for a Promised Land in Nova Scotia and Sierra Leone 1783-1870*, particularly chapter one, "Origin of the Black Loyalists".

reft of another child, Aminata helps set up the move of 1,200 Blacks from Nova Scotia to Sierra Leone, where the Sierra Leone Company plans to establish a colony in which Blacks "would enjoy political and racial equality" (BN 356). Aminata thus becomes the chronicler of a voluntary exodus for the second time. When she learns that Chekura has died, there is nothing to keep her in Nova Scotia, so she joins the "Adventurers", as the Blacks going to Sierra Leone are called. After an abortive attempt in 1800 to go back inland to visit the place of her birth and childhood, Aminata resolves to go to London with one of the leading abolitionists of the time. In London, she is supposed to plead the case of the abolitionists before the King and before Parliament, which she does. It is in London that Aminata finally begins to write her memoirs – presented to us in Lawrence Hill's *The Book of Negroes*.

5.1.2. Narrative mode and structure

The writing of Aminata's memoirs also structures the novel formally. The first-person narration is divided into four "Books", each describing a station in Aminata's life, concluded by passages over water which coincide with an (attempted or enforced) passage in status. "Book One" deals with Aminata's life in Mali, her abduction and the Middle Passage to North America; Aminata is thus stripped of her freedom and the status of self-determined 'subject' and relegated to her new status of property. "Book Two" accordingly comprises Aminata's life as a slave on the indigo plantation in South Carolina and closes with her new master's preparations for their journey to New York City. Aminata's time in New York, described in "Book Three", is signified by her status as a fugitive slave – a limbo between being rid of her master and thus free to a certain extent, yet heavily constricted by poverty and continuing racism. Another passage over water, her joining the Black Loyalists on their way to Canada, only prolongs this limbo and is thus also included in "Book Three". Though formally free, Aminata realizes that her status is hardly different from her life as a fugitive slave in New York. "Book Four" comprises Aminata's return to Africa and her wish to reverse the Middle Passage by participating in the Sierra Leone experiment. As Aminata has realized that going to Nova Scotia did not fully invest her with her former regalia of freedom and equality, the passage to Africa might be conceived as the endeavor to nullify her abduction and return to her former self and status, though again, she is unable to complete the reversal. Understanding that her former status will not be restored until slavery is completely brought to an end, she travels to London to support the abolitionist movement, crossing the ocean one last time.

Books "One" through "Three" are introduced by parts of the frame setting, i.e. by scenes set in 1802-1804 describing Aminata in the process of writing her memoirs. These are sequenced chronologically: The frame setting of "Book One" is set in 1802, "Book Two" in 1803 and "Book Three" in 1804. In "Book Four", the time of the frame setting and the time level reported by Aminata merge. Consequently, there is no introductory segment for the last chapter of the novel. The very ending of the novel, however, surpasses the frame setting chronologically described in Books "One" through "Three", so that the final part of the narrative is not predictable.[109] Aminata, in writing the last pages of her memoirs, moves from writing from memory to eyewitness writing; her metanarrative (though not metafictional) comments do not introduce accounts fetched from memory anymore but become 'real time' writing. From casting her glance backwards (thus creating a diachronic narrative perspective), Aminata moves on to a more synchronic description, delayed only by the writing process (much as in epistolary novels). Narrating I and experiencing I converge. In terms of focalization (Genette), the distinction created by alternately focalizing through the – limited – eyes of the young and the – more knowledgeable – eyes of the old Aminata is thus successively reduced.

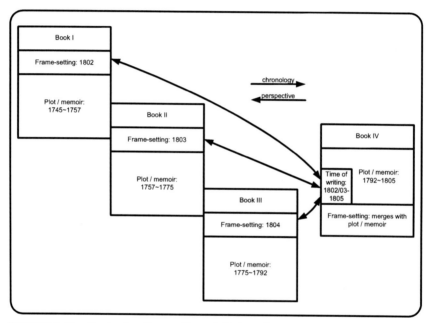

Illustration 2: Narrative structure: Frame setting and plot / memoir

The single frame tale (*Einzelrahmen*), which consists of Aminata's writing down the story of her life – turning the novel's protagonist into the familiar figure of the autobiographical writer within a story –, serves both a literary and a 'mnemopolitical' function. The literary function is obvious: through the frame setting, Hill is able to structure the story, provide incentives (such as foreshadowing, of which he makes liberal use), and create suspense. The reader is

---

109 Accordingly, the beginning of *The Book of Negroes* is strictly speaking neither completely *ab ovo* nor *in ultimas res*. The introductory frame setting is not the very ending, nor is the imbedded story (which begins *ab ovo* with Aminata's childhood in Bayo) the very beginning of the novel.

made to realize from the very beginning that he or she is reading Aminata's memoirs.[110] On a mnemonic or 'mnemopolitical' level, then, it is important that Aminata's task is fulfilled, that she indeed manages to compile the story of her life. Throughout the text, the importance of passing on the knowledge of what she has witnessed is Aminata's prevalent motivation to survive. Through this passing on, the greater task of remembering and keeping alive the memories of actions and, in particular, of people, is performed.[111] Literature in this respect is part of the construction of a collective memory and as such is 'political' in its ability to inform processes of self-identification. Making the reader aware from the very beginning of the novel that Aminata's report has a relevance beyond the cursory literary realm and beyond the human-interest perspective of an autobiographical account is at the core of *The Book of Negroes*. In the introductory frame setting (London, 1802), Aminata states:

> Let me begin with a caveat to any and all who find these pages. Do not trust large bodies of water, and do not cross them. If you, dear reader, have an African hue and find yourself led toward water with vanishing shores, seize freedom by any means necessary. (*The Book of Negroes*, 7)

Hill thus creates a narratee who is explicitly not part of Aminata's time frame or immediate surroundings; this conceptualization of a narratee presumes a time shift and thus an audience removed from Aminata's own life span. Her memoirs are unequivocally perceived and projected as a legacy, not a document intended for Aminata's contemporaries.[112] Hill emphasizes this notion at a later point in the novel, when Aminata (writing her memoir in 1803) points out:

> But I have long loved the written word, and come to see in it the power of the sleeping lion. *This is my name. This is who I am. This is how I got here.* In the absence of an audience, I

---

110 One could argue that this fictionalized autobiographical frame tale construction is traditionally supposed to create authenticity as well. Today's readers, however, are so accustomed to 'unreliable narrators' that the mere implementation of a (fictional) autobiographical, homodiegetic narrator does not in itself foster credibility – quite the opposite. Mechanisms of remembering and forgetting, conceptualized here as both neural *and* self-identifying processes, have become so prevalent that the pseudo-autobiography (first-person, fictional biography) has come under the educated readership's general suspicion. Cf. for instance discussions revolving around the contemporary interest in aging and its effects on memory (e.g. Mordecai Richler's *Barney's Version*, 1997, or Philip Roth's *Exit Ghost*, 2007). For a closer look at the narrative mode of *The Book of Negroes*, cf. section 4.1., "Lawrence Hill's Explorations in Faction".

111 Cf. the discussion of anonymity in the section on "Name changes: Autonomy vs. heteronomy", p. 100.

112 This notion will be corroborated and acquires additional significance in the course of discussing the abolitionists' attempts to control and censor the publication of Aminata's account; cf. section "Representation, appropriation, authentication", p. 127ff.; the abolitionists – with good intentions but a distinct lack of understanding of the importance of Aminata's story being told on her own terms – wish to have an account they can use (in a utilitarian sense) for political purposes. Consequently, they press for a report addressing a contemporary audience, a wish which Aminata refutes.

will write down my story so that it waits like a restful beast with lungs breathing and heart
beating. (BN 101; emphasis in the original)

Aminata clearly perceives an "absence of [a contemporary] audience" so that her story will
sleep "like a restful beast". Lacking a contemporary readership, Aminata's account is indeed
aimed at a future narratee – which, of course, is realized in today's readership. Hill's narratee
is thus closely linked to the extra-textual readership of *The Book of Negroes*. A telling metaphorical shift occurs in the passage quoted above: Before this passage, the recurring image of
the beast (particularly the lion) connotes loss and abduction. Aminata describes the slave ship
as a beast devouring the Africans: "The animal had an endless appetite and consumed us all:
men, women and babies." (BN 57) The hatch through which the slaves are led below deck is
described as a "crocodile's mouth" (BN 60), equally conjuring up the image of a beast swal-
lowing the slaves. The lion itself, however, provides the most unsettling metaphor for the
slave ship: "I imagined the biggest lion of my land – as big as the lion mountain on shore, but
living and breathing and hungry. It seemed as if we were being taken straight into its anus."
(BN 63) Aminata's description is picked up by the other slaves and turned into a call-and-
response pattern interwoven with notions of surpassing the enforced anonymity of slavery (cf.
BN 66). It thus reverberates in the inverted imagery of the lion as a story waiting like a "restful beast" (BN 101) revived by the narratee's reading. The liberating effect of Aminata's account actually being read by a future audience insinuates notions of Jonah's liberation from
the belly of the whale – while at first, the descend into the 'intestines' of the slave ship seems
to signify a consumption without hope of deliverance, Aminata hints at a possible liberation
when she says: "'Now we must all live [...]. Who wants to die in the anus of a lion?'" (BN
66) The imagery used to suggest departure, loss and hopelessness in the beginning[113] is turned
into a sign of hope – a hope which rests on the conjecture that a future narratee (again, closely
connected to the assumption of a future readership) will awaken the power of the lion by 'discovering' ("any and all who find these pages", BN 7) Aminata's account.

---

113 While being led onto the slave ship, Aminata turns around and looks back at the African coast
    line, discerning "mountains in the distance. One of them rose like an enormous lion. But all its
    power was trapped on the land. It could do nothing for any of us out on the water." (BN 54)

5.2. Narrative, Memory, Authenticity I:
The Book of Negroes and the (Neo-) Slave Narrative

> As a historical novel the modern slave narrative novel
> tries to bring to life a past that is still waiting for its
> redemption in the present. *(Link 1993, 286)*

Both Henry Louis Gates in his introduction to *The Slave's Narrative* and Maria Diedrich in her study of the ante-bellum slave narrative *Ausbruch aus der Knechtschaft*[114] discuss Hegel's notion that Africans – including, based on an essentialist racial extension of alleged African characteristics, African-Americans – have been unable to provide a written legacy and as such were excluded from the most eminent marker of civilization and humanity: a meaningful history.[115]

> Hegel's strictures on the African about the absence of 'history' presume a crucial role of memory – of a collective, cultural memory – in the estimation of a civilization. [...] Without writing, there could exist no repeatable sign of the workings of reason, of mind; without memory or mind, there could exist no history; without history, there could exist no 'humanity,' as defined consistently from Vico to Hegel. (Gates 1989, 20f.)

The voicelessness thus perceived by Hegel is remedied by the first slave narratives to be published by ex-slaves.[116] Contemporary African-*Canadian* literature does not have to establish

---

114 Two indispensable volumes on the subject; *The Slave's Narrative* is still what Kawash ·described in 1997 as "the most significant contemporary anthology of criticism on the slave narrative" (1997, 26). Diedrich and Gates also have jointly edited a significant collection of conference papers on the Middle Passage (in cooperation with Carl Pedersen; Diedrich et al. 1999).

115 Cf. Davis/Gates 1989, xxviii and Diedrich 1986, 291. Rinaldo Walcott adds that "historically speaking", the novel as a literary form of course also "was said to be beyond the capacities of Black people" (2003, 69).

116 The conception of an absence of meaningful history based on a lack of written testimony has of course been rendered void for decades, mainly so by the study of 'oral literature', or *orature* (as Eva-Marie Kröller succinctly puts it, "'[o]rature is a term widely used to refer to forms of oral discourse such as stories, songs, and various kinds of ritual utterance. The word was coined because 'oral literature' was a contradiction in terms." (2004, 24) The term orature was *not* coined, however, as Charles Saunders claims (1992, 13), by George Elliott Clarke, though he uses the term in a number of publications (cf. Clarke 1991, 9 for the instance Saunders likely refers to). Wayde Compton equally uses the term 'orature' for his collection *Bluesprint: Black British Columbian Literature and Orature* (2001), which is in many ways the West Coast equivalent of George Elliott Clarke's *Fire on the Water* anthologies (1991, 1992a).

The study of orature has particularly thrived in African and/or postcolonial contexts. Cf. for instance Susan Arndt's 1998 study, which combines both aspects by linking African orature and postcolonial writing back; for a comprehensive study of African orature, cf. Isidore Okpewho 1992 (the first four sections of chapter one provide a good overview, cf. ibid., 3-17); in certain contexts, oral and written literature has been collapsed entirely ("Language carries culture, and culture carries, particularly through orature and literature, the entire body of values by which we

the humanity of Black Canadians *per se*. It does, however, equally aim to insert Black Canadian history into the general process of historiography. Insofar, the classic slave narrative and contemporary African-Canadian literature share the aim of establishing, against mainstream thought, the notion of a meaningful historical participation of Blacks. While the ex-slaves had to bring to the fore the mere fact that they and their brethren did indeed possess humanity and were capable of constructing a history of their own, today's African-Canadian authors start from a more complex vantage point, although one that is strikingly similar in its exclusion and obliteration of Blacks from mainstream perception.

The "outsider", Diedrich observes regarding the slave narrative, writes in order to become an "insider" (1986, 292). While it was the goal of the (ex-)slaves to write themselves into humanity,[117] African-Canadian authors fulfill the task of writing their version of the experience of Black Canadians into the collective memory. Just as the slave narrative was supposed to bring the African from the shadow of an alleged inhumanity into the light of being a commonly accepted member of society, African-Canadian literature brings the muted memories of Black Canadians from the storage memory into the functional memory – and thus to the fore, where it can exert influence on processes of identity formation. *The Book of Negroes* is a case in point. It does not only conform to the overall pattern and intent just outlined: it reflects the slave narrative in both form and content, examining and re-evaluating topics, stylistics, narrative patterns and structural features of this particular genre.

The slave narrative constitutes what Theodore Parker more than one hundred years ago identified as "one series of literary productions that could be written by none but Americans, and only here; I mean the Lives of the Fugitive Slaves" (1907, 37).[118] This assessment, which has become a stock ingredient of discussions of the slave narrative,[119] is supplemented by the observation that the slave narrative has, more so than any other genre, contributed to

---

come to perceive ourselves and our place in the world." Thiong'o 1986, 16). For an African perspective that encompasses French language aspects, cf. the papers in Ricard/Veit-Wild 2005.

In a Canadian (postcolonial) context, the study of orature often concentrates on Native Canadian issues, e.g. Gingell 2004 or Shackleton 2007 (particularly 85-88). For an African-Canadian perspective, cf. the Canadian Oral History Association's journal *Oral History Forum*, double issue 21-22 (2001-2002).

117 "If blacks could write and publish imaginative literature, then they could, in effect, take a few giant steps up the Chain of Being..." (Gates 1986, 8; slightly revised in Gates 1993, 55)

118 Gates comments on the genesis of African-American literature when he claims that, "Ironically, Anglo-African writing arose as a response to allegations of its absence. Black people responded to these profoundly serious allegations about their 'nature' as directly as they could; they wrote books: poetry, autobiographical narrative, political and philosophical discourse were the predominant forms of writing." (Davis/Gates 1985b, xxvi) It might be noted, however, that Gates is slightly arbitrary in his classification of certain genres as "predominant", as a comparison with a later publication shows: "Black people responded to these profoundly serious allegations about their 'nature' as directly as they could: they wrote books, poetry, autobiographical narratives. Political and philosophical discourse were the predominant forms of writing." (Gates 1993, 62)

119 Cf. for instance Baker/Redmond 1989, 31; Davis/Gates 1985b, xxi; Ellis 2003, 68.

the development of a distinct African-American literature (cf. e.g. Diedrich 1997). The slave narrative derives its strength from the destruction of the vicious circle of illiteracy as a marker of inferiority and the denial of literacy through White slave masters (cf. e.g. Davis/Gates 1985b). Its political aim is thus two-fold: to lay bare the inhumanity enshrined in the 'peculiar institution' on a surface or immediate level and to undermine the underlying suppositions that relegated Blacks to the lowest ranks of the social hierarchy. Beginning around 1760, narratives of the lives of former slaves are published, written either by themselves or orally related to White amanuenses. Combining elements of the spiritual autobiography and the captivity narratives (though, of course, with reversed racial roles), the slave narrative became a best-selling genre with Olaudah Equiano's 1789 autobiography, *The Interesting Narrative of the Life of Olaudah Equiano; or, Gustavus Vassa, the African, Written by Himself* (Equiano 1995).

Most slave narratives were published under the auspices of White abolitionists and intended as propaganda against the trade in slaves (later on also against the institution of slavery itself). The influence of the abolitionists created a formulaic approach towards the form and the content of the slave narrative:[120] the fugitive or freed slaves had to ascertain their authenticity; they had to maintain their innate humaneness; they had to embed their personal stories within the larger political framework, almost always employing biblical allegories. As such, the slave narrative conventionally encompasses the three stages of slavery, escape, and freedom, which are nearly inadvertently linked to the triad of hell (or the biblical captivity of Israelites in Egypt), the search for redemption (or the Exodus), finally deliverance (or the arrival in Canaan); cf. e.g. Diedrich 1997.[121] Aspects to be covered included abhorrent violence,

---

120 Olney describes the slave narratives as "so cumulative and so invariant, so repetitive and so much alike", 1985, 148. Chaney holds: "Indeed, if the format of the standard slave narrative were not routine enough, the iconography of abolitionism offered no variety of expression." (2008, 6)

121 It has to be pointed out that while comparing the original, African-*American* slave narrative to a contemporary, African-*Canadian* Neo-slave narrative such as *The Book of Negroes*, one significant aspect has to be kept in mind from the start: in the original fugitive slave's account, Canada figures as an almost transcendental entity, 'Canaan'. Canada, particularly after the passing of the Fugitive Slave Law in 1850, attains the status of the sole terminal (exemplified by its connection to the Underground Railroad, whose terminals were often on Canadian soil). After 1850, the Northern United States ceased to present a safe haven for runaway slaves, making Canada their only viable route of escape. Before the Fugitive Slave Law, a US-American Canaan existed in the Northern States; after 1850, slaves could not rely on intra-US redemption any more. On the US and what Greene calls the America-as-"Eden trope" (7), cf. Greene 1996.

The resulting dichotomy between the US and Canada (metaphorically, hell vs. heaven) had to be highlighted in order to achieve maximum propagandistic effect. African-Canadian literature, however, as will be pointed out numerous times in this thesis, has not been and cannot be content with the simple dualism thus construed, lest Canadian shortcomings regarding its Black population be glossed over. Consequently, while the slave narrative has proved to be constitutive for African-American literature as a genre to be adopted and developed, it has been constitutive for African-Canadian literature as a genre to be ad*a*pted and *disputed*.

The reflection of the slave narrative in Black Canadian literature is thus a more complex and intellectualized one, necessarily becoming more elusive; while the overall intention of showcasing the

an inhumane workload (enforced by the whip), the destruction of families, and sexual abuse. Topics to be avoided, on the other hand, were lust for White women as well as violence of slaves against Whites; after all, the authors of slave narratives were to establish the racial equality and civility of Blacks, not foster existing stereotypical fears among the Whites. Under the abolitionists' patronage, the slave narrative became a mass publication business by the late 1830s. Large readerships in both the United States and England indulged in the subsequent accounts of Frederick Douglass (1845), William Wells Brown (1847), Henry Bibb (1849), Sojourner Truth (1850), or Solomon Northup (1853). Douglass, who followed up his 1845 *Narrative of the Life of Frederick Douglass, An American Slave, Written by Himself* ten years later with *My Bondage and Freedom* [2000] to include more of his post-slavery experiences, created the genre's epitome by stressing the connection between freedom and literacy and by creating the prototypical "loner" hero (cf. Diedrich 1997, 408),[122] while Jacobs's influential *Incidents in the Life of a Slave Girl*, self-published in 1861, underlines the double discrimination endured by female slaves. Jacobs thus establishes an audibly female voice in the canon of a mostly male-dominated genre, influencing later high-profile African-American women writers such as Zora Neale Hurston, Alice Walker or Toni Morrison. Most African-American writers have since acknowledged the impact of the slave narrative on their writings. A wide range of "Neo-slave narratives", among them best-sellers such as Toni Morrison's *Beloved* (1987), have consciously embraced or (as in the case of Ishmael Reed's satirical 1976 novel *Flight to Canada*) irreverently grappled with the influence of the slave narrative on contemporary literature.

The term "neoslave narrative" has been coined by Bernard W. Bell in his 1989 study *The Afro-American Novel and its Tradition.* Ashraf A. H. Rushdy is generally credited with reinvigorating the term (which he acknowledges to have borrowed from Bell, cf. Rushdy 1999, 233), albeit with a slightly different spelling ("Neo-slave narrative") and a more specific definition. Conventionally, studies of "contemporary narratives of slavery" (a more encompassing term used by Arlene R. Keizer 2004, 2) begin by quoting two aspects of Bell's early

---

evils of slavery of course has to be maintained, one of the slave narrative's central tenets, the moral opposition between the United States and Canada has to be deconstructed. Another aspect to be minded is the fact that the original slave narrative was at all times (African-) *American* in its impetus. Even though Canada may feature as the new home of former slaves such as Henry Bibb (cf. Bibb 2000), Canada's intrinsic value is limited to its function as a contrast to the slave-ridden United States in their accounts. As such, it is not a direct (in the sense of strictly national) predecessor or model for African-Canadian literature. However, the slave narrative, just like African-American literature in general – and even more so, African-American thought in terms of racial, social and political philosophy –, has heavily influenced African-Canadian literature as well.

122 Olney argues that in some respects, however, Douglass is more of an exception than the role model: "... Douglass regularly reflects back and forth (and here he is very much the exception) from the person written about to the person writing, from a narrative of past events to a present narrator grown out of these events." (1985, 158) In terms of perspective, Douglass is thus more closely related to *The Book of Negroes* than to his contemporaries. For a discussion of Douglass's unrepresentativeness in terms of the classic slave narrative (particularly by virtue of being a 'lone male hero'), also cf. Heglar 2001, 149-152.

definition: neoslave narratives, Charles J. Heglar summarizes, "are 'based primarily on folk material' (286); they are 'residually oral, modern narratives of escape from bondage to freedom' (289)." (2001, 148) This definition has two grave flaws, the first one being that Heglar simply quotes Bell out of context. The criterion of being "based primarily on folk material" is not part of some sort of general definition of the neoslave narrative but a concrete description of Margaret Walker's 1966 novel *Jubilee* [1999], which reads, in full: "As its structure and style reveal, *Jubilee* is a neoslave narrative based primarily on folk material and Vyry's quest for freedom." (Bell 1989, 286) Logically, Heglar thus also ought to argue that it is characteristic of the neoslave narrative to include "Vyry's quest". The second flaw – genuinely Bell's – is the extensive, even sweeping, scope of literature falling under the category of "residually oral, modern narratives of escape from bondage to freedom." As Valerie Smith – while incorrectly attributing Bell with Rushdy's later, hyphenated and lowercase version of the term 'neo-slave narrative' – has noted, "over time that definition has expanded to include a more diverse set of texts than Bell's initial description could have anticipated." (V. Smith 2007, 168) Although it is hard to see how such a broad definition could be expanded beyond anticipation, Arlene Keizer goes even further, claiming:

> Though Bell's definition is more inclusive than Rushdy's, it nevertheless limits the scope of these works because of its focus on the movement from enslavement to freedom, the trajectory of the traditional slave narrative. (Keizer 2004, 3)

As she, too, cites Bell's definition, which rests on the three aspects of 1) being residually oral, 2) being modern, 3) dealing with the escape from slavery to freedom, her proposed definition, if it indeed was to sidestep the 'narrowness' of Bell's conception, would consequently have to position the neoslave narrative simply as modern, residually oral fiction. Assuming that a reference to slavery should still be included (even though shunning the original slave narrative's "trajectory"), one might thus define the neoslave narrative, *à la manière de* Keizer, as a modern, residually oral fiction referencing slavery – a definition whose limiting, and thus defining, power is rather doubtful. Thankfully, Keizer acknowledges the broadness of her approach and reclassifies the neoslave narratives, rephrases her use of the overall genre as "the contemporary narrative of slavery" and breaks what she correctly identifies as "a wide variety of works" down into three categories:

> (1) the historical novel of slavery (*Beloved, Cambridge, Oxherding Tale*); (2) works set in the present which explicitly connect African American/Afro-Caribbean [Keizer's area of study] life in the present with US/Caribbean slavery (*The Chosen Place, The Timeless People, Corregidora, Dream on Monkey Mountain*); and (3) hybrid works in which scenes from the past are juxtaposed with scenes set in the present (*An Echo in the Bone, Thereafter Johnnie*). (Keizer 2004, 2)[123]

---

123 Ashraf Rushdy arrives at a slightly different threefold categorization, identifying "three major forms that these novels [Neo-slave narratives] employ: the historical novel, the pseudo-autobiographical slave narrative, and the novel of remembered generations", which focuses on intergenerational traumatic legacies (Rushdy 2004, 90).

Ashraf Rushdy's own definition of the Neo-slave narrative, by far the most quoted one in the study of the genre as he is widely credited with establishing it as a convincing category of analysis in the first place (cf. e.g. Brodzki 2007, Dickson-Carr 2005, Mitchell 2002, Spaulding 2005) "focuses even more narrowly [than Bell] on the influence of the antebellum slave narrative, analyzing only those contemporary novels that clearly and explicitly reference nineteenth-century, first-person, literate slave testimony" (Keizer 2004, 3).[124] As Tim A. Ryan has duly noted (2008, cf. 187f.), this statement is true in terms of Rushdy's definition, yet misleading in terms of the actual corpus. Ishmael Reed's *Flight to Canada* is one of the four novels studied in Rushdy's *Neo-Slave Narratives* (1999), yet it does in fact not adhere to Rushdy's own definition, which explicitly includes the phrase "first-person voice" (ibid., 3). *Flight to Canada*, however, is not told by a first-person (slave) narrator except for very brief introductory and concluding passages (which are visibly set apart by italics, cf. Reed 1998, 11 and 178). In contrast to Ryan, who is generally critical of Rushdy's approach, Keizer does not notice this error and thus simply echoes Rushdy's inconsistency.

In full, Rushdy's introductory definition of the genre reads as follows: Neo-slave narratives are "contemporary novels that assume the form, adopt the conventions, and take on the first-person voice of the ante-bellum slave narrative." (Rushdy 1999, 3) Based on this definition, which leaves enough room to be inclusive – cf. the flexibility of the phrases "assume the form" and "adopt the conventions" – yet is decisive enough to be limiting – cf. the necessity of a first-person narrator –, it is indeed possible to assess contemporary varieties of the original slave narrative. While Rushdy's criteria might appear slightly formalistic at first glance, they are indeed useful yardsticks for an approach not only taking account of, but moving beyond the purely formal aspects of the Neo-slave narrative. Rushdy himself conceptualizes the uses and the goals of an analysis of the form in order to arrive at conclusions concerning, *inter alia*, Black subjectivity, identity constructions, and the structuring of historiography:

> The authors of the Neo-slave narrative raise questions concerning the possibility for subjective knowledge within a predetermined form of writing, especially as regards the construction and dismantling of 'racial' identity. They ask questions about and demonstrate the process through which a historical subject constitutes itself by employing or revising a set of ideologically charged textual structures.[125] [...] Most important, they ask what it means for a postmodern author to negotiate and reconstruct what is essentially a premodern form, one in which 'race' was both a presupposition of authenticity for the author and yet a necessary absence for the primarily white, northern readership. [The Neo-slave narrative contains a] complex interplay among literary texts, social processes, and cultural imperatives, showing how literary form contributes to and is partially derived from the processes of racial formation... (Rushdy 1999, 7)

---

124 Like Keizer, Pilar Cuder-Domínguez laments Rushdy's definition to be "too restrictive" for her purposes (2003, 73).

125 Though Rushdy does not explicitly reference Foucault here, it should be obvious that the termini and the notions used here – connection between knowledge and power; self-assertion within a given discursive frame – in fact rely on his works (cf. particularly Foucault 1980 and 2002).

It should be obvious from this quote that Rushdy accordingly devotes a chapter to conceptualizing a theory of intertextuality which he applies to the four novels he investigates. His intertextual approach – largely based on Julia Kristeva and Hortense Spillers[126] – includes intraliterary linkages but also, and more centrally so, connections between the literary and the social text while particularly paying attention to the "intertextual relations between 'mainstream' and 'minority' discourses and traditions" (Rushdy 1999, 16). In terms of the Neo-slave narrative, the most important influences from the 'social text' are, as Rushdy argues, the New Left, the Civil Rights Movement, and the Black Power Movement. Superficially often perceived as a disputation of William Styron's *The Confessions of Nat Turner*, a highly controversial novel criticized most prominently for its alleged appropriation of the Black slaves' voice,[127] the Neo-slave narratives of the 1970s and 1980s react not so much toward Styron's novel *per se* but toward its genesis in the 1960s (cf. Rushdy 1999, 18).

In his 2004 article "The Neo-Slave Narrative", Rushdy provides a concise explanation for the rise of the Neo-slave narrative, expounding the genre's genesis and ambitions in what María Frías calls "a more militant attitude" than Bell and Elizabeth Beaulieu (1999) adopt.[128] According to this analysis, the Civil Rights Movement led to a more nuanced and more individual depiction of slavery in scholarly work, as it underscored the approach of the New Left to present history 'from the bottom up' by attesting to the fact that the ostensibly powerless may in fact 'make history'. This led to a revived interest in the slave narrative (which of course, focusing on the slave as the paragon of powerlessness, provide prototypical examples of these trends) and thus to a rise in fictional accounts of slavery. Furthermore, the Black Power Movement incited college programs in Black Studies and excited writers, which in turn also piqued the interest of publishers.[129] Consequently, more fictional accounts referencing

---

126 Combined, Kristeva 1986 (*The Kristeva Reader*) and 2002 (*The Portable Kristeva*) offer the bulk of work by the Bulgarian-born thinker. The recent collection *Black, White, and in Color: Essays on American Literature and Culture* (Spillers 2003) provides a good overview of African-American feminist Hortense J. Spillers's writings; in this context, it is interesting to note that she is an expert not only on Toni Morrison in general, but also on reverberations of the slave narrative in the Nobel laureate's work.

127 For criticism on Styron's novel, cf. J. H. Clarke's 1968 *William Styron's* Nat Turner: *Ten Black Writers Respond* as well as Byerman 2005, 54-57; cf. Hadaller 1996, 113-139 on Styron's female characters; also cf. Henderson 2002, 62, and Ryan 2008, part. 83-111.

128 Frías's comment refers to Rushdy's earlier work. In the 2004 article, which otherwise largely reflects his previous studies, Rushdy acknowledges having included in his analysis works that diverge from his initial definition of the Neo-slave narrative, which calls for a first-person narrator; cf. Rushdy 2004, 98 (as an aside, he also reverts to the minuscule in 'neo-slave narrative', a change I will abstain from as it further complicates the distinction between Bell's "neoslave narrative" and Rushdy's original "Neo-slave narrative"; the majuscule also fittingly indicates, I believe, the indebtedness of this specific form of postslavery literature to conscious theoretical notions of adaptation).

129 Rushdy admits that there was also considerable skepticism among the adherents of the Black Power Movement concerning such an apparently 'backwards', almost 'reactionary' gaze, yet claims that "the reclamation of 'blackness' as a political category and an ethnic identity necessitated such an archeological project" (Rushdy 2004, 102).

slavery were written, published, and studied. The variously rejuvenated study of the slave narrative and the emergence of the Neo-slave narrative have thus coincided chronologically, a fact which Rushdy and others have understood also as a causal, not only a correlating relationship. This adds to the broadly held opinion that the slave narrative is the very basis of much of African-American (and, transnationally, African-Canadian) literature: "The narratives of ex-slaves are, for the literary critic, the very foundation upon which most subsequent Afro-American fictional and nonfictional narrative forms are based." (Gates 2002, 5)

The exact extent to which the slave narrative as a literary genre has indeed had an effect on Black North American writing, however, has been disputed. Ralph Ellison, for instance – in contrast to Gates and others – argues that African-American writers could hardly *fail* to include elements of the slave narrative in their writings. The general themes of exploitation, injustice, maltreatment and the search for freedom have, according to his logic, simply been quite unavoidable for African-American writers concerned with the fate of Blacks in North America (cf. Ellison 1995a, 372f.; also cf. this thesis' section on "Representation, appropriation, authentication", p 129ff.). He additionally claims that novelists are inspired not primarily by autobiographies or historical works but by other *novels*, which he calls "a cultural, literary reality" (ibid., 373). Regarding the latter assertion, though the degree of influence of either fiction, historical accounts or autobiographies can evidently not be determined in an *overall* way, Lawrence Hill distinctly points out *his* interest in history and (auto-) biography.[130] Moreover, the strict distinction between fictional and historical accounts underlying Ellison's argument has repeatedly been debated.[131] Regarding Ellison's first line of reasoning, an assessment pertaining to the actual influence of slave narratives upon particular literary works is empowered by the wealth of scholarly literature on the topic blossoming since World War II and further invigorated by the Civil Rights and Black Power Movements.[132] Hence, we do not have to content ourselves with the identification of broad thematic correlatives *à la* Bell (or even flimsier thematic links *à la* Keizer).[133] Instead, a host of criteria has been developed to characterize and define the genre of the slave narrative in a detailed and concrete way.

---

130 Cf. his afterword to *The Book of Negroes* (BN 471-479) as well as the interview reprinted in this thesis. Also cf. the discussion of his concept of 'faction' (p. 55ff.).

131 Cf. section 4.2., "Hill's Faction and Historiographic Metafiction" above; for the time being, I maintain here, in regard to the (Neo-) slave narrative, a rough division between largely *non*-fictional, *original* slave narratives and predominantly *fictional, Neo*-slave narratives – a distinction which more or less corresponds to the overt retention or suspension of the autobiographical pact (cf. below).

132 An extensive list of early studies can be found in Davis/Gates 1985b, xiv, as well as in Diedrich's thematic bibliography (1986). An explanation of *current* interest in the slave narrative can be found in Spaulding 2005, particularly 8ff.

133 For the mere thematic incorporation of the slavery topos in contemporary (in fact, all post-slavery) literature, the very terms 'postslavery literature' or 'postslavery fiction' might be more appropriate than 'Neo-slave narrative', 'neo-slave narrative' or even 'neoslave narrative'. As in 'postcolonial' literature, the 'post' prefix in 'postslavery literature' would not indicate the mere dealing with a chronologically post-slavery situation but with the discourses surrounding slavery

Accordingly, what will be undertaken in this section is the dissection of *The Book of Negroes* according to a range of these criteria. In order to do so, I will classify the criteria (which of course logically are characteristics rather than criteria given their *a posteriori* genesis) into categories, then apply them to *The Book of Negroes*. The categories I will be using are: 1) layout, structure, publication, 2) thematic characteristics, recurrent phrases and images, and 3) goals – thus dealing with three essential elements of narrative: form or composition, content, impact or goal (the latter element translating as 'intention' or 'meaning' in a traditional sense). Evidently, the comparison of Hill's novel with the established literary mould of the slave narrative is not an end in itself, lest it be what Rushdy would, disparagingly, call a mere "'influence' or 'revisionist' study" (Rushdy 1999, 14). Instead, as has been pointed out above, the comparative approach will facilitate the contextualization of Hill's novel, clarify its approach and trajectory, draw attention to its structure and narrative configuration, and, last but not least, provide an organizing principle to its analysis. Valerie Smith, in her introduction to the Neo-slave narrative, sums up the merits of this genre:

> [The Neo-slave narratives'] differences notwithstanding, these texts illustrate the centrality of the history and the memory of slavery to our individual, racial, gender, cultural, and national identities. Further, they provide a perspective on a host of issues that resonate in contemporary cultural, historical, critical, and literary discourses, among them: the challenges of representing trauma and traumatic memories; the legacy of slavery (and other atrocities) for subsequent generations; the interconnectedness of constructions of race and gender; the relationship of the body to memory; the agency of the enslaved; the power of orality and of literacy; the ambiguous role of religion; the commodification of black bodies and experiences; and the elusive nature of freedom. (V. Smith 2007, 168f.)

As Hill's novel likewise deals with all of the aspects listed in Smith's remarks, the following sections will look at Aminata's story as a Neo-slave narrative in more detail. It is my claim that without the juxtaposition of slave narrative and *The Book of Negroes,* a number of the novel's qualities (double meaning intended) would not even surface; the question of the narrator's constant renaming is one example, the inverted use of the Exodus motif another. Thus, the three analytical subcategories of comparison (composition, content and goals) serve both as a structuring and a theoretical framework in the analysis of *The Book of Negroes* in the light of the slave narrative.

5.2.1. *Category one: Composition*

Concerning layout, structure and publication, one of the overriding features of the slave narrative is its "hetero*generic*" nature (Olney 1985, 152; his emphasis). Somewhat confusingly, Olney's term does not strictly refer to the closeness to other genres (which is indeed another

---

and/or its aftermath. Handley (2000) employs the term 'postslavery literature' (and also discusses its possible weaknesses, cf. 2ff.), yet it is not a widely used designation, which would facilitate a usage that indicates fictions *dealing with* slavery, while the term Neo-slave narrative (or neo-slave narrative) could be reserved for texts more closely (e.g. also formally) connected to the slave narrative – which, after all, it is terminologically, qua its prefix, supposed to revive or emulate.

characteristic of the slave narrative),[134] but to the heterogeneity of modes, literary styles and the structural closeness to collage techniques: the slave narrative includes elements of testimonials, epigraphs, poetry, illustrations, documents and legislation, to name the most common ones. George Elliott Clarke employs this *modus operandi* in *George & Rue* (2005) as well as in his poetry. Afua Cooper, in *The Hanging of Angélique* (2006), approaches the collage technique from its reverse side, inserting narrative elements into a non-fictional account of Quebec's most famous slave, which is largely based on trial records. Claire Harris works extensively with 'found pieces' in her poetry. In *Childhood* (1998), André Alexis inserts maps, poetry by Archibald Lampman, diary entries, mathematical equations and the like, yet uses them to a very different purpose, viz. to *question* authority, coherence and memory (just as Joy Kogawa's epitomic novel *Obasan* does for the context of a different Canadian visible minority). The purpose of the heterogeneous mode of the original slave narrative is quite the opposite: the authentication of the ex-slave's account.

As Hegel's notion of the absence of humanity and the alleged voicelessness of Africans suggests, it was essential for the slave narrative to initially establish the plain *existence* of their authors. Furthermore, if political action was to derive from their accounts, they had to be credible at all costs (one of the literary shortcomings resulting from this urge was then the streamlining into formulae that allowed little originality). No doubt could be afforded as to whether the author had 'meddled' with his story: the suspicion of willful fictionality would have rendered the narrative useless for the abolitionists' political purposes. From the start, however, the slave narrative's authenticity was under racially charged scrutiny by its White readership: How could Black people write the stories of their lives, given their 'obvious' cognitive inferiority? Moreover, even if the readership was prepared to accept the slaves' mental *ability* to pen their accounts (which, for the most part, the audience was not prepared to do), hadn't the institution of slavery, given its ban on acquiring literacy, obliterated the basic skills to do so? The mere existence of the slave author, his intellectual capacity and his literacy thus had to be ascertained and verified before any slave narrative could exert its political impact. The heterogeneous, collage-like technique provided the means to do so. The existence of the slave author, for instance, was illustrated by certificates of ownership, testimonies by White abolitionists confirming their personal acquaintance with the author, an engraved portrait of the ex-slave on the title page as well as other documentary such as proof of manumission. The ability of the ex-slaves to indeed tell their own story is demonstrated through essentialist claims ("Written by himself", for instance, is a common addition to the title of the narratives, cf. Olney 1985)[135] and/or the testimony of White amanuenses claiming to have faithfully rec-

---

134 Cf. on the influence of the picaresque novel e.g Nichols 1985, Píccinato 1994, and Reinhart 2001 (who does not come from an African-American studies background but focuses on the picaresque novel itself, also briefly commenting on both aforementioned articles); for the sentimental novel, cf. Weinstein 2007; for the captivity narrative and the spiritual autobiography, cf. Pierce 2007; also cf. Greene 1996 (who includes – in addition to the standard genres – the fairy tale as an influence, cf. 89), and Gates 1989, 81f.

135 Of the ten narratives collected in the canonical anthology *Slave Narratives* by William L. Andrews and Henry Louis Gates, Jr. (2000), six titles contain the addition 'Written/related by him-

orded what the ex-slave orally reported. Through amanuenses, the stereotype of White superiority is maintained, while at the same time the authenticity of the narrative is established.

However, many slave narratives in fact also include fictional elements, often induced by the existence of prior slave narratives or other readings (e.g. Biblical ones) on which they are modeled. A number of narratives have been under re-evaluation regarding their authenticity; most recently, Olaudah Equiano's account has been questioned.[136] Moreover, slave narratives such as *The Bondwoman's Narrative*, allegedly written by one Hannah Craft and recently edited by Henry Louis Gates, Jr. in a remarkable facsimile edition, are arguably fictionalized versions of autobiographies (for a summary of the debate revolving around the *Bondwoman's* authenticity, cf. e.g. Reid-Pharr 2007; comprehensively and centrally: Gates/Robbins 2004). Nonetheless, the original slave narrative, in contrast to Neo-slave narratives, lays claim to the presentation of an authentic autobiography (even though, based on the fluctuation of authors' names, the "autobiographical pact" in its stricter sense is suspended; cf. Casmier-Paz 2001, 216).[137] It is surprising, then, to find that Hill to a certain degree adheres to the modes of authenticating Aminata's account through structural means such as the inclusion of heterogeneous, 'heterogeneric' elements.[138] *The Book of Negroes* includes a va-

---

self/herself (Harriet Ann Jacobs, Henry Bibb, William Wells Brown, Frederick Douglass, Olaudah Equiano, James Albert Ukawsaw Gronniosaw).

136 A theory proposed by Vincent Carretta (2005; also cf. 2007); also cf. Hochschild 2005, 369ff., Eckstein 2006, 28ff., and Mackenthun 2004, chapter 2 ("The Emergence of the 'Postcolonial' Atlantic", 23-47).

137 Casmier-Paz refers to what is also variously termed the "autobiographical contract". Philippe Lejeune (2005 [1975]) has devised what he termed the *pacte autographique* as a mode of emphasizing the unity of author/narrator/protagonist in autobiographical writing. The *signature* (the author's proper name) guarantees the autobiographical contract, while readers do not necessarily assume the entirety of the work to be factually correct; they take for granted, however, that the author has striven to maintain the highest level of veracity possible. The autobiographical contract is signaled by *para*textual elements alone (cf. for instance the usage of frontispieces depicting the authors/narrators) and cannot be determined text-immanently.

In *The Book of Negroes*, as in the Neo-slave narrative in general, the autobiographical contract is evidently revoked, which is visible paratextually (by Hill's name on the title) as well as immanently by minor glitches such as using the word 'trauma' in an anachronistic way (cf. footnote 143, p. 96). Lejeune's structuralist and referential conception has come under severe criticism (mostly, though not surprisingly, by poststructuralism) for its adherence to a strict division between autobiography and fiction (cf. Marcus 1994). Lejeune himself, however, has softened his stance in later works to accommodate the fictional aspects of autobiography. For a Canadian perspective on autobiography, cf. e.g. the essays in Rak 2005. On the slave narrative *not* being a standard autobiographical work according to Western notions of highly *individualized* stories, cf. Olney 1985, 154.

138 In terms of layout, *The Book of Negroes* extensively deviates from the slave narrative's model. There is, for instance, no frontispiece engraving of the author (in this case, the narrator). The novel's original cover, as opposed to the US-American edition, does however offer the head shot of a person obviously meant to resemble Aminata (cf. for instance the crescent moons carved into her cheeks). The slave narrative's appendix of sermons, reflections on slavery, appeals, speeches, and poems (cf. Olney 1985, 153) is not mirrored in Hill's novel, even though we do find "A Word

riety of these collage elements, many of them explicitly listed in Olney's inventory of essential slave narrative components (cf. Olney 1985). Thus, we find a poetic epigraph as well as a biblical one; Swift's poem is taken up time and again throughout the text, as are other bits from Swift's works (cf. e.g. BN 204, when Aminata is given a copy of *Gulliver's Travels* by her master Solomon Lindo). Pieces of legislation are quoted, such as the Lord Dunmore and the Philipsburg Proclamations (BN 268 and 279), the Birch Certificate granting Black Loyalists passage to and freedom in Nova Scotia (BN 302) or the Peace Treaty ending hostilities in the War of Independence (BN 282f.). Letters (e.g. BN 207)[139] are reprinted alongside text excerpts from actual slave narratives (BN 443),[140] prayers (Koran verses, for instance; e.g. BN 33f.) and songs ("Rule Britannia" during a church service, for example; BN 236f.; or a gospel chorus sung at a funeral; BN 267). Advertisements for runaway slaves are cited twice (cf. BN 208, 321), underlining the continuous danger of recapture and re-enslavement even in the Northern United States and the 'Promised Land' of Canada.[141]

The extent to which Hill relies on heterogeneric elements does not amount to the heterogeneity of Alexis's *Childhood* or Harris's poetry in terms of quantity. Two key elements, however, underline the conscious and prominent usage of this characteristic. The overt element is constituted by the explicit reference to actual slave narratives, whereas in terms of literary impact, the most important heterogeneric element is the portrayal of the actual Book of Negroes and the entries Aminata makes in this ledger. The direct references to historic slave narratives provide a conscious intertextual acknowledgment of this genre's influence on

---

about History" and an annotated bibliography "For Further Reading" annexed to the novel, which might be used as stepping stones to the acquisition of such material. The obligatory poetic epigraph, of which Olney ironically comments it should be "by preference from William Cowper" (cf. ibid., 152), exists in the form of a poem by Jonathan Swift. Hill does not include any illustrations, either; maps, for instance, are described in detail rather than reprinted. The convergences and divergences in layout, however, certainly do not constitute the main comparative criteria here – after all, publication conventions have drastically altered within the last 200 years. If they had not, the title of Hill's novel would possibly not have read *The Book of Negroes* or *Someone Knows My Name*, but *The Trials of Tribulations of Aminata Diallo, or Meena Dee, Born and Captured in Africa and Abducted to America. Containing the Account of her Life in New York, Canada, and Sierra Leone, as Told in her Own Words.*

139 These constitute a minor element in the novel, whereas a small number of slave narratives was in fact written in epistolary form; cf. Link 1985, 291, who quotes M. Walker in this regard.

140 Somewhat oddly, Hill employs this intertextual reference in more of a scholarly than a novelistic style, reprinting the passage from Equiano's narrative using triple dots and square brackets to indicate omissions – even though the passage is supposedly read by Aminata to a group of African villagers (cf. ibid.).

141 These kinds of advertisements have become a standard ingredient of historical accounts of the Black presence in Canada (cf. e.g. Spray 1997, 342f.; Elgersman 1999, part. chapter 2; Winks 1997, 107; Hamilton 1994, 14f.), being used to the exact same effect as Lawrence Hill employs them, viz. the presentation of irrefutable proof that the conception of Canada as a safe haven for runaways is an, albeit common, misconception. (For the – of course also existent – opposite advertisement, cf. Collison 1998, 178, who reprints an ad in a Canadian newspaper by fugitive slaves looking for employment in "the True Land of Liberty".)

Hill's writing and a heterogeneric aspect, with nods towards Equiano's account being the most common reference. When talking to Anna Maria Falconbridge, wife of the former slave-ship's doctor who assists Aminata in her attempt to return to her native village of Bayo, Aminata admits to not having read his account yet. In a casual comment on the importance of authenticity, Hill has Mrs Falconbridge declare that she has "no idea if [Equiano's] account is entirely true. But no matter." (BN 409) This comment harks back to both the fictional character of Hill's own work and the discussion that has evolved around the authenticity of Equiano's narrative, and strongly suggests that such a dispute may have intrinsic value to historical studies but not to the fate of the author or the impact of such a work. Falconbridge continues: "His book has sold everywhere in England. There is many a white Englishman poorer than he." (Ibid.) Falconbridge gives Aminata her copy of the *Interesting Narrative*, from which Aminata, in a double irony – given the fact that she is both an ex-slave and kept from returning to Bayo by fear of re-capture –, reads to the villagers accommodating her after she has fled from the slave traders who had agreed to take her inland to her native village. Aminata uses this English-language passage (which is reprinted in *The Book of Negroes* with editorial changes) to authenticate her *own* tale, as the villagers had questioned her story and demanded that she speak the language of the toubabu, the Whites, to prove her account. The *mise en abyme* is completed when Aminata summarizes the narrative for the Africans, describing of course her own story in the process:

> I told them that Equiano was an African, kidnapped and taken to the land of the toubabu, and that he had survived and recaptured his freedom and written a book about his life. (BN 443)

In accordance with the conventions of the slave narrative, Aminata furthermore dismisses the use of violence; when asked by the Africans whether Equiano took revenge once he had regained his freedom, Aminata explains that he "was too busy surviving to go back and kill his enemies." (BN 444) Having aborted her African quest and gone to London with Clarkson, Aminata once more discusses Equiano's writing. Speaking with Dante, Clarkson's suggestively named Black butler, she learns that Equiano is famous among London's Black community. When she expresses her desire to meet the writer, however, Dante has to disappoint Aminata: "He died a few years ago", (BN 454) a statement which within the novel's chronology corresponds to Equiano's actual date of death in 1797. It is salient for the authenticity of her memoirs that Aminata does not meet Equiano as a fictional character. If she had, the parallels between *The Interesting Narrative* and *The Book of Negroes* would have been overriding, dominating her own tale both in terms of her fictional writing process and in terms of contemporary assessments of the novel. Hill makes abundantly clear that Aminata has to come up with her own technique of grappling with her past, even though he acknowledges her familiarity with Equiano's work. Her memoirs will thus by necessity not be limited to a mere allegory of *The Interesting Life*; they will be indebted but independent:

> I felt deflated. Equiano was the one man I would have liked to meet. I felt I already knew him after reading his story, and had hoped to ask how he had gone about writing the account of his life. (BN 454)

The insertion and discussion of actual slave narratives in *The Book of Negroes* thus conforms to the overall impact of the slave narrative's genre on both this work and Black North American literature in general, as in a nutshell, 'indebted but independent' is the prevailing contemporary stance towards the literary heritage provided by the ex-slaves' accounts. Hill very offensively recognizes the influence and the parallels while at the same time twisting and reconfiguring some of the genre's main tenets.[142] The inclusion of original slave narratives in Hill's novel represents both an authentic technique of this genre – 'heterogenerity' – and a metafictional comment on its literary impact.[143]

The same holds true for the inclusion of the historical Book of Negroes, the British military ledger containing the records of about 3,000 Blacks deemed worthy of passage to

---

142 This position is characteristic of the approach taken by authors of Neo-slave narratives, as Spaulding observes: "As a result [of the original slave narrative's conventions forcing it to leave certain aspects of the slaves lives' out], the contemporary writers' relationship to the original slave narrative is complex, evoking both vexation at the forces which constrained the form and admiration for the ways the writers were able to negotiate these constraints. For writers of the postmodern slave narrative, simply recovering the voices of those who endured slavery is not enough. They set out to re-form the slave narrative itself..." (Spaulding 2005, 8).

143 In addition to repeatedly mentioning the ex-slave Olaudah Equiano's narrative, Hill includes references to two non-fictional accounts written by Whites at the time of slavery. Alexander Falconbridge, who features as a character in *The Book of Negroes* – enabling Aminata to go inland in search of Bayo – is, according to his own standards, "a complex failure" (BN 407) who regrets his involvement in the slave trade. His document (entitled *An Account of the Slave Trade on the Coast of Africa, by Alexander Falconbridge. Late Surgeon in the African Trade. London, 1788.* BN 407) is hence committed to the abolitionist cause. The actual document is provided in Falconbridge/Falconbridge 2000.

As a side note, Hill has Mrs Falconbridge make an anachronistic remark in regard to her husband's report: reading Mr Falconbridge's account, Aminata has to put the book away, overwhelmed by flashbacks of her own passage onboard the slave ship (intensified by her conjuring up the stench of the vessel, which "smelled like death itself," BN 408. Cf. discussions of sensory impressions in mnemonic processes, section 5.3.1., "Expository frame setting"). Mrs Falconbridge then comments: "I can see that the reading is traumatic," (ibid.) employing the term 'trauma' in its psychological meaning, which it had not yet acquired in the early 1800s. This mishap vividly underlines that the concepts of trauma and of traumatic reading are notions that have been vital to Hill's writing of *The Book of Negroes* – so prevalent indeed that they have slipped into the novel's pre-psychoanalytical terminology.

Hill also mentions John Newton's *Journal of a Slave Trader, 1750-1754* (cf. BN 418), thus adding to Aminata's memoir (which poses as a slave narrative, but actually constitutes a fictional, Neo-slave narrative) an original, though possibly fictional, slave narrative (Equiano), the non-fictional report of an ex-ship's doctor in the slave trade (Falconbridge) and the non-fictional work of an ex-slave trader (Newton), again authenticating his story as well as his research and adding the perspectives of several parties involved in the transatlantic slave trade. Hence, Hill deals with the legacy of historical accounts in the same way he deals with other issues, such as intra-African slavery or professed 'justifications' of slavery: by including multiple perspectives and providing a complex, multi-faceted and encompassing approach.

Nova Scotia.[144] The historical file, whose eminent importance for Hill's work is most obviously illustrated by the literal repercussion in the novel's title, serves as a cornerstone of several
key topics. These include concepts of anonymity and identity, forgetfulness and remembrance, promise and reality, hypocrisy and truthfulness, individual and collective memory,
oral and written history, as well as, in the most general take, bondage and freedom. At first
sight, the Book of Negroes should indeed be the epitome of the dichotomy between bondage
and freedom, and should serve to illustrate the opposition between the benevolent British Empire and the malicious slave system of the United States. After all, the people registered in it
were, historically as well as in Hill's work, promised freedom and equality in the British colonies north of the 49th parallel based on their duties rendered to the Loyalist cause during the
War of Independence.

Naturally, such a crude dichotomy between slavery in the US and British benevolence
in Canada is not supported by a close reading of Aminata's role in the process of registering
the Black Loyalists. Aminata, true to her characteristic position of intermediary,[145] agrees to
help the British military record the names of those eligible for passage from New York, beginning her duty on April 21, 1783 (cf. BN 291). Aminata describes her task in a perfunctory
way,[146] yet it is clear from the onset that there are darker notions lurking underneath the surface of the automated liberation ostensibly performed in the act of registering the Black Loyalists for their passage to freedom. Even though the journey to Nova Scotia entails, in principle, the exact opposite of the Middle Passage, people are suggestively "kept in a waiting area
below" deck (BN 292) when Aminata embarks, reminding the attentive reader of her arrival
on board the slave vessel that brought her to America in the first place.[147] As the registering
process and its implications for collective memory processes in particular are discussed in
more detail later on, it should suffice here to say that even though Aminata is hired as a mere

---

144 Not all of the Blacks registered in the Book of Negroes actually sailed to Nova Scotia. A minority
went to other British colonies or to Europe (cf. BN afterword, 471; also cf. Robert-Johnson 2009,
30, or Walker 1992, 11f.).

145 Not only is Aminata an interpreter for both the Africans and the Europeans; speaking two African
languages, she is even an interpreter between different African language groups. She is also a
midwife, acting as intermediary between the pre- and postnatal world of the infants. Furthermore,
she acts as a news broker in Birchtown and Canvas Town, transforming official written an-
nouncements into oral reports for the illiterate inhabitants of the Black communities. Later on, she
also serves as a go-between for the abolitionists in their efforts before the Parliament and the
King. Of course she also serves the reader as an intermediary by narrating her (and her fellows')
experiences.

146 "We were there to inspect the Negroes. My job was to listen to the officers interview the refugees
and to enter details into a two-page ledger." (BN 292) Hill, in the afterword, acknowledges that
Aminata's employment is most likely inauthentic, as the British military did not hire scribes to
perform this task, but simply used their own staff (cf. BN 473).

147 This notion is emphasized when Aminata and Chekura board the ship. Their (ostensible) freedom
is immediately linked to the memory of the Middle Passage and its inspection and shipment of
slaves: "With a few businesslike scratches of the quill on paper, we were free. Chekura and I
moved below deck with the last of the inspected Negroes." (BN 303)

tool by the British, she by far surpasses this function and becomes a chronicler and safe-keeper of memories and identities.

In the context of slave narrative characteristics, the record-keeping that is performed by the filing of names – several entries are quoted, with or without changes, from the original Book of Negroes – adds to the authentication of Aminata's tale and of course provides another heterogeneric element. The heterogenerity of written texts supplemented by the inclusion of yet another reference to an authentic document of course only applies to the North American context, which is steeped in a tradition of literacy. Thus, we are faced with a heterogeneous structure that encompasses both oral (African) as well as written (North American) aspects, adding to the multiplicity of elements constituting the novel's closeness to the original slave narrative in terms of the inclusion of various and disparate styles, modes and techniques. It must be reemphasized, however, that *The Book of Negroes* is not representative of an exceedingly heterogeneric style. Hill does indeed include a fair number of heterogeneous elements – among them epigraphs, poems, legislation, prayers, letters, ads, certificates, songs, files, other narratives –, but he does not compile a novel that approximates the actual quantitative level of heterogenerity which is distinctive for the original slave narrative. In this, he is consistent with the overall approach of consciously employing references and a certain degree of the stylistics and characteristics of the slave narrative without blatantly and epigonically emulating it in terms of layout, structure and publication (the first category of comparison).

5.2.2. *Category two: Content*

The second category of criteria focuses on content rather than layout or structure and encompasses thematic characteristics, recurrent phrases and images. These criteria of the slave narrative are empirically derived at, as their frequency is soundly documented (e.g. in Davis/Gates 1985a). Empirical analysis in this case is facilitated and fostered by the streamlining process undertaken by the abolitionists and/or White amanuenses, who made sure that a certain set of recurrent elements, particularly those exerting a strong political impact, would be included in most of the ex-slaves' tales. In a very basic way, the general plotline of course is such a staple ingredient: the slave narratives "concern the past sufferings, escape, and freedom of a former slave" (Casmier-Paz 2001, 215). The narrative is evidently teleological as it is geared towards escape into freedom (cf. Link 1993, 283; Minter 1974, 65). This fundamental plotline is of course mirrored in Hill's novel. Being such a general and thus indeed slightly spongy criterion, the general plotline can thus only account for a very broad thematic classification (cf. Ralph Ellison's critique, discussed above), yet however plain and obvious this criterion may be, it is still one of the crucial elements of the slave narrative in terms of its propagandistic impact: the transition from slavery to freedom must be present in order to illustrate the innate humanity of the slaves as well their natural ability to live outside of slavery – an underlying, vital concept that in its urgency and profoundness is often lost on a modern reader.

Having established that on this general level, *The Book of Negroes* does comply with the basic plotline of the slave narrative, it must be added that of course there are a number of variations of this basic scheme even in the original narratives. Whether the slave has been born into slavery or captured in Africa; whether he escapes by running away, pays for his manumission or seizes some other opportunity; whether his life in freedom is satisfying or not – all of these options are of course available to vary the basic plot scheme. In the case of *The Book of Negroes*, Hill has opted to include as many stations as possible, going from Aminata's African roots through her capture, the Middle Passage, her plantation life, her 'servant' days, to her flight and subsequent manumission as a Black Loyalist. It is noteworthy that the last stage in the classic triad of slavery, escape and freedom takes up such an extensive amount of the novel. In the original slave narrative, the part that most appealed to the audience – as well as best underlined its political aim – was the reality of slavery and the 'adventures' of the slave's escape.

Hill, however, needs to prolong Aminata's account of her time as a free person for a two-fold reason in particular: first, to add, in a manner of speaking, inverted commas to the term 'freedom' by showing the limits imposed on the former slaves even after their escape, which is something that the original slave narrative could only do to a certain extent, not wanting to challenge the idea that Black and White would live harmoniously side by side if only slavery would be abolished. Second, for an African-*Canadian* author, the extensive treatment of the post-slavery time of a character provides the opportunity to include a more comprehensive account of Black history *north* of the 49th parallel. Hill – in contrast to the slave narratives' authors – is able to spend a great amount of time looking at the not-so-heavenly aspects of Black Canadian history through Aminata's eyes, while the slave narrative, for obvious reasons, had to stop short of criticizing the North (after the Fugitive Slave Law, this means Canada exclusively) it was praising as the counter-model to the hellish South of the United States. Thus, again, one of the most basic generic definitions of the slave narrative does apply to Hill's writing, yet with a certain modulation in emphasis: the triad of slavery-escape-freedom is clearly employed, yet the focus is extended in terms of the protagonist's life in freedom in order to more comprehensively accommodate a distinctly Canadian perspective.[148]

---

148 Rachel Adams notes on a further distortion of the historical picture based on the slave narrative's insistence of the 'North' as a Canaan when she criticizes that the 'southern alternative' has been largely neglected in contemporary constructions: "In the history of North American slavery, Canada has been enshrined as the terminus of the Underground Railroad, a bastion of freedom that welcomed fugitives at the end of a long and arduous journey. Although significant numbers of slaves escaped by running south to Mexico or elsewhere in the Americas, 'the South' is persistently held up as the epicentre of unfreedom in contrast to the northern states and Canada. This directional bias has much to do with the authority granted to slave narratives as a form of historical evidence. Produced under the auspices of white abolitionists in Canada and the northern United States, the slave narrative is the most formulaic of genres. One of its primary conventions is the story of the harrowing passage from south to north." (Adams 2007, 217)

a) Name changes: Autonomy vs. heteronomy[149]

There are a number of content-related characteristics far more specific than the general plot structure, such as recurrent motifs, phrases and images. It should not be coincidental – in fact cannot be coincidental given the number of parallels – that Hill employs a multitude of these components in his own writing. One of the plainest and simultaneously most potent recurrent motifs is the usage of multiple names identifying the (ex-)slaves. The most common change of names that occurs in the slave narrative signifies the hierarchical structure, the concept of complete ownership, the heteronomous allocation of identity (consequently a lack of autonomous self-identification) as well as Eurocentric and racist notions of White supremacy: slave masters would impose new names upon their 'property', the slaves. Frequently, this change of names is reflected in the titles of the slave narratives themselves, identifying, for instance, both the original name "Olaudah Equiano" and the enforced label "Gustavus Vassa" (Equiano 1995).[150] The heteronomy of the imposed change of names is obvious: the new denomination is an act of willful assertion of a power structure that allows the master to (re-)define a slave, while the slave is severed from his original identity. Often, slave masters would give their slaves patronymic names, adding for instance a new last name that matches or resembles their own (cf. Casmier-Paz 2001, 217). After gaining freedom, the ex-slave would sometimes convert his name once more – though, surprisingly, they would often assume another *new* name instead of reverting to the original African one, which they may have considered as 'blemished' because of their enslavement. It is an illustration of the abolitionists' influence and the difficulties of simultaneously maintaining and altering their identities that the authors would "frequently [adopt a name] suggested by a white abolitionist" in order to signify their "new social identity as a free man, but [retain their] first name as a mark of continuity of individual identity" (Olney 1985, 153). Hill gives an example of this process when, in *The Book of Negroes*, he depicts Aminata teaching illiterate dwellers of Canvas Town:[151]

> 'What's that?' asked a tall thin man of about twenty [who is observing Aminata enter his name into a list of participants]. 'Your name,' [Aminata said,] 'Claybourne Mitchell.' 'Well, I can't read, so how do I know it from any other name?' [he asked.] 'I'll teach you,' [Aminata] said. 'I can cooper a barrel of any size,' he said, 'but I ain't teachable.' 'Sure you are,' [Aminata] said. 'Ain't not. My master saw to that. It's why I run from him. [...] Claybourne the only name they done give me,' he said. 'Mitchell is a name I done took. Heard a man called that once, and liked it so much I decided when I got here I was gonna be a new man. Free man. With two names, both for myself.' (BN 259)

---

149 Excerpts from this section have appeared in Krampe 2010.

150 The name "Gustavus Vassa" is practically beaten into Olaudah Equiano, enforcing the submission into his new identity by the fist. Moreover, he had been called Michael and Jacob before, so his external re-definition through labeling is a repeated event – as it is for other authors (cf. Casmier-Paz 2001, 216 and 222).

151 It is interesting to note that teaching takes place in a church; in terms of the question whether or not the church had a positive impact on the Black Canadian population, Hill seems to suggest a positive assessment at least in terms of education.

While Hill consciously acknowledges the practice of adding a new name to the existing slave name in order to reconcile the past identity as a slave with the new identity as a free man, he does not use this technique for Aminata herself, who clings to her original African name throughout the story, just as she clings to the dream of returning to Africa and restoring her old, unified self almost until the very end of her life. The quotation above, however, illustrates another important point that is part and parcel of the slave narrative itself: the enforced name change of the slave is closely connected to the obstruction of literacy and education. Both measures indicate and perpetuate the major power imbalance and underlying notions of racial supremacy which are at the core of slavery. Here, pragmatic reasons merge with ideological ones. By keeping the slaves illiterate and uneducated, mutinies and escapes could be impeded, which is pragmatic reasoning given the fact that slaves were precious property in terms of commercial value.

Ideologically, of course, the suppression of literacy fuels the vicious circle of the alleged absence of the slaves' humanity, the alleged right of Whites to enslave Blacks, the imposed illiteracy of the slaves, and the professed absence of their humanity due to a lack of written history (cf. p. 85f. of this thesis). As for name changes, the pragmatic aspect is quite simply convenience, as "Michael" or "Jacob" rolls more easily off the tongue of a slave master than "Olaudah"; "Meena" or "Mary" more easily than "Aminata". In unison with the imposed ban on literacy, the ideological foundation of name changes is based on notions of racial supremacy – to rid the slaves of 'primitive' or 'barbarian names' – and to vividly assert the power structure that allowed the slave master to call their 'property' any name they pleased. By re-identifying their slaves, slave masters of course fostered the process (or at least hoped to foster the process) of the slaves self-identifying with their new role as property (a process whose negative inversion is known in theories of juvenile delinquency as the "labeling approach", cf. e.g. Griese/Mansel 2003 or Paternoster/Ioavanni 1996).

Aminata herself undergoes several name changes. Her original African name is used in the variations Aminata Diallo, Miss Diallo, or simply Aminata.[152] On board the slave vessel, she is given the name Mary by the ship's doctor. Her slave name is Meena Dee, varied as Miss Dee or simply Meena. Aminata's first change of name signifies the characteristic imposition of a heteronomous identity which rests upon a major power imbalance. The pressure involved in this act is emphasized by the doctor's pushing Aminata down – a highly symbolic gesture of submission, which conjures up the will to resist in her (though to no avail, which is also typical of the enforced name change):

---

152 "Aminata" means "the peaceful one", an explanation provided by Hill in *Any Known Blood* (Langston the Fifth "would have tendered the name Aminata" for the baby his wife lost the very day he cheated on her in Mali, cf. ibid. 210). "Amina" is the term used in Mali to designate gratefulness (AKB 203). Aminata's last name, "Diallo", may possibly refer to the 1999 shooting of a 22-year-old immigrant from Guinea named Amadou Diallo in New York City – he was shot at 41 times and hit 19 times; four police officers said they mistook his wallet for a gun. Rev. Al Sharpton spoke of a "firing squad" (cf. Cashmore 2005, 49; also cf. Gutiérrez-Jones 2001, 3ff.; Kassin/Fein/ Hazel 2011, 182ff.; Roy 2009; Taylor 2004, 100).

> Then [the ship's doctor] pointed at me. I said my name. He scrunched up his face. 'Aminata,' I said once more. But he pointed at me and said something else. Over and over. He wanted me to repeat it. 'Mary,' I finally said. He pointed to me again, and I did it to. I used my thumb, just like him. 'Mary,' I said softly. I pushed the word through my lips and told myself it would be the last time I would ever say it, or his name. He jumped up and clapped his hands. 'Mary,' he said, over and over. I got up too. I wanted to be with the women again. But he put his hand on my shoulder and pushed me back down, leaning his face too close to mine. (BN 72)

Of course the close linkage between the enforced name change and the physical act of being pushed back by the ship's doctor underlines the encompassing powerlessness Aminata experiences. Racial and colonial hierarchies are enforced on all levels of her existence, limiting not only her physical autonomy but also obstructing her freedom of self-identification. Furthermore, the combination of the name "Mary" and the early insinuation of sexual violence ("pushed me back down", "too close to mine") add another sinister dimension to the heteronomy and subjugation experienced by the slaves aboard the slave vessel. It also hints at the fact that the surgeon does indeed later on try to sexually assault Aminata, but is temporarily deterred by Aminata's ferocity and by bouts of guilt induced by his religion (whenever Aminata rejects his groping, he turns to prayer or clutches a cross to his body, cf. BN 74 and 76). Again, however, Hill emphasizes that other slaves are not as lucky as Aminata: the doctor may leave Aminata largely alone, yet sexually abuses a number of other women slaves in her presence. The use of the name "Mary," cynically given to Aminata by a man who in fact wants to *take* her virginity in a violent way, is discontinued after she leaves the slave ship.

When Aminata arrives at Appleby's indigo plantation in South Carolina, she is given a new name: Meena Dee. While the enforced name change aboard the ship fully complies with the standards of the slave narrative (the White master imposes a 'Europeanized' name on the slave), the conversion to Meena Dee involves a slight deviation from the established blueprint, once more illustrating Hill's usage of a standardized slave narrative pattern but twisting it to a degree that keeps his story from over-conforming to a generic model. Once Aminata has arrived at the plantation, she is handed over to Georgia, a slave who later on becomes a surrogate mother to her, which is alluded to from the very beginning of their relationship by the fact that Georgia, like Aminata's dead mother, is a midwife. Georgia gives Aminata the name "Meena":

> She dug a finger into her own breast, said 'Georgia,' and opened her hands toward me. 'Aminata,' I told her. Three times, Georgia made me repeat it, but the best she could do was to say 'Meena.' In this new land, I was an African.[153] In this new land, I had a different name, given by someone who did not even know me. A new name for the second life of a girl who survived the great river crossing. (BN 127)

---

153 Prior to being shipped to America, Aminata had of course not considered herself an "African" (neither linguistically, i.e. by that term, nor in the wider sense of a self-identification based on any concept of a continental 'belonging' or 'community' – after all, Aminata was not even aware of the extent of the land mass the term 'Africa' refers to, instead working with (socio-)topological determinants such as villages, tribes and language groups. Hill dedicates ample space to this phenomenon, particularly in the aptly titled chapter "They call me an 'African'" (BN 104-123).

Both the parallels and the differences between the renaming by the surgeon and Georgia are noteworthy. Both indeed call Aminata by a name other than her original one, and both use gestures to underpin their doing so. Moreover, the name change in both situations signifies a new episode, a drastically different station in Aminata's life. There are some constitutive differences, however: Georgia, in contrast to the ship's doctor, at least attempts to enunciate and thus initially tries to accept Aminata's African name.[154] That she is unable to do so is likely based on the fact that Georgia, as an American-born slave, is neither from the Bamana nor Fula language group and thus might not be used to or proficient in the linguistic particularities of Aminata's name. Whereas the doctor immediately "scrunched up his face" (BN 72) in disapproval, plainly showing his disgust for the 'barbarian' African name, Georgia is ready to grant Aminata the right to her own name, yet proves unable to do so linguistically (Aminata quickly realizes that Georgia is not as intellectually capable as herself and thus immediately grants her the explanation of 'inability' instead of mere 'unwillingness').

Consequently, it is Georgia's own station in life, including the fact that she is a slave who is deliberately kept uneducated, that makes her rename her fellow slave, not the willful subjugation of an allegedly inferior human being. The gestures employed by Georgia and the surgeon vividly illustrate this contrast. While the surgeon points at Aminata, *ap*pointing her new identifier and clarifying the power relation between the two, Georgia "open[s] her hands toward" Aminata (BN 127), thus literally extending and exhibiting her openness and offering her recognition. Although Aminata acknowledges that her new name on the indigo plantation, which would become her slave name for the rest of her life, has been externally attributed – by a stranger, to boot, "someone who did not even know" her (ibid.) –, the repetition of "in this new land" (ibid.) stresses the formative environmental constraints which in fact determine her fate and the name change which signifies this fate. Aminata accepts the name "Meena" more easily (or: more wearily) than the one given to her aboard the slave vessel. She has realized that the resistance she professed aboard the ship ("I pushed the word through my lips and told myself it would be the last time I would ever say it, or his name," BN 72) is futile. Her "second life" (BN 127) comes with a change of names, and there is little she can do about it.

Aminata's name changes thus do not adhere to the strict sequence prototypical for the genre of the slave narrative, viz. 1) original African name, 2) imposed slave name/s, 3) self-chosen name in freedom, often influenced by abolitionists. Instead, her original African name and her slave name[155] are used interchangeably and simultaneously, depending on the person who addresses her rather than on her overall status – it becomes interdependent on the social interaction she is involved in. Thus, her name is a much more fine-tuned and complex indicator of Aminata's status than might be expected: it indicates not merely her general, essentialist status – slave or free woman – but her status *vis à vis* different people. Her African compan-

---

154 Also cf. Sam Fraunces, a New York tavern and hotel keeper, who aids Aminata in her escape later on. He equally attempts to pronounce Aminata's name but likewise fails. Aminata then offers him to call her "Meena" (cf. BN 244).

155 In fact, slave name*s*, but the name "Mary" is in actual use only for a very limited period of time, viz. the Middle Passage.

ions, Fanta and Fomba for example, who have known her from the very beginning, of course use her original African name throughout. Biton, the African chief she meets aboard the slave ship,[156] even uses her full name, thereby expressing respect even though Aminata is a mere child when abducted (cf. BN 112). The same holds true for Chekura, with whom she shares the closest bond. Consequently, his usage of Aminata's name is particularly significant. Aboard the slave ship, Aminata has Chekura affirm her identity by having him reiterate her name, which in turn she does for him:

> He repeated my name over and over, and then added, 'I must hear you say it. Please. Say it. Say my name.' 'Chekura,' I said. 'Someone knows my name. Seeing you makes me want to live.' (BN 66)

Mutually confirming each other's existence as individual persons by breaking the anonymity of slavery, Chekura and Aminata assure each other of their subjectivities and identities.[157] It is obvious that both use the enunciation of their names as a source of strength. Chekura later on maintains the habit of speaking out Aminata's name, often in full, which greatly pleases her ("I loved it when Chekura said my name. All of it."[158] BN 182). During her time on the indigo plantation, Chekura is the only person to consistently (though infrequently, due to his rare visits) use Aminata's original name. The time Aminata spends in South Carolina is the part of her life that is most closely associated with a mainstream conception of Black slavery, involving plantation work, whippings, harassment of slaves and the like. The usage of her slave

---

156 Chief Biton himself might in fact be named after Biton (Mamari) Coulibaly, an African king who established the Bambara kingdom of Ségou in Mali (Ségou, or Segu, is a place close to Aminata's birthplace Bayo, cf. BN 66); cf. Imperato 1986, 3 and 30.

157 Notions of anonymity will be discussed in more detail later on in the context of transferring the retention and transmission of individual memory to a collective level. It will be shown that Aminata's experience of overcoming the loss of individual memory and identity, which is indicated by the loss of a person's name, serves as a model for the perpetuation of collective memory through narratives. What starts out as a dialogue between Aminata and Chekura consequently provides a meta-fictional comment on the power of stories to mediate collective memories.

It might be noted here again that *The Book of Negroes* has been published in the US under the title *Someone Knows my Name* (2007b), which of course alludes to James Baldwin's *Nobody Knows my Name* (1993, originally published in 1961). However aptly the US title may be chosen, the quote above demonstrates that, curiously, the personal pronoun in *Someone Knows* my *Name* does, strictly speaking, not refer to the novel's protagonist herself, but to her lover and later husband, Chekura. It does, however, refer to Aminata's role as a keeper of memories (a *djeli*) and her salient role in overcoming the anonymity so characteristic of slavery.

158 In fact, Chekura had only said "Aminata", not "Aminata Diallo" in this scene (thus *not* "all of it", ibid.), which may be taken either as a mishap on the author's side or as indicating the assumption that Aminata considers her first name to be fully sufficient – as long as it is her original one instead of her slave name. Chekura does, however, on occasion use Aminata's full name (cf. e.g. two instances when Chekura returns to Aminata in Canvas Town, BN 289). When Chekura is not around, Aminata misses his saying her name in particular (e.g.: "Against all reason and logic, I waited and hoped for Chekura's return. [...] But no voice called out my African name..." BN 228).

name thus corresponds to her status there, being used more consistently on St. Helena Island than during any other part of her life. The only one to use Aminata's African name besides Chekura is Mamed, the plantation's overseer, who has taken a liking to Aminata, furthers her education (in spite of risking punishment), and uses both her names interchangeably, according to the given situation:

> Mamed was the only person in South Carolina who ever asked for my whole name. He spoke it properly, and then taught me how to write it. But on the plantation he would always call me Meena. (BN 155)

Small wonder that Mamed, a surrogate father figure[159] and a teacher, recognizes Aminata's need and the implication of being called by her real, her original name. His alternating usage underlines both his grasp of their social reality with its underlying impositions (thus, it was dangerous to use an African name instead of the slave name, as only the latter indicated the obligatory submission) and the dualistic construction of Aminata's identity: though she might be a slave and might endure the heteronomous labeling that relegates her to the rank of 'property', there is also the remnant of her former identity as a free-born African. The self-determined human is suppressed, but not eradicated. For others, such as Georgia, the problem of a dualistic identity structure is not as prevalent; being born on the plantation and into slavery, she has a mostly unified self-conception based on the resigned understanding that if you "[g]ot a slave mama, then you is slave. Got a slave daddy, then you is slave. Any nigger in you at all, then you is slave clear as day." (BN 134)[160] Georgia's comment accordingly lays bare 1) essentialist, biologist constructions of race based on 'heredity' or genetics, 2) the un-

---

159 Also note the alliterative linguistic closeness of the name "Mamed" to "Mamadu", Aminata's father.

160 Note the absence of an indefinite pronoun in Georgia's statement ("then you is [a] slave"), which has a reason beyond vernacular representation. Georgia, born into slavery, does not refer to any one individual person's status or fate, but to the broad category of *existence as (a) slave*. 'To be slave' – rather than 'to be *a* slave' – indicates an all-encompassing status, synonymous with 'to be inhuman'. It is not an individual role that one adopts ('to be *a* teacher/father etc.) but an essentialist, collectivized marker ('to be White/Black').

In terms of the linkage of slavery and conceptions of race, this remark also offers a comment on the then-prevailing one-drop rule according to which a single drop of 'Black blood' would 'spoil' the 'purity' of a White person. Hill has observed, in *Black Berry, Sweet Juice*: "For centuries in Canada and the United States, if you were known to have black ancestry, you were black. And that was that. The laws of slavery and segregation made it so, as did regulated customs such as where you could live, eat, work, and worship, and at whom you could direct the lustful eyeball." (BBSJ, 39) On the close linkage of racial thinking and the institution of slavery, which is often denied based on an assessment of Greek slavery as racially unbiased, cf. Charles W. Mills'S compellingly argued *The Racial Contract* (1997), which is based on Carol Pateman's *The Sexual Contract* (1988) and harks back to political theories of contractualists like Thomas Hobbes, John Locke, Jean-Jacques Rousseau, Immanuel Kant and the contemporary John Rawls.

contested equation of 'slave' and 'Black person', and 3) the internalization of these constructions by Black slaves themselves.[161]

Up until that point in the novel, there are few surprises in terms of which characters
use Aminata's African and/or slave name. Needless to say, the plantation owner, Appleby,
uses her slave name. Georgia's usage – indeed, the creation – of "Meena" comes a little unex-
pected at first, but is quickly explained by her status, as Georgia is "a Negro, but not a
homelander", as Aminata phrases it (BN 126). Mamed, versed in the rules of plantation di-
plomacy, aware of Aminata's dualistic identity, sympathetic, understanding and, moreover, of
mixed racial origin, employs both variants according to social situation. Aminata's subsequent master, Solomon Lindo, uses the slave name by which he has acquainted – and acquired
– Aminata (cf. BN 188). So does his wife, who, however, is "the first white person to know
my name before we met," as Aminata observes (BN 190). This slight improvement in terms
of her name corresponds with a slight improvement in Aminata's status; the Lindos prove to
be kinder than her former master, Appleby.[162] As with Appleby's staff, excepting Mamed,
Lindo's staff adopts their master's usage and calls Aminata by her slave name.

In New York City, Lindo's more lenient character is underlined by the fact that he allows Aminata, for the first time since her abduction, to officially self-identify herself. In addition, she is allowed to freely and proudly exhibit her writing skills, which on Appleby's plantation would naturally have been dangerous. Again, however, Lindo's lenience is not unconditional and does not seem to be rooted in any truly profound belief in equality. Rather, it is
his impatience which makes him ask Aminata to put down her own name in a New York City
hotel's register (cf. BN 243). Lindo could not possibly have suspected that it is this act which
prompts Aminata's final decision to run away from her owner. When writing her own name in
the hotel registry, Aminata realizes that in New York City, there might be a chance to reassert
her personhood by liberating herself: "I had now written my name on a public document, and
I was a person, with just as much right to life and liberty as the man who claimed to own me."
(BN 244) The close linkage of the act of writing to the claim of freedom and personhood, as

---

161 Cf. of course W.E.B. DuBois's famous 'double consciousness' here (DuBois 2003, 9f.), but also
Franz Fanon's notions (his two major works are available in new translations with forewords by
Anthony Appiah and Homi Bhabha respectively; Fanon 2008a and 2008b).

162 Actually, the situation is of course more complicated than that, involving a double plot turn: At
first, the Lindos seem to be kinder indeed, which is illustrated by their usage of the term "servant"
instead of "slave" (cf. BN 187; Lindo adds: "And we don't treat our servants rudely. In our home,
you will find none of the barbarism of St. Helena Island [Appleby's plantation]." Ibid.). Lindo believes to be able to relate to Aminata, since, as he claims, "I am not a white man. I am a Jew, and
that is very different. You and I are both outsiders." (BN 188) Later on, however, Aminata discovers that mood swings, a flailing economy, the death of Mrs Lindo and other factors worsen the
servant-master relationship so that finally, Aminata is compelled to ask Lindo, "So will you now
start saying 'slave,' instead of 'servant'?" (BN 227) Yet it is not until Aminata learns that Lindo
had been instrumental in the sale of Mamadu, her first-born child, that she decides to run away
from him. A second plot turn then partly redeems Lindo, as he appears in a New York City court
to manumit Aminata, who is claimed as a fugitive slave by her former owner Appleby. Also cf.
section 5.3.3.

well as the textual allusion to the Declaration of Independence, signify that Aminata cannot revert to her role as a slave. Once she has reclaimed her humanity by establishing her own identity in writing (the assertive metanarrative allusion could not be more pronounced here), there is no turning back: "I would not submit again to ownership by any man", Aminata vows (ibid.).

Once she has fled her master and lives in Canvas Town, the ramshackle Black settlement outside New York City, the indicative use of her two names continues – which, considering her avowed self-liberation, turns out to be slightly disillusioning. Though usage of her original name increases, some Canvas Town residents face the same difficulties as her surrogate mother Georgia or Sam Fraunces, the New York hotel-keeper; they cannot pronounce Aminata's name and revert to "Meena" (Jason Wood, a Birchtown, Nova Scotia, resident, and Daddy Moses, the blind priest who becomes a close confident of Aminata's, are examples of this phenomenon; cf. BN 318). Aminata's shifting status is indicated by the varying degrees of her original name being accepted in official contexts. While her General Birch's certificate, which grants her freedom and passage to Nova Scotia, idiosyncratically labels her "Meena Dee, a Negro of Mandingo extraction" (BN 302) and thus uses her slave name and a racially charged description to document her manumission, the British military officials hiring her for the registering process involving the Book of Negroes respectfully refer to her African name by calling her "Miss Diallo" (BN 286). In Canvas Town as well as later on in Birchtown, the fluctuating usage of the protagonist's two designations reflects the volatile status to which Aminata is relegated. As a runaway slave, she considers herself free, yet she is keenly aware of the fact that she is under constant threat of recapture. Hill thus employs the labeling of his protagonist in order to underline the lingering residues of slavery; conversion to her own, entirely self-determined self is not achieved in North America, where she is still identified as a 'racial other' burdened by the history of slavery and the ongoing (socioeconomic) power imbalance *vis à vis* Whites.[163]

It is only in Africa that Aminata can fully revert to her former name, even though she cannot escape her (individual and collective) past even there. In Sierra Leone, she identifies herself by her African name to the people she encounters; given their linguistic abilities on the one hand and the absence of the racist impulse to showcase their alleged superiority by heteronomously labeling her on the other, the Africans in Sierra Leone unquestioningly accept her denomination (e.g. King Jimmy;[164] BN 381). After having fled from the trek of slave traders who were supposed to take her back to Bayo (but who in fact planned on re-enslaving

---

163 As soon as Aminata resolves to run away from Lindo, thereby effectively ending her slavery, she witnesses a Black fiddler in a New York City street trying to coerce some coins from White passers-by. This scene vividly highlights the continuing dependence of Blacks on Whites in terms of economic sustenance, created by the institution of slavery and the continuing asymmetrical socioeconomic structure. Hill thus foreshadows on an individual level the difficulties Aminata will continue to face as well as, on a social level, the ongoing struggles of an ostensibly liberated Black population.

164 King Jimmy is another character with a real-life model, a Temne chief (cf. Walker 1992, 104; Wilson 1976, 169; Schama 2005, 7, 212, 339).

her), Aminata finds shelter in an African village, where she assumes a position resembling that of a *djeli*.[165] Again, her name is accepted without the slightest irritation; what is more, there are two children named Aminata in that village, emphasizing both her 'belonging' and the rootedness of her identity within Africa (cf. BN 441, 446) as well as adding two more *alter egos* to the one established by the child whom Aminata encounters in the slave coffle that is marched through Freetown.[166]

After the abortive attempt to return to her native village and after she has left Africa for England in order to support the abolitionist cause, Aminata gets to speak before the British Parliament and before the King and Queen. Here, Hill employs an almost tongue-in-cheek usage of Aminata's names. As could be expected, she is called by her slave name before (White) Parliament (cf. BN 459). Queen Charlotte Sophia, however, addresses her as "Aminata", which prompts the ex-slave to ponder that the Queen was "the first white person to use it [her real name] on first greeting. But then again, perhaps she wasn't white after all." (BN 464) Queen Charlotte has long been considered 'the Black Queen'.[167] As Aminata notes in an ekphrastic account, however, Charlotte's artistic depiction has not always reflected this ancestry: looking at a portrait of the Queen, Aminata reasons that she "couldn't understand why anyone had called her black: her skin looked light, and her features white." (BN 414; on ekphrasis as a means to represent visual arts in literature, cf. for instance Heffernan 2004; Mitchell 1995, 151-182; Wandhoff 2003, esp. 2-12.) When meeting Charlotte in person, Aminata notices her peculiar features, "a woman with a broad nose and full lips, and skin much richer than in any painter's rendition." (BN 463) The reference to portraits of Queen Charlotte ties into issues of (imposed?) passing and of (willful?) external misrepresentation, as different painters have provided vastly different renditions of Queen Charlotte (with, e.g., Thomas Lawrence's 1789 portrait betraying not even a hint of African ancestry, while Ester Denner's 1761 painting as well as renditions by Allan Ramsay, a known abolitionist, clearly depict the African features described by Aminata).

---

165 Throughout *The Book of Negroes*, the conception of Aminata acting as a *djeli* is of central importance. A *djeli*, occasionally written *jeli* or *jali*, is a West African storyteller; *griot* is the term predominantly used in Francophone contexts (cf. for instance the brief explanation in Richardson/Green 2004, ii). His – it is commonly held that the *djeli* must be male, though Hale (1998, 16) disagrees to some extent – obligation is to relate and pass on oral history (cf. Belcher 1999, 7ff. and 91; Schulz 2001, 240f.). As such, he is the quintessential specialist in the field of preserving and transmitting identity-informing collective memories (cf. on the disputed nature of the oral transmission of collective memory distinctions between cultural and communicative memory, e.g. J. Assmann 1992, 50ff.; also cf. section 2.3. of this study on the difficulties of distinguishing between communicative and cultural memory in the given context).

166 The usage of several *alter egos* of course again underlines the collectivization of Aminata's experience (cf. p. 136ff. of this thesis).

167 The Black Cultural Centre for Nova Scotia, for instance, has an exhibition section devoted to Queen Charlotte's possible African ancestry. Walter Borden makes the same claim in *Tightrope Time:* "... it is my duty to tell you that Charlotte was a lady of colour." (1987, 61f.) Clarke aptly describes the reclamation of Queen Charlotte (and others, among them "Ludwig von [sic] Beethoven") by Borden as a 'poetical re-borrowing' (cf. 2002a, 79).

In *The Book of Negroes*, Aminata had been made aware of Queen Charlotte's possible African roots both by a fellow slave in South Carolina and by Sam Fraunces[168] in New York City well before meeting her in person (cf. BN 194, 246). The ship that takes Lindo and Aminata to New York City is likewise called "Queen Charlotte" (BN 240). Possibly, Hill devotes so much attention to the case of the purportedly Black Queen because of the significance of her 'whitewashing' in official and popular perception. Aminata, when she first learns of the Queen's ancestry, gives the following reason for this lack of acknowledgment: "I didn't believe [my fellow slave's claim that Queen Charlotte has African roots]. Nobody would let an African become boss woman of the whole land." (BN 194)

In her still-naïve way (it has been pointed out before that when focalizing through Aminata in her youth, Hill frequently employs terms he considers linguistically representative for her given age), Aminata discovers an important principle of racial constructions: that they are *in fact* constructions. Any possible African ancestry, it is suggested in the passages of the novel referring to the wife of George III, is denied in official discourse and artistic representation, thereby construing a 'racially pure' image of the queen, reflected in the portraits that have erased Charlotte's African heritage. The parallels between the example of Queen Charlotte and the whitewashing of the Canadian collective memory (as exposed by African-Canadian literature, cf. Clarke 2004) are clearly visible – pun intended. In order to preserve an image of an 'all-White heritage', mainstream (artistic) renditions misrepresent and downplay the African influence that should be apparent. Aminata, however, recognizes the African hues and brings them to the fore – regarding both the case of the Black Queen and, through her account, the case of Black Canadian history.

The question of name changes thus provides insights not only into the analogies between the original slave narrative and *The Book of Negroes*. While Hill acknowledges the standardized chronological name changes that enslaved Africans undergo in most ex-slaves' accounts (sequence of African name, slave name, freeman's name) by structuring some of the novel's minor characters' designations according to this model, Aminata's name changes adhere to a more complex model. The aspects of external designation and thus heteronomous identification, which reflect the enforcement of hierarchical structures, are illustrated in Aminata's imposed name change aboard the slave vessel and on Appleby's plantation. Her identification, however, depends as much on the individual personal relationships that are dealt with as it depends on the mere chronological sequence of her status (freeborn African, slave, free/d person). The volatility expressed in this limbo reflects the constructivist and malleable character of name assignations and thus of identity constructions, whether self-determined or external.

While a majority of Aminata's assignations complies with the reader's expectations (e.g. Africans during the Middle Passage and in Sierra Leone calling her "Aminata"; her own-

---

168 Another character with a namesake in Black American history: "Black Sam" Fraunces's tavern was located in New York City's Vauxhall Gardens (cf. Davis 2001, 31, who includes the site of Fraunces's tavern in Barton's volume *Sites of Memory. Perspectives on Architecture and Race*).

ers calling her "Meena"), Hill also introduces some surprising combinations in order to under-line more complex aspects than might have been discussed in the highly conventionalized original slave narrative. Her fellow slaves' usage – indeed, introduction – of her slave name indicates both their immersion in the rules of institutionalized slavery and the pervasiveness of the ban on education. The British abolitionists, on the other hand, at first actually "do not say [Aminata's] name" at all, though they profess to be steeped in racial equality (BN 101). Queen Charlotte's usage of Aminata's African name finally illustrates the racial constructions that underlie not only the usage of names as identifying labels, but also the racial whitewash-ing which has informed (artistic) representations. Both external labeling and heteronomous artistic depiction are therefore identified as discursive projections, which are critically ques-tioned and thus challenged. "The very act of naming a slave powerfully demonstrates a slave owner's hold upon slave identity," as Casmier-Paz observes (2001, 222) – the same holds true for constructions of a collective memory through artistic representations, which equally demonstrates the hegemonic definitions' (and definers') hold upon identity.[169]

b) Literacy: Gaining Agency and humanity

In terms of the *emphasis* that slave narratives place on the acquisition of literacy, *The Book of Negroes* fully conforms to the established model. Aminata's development, her professional skills and her actual as well as psychological and emotional survival are closely linked to her ability to read and write. Davis/Gates (1985b) distinguish three aspects concerning the litera-cy of slaves: first, the learning process and instruction; second, the ban on attaining literacy; third, 'discursive', ironic apologia justifying the ostensibly substandard writing by contem-plating the apparently 'limited' capabilities of the authors. The first element constitutes one of Aminata's central traits, setting her distinctly apart from other slaves originally occupying the same stratum in the hierarchy of slaves as herself. Her instruction begins in Africa, where she

---

169 While African-Canadian literature in this regard can be classified as 'subversive' and conscious of the literary strategies it has at its disposal, it is doubtful that the original slave narratives' authors were allowed (by their editors and/or the conventions of their genre) quite this level of subversive tactics; Casmier-Paz, in "Footprint of the Fugitive: Slave Narrative Discourse and the Trace of Autobiography" (2001), claims that "tactical manipulations of slave narrative discourse use mul-tiple names to evidence the fugitive's problematic relationship to the laws of racified identity – laws which the published texts must resist and yet engage to persuade a reading public" (220). Casmier-Paz herself exemplifies these "tactical manipulations" using Douglass's account, grant-ing that his chosen name "identifies him as the willing property of abolitionism's work" (221). Given that his slave name was not of his own choosing either, the heteronomous attribution of his name(s) hardly seems a 'tactical manipulation' on *his* account; rather, it adheres to the standard-ized characteristics identified by Olney (1985) and illustrates the *opposite* of autonomous, self-determined identification (let alone 'manipulation'). In regard to name changes, the ex-slaves conventionally do not manipulate, but are in fact the ones who are – qua external assignation of identity – variously manipulated. While it is certainly laudable to avoid the overuse of stereotypi-cal conceptions of victimization and to expose (Black / subversive) agency where it is indeed im-plied, Casmier-Paz in this case seems to be overly driven by political correctness or the will to unveil (literary) resistance.

is taught some basic writing skills by her father. Even then, writing is closely connected to her religious education (she is taught Koran verses, while later on, she hones her skills using a Bible provided by Mamed, the overseer on Appleby's plantation and a surrogate father to Aminata).[170] Aminata's own instruction is furthered in particular by Mamed and by Mrs Lindo in Charles Town. Aminata is then able to profitably employ these skills to sustain or enhance her living standards: just as she was able to improve her position aboard the slave ship by acting as a translator for individual African languages, she rises to tasks such as bookkeeping in the Lindos' household. In Birchtown, she is even able to work for a newspaper as a corrector, a position which underlines her thorough command of the English language and ridicules underlying stereotypes and preconceptions of Africans' alleged cognitive inferiority prevalent at the time.

What is more, Aminata becomes an instructor herself, now passing on to the Black community what she has received from father, courageous overseer and sympathetic owner (note the shift from Black to mixed-race to White instructor as Aminata becomes immersed in Western culture). In the Black settlements of Canvas Town and Birchtown, Aminata acts as a teacher to the Black community, spreading literacy among the socioeconomically and culturally underprivileged. She thus rises from recipient to agent, exhibiting a shift from passivity to activity. An acquisition of agency hence lies at the core of Aminata's development in terms of literacy, which correlates with her overall progression from slavery to freedom.[171] From finding her voice, she proceeds to multiplying it, which constitutes a metadiscursive element harking back to Black literature itself; as Rushdy states for a US-American context: "And it is by sharing those stories and that history with their readers that the neo-slave narrative authors perhaps hope to heal a nation that in many ways still denies its original wound." (Rushdy 2004, 103). Given that, as Cooper asserts, "[s]lavery is Canada's best-kept secret, locked within the national closet. And because it is a secret it is written out of the official history"

---

170 Hill uses the contrast between Aminata's original writing skills, which are based on Arabic writing, and her subsequent acquisition of the Roman writing system, to underline equivalence through emphasizing difference: Aminata expresses tremendous surprise when discovering that the *toubabu*, the White men, write from left to right, which in turn of course questions Westernized preconceptions such as taking the Roman writing mode for granted. By laying bare culturally and socially instilled notions (which we, however, conventionally take to be self-evident rather than constructed), Hill thus forces us to revalue the cultural other. Here, the reader has to arrive at the conclusion that even though Westernized mental scripts do not immediately take into account non-Western cultural achievements (e.g. Arabic script), there is no given hierarchy that delegates certain cultural achievements to superior or inferior ranks. Indirectly, Aminata's being steeped in a 'foreign' writing system thus emphasizes that there is no *a priori* distinction between a 'culturally superior' Europe and a 'culturally inferior' Africa (a presupposition embedded in the slave narratives' insistence on the cognitive equality between Africans and Europeans, which is, ironically, thwarted by the genre's extensive reliance on White authentication so adamantly avoided by Hill).

171 The fact that her progression towards freedom is not a stringent, linear movement (she falls from freedom into slavery and remains dependent on Whites and/or threatened by recapture for a long period of time) is paralleled by the non-linear development of her writing skills, which she is kept from exhibiting over extended periods as well.

(Cooper 2006, 68), Rushdy's remark pertaining to a denial is even more valid in a Canadian context. The move from voicelessness towards being heard and recognized has long been acknowledged as one of the central tenets of Black North American writing – indeed, of all writing from the margins (cf. e.g. Woods 1999, 63f., or George's discussion of Vassanji, Bhabha and Spivak, 1996, 187ff.).[172] One concession has to be made here: Aminata does not actually *find* her voice when she acquires a certain level of literacy; she finds a *durable medium* for her voice. This distinction is important in terms of conceptions of oral literature as well as in regard to the transmission of collective memories.[173] Even before Aminata has honed her writing skills to a degree that allows her to teach others and to pass on her narrative in writing, she has an acute understanding of the importance of oral story-telling. Beginning, again, with her parents in Bayo, Aminata uses the oral transmission of memories as a means to avoid their loss; the naming-games aboard the slave vessel is an essential element in this regard (cf. BN 66; 80). Later on, Aminata retains the use of oral story-telling, whether to school children in London or to African villagers. Yet she *adds* another medium to her repertoire.

Current approaches to collective memory theory acknowledge the fact that orality is one of the media employed in the construction of collective memories;[174] more durable media, however, tend to preserve memories more effectively in terms of both permanence and ease of dissemination or circulation. Consequently, Aminata is able to supplement the initial medium of narrative, which (both in historical, evolutionary terms and in terms of the novel's progression) is orality, with a more effective medium: writing. Rendering memories and oral (hi)stories into written form, thus attaining higher levels of permanence, denotes both the narrative process in *The Book of Negroes* and the more general process of integrating (neglected) elements into the collective memory using the medium of literature. Accordingly, Aminata's task (simultaneously: the task of African-Canadian literature) is not only to *find* a voice; the voice, once found, has to be established as well, to be rendered permanent and to be made heard/read. Aminata's understanding and tackling of this task are clear: from the beginning, she vows to bear witness lest the memories be lost. After her trip to Africa, however, she realizes that the position of a village *djeli*, who orally hands down her story to a limited number of people, may be fulfilling for her personally, but would prove to be socially and politically ineffective. Her written account, in contrast, could indeed turn out to make a difference due to the increased impact of written over oral transmission in terms of agenda setting and the construction of a collective memory. That is why she decides to travel to England, giving testi-

---

172 On African-Canadian literature's search for a voice in particular, cf. e.g. Clarke 2002a, 97 on the regaining of a specifically Africadian voice, or discussions of Marlene NourbeSe Philip's *She Tries Her Tongue, Her Silence Softly Breaks* (which deals *in extenso* with issues of finding a voice and (re-)claiming English/language for Black authors) in Quashie 2004; 130ff.; McCallum 2003; Cohen 2001, 134ff.; or Richards 1994, 249ff.

173 Cf. J. Assmann 2006, 101-121 on oral and/vs. written transmission of (cultural) memories.

174 Cf. on this aspect the discussion of orality and the slave narrative above (p. 83ff.).

mony both spoken and written, knowing that though she has found her voice, she still has to make it widely acknowledged.[175]

The focus placed on the acquisition of literacy in the original slave narrative hence proves to be a major constituent of *The Book of Negroes* as well; Aminata not only acquires literacy, she also spreads her knowledge, thereby gaining agency by progressing from recipient to instructor. Finding her voice and solidifying it in writing offer an opportunity for her to perpetuate her memories and thus contribute to the creation of a collective memory. Acquiring literacy, however, is never an easy task for an (ex-)slave, a fact which is underlined in the analysis by Davis/Gates (1985b), who identify the *ban* on learning as one of three major aspects concerning the discussion and representation of literacy in slave narratives. It has been pointed out that the learning process is an integral part of the slaves' emancipation, and that "[t]he slave narrative arose as a response to and a refutation of claims that the slaves *could* not write." (Davis/Gates 1985b, xv; emphasis in the original.) This pertains first of all to their immediate emancipation in terms of social acceptance and contribution, as Aminata exemplifies through her ability to perform tasks and hold jobs that would normally have been reserved for (literate) Whites. Aminata – as well as any slave narrative author not enlisting the assistance of an amanuensis – demonstrates the most basic of emancipatory assertions: Blacks were fully able, cognitively, to perform tasks for which they were commonly believed unfit.

The reactions Aminata's skills evoke are pervasive throughout the novel. They are succinctly summarized by a patron of a London coffee house, who remarks incredulously: "You kin read, kin ya? I'll buy ya coffee with my own wages, and one for each of the gentlemen what brung ya, if ya can read me a piece from this newspaper." (BN 450)[176] Furthermore, however, the former slaves' literacy also enables them to deconstruct and overcome the vicious circle of illiteracy and the alleged inhumanity which their lack of a written history was supposed to illustrate. Emancipation from an imposed voicelessness and invisibility is at the core of a larger emancipation process. Since the vicious circle enforced upon the slaves of course proves profitable for the White mainstream (and slave masters in particular) in economic and socio-psychological terms by ensuring White supremacy in both regards, slave masters as well as a high percentage of the White population professed an intense interest in perpetuating the *status quo* and keeping the slaves 'in their place.' One of the least conspicuous yet most effective ways to do so was the exertion of a ban on literacy.[177] Overcoming this

---

175 It seems important to Hill not to devalue the oral aspect of story-telling and transmission of memories in this process; throughout the chronology of the novel, Aminata also exerts and underlines her role as a *teller* of stories in the literal sense of *raconteur*, even when she is in England.

176 A similar scene takes place when Aminata meets the abolitionists in London and one of them "has a chuckle over" the idea that Aminata visits the library to stock up on books (cf. BN 102).

177 For slave masters, it was foremost of practical consequence that the slave should not learn to read and write in order to quell any ambition that might thus arise; in addition, as Davis/Gates point out (citing a 1740 South Carolina statute), the acquisition of literacy by Blacks was not merely discouraged or prohibited by slave owners, "it was a violation of law" (Davis/Gates 1985b, xxv). Also cf. Olney 1985.

obstacle has hence become one of the slave narratives' key issues (cf. e.g. Diedrich 1997). In *The Book of Negroes*, the hurdles erected against the acquisition of literacy are manifold, ranging from the comprehensive and explicit ban on Appleby's plantation to more subtle impediments such as libraries reserved exclusively for Whites.[178] Hill's writing thus conforms with this aspect of the slaves' acquisition of literacy, yet he diverges from what Davis/Gates categorize as a third facet of the issue:

> Almost all of the narratives [...] are prefaced by ironic apologia, in which the black author transforms the convention of the author's confession of the faults of his tale, by interweaving into this statement strident denunciation of that system that limited the development of his capacities. (1985b, xxviii)

The authors of the original slave narratives often introduce their works by admitting to faulty English or bad grammar, to poor prose or deficient vocabulary. In turn, they ask the reader to understand that these faults should not be blamed on their cognitive limitations, for this would have strengthened the stereotype of Blacks' mental inferiority; instead, they ask the audience to take into account the evils of the institution of slavery, which have interfered with their learning process and consequently impeded their writing skills. Hill could have done the same by having Aminata ask the reader for indulgence and leniency with her writing while revealing the intellectually crippling effects of slavery and highlighting the achievement of acquiring basic literacy in the first place, but he refrains from doing so. Instead, he frequently underlines the fact that Aminata employs no help – in fact, squarely refuses any such attempt – in writing her memoirs. Her impressive capabilities in terms of reading and writing are underlined numerous times; she does not require a proof reader, for instance, but is one herself (cf. BN 314f. and 332). By the same token Aminata does not question her memory, which is presented to be as infallible as her writing (cf. e.g. BN 1).

Hill pits utter confidence against the subversive apologia of the slave narrative, thus circumventing the exploitation of Aminata's recurring victimization in this regard; instead of pleading guilty of bad writing and then blaming it on slavery, Aminata expresses confidence in her skills, particularly so *vis à vis* the abolitionists: "Make the arguments that you must, I tell them, and let me make mine." (BN 101) It is important for Aminata's tale that it is self-authenticating, thus the detour via ironic apologia or White authentication suits neither her character, nor her writing style, nor the novel's narrative mode.[179] Focalization equally requires no meta-commentary; when Aminata recalls her childhood, she inserts linguistic markers of her age and education, such as using the word "moons" during her early childhood,

---

178 When Aminata asks Solomon Lindo to take her to the Charles Town library, the librarian lets Lindo know that "we don't allow Negroes here" (BN 210). Lindo has to blackmail the clerk in order to have Aminata admitted to the reading rooms even as his servant; it is revealing of Lindo's ambivalent character that he has Aminata fan him to alleviate the heat first for the sake of appearance, but keeps her going even when the librarian is not watching (cf. ibid.).

179 Cf. the discussion in section 4.2., "Hill's Faction and Historiographic Metafiction", p. 61ff.

which is then replaced by the term "months" later on.[180] This is done in ways as not to convey self-consciousness but a natural, confident choice of vocabulary suitable for the situation Aminata describes in retrospect. Consequently, there are no apologia for terms such as "moons", there is only a natural shift towards "months" as Aminata – in the chronology she narrates – grows more accustomed to her Europeanized environment.

In short, literacy is as significant for Hill's novel as it is for the slave narrative in general. Instruction is a key motif; yet while the slave narrative conventionally focuses on the 'passive' side of the instruction process, Aminata gains an extended measure of agency and adopts the role of instructor herself, therefore being able to act as a multiplier. *The Book of Negroes* heavily relies on its protagonist achieving literacy in spite of numerous obstacles, thereby disrupting the vicious circle of illiteracy and the imputation of inferiority and sub-humanity. In the end, Aminata is able to transform the voice she has found in oral story-telling into writing, hence consolidating her memories by using a more durable medium, which is the fundamental triumph of the slave narrative as well, "the first achievement in the [slaves'] struggle for literacy" (Link 1993, 278). Aminata's skills in this regard are presented as being beyond reproach, so Hill does not exploit any imperfections nor does he explicitly include any for the purpose of exploiting 'bad English' in deceptive excuses. In terms of the difficulties, the importance and the impact of the acquisition of literacy, *The Book of Negroes* thus fully conforms to the generic model, while – again – in terms of authentication, Hill obviously diverges. Elevating Aminata to full agency underlines an approach which does not take the Black North American experience as a story of victimization or insufficiency; as James Walker observes in regard to African-Canadian history: "That story resonated with pride, independence, sense of freedom, self-determination – with what we have come to call *agency*." (2007, 4; italics in the original)

c) Ham's children: Israelites in Egypt?

The extensive metaphorical use of the Israelites' biblical Exodus from Egypt is a common-place in the slave narrative and its study (cf. for instance the succinct equation provided by Diedrich 1997, 407). There is hardly a motif more commonly employed in the slave narrative than the one linking the American slaves' struggle to the biblical triad of slavery in Egypt, Exodus (led by Moses) and arrival in the Promised Land of Canaan. Franz Link writes of Styron's 1967 [1993] "slave narrative novel" (1993, 281; in Rushdy's terminology, a "Neo-slave narrative"; cf. discussion above) *The Confessions of Nat Turner* that its "biblical example is, *of course*, as in most slave narratives Israel in Egypt" (ibid., 284, emphasis added). The same can be said about *The Book of Negroes*: 'of course,' Hill employs the leitmotif of the biblical escape from slavery, and 'of course,' he uses the image of the promised land. The effect to which he uses these well-established tropes, however, diverges from the mostly imitative use displayed by the original slave narratives (as well as, one might add, by Styron's novel,

---

180 The same mechanism applies to terms such as "suns" for "days" or "rains" for "years"; "toubabu" becomes "buckra", then "whites"; from "homelanders", there is a shift to "Negroes" / "Africans".

though it has been criticized for an 'un-heroic' portrayal of Nat Turner, cf. Link 1993). The original usage provides a very clear-cut sequence of slavery–Exodus–Canaan, illustrating a stringent process propelled by God's wish to deliver the enslaved Israelites (read: American slaves) from their misery. Melvin Dixon notes:

> Using the Bible as a storehouse of myth and history that could be appropriated for religious syncretism and a practical philosophy based on historical immediacy, the slave community identified with the children of Israel; but they did not stop there. Slaves knew that deliverance would come, as proven by their African assurance of intimacy and immortality with the Supreme Being, and by the wider implications of the biblical past. (Dixon 1985, 300)

Though the journey itself, biblical as well as allegorical, might test and try the former slaves throughout their meanderings, final deliverance is promised and achieved. With Hill's novel, things are not quite as straightforward. Again, the reason might be found in the conventions imposed upon the original slave narrative: the abolitionists needed an image that both stressed the Christian duty of delivering the slaves and had at its teleological (and theological) terminus a paradisiacal state of being. To the Blacks had to be attributed the right and the ability to live in a state of harmony with Whites – in freedom, self-reliance and self-governance. Hill, of course, is not limited by this political aim; he no longer has to demonstrate Black people's ability to indeed live useful and fulfilled lives outside the restrictions of slavery. Thus, he is able to look at the biblical triad in a more complex and critical, even a subversive way.

Throughout *The Book of Negroes*, Hill incorporates more than twenty direct and explicit references to the Exodus and the Promised Land. These direct, literal references constitute the first way in which Hill, through his narrator Aminata, employs (and reconstructs) the collective memory of the Israelites' flight from Egypt in the context of the Black North American experience. The second way in which the Exodus is implemented in the novel is through the linkage between (biblical) Jews and Africans in the Americas repeatedly conjured up by Solomon Lindo, the Jewish indigo inspector and owner of Aminata in Charles Town. A third variant of the theme can be found in the recurring self-association of Black characters with Israelites fleeing from Egyptian slavery; these characters frequently describe (and thus narrate to instill meaning in) their own lives modeled on the biblical example. Just as Lindo perceives the Africans to be linked to his own forbears, the Blacks thus also *self*-identify with the Israelites. Finally, a fourth usage of the biblical mould is provided by the British promise of liberty and passage to Canada to the Black Loyalists, which explicitly employs biblical terminology and proclaims the Blacks' departure from New York City their 'Exodus' to the 'Promised Land'.[181] The heteronomous *and* autonomous identification of North American Blacks with

---

181 The analysis of the central motif of the exodus is split into three distinct sections: Here, I will deal with the first approach (direct references) only, discussing one exemplary instance of direct references made in the frame narrative, as these are the conclusions Aminata draws *in retrospect*, i.e. in her capacity as a free woman in London. The remaining strategies of implementing the exodus will be discussed in the chapters concerned with the respective stage of Aminata's journey. Thus, a thorough discussion of the linkage between biblical Israelites and African slaves established by Lindo is provided in the chapter dealing with Aminata's status *after* plantation slavery, i.e. in the Lindo household in Charles Town (section "Slaves and servants", p. 162ff.). Notions of Black

the Israelites in Egypt is thus pervasive in *The Book of Negroes*, just as it is throughout the genre of the slave narrative. In tune with his overall implementation of the generic model, however, Hill acknowledges the epitome – and then bends it. In terms of the slave narrative's most central image, the triad of slavery–Exodus–Canaan, Hill even bends the usage by just about 180 degrees, almost completely reversing the implications of both the biblical model and its epigone in this regard, the slave narrative.[182]

As an illustration of the explicit allusions to the Exodus throughout the novel, we may, for instance, consider the respective references within the frame narrative (Aminata writing her memoirs in London, 1802-1804). When Aminata is coaxed by the abolitionists into attending an Anglican church service, she finds the service to be intolerable – sitting on hard benches and quietly listening to the mumbling bishop seems excruciating to her, particularly in comparison with (African) Baptist services such as the ones she experienced in Nova Scotia or Sierra Leone (cf. BN 236). In this scene, Hill apparently does not engage in any particularly complex debates, and the plot is limited to Aminata fainting during the service and being carried outside after she has regained consciousness. Accordingly, Hill quite innocently pokes a little fun at the contrast between the stiff (White) Anglican and the lively (Black) Baptist church services.[183] Yet even in this lighthearted scene, Hill inserts references to collective

---

Loyalists self-identifying with the slaves fleeing from Egyptian slavery as well as British promises of a Canaan in Nova Scotia will be discussed in the section "The Canadian perspective: Canaan denied", p. 168ff.).

182   We have to keep in mind that, intertextually, Hill has to work with a repeatedly 'preconfigured' collective memory; while the original slave narrative invoked the biblical Exodus (which, of course, is itself a textualized memory), Hill, when referring to the Israelites' escape, necessarily considers both texts and thus employs a collective memory which has undergone two major (re-)writings in the given context: the original biblical one and the one adopted/adapted for the slave narrative. Hill's usage must thus be seen as a 'third level' reconstruction incorporating at least two prominent and forceful literary strands.

183   The comparison here is lighthearted, yet the issues of Black Baptist church services and the Black Baptist Church in general are important literary and social factors. They resurface variously in *Any Known Blood*, where they are used in particular to highlight – in the end, partly mend – the estrangement of Langston Cane V from Black grassroots institutions such as the church and to discuss sociopolitical movements either involved with or opposed to the established churches, such as the Black Panthers (cf. various scenes involving Millicent Cane's church, the Bethel A.M.E. in Baltimore).

G. E. Clarke also makes extensive use of both the image and the role of the Black Baptist Church, *inter alia* incorporating sermons, spirituals and gospels. Instances of Clarke referring to the (importance of) the Black Baptist (in his case, the African United Baptist church and the respective AUB Association of Nova Scotia) are legion. It suffices to open the first page of his anthology *Fire on the Water, Vol. 2* (which depicts a full-page dedication to the AUBA) or watch the first minutes of the ABC "Heart of a Poet" documentary series' episode on Clarke.

Others have disputed the church's positive influence; according to Winks, Black churches have kept African-Canadians from integrating by pointing to the transcendental instead of the worldly issues (cf. Winks 1997, chapter "Source of Strength? – The Church", 337-362). G. E. Clarke repeatedly bashes Winks; the historian's slightly unfavorable view of the Black Baptist church is likely one of the reasons for Clarke's anger (cf. e.g. 2002a, 68: "Characteristically, Winks puts the

traumata and to collective memories which he attempts to recontextualize and redefine. While quietly cursing the hard bench she has to sit on, Aminata for instance uses the term "children of Ham" to refer to the Africans who suffer from the hands of the British (BN 234). This biblical reference signifies the alleged biblical endorsement of slavery[184] and thus poses a counter-model to the conception of the Exodus – which, in turn, is alluded to only shortly after: "I heard something about the Israelites and the Promised Land, but my body ached for a horizontal position." (BN 235) Supplementing the reference to the Exodus, which could easily be taken as a promise of salvation to the Africans in slavery, with the reference to the supposed Christian approval of African slavery of course creates a tension from which critical questions emanate. Hill further underscores his critical approach by framing the allusion to the biblical flight from Egypt with another reference to the justification of slavery. Towards the end of the Sunday service, a song brings "rousing passion to the good Anglican churchgoers and made them sing as lustily as I had ever heard white people sing," as Aminata reports (BN 237). This song is "Rule, Britannia!", and it includes the line "Britons never never never shall be slaves". The song stirs up a recollection in Aminata, and when she can finally put her finger on it, the recollection of that memory makes her lose consciousness. What happens is that the song conjures up a personally and collectively traumatic situation. On a personal level, she recalls the slave ship's doctor softly singing "Rule, Britannia!" after sexually abusing Aminata's fellow slaves in the presence of Aminata (cf. BN 237f.).

We have to keep in mind that the surgeon's raping of the African women takes place when Aminata is still very young (barely eleven years old). The painful memory is thus triggered by a song almost fifty years later, but it is still powerful enough to make her faint.[185]

---

matter more negatively [...]. His prose is always only one step removed from propaganda."). James Walker, in contrast, emphasizes the church's importance in terms of community-building (Walker 1982). Lawrence Hill's father, Daniel Hill, according to David Este agrees with Walker and argues that the churches have helped African-Canadians maintain a distinct culture (cf. Este 2008, 395, who, however, constantly misspells James W. St. G. Walker as 'Walker, J. S. G.' in his bibliography).

184 According to the Old Testament, all mankind has descended from the three sons of Noah ("and the sons of Noah, that went forth of the ark, were Shem, and Ham, and Japheth: and Ham is the father of Canaan. These are the three sons of Noah: and of them was the whole earth overspread." Gen. 9:18-19). Ham is usually associated with Africa, while Shem is associated with Europe and the North, and Japheth with Asia. Ham is also the father of Canaan, and for centuries, the curse of Ham (he had behaved indecently towards his – drunken – father Noah, cf. Gen. 9:21-27) was believed to have befallen Africans in guise of their dark skin color (cf. Brow 2009 [1973]). The name "Ham" may be derived from the Hebrew word for "Black", and the curse upon Ham's son Canaan (he was to serve Ham's brothers and their offspring) was frequently taken to be a biblical endorsement of slavery (cf. Goldenberg 2003, part. 104-110).

185 On the ability of music to trigger 'lost' memories, cf. Bielefeldt 2001 (cursory) and Luban-Plozza et al. 1988 (in depth). When Aminata heard the song for the first time, viz. aboard the slave ship in 1757, she was of course unable to make out the lyrics because she was still unfamiliar with the English language. The memory is thus triggered by the melody alone, while Aminata consciously listens to the *lyrics* for the first time in 1804. In terms of the lyrics, the repeated reference to the sea and to waves would certainly have stimulated the process of vividly recollecting the time

Moreover, Aminata is able to grasp the social dimension of the traumatic situation she recollects: "Let him [the surgeon] sing, I thought [when aboard the slave vessel], ashamed that he spent himself on women from my homeland. The misfortune of those women was my good luck, their misery my escape." (BN 238) Aminata thus realizes that even though she herself had been spared some of the ultimate brutalities of slavery, these evils did indeed befall her fellow slaves. Accordingly, she collectivizes the traumatic situation she recalls and thus remembers the pain of others as well.

Additionally, "Rule, Britannia!" also includes a political claim which Aminata is quite aware of, as she asks herself "Britons? Slaves? What nonsense was this?" (BN 237) The political claim that "Britons never never never shall be slaves" seems cynical to Aminata given the fact that the British had been her enslavers and were nowhere near running the risk of being enslaved themselves. On what grounds then should the British ask to be spared slavery but inflict it on others? It is the same ambivalence and hypocrisy that Aminata had encountered in the United States, where Americans complained "about being enslaved by the King of England" (BN 228), while at the same time enslaving Africans.[186] For Aminata, "Rule, Britannia!" triggers the recollection of the concrete traumatic situation of sexual violence in slavery, but it also signifies the double standard employed by Whites as far as notions such as freedom and liberty are concerned – double standards, Aminata knows, that are clearly based on notions of European superiority and White supremacy.[187]

Consequently, the reference to the Exodus made by the Anglican bishop during the Sunday service is revealed as pure hypocrisy. Hill places this reference – which without further context could be considered a God-given promise to Africans to deliver them the way he delivered the Israelites from Egypt – between two references that lead to a complete reversal of the original collective memory, thus thwarting the entailed hope (even the promise) of de-

---

Aminata spent aboard the slave ship (as she had been on the ocean for the first time in her life, the waves of course would have made a lasting impression).

186 Aminata also remembers that the Canvas Town residents would "boo and hiss" when she read them Thomas Paine's *Common Sense*, because they "thought it absurd for any white man in the Thirteen Colonies to be complaining of slavery at the hands of the British." (BN 280)

187 The singing of 'Rule, Britannia!' of course alludes to Britain's (and therefore also Canada's) colonial past. Although Canada has repeatedly been characterized as a 'settler society' rather than a 'full-fledged' colony, the imperial attitude of "Rule, Britannia!" certainly also extended to the then-British colony (discussions of postcolonialism in a Canadian context are fruitful and extensive; cf. primarily Moss 2003a and Sugars 2004; for a concise and reliable introduction cf. Genetsch 2007, 12-21). The British sense of mission encapsulated in the phrase of the 'White man's burden' applied to Canada in equal measure, as mainstream White Canadians' attitudes and policies towards African-Canadians underline. (The phrase 'White man's burden' itself originally even refers to a North American context, specifically to an act of *US* imperialism – posing as imperialism-cum-humanism –, but generally implies Eurocentrism and an apparent civilizing mission of Whites. It is the title of a poem composed by Rudyard Kipling in 1899 in reaction to the US invasion of part of the Philippines; cf. Kipling 1999; also cf. Mama 1995, part. the chapter "Enslaving the soul of the Other", 17-42, for a discussion of the racial concepts underlying the poem.)

liverance. The first reference is to the "children of Ham", which indicates the involvement in and justifications of the institution of slavery by the church as well as ancient conceptions of an alleged biological inferiority of Africans, signified by darker skin and caused by the hand of God (Ham's curse). The second reference is to a song which triggers Aminata's recollection of the Middle Passage and its bestialities; it also points to the theoretical assumption that slavery was somehow justified by racial or cultural superiority. In this ostensibly breezy scene, it hence becomes clear that the African slaves cannot hope to be delivered like the Israelites; consequently, the collective memory of the Exodus from Egypt, which is so frequently employed by the slave narrative, is given a cynical connotation which replaces its originally hopeful one. Its impact is hence reversed: the slave narrative's almost naïve implication (coerced, if not enforced by the abolitionist editors) of the inevitable and imminent divine deliverance has been shattered by disillusionment. The key memory of the Exodus is given the same prominence in *The Book of Negroes* that it receives in the slave narrative, yet its implications are largely inverted.[188]

d) Secondary criteria of the slave narrative

Multiple names signifying multiple identities – whether autonomously or heteronomously assigned – constitute one of the most frequently used content-related elements characterizing the original slave narrative; *The Book of Negroes* makes extensive use of this constituent as well, though modifying it to reflect a more complex development of its protagonist. Literacy is used as a central means of improvement in both the original slave narrative and Hill's novel: for Aminata, it provides personal opportunities in regard to her standard of living and her desire to preserve her individual memories. In terms of collective memory, literacy establishes the solid and enduring externalization of memories and thus – via construction of a viable history of Africans in North America – implodes the vicious circle of illiteracy, alleged absence of history, denial of humanity, and obstruction of literacy. The extensive usage of the collective memory of the Exodus and the Promised Land[189] is characteristic of both the original slave narrative and Neo-slave narratives such as *The Book of Negroes,* which adopts yet adapts the original usage to convey a harsher and less comforting conception. The criteria of multiple names, literacy and the image of the Exodus are salient and central criteria in establishing parallels and differences between the original slave narrative and its possible epigone. They are, however, only three among a host of criteria which have been developed in studies of the slave narrative.

The author's uncertainty about his or her date of birth is one of these additional staple ingredients in terms of conventionalized, genre-specific markers. Often, authors only give a place of birth, but are either very vague about their date of birth, calculate it *ex post*, or skip it

---

188 As will be discussed later on, the same applies to Lindo's comparison between biblical Israelites and enslaved Africans in America as well as to the British promises of finding a Promised Land in Canada.

189 Cf. the example above as well as others in section 5.3.3., "Slaves and servants".

altogether (cf. Diedrich 1986, 193; Olney 1985, 153). Usually, the very first sentence would provide the (lack of) information on the authors' births, conventionally beginning with the famous phrase "I was born..." (cf. e.g. Davis/Gates 1985b, xiii). What is captured in this phrase – which is commonly followed by a place, but not a date – is a twofold message: 'I might not know exactly *when* I was born, but I *was*, so I *do* exist.' Again, what is underlined is the notion of authentication and of establishing the authors' plain existence – there could hardly be a more essentialist claim than "I was born", offered by the ex-slaves writing/dictating their memoirs. What conventionally follows this statement is a "sketchy account of parentage, often involving a white father" (Olney 1985, 153). *The Book of Negroes* closely follows the existentialist claims as well as the uncertainty expressed in the slave narratives' standardized introductory phrase. The novel's very first sentence asserts the bare existence of its narrator ("I seem to have trouble dying." BN 1), while in a very early scene, Aminata states, "I am Aminata Diallo, daughter of Mamadu Diallo and Sira Kulibali, born in the village of Bayo [...]. I suspect that I was born in 1745, or close to it." (BN 4) Hill thus closely follows the slave narratives' standard introduction by providing a place of birth and a vaguely recomputed birth date.

Hill deviates from the model, however, by supplying a rather detailed account of Aminata's parents, as their role of guidance *in absentia* constitutes an important element of Aminata's recollection process later on. The detailed description of her parents also lends itself to a more dramatic abduction scene, when the continuing chain of Aminata's loss of family members and loved ones is begun. Aminata's upbringing, both in terms of her character and her skills, such as midwifery and basic literacy, preordains part of her development and in dramaturgical terms necessitates a closer look at her parents. A second deviation from the slave narrative's introductory constituents is found in the fact that Aminata is not of mixed racial origin (cf. Sekora 1993, Olney 1985, 153). Even though Lawrence Hill himself is the son of a Black father and a White mother and explores this theme in most of his other writings,[190] Aminata is conceived of as a person of mixed *African* origin (Fula and Bamana), not of mixed race.[191] The reason, of course, is obvious: if Hill wanted to include Aminata's abduction from Africa, a mixed-race identity would have been extremely unlikely given the fact that Whites at that time had not yet advanced to Mali, where Aminata is kidnapped.[192] Thus, while

---

190 Langston Cane V in Hill's *Any Known Blood* is the son of a White mother and Black father; Mahatma Grafton in *Some Great Thing* could pass for an Indian, and *Black Berry, Sweet Juice* is largely devoted to the issue of biraciality. Other African-Canadian authors of course deal extensively with mixed-race identities as well: Suzette Mayr, for instance, grapples with these issues to a large extent (partly based on her own experiences); Beatrice Chancy, in George Elliott Clarke's libretto of the same name (1999), is the slave narrative's prototypical offspring of a Black slave mother and a White slave master, as is Mary-Mathilda, the protagonist of Austin Clarke's 2002 bestseller *The Polished Hoe* (winner of the 2002 Giller Prize).

191 Cf. Belcher 1999 for background information on the two sides of Aminata's African heritage, Bamana (chapter 6) and Fula (chapter 7).

192 In the words of Hill: "At the time when my characters were abducted, around 1756, Europeans were not in any number traveling deep into the heart of West Africa. They had explored and mapped the coast in detail, but they did not know what the interior looked like. Their maps betray

conforming to the central tenets of the essentialist 'I am', also providing a place of birth and a vaguely remembered or recalculated date of birth, Hill deviates in terms of the parents' presentation and the mixed-race origin of the protagonist.

A number of minor aspects can be added to the ones already presented.[193] Link (1993) and Olney (1985) provide extensive lists of recurrent motifs, phrases and plot elements that characterize the slave narrative in terms of content; most of these criteria are met by *The Book of Negroes*, though some are varied and modified, e.g. through displaying them in minor characters instead of the protagonist. Accounted for separately, these criteria may appear trivial and inconsequential, yet amassed, they are indicative of the closeness between the slave narrative and *The Book of Negroes* in terms of content. Consequently, a number of additional secondary criteria will be considered summarily and in brief here:

Characteristic (cf. Link 1993, Olney 1985)	Fully met by *BN*	Partly met by *BN*	Not met by *BN*	Comment
Hierarchy between slaves depicted	x			Examples: Aboard the slave ship: Biton > Fanta > Aminata; Appleby's indigo plantation: Mamed > Georgia > Aminata
Good and bad masters depicted	x			Appleby contrasted with Solomon Lindo (even though Lindo is a somewhat ambivalent character ultimately redeemed only towards the end, he almost always treats his 'servants' kindly)
Separation from family	x			Pivotal experience; Aminata's greatest regret is not having "children and grandchildren to love, and parents to care for me" (BN 3); Aminata experiences this trauma four times: separation from her parents, from both of her children, from her husband Chekura
Lust for White women off-topic[194]	x			Conversely, Aminata does not crave the companionship of White men (she is close to Clarkson, but in a platonic way)[195]

an ignorance of the interior of Africa. One of the first Europeans to travel far into the interior of West Africa is the Scottish doctor Mungo Park in 1799, which is after my characters were abducted. He becomes the first European to say that these old maps of Africa show the Niger River flowing in the wrong direction." (Hill, Appendix 297)

193 An additional, though tongue-in-cheek, characteristic could be derived from Link's statement that the slave narrative was the "most popular black literature of the ante-bellum period" (1985, 277). Davis and Gates similarly observe that Douglass, Equiano, Henson, Brown and others wrote actual bestsellers (cf. 1985b; also cf. Kawash 1997, 15f.). Likewise, *The Book of Negroes* has been published not only to great acclaim, but also with great popular success in Canada, the United States, Great Britain, and Australia. Winning the 2008 Commonwealth Writers' Prize has further fostered sales and added to the novel's commercial success so that it indeed stands in the tradition of bestselling slave narratives.

194 It was considered counterproductive for the slave narrative's political agenda to foster stereotypes and fears that pre-existed among the White population, therefore mixed-race relationships (partic-

Characteristic (cf. Link 1993, Olney 1985)	Fully met by *BN*	Partly met by *BN*	Not met by *BN*	Comment
Detailed description of the brutalities of slavery	x			A staple ingredient in *BN* as well; cf. e.g. the cruelties aboard the slave ship, the slave auction in South Carolina or Aminata's being humiliated and raped by Appleby
Cruel master / mistress / overseer	x			Cf. above; a cruel mistress (Lindo's sister) replaces Mrs Lindo after she dies; the cruel overseer on Appleby's plantation is replaced by Mamed after he dies (consequently, there is also an antipode for each cruel master / mistress / overseer)
'Everyday life' (food, clothing, daily / weekly routine etc.)	x			Food and clothing play important roles and are used to contrast life in freedom (Africa) with life on the indigo plantation; also: detailed descriptions of Aminata's tasks (e.g. indigo harvesting and processing)
One extraordinarily industrious and strong slave who is not whipped		x		Fomba is indeed the prototypical drudge slave (strong and dexterous but slow-minded); he is indeed spared the whip, though not because he is so obedient and useful, but because Aminata takes care of him and steers him clear of trouble
One 'Christian' slaveholder, usu. worse than a non-Christian one		x		Appleby indeed treats his slaves worse than Lindo, a Jew; however, Appleby's Christianity is not emphasized and tasks at Lindo's place are household chores rather than plantation work; the ship's doctor, though not a slaveholder *per se*, is even mollified by his Christian faith
Slave auction (families separated, weeping mothers, slave coffles)		x		Aminata is brought to the slave auction in a coffle, but family separation takes place *before* the auction (except for Chekura, but he is not family yet); consequently, Aminata's mother cannot not weep at the slave auction; however, all elements are present at some point in the novel without being conflated at the slave auction
Failed attempts to escape; patrols; chase by men and dogs		x		Aminata tries to escape only once and is not chased (her escape illustrates willpower and is not structured along the lines of 'adventure stories'); Chekura fills in the stories of dog chases, patrols and the like (he loses several fingers as a punishment for repeatedly running away)

ularly Black men desiring White women) were anathema. In *The Book of Negroes*, Aminata does not long for a White companion; this however, is mainly due to her portrayal as fiercely loyal to her (often absent) husband Chekura. In *Any Known Blood,* however, Hill extensively deals with interracial sexual relationships, introducing the novel with a scene in which an interracial couple is attacked with stones. In *Black Berry, Sweet Juice*, Hill discusses the issue as well (particularly in the chapter "But for the Interference with His Arrangement").

195 It is ever so slightly insinuated in *The Book of Negroes* that Mrs Falconbridge, wife of a former slave ship surgeon, might have desired African men ("On her way out, she took another look at the Temne roof workers next door." BN 411; this possible allusion, however, is far too subtle to provide a counter-example of the characteristic in question).

Characteristic (cf. Link 1993, Olney 1985)	Fully met by *BN*	Partly met by *BN*	Not met by *BN*	Comment
Lincoln figures as Moses			x	There are several figures modeled on Mosaic traits as well as a character explicitly named "Daddy Moses"; Lincoln, however, is born five years after the fictional Aminata finishes her memoirs[196]
Successful escape, aided by the North Star and Quakers			x	Aminata's escape is explicitly not modeled on flight via the Underground Railroad or other secret routes; no Quakers aid her[197]

Table 2: Additional slave narrative characteristics, compiled from Olney 1985, Link 1993

It is obvious from the collected secondary criteria that there is a large concurrence between the slave narrative's characteristics and *The Book of Negroes*. Hill's novel fully conforms with seven out of the thirteen criteria, partly meets an additional four and significantly diverges only on two accounts. While this is of course only a superficial attempt at literary bookkeeping, it underlines the close kinship that has been demonstrated in the in-depth analyses above. Equally, however, it shows that there is no *strict* adherence to the slave narrative's conventions, which should be obvious by taking into account that a) *The Book of Negroes* is of course *not* a slave narrative *per se* but a generic successor and b) quite plainly, not even *all* of the slave narratives fully complied with *all* of the genre's prototypical characteristics. Yet combined with the more encompassing and significant characteristics such as the issues of name changes, the importance of literacy, and the usage of the Exodus motif, it is apparent that *The Book of Negroes* shares with the classic slave narrative more than the sketchy familiarity attributed to the Neo-slave narrative by various scholars (cf. the introductory discussions of this chapter, 88ff.). In addition to the general description of Neo-slave narratives as "contemporary novels that assume the form, adopt the conventions, and take on the first-person voice of the ante-bellum slave narrative" (Rushdy 1999, 3), we may thus add a significant number of concrete correspondences.

---

196 Moses can be embodied by other persons in the original slave narrative; Dixon, for instance, notes: "Moses very often came to the slaves in the person of Harriet Tubman and other ex-slaves who went back into Egypt, heard the children of 'yowlin',' and led them to the promised land in the North." (1985, 300)

197 This escape mode is employed at length in *Any Known Blood*, which includes Quaker abolitionists and their prominent involvement in hiding and smuggling fugitive slaves to the North. Yet if Aminata, in *The Book of Negroes*, had escaped via the Underground Railroad, the vital theme of broken British/Canadian promises could not have been implemented adequately. Aminata's escape is thus constructed in opposition to the (almost stereotypical) adventurous and dangerous flight ending in 'deliverance'.

5.2.3. Category three: Goals

If *The Book of Negroes*, as has been shown above, does in fact emulate as well as re-modulate the classic slave narrative, to which end does Hill employ these literary and generic moulds? Why should a Black Canadian author, removed almost two hundred years from the factual ending of slavery in Canada,[198] take possession of an outdated, overly conventionalized and indeed predominantly *US*-American literary form?[199] First of all, because the slave narrative is simply not an outdated genre, as we have seen. In the United States, it has enjoyed a celebrated revival through the Neo-slave narrative following the Civil Rights and the Black Power Movements, producing in its wake such works as Margaret Walker's *Jubilee* (1966), Ernest Gaines's *The Autobiography of Miss Jane Pittman* (1971) and the hugely successful *Beloved* by Toni Morrison (1987), to name but a few.[200] Second of all, Canada has in fact figured in most of the classic slave narratives, yet in a way highly contested by Black *Canadian* literature.[201] As such, African-American slave narratives have constructed an image of Canada which mainstream discourse in the 'true North' has eagerly adopted and which is now vehemently challenged in African-Canadian literary writing. It is imperative in regard to Black Canadian issues, and I believe it is indeed one of the central claims that can be made about African-Canadian literature, that in contrast to the United States, the realm of literature indeed spearheads social and political movements instead of vice versa. It is my argument here that a comparative analysis of the goals of the original slave narrative, the US-American Neo-slave narrative and *The Book of Negroes* reveal one of the main characteristics of Black Canadian writing: it lacks the background of political and social developments its southern counterpart has been able to draw upon; consequently, it has to make up for this absence. Black Canadian writers are thus forced to *initiate*, not merely mirror, evolve or comment, shifts in the society they are embedded in.

Leaning on notions of intertextuality as an interplay between literary and social text/s,[202] one could in fact argue that – although of course both systems are mutually interde-

---

198 Throughout the British Empire, slavery was abolished in 1834; in Canada, however, African slavery had ceased to be a factor some time before (cf. section 3.1.4., "The decline of slavery").

199 In spite of G. E. Clarke's valiant efforts to 'repatriate' a number of American slave narratives as belonging to the African-Canadian literary corpus (Clarke 2008a), there can be no doubt as to the dominance exerted by the US in regard to the slave narrative.

200 For more examples, cf. the introductory discussion in this chapter as well as e.g. Beaulieu 1999, 27; Rodgers 1997, 182; Rushdy 1999, 3 and 2004, 92f.

201 Canada has also figured in numerous US-American *Neo*-slave narratives, yet its depiction has logically been far less streamlined and more open to reconsideration, even to satire (the most obvious example being Ishmael Reed's *Flight to Canada*).

202 A usage I refrain from elsewhere in this study, but have adapted here from Rushdy (cf. 1999, 14ff.); I generally rely on a conception of intertextuality in a stricter and more descriptive, not a universal and ontological sense. Hence, what I habitually refer to as intertextuality is the (intentional) incorporation of texts in other texts (again, in its stricter sense of a written text: in the discussion of an ekphrastic description, for instance in section 5.2.2.a), I abstain from referring to

pendent – in the context of Canadian literature, a minority *literature* indeed leads (i.e. must by necessity lead) the way for a more general socio-cultural reassessment. In short, Black Canadian fiction could thus be considered the pretext of social text. In absence of activists of the stature of Martin Luther King, Jr. or Malcolm X, and in the face of the clear absence of any truly revolutionary moments in Black Canadian history,[203] literature serves as the prime medium of a *social* re-writing as well.[204] The Canadian policy of multiculturalism has clearly contributed to pacify the concerns of the nation's Black minority and to deflect hegemonic discourse away from racial issues by proclaiming Canada's appreciation and benevolence in regard to race/ethnicity (cf. for instance Laura Moss's synopsis of criticism brought forward by Bissoondath, G. E. Clarke, and R. Walcott; 2003b, 13; also cf. Foster 2007, particularly Part Two). Multiculturalism in this case has thus served as an additional obscurer of the social realities perceived by Black authors – concomitantly with the traditional and historiographical (mis-)reading of Canada as a safe haven.

It is obvious, and it has been pointed out before, that neither Hill's novel nor any other North American Neo-slave narrative shares with the classic slave narrative its overt and main goal: the abolition of slavery.[205] However, as has been shown in the section on literacy and its

---

intertextuality, whereas I employ a clearly intertextual approach when dealing with Hill's references to e.g. Equiano's slave narrative). What I do *not* usually refer to, then, are more encompassing poststructuralist notions of intertextuality such as Bakhtin's dialogic principle (cf. Bakhtin 1986), Kristeva's subsequent introduction of the term itself (while marginalizing the knowable, static subject, replacing intersubjectivity with intertextuality; cf. Kristeva 1972), Barthes's death of the author (cf. Barthes 2000), or Derrida's "texte général" (cf. Derrida 1992). There is an overall tendency in poststructuralist literary studies to stress *general* intertextuality, yet proceed to study *specific* instances. Cf. as a possible 'remedy' that reintroduces a discussion of specific influence as well as (inter)subjectivity Bloom's 'anxiety of influence' (cf. Bloom 1997). What is generally referred to as 'intertextuality' here are thus Genette's 'meta-' and 'hypertextuality', not the 'transtextual' nature that is inherent in every text (cf. Genette's five-fold typology of intertextuality, 1997). Allen (2000) provides a fine introduction to the discussion of intertextuality.

203 In this, as in many other regards, African-Canadian literature mirrors a more general Canadian tendency; cf. Frye 2003c.

204 Joy Kogawa's *Obasan* (1994) has – for a more narrowly limited historical and social context as well as a different minority group – achieved a similar feat, initiating a nationwide discussion about possible reparations for the evacuation and other atrocities Japanese Canadians had to endure around the time of World War II (cf. for instance Lutz 2005, 321f.; Hammill 2007, 43ff.). Kogawa's fiction is likely the most prominent example of unearthing and rewriting history in Canadian literature; in an African-American context, this rank is arguably occupied by Morrison's *Beloved*. Hill himself cites Kogawa as an example of how literature can create sociopolitical momentum. In an interview, H. Nigel Thomas refers to Barbara Kingsolver's comment that she was able to reach a much larger audience through fiction than she would have been able to by writing scientifically, to which Hill replies, "I think it's true. Dramatizing critical moments of our past can produce excellent fiction. Joy Kogawa comes to mind." (Hill 2006, 135)

205 As Valerie Smith observes, "the notion of the neo-slave narrative may need to be expanded to include slave narratives by former slaves written (and not merely reprinted) in the twenty-first century", as "slavery is not an obsolete practice" (2007, 184). While this is of course a valid ob-

attempted suppression in the context of slavery, the classic slave narratives indeed had agendas that went far beyond and far deeper than this obvious political aim. First of all, they offered a venue for personal authentication. Fugitive slaves through the slave narrative were able to reestablish their individual, personal subjectivity and humanity. They were offered a chance to re-write, re-create their lives and through a literary venue affirm their existence as human beings. The ability to de-commodify the self is an important part of the classic slave narrative, to which the autobiographical pact of course still largely applied.[206] Today, the slave narrative is known to include examples of fictional accounts and/or intertextual elements, a fact which might be considered to subtract from the narratives' veracity.[207] On the other hand, 'life writing' by necessity includes fictionalized, constructed elements in order to arrive at a 'usable past' which may thus lend structure and purpose to the life of the author.[208] As such, the slave narrative offered the possibility to enrich the individual author's life in ways largely unseen before: not only did the writer of a fugitive slave narrative establish his fundamental existence; he could furthermore lend it an aura of purposefulness, which is reflected as well as performed in the slave narrative. All of a sudden, a supposedly sub-human, commodified slave emerges as a subject, an agent, and – possibly – a political mover.

a) Representation, appropriation, authentication

In order to validate the individual narratives and their authors' existence, the classic slave narrative went to great lengths of authentication. This changed with the arrival of the Neo-slave narrative, which was attacked on these very grounds: the appropriation of the slave's

---

jection, all references to the (Neo-) slave narrative in this study point to the literary dealings with the *historical, transatlantic* slave trade, not contemporary global exploitation.

206 Cf. the discussion of the *pacte autobiographique* at the beginning of section 5.2.1., "Category one: Composition".

207 Cf. e.g. Ring 1994 or Sinanan 2007, 65 on Equiano and intertextuality ("While this [intertextuality] may seem to compromise the authenticity of Equiano's own account, it is most useful to read this intertextuality as a necessary responsiveness that strategically amplified the antislavery agenda." Ibid.). On the validity of (and the problems involved in considering) the slave narrative as historical sources, see for example the section "The Slave Narrative as History" in Davis/Gates 1985, particularly C. Vann Woodward, "History From Slave Sources" and John W. Blassingame, "Using the Testimony of Ex-Slaves: Approaches and Problems."

208 The term 'life writing' has come to be regarded as an equivalent to or as a substitute for the term 'autobiographical'; cf. theoretically dense Wagner-Egelhaaf 2000; thoroughly Olney 1998; for a Canadian context, Egan/Helms 2004. On 'usable pasts' in connection to collective memory cf. for instance Neumann 2005, 73; more extensively Wertsch 2002, part. 31-46; also cf. Zamora's 1997 *The Usable Past: The Imagination of History in Recent Fiction of the Americas*, which explores the connections between fiction and past – past influencing fiction and vice versa – in a comparative Latin and North American context; Zamora, in turn, also reflects briefly on collective memory, namely Walter Benjamin's thoughts (ibid. 174).

voice.[209] The suspension of the autobiographical pact in the Neo-slave narrative is of course self-evident, as no ex-slave would still be alive to write his memoirs in, say, 1976; patently, the same then holds true for *The Book of Negroes*. Yet, in contrast to Ishmael Reed's *Flight to Canada*, for instance, Hill uses a different way of authentication, not undermining but under-*lining* the historical veracity of his story. In this regard, Hill follows the classic slave narrative more closely than their emulation, the Neo-slave narrative. For propagandistic reasons, i.e. in order to ensure the greatest political impact possible, the classic slave narratives had to ensure that their depictions of the evils of slavery were believable. *The Book of Negroes* follows suit, yet for a slightly different reason: Hill does not have to unveil the evils of (US-American) slavery as an institution, which is a task thoroughly completed on a literary as well as a formal historiographic level. What is perceived to be missing, however – perceived by Hill as well as other African-Canadian authors – is the incorporation of the history of Canadian (post-)slavery, indeed also the history of the Canadian Black presence in general, into the Canadian collective memory in any faithful or representative way.

The issue of representation is in fact a central aspect: As the classic slave narrative strove to represent, for the first time, the Black subject(ivity), and the Neo-slave narrative aimed at a reclaiming of an appropriated literary tradition which was then reinvigorated as to represent, again, the Black subject in his or her current position, *The Book of Negroes* lays claim to faithfully representing a neglected part of Canadian history, hence historically re-building Black Canadian subjects/subjectivity. It is one of the arguments of this thesis that in fact, these building blocks have not been 'forgotten' or 'neglected' in the construction of a hegemonic collective memory, but (un-)consciously *de*selected in order to arrive at a more streamlined and fissure-free self-identification. Unconscious as these processes of memory construction may often be – particularly for the individual persons unaware of the discourses, the larger processes and mechanisms of agenda setting and memory constructions they are involved in – they are not arbitrary or haphazard. Representation thus lies at the core of the classic and the Neo-slave narrative as well as *The Book of Negroes*. Hill then authenticates his tale in numerous ways, among them the inclusion of intertextual references (explicated in section 5.2.1., p. 93). He furthermore verifies his writing by supplying an outline of the histor-ical research he conducted as an afterword in which he also comments on the liberties he has taken with the novel's (numerous) characters which are modeled on historical persons.[210]

The main device of authentication in *The Book of Negroes*, however, is a narrative one: Hill creates what Neumann would call a *Gedächtnisroman* as opposed to an *Erinnerungsroman*, the latter combining past and present levels and incorporating a metafictional level on which the very memories presented are challenged (2005, 208-237).

---

209 Quite obviously, the debate over appropriation focused mainly on *White* appropriations, most famously – and most controversially so – regarding Styron's *The Confessions of Nat Turner*; cf. above.

210 Examples range from Queen Charlotte Sophia through the ex-slave trader Alexander Falcon-bridge to the abolitionists John Clarkson and Thomas Peters (cf. the – incomplete – list provided in the appendix "A Word About History", BN 473).

Hill refrains from any of these doubts; cf. the discussion of his 'faction'. Aminata's story is presented as unchallenged by failing memory, by external influences or characters' anxieties. No postmodern complications offer competing memory versions and the narrator happily and without a trace of irony declares that her memory is unperturbed – her mind is not, as it seems to have occasionally been inferred from her old age, "like pumpkin mush." (BN 1)[211] Time and again, Hill underlines the reliability of Aminata's account, but stops short of creating suspicion by over-repetition. Why, then, does he go to these lengths to implement what is in academic circles today often viewed as a less refined literary strategy, viz. creating a fictional autobiography lacking the doubts and challenges that shape not only postmodern literature but which are an inherent part of any memory constructions that humans undertake?[212] A possible reason is that the time may not be ripe in Canadian literature yet for a deliberately open, protean treatment of the issues brought forward by *The Book of Negroes* – not before public discourse and constructions of mainstream collective memory have been altered to faithfully reflect the Black Canadian experience.

What might sound depreciatory at first is not at all intended as a commentary on the literary *quality* of Black writing north of the 49th parallel. At least a good handful of African-Canadian authors would be able to transfer brilliantly, for instance, the highly postmodern mode of *The Polished Hoe* to an entirely Canadian context (including, of course, Austin Clarke himself).[213] Yet the goal of *Canadian* postslavery literature is more closely related to the classic fugitive slave story's than to the US-American Neo-slave narrative's in its urge to

---

211 Examples for these modes would prominently include Mordecai Richler's 1997 *Barney's Version* (Canadian context) and Caryl Phillips's 1991 *Cambridge* (Black – British – context). Generally, as has been explicated in sections 4.1. and 5.1., Hill does not consider himself a writer prone to avant-garde writing; in an interview, he claims: "I don't see myself experimenting with form [as was suggested by the interviewer]. So far, at least, I write in a fairly traditional manner." (Hill 2006, 135)

212 Cf. for succinct overviews Erdfelder 2001 and Keller 2001. Far more comprehensive, and often written in the light of the false memory debates surrounding child abuse cases in the 1980s, which revitalized a field scientifically dealt with as early as the 1930s (by Frederic C. Bartlett): Schacter's important 1997 collection *Memory Distortion* (both on individual, i.e. neurological/psychological and social, i.e. collective/cultural, aspects), Schacter 1996 (also authoritative on recovered memory), Brainerd/Reyna 2005 (part. 3-96), and Aleida Assmann 2006 (part. 119-182).

213 It is indicative in this regard that earlier Canadian postslavery novels, such as Austin Clarke's *The Polished Hoe* or Brand's *At the Full and Change of the Moon* and *In Another Place, Not Here* (the latter in a more remotely derived way), conventionally set the slave characters' existence and the site of slavery itself *outside* of Canada (e.g. in Trinidad). By and large, the slaves themselves do not come – forcibly or otherwise – to Canada so that slavery remains, geographically, an extra-Canadian phenomenon. In *At the Full and Change of the Moon*, the *legacy* of slavery is explored in Canadian terms through one of Marie Ursule's descendants, yet this is done in a chronologically post-slavery setting. Austin Clarke's Mary-Mathilda does not leave Barbados either. It is only in *recent* African-Canadian literature that the issue of slavery is brought to Canada and 'repatriated' in direct, unmediated ways. Cf. for instance – next to *The Book of Negroes* – G. E. Clarke's *Beatrice Chancy* (a libretto) or Afua Cooper's *The Hanging of Angélique* (a history/novel amalgam). This assertion does not apply to Black Canadian poetry, which has been incorporating issues of the (ex-)slaves' existence in Canada for a long time.

authenticate rather than question and undermine. For the classic slave narrative, it was of the utmost importance to avoid any semblance that they might *not* be trustworthy and believable lest they lose their political impact as revelations of a social reality; the Canadian Neo-slave narrative is in a similar position: if it challenges, questions or undermines its representation of the Black presence in Canada, it risks the effectiveness of its own counter-hegemonic constructions. Questioning its own claims – e.g. that of a lopsided and curtailed (re-)presentation of Black history in Canada – would lead to a consolidation of hegemonic discourse, which holds that Canada has been and continues to be an outright benefactor of Blacks.

Hill places particular emphasis on the aspect of authentication, using the classic slave narrative's weak spot as an intertextual point of reference. The classic slave narrative relied heavily on external authentication, incorporating a wide range of means to prove their authenticity. These means, however, were almost exclusively 'White' – given the prevailing attitudes, the narratives' intended audience, the publishers themselves, and the narratives' political aims, one has to add: *unsurprisingly*, these means were almost exclusively 'White'. Through the credibility provided by White abolitionists who 'streamlined' the classic slave narrative, the genre's political impact at the time of their publication was ensured.[214] Today, however, the fact that most of the slave narratives were heavily edited by abolitionists seems to subtract instead of add to their credibility. What is more, the need to authenticate via *Whites* obviously speaks to the fact that hegemonic antebellum notions of credibility did not include Blacks as particularly trustworthy – the Black subject was not allowed to fulfill the role of witness (what is referred to throughout *The Book of Negroes* as a *djeli*), thus Black memories were rendered questionable, if not invalid. This, of course, is a mechanism and an implication which Hill has the liberty to avoid by merely refraining from the conventionalized addition of White authentication. In fact, however, he makes an explicit point of the fact that Aminata possesses credibility *beyond* any external authentication. To quote one of several examples:[215]

---

214 Some critics have argued that the classic slave narrative is indeed *not* as formulaic as the vast majority of research assesses: "A perception of automatization in slave narratives – the perception of a lack of originality and so forth in the slave narratives – can be traced to faulty perceptions and emphases of the dominant culture." (Flagel 2005, 18) Given the comprehensive evidence compiled by Olney, Gates, and others, however, I must agree with the position that claims a predominantly formulaic nature for the original slave narrative. As Henry Louis Gates, Jr. puts it: "These slave narratives came to resemble each other, both in their content and in their formal shape. So similar was the structure of these narratives that it sometimes seems to the modern reader that the slave authors were tracing a shared pattern, and then cutting that pattern from similar pieces of cloth." (Gates 2002, 2) Even the narratives' 'hybrid' status has been highly conventionalized, so that "all the mixed, heterogeneous, hetero*generic* elements in slave narratives come to be so regular, so constant, so indispensable to the mode that they finally establish a set of conventions – a series of observances that become virtually *de rigueur* – for slave narratives unto themselves." (Olney 1985, 152; italics in the original)

215 For further instances of Aminata's insistence on relating her own story, in her own words, cf. BN 4, 101, 234, 451, 454, 457.

'I have decided to write the story of my life,' [Aminata said]. 'Certainly,' Hastings [an influential abolitionist] said, 'but you will require our guidance to ensure–' 'Without guidance, thank you very much,' I said. 'My life. My words. My pen. I am capable of writing.' A slender, well-dressed man stood and introduced himself as William Wilberforce, member of Parliament. He asked if he might clarify the matter. 'Please do,' I said. 'This is not a question of your literacy,' Wilberforce said. 'It is rather an issue of ensuring its authenticity.' 'That is precisely why nobody will tell my story but me.' (BN 455)

Ironically, the abolitionists had decided to 'ensure the authenticity' of Aminata's story by deliberately keeping her separated from London's Black community, thus avoiding "Londoners saying that the blacks of London made up [Aminata's] story." (BN 454) Hill, by laying bare the possible influence of a communal, diasporic Black voice which could in fact have supplemented ('distorted'?) Aminata's story, renders void the abolitionists' concerns. Aminata is aware of possible influences – including intertextual ones such as Equiano's narrative (cf. ibid.) – yet consciously focuses on her own experiences.[216] The novel's very ending is an insistence on the authenticity, autonomy and self-reliance of Aminata's tale. Aminata has come within reach of finishing her manuscript when the issue of publication comes up again:

May [Aminata's abducted daughter with whom she is miraculously reunited in London] tells me that she has found a publisher for my story. But the abolitionists have their own publisher and insist on correcting 'allegations that cannot be proved' and she doesn't know whether to give in or to use the man she has chosen. (BN 469)

May's publisher is her fiancé and – of course – Aminata's manuscript goes to him for publication.[217] Aminata's insistence that "my story is my story and it will be published by the one who lets my words stand" (ibid.) is thus clearly heeded. In fact, it is only after her story has in this way been passed on to Aminata's daughter and her fiancé, only after Aminata has stated that she is "finally done", her "story is told" (ibid.), that her old age eventually takes its toll and begins to cloud her memory (cf. BN 470).

The discussion revolving around the publication of Aminata's memoirs in an undiluted and non-appropriated way of course speaks loudly to the self-reliance of Black North Americans in telling their story. As Aminata resolves to have her story told by the people she trusts

---

216 Additionally, Hill resolves all doubt by relating that Equiano's death prevents a personal meeting with Aminata, while her physical frailty keeps her from visiting London's Black neighborhood in the first place (cf. BN 457) – consequently, not even the slightest opportunity of altering influences remains. Obviously, we need to keep in mind here that of course the *writer* Lawrence Hill is strongly influenced by Equiano's and other ex-slaves' narratives. The repeated allusion to Equiano's account underlines the importance of this inter- (or hypo-)text (Genette) for the novel *as such*.

217 There is also a short reference to the issue of (White) appropriation here, as Aminata asks May whether the man she intends as a publisher "know[s] the story of our people" (BN 469), which is quite clearly a masked allusion to the question of his race. If taken literally, Aminata's question would of course also have included the abolitionists, as they were plainly also familiar with the 'story' of Africans in North America; consequently, the issue is in fact not *knowledge* but *experience*, and as such, the question is obviously aimed at racial affiliation.

and who 'let her words stand', *The Book of Negroes* in general, but specifically in regard to the publication of the narrator's autobiography, advocates the autonomy of constructions of Black Canadian historical discourse. The power/knowledge nexus has, as the slave narrative underlines, too long been appropriated by White 'translators' – be they scribes, amanuenses, publishers, or scholars – and distorted in the process.[218] *The Book of Negroes* does not necessarily ascribe bad intentions to these appropriations. The abolitionists are presented as well-meaning, but also as ambivalent up to the point of being hypocritical. While the abolitionists ostentatiously refrain from using sugar in their tea as to boycott the sugar trade and its exploitative system (cf. BN 99f.), John Clarkson, for instance, has in his household Black servants (cf. BN 452) and the abolitionists put forth a string of racial stereotypes – summarily without intending malice (cf. e.g. BN 102).

> The abolitionists call me their equal and say that we all conspire to end tyranny against mankind [i.e. slavery]. 'Then why –' I began to ask. But they don't let me finish. [...] Sir Hastings murmurs to his neighbour that I can't be expected to grasp the details in their complexity. [...] The abolitionists may well call me their equal, but their lips do not say my name and their ears do not hear my story. Not the way I tell it. But I have long loved the written word, and come to see in it the power of the sleeping lion. *This is my name. This is who I am. This is how I got here.* (BN 100f., italics in the original)

---

218 George Elliott Clarke's poem "Milk" (2001) exemplifies this point, criticizing 'anemic' scholarly criticism of Black literature:

> *Milk*
> Garbage Day is Thursday, not quite today.
> There's time left for letters and defecation,
>
> Repair of deficits, undertaking
> The milking of a poem. I am, I think,
>
> A pagan suckered by a creed stillborn,
> Obsessed by Impressionists, symbolists,
>
> Exhibitionists, and their obsessions
> With light. Only milk is natural light –
>
> A melted snow that keeps its colour
> And gleams healthily as a line of surf
>
> Washing away verse that is like child's play –
> Just as parasites milk these words to white.

Also cf. Dionne Brand's "Eurocentric" (1995) on the supposed difficulties – even incapability – of White men to grasp the full meaning of Black women's experience in North America ("There are things you do not believe / there are things you cannot believe / (in fairness I do not mean women here except / jean kirkpatrick and the like) / these things / they include items such as / [...] / percussive piano solos, squawking saxophones / rosa parks' life, bessie smith's life and any life / that is not your own, / ripe oranges with green skins, / blacks lynched in the american way, / [...] / chains other than ornamental ones, [...]").

It is obvious from this passage that the issues of (enforced) voicelessness, appropriation, the struggle for the dominion over discourse formation and collective memory constructions as well as the acknowledgement of (a) Black subjectivity are closely interconnected (and exemplified here by Aminata's memoirs as well as by references to the slave narrative). The silencing of the Black voice is demonstrated in *The Book of Negroes* on two levels: the violently enforced silence of slavery *and* the 'benign', self-congratulatory silencing that occurs with the hegemony of White discursive constructions. Quite plainly, the abolitionists refuse to grant Aminata the right to determine the representation of her own (hi)story. Their refusal to even *listen* to Aminata's version is highly indicative of the way in which African-Canadian history has been dealt with in the 'benevolent' but equally self-congratulatory way of Canadian mainstream.[219] Hill uses a parallelism to underline that the abolitionists merely pay lip service to their high ideals: the phrase "call me their equal" (ibid.) is followed in both instances by the silencing of Aminata. Her subjectivity, though abstractly granted, is not heeded in fact: the abolitionists cloud her in anonymity ("do not say my name", ibid.) and an inferior (cognitive) status ("I can't be expected to grasp", ibid.).

The correspondence to the shortcomings of multicultural Canada as portrayed by Hill's writing, and likewise by many other African-Canadian writers, is almost tangible here: in an often well-meaning fashion, predominantly 'White' Canada has proclaimed its veneration for 'its' Black minority and of course 'considers Black Canadians their equal', to paraphrase Aminata; yet it refuses to listen to their story – 'not the way they tell it', to rephrase Hill's words again. Yet Aminata, in *The Book of Negroes,* supplies the solution to her plight, as she has "long loved the written word, and come to see in it the power of the sleeping lion." (Ibid.) As nobody else will tell her story the way it is supposed to be told, she has to take care of that herself. Consequently, she insists on determining the discourse that is, in turn, defining herself (and her self). Likewise, it is up to African-Canadian authors to represent the story and history of the Black presence in an effort to determine the discourse revolving around – and subsequently identifying! – their own history. These efforts at self-definition must thus be counter-hegemonic in impetus. The collective memory version advanced by Black Canadian authors necessarily runs counter to current hegemonic versions as it aims at either filling a blank (as when Aminata's name is not spoken, her story not heard) or righting a distorted picture (as when Aminata's story is *mis*represented by White abolitionists in the position of discursive hegemony). If the abolitionists do not say Aminata's name, she will.

---

219 Cf. the explicit contrast between the story-telling Aminata is supposed to perform for the *abolitionists* (with all its restrictions and 'White' supervision) and Aminata's position in the *African village* she finds refuge in after she runs away from the slave traders on her return to Africa: "For one revolution of the moon [note here that she relapses into her childhood usage of 'moons' instead of 'months'], I told my stories each night to people who had come from other villages, sometimes walking hours to hear me. […] I told my stories to people who were willing to sit half the night, listening to me and asking questions." (BN 446)

Read in the context of the classic slave narrative,[220] Aminata's desire to autonomously self-authenticate the story of her life comments on the fact that, contrary to the (fictional as well as factual) abolitionists' opinion in 1805, a Black author does in fact not need external authentication – something that could hardly be more obvious to a contemporary reader, yet which is a definite revision of the original slave narrative's formulaic approach. In the context of memory constructions, however, Hill's insistence is also an important comment on the *reliability* of his narrator – and, in extension, of his narrative. The doggedness with which Aminata claims her story to be her own and no one's but her own (again, *sans* the slightest irony or doubt) establishes the veracity of her account in a twofold way: first, in personal terms, Aminata's self-assertion, her life-writing, is an endeavor that she conducts on her own, without White people's assistance – indeed, expressly against any attempts on their behalf to temper with her story.

This of course speaks loudly to the notion of personal autonomy and individual subjectivity not only irrespective of but *in spite of* her race. Aminata thus constitutes an example which the classic slave narrative was yet unable to provide: the self-reliant, fully de-commodified Black subject in charge of her own self-narration and thus self-identification. Second, in terms of establishing a (historical) counter-memory, Hill insists on the truthfulness and validity of his representation *vis à vis* hegemonic constructions. While the classic slave narrative had to insist on the author's *mere* existence ('I was born'), Hill insists on the *full* existence of his narrator, including her right to self-identify *and* to present her narrative without any form of external, heteronomous representation (in contrast to the slave narrative, which established Black subjectivity but still depended on White verification – and, of course, publication).[221] In this regard, Aminata's story is a 'postcolonial Neo-slave narrative';[222] it has

---

220 In the passage quoted above, the direct reference to the slave narrative is of course achieved by quoting the introductory elements so characteristic of the genre (*"This is my name. This is who I am. This is how I got here"*, ibid., italics in the original).

221 It is interesting to note that until very recently, most Black Canadian literature was largely either self-published or published by small presses specializing in minority literatures (cf. Black 2006, 12, and Mordecai 2006, 195f.). Publishing opportunities have now altered dramatically for some African-Canadian authors, as Lawrence Hill attests to while warning against a possible end of what might still turn out to be a momentary hype: "[QUESTION:] '*Is there a danger in this renaissance of the same kind of showcasing that happened during the Harlem Renaissance? You said that publishers are taking a huge interest in African-Canadian literature – which they do, that's obvious...*' [HILL:] '... the danger of a fad that will burn out in the end? Yes. I fear a situation where a publisher might say, 'Well, Black writers? We already got a Black writer, I don't see why we'd need another one.' You would never say that about a White writer. It could be that in a few years, books about the Black experience will no longer be fashionable, marketable, or interesting to Canadian publishers. For the time being, Canadian publishers are snapping up books by and about Blacks in Canada. For the time being, some of these books are selling like hotcakes. As for what will happen next, who knows? But I'm optimistic that we will never turn entirely back to the past, now that Canadian writing and publishing has become so thoroughly diversified.'" (Hill, Appendix 303)

222 Albert Paolino delineates the nexus between postcolonial rewriting and the extensive examination of historical matters as a way to influence present identity constructions when he states: "The

moved beyond the slave narrative's mimicry and has fully appropriated the slave narrative, taken possession of and responsibility for a genre that is both the basis for a self-confident, independent Black North American literature but also an illustration of the restrictions imposed by racial and colonial boundaries.

Aminata's narrative is not subversive or particularly challenging in any formal or narratological way, i.e. in the way the story and Aminata's memory constructions are presented; it does not rely on different levels of memory, it does not implement contested memories, contrasting memory versions, or the like. Instead, it is subversive in what it establishes in terms of 'content', i.e. by providing a novel reading of the historical aspects covered in *The Book of Negroes*. Thus, questioning the reliability and autarchy of Aminata's recollection would weaken her tale on two levels: It would a) question her ability to independently present her life story and b) challenge the historical account that is presented through and alongside her account. The latter in turn would directly translate into a weakening of the counter-hegemonic collective memory presented by *The Book of Negroes* (and other Black Canadian writing). While the US-American Neo-slave narrative may indulge in challenging and reformulating the established (literary and collective) memory of slavery, Hill's novel, in concert with other Black Canadian works, has to *establish* such a memory in the first place; it must thus revert to the original slave narratives' claims of authenticity while at the same time actualizing the slave narratives' authentication on a completely different basis: the self-reliant and autonomous construction of (African-Canadian) counter-hegemonic memory.

In a very concrete way, Ishmael Reed may satirize a slave's flight to Canada in his novel of the same name – introducing jumbo jets and the like in this exodus – because the history of slavery in the US is already irreducibly incorporated into the US-American collective memory. Consequently, it is available for review, even satire. Satirizing or questioning the *Canadian* history of slavery or the experience of fugitive slaves who came to Canada as Black Loyalists, however, would be counterproductive regarding the introduction of these memories into Canadian hegemonic discourse, as it would hinder the serious consideration of these elements as unquestionable parts of Canadian history. In Aleida Assmann's terminology, I would argue that only through assertion and insistence may the repressed memories, which of course lack official authority and must therefore find authority through other devic-

---

Fanonian spirit that inhabits Said is filtered through Antonio Gramsci and Michel Foucault, so resistance becomes a matter of constructing a counterhegemonic discourse in which the postcolonial writer needs to revise the colonial past and uncover resistance in the historiographical record as a prelude to recovering contemporary identity. The change in emphasis is significant: Not only does resistance become almost exclusively discursive, it looks backward for its redemptive ethic." (1999, 69) Note, however, that the delegation of resistance to an almost exclusively discursive practice is not undisputed; activism might thus be relegated to the back benches and social change can thus be postponed. To quote Paolino again: "Ironically, the common effort to invoke and rewrite the past in order to uncover the voice of subaltern resistance places Said and these other writers [Gramsci, Foucault] potentially at odds with Fanon. Near the end of *BSWM* [*Black Skin, White Masks*], Fanon reflects that the desire to uncover a past Negro civilization, literature, or architecture, though of inherent interest, would not 'change anything in the lives of the eight-year-old children who labor in the cane fields of Martinique or Guadeloupe.'" (Paolini 1999, 70)

es, be brought from the storage memory (background) to the functional memory (foreground) and thus be made available for processes of identity formation.

b) Creating a collective voice

Despite the contrast established between the slave narrative and *The Book of Negroes* by the somewhat facile distinction between fact and fiction[223] (which – as we have seen – in this case is still largely valid but not quite as unambiguous as might be expected given the strictly autobiographical pretence of the slave narrative and the overtly fictional character of Neo-slave narratives such as Hill's novel), both extensively use and aim at a collectivization of the experiences they describe. In this, the slave narrative is communal rather than personal autobiography,[224] even though it has to maintain the façade of the latter in order to achieve the first.[225] *The Book of Negroes*, in turn, is a fictional account highly infused with documentary elements – historical novel-writing, that is, with a high degree of authenticity (cf. section "Hill's Faction and Historiographic Metafiction", p. 63ff.). Both approaches leave plenty of room for elaborations of *communal* issues over and above – in fact, more prominently than – individual lots. For the original slave narrative, such classics of the scholarly field as the collection *The Slave's Narrative* by Davis/Gates or Diedrich's monograph *Ausbruch aus der Knechtschaft* establish as much: Diedrich, for instance, maintains that the 'representational function of the I' is characteristic of the original slave narrative ("Repräsentativfunktion des Ich", Diedrich 1986, 28). Davis/Gates speak of the "chaos of individual memories" which is rendered into "collective texts" (1985b, xx). Ralph Ellison comments on his *Invisible Man* (1952), which may be read – among several other legitimate approaches – as a Neo-slave narrative (cf. e.g. Rushdy 2004, 103; Hedin 1982):

> Experience tends to mould itself into certain repetitive patterns, and one of the reasons we exchange experiences is in order to discover the repetitions and coincidences which amount

---

223 See for instance Stephanie A. Smith's discussion of the fluctuating status – the "loss and rebirth," as she calls it (2007, 199) – of Harriet Jacobs's slave narrative *Incidents in the Life of a Slave Girl*, which used to be considered inauthentic by a vast majority of scholars, including renowned experts such as John Blassingame and Robert Stepto. Similarly, Equiano's narrative has been negotiated; cf. discussion above (section 5.2.1., "Category one: Composition").

224 What Neumann would call in her classification of Canadian fictions of memory *kommunaler Gedächtnisroman* (cf. Neumann 2005); also cf. Couser 1989, who discusses aspects of the communal and/or personal in autobiography and includes a lengthy section discussing authority in the "(En)Slave(d) Narrative" (Couser's chapter heading). Rushdy likewise holds for a number of Neo-slave narratives: "Against this kind of arrogance [found in Styron's egocentric narrator], and in respect to the importance of the historical task they are undertaking, Gaines, Reed, Williams, and Johnson produce choral and communal voices in an effort to capture the kind of spirit also evinced in those antebellum slave narratives where the authors realized that they spoke not only for themselves but for a captive community whose voices the represented." (Rushdy 2004, 99)

225 Only through the individual authentication is the communal aspect acceptable, i.e.: only if the slave narrative is accepted as a bona fide account of an individual slave's life may the narrative's collective or communal aspects exert their socio-political influence.

to a common group experience. We tell ourselves our individual stories so as to become aware of our *general* story. (Ellison 1995a, 372; emphasis in the original)

Ellison's remarks pertain to his own 1952 novel, yet Davis/Gates quote his statement as if pertaining to the slave narrative:

> Accused of having no collective history by Hegel, blacks responded by publishing hundreds of individual histories [slave narratives]. As Ellison defined this relationship of the particular to the general, to Steve Cannon, 'We tell ourselves our individual stories so as to become aware of our *general* story.' (Davis/Gates 1985, xxiii)

Gates some years later reprints this statement with only minor changes, still subtly suggesting that Ellison meant to imply that the slave narrative has served to present[226] 'the' collective/collected history[227] of African-American slavery:

> Accused of having no collective history by Hegel, blacks effectively responded by publishing hundreds of individual histories [slave narratives] which functioned as the part standing for the whole. As Ralph Ellison defined this relation, 'We tell ourselves our individual stories so as to become aware of our *general* story.' (Gates 1993, 57)

In fact, Ellison – in the very same breath the statement in question was made during an interview – denounces the slave narrative as a major influence on his own writing, instead suggesting that it was not the slave narrative as a literary genre that influenced his writing of *Invisible Man* but an almost inescapable (collective) experience *per se,* which needed either no mediation at all or a literary one at best (here, literary is taken as opposed to autobiographic by Ellison).[228] Ellison's logic suggests that there is hardly a need for intertextuality in the stricter

---

226 Note the (slightly offbeat) double imagery used in the following excerpt; the slave narratives are explicitly *pars pro toto* or metonymically representative of "the whole" (ibid.) but also, due to their sheer number, serve as a mosaic of individual pieces representing a larger picture.

227 Regarding the opposition as well as the transition between collected and collective *memory,* cf. Olick 2007, 24f.; Erll 2005, 250f.; Neumann 2005, 53. The differential explanatory power of the two concepts is often lost when the two terms are illegitimately/unwittingly conflated or confused (cf. e.g. O'Keeffe 2007, 5f.).

228 Ellison even questions, as has been pointed out before, the importance of the slave narrative for African-American literature in general: "No, [the structural similarity between *Invisible Man* and the slave narrative,] that's coincidental. And frankly, I think too much has been made of the slave narrative as an influence on contemporary writing. [...] I had no need of slave narratives to grasp either its [the northward movement's] significance or its potential for organizing a fictional narrative. I would have used the same device if I had been writing an autobiography." (Ellison 1995a, 372f.) Davis/Gates reprint this passage as well, thereby correcting the impression that Ellison might have meant to attribute foundational value to the slave narrative. David Blight, however, delivers a slight misreading of the exact same quote when he applies Ellison's statement to autobiography (2002, 17), while in fact, Ellison stresses the *fictional* character of the writing in question ("*as if* I had been writing an autobiography", cf. above; my emphasis). Also cf. Rodgers 1997, 118f.

sense of the word – the 'Black experience', be it individual or collective, is so pressing that it shapes his writing in an unmediated way. Though downplaying the influence of the slave narrative, Ellison's comment indeed – involuntarily – describes the effect of the slave narrative quite accurately. What Ellison claims for postslavery literature, though of course rejecting the very notion of a generic *Neo*-slave narrative, applies to the slave narrative as well, as Davis/Gates have realized: the patching together of individual stories to be woven[229] into a larger, collective, story which supplants an (allegedly) absent *hi*story, so that Link holds that the "narrator does not speak for him- or herself but for all who share a similar destiny." (Link 1993, 287)

If this is taken as an inter-textual process (here, as almost persistently, understood in a narrow sense as a process encompassing a number of written texts), there is also an intra-textual side to this collectivization device within the respective works. In the (Neo-) slave narrative, we can thus discern a common textual strategy of collectivizing individual characters' experiences or incorporating larger, i.e. communal, experiences in order to arrive at a portrayal valid on two levels, the personal and the social.[230] The writers become "part of the history of the author's people" (Link 1993, 278). In this context, Davis/Gates indeed go as far as to speak of a "collective 'I' of the race", brought into being through the slave narratives (Davis/Gates 1985, xxvi; also cf. Gates 1986, 11 and Gates 1993, 62f.). While the latter notion might be taken as too essentialist for the given purpose,[231] it is clear that there are both a horizontal and a vertical dimension to the collectivization processes involved, i.e. the stressing of a communal experience both through the existence of a number of individual literary works, which form a 'horizontal network', and the representation of collective experiences

---

In terms of the *validity* of Ellison's argument, it might suffice to point out that even though I approve of Ellison's general skepticism, a strong intertextual relationship with the (largely autobiographical) slave narrative cannot possibly be denied regarding the concrete example of *The Book of Negroes*. Consequently, even though one might refute Ellison's argument that certain aspects of African-American literature are driven by experience rather than intertextuality by means of merely employing a more flexible definition of intertextuality and hence simply extending the definition of 'text' to include realms other than and beyond the written text, it is possible to counter his underplaying of the slave narrative's influence with concrete, descriptive intertextual analyses as well (which might require more 'technical' effort, however, than simply employing broader concepts of intertextuality).

229 It would be almost a cliché to speak of the quilt here, which has so often be taken as a metaphor of (Black) history (cf. for instance, from a feminist stance, bell hooks 1990, 115-122).

230 William Zinsser, for example, applauds instances when, in memoirs, writers are simultaneously "catching a distinctive moment in the life of both a person *and* a society" (quoted in Blight 2002, 17; emphasis added).

231 Terminology suggesting a racial 'personification', however, is not uncommon in a general African-Canadian context either. Jan Carew, for instance, uses the term "racial memories" (2009 [1978]), which is then taken up as an epigraph by Afua Cooper for her poem "Roots and Branches" (1992). Also cf. Olive Senior's usage of "memories / of his race" in her "Ancestral Poem" (Senior 1980, 77f.). While these metaphors are commanding and – in terms of collective memory theory – even illustrative, the presentation of a 'collective Black body' is of course questionable.

within the individual works themselves. While being part of the generic 'network' of Neo-slave narratives, *The Book of Negroes* also engages in relating/creating a distinctly collective experience through a number of literary strategies.

The collectivization of Aminata's story proceeds on two levels, similar to the collec-tivization process of the slave narrative genre: on the one hand, Aminata clearly stands *pars pro toto* for the Black Canadian experience; Hill states that, plainly, Aminata's "personal sto-ry, her loves, her losses and her victories are unique, but they reflect the experiences of thou-sands of other Blacks in the same time and places." (Hill, Appendix 294) On the other hand, Aminata of course, by virtue of being a *djeli*,[232] collects the stories of her fellow Africans, slaves, servants, fugitives, Black Loyalists, Sierra Leone adventurers, abolitionists. Her status as a quintessential preserver and mediator of collective memories cannot be overstated in this regard, and Aminata is explicitly conscious of her role (though Hill naturally abstains from the theory-based vocabulary and resorts to terms such as 'story-teller', 'remember', 'relate', instead of the more technical lingo such as 'externalization', 'mediation' etc.).

Aminata's position as a keeper of memories is shown to be that of a prototypical spe-cialist as described by collective memory theory (cf. J. Assmann 2006, 106f.; Breyer 2007, 60f.), yet her role also harks back to more common and traditional notions of memory trans-mission. Conceptions of generational memory have, after all, been elaborated since antiquity, and Hill underlines Aminata's indebtedness to her parents right alongside the discussion of her position as *djeli* (cf. BN 56).[233] Aminata thus combines the everyday passing on with the specialized conservation performed by professional record-keepers; in the same vein, neither mode of mediation (oral or written) is clearly favored by her. Obviously, Aminata's responsi-bility stretches beyond the preservation of her own, highly individual story, and in this, she is the recorder of a group memory and thus, as a *djeli*, the emblem of collectivization via the handing down of memories: "It was said that when a *djeli* passed away, the knowledge of one hundred men died with him." (BN 55)With her narrative, Aminata literally saves the "knowledge of one hundred men" which would have been lost if she, like so many of her fel-low slaves, had not survived the Middle Passage. The term 'knowledge of' in this regard un-folds its grammatical ambivalence; a *djeli* indeed unites the knowledge of a number of people

---

232 Following her life-saving longing to become a *djeli* when she commences her first involuntary voyage over the ocean, she is, as has been pointed out, indeed accepted as an 'honorary' *djeli* first in African and then in England as well.

233 These conceptions are also exemplified in African conceptions of a *djeli*; Aminata, about to marry Chekura on the South Carolina plantation, for instance notes: "We wouldn't be able to have a marriage like in my homeland, with village elders and a *djeli* to witness the event and describe it to the next generations." (BN 174) Cf. Beaulieu's characterization of the Neo-slave narrative, in which she likewise stresses the oral transmission of generational memories: "Other elements in-clude uses of the spiritual and the folkloric, and the [Neo-slave] narratives usually evoke the Afri-can tradition of storytelling, with importance being placed on passing the story to future genera-tions." (2002, 535)

in his[234] reservoir of memories, but he also *knows* the people themselves, thus preserving not only the knowledge they possessed but their personhoods as well.

Notions of preserved personhood of course tie in with issues of anonymity and name changes – two modes of *erasing* a slave's subjectivity. Aminata, acting as a *djeli* onboard the slave vessel, retains the slaves' subjectivity even under their greatest humiliation. Thus, when the slaves are made to dance over a whip swung by the *toubabu*, Aminata graces them by calling out their names in a chant: "'Chekura,' I sang, 'of Kinta. And Isa, of Sirakoro. Ngolo, of Jelibugu. Fanta, of Bayo.'" (BN 80) Likewise, Aminata, after a failed slave revolt which results in a number of slaves being killed, reports: "We called their names as they were pulled from the hold. *Makeda, of Segu. Salima, of Kambolo.*" (BN 93; italics in the original) Preserving their names saves the memory of these men from being forgotten, from being buried with their depersonalized, enslaved selves under the ocean. That Aminata herself survives – indeed, survives as a *person* – is summarized in a statement made by Chekura at the end of the Middle Passage: "'We still live, Aminata of Bayo,' Chekura said. 'We have crossed the water. We have survived.'" (BN 94) With Aminata of Bayo, "*Makeda, of Segu [;] Salima, of Kambolo*" and indeed, the "knowledge of one hundred men" has survived (BN 93, 55).[235] Aminata herself thus embodies a collective, she serves as the voice of those who could not speak for themselves. This idea is likewise expressed in the pivotal passage in which Aminata explains her witnessing in lieu of those who cannot bear witness: "In telling my story, I remember all those who never made it through the musket balls and the sharks and the nightmares, all those who never found a group of listeners, and those who never touched a quill to an inkpot." (BN 56f.) Interestingly, Aminata not only speaks for those who have died but also for those whose stories are ignored or who are unable to record their story in the first place – this of course closely connects to issues of (historiographic) erasure and invisibility as well as to (enforced) illiteracy. Her feeling of belonging, of being part of the collective whose story she tells, is further underlined in a scene taking place at the burial of a Black infant child in Canvas Town outside New York City immediately after her arrival in that segregated community:

> They [the Blacks of Canvas Town] took me into their dancing, and did not ask where I came from, for all they had to do was look at me and hear my own sobs in my maternal tongue and they knew I was one of them. The dead infant was the child I had once been; it was my own lost [son] Mamadu; it was every person who had been tossed into the unforgiving sea on the endless journeys across the big river [the Atlantic]. (BN 256)

A further literary device used by Hill to underline the shared, collective element of Aminata's voice is his introduction of a number of *alter egos*. Two of these *alter egos* explicitly carry

---

234 A *djeli* is *per definitionem* male (cf. the brief discussion on p. 108); Aminata acknowledges this fact and hopes for an exception (cf. BN 55; her doubts also relate to the fact that the position of a *djeli* is usually hereditary and that she herself is not from a *djeli* family).

235 While being a *djeli* in an African village, Aminata also experiences the intense interest her audience has in the actual names of her story's characters ("Always, with each story, I was asked for names." BN 446).

Aminata's name. The first is named in honor of Aminata's midwifery skills: aboard the slave ship, Aminata performs her first assistance at birth (though we learn only later that Sanu, the woman whom Aminata helped, named her child after her midwife). The second child named Aminata is an eight-year-old girl in the African village Aminata Diallo rescues herself to when she runs the danger of being sold into slavery once more. Apart from these two, there is a girl in a slave coffle that is walked through Freetown, Sierra Leone, when Aminata and her fellow 'adventurers' are setting up residence there.[236]

> I watched [the coffle] coming, captives of all ages and sizes, and wondered how I could set them free. A girl in the coffle looked at me pleadingly. She wasn't a woman yet, but she was close to becoming one. As she came near, I could see the traces of blue dye in two vertical lines carved high up on her cheeks. [...] I tugged at her yoke, but it was bound fast. (396f.)

The only thing Aminata can do for the girl in the coffle is to give her the bandana she is wearing, just like she experienced tiny acts of empathy and sympathy when she herself was marched to the ocean as a child (cf. e.g. BN 38). The parallels between the young Aminata and the girl in the Sierra Leone coffle are evident: when she was abducted, Aminata was about to experience her first menstruation ("close to becoming" a woman; cf. above) and the crescent moons carved in their cheeks are an obvious commonality. What they share moreover is their total disbelief regarding the passivity of their fellow Africans. When she herself marched in a slave coffle as a child, Aminata could not understand why the villagers they were walked by did not come to their rescue: "But if we had seen men, women and children yoked and forced to march like *woloso*, only worse, I hoped that we would have fought for them and freed them." (BN 38) Now, more than 35 years later, Aminata feels with the captive girl: "I imagined that she felt that we could save her if we truly wanted to do so." (BN 398) When the newly-arrived Africadians indeed interfere with the coffle's march, however, the Sierra Leone Company men, fearing a war with the Temne tribe supervising the procession, keep them at bay. A leading abolitionist, Thomas Peters, is stabbed by a slave trader, another colonist is shot, paving the way for the captives to be shipped off to Bance Island (cf. BN 399f.).

Bance Island itself becomes another mirror image of Aminata's experiences and thus a device of turning her voice into a collective one. Alexander Falconbridge, a former ship doctor aboard a slave vessel, is able to bring Aminata into contact with slave traders going into the interior of Africa. For years, Aminata had been trying to enlist help in journeying to her native village of Bayo, so she is willing to make a deal with the slave traders. In order to ne-

---

236 Sierra Leone, though itself a slave-free colony, was established at the end of the 18th century on the North Atlantic African coast – hence right in the middle of the ongoing slave trade. This realization hits Aminata hard, as does her own feeling of helplessness. The Sierra Leone Company had variously made agreements with the surrounding African tribes that the newcomers would not interfere with the established practices of slave transport (which of course was routinely executed by Africans themselves; the Europeans then received their 'goods' at the coast to ship the slaves off, most of the time to the Americas). On the historical record underlying Hill's description, cf., elaborately, Walker 1992, 145ff.

gotiate the terms of her journey, she is taken by Falconbridge to the slave castle at Bance Island to meet the second-in-command of the local forts, William Armstrong. Some thirty-six years ago, it was at this very slave castle that Aminata herself was kept in a pen until the slave vessel left for America. Now, as Aminata peers out of one of the slave castle's windows down into a slave pen, she comes full circle to her traumatic experience, feeling transported back into her childhood: "For a moment, I forgot how long it had been since I lived in Bayo, and I strained to see if I could recognize any of the faces of the men." (BN 417) Moments later, Aminata experiences again the powerlessness she had felt when the slave coffle was driven through Freetown: "I hated myself for doing nothing to help the captives escape their wretched confines. [...] The only moral course of action was to lay down my life to stop the theft of men." (BN 417) Of course, Aminata quickly realizes that in the given circumstances, there is nothing she could do. It would take the abortive attempt to reach her native village of Bayo to make her fully understand that it is the institution of slavery itself that she needs to tackle – and which she indeed can tackle. As Clarkson tells her, her account "could move thousands of people. And when it comes time for Parliament to deliberate on the matter, [Aminata's] voice could swing the vote." (BN 426) For this goal, she lets her ultimate dream – returning to Bayo – go. For Hill, the emphasis on the little agency Aminata has left is important:

> She [Aminata] just couldn't get her head around the reality that of all these Black people, all these villagers, nobody came out to save her from the slave coffle [when she was abducted]. It was heartbreaking, for her as a child. As a much older woman in Freetown, when she herself witnesses a child slave being led to the coast, she cannot stop what she sees. But she is not entirely powerless. She can't save this girl who is passing through Freetown, but she goes to fight for the abolition of slavery. She writes her story. She loves and helps the people around her. A powerless victim is an uninteresting character. A character does not become interesting by dint of being stomped on, but by asserting her humanity, even in the smallest ways. Aminata can't snap her fingers and save someone from a terrible fate, but she tries to make a better world, and she succeeds. (Hill, Appendix 300)

It is thus vitally important for Aminata's survival and her sense of purpose that she be able to remember and to tell her story with a good deal of certainty (just as it is for the novel's appeal, as Hill underlines, because it lends a small degree of agency to its protagonist). Aminata, at the slave castle on Bance Island, is submerged in recollection, remembering sight and sound of her captivity: "I remember this place. [...] During night storms, after the lightning flashed, thunder echoed out of the mountain caves." When Armstrong tells her that she "certainly [has] the details right", Aminata replies, with utter confidence in her recollection of the traumatic experience, that there "is no need to test a woman about her own life" (BN 419). Thus, we are presented with, again, an illustration of Aminata's believability and the accuracy of her account. Coming practically full circle to the beginning of her ordeal, Aminata almost merges with the slaves *currently* held at the castle ("I forgot how long it had been", cf. above) – her history is mirrored, repeated, ongoing, collective. The one thing she can do to assist in the interruption of the circle is to give testimony, just as Clarkson, Mrs Falconbridge and others suggest. Which, of course, is what she does in the end, though it takes the detour via her near re-enslavement in the interior of Africa.

5.3. Movements I:
Water Crossings and Shifts of Status

Aminata undergoes a number of substantial, even existential, shifts of status, most of which coincide with a change of locale involving a passage over water. This chapter focuses most intensely on the transitions themselves; the Middle Passage, for instance, is read as a traumatic passage into chattel slavery on several levels (personal, social, and in terms of collective memory), while there will be no detailed discussion of her life on the plantation itself. An in-depth look at the fate of the Black Loyalists in Nova Scotia will be the exception to this approach. In broad terms, four (sets of) shifts will be more closely examined: first, the ones reflected and/or introduced in the frame-setting, which is written in retrospect and thus offers an outline of the most significant stages in Aminata's life; second, the shift towards slavery enforced through her abduction and the gruesome Middle Passage, in which Aminata is forcibly turned from free-born African into chattel slave; third, the in-betweenness of her life as a 'servant' and a fugitive slave, *de jure* commodity but *de facto* suspended in a limbo of freedoms granted and freedoms won; fourth, Aminata's journey into what is made to appear as a Canaan for her and her fellow Black Loyalists (here, an aperçu is added regarding the second exodus, in 1792, to Sierra Leone). The approach taken here mirrors the chronology of the novel and delineates the ways in which Hill creates a coherent tale of selfhood for Aminata, who is able to maintain a usable past, hence a stable version of her identity in spite of the many ruptures, both enforced and voluntary, in the fabric of her life.

5.3.1. Expository frame setting

The Book of Negroes' first chapter, "Book One", comprises, as has been pointed out before, two distinct time layers: 1802 (expository frame setting: writing process of Aminata's memoirs) and 1745-1757 (embedded narrative: childhood memories). The introductory sentence, "I seem to have trouble dying" (BN 1), written by Aminata in 1802, indicates not only her old age and declining health, but also signifies the continuation of her own story as well as the story of North American Blacks – stories that refuse to fade away. In the same vein, Aminata tells one of the "society ladies" associated with the abolitionists who take care of her: "I may outlast you!" (BN 1) Accordingly, what may at first glance be read as a frail statement is in fact an assertive one: Aminata does not *wish* to die. On the contrary, she *should* in all likelihood be dead already but she is not.

In the novel's introductory pages, Lawrence Hill creates an almost 'archetypal' exposition, introducing – next, of course, to the setting – both his protagonist Aminata Diallo and a large number of issues featuring prominently throughout the novel.[237] Within the first seven pages of the book, the reader is thus confronted with innuendos of a majority of the text's major topics. Even though the perspective is almost *ex post*, and even though already foretelling several of the potentially suspense-creating elements (e.g. Aminata's survival and the death of her parents), Hill here withholds one of the central plot turns of the novel's very ending: the somewhat melodramatic reunion of Aminata and her daughter May. Quite contrary to insinuating a possible reunion, Hill stresses Aminata's anguish over having lost her entire family, parents and children alike. It seems to Aminata that she misses her children "the way I'd miss limbs from my own body." (BN 2) Hill comments quite explicitly on the interrupted chain of passing down memories (at least Aminata at the point of setting out to write her memoirs believes it is interrupted; we later learn that the chain will be restored by the re-emergence of May) when Aminata laments the fact that she will not experience the feeling of her and her children's "shared moments [growing] like corn stalks in damp soil" (BN 2).

The disruption of family ties pertaining to both the preceding and the subsequent generation[238] indicates a multi-generational injustice and trauma, which the reader can easily abstract and prolong beyond the limitations of Aminata's immediate family. Her family tragedy thus becomes a comment on collective and intergenerational trauma. The intense feeling of loss concerning the absence of her parents is particularly noteworthy, as Aminata at the time of writing down her memoirs is already in her late fifties. Her regret at not having "parents to care for [her]" (BN 3) in her own old age indeed seems idiosyncratic at first.[239] This sentiment, however, paves the way for two notions that are important in the course of the novel: first, it allows for a more or less seamless transition to her childhood memories, in which, naturally, the loss of her parents' protection is an almost unbearable experience. Second, it stresses the need for intergenerational communication and the intergenerational sharing of memories. As such, Aminata compensates for the loss of her parents by including them 'virtually', i.e. *in absentia*, in her current situation:

> Most of my life-time has come and gone, but I still think of them as my parents, older and wiser than I, and still hear their voices, sometimes deep-chested, at other moments floating like musical notes. I imagine their hands steering me from trouble, guiding me around cooking fires and leading me to the mat in the cool shade of our home. I can still picture my fa-

---

237 This section can accordingly be read as a very brief outline of salient issues in *The Book of Negroes*. All of the issues raised here are explicated in more detail at other places in this thesis.

238 Aminata directly or indirectly has lost her parents and both of her children to the *buckra*, the Whites. Her parents were killed in the slave-traders' raid on her village; her first child, a son, was sold by her first master and died in his infancy; her second child was abducted by a White couple for whom Aminata worked.

239 The chapter heading "And Now I Am Old" as well as my own reference to a lady in her late fifties as being of 'old age' takes into account that at the time of the setting, viz. the late 1700s and very early 1800s, demographic probabilities were hardly in favor of reaching such an age; of course, the additional fact that Aminata is an ex-slave makes the age of 57 indeed appear almost biblical. Aminata consequently is taken aback when a student tells her of her own grandparents ("I replied that it amazed me that she still had grandparents in her life." BN 3).

ther with a sharp stick over hard earth, scratching out Arabic in flowing lines and speaking of the distant Timbuktu. (BN 3)

Compared to an excerpt from Maurice Halbwachs's famous 'walk through London', the analogies become obvious immediately:[240]

> Don't we believe that we relive the past more fully because we no longer represent it alone, because we see it now as we saw it then, but through the eyes of another as well? Our memories remain collective, however, and are recalled to us through others even though only we were participants in the events or saw the things concerned. In reality, we are never alone. Other men need not be physically present, since we always carry with us and in us a number of distinct persons. I arrive for the first time in London and take walks with different companions. An architect directs my attention to the character and arrangement of city buildings. A historian tells me why a certain street, house, or other spot is historically noteworthy. A painter alerts me to the colors in the parks [...]. Even if I were unaccompanied, I need only have read their varying descriptions of the city, been given advice on what aspects to see, or merely studied a map. Now suppose I went walking alone. Could it be said that I preserve of that tour only individual remembrances, belonging solely to me? Only in appearance did I take a walk alone. Passing before Westminster, I thought about my historian friend's comments (or, what amounts to the same thing, what I have read in history books). Crossing a bridge, I noticed the effects of perspective that were pointed out by my painter friend (or struck me in a picture or engraving). Or I conducted my tour with the aid of a map. Many impressions during my first visit to London – St. Paul's, Mansion House, the Strand, or the Inns of Court – reminded me of Dickens' novels read in childhood, so I took my walk with Dickens. In each of these moments I cannot say that I was alone, that I reflected alone, because I had put myself in thought into this or that group [...]. (Halbwachs 1980, 23)

Humans both *en*code and *de*code memories conversationally – Aminata, for instance, holds imaginary conversations with her parents when facing difficult situations; she feels that they still 'steer', 'guide' and 'lead' her. Though being physically absent, they are (just like the architect or the historian in Halbwachs's example) still a part of both her recollection and – crucially – part of her *current* experiences and patterns of thought. In Halbwachs's terms, Aminata's father and mother "need not be physically present, since we always carry with us and in us a number of distinct persons" (ibid.).

In addition to exemplifying that "memories remain collective, however, and are recalled to us through others even though only we were participants in the events" (ibid.), the given excerpt from the opening of *The Book of Negroes* also illustrates another important aspect in mnemonic and collective memory contexts: the use of multi-sensory perception. Hill's usage of auditory ("hear"), tactile ("hands steering me", "leading me"), and visual perception ("picture", BN 3) creates a mnemonic closeness and actuality that corresponds to the virtual conversations Aminata repeatedly holds with her parents (cf. e.g. BN 28, 82, 132f.).[241] Ac-

---

240 Also cf. chapter 2.1. of this thesis ("Basic Principles of Collective Memory Theory: Maurice Halbwachs", p. 22ff.).

241 Olfactory perception is addressed through the mentioning of "cooking fires" in the above quote. Additionally, the novel's very first paragraph makes explicit use of the olfactory sense: "I still can smell trouble riding on any wind, just as surely as I could tell you whether it is a stew of chicken

cordingly, in absence of the living parents, her memory of them guides and advises her. The imaginary conversations serve, in Halbwachs's terminology, as *cadres sociaux*, the social framings exemplified in the London walk with physically absent friends. This psychological mechanism is preserved in Aminata up to her old age. Consequently, Aminata's recollection is thus shaped not only by the *cadres sociaux* that are part of her *actual* social surroundings; her genealogy is part of the self-identification process as well. The importance placed on the preceding generation in terms of current self-definitions and in terms of guidance is a persistent feature of memory constructions in *The Book of Negroes*.[242]

A variety of other equally persistent issues is presented in the exceptionally dense expository section, including survival, beauty and bodily markers, appropriation, abolitionism, education, the importance and modes of story-telling, status and personhood, and religion. Survival (physical as well as mental) as one of the pivotal themes is introduced in the novel's very first sentence, "I seem to have trouble dying." (BN 1) It is augmented by Aminata's comment that she "may outlast" the society ladies (BN 1, quoted above) and her musings that there "must be a reason why I have [...] survived all those water crossings" (BN 1). Aminata contrasts her aging body and declining beauty with her former, her younger self. She does, however, emphasize two positive aspects of or in spite of her declining physical appearance:

---

necks or pigs' feet bubbling in the iron pot on the fire." (BN 1) As this quote exemplifies as well, sensual perception is used to minimize the distance between memory and present (as Aminata's current status as a guest of the abolitionists in London would certainly warrant that she is not in fact in the vicinity of 'slave food' such as chicken necks or pigs' feet).

When she is brought to Charles Town by Solomon Lindo, she perceives the smell of a slave ship, thereby directly linking her memory of the Middle Passage with her new, ostensibly superior status as 'servant'. Hill thus reminds the reader that even though Aminata personally may have fared better, the institution of chattel slavery is far from over. The smell lingers invisibly like a ghostly, suffocating memory: "Without even looking [...] anyone could detect the presence of a slave ship. The odour of the dead and dying lifted into the air, growing so thick that it made you choke." (BN 193)

The beginning of Aminata's reminiscence of her childhood in Bayo is likewise related to a specific, albeit far more positively connotated, smell – in a way the reversal of the smell of the slave ship: "No matter the time of life or the continent, the pungent, *liberating* smell of mint tea has always brought me back to my childhood in Bayo." (BN 8; emphasis added) (The memory of mint tea is held sacred by Aminata; even when she develops a trusting relationship towards the abolitionist John Clarkson, she postpones telling him about that memory to a later day as it is too personal to share with a stranger; cf. BN 361.)

On the importance of sensual perception in mnemonic contexts, cf. van der Kolk and van der Hart 1995, particularly p. 173. Also cf. e.g. Kölbl 2001 on olfactory memory and A. Hartmann 2001 on taste. Interestingly, Aminata uses reading to consciously trigger memories of her absent (mostly deceased) friends and family: "When I couldn't sleep, I would stay up late into the night, rereading books and thinking of the people – Georgia, Chekura, Mamed, Dolly, and Mrs. Lindo – who had been in my life when I had first read them." (BN 219) Literature is thus not only a medium or 'container' but also a trigger of memories.

---

242 Cf. for instance, on a very pragmatic level, Aminata's advice to honor one's grandparents: "Love them good, I told [a student], and love them big. Love them every day." (BN 3)

first, she stresses her remaining vigor and the remnants of her abilities: "People assume that just because you don't stand as straight as a sapling, you're deaf. Or that your mind is like pumpkin mush." (BN 1) Of course, both assumptions are untrue, as Aminata demonstrates by quickly grabbing the impolite society lady as well as by fluently and studiously writing her account (cf. BN 7).[243] The assertion and demonstration of her remaining physical and especially her cognitive skills can be read as a comment on the authenticity of her memoirs, as her recollection is apparently unhampered by her age.

The second positive aspect of her aging and the accompanying loss of her former beauty is the reduction of male covetousness regarding her body. Throughout her memoirs, Aminata stresses the point that too much beauty is dangerous in face of a hierarchical structure that positions the female (slave) body as property and as such assigns an omni-availability to it.[244] This aspect is part and parcel of the larger issue of the significance of Aminata's body. In the exposition, Hill establishes some general features of his protagonist's physical appearance: First of all, "rich, dark skin", which some "people have described as blue black" (BN 4). In concurrence with her (former) feminine beauty ("round, rising buttocks", breasts that once "soared like proud birds", BN 5), it is obvious that her body alone has strongly influenced, often even determined, her fate and placed her in a position in which she has had to endure the double discrimination of sexual and racial inequity. Accordingly, the description of her body in the introductory section of "Book One" alludes to important parts of Aminata's story – it can be read as a map of her history. Aminata for instance mentions both the carvings of crescent moons on her cheeks (a signifier of her former freedom and the vain hope of being sheltered from capture and enslavement) and the "GO" branding that is the irreversible marker of this hope's futility and of her interim status as slave: "Alas, I am branded, and can do nothing to cleanse myself of the scar." (BN 5)[245]

---

243 This assertion also ties in with another topic, namely different reactions to trauma; in this respect, Aminata's relative mental health, which has been emphasized, is contrasted with the 'snapping' of slaves during the Middle Passage (cf. section "Traumatic memory: The Middle Passage", p. 154ff.).

244 "Some say that I was uncommonly beautiful, but I wouldn't wish beauty on any woman who has not her own freedom, and who chooses not the hands that claim her." (BN 4) Cf. Rushdy's linkage of the availability of the slave's body to cultural dominance: "Another means by which the writers of contemporary narratives of slavery talk about cultural appropriation is by focusing on the physical appropriation of the slave's body." (Rushdy 2004, 101)

245 As we learn later on, the "GO" branding marks Aminata as property of "Grant, Oswald", the company that runs a slave trading post on Bance Island, just off the African coast (cf. BN 422). In G. E. Clarke's *Beatrice Chancy*, the protagonist's ill-fated lover Lead, a slave himself, attempts to rid himself of a branding just like Aminata's, trying to erase the visualization of his status as property with "a found blade" consisting of "a shard of glass" (Clarke 1999, 100). After having been raped by her father – and owner – Beatrice herself feels she must remove her skin with a razor as she "can't be cleansed" by water alone (ibid., 93). She describes her own body as an "atlas of pain" (ibid., 71), just like Aminata's body can be read as a map to her own suffering (yet also to her triumphs, however small they are; cf. for instance her suppleness even in old age). On Beatrice Chancy and the importance of her body, cf. the feminist readings in Wilson 2001 and

Aminata's status in 1802 is determined by her new role and newly acquired importance in the abolitionist movement (the abolitionists plan to use Aminata's account to argue in favor of the abolition of the slave trade – not slavery itself – before Parliament and the King and Queen). The introductory narrative frame setting already establishes the nuanced treatment Hill employs in reference to the abolitionists and their goals. While they cater to Aminata's physical needs, their initial characterization already also includes traits that allude to their political and personal shortcomings and hypocrisy. The exposition and reversal of Eurocentric stereotypes are fostered by the depiction of Aminata's hosts in London: while Aminata has a "white, full, glowing set of teeth", she concludes that the "more fervent the abolitionist, it seems, the more foul the breath" (BN 5).[246] Hill thus thwarts stereotypical assumptions about European vs. African hygiene in the early 1800s. The same holds true for literacy as a pervasive topic in *The Book of Negroes*; while Aminata's literacy is emphasized from the very beginning, the abolitionists (and Whites in general) repeatedly react with incredulity and shock to her abilities.

The reversal of Eurocentric assumptions is also displayed when Aminata recalls a visit to a London school, where she is asked if Africans ate elephants. She reacts with mild and witty irony to the student's question, exposing the alleged inequality between Europeans and African; she does the same when she responds to a student who comments that she "must have been very pretty, even though [she is] so very dark" (BN 4).[247] It is an indication of this inversion that Aminata speaks of Africa as the "old country" (BN 6), while a Eurocentric perspective would commonly consider Europe the 'old country' *vis à vis* the 'New World' of the North American continent. The abolitionists' air of superiority and their lack of an unbiased perspective are demonstrated by the fact that they – disregarding Aminata's literary skills out of prejudice – plan to edit her written account, so that Aminata has had to arrange for one of the abolitionists, John Clarkson, ("the only one I trust", BN 4) to "change nothing" (BN 4) and ensure that her memoirs be published in an *un*corrupted edition. Issues of appropriation are thus alluded to, and Aminata strongly asserts her autonomous authorship: "I am writing this account. All of it." (BN 4) Yet Aminata's own perspective and her approach toward the abolitionists cannot be unbiased either, given her experience with the people she successively

---

Moynagh 2002 (reprinted in Moynagh 2005a); the latter explicitly refers to Jan Assmann as a source in terms of collective memory theory.

246 Through the description of their foul breath, the abolitionists are linked to the slave traders; the slave inspector on Bance Island is said to smell like "rotting from the inside out" and reveals "black teeth" (BN 61), just like the abolitionists ("But in England, the abolitionists do much worse [to their teeth than the Africans who chew kola nut], with coffee, tea and tobacco." BN 5). The same (literally) rotten smell is attributed to the slave ship itself: "It smelled like rotting food." (BN 50)

247 In this scene at a London school, another important aspect is alluded to: Aminata teaches the students to pronounce her original name, Aminata Diallo, instead of the 'whitewashed' version "Meena Dee" (cf. BN 3). The issue of heteronomous name assignation ties into the larger issue of anonymity vs. 'being known', i.e. being accepted and acknowledged as an individual human being. Cf. discussion of this point in section "Name changes: Autonomy vs. heteronomy", p. 100ff.

calls *toubabu*, *buckra* and *whites*.[248] In a remarkable very early passage of the novel, Aminata states:

> These days, the men who want to end the slave trade are feeding me. [...] Not having to think about food, or shelter, or clothing is a rare thing indeed. What does a person do, when survival is not an issue? Well, there is the abolitionist cause, which takes time and fatigues me greatly. *At times, I still panic when surrounded by big white men with a purpose. When they swell around me to ask questions, I remember the hot iron smoking above my breast.*
> (BN 6; emphasis added)

Aminata's traumatic memories are triggered in situations when she is confronted with a buzz of white males – irrespective of their actual intentions. It is a defining feature of psychological trauma that the traumatic memory is invoked in situations resembling the 'physiological conditions' (cf. Eggers 2001, 603) of the original traumatic situation. While traumatic memories are often suppressed and therefore unavailable to the traumatized person on a conscious level (cf. ibid., 602; for a critical stance cf. Loftus/Ketcham 1994), a recreation or approximation of the original situation may trigger the involuntary invocation of such a memory. Hill links the triggering process to the bodily marker discussed above (the "GO" branding), thus emphasizing the fundamental and indelible impact of the de-humanization as a traumatic experience. Closely linked to the invocation of the visual image (the two letters "GO" burned into Aminata's flesh), the "smoking" of the branding iron also evokes an olfactory element, which creates a sensory closeness to the original traumatic situation.[249] Underlined by the use of the adjective "hot" (sense of touch, tactile aspect), Aminata's recollection acquires the qualities of both a flashback and an experience almost contemporaneous to her narrative situation.

Aminata's recollected trauma furthermore reinvigorates the aspect of double discrimination evoked by her self-description, which focuses prominently on her skin color and gender: the 'physical situation' has as its agents – the notion of agents vs. 'objects' acquires additional severeness and heft in light of the 'objectification' of slaves – White males. The abolitionists, qua male Whiteness, are hence connected, however loosely and however feebly and carefully in terms of suggesting a 'collective guilt', to the slave traders who branded Aminata as property of "Grant, Oswald" on Bance Island.[250] Five main aspects are thus alluded to in

---

248 Likewise, Aminata switches from *homelanders* through *Negroes* to *blacks*.

249 Also cf. the triggering of Aminata's recollection by a sound: "While I considered an answer, the two men clinked glasses. Something about that sound reminded me of tapping chains. I fell into a moment of utter dread." (BN, 415)

250 Both the spelling "Bance Island", as used by Hill, and the alternative – contemporary – spelling "Bunce Island" are accepted variations; the original spelling was in fact "Bence" Island (cf. Shaw 2002, 29); Bunce/Bance Island was the largest British slave trading post in West Africa: an estimated total of 30,000 slaves passed through this post; cf. Cross 2008, 225. For a brief introductory passage, cf. LeVert 2007, 10; also cf. Clifford 2006, part. chapters 15 and 22-23 for details. An early documentation is provided in a reprint of Thomas Clarkson's journal, cf. Ingham 1968 (Thomas Clarkson, the brother of John Clarkson, who becomes a close ally of Aminata's, also briefly features as a character in *The Book of Negroes*).

this text passage: one, traumatic memories endure and may be invoked or resuscitated by analogous or similar situations in the present. Two, the double discrimination of female African slaves is underlined. Three, in Aminata's case, the traumatic experience of abduction and dehumanization (objectification) understandingly hampers and impairs an 'unbiased' approach to certain situations and groups of people (in this case, White males). Four, the traumatic memories, frequently triggered through and in connection with sensory perceptions, are particularly apt to have an effect on a collective memory, which heavily relies on the emotional impact of certain recollections in order to keep them 'inhabited' or 'alive'. Five, the depiction of the role of the abolitionist movement in *The Book of Negroes* is a nuanced one which neither glorifies nor condemns the efforts and approaches of British abolitionists around the turn of the 18th century. This point, viz. the aspect of possible appropriation, is repeatedly taken up in the novel, particularly towards the very end, when Aminata negotiates the terms of her memoirs' publication (an aspect discussed in section 5.2.3.a).

Three more essential elements are touched upon in the novel's introductory passage: the topics of religion and education as well as one of the overarching images, the passage over water. It is an indicator of Aminata's newly gained importance that she, in her (and the abolitionists') efforts to work against the slave trade, has met an Anglican bishop in London. Aminata mentions this meeting very early on, underlining both her recent change in status and the importance of religion in this regard, which of course is also a question of considerable theological and moral heft. Religion is one of the recurrent themes in *The Book of Negroes* in general, beginning with the *Qu'ran* (the spelling variant of the Muslim scripture employed by Hill) of Aminata's father, going through the discussion of the social hierarchy of religions (personified in Solomon Lindo, the Jewish indigo inspector) and dealing in depth with issues of theodicy.[251] Aminata already hints at the import of this subject when she says that

---

251 Issues of theodicy not only permeate *The Book of Negroes*. In *Any Known Blood*, Hill incorporates the question of God's existence in the face of human evil as well: Langston the First, for instance, doubts the existence of God in the face of evil (cf. AKB 432; also cf. p. 264ff. of this study). Ironically, Langston I would eventually beget two generations of pastors. In *The Book of Negroes*, theodicy is not an exclusively Christian issue; as Aminata is a Muslim, the same questions Langston I ponders are asked in regard to Allah. Fanta, for instance, confronts Aminata on the issue: "Can't you see that Allah doesn't exist? The toubabu [Whites] are in charge, and there is only madness here." (BN 86) Given the atrocities Aminata witnesses aboard the slave ship, she becomes increasingly insecure about the existence of God herself ("But maybe Fanta had been right. Maybe God was impossible here." BN 92). When asked by blind priest Daddy Moses in Nova Scotia whether she has embraced Jesus as her savior yet, she replies, drily, "My arms have been busy, and Jesus hasn't come looking." (BN 317; in *Any Known Blood*, Langston the Fifth reveals a similar attitude: when asked whether Jesus has entered his soul yet, he answers, "Not to my knowledge." AKB 118) Later on, Aminata tells Daddy Moses that she indeed used to have faith but that she "had had to give it up" in face of what she experienced (BN 350).

Hill is by far not the only African-Canadian author who employs the trope of the theodicy in his works. George Elliott Clarke, for instance, equally discusses the role of religion for early Black Canadians in *Beatrice Chancy*. Pitting Father Ezra Moses, enslaved on Chancy's orchard, against the disillusionment and hypocrisy which characterize the slaves' experience, Clarke is able to oscillate between dreams and promises on the one hand (Moses of course advocates temperance and

[s]ome people call the sunset a creation of extraordinary beauty, and proof of God's existence. But what benevolent force would bewitch the human spirit by choosing pink to light
the path of a slave vessel? (BN 7)

However, religion is also a resource of instruction; the Koran of Aminata's father is repeatedly linked to her instruction, particularly her literacy: said book is the only one in the entire
village of Bayo (cf. BN 2). The Muslim faith is thus connoted as a source of knowledge and
one of the bases of Aminata's learning – which, in turn, subsequently ensures both her physical survival (as she is useful to her captors and later on to her masters Appleby and Lindo as
well as to the British military) and the writing down of her memoirs. The inherent logic of the
(pseudo-) autobiographical account thus suggests that without the education administered to
Aminata by her father – based on the Koran –, the story of her life would not have been
passed on in written form and consequently not be available to 'us', the readership (more specifically, of course, the narratee). The significance of Aminata's literacy is corroborated by
her comment that she is "addicted" to reading "like some are to drink or to tobacco" (BN 7).
Later on, Aminata will both receive and pass on (further) lessons in reading and writing.

The fact that Aminata is able, in a very basic sense, to write down her memoirs gains
particular importance in discussions of the oral and written transmission of memories. Collective memory theory has for some time discovered this issue to be a prevalent (though previously underestimated) one.[252] The media through which memories are related play a decisive

---

faith, predicting an exodus and assuring his fellow slaves of God's presence), and the dire reality
under Chancy's rule. Thus, while Moses promises deliverance ("Ma Lawd's gonna hail down
flame, / Pitch snow-face pharaoh's grief", Clarke 1999, 16) and God's closeness ("God ain't fled;
[…] He's in the fields, / Stooped low in the fields, / Where us toilers are", ibid., 20), Clarke introduces Reverend Ezra Love Peacock as an antipode.

Peacock, true to his name, turns out to be vain, hypocritical and lecherous. He represents the
church's ambivalent stance towards slavery – condemning it on theological grounds but in fact
tolerating it. As the Reverend tells Chancy: "Negroes are still God's loved children" – even
though they might be "benighted, foolish, errant" (ibid., 26). The same hypocrisy is revealed
when Peacock suggests Chancy should abandon slavery: "Chancy, the Bishop seeks / But the *look*
of freedom. Free / Your slaves, then work them / At cheaper cost. Appearances / Are made to de-
ceive." (ibid.; emphasis added.)

Beatrice, who has spent three years in a convent to learn the 'White ways' (cf. ibid., 52), points to
this hypocrisy when she tells her fellow slaves: "Nuns tore Exodus from our books; they feared /
Moses speaks satanic as Robespierre. / Slavery bedevils and chains our Christ." (ibid., 32)
Though Methodists and Baptists might fight for emancipation in *this* world (cf. ibid., 50), Lead
resolves not to wait for deliverance in the beyond suggested by Moses ("Vengeance be God's
luxury", ibid., 80): "When we bow down, our eyes blind with prayer, / White men taste our
daughters and our wives, / Spreadin them in milkweed." (ibid., 79) Ultimately, Beatrice is raped
by her own father inside a chapel – prompting her to speak her final verdict on the issue of theodicy ("Did you spy God, lynched, dangling from a tree?" ibid., 91) and submerging in bitter cyni-
cism ("[Christ?] Sweet? By Lucifer, I'm sure he winked / While someone stubbed twixt my legs,
Pleasuring himself in my pain." ibid., 95).

252 The early proponents of theories of collective memory did not yet account for the influence that
different media may have on the contents and modes of memory and remembering. Pierre Nora,

role in the concrete construction processes of collective memories: "Especially when it comes to collective remembering, media – such as books, monuments, films, and the internet – display their constructive, world-(and memory-)making nature." (Erll 2005, 249) In short, the vehicle influences the message transported, so that the mode of its relation, whether as an oral, a painted, a written or otherwise mediated account, affects the memory in question. In *The Book of Negroes*, we are faced with both oral and written modes of story-telling and passing on of memories. Hill is careful not to devaluate or exalt any one of these modes. In "Book One", therefore, he introduces both media, literature as well as orature, making sure that both receive their due credit. While the written account is of course clearly foregrounded here (after all, the narrative frame setting is explicitly based on Aminata's writing process), Hill also early on includes a scene that highlights the value of oral accounts: Aminata, in 1802, is invited to speak at a school in London. Stylistically, Hill underlines the oral aspect of Aminata's conversation with the British students, extensively using markers of oral communication (cf. BN 3f.).[253] In a clever ruse, Hill then inserts a transition from oral to written account:[254]

> [One girl] said she was an excellent listener and wanted me to please tell her a ghost story. Honey, I said, my life is a ghost story. Then tell it to me, she said.
> As I told her, I am Aminata Diallo, daughter of Mamadu Diallo and Sira Kulibali, born in the village of Bayo, three moons by foot from the Grain Coast in West Africa. [...] And I am writing this account. (BN 4)

Aminata's story thus fluently passes from oral to written account. The addressee simultaneously slips from a listening to a reading position, a feat facilitated by the absence of quotation marks in direct speech in this passage, which renders the shift from oral to written report less noticeable (the lack of quotation marks is a deviation from the mode used elsewhere in *The Book of Negroes*). The unobtrusive transition from oral to written account is paralleled by the equally subtle, fluid shifts between the present and the past of Aminata's recollections, i.e. between the frame setting and the embedded main narrative (shifts which are, as mentioned above, often aided by sensory perceptions that link the past and the present). From telling the

---

for instance, subsumed literature, photography, architecture, memorials, painting and the entire spectrum of artistic forms of expression under the term of *lieux de mémoire* (cf. P. Schmidt 2004, 35f.). Likewise, Aby Warburg's concept of 'pathos formula' applies to both the literary and the visual arts (it actually derives from the visual arts, as Warburg himself was an art historian; cf. Erll 2003, 161f.). Yet, recent studies have argued that no medium is neutral towards the things it contains and transports (cf. Erll 2004, 5f.; Erll 2009 – particularly part I: "Mediations" – assembles an array of papers on the topic).

253 Her visit to the London school also foreshadows her status as "Grand *djeli* of the academy" (BN 448), when a school is named in her honor; it also alludes to her status as *djeli* in an African village she flees to after escaping the slave-traders who had promised to take her back inland to find her native village. The function of the *djeli*, or African story-teller, is performed through oral communication exclusively. Again, the expository frame setting thus prefigures topics dealt with *in extenso* later on.

254 Cf. discussions of the shift from oral to literary art in the section on *The Book of Negroes* and the slave narrative; also cf. Link 1993, 277 and Gates 2002, 4.

"ghost story" of her life to the London schoolchildren, Aminata almost imperceptibly proceeds to telling – in writing – her account to the narratee. The narratee is subsequently addressed directly, which of course is an additional extension of the direct oral communication employed in the London classroom ("If you, dear reader,…" BN 7).

The direct appeal to the narratee employed in this passage ("Let me begin with a caveat to any and all who find these pages." BN 7) marks the reference to one of the paradigmatic and structuring images of Hill's work: the passage over water. Aminata explicitly warns against the crossing of "large bodies of water" (BN 7), which for her have signified passages in status, both attempted and involuntary. The most dramatic sea travel of course is the Middle Passage, indicating Aminata's conversion from self-determined subject to heteronomous, commodified 'object'. Aminata is referring to the experience of the Middle Passage when she states that under the water surface,

> [t]here, right underneath, lies a bottomless graveyard of children, mothers and men. I shudder to imagine all the Africans rocking in the deep. Every time I have sailed the seas, I have had the sense of gliding over the unburied. (BN 7)[255]

Aminata's numerous water crossings are thus a reminder of the abduction, exploitation and enslavement that have shaped her life – and prematurely cut short the lives of so many of her fellow Africans. It is a trauma that reverberates in Aminata, and of course, the recollection of this trauma is forced upon Aminata whenever she crosses the sea, i.e. when the 'physical conditions' resemble that of the original traumatic situation. Aminata herself admits that she "crossed more water than [she cares] to remember" (BN 3). Remembering the Middle Passage – both as the actual, horrifying journey and as the signifier of her enslavement – is so hurtful that she would rather leave the memory behind (cf. Toni Morrison's notions of disremembering and rememory; Morrison 2008, 70; also cf. Rider 1995, 120f.). Yet she knows that she will have to pass on her "ghost story" nonetheless: "I have my life to tell, my own private ghost story, and what purpose would there be to this life I have lived, if I could not take this opportunity to relate it?" (BN 7) There is, however, one concession that Aminata makes – she vows to never again cross the ocean.

> Once I have met with the King and told my story, I desire to be interred right here, in the soil of London. Africa is my homeland. But I have weathered enough migrations for five lifetimes, thank you very much, and I don't care to be moved again. (BN 7)

The expository narrative framework of "Book One" appropriately concludes with this statement, completing the circular structure of the novel's introductory passage, which opens with the words "I seem to have trouble dying." (BN 1) At the outset of the novel, Aminata has al-

---

255 Aminata believes that those Africans simply thrown overboard will not find their final rest and thus lie, unburied and restless, at the bottom of the sea: "The [slave] boat terrified me, but I was even more afraid of sinking deep into the salty water, with no possibility for my spirit to return to my ancestors." (BN 53; also cf. BN 81, 7)

most completed her life cycle, but her story will live on – a story whose pivotal themes are, in a nutshell, introduced in the very first pages of *The Book of Negroes*.

In the following three sections, I will provide closer readings of several of these pivotal themes, which include the memory of the Middle Passage, the shift from 'slave' to 'servant' (and Aminata's subsequent escape from bondage altogether), and, crucially of course, the particularities of the *Canadian* experience, viz. the promise and ensuing denial of a Canaan for Blacks in the True North.

5.3.2. Traumatic memory: The Middle Passage[256]

> *When I was carried up the ladder and dropped like a sack of meal on the deck of the toubabu's [Whites'] ship, I sought comfort by imagining that I had been made a djeli, and was required to see and remember everything. My purpose would be to witness, to prepare to testify.* (BN 56)

The story of Aminata's life explores traumata in a variety of constellations and levels of intensity. *The Book of Negroes* furthermore includes discussions of coping with trauma and the inability to do so, thus confronting the reader with an intricate treatment of issues revolving around remembering and forgetting, suffering and surviving.[257]

At the age of eleven, Aminata is captured by African slave traders (whom she initially refers to, in the slightly age- and locale-adapted language discussed before, as "man-stealers", e.g. BN 56), marched to the coast of Sierra Leone and briefly imprisoned in a slave castle at Bance Island. She is then brought aboard the slave ship that will take her to South Carolina. After a three-month coffle march, what begins is the two-month crossing of the Atlantic that we know today as the Middle Passage (being the middle leg in the triangular slave trade; cf. for instance the very useful *Encyclopedia of the Middle Passage* compiled by Falola and Warnock; 2007). The Middle Passage has served as an almost archetypical, hyperbolic image of both slavery's concrete, physical brutalities and of the commodification of humans. As such, it has been rendered in numerous literary accounts and other artistic expressions (cf. e.g.

---

256 Excerpts from this section have appeared in Krampe 2009.

257 *The Book of Negroes* deals with trauma both in detail and in broad scope. Instances of trauma include – but are not limited to – racial and sexual violence, dehumanization, impotence *vis à vis* cruelty and humiliation, loss of family and friends, loss of identity, disillusionment and broken promises, subhuman living conditions and preventable sickness, total heteronomy and dispossession of self, and structural violence in general. Given the fact that the 486-page novel spans, among others, the histories of the abduction of Africans by slave-traders, the Middle Passage, plantation slavery, indentured labor, broken promises in Nova Scotia, and the impossibility to return 'home', it should be obvious that the reading offered here will by necessity remain selective. What I will focus on in this section is thus the 'archetypal' trauma of the Middle Passage, which in *The Book of Negroes* is closely connected to issues of anonymity, remembering and storytelling.

the essays in Diedrich/Gates/Pedersen 1999 or Haehnel/Ulz 2010). Accordingly, while Hill's depiction of plantation slavery – which includes the slave narrative's staple ingredients of cruel whippings, rape and other atrocities (cf. Link 1993, 46) – is vividly outspoken in its account of the dehumanization of slaves in the southern United States' system of exploitation, it is the description of the Middle Passage which sticks out for its intensity and graphic portrayal.

The respective chapter, entitled "We Glide Over the Unburied" in reference to those slaves who died and were hauled overboard, is central for another reason, too. The very moment Aminata sets foot upon the slave ship, she resolves to witness, to remember, and to tell (cf. BN 55f.). Essentially, of course, this is the credo of collective memory transmission – Aminata thus vows to pass on the stories of what she and her fellow slaves experience lest it be excluded from memory. It has been discussed before that she, by the very act of remembering her fellow captives' names, restores subjectivity to the commodified, depersonalized, anonymous slaves. On the level of historiography and identity formation, of course, the remembrance of the Middle Passage keeps these memories alive and at the forefront, i.e. available for processes of identity construction fed by functional memory. Thus, telling her/their story, Aminata achieves a threefold effect: she keeps herself alive, she keeps the subjectivity of her fellow Africans alive and she keeps alive the memory of the Middle Passage as a whole.[258] On the first level, it is Aminata's good fortune that she elects herself to bear witness and to go on living in order to testify; her wish to be a *djeli* lends purpose to her otherwise largely senseless (slave) life. Others are not as fortunate, as Hill shows; there is a pivotal scene in the novel in which the African captives' reaction to their enslavement is drastically visualized. This scene also illustrates the differential reaction of individuals to the trauma of their commodification: while some might retreat or break down, others may go berserk.

Alongside Aminata, several people from her home village of Bayo are abducted, among them the fourth wife of the village chief, Fanta, and the chief's *woloso*, Fomba.[259] Their difference in status and personality is explored from the very beginning of Aminata's story, as she recounts several instances of Fanta mistreating Fomba (e.g. BN 21f.). Fanta has, during the coffle march to the African coast from where the group of captives is to be shipped overseas, by and large proved to be an obstinate, exceedingly proud woman. Onboard the slave ship, Fanta realizes that there is no escape for her – and neither is there hope for her newborn baby, whom Aminata helps to bring into the world aboard the slave vessel. It is obvious from the very birth of her baby boy that Fanta is so traumatized that she is emotionally

---

258 On an extraliterary level, the latter aspect is of course one that applies to *The Book of Negroes* as well, which – in literary/fictional form – keeps the memory of the Middle Passage at the forefront and thus available for collective memory constructions.

259 *Woloso* (plural: *wolosow*) designates, put simply, a 'houseborn', often second-generation intra-African slave (cf. Hoffman 2000, 244; Mann 2006, 1f.; Roberts 1987, 122f.). The inclusion of a *woloso* character underlines Hill's intricate and multi-perspective treatment of his (historical) subject; he does indeed include issues of intra-African slavery, female circumcision, African cooperation (collaboration) in the transatlantic slave trade and other 'sensitive' topics (cf. Hill, Appendix 297f.).

crippled; Aminata, for instance, observes: "She was not a proud mother, but an angry one." (BN 87) The birth of Fanta's child is closely linked to violence and death, as Fanta immediately after giving birth kills the ship doctor's pet parrot with a knife she stole[260] (Fanta "stabbed and stabbed until the claws stopped scraping at her and the body stopped quivering", BN 87); moreover, the news of the baby's birth – delivered by Aminata at the surgeon's command – serves as the signal for a slave revolt that ends in a bloodbath. It is obvious from the progression of the mutiny that there is no chance of escape or successful resistance. The very thought that her status as a slave will be entailed to her child, that the trauma of her objectification will be passed on, subsequently makes Fanta kill her own baby as well as the child of a fellow slave.[261] Aminata recalls the foreshadowing of the infanticide as well as the gruesome murder itself:

> I put my hand on [Fanta's] shoulder and told her to think about the baby. She grunted. 'I stopped caring about that a long time ago. No toubab will do to this baby what they have done to us.' A shiver ran through my body. (BN 82f.)

> Fanta brought out the knife from the medicine man's room, placed a hand over the baby's face and jerked up his chin. She dug the tip of the knife into the baby's neck and ripped his throat open. Then she pulled the blue cloth over him, stood and heaved him overboard. (BN 90)

While Aminata's reaction to the trauma of the Middle Passage is to survive in order to testify, thus reconstructing human subjects through narration, Fanta can see no other way of escape than to disrupt the chain of objectified, commodified and depersonalized selves by murder. Hill explains his pursuit of these differential individual reactions towards the pressures and the traumatizing effects of enslavement and the Middle Passage in an interview:

> I was interested in the different ways that people respond to this pressure. We react in different ways. Aminata becomes an astounding survivor. She survives physically and emotionally. She does not become engulfed in hatred – which is a miracle. She might easily become engulfed in hatred and bitterness and become murderously vengeful, but she does not. Fanta is another kettle of fish, reacting in different ways to similar pressures. Fanta is so overcome by the horrors visited upon her that she has to lash out. She doesn't want anybody else to go

---

260 The doctor's parrot stands for the slaves' status aboard the slave ship, which is characterized by the captives' subjugation under animal rather than human conditions: "It [the parrot] could not escape, and it could not get me, for it was locked in that cage just as surely as I was locked in the ship." (BN 72)

261 Although Aminata herself does not kill either one of her children, it is evident that trauma does indeed tend to breed trauma, that Aminata entails to her children some of the experiences she herself has made, thus shaping their character (not in a conscious way of education, that is, but rather in an emotional way); "I loved every inch of my daughter and worshipped every beat of her heart, but I was not a playful mother. I did not have a lot of fun in me", Aminata confesses (BN 336). As for her daughter May, Aminata "didn't know what to make of her temper [as an infant]. Sometimes it seemed that all the wrongs of the world were pent up in her soul, waiting for an excuse to erupt. Before she turned one, she howled and pounded my back to be let down and allowed to stumble about on her own." (BN 331)

through this, and so she takes down other people, including babies, rather than have them endure slavery. And also, I think it is common that when we are terribly abused, we often lash out against our own people. It is hard to lash out successfully against those who oppress us. So it is easier for Fanta to kill Black babies than it is to kill White adults who are armed and fight back. (Hill, Appendix 299)

Fomba, the *woloso*, reacts in another vastly different way to the humiliation and pain of the Middle Passage. In contrast to Aminata, who witnesses to testify, and to Fanta, who kills to break the chain of entailing subhuman status to her offspring, Fomba completely retreats and falls silent. At the slave auction in South Carolina, Fomba is among the 'surplus' slaves – the old, sickly and useless – just as Aminata, who remembers:

I caught a glimpse of Fomba, sitting on the ground, elbows around his knees, palms over his ears, eyes shut, rocking back and forth. [...] Dead weight, but not dead. [...] Fomba opened his mouth, but nothing – not one sound – came from his lips. (BN 115)

Aminata claims that Fomba's mind is "gone" (BN 114); he refuses to interact with the world of cruelty that surrounds him. The scene described above is an almost clichéd depiction of a deeply traumatized person. Later on, Fomba is able to work again, but he never recovers his ability to communicate. Tragically, his social death[262] also precipitates physical death: Fomba is shot by a guard when he fails to identify himself (BN 214). It is no accident that Fomba's inability to identify himself coincides with both his inability to communicate and his death; without being able to put forward, to verbally supply and express an individual self, Fomba has become an anonymous, empty shell. His inability to bear witness and, in its double meaning, identify himself results in an inability to 'tell himself into being' (to adapt a well-worn phrase by Davis/Gates in the introduction to *The Slave's Narrative*, who argue that the slave narratives are attempts of "blacks to *write themselves into being*", 1985b, xxii; emphasis in the original). Slavery kills Fomba by taking his identity and silencing him. What is furthermore underlined by the fact that Fomba, of all people, succumbs and is silenced by his traumatic enslavement is the quality of the Atlantic slave trade as opposed to the quality of intra-African slavery: while Fomba had been a *woloso* slave all of his life, half a year under the objectifying institution of transatlantic slavery suffices to fully crush him.[263]

Aminata, in contrast, in a limbo of wanting to witness and having to suffer terribly throughout the process of witnessing, cannot and will not shut herself off from the pain the way Fomba does, even though she momentarily tries to: "I shut my eyes and plugged my ears, but could not block out all the shrieking." (BN 93) There are two major factors that secure

---

262 Cf. the widely discussed work of Orlando Patterson (1982) as well as newer writings (e.g. Patterson 2003).

263 In fact, Fomba falls silent at the beginning of the Middle Passage; his last utterance is a weak 'yes' when Aminata asks him if his ribs are broken. Shortly after – when the slave inspector prods at his genitals – "Fomba's mouth opened wide, but no sound came out." (BN 59) Chief Biton subsequently tells Aminata not to focus her energies on Fomba: "He can't even speak. His mind is departed." (BN 70)

Aminata's psychological survival (though a mere 'survival' it is indeed): her young age and the notion of being a *djeli*. As a *djeli*, she passes on what she has witnessed in various ways. On the plantation, in Charles Town and in the segregated communities of Canvas Town and Birchtown, she relates her story to varying audiences. In the African village where she is awarded an honorary position of *djeli*, she repeats her account over and over again. After her passage to London almost forty-five years after her abduction, Aminata tells her story to school children and bears witness before the King and Queen as well as before Parliament. By subsequently writing her memoirs, thus rendering her story into a durable medium, Aminata – as a *djeli*-cum-writer – externalizes and spreads those memories. In extension, of course, the extra-literary readership of *The Book of Negroes* is, on a non-fictional level, confronted with the memories of its fictional protagonist, who tells a story that had arguably come to the brink of forgetfulness. Thus, when Aminata comments on the fact that there are people completely unaware of the history she is conveying alongside and through her story, her remarks relate just as much to a current extra-literary ('real') phenomenon, namely the (perceived) sinking into oblivion of the history of slavery and, importantly, its aftermath:

> Some of us still scream out in the middle of the night. But there are men, women and chil-
> dren walking about the streets without the faintest idea of our nightmares. They cannot know
> what we endured if we never find anyone to listen. In telling my story, I remember all those
> who never made it through the musket balls and the sharks and the nightmares, all those who
> never found a group of listeners, and those who never touched a quill to an inkpot.   (BN
> 56f.)

Aminata wants to share her pain (or rather: *their* pain, as she explicitly speaks for a collective, including those who have died), she must pass on her/their memories lest the nightmares of the abducted Africans die with the slaves themselves and be forgotten. The fact that Hill in-cludes in the list of lethal things not only "musket balls and sharks" but also "nightmares" (ibid.) not only stresses, through repetition, the significance of nightmares.[264] It also under-lines that the stress, the trauma of commodification itself can be crippling, even lethal. Aminata's way out of being overwhelmed by the trauma is to remember, to structure and to derive purpose from the most dreary experiences. Again, two levels of dealing with trauma are reflected in this quotation: the immediate, individual reaction to trauma (which is com-monly associated with PTSD nightmares) and the need to keep alive the traumatic memory, which can take place either orally (through "listeners") or through writing ("quill to an ink-pot"). Consequently, Aminata – in contrast to Fanta or Fomba – has both the predisposition, viz. her young age, and a reason to survive physically as well as mentally. She brings herself to channel her traumatic experiences and renders the process of witnessing usable against cav-

---

264 A wealth of research is available relating nightmares to Post-Traumatic Stress Disorder (PTSD).
   Cf. for instance comprehensively McNally 2003 (who argues, against a bulk of previous studies,
   that traumata are more effortlessly and more often remembered than forgotten); Cash 2006, 39ff.
   on nightmares as a defining criterion of PTSD; Barrett's 2001 collection *Trauma and Dreams*
   (particularly E. Hartmann and Lavie/Kaminer); also cf. Revonsuo 2003, 284ff. on PTSD nightmares from an anthropological and evolutionary perspective.

ing in: "*No*, I told myself. *Be a djeli. See, and remember.*" (BN 64) Significantly, there is an almost literal repetition of this phrase when Aminata is brought to Charles Town by Solomon Lindo as a so-called 'servant', though she is fully aware of the fact that she is still considered property, and thus in effect still a slave.

> I missed the nonstop crying of the cicadas, which I imagined to be the voices of my ances-
> tors, saying, *We will cry out like this always always always just so you don't forget us.* [...] I
> vowed not to let the noises of the city drown out their voices or rob me of my past. It was
> less painful to forget, but I would look and I would remember. (BN 190; italics in the origi-
> nal)

For African-Canadian literature in general, this of course points to the importance of telling the story of slavery. While this may sound superficial, one has to bear in mind the distinction between African-*American* and African-*Canadian* literature in this regard. In Black *Canadian* literature, as has been elaborated before, there is a distinct perception of absence or negligence. Therefore, it is a pressing task to come up with the respective narratives, which for the last couple of years has indeed proven to be a main focus of interest. In the foreword to the collection *T-Dot Griots*, Afua Cooper, a Black Canadian poet, scholar, and historian, elucidates the connection between the ancient tradition of African *djelis* (or griots) and the position of today's African-Canadian writers (here, Cooper speaks of poets and spoken word artists in particular, whose voices are assembled in the collection she introduces):

> For example, in the Manding culture of West Africa,[265] the griot (the Manding word is *djeli*)
> was the historian, the bard, the moralist, and also an entertainer. The griot knew law, the
> griot knew tradition, the griot knew history, and s/he had the responsibility to pass these tra-
> ditions on through words and performance to the rest of the community. The griot was also
> the conscience of the community. [...] No community was complete without the griots for
> they were the ones who knew, they were the ones who had the responsibility to tell, instruct,
> and make whole. [...] By using the word griot to call the African Canadian practitioners of
> the word, the editors of this volume tell us they believed that the Middle Passage did not de-
> stroy all the traditions of the captive Africans who were taken from their homelands, dragged
> across the Atlantic Ocean in the stinking bottom of slave ships, and made into slaves on New
> World plantations. It is this captivity of Africans and their dispersal throughout the world
> and the Americas that led to the formation of the African diaspora that produced us – de-
> scendants of those who endured enslavement. Our ancestors lost much in captivity but not
> everything. In their heads they carried the words, songs, stories, poems, and their meaning.
> They remembered. And they passed on their remembrances to their children, and their chil-
> dren's children. [...] As black Torontonians we live the daily experience of police brutality,
> racial profiling, educational inequities, inadequate healthcare (including mental health) fa-
> cilities, and other forms of discriminations. Marginalization is our daily fare. But we fight
> back. One of our main weapons is culture and art. (Cooper 2004, ii)

---

265 This is the native culture of *The Book of Negroes'* Aminata. The slave trader William King, who
    sells Aminata to her first owner, Robinson Appleby, claims to be able to tell by her physical ap-
    pearance that she is from today's Mali (his skill is to classify Africans according to their 'breed'
    like cattle), cf. BN 171f.

Cooper of course reads African-Canadian authors in terms of the African paragon of the griot, and even though she focuses on spoken word artists, her remarks extend to the bulk of Black Canadian authors.[266] If anyone has ever heard George Elliott Clarke recite his poetry, there can be no doubt in his or her mind that Clarke – to a degree verging on cliché – embodies the griot, or *djeli*: historian, bard, moralist, entertainer.[267] It is evident that Black Canadian literature in its entirety aims at "passing on through words and performance" (this and the following quotes ibid.) what the griot passes on, viz. tradition and the (inhabited parts of) history in particular – read: collective memory. Cooper explicitly refers to the Middle Passage and sees in the African diaspora "descendants of those who endured enslavement." Of course, her identification thus assumes pivotally the existence of a memory group or *Erinnerungskultur* which bases its existence on a set of shared, i.e. collective memories; predominantly, of course, slavery and the Middle Passage. Remembering these traumatic experiences is understood here as the foundation of identity, and it is the griots/*djelis* who not only "knew" but have "the responsibility to tell, instruct". What has survived the Middle Passage, commodification and captivity, the editors of *T-Dot Griots* claim according to Cooper, are the *narratives*, the memories enshrined in "words, songs, stories, poems". The survivors "passed on their remembrances" through the generations. Now, they have been handed down to the current generation of griots, "African Canadian practitioners of the word". Surviving the Middle Passage is thus inextricably linked to the survival of memories externalized in artistic – linguistic – expression, which of course is exactly what Aminata in *The Book of Negroes* embodies. She is thus the (fictional) paragon of those "captive Africans who were taken from their homelands, dragged across the Atlantic Ocean in the stinking bottom of slave ships, and made into slaves on New World plantations," the archetypal *djeli* who remembers and passes on.

Cooper then links the African slaves and traditional griots to contemporary urban Canadian reality: "we live the daily experience of police brutality, racial profiling [...] and other

---

266 Spoken word artists like Wendy Brathwaite (a.k.a. Motion) have found their way into the realm of the written publication as well, cf. e.g. *Motion in Poetry* (2002); G. E. Clarke introduces her in his foreword as among the next generation of African-Canadian poets to pass on the tradition of orature and performance ("Us old-school poets set the stage, uh huh, / And Motion, she study our page, uh huh, / Givin' props to her peeps and agitation to the age." (Clarke 2002b, 6) Brathwaite herself describes her own art as rooted in the hiphop constituents of "DJing, Breakdancing, Graffiti Art, and *the modern day Griot* – the MC" (2002, 9; emphasis added).

267 When asked whether he personally sees himself as a kind of griot or *djeli*, Lawrence Hill modestly dismisses an immediate affinity, claiming a direct identification "would be taking it too far. I see myself as a writer who is interested in mining specific aspects of the Black experience that will translate into drama of universal appeal. [...] I find it interesting to note that stories arising from specific socio-geographic locations often hold the most universal appeal for readers." (Hill, Appendix 293) Clarke might be more accommodating regarding the comparison to the *djeli* as historian, moralist, bard, entertainer; obviously, he is a historian in his own right, excavating not only forgotten (Africadian) literature but the history conveyed alongside as well; every preacher is necessarily a moralist, so Clarke's poetic sermons are certainly those of a moralist; an entertainer can be found in Clarke's verse as much as in his presence; as for the bard, Clarke certainly is Africadia's foremost lyricist – anecdotally, Knutson (2007a and 2007b) even reads Clarke in conjunction with the English "'National Bard'" (2007b, 157), Shakespeare.

forms of discrimination." Racism, the pattern underlying the atrocities of the Atlantic slave trade, is still virulent; in this, the past is present as much as through the generational passing on of memories. Yet both presences are habitually ignored and rendered invisible by mainstream hegemonic (memory) constructions: "Marginalization is our daily fare." Even so, Cooper does not abide by the position of the liminal victim. She thus mirrors a stance that is prevalent in African-Canadian literature as a whole: just like Aminata, in *The Book of Negroes,* evades and overcomes the erasure of her subjectivity and her history by remembering and telling,[268] the position of the marginalized, erased victim is not the terminal position in most of Black Canadian literature. Instead, what we are facing is the empowered Black subject who, through autonomous, narrative identification and the will to change current, heteronomous, hegemonic definitions, aims to insert *his/her/their* story into the larger collective memory.

The characters in contemporary Black Canadian postslavery writing are usually not pathetically helpless victims, even though they *do* face the danger of erasure and subjugation. Langston Cane I, in *Any Known Blood*, is enslaved but escapes slavery; his descendant Langston IV is denied rent but begins a moral and political crusade; Langston V is discriminated against and begins to assemble his family history. Beatrice Chancy, in George Elliott Clarke's libretto of the same name, is a slave subjugated and raped by her owner (who is her own father), yet she rebels and displays an indomitable will even in the face of execution (as does Angélique in Cooper's *The Hanging of Angélique*); George and Rue (of George Elliott Clarke's novel named after them) may be at the receiving end of the history of discrimination, yet at least one of them is willing to be redeemed. Marie Ursule of Dionne Brand's *At the Full and Change of the Moon* (2000) certainly is desperate along the lines of Fanta in *The Book of Negroes,* and she is likewise taking her life (and death) in her own hands. Mary-Mathilda, narrator and protagonist of Austin Clarke's *The Polished Hoe* is subjected to slavery and sexual exploitation but subjects her master to the blade of her hoe.

---

268 In an interview, Lawrence Hill emphasizes that Aminata also succeeds in retaining her ability to love, which he sees as another instance where she supersedes her victimization: "[QUESTION:] *Just the mere fact of surviving the Middle Passage, slavery, her migrations back and forth over this great body of water, which she loathes, is very courageous...*[HILL:] ...yes, but she does more than survive. She loves. She has the courage to love. How easy it is to shut down love if one has endured horrors. But still she risks love. I feel that she is heroic in her own way." (Hill, Appendix 300) One of the more clichéd scenes in *The Book of Negroes* underlines this notion: In a discussion between Chekura and Aminata shortly before boarding their ships to sail to Nova Scotia (a journey Chekura does not survive and Aminata only embarks on with some delay), Chekura warns Aminata that the Canaan she and the others are expecting in Canada may not materialize. What will survive all the hardships, disillusionments, pain, and broken promises, however, is love and passion: "'But the British promise that we will be free in Nova Scotia,' [Aminata] said. 'Don't forget all the slaves and indentured folk you have put in that ledger [the Book of Negroes]. They were stolen from the rebels and re-enslaved by the British. We may get to the promised land and we may not, but wherever we are, life won't be easy. But that has never stopped us.' 'Stopped us from what?' 'From this,' he said, once more pressing his lips to mine.'" (BN 297)

Most of these characters not only escape their marginalization in terms of power structures that also determine their very status as humans (albeit many through fatal, often suicidal actions – a fate Aminata escapes), they also directly or indirectly *tell their own story*. Their narrative survives, and with it, their memories do. It is one of Black Canadian authors' most prominent goals, I claim, to achieve what their characters achieve: to put forward narratives that reclaim a place for the Black presence in what is perceived as a whitewashed representation of Canada. Aminata, in *The Book of Negroes*, states that she has "long loved the written word, and come to see in it the power of the sleeping lion." (BN 101) In Cooper's words, this translates as: "But we fight back. One of our main weapons is culture and art." (2004, ii)

5.3.3. *Slaves and servants*

In 1762, Robinson Appleby, the South Carolina plantation owner who is Aminata's first master, sells her and her infant son Mamadu, partly because Aminata had shown a certain degree of obstinacy. Solomon Lindo, an indigo inspector from the state capital of Charles Town, buys Aminata and – as we learn later on – arranges the sale of Mamadu to another White couple as Appleby refuses to sell him both Aminata and her son. In the Lindo home, Aminata is mainly put to household chores, which are progressively supplemented by bookkeeping and other more learned duties (Lindo in fact had first expressed interest in buying Aminata from Appleby after finding out that she is indeed literate). It is in the context of the Lindo household that, in terms of Aminata's biography, the story of the Exodus is first explicitly discussed.[269] Aminata had, secretly, read the Bible on Appleby's St. Helena Island plantation and is accordingly acquainted with the biblical narrative of Moses leading the Israelites out of Egypt. Even though Aminata has already proven to Lindo that she is an avid reader and a quick learner (though she tends to be dangerously cheeky at times, considering her position), he is quite taken by surprise when he finds out that Aminata is indeed familiar with the text of the Holy Scripture.

When Lindo gives Aminata a gift of *Gulliver's Travels* by Jonathan Swift, Aminata – in a bout of double intertextuality within the story[270] – is reminded of the Exodus by a certain scene she comes across. The scene describes Gulliver waking up and finding himself bound so that he cannot move his limbs or his head. The connection to the biblical Exodus might not

---

269 As has been explicated in section, "Ham's children: Israelites in Egypt?" (p. 115ff.), this aspect is the second way of approaching the topic of an allegorical exodus; the first approach in terms of the *novel's* narrative chronology (as opposed to the chronology of Aminata's life provided in the embedded narrative sections) can be found in the direct references made in the frame narrative.

270 The double intertextuality – Aminata (a fictional character) being reminded of a certain text by another text – exemplifies Hill's own general take on the biblical Exodus, which he reflects not only as a direct reference, but also *through* the original slave narrative's conception of this prototype. What we end up with on the level of the novelist Lawrence Hill is thus a triple intertextuality, yet without over(t)ly highlighting it (which is in line with both the novel's and Hill's overall non-pompous style).

be immediately clear (and Hill uses a somewhat labored transition to shift from Swift to the Exodus: "I was instantly full of desire to read the book. 'It looks as good as Exodus," I told [Lindo]." BN 204). Yet given the fact that Hill repeatedly uses Swift to comment on the situation of Africa and Africans in colonial times,[271] it is the aspect of finding oneself bound and incapacitated that connects Gulliver's experience ("I attempted to rise, but was unable to stir", quoted ibid.) to the memory of the Israelites' slavery in Egypt. Lindo then assures Aminata of what he considers their mutual heritage:

> 'And what do you know of [the Exodus]?' he asked. I explained that I had been reading the Bible on St. Helena Island. 'We all talk about the Exodus, did you know that?' he said. It seemed foolish to say too much, but I could not stop myself from blurting out a question: 'What do you mean?' 'What I mean is that Jews and Muslims and Christians all have the story of the Exodus in our religious books,' Lindo said. 'The Israelites are my people and Exodus is the story of our escape from slavery.' I listened carefully to Lindo, and thought about what he was saying. The discovery was fascinating, yet confusing. Perhaps Lindo could explain why Christians and Jews kept Muslims as slaves if we all had the same God and if we all celebrated the flight of the Hebrews from Egypt. (BN 204f.)

It is obvious that Lindo assumes an ostensibly egalitarian position, claiming the similarity of the three major monotheistic religions in terms of their reverence for the memory of the Exodus. While not in fact wrong (the Exodus is indeed part of all three religions' sacred texts), the implication of Lindo's lecture is that Aminata's and his religions, their people's traditions and histories are not so dissimilar after all – and that consequently, neither are their people themselves as disparate as one could assume. Lindo hence indirectly equates his ancestors' (i.e. the Israelites') history and historical experience with that of Aminata's people. Interestingly, his comment starts out as a religious treatise but ends up as a slightly lopsided equation involving two 'peoples' rather than two religions (Lindo switches from Islam, Aminata's original religious affiliation,[272] to Africa, Aminata's geographical roots, here). Aminata reports:

---

271 It can be presumed that Swift in particular is used as an occasional comment on *today's* social, economic and political situation as well. It is clear that Lawrence Hill is highly interested not only in the historical dimension of African–European (or African–'Western'/'Northern') relations; cf. for instance his 2005 essay "Is Africa's Pain America's Burden?" Hill both quotes from Swift's *Gulliver's Travels* and repeats the novel's epigraph by Swift (a poem first published in 1733) within the text, the latter stressing the notion of (Western) ignorance about the 'dark continent'. By situating the text excerpt from *Gulliver's Travels* in a context that revolves around economic issues, Hill also stresses the fact that the West has repeatedly 'bound' Africa economically (just as Gulliver discovers he is tied to the ground). On Swift's poem, cf. Löffler 1982, part. 87f.; on the mapping of Africa cf. Kuba 2004 (who also chooses Swift's poem as an epigraph); also cf. the interview with Lawrence Hill in the appendix on Hill's interest in the general lack of knowledge about the interior of Africa in colonial times, especially the lack of reliable maps.

272 As has been discussed before, we witness Aminata's insecurities, doubts, rapprochements and departures in terms of both her religious upbringing and her overall religious attitude throughout her story. Her original, strong Islamic faith (cf. for instance her unwavering belief in the power of her symbolic cheek carvings, the crescent moons that are supposed to show her as a free-born Muslim and thus ought to protect her from enslavement) is deeply shaken during the coffle march

> Mr. Lindo had mentioned a few times that Jews had been slaves in ancient Egypt and that his own ancestors had been driven from Spain. He had told me that Jews and Africans could understand each other because we were both outsiders, but even though the man preferred the term *servant* to *slave*, he owned me and [his servant] Dolly and now he owned Dolly's baby boy. (BN 209)

The groups described by Lindo are clearly based on shared sets of collective memories and should be analyzed as such. At first sight, the groups Lindo initially defines and then puts on a level with each other are categorized on mismatched criteria; in his second comparison, he uses a geographical marker for Aminata's people, while using religion for his own. In fact, however, the groups are compared on the basis of a concrete collective memory, namely the remembrance of the Exodus. This key memory (*Erinnerungsfigur*) is an emblematic example of a collective memory, as it is highly ritualized (being an integral part of institutionalized religion's stack of prototypical narratives, this fact is not surprising), solidified through constant repetition, and externalized in the respective sacred texts. Lindo thus recurs to a memory that is highly identity-shaping. His self-perception is based on the historical experience of being "driven from Spain" (ibid.), so he considers himself part of a victimized group. Interestingly, Lindo himself expresses the linkage of past and present here, because although his example is historical, he still identifies himself as strongly influenced by that collective experience. Aminata reports: "He had told me that Jews and Africans [...] *were* both outsiders" – not '*had* both been outsiders' (ibid., emphasis added). The workings of collective memories as founding *current* identity-constructions is vividly illustrated here.

Lindo's self-perception is that of a victim, yet it is built on a *collective*, not a personal memory. On the same level, he identifies Africans as an equally victimized people, enslaved just as the Israelites in Egypt had been. Indeed, he thus denotes and refers to two immensely established and powerful strands of identity constructions: both the 'Hebrew children' and the

---

and the Middle Passage. During the coffle march, the slave traders keep Aminata from praying properly, thus suppressing her faith: "The next night, after another trashing [because of praying aloud], I gave up the prayers. [...] Praying inside the head was no good. I was worse than a captive. I was becoming an unbeliever." (BN 34) While at first, Aminata's faith does not suffer from her questioning God's very existence but from external repression of the Islamic rituals (also cf. another instance, BN 122), the same sort of subjugation soon makes her ponder questions of theodicy. When Fanta tells her that "Allah doesn't exist" and that instead, "the toubabu are in charge" aboard the slave ship, Aminata begins to doubt her faith: "Perhaps it was true. Maybe Allah lived only in my land, with the homelanders." (BN 86)

At times, Aminata's skepticism is clad in metaphorical terms ("If the sky was so perfect, why was the earth all wrong?", BN 142), at times Aminata explicitly states that she has "not embraced God as might be imagined by a Muslim, Jew or Christian" (BN 233). Particularly in conversations with Blind Daddy Moses, Birchtown's preacher, Aminata's attitude is explicated (e.g. when she tells him after the abduction of May that she "wasn't thirsting for another God in [her] life." (BN 350) Aminata attends the Christian services held by Daddy Moses and largely abstains from the conventions of her original Muslim faith (she drinks alcohol, for instance), but she does not convert to Christianity either; the atrocities she has witnessed do not allow her to overcome the questions of theodicy that she ponders. (Also cf. the brief discussion of theodicy in *The Book of Negroes, Any Known Blood*, and *Beatrice Chancy* on p. 150f. of this thesis.)

'children of Ham', Jews and diasporic Blacks, have long adopted the Exodus as one of their central identity-shaping collective memories. For the African diasporic tradition, the slave narrative vividly illustrates this notion: it has been pointed out numerous times that it is indeed one of the central claims of the slave narrative that the Africans enslaved in the Americas resemble the Israelites in their escape from slavery. Accordingly, Lindo underscores the slave narrative's depiction of the evils of slavery and the hope of deliverance thus propounded. What he fails to notice, however, is the reversal of roles which Aminata immediately recognizes: While assuming that he and Aminata, representing their respective 'people' (memory groups), are on a par in terms of being victimized, he disregards the fact that he has indeed taken on the role of the enslaver, not the enslaved. 'Objectively', the selection process is thus a lopsided one, as the memory chosen does not match the current social situation of Lindo. In memory selection processes, however, the criterion 'objective' is questionable. What we are faced with here, then, is the illustration of the selectivity of collective memories and the notion that collective memories are chosen *a posteriori*, i.e. from a *current* perspective to serve a *present* need. Lindo selects the collective memory (Exodus) that he thinks appropriately characterizes both Jews and Africans, but his choice is based on the urge to be perceived not as a victimizer, but a victim himself.[273] *Vis à vis* Aminata, Lindo foregrounds (i.e. he narrates and thus establishes an identity) the collective memory of being enslaved as part of *his* identity in order to both appear more sympathetic in the eyes of his 'servant' and – it can safely be assumed – in order to more easily come to terms with the fact that he has become a slave master himself (even though he in various ways tries to soften this fact and/or to cover it up; cf. for instance the liberties extended towards his slaves in terms of self-hire, his lenience and his calling them 'servants' instead of slaves).[274]

Aminata instinctively recognizes the attempt by Lindo to construct not only a usable past, but a utilitarian one. She instantly challenges his egalitarian postulations: "The discovery was fascinating, yet confusing. Perhaps Lindo could explain why Christians and Jews kept Muslims as slaves if we all had the same God and if we all celebrated the flight of the He-

---

273 When Aminata learns of Lindo's complicity in the sale of Mamadu, her first-born son, she confronts him with his pretence, saying "Some Hebrew you are. And you say you're not a white man." (BN 227; his claim is repeatedly mentioned, cf. e.g. BN 229.) Lindo's claim not to be White of course indicates that he positions himself as part of a marginalized group, not part of the hegemonic White population (and as such, he considers himself akin to Aminata). Throughout the novel, Hill is particularly concerned with the different kinds of hypocrisy towards slavery. He criticizes the abolitionists' air of superiority, Lindo's hypocritical stance to define himself as suppressed but indeed keeping slaves, and he also criticizes the American Independence movement for its partial blindness to the problem of slavery: "White people in the markets mumbled about being enslaved by the King of England, but I had stopped listening to their complaints. *Liberty to the Americans. Down with slavery.* They weren't talking about the slavery I knew or the liberty I wanted, and it all seemed ludicrous to me." (BN 228, italics in the original)

274 The relabeling of his slaves is a good case in point when it comes to Lindo's need to externally affirm how kind and caring he is towards his 'staff'. He seems to feel an urge to *postulate* what he is doing in order to give it more significance and to construct and present (both processes are interdependent and recursive) a benevolent identity.

brews from Egypt." (BN 205) Hill uses, as he is prone to do, the semi-naïve voice of the young Aminata to offer doubts and to undermine in a slightly ironic way the idiosyncratic claims and strange ways of the adults.[275] By having Aminata innocently ask for further explanation, Hill lets the reader know that Lindo's theories are not as sound as his superior posture would initially suggest. Aminata's request also provides a very real and concrete question, viz. why indeed have Jews and Christians, if they revere the collective memory of the Exodus and have incorporated this experience into their current identity – as Lindo suggests – not learned from this experience, which is undoubtedly anything but forgotten? Aminata thus exposes the tendency of collective memories not to be deterministic, even though they might seem to be; selection and interpretation are, after all, essential processes in the constructions of usable pasts.

Although Lindo has incorporated the victimization of his people into his own identity construction, he does not deduce from this the need to set his slaves free; it suffices to postulate a position sympathetic with his 'servants' in order to arrive at a unified self-perception free from internal contradictions. It could be argued that, in the end, Lindo does indeed realize the illogical conclusion he has drawn based on the proposed likeness of the Jews' and the enslaved Africans' fates.[276] When he finally returns to New York City to manumit Aminata, he does so at great financial expense and risks personal prestige. Yet at this early stage of their relationship, Lindo still upholds the incredulous notion that he is somehow in a position similar to Aminata's, as they are both "outsiders" (BN 209). Aminata immediately sees through Lindo's construction of a victimized (and thus sympathetic and benevolent) self and questions this construction.[277] She exposes Lindo's identity to be built not only on a usable, but a utili-

---

275 A number of examples could be mentioned, such as Aminata's comment on the 'Black Queen Charlotte' that certainly nobody "would let an African become boss woman of the whole land" (BN 194), which has been discussed earlier, or Aminata's surprise when discovering that men could indeed work as hard as women (cf. BN 13).

276 When manumitting Aminata, Lindo claims that he does so to "make peace with [his] past." (BN 310) Aminata, however, is not willing to forget nor to forgive his wrongs. Fully aware of her autonomy and the fact that her freedom and humanity should rightfully never have been subject to anyone else's will, she declares her emancipation and thus her refusal to accept Lindo's apology, even though she does acknowledge the different quality of plantation slavery and servitude in the Lindo household: "I wasn't ready to receive Lindo's sorrow, or to thank him for giving back what had always been mine. I could see that Solomon Lindo was a better class of man than Robinson Appleby. But he was tainted by the very world in which he lived, and from which he too richly profited. I did not want to hate him, but neither could I forget him." (BN 311) What is emphasized in this passage is the fact that even though a 'milder' form of slavery, consisting mostly of household services, has existed, there is a decisive structural similarity between plantation slavery and the more subtle forms of servitude in that both regarded Blacks as property and thus deprived them of their freedom. This aspect of course refers to the character of Solomon Lindo as much as to the historical realities in Canada with its historically more 'subtle' forms of subjugation.

277 Aminata corroborates her critique by contrasting Lindo's socioeconomic position with her own, concluding that even though Lindo, who, in contrast to his 'servants', "wore fine clothes and came and went as he pleased" (BN 210), might not be eligible for the board of the local Library Society, he at least was in a position to visit the library any time he pleased – a privilege not afforded to Blacks (cf. ibid.).

tarian past, probably geared towards a reduction of possible pangs of conscience. The incorporation of the collective memory of the Exodus into Lindo's self-perception is thus imploded. Later on, Aminata also exposes the slave narrative's usage of the Exodus as one of its central images to be equally manipulative; she does so by presenting an alternative version of her (and her people's) story, one that does not conform unquestioningly to the schemata established by the biblical Exodus.

Aminata thus reconfigures the collective memory of the Exodus and applies it to her own life and her own story very much as dystopian writers employ utopian models – to present an alternative version to replace a usage that is perceived to be inaccurate or misleading. Thus, Aminata shows the Africans' exodus to be anything but a parallel to its biblical model: while after their meanderings, the Israelites found their Canaan and successfully finished their trek, Aminata shows that the slave narrative's claim that the Blacks could, and indeed *had* done the same (i.e. completed their exodus North and found freedom and prosperity in the British colonies) must be refuted if any level of veracity should be achieved. She thus re-interprets, i.e. re-constructs the collective memory of the biblical Exodus: instead of being a model that is claimed to be constitutive and fully emulated, it is perceived by Aminata as a foil against which the fate of Africans in North America can be *contrasted*. Hill thus takes up the slave narrative's central image, but reverses it: to him, the Exodus does not signify deliverance for the African slaves, it signifies what they had hoped for – what they had even been promised –, yet it stands for a hope and a promise not fulfilled.[278] If the Exodus should indeed be an experience that unifies the different religions and races, Aminata asks, why do Christians and Jews keep slaves (cf. BN 204f.), and why does Lindo own Aminata herself and even the children of his slaves (cf. BN 209)? Consequently, Hill accords the collective memory of the biblical Exodus a prominent position – as prominent a position as *The Book of Negroes'* generic model, the slave narrative, accords it – yet he deconstructs and reconstructs its meaning for North American Blacks, particularly for those groups represented in his novel, such as the Black Loyalists.

Lindo's discussion of the Exodus, however, is only the beginning of an extensive usage of this collective memory in *The Book of Negroes*. Even while still in Lindo's household – and thus still *de facto* and *de jure* enslaved even though Lindo pretends she is *de jure* a slave but *de facto* a free woman –, Aminata begins to conceive of her own life as an allegory of the biblical escape from slavery. When she is asked to accompany Lindo on a business trip to New York City, she hopes never to return to Charles Town: "I decided to travel with him in the morning. It would be my Exodus." (BN 229) With the expression of this hope, Hill closes "Book Two" of his novel, using Aminata's intent as the starting point of "Book Three", in which she indeed travels North with Lindo – towards what to her still is, but soon ceases to be, the Promised Land.

---

278 Some forty-five years before the publication of *The Book of Negroes* and some two hundred years after its fictional protagonist's abduction, Rev. Martin Luther King would use a similar image in his famous speech in Washington D.C., in which he speaks of a check the African-Americans have come to cash because it has not been redeemed yet (cf. King 1997, 533).

5.3.4. The Canadian perspective: Canaan denied

In 1783, Aminata is asked to work for the British Army – by then preparing to retreat from New York City, their last stronghold south of the 49th parallel separating the two North American countries – by helping to compile the Book of Negroes. This list of Black Loyalists signifies, so Aminata and her fellow Canvas Town residents are promised, their ticket to a life in freedom and equality under the lion's paw of British rule in the North. "Nova Scotia, Miss Diallo, will be your promised land," Aminata is told by a British officer (BN 286). All Blacks registered in the Book of Negroes (an actual historical document that has survived and is available to the public today; cf. Library and Archives Canada, 2009) were guaranteed to be "as free as any [White] Loyalist" (ibid.) in the British colony of Nova Scotia.

The British officers in Canvas Town, representing and advertising the Promised Land in Nova Scotia, already inscribe in the construction of what is termed another 'Exodus' the stark contrast between the United States and Canada. Explaining the geographical location of Nova Scotia, a British colonel explains to Aminata that "Nova Scotia is a British colony, *untouched and unsullied by the Americans*, at a distance of two weeks by ship from the New York harbour." (BN 285; emphasis added) Aminata, however, again using the half-naïve voice often characterizing her when questioning the conceptions she is presented with by Whites, foreshadows the disillusionment that awaits the Black Loyalists: "I hoped it wasn't a penal colony." (ibid.) The officer who initially acquainted Aminata and enlists her for the British, Captain Waters, serves as a close emulation of John Clarkson, the trustworthy abolitionist, in representing the voice of doubt even among the hegemonic power; when he is asked the name of the ledger in which the Black Loyalists are to be entered, he equally suggests that the Blacks' journey might not turn out to be what the Canvas Town residents may hope for. "Waters gave me a dry smile. 'How about [calling the ledger] Exodus from Holy Ground?'" (BN 287)[279] Referring to the most *un*holy place of Canvas Town, the red-light district entitled Holy Ground for its location close to a church yard, Waters makes clear that the Blacks may escape slavery – as they had ostensibly done by coming to Canvas Town, a settlement of Black refugees – but that further dependence and exploitation may lie ahead. Colonel Baker, in contrast, had warned that being in Nova Scotia "will be hard work", but vowed that there "will be plenty for everyone in the vastness of Nova Scotia." (BN 286)

Evidently, the inclusion in an official, written document meant for the (mostly illiterate) Blacks the irrefutable proof that they would indeed find their Canaan in the north. For Aminata, the writing of her name in a New York City hotel register had proven to be the catalyst for her decision to run away from Solomon Lindo, even though her status at the time designated her as 'property' (cf. BN 244). Similarly, the externalization of the captives' names

---

279 Though the British *policy* will be focused on in the following discussion, Hill also clarifies that there was, somewhat analogous to the abolitionists, also a certain amount of personal or individual shortcomings involved on the side of the British military. Aminata, for instance, works as a midwife in Holy Ground, where she assists Black prostitutes giving birth to the illegitimate children of British officers. As she gets paid for this work by the British officers, she becomes known as "one-pound Meena" for her standard rate (BN 277).

onboard the slave ship – in the form of call-and-response chants repeated and remembered by the '*djeli*' Aminata – had held the promise of being saved from anonymity, of being remembered and thus of subjectivity restored. Likewise, it is Aminata's job not only to register the Black Loyalists when they actually present themselves at the registrar; she is also supposed to spread the word of the promise of Nova Scotia among the Canvas Town residents and to collect the names of those willing to go in the first place. Initially, Aminata is excited about her new work. She feels connected to her community and feels she is of service to her fellow prospective Africadians. Hill uses this short phase of happiness (incidentally, her long-lost husband Chekura also turns up and is willing to go to Nova Scotia with Aminata) to once more underline the collective experience Aminata records:[280]

> I felt that I was giving something special to the Negroes seeking asylum in Nova Scotia, and that they were giving something special to me. They were telling me that I was not alone. I had imagined, somehow, that my life was unique in its unexpected migrations. I wasn't different at all, I learned. Each person who stood before me had a story every bit as unbelievable as mine. (BN 291)

Clearly, then, what we are presented with in Aminata's account – and in Hill's novel – is a collective memory rather than merely an individual recollection, as has been variously pointed out before. As Aminata cannot expand her entries in the Book of Negroes beyond the merest basics, she postpones a more detailed report to a later day: "I wanted to write more about them [the Black Loyalists], but the ledger was cramped." (BN 294) The official record, provided and monitored by Whites, allows only for a certain amount of information[281] – a limitation which Aminata remedies by writing her memoirs granting the personality and subjectivity of the Black Loyalists ample space. (Hill indeed includes a number of semi-round characters at every station of Aminata's life, often also interspersing the narration with bits and pieces of romantic and/or other emotional aspects both regarding minor characters and Aminata and her family, thus not reducing his personages to the short physical descriptions of the White hegemonic definition exerted in the Book of Negroes.) Even in the process of registering the potential Africadians, Aminata is fully aware of the ledger's power in terms of genealogical evidence and collective memory in spite of its limitations: "It excited me to imag-

---

280 Of course, in connection with the Book of Negroes in which Aminata makes entries, the meaning of Aminata's recording is always two-fold: she registers the Black Loyalists and their history (though in the very brief way of only a few phrases) in the ledger itself and – by relating this recording in her narrative – to the narratee. The narratee, being deferred by Aminata to a future audience (cf. section "Narrative mode and structure" 79 91ff.), is closely connected to the extraliterary contemporary readership, so that we are presented with a triple recording (the Book of Negroes, Aminata's memoir, and – on an extra-narrative level – *The Book of Negroes*).

281 Decidedly racist information to boot, designating Blacks with phrases such as "*worn out, one-eyed, lusty wench, incurably lame, little fellow, likely boy*", "*squat wench, quadroon*" and the like (BN 295, italics in the original). Also cf. in this regard the discussion Aminata leads with Lindo concerning the usage of the term 'wench', which, incomprehensibly to Aminata, could be attributed to Black women but not to Mrs Lindo (BN 200).

ine that fifty years later, someone might find an ancestor in the Book of Negroes and say, 'That was my grandmother.'" (BN 295)

As a voice both of and for her community, Aminata spreads the word among Canvas Town's population that everyone who had served the British in any conceivable position (under a former proclamation, only those Blacks actually involved in the armed struggle were eligible) for more than one year had basically already earned their freedom – although she herself has her doubts.[282] When she sees the "disconsolate face" of a girl approaching her registrar table, Aminata "could see that nothing about this trip suggested freedom." (BN 293) The history of Black Canadians, as Aminata already suspects, is characterized by a succession of broken promises. Consequently, Hill describes Aminata's first day of recording the names of those ready to leave New York City for Nova Scotia as a thoroughly disillusioning experience:

> A group of ten Negroes was called up to the deck [where Aminata logs the names of those Blacks wishing to sail for Nova Scotia]. I had never seen them before. 'Who are they?' I asked [Captain] Waters. 'Slaves and indentured servants,' he said. 'But I thought...' 'We will get around to evacuating the refugees in Canvas Town,' Waters said. 'But first, we register the property of white Loyalists.' [...] A girl appeared before me. [...] I could see that nothing about this trip suggested freedom. *Hana Palmer*, I wrote, again taking down the colonel's words. *15, stout wench. Ben Palmer of Frog's Neck, Claimant.* 'Claimant?' I asked the colonel when the white man had taken away the girl. 'It means that he owns her,' the colonel said. (BN 293; italics in the original)[283]

In a twist of sardonic irony, Hill has Aminata even record the name of a slave once belonging to Lord Dunmore, the British governor who issued the very declaration promising Blacks freedom if they joined the British ranks. The entry Hill uses is an actual excerpt from the Book of Negroes, where several slaves are listed as (formerly) belonging to Lord Dunmore.[284] "Virginia governor got to have his slaves," Dunmore's blind ex-slave squarely comments (BN 299). Through Aminata's entries in the Book of Negroes, Hill thus discerns the fact that slavery – contrary to popular opinion – indeed existed in Canada. The text also cites advertisements for runaway slaves (slave-owners promised rewards for captured and re-enslaved fugi-

---

282 When told by Colonel Baker that Chekura and herself were already technically free (the Peace Treaty between the British and the Americans explicitly states that no 'Negroes or other property' may be taken by the British – and the British subsequently simply claim that they do not consider Negroes property in the first place), Aminata doubts that reality indeed matches rhetoric in this regard: "That was easy for him to say, since he didn't have to fend off slave catchers in Canvas Town." (BN 285)

283 Note the patronymic name of the slave girl, which is the predominant variation of name changes depicted in the slave narrative, though Hill deviates from this pattern with his protagonist (cf. section "Category two: Content", p. 98ff.).

284 The entry listing Hana Palmer quoted above is likewise an original quote from the historical ledger. It must be emphasized that Hill reprints entries from the Book of Negroes in balanced and truthful proportion, citing more examples of *former* slaves than of actual 'property' instead of hyperbolically presenting entries of *slaves* in Nova Scotia exclusively or as the majority of instances.

tives) and describes raids for these fugitives. These raids, which led to an all-encompassing feeling of insecurity, were executed in order to return fugitive slaves to their owners. Aminata herself, already aboard the ship leaving to Nova Scotia, is called back because Robinson Appleby, her former owner, had filed a claim for her. The British practice of letting slave owners recapture – even judicially reclaim – their (former) property turns out to be one of Aminata's greatest disappointments and disillusionments. Aminata herself is brought before court to face the claim by Appleby, clearly bearing the concrete visual – and today, metaphorical – signs of enslavement under the auspices of the alleged liberators ("I was taken – wrists tied and legs shackled", BN 306). Aminata recapitulates her experience with the British and their promises of liberty and a Black Canaan:

> I despised the Americans for taking the Negroes [they claimed as their property], but my greatest contempt was for the British. They had used us in every way in their war. Cooks. Whores. Midwives. Soldiers. We had given them our food, our beds, our blood and our lives. And when slave owners showed up with their stories and their paperwork, the British turned their backs and allowed us to be seized like chattel. Our humiliation meant nothing to them, nor did our lives. (BN 307)

It is interesting to note that the White narrative is supplemented by official papers here, an indication of a formalized rendering of 'facts'. The British regard the "stories" of their enemies, the Americans, as unquestionably more believable than the ones presented by the Blacks, which consequently "meant nothing to them" (ibid.). This illustrates the fact that White (narrative) constructions and memory versions are hegemonic ones qua *Whiteness* – transcending even the cleavages created by war and lending the representations of wartime enemies more weight than those by Blacks. Aminata summarizes the British policy which so blatantly violates the promises made to the Black Loyalists:

> I came to understand that if you had come to Nova Scotia free, you stayed free – although that didn't prevent American slave owners from sailing into town and attempting to snatch back their property. However, if you came to Nova Scotia as a slave, you were bound as fast as our brothers and sisters in the United States. (BN 321)

The first crucial revision of hegemonic collective memory constructions in *The Book of Negroes* is thus: slavery existed in Canada as well as in the United States. Canadian slavery certainly remained *comparatively* small-scale in terms of numbers, economic and social enmeshment (particularly due, of course, to the absence of an extensive plantation economy in Canada).[285] Yet there is a certain percentage of slaves among the Black Canadian population, a fact both revealed by the – largely ignored – historical record and depicted in the fictional autobiography of Aminata Diallo. What Hill is clearly achieving in his rendering is to "exca-

---

285 In her compelling reasoning (posing as semi-naïvety), the young Aminata had very early on questioned the economic motives of the Atlantic slave trade, ostentatiously unaware of the will to exploit others (or rather: the Other) in order to ensure one's own superior wealth: "It struck me as unbelievable that the toubabu would go to all this trouble to make us work in their land. [...] Surely they could gather their own mangoes and pound their own millet." (BN 62)

vate and dramatize aspects of Canadian history that are little known, undervalued, misunderstood or forgotten" (Hill, Appendix 292).

In this venture, as numerous examples show, Hill's approach is scrupulously differentiated in order to conform to (his reading of) historical research, so that a multitude of angles and perspectives are covered.[286] As Aminata observes in her summary quoted above, there are indeed also those Blacks for whom the promised land actually meant freedom. Freedom, it turns out, however, that was dearly paid for – and attained only by a small fraction of the Black population in any exhaustive way. Even for those Blacks who had come as free/d people and managed to evade capture, Nova Scotia turned out to be anything but the Canaan they had hoped for. First of all, due to the economic dependence of Blacks on the White population, the institution of indentured labor constituted a prolongation of slavery under only marginally better terms. Aminata, discussing the difference between slavery and indenture with a British officer, resolves: "After such a long journey to freedom, I couldn't imagine agreeing to that [indenture]" (BN 295), yet many of her fellow exiles hardly had a choice: "A woman [...] found herself so hungry and cold that she placed her x mark on indenture papers" (BN 324). And for those Blacks who, like Aminata, avoided both (re-)enslavement and indenture, Nova Scotia did not materialize as the land of milk and honey ("plenty for everyone", BN 286) they had been led to anticipate either.

Just as Queen Charlotte's African roots have come under erasure (or so Aminata's account suggests) and just as the slaves' original names, including Aminata's in *The Book of Negroes*, have been either exterminated or distorted, Aminata's self and subjectivity comes under erasure once more even *after* her escape into the alleged Promised Land that, to her, was to be Canada. When Aminata arrives in Canada, it is near Shelburne, Nova Scotia (which in itself constitutes the first broken promise and/or misnomer, as the former slaves "had been told [they] were sailing to Port Roseway", Shelburne's more poetic former name; BN 312; also cf. BN 314). The reception could not be any chillier, as Aminata recalls, again employing strongly tactile descriptions which underline the climatic cold, yet which even more so emphasize the whiteness (viz. Whiteness) and tangibly cool, denying character of the Black Loyalists' new home: "Sailing into the port at the end of a nine-mile bay, I felt the snow on my face and a film of ice gathering above my lips, and I saw the granite spilling onto the shores." (BN 312)[287] Making a brief reference to King George III, after whom Aminata's ship is named, conjures up the Black Queen Charlotte Sophia once more (when Aminata sailed from

---

286 Examples range from the presentation of *wolosow* and African compliance with European slave traders through the discussion of a possible 'White man's burden' in Africa which Aminata leads with Mr and Mrs Falconbridge to the depiction of the intermittent (racial) hypocrisy of otherwise venerable abolitionists.

287 Before leaving for Nova Scotia, Aminata had hoped for Canada's mild climate – a hope that was quite clearly prone to be disappointed ("Huddling together under a freezing rain [in New York City], we hoped that Annapolis Royal would offer gentler winters than the biting cold and snow of Manhattan." BN 302) There is of course an almost self-evident metaphorical aspect to this description, which emphasizes the hope for a warmer, milder welcome than the Black Loyalists would in fact receive.

the slave-ridden south to the north of the US, her ship was tellingly called "Queen Charlotte", cf. BN 240), whose Blackness was rendered invisible. Aminata's first experiences in her new homeland are, accordingly, feelings not only of chill up to the point of voicelessness ("ice gathering above my lips", cf. above) but of invisibility as well:[288]

> ... I saw no familiar faces. Most of the people were white, and they walked past as if I didn't exist. A white woman in a cap and a long coat approached me on Water Street. 'Is this Port Roseway?' I asked. She walked right by without stopping to look at me. (BN 313)

Aminata is quick to discover that her invisibility, however, does plainly not imply equality. She does not fit in. This is an experience she had made in Charles Town before, when she was brought there by Solomon Lindo. Experiencing a *déjà vu* of her own slave auction there, she resolves that although nobody stares at her, it is this very ignorance that marks her as inferior – even though she is told she is a 'servant' now, not a 'slave': "That, I decided, was what it meant to be a slave: your past didn't matter; in the present you were invisible and you had no claim on the future." (BN 189) In this, she is at once invisible and hypervisible, ignored but sticking out, irrelevant and a slave. Even the man who had originally sold her to Robinson Appleby, the slave trader William King, "glanced at [Aminata] but looked right past [her]." (BN 195) In Nova Scotia, allegedly beyond even the status of 'servant', she is refused service in a coffee house ("We don't serve niggers", BN 313), pelted with nuts, and spat at. "Birchtown is the place for your kind", she is told (ibid.). Segregation and racial hostility turn out to be the bottom line of the Black Loyalists' history.

In terms of collective traumatizing events, the disillusionment that a vast majority of Black Loyalists experienced has left obvious scars that still reverberate in contemporary African-Canadian literature. In general, this aspect of the Black presence is the most distinctly *Canadian* one – in tandem with the sheer denial of the existence of slavery and (historical as well as contemporary) racism. Slavery, indenture, racism, and segregation all existed in the United States, and most of the time more harshly so than in Canada. But Canadian Blacks *expected otherwise*. They had been promised a refuge but got only a continuation of their suffering and hardships on a lesser scale.[289] In Birchtown, the segregated Black community halfway between Yarmouth and Annapolis Royal, Nova Scotia, Aminata lives among the disappointed and disgruntled Black Loyalists waiting for the land allocations promised by the British.

---

288 Cf. on the invisibility of the visible (Black) minority both in American literature as well as in "Canadian public affairs" Clarke 2002a, 34f. The invisibility motif is, of course, a pivotal African-American one; cf. centrally Ellison's 1952 *Invisible Man* (1995b) and its reception: primarily the essays in Posnock 2006 and Callahan 2004; the essays in O'Meally 1988 for introductory purposes; Mellard 2006 (chapter 3) for a contemporary psychoanalytical approach.

289 Disillusionment is one of the most pervasive overall themes in African-Canadian literature. It has been explored from the onset of the Black Canadian literary landscape in the 1960s (by Austin Clarke, cf. Nurse 2006a, XIV f.) and is applied to historical as well as to contemporary issues (cf. ibid.). For a concise but instructive survey of the African-Canadian literary field, cf. Lutz 2005, 313-319.

> Nova Scotia had more land than God could sneeze at, [the blind and paralyzed pastor] Daddy
> Moses said, but hardly any of it was being parcelled out at black folk. 'But the British said
> we could have land,' I said. 'Get good and comfortable at the back of the line,' he said.
> 'There are a thousand coloured folks waiting before you. And, ahead of them, a few thou-
> sand white people. They call this place Nova Scotia, but folks in Birchtown have another
> name for it.' 'What's that?' I asked. 'Nova Scarcity.' I thought of Chekura warning me to be
> realistic about the promised land. (BN 316f.) [290]

As the ironic usage of the name "Moses" suggests, the Black exodus to Nova Scotia has thus
turned out to be a continuation of the structural racism experienced by Blacks in the United
States. The scale or force of traumatic experiences has been reduced, yet their underlying factors, such as assumptions of racial superiority, persist. Those African-Canadians who were
granted freedom – and thus, at least superficially, humanity and the status of subject, not
commodity – still remain second-class citizens as well as second-class humans. [291] There is an
image which illustrates this distinction between overt slavery and more subtle Canadian racism in a semi-tongue-in-cheek, semi-bitter way: aboard the slave ship, *en route* to South Carolina, Aminata describes the slave ship as a lion and perceives the Africans' descent below
deck "as if we were being taken straight into [the lion's] anus." (BN 63) In Nova Scotia, the
Blacks' segregated, ramshackle settlement of Birchtown lies, according to Daddy Moses, "in
the *dog's ass* of the harbour." (BN 316, emphasis added) As the slightly gritty imagery suggests, the level of suppression and exploitation may have changed, but the overall wretched-
ness remains.

Formally free, Aminata discovers that the Canaan she was promised offers more
harshness than she could have expected even in her most skeptical moments: "I had less food
and fewer comforts than at any other time in my life. But I was in Nova Scotia and I was
free." (BN 321) While Hill also emphasizes that, personally, Aminata is indeed granted freedom, Nova Scotia is a home which deals out "a flogging here for dancing a Negro frolick, a
lashing there for drunkenness", where "crowds formed to cheer and throw peanuts as [a]
man's back was whipped to all corruption." (BN 323) Against all promises, runaway slaves
are sought out and returned to their owners just as in Canvas Town, and a Black woman is
hanged for mere stealing (cf. ibid.). Yet there is solidarity, too, in Birchtown, as Aminata recalls, as well as "music and laughter in our churches" (BN 324f.). Birchtown is not a settlement without its sins and vices, either (cf. e.g. BN 325). The (recent) Africadians are thus not
completely victimized, yet the bottom line is still personified by handicapped Daddy Moses:

---

290 If land plots were allotted to Blacks at all, they were indeed second-rate or worse. Boyko summarizes: "Freed slaves fared little better than those still in bondage. [...] Whites were afforded land
grants of fifteen to 150 acres and given their choice of location. Freed Blacks were given an average of less than twenty acres and were assigned land that was nearly all rocky, swampy or far
from fresh water." (Boyko 1998, 159)

291 This treatment of the newly-arrived Black Loyalists is well-documented, but habitually overpow-
ered by the positive images produced and established in the context of the Underground Railroad
and the assumption that Blacks were of course given their promised share; cf. e.g. the seminal
works of Winks (1997) and Walker (1982) and particularly Walker's *The Black Loyalists* (1992).

when Aminata comes to him for assistance in the birth of her second baby, she finds him alone, helpless and "vulnerable at home" (BN 327) – a stark contrast to his usual rhetoric, which is intended to lift the spirits of his parishioners:

> In church, the man was so vivid and alive that people could not contain themselves when he thumped the pulpit and cried about Moses taking the Hebrews to freedom. *They were chosen to settle in Palestine, and we too are the chosen people. We too, brothers and sisters, are chosen for freedom, right here in Birchtown.'* (BN 327)

For all its biblical rhetoric – and for the intertextual reference to Langston Hughes's "I, Too", which embodies a similar spirit, but must be read in conjunction with his poem "Harlem" in order to relate to the early Africadians' situation as well[292] –, it is obvious that Blind Daddy Moses literally cannot see the truth. True freedom is still a long way coming in Nova Scotia's Black community. An economic recession subsequently even increases the violence against the Black minority. Aminata, accompanied by her daughter May, witnesses the murder of a Black boy by a mob of Whites which, after killing another Black man, proceeds to raid Birchtown, tearing down a number of shacks and burning others.[293] The Black population in Nova Scotia is blatantly deprived of their full freedom and their security. In addition to the more subtle racism that is expressed in segregation, the asymmetrical allocation of land, and the lack of educational opportunities, violence also dominates the Black Loyalists' reality in

---

292 It goes almost without saying that African-Canadian literature has taken up many motifs, images and metaphors from African-American literature – both out of an intertextual impulse and out of a shared collective experience. The mood of "Harlem" ("What happens to a dream deferred?", Hughes 1958), so intensely reproduced in Loraine Hansberry's *Raisin in the Sun* (which, fittingly, is prefaced by Hughes's poem), is a central element of both Black North American literatures. It must be emphasized, however, that despite the various deferrals in *The Book of Negroes* (e.g. the broken promises of freedom and equality in Nova Scotia, the unfulfilled dream of a self-governing Black colony in Sierra Leone, Aminata's dream of returning to her native village of Bayo), the final line of "Harlem" with its threatening undertone ("Or does it explode?", Hughes 1958) is hardly reflected in Hill's novel, which offers a more conciliatory – though by no means merely appeasing – tenor.

Another, albeit possibly coincidental, intertextual reference to Langston Hughes (who is also in all likelihood the namesake of Hill's line of protagonists in *Any Known Blood*) can be found in the novel's title, which does not only echo the historical ledger it is so crucially concerned with, but also Hughes's *The First Book of Negroes* (1952), the first volume in a series of five educational books written for a young audience.

293 The 1787 Shelburne race riots are historically recorded, as is the murder of Ben Henson, whose death is described as the day's second killing (cf. BN 338ff.). In regard to the underlying economic tensions, Hill has remarked that of course, the economic desperation of Whites did play a role in their violence, but that there was no justification of race violence inherent in that fact. "I observe in both novels [*Any Known Blood* and *The Book of Negroes*] that racial hatred can arise in the context of economic insecurity, but the latter does not justify the former. Often, groups that feel most threatened economically are the ones who rise up against their perceived competitors. In Loyalist Nova Scotia, black settlers faced the violent anger of unemployed or underemployed White former soldiers who believed that Blacks were undercutting their salaries." (Hill, Appendix 295)

Nova Scotia: "on this day [Aminata] saw only one Negro [on her way], and he was dead – hanging from a tree to the side of the path." (BN 341)

The insecurity that pervades the Africadians' situation is reflected in the abduction of Aminata's own daughter May, who is kidnapped and taken to Boston by Aminata's White employers. When Aminata finds out about May's abduction, she asks a witness, "Did my daughter go on that ship?" (BN 347), which of course provides a clear parallel to Aminata's own experience of enslavement and the Middle Passage, thus underlining the persistence of underlying power structures and overt abuses. When her own child is seized, Aminata's feelings in fact mirror those of Fanta aboard the slave vessel: "I feared that if I expressed my feelings, so much pain would erupt from within that I'd lash out and kill somebody." (BN 349) The traumatic experience of losing her daughter brings Aminata close to caving in, and "the pain of my losses never really went away. The limbs had been severed, and they would forever after be missing. But I kept going. Somehow, I just kept going." (BN 352)[294] In the light of Aminata's traumatic experiences in Nova Scotia and given the fact that the Black population lives not only in (economic) dependence and segregation, but in fear for their lives as well as in fear of recapture, the Black Loyalists' self-identification with the Exodus of the biblical Israelites from Egypt seems quite ironic, as their exodus has yielded anything but a Canaan. Any allusion to the Promised Land turns out to be an empty one. In view of the stark contrast between the promises made by the British (promises which are, it has to be added, eagerly absorbed by the vast majority of Blacks Loyalists) and the actual situation in Nova Scotia, blind Daddy Moses' words that "*We too, brothers and sisters, are chosen for freedom, right here in Birchtown*" (BN 327; italics in the original) seem almost cynical.

Clearly, *The Book of Negroes* thus presents a picture of the exodus of Blacks to Canada in terms of a Canaan *not* secured, accordingly contradicting common notions of Canada's paradisiacal character regarding its Black minority and of Canadian moral superiority *vis à vis* the slave-ridden United States. Hill seems to discern a need to correct the lopsided perception of Canadian history and constructions of national identity derived from the unbalanced composition of mainstream collective memory – in unison so with a large number of African-Canadian writers. The question Aminata asks herself, "Was this the promised land?", turns out to be a rhetorical one for her as well as for her community both past and present.

---

294 Severed limbs and the ensuing phantom pain are a recurrent image for the loss of Aminata's family, e.g. BN 2, 331.

6. Any Known Blood: 1828-1995

He said he wrote it. He said it would explain some things. He said that I should preserve it, and share it with those who might want to preserve his record of things past. (Any Known Blood, 423)

Any Known Blood rewrites Canada's history [...]. In Any Known Blood remembering is not merely nostalgic as official multiculturalism would have it be. Remembering is the active process of making present the gaps and silences in official histories of the nation. (Walcott 2003, 68)

6.1. Preliminaries

6.1.1. Structure and paratextual additions

Any Known Blood (1997, abbreviated AKB) is Lawrence Hill's second novel and tells the story of five generations of Langston Canes, a genealogy that runs from Langston Cane the First, a Black American slave, through Langston Cane the Fifth, an African-Canadian, mixed-race ex-speechwriter who is researching the family history and writing the story we are presented with. The novel is, as has been pointed out before, highly autobiographical. In the acknowledgments, Hill unostentatiously explains: "My family history inspired much of his novel." (AKB 507) He goes on to thank individual family members for their assistance in compiling, very much like the novel's narrator(-cum-writer), the family history. In a brief appendix called "A Word About History",[295] Hill also points to his ambition to truthfully represent his

---

295 Cf. here a comparable paratextual addition in *The Book of Negroes* and its discussion in section 4.2. ("Hill's Faction and Historiographic Metafiction") of this thesis. In the addendum to *Any Known Blood*, Hill at length discloses the material he has consulted, down to the information on rats which he includes in his narrative (Langston the First turns into a veritable rat-catcher in Oakville, hence expounding on the topic of rodents).

understanding of the historical aspects of his novel – even though he is, unsurprisingly, keenly aware of the prevalent fictionality of his work (cf. AKB 507). "I have attempted to provide a generally faithful reckoning of [John] Brown and [Frederick] Douglass", Hill states (AKB 511f.), adding those instances where he has taken dialogue or quotations from historical personages' actual words and pointing out those instances where he has clearly invented or added major aspects. Hill also explicates other historical role models and the extent to which he has reproduced them in either unaltered or modified ways. Another paratextual addition is provided by the prefixed family tree which handily lists Langston the Fifth's paternal lineage from Langston Cane the First's birth in 1828 to the present (the story is set in 1995).[296]

As in *The Book of Negroes*, Hill employs a writer-cum-narrator who presents both a frame narrative and several embedded narratives representing different time levels. These layers, though generally going backwards chronologically, are not as strictly arranged as in Aminata's account; while Aminata's story is told *ex post* in a strictly chronological arrangement with interspersed frame narrative sequences, using first-person narration and focalization through Aminata throughout, *Any Known Blood* is slightly more complex in narratological terms. As we will see, Langston the Fifth is not the only first-person narrative voice: chapter 22 of the novel (unlike in *The Book of Negroes*, there are no chapter headings in *Any Known Blood*) presents an embedded (Neo-) slave narrative, which is told from the first-person perspective of Langston the First because it is a fictional 'reprint' of his memoirs by his great-great-grandson Langston the Fifth, who had recovered the document at a museum. As will be discussed in detail later on, Hill uses a number of techniques to bestow fluency and coherence on the transitions between the frame narrative and the embedded narratives, yet he often leaves the reader puzzled for some time about which of the possible five Langstons he or she is currently facing – a modus operandi which underlines from the very beginning the interconnectedness and genealogical 'pooling' of memories shared by the Cane family members.

The *very* beginning, in fact, underlines, as has been pointed out by virtually every review and scholarly discussion, both the significance of the novel's title and the protagonist's/protagonists' name/s.[297] Hill uses two epigraphs; the first one, by Nobel laureate Gunnar Myrdal, explicates the 'one-drop rule' according to which "a known trace of Negro blood" will 'spoil' the Whiteness of a person and will thus prevent "entrance to the white race." (AKB ix)[298] The second epigraph, drawn from a poem by Langston Hughes, takes up the

---

296 Another addition, the reprint of an historical map of 1835 Oakville, Ontario, seems quite superfluous in contrast (AKB xi), as it does not foster the reader's understanding in any major way.

297 Cf. for instance the sound article by Siemerling (2004, 33f.), Walcott's opinioned essay in *Black Like Who?* (2003, 67; the chapter "Desiring to Belong?" has previously been published as Walcott 1999), Nurse's *Globe and Mail* review (2003, 173f.) or the dissertation by Nadine Flagel (2005, 279).

298 In full, the epigraph reads: "Everybody having a known trace of Negro blood in his veins – no matter how far back it was acquired – is classified as a Negro. No amount of white ancestry, except one hundred percent, will permit entrance to the white race." (AKB ix)

theme of mixed-race identities, though postulating a more complex and ambivalent identification that emphasizes displacement and a lack of belonging: "I wonder where I'm gonna die, /
Being neither white nor black?" (ibid.) The poet's name, of course, is a namesake one for
Hill's protagonists, whose last name celebrates the "signature novel of the Harlem Renaissance" (Clarke 2002a, 311), Jean Toomer's *Cane* (1993, originally published in 1923).

A prologue then takes up the issue of interracial (sexual) relationships – which of
course is most obviously the biological basis for any ensuing mixed-race offspring – and sets
the tone for the novel in general: in the midst of love-making, an unidentified interracial couple is assaulted by racial slurs and a rock hurled through a window. The underlying notion of
the contrast between a deracialized love ("they noticed that the shadows revealed nothing of
her whiteness, or his blackness", xiv) and the pervasiveness of racialization based on skin
color in being targeted by racists (or, more abstractly, by rac*ism* as a type of structural or cultural violence; cf. Galtung 1996) is a determinant in the discussion of 'race' as a concept in
Any Known Blood. More precisely, the negotiations of race that take place in the novel follow
what Hill has subsequently put forward in *Black Berry, Sweet Juice* (2001; abbreviated BBSJ)
as well: race might be a socially constructed concept, and it might or might not be absent from
the conscious self-conception of a person, but it will *not* be absent from *social* perception.

As will be further discussed, Langston the Fourth and his wife Dorothy are a case in
point and an illuminating example: while they themselves deal admirably (in a positively
nonchalant but still highly conscious manner) with their interracial relationship, in public they
prove to be head-turners at best, victims of overt discrimination at worst. The novel's prologue, though not identifying any of the novel's characters, thus exemplifies the underlying
difficulties of claiming race – and the impossibility of *not* claiming a 'non-default' race if
your skin tone does not permit you to do so; only Whiteness is considered an absence of race

It might be added that in the quotation's original context, Myrdal in fact places an additional emphasis on the heteronomous identification of Blackness, beginning Chapter 5 of *The American Dilemma*, "Race and Ancestry", from which the epigraph is taken, with the following passage: "The
'Negro race' is defined in America by the white people. It is defined in terms of parentage. Everybody having a *known* trace of Negro blood in his veins [...]." (1996 [1944], 113) The emphasis
on *known* (which in the epigraph to *Any Known Blood* is not reproduced) underlines the importance of the chapter's first sentence: while a "trace of Negro blood" alone would not necessarily define one's race as 'Black', any *known* trace actually would; *known*, that is, by the ones actively defining: "the white people" (ibid.). Hill of course incorporates the issue of self- vs. heteronomous definitions of race as a salient topic in *Any Known Blood* as well as, extensively so, in
the non-fictional *Black Berry, Sweet Juice*.

Within the novel proper, Hill employs the term "any known blood" twice. In an article published
in the *Toronto Times*, which is taken as satire by everyone but the author himself, the Cameroonian Yoyo discusses current fluctuations and trends in race terminology, arguing that "*Colored
people* used to be a term sympathetic to people of Any Known Blood, but no longer." (AKB 258;
capitals and italics in the original) During the Klan raid on the home of Langston the Fourth, his
mother-in-law refuses to leave the house, arguing that the Klan is "looking for any known blood
they can find." (AKB 317) The term "any known blood" thus designates people falling under the
one-drop-rule; in both instances, the term is used in a context that signifies heteronomous identification.

(cf. Wang 2006 on White as the "default race" in North America). Hill demonstrates the pervasiveness of this notion when he has Langston the Fifth 'feel White' during a trip to Mali[299] and at an all-Black church;[300] also cf. the discussion between one of Langston V's acquaintances, the Cameroonian Yoyo, and a Nation of Islam member at a party (cf. AKB 243ff.). When Yoyo is detained by a police officer for working illegally at a local bakery, the owner tells Langston V: "We had a[n illegal] Russian woman working for us for three years, we never had any trouble. But it's too risky, when you're black, and when you're illegal." (AKB 230) Visibility thus sets the limits of racial self-assignation: while Langston the Fifth, like Mahatma Grafton in *Some Great Thing*, deliberately plays with his identification by others, passing for all sorts of nationalities, neither passes for White except (unintentionally so) in all-Black and/or African contexts. Race, as socially constructed as it may be, is essential in that it is inescapable (as either 'default' or 'non-default'); it *is* about skin color in the end. Discrimination, racial profiling, racially motivated assaults etc. may be based, ideologically, on a social conception, but they are still dispersed and carried out on the basis of outward appearance.

---

299 Again, a highly autobiographical passage: "Suddenly, I heard the girl say *toubab*, the word for white man, which was the way Malians described me, although they knew I wasn't really white, or not entirely so." (AKB 201) Hill writes about this experience in *Black Berry, Sweet Juice* when he recounts being considered a *toubab*, a White person, in Niger (cf. BBSJ 63ff.). Also cf. *The Book of Negroes*, where Aminata is considered a *toubab* "with black face" in Sierra Leone based not on skin color but on acculturation (BN 375ff.; 394). Mixed-race Mahatma Grafton, in *Some Great Thing*, shares Langston's experience when he is told in Cameroon that he certainly has "an odd pigmentation" (SGT 211). Note how Hill covers various West African countries both biographically (he has worked for an international non-governmental organization in Niger) and fictionally (Aminata in Sierra Leone; Mahatma in Cameroon; Langston the Fifth in Mali).

300 "I was glad that my hair was longer than usual, and combed out into an afro, because I didn't want to be seen as a white visitor. I wanted my race clearly marked." (AKB 119) The insecurity exhibited by Langston at A.M.E. Bethel is repeatedly taken up later on, focusing on Langston's experiences in Baltimore. When addressed as an 'African' ("We're all Africans, aren't we? Aren't we, brother?" AKB 120f.), Langston for instance identifies himself as one of the "half brothers"; similarly, he rejects the label of "octoroon" (AKB 94) but is made keenly aware of his mixed-race status by the remark. Siemerling's assessment that Langston the Fourth travels north "into politeness and ambiguity, [but] his son's trip south moves into disambiguation" (2004, 37) hence does not account for the heightened level of ambiguity which runs parallel to the heightened sense of racial awareness Langston the Fifth develops in the US. Cuder-Domínguez equally argues that in the US, Langston's racial identity is cured and disambiguated: "Moreover, it is in US territory that the answers lie; it is there that the fractured African Canadian self can heal and be reconstructed." (2003, 61) This view, again suggesting African-*Américanité* as a ready cure for an ailing African-*Canadianité*, disregards the fact that Langston does not find definite answers in the US either; it also neglects the notion that he does not go to Baltimore without being pre-equipped with (his father's as well as his old friend Aberdeen's) orature. He does not return to Canada "reconstructed", but enriched, having added further aspects to his still-"fractured self". While Langston's story is written in the US, it is brought 'home' to Canada in the end (in fact, Cuder-Domínguez states as much when noting that at story's end, Langston brings "the many trends of his mixed origins and identity" home; 2003, 61).

6.1.2. Plot synopsis

> Any Known Blood *is a serious recounting of black Canadian*
> *history that has been largely absent from imaginative writing*
> *by black Canadians.* (Walcott 2003, 68)

Any Known Blood presents the reader with a family novel written by Langston Cane the Fifth
in 1995. The story covers his paternal forebears of the preceding four generations and thus
chronologically begins with Langston the First (though the structure of the novel itself applies
a mostly inverted sequence), an American slave who flees from Maryland to Oakville, Ontario, via the Underground Railroad. A part of his journey consists of a passage over Lake Ontario onboard a schooner owned by Captain Robert Wilson (who is modeled on a historical figure, cf. Winks 1997, 245) in 1850. Marrying the ship's hand Mattie, Langston Cane the First
fathers three sons, among them Langston the Second.[301] Langston the First makes a decent
living working odd jobs in Oakville and becoming an expert rat catcher. He is, however (as
we learn late into the novel from a document saved and passed on by Langston Cane the Second) accused of bigamy and decides to join John Brown in his raid on Harpers Ferry, a US
armory, in 1859. Langston the Second, the story holds, had acquainted John Brown – and,
incidentally, Frederick Douglass, who also makes an intertextual appearance via his narrative
in *The Book of Negroes* – at Captain Wilson's home. John Brown's raid is supposed to instigate a nationwide slave revolt but fails. Langston the First manages to escape and subsequently writes the short memoirs which are eventually recovered and 'reprinted' by Langston the
Fifth in his novel (these memoirs are, like Langston Cane the First's involvement in the raid
on Harpers Ferry, inspired by an actual account by a Black Canadian participant in the raid
named Osborne Anderson).[302]

---

301 Langston the First starts the tradition of homonymic Langston Canes with a smirk: When Captain
Wilson asks him, "'What did you say your name was, again?' [he answers:] 'Cane. Langston the
First.' 'The First? Meaning?' 'Meaning that there will be a second. After I get to know Mattie better.'" AKB 454) In fact, Langston the First hyperbolically even names *each one* of his three sons
Langston Cane: Langston Senior, Langston Junior and Langston the Second. (Siemerling only
slightly simplifies this naming when he claims that Langston the First "has fathered, at this point
in the novel, not one but three Langston Canes II"; 2004, 40.)

302 Flagel deals at length with what she identifies as 'intertexts' for *Any Known Blood* and claims that
the novel's "relationship with contemporary memoirs and its evocations and revisions of Alex
Haley's *Roots* and Osborne Anderson's narrative have gone unnoticed until now." (2005, 291)
This, however, is not the case. First of all, Hill himself explains his indebtedness to Osborne Anderson's account and explicitly calls Anderson's *A Voice From Harper's Ferry* the "most important of all" his sources on the raid (AKB 508; Anderson's account is also mentioned in *Some
Great Thing*, where he figures among the Black Canadians on whom Mahatma Grafton's father
Ben has collected documentation; cf. SGT 58f.). Lawrence Hill's father, Daniel G. Hill, wrote
about Osborne Anderson in *The Freedom-Seekers* (1981, cf. 214). Furthermore, Siemerling 2004
also comments on Anderson's model (even quoting W.E.B. DuBois on Anderson and G. E.
Clarke on the literary quality of the novel's embedded slave narrative in the process). In fact,

Langston Cane the Second is adopted by a White abolitionist, Nathan Shoemaker, through whose journal we learn that Langston the Second, too, is acquainted with Frederick Douglass – who in turn confirms to him the participation of Langston the First in John Brown's attack. Langston the Second studies at Storer College and moves on to become an African Methodist Episcopal (A.M.E.) Church minister in Baltimore, where his mother had taken the three sons of Langston the First after his disappearance and shortly before she herself dies and Langston the Second's brothers are kidnapped into neo-slavery. In narrative terms, Langston the Second remains the novel's most neglected Langston Cane. He does, however, father nine children, among them Langston the Third, and provides a 'bridge' between the immensely interesting and well-rounded characters Langston Cane I and III. Langston the Second himself writes a brief memoir of about six pages and, importantly, is visited by his father (who was presumed dead) and handed the ex-slave's autobiography, which Langston the Second later passes on to a museum. There, Langston the Fifth ultimately discovers the memoirs and subsequently uses them in his novel; they thus feature as an embedded (Neo-) slave narrative[303] in Hill's *Any Known Blood*.

Langston Cane the Third is dealt with extensively, particularly (because of) his intricate love and marital life, the two of which do not always correspond – an inclination which links him to both his grandfather and his grandson (Langston I and V). Langston III joins a segregated army battalion in 1917 and is sent to fight in Europe a year later; his battalion is among the last to be pulled from Europe after the end of World War I. Langston's relation to his wife Rose and her family – who dislikes him on grounds of his not being a Catholic and his being too Black and too poor for their taste – offers a human interest aspect; Rose's serious illness provides additional suspense in this regard. Langston the Third moves back to Oakville with his family, where he is offered a well-paid position as a minister. It is in Oakville that he becomes the victim of a Ku Klux Klan raid aimed at an interracial couple he shelters in his home. During the Great Depression, his parish dwindles and Langston the Third is forced to relocate back to Baltimore, where Langston the Fourth grows up.

Langston Cane the Fourth, loosely modeled on Lawrence Hill's father, Daniel G. Hill,[304] is a highly educated, though often snobbish and stubborn doctor who moved to Canada

---

Siemerling closes his article by commenting on the notion that Hill, by using Anderson's account, asserts the Canadian perspective on the Harpers Ferry raid. Flagel, in turn, repeatedly cites Siemerling on other issues but does not credit him with 'noticing' *Any Known Blood's* "evocations and revisions of [...] Anderson's narrative" (cf. above). G. E. Clarke, incidentally, mentions Anderson's writing as an example of early Black Canadian autobiography (2002a, 328) and points out its "sympathetic account" of the Harpers Ferry raid. For easy-to-digest information on John Brown, the Harpers Ferry raid and Osborne Anderson, cf. Horton 2005, 76-89. Peterson 2004 is more thorough, though at times laborious.

303 Langston the First's memoir of course is, within Hill's novel, presented as a slave narrative proper. The fact that it is an invention of Hill's, however, classifies it as a Neo-slave narrative.

304 Winfried Siemerling has remarked on the differential numbering of Canes and Hills; novelist Lawrence Hill has had to add, with Langston the First, one generation of Canes to the mould provided by his own family for various reasons (cf. 2004, 47n12).

in order to study medicine. He had served in the US Army in World War II, where Blacks had been treated in a way that "was enough to make any black soldier hate America, [so he] left the United States and came to study at the University of Toronto." (AKB 62; also cf. Siemerling 2004, 36) In Canada, Langston the Fourth meets his future wife Dorothy, a White sociology student from Winnipeg, and becomes a vocal and well-known civil rights activist. Langston IV for years suspends communication with his sister Mill(icent), who was born, three years before him, in 1920. As we learn at a late point in the novel, Langston still sends Mill, who has remained in Baltimore, checks, but both have discontinued any personal contact, primarily because Mill is ashamed for having been a prostitute and because she objects to Langston the Fourth's interracial marriage.[305]

Successful and reputable, Langston Cane the Fourth has two sons: Sean, a lawyer, is two years younger than Langston, but eminently more successful. Langston the Fifth, recently divorced, is a speech writer at a provincial ministry; at least he is so to the day he tampers with a minister's speech so that a secret plan to cut funds for human rights issues is leaked. Langston V, who is of mixed race to a degree that he can pass, at will, for a number of different nationalities, is fired from his job and decides to go to Baltimore to research his family history, a task he had meant to give a try for years but lacked the vim to actually tackle. In Baltimore, he contacts his aunt Mill(icent) and slowly but steadily compiles the pieces that make up his family's portrait over the last 167 years, beginning with the birth of Langston the First in 1828 and ending – for the time being – with his assemblage of the family (hi)story in 1995. Needless to say that the frame narrative involving Langston the Fifth constitutes a major part of the novel's composition. Along the way of searching for the puzzle pieces of genealogical history that are waiting for him to be found and assembled, Langston the Fifth also tells the story of his own life, which, combined with the stories of his ancestors, then makes up the novel that we are presented with in Hill's *Any Known Blood*.[306]

---

305 In the course of the KKK incident in Oakville, Mill had lost her beloved caretaker Ab(erdeen) Williams, who, scared by the Klansmen's threats, leaves Oakville to live with his White girl-friend. This incident plants in her a deep-seated aversion to interracial relationships; instead of blaming the Klansmen for Ab's flight, it is the fact that Aberdeen had chosen a White girl (or vice versa) that she considers the core issue. It is only towards the very ending of Langston's narrative that Mill overcomes her anxieties; as Rinaldo Walcott summarizes: Mill's resistance against "her bother's [sic] marriage is founded in a traumatic experience which she will eventually work through and recover from." (2003, 69)

306 Pilar Cuder-Domínguez argues that in Brand's *At the Full and Change of the Moon*, "the figure of the ancestor [is] (as in the case of much black literature) the cornerstone" of the story and "central to the definition of genealogy" (2003, 69). The same indeed applies to *Any Known Blood*. Similarly, Maureen Moynagh writes regarding Brand's novel: "The novel traces the uneven and contradictory processes by which the history of slavery maintains a legacy, so that some 160 years later its diasporic offspring experience its trauma in a way akin to the aching of a limb long since amputated." (2001, 195) This comment is equally applicable to *Any Known Blood*. Note, however, the particular metaphorical closeness to *The Book of Negroes*, in which Aminata's loss of her family is repeatedly linked to "phantom limbs" (cf. for instance the chapter heading "My Children Were Like Phantom Limbs", BN 331), emphasizing the traumatic recollection which Aminata experiences on a personal level but which, as Moynagh observes (and as I argue in section 5.3.2., "Traumatic memory: The Middle Passage"), finds its continuation in collective memory so that it is still 'felt' more than 200 years after the fictional Aminata writes down her story.

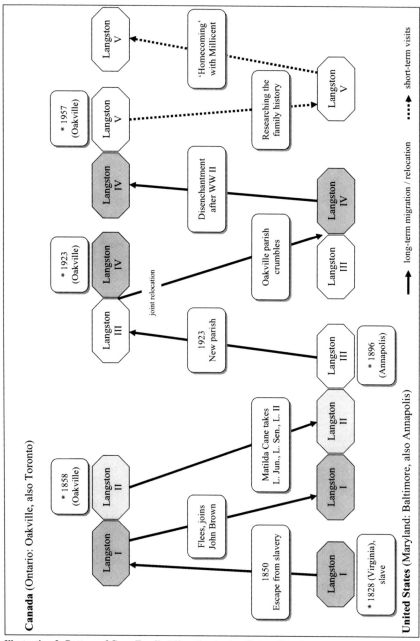

Illustration 3: Pattern of Cane Family Migration in *Any Known Blood*

6.2. Narrative, Memory, Authenticity II: Assertive Genealogy

> *The archive cannot be described in its totality; and in its presence it is unavoidable. It emerges in fragments, regions, and levels, more fully, no doubt, and with greater sharpness, the greater the time that separates us from it: at most, were it not for the rarity of the documents, the greater chronological distance would be necessary to analyse it. And yet could this description of the archive be justified [...] if it persisted in describing only the most distant horizons? (Foucault 2002,147)*

> *'That's what colored people do, son. They shut down a building and leave all the papers alone, instead of throwing them out. That way, if some fool like you wants to come along once every hundred years and waste three good days digging through it, he's welcome to do so.' (Millicent Cane, AKB 399)*

6.2.1. Authorship

In *The Book of Negroes*, Hill has his narrator Aminata Diallo write the story of her life and presents this fictional autobiography in and as his novel. In *Some Great Thing*, Hill uses the protagonist Mahatma Grafton to achieve a similar structural effect, concluding the novel with the beginning of Grafton's writing process, which apparently leads to the compilation of the story we as an extraliterary readership have just finished reading:

> And he [Mahatma] started writing a novel at night. He said he was looking forward to showing it to [his father] Ben. Wouldn't talk about it, though, wouldn't even give the name of the title, except to say that it had something to do with one of Ben's favourite lines [viz. 'go do some great thing'].[307]   (SGT 240)

In *Some Great Thing*, it is palpable that Mahatma Grafton will eventually – finally – be able to satisfy his father's desire to have his son achieve great things. Mahatma's turning towards chronicling and writing is clearly something that qualifies as a great achievement in the matrix of his father's approval, as Ben himself is a chronicler and writer *manqué*. From the very birth of Mahatma, it is clear that his father will make it close to impossible for Mahatma to live up to his expectations; in the nursery, thinking about a suitable name for his first-born, Ben resolves that he needs a "*good* one. This child was destined for great things. No ordinary

---

307 Note that the title of *Some Great Thing* is based on Crawford Kilian's *Go Do Some Great Thing: The Black Pioneers of British Columbia* (1978; now available in a 2008 edition). Hill thus immediately references the importance of African-Canadian *history* in his work. Ironically, British Columbia is one of the few main Anglophone Canadian regions not receiving any attention at all in Hill's novels (*The Book of Negroes* deals with the Maritimes, *Any Known Blood* covers Ontario, *Some Great Thing* focuses on Manitoba, so that Canada's east, 'center' and the prairie provinces are covered).

name would do." (SGT 2; emphasis in the original)[308] Ben in fact comes up with the name "Mahatma Lennox", combining the remembrance of one of the world's greatest leaders with the memory of one of African America's culturally most productive periods, the Harlem Renaissance (which centered, in the 1920s, around Lennox Avenue in Harlem, New York City).[309] Ben combines his ambitions regarding his son with his interest in (really, an obsession with) Black history, which in fact alienates Mahatma from both ideas, viz. serious writing as well as Black history:

> [Ben:] 'You have to stay on that job and show them all you're better than they are. You are going to be a great writer, son. You can write circles around those people. You have it in your blood. [...]' Mahatma felt a trace of revulsion at the speech. It seemed he'd heard it a million times. [...] Ben had so sickened him with black history that Mahatma gladly forgot the whole subject, avoided books about race issues and avoided people who talked about them, or any causes. (SGT 56f.)

Consequently, when Mahatma in the end redeems himself by writing a story for which he really cares (it might be argued that Hill's entire novel is structured around that very quest), making use of Ben's collection of Black history and family documents to boot, it is evident that he will convert from under- to overachiever in his father's eyes.

Not so Langston Cane the Fifth in *Any Known Blood.* Quite plainly, Langston the Fifth in his position as speech writer at a provincial government does not win any parental recognition.[310] On his first – and last – visit to his son's office, Langston the Fourth, in his slightly pretentious, usually off-hand way, tells his son: "Office? You call this an office? It's a water closet. A coffin. At best, a measly nook in a rabbit warren. Son, can't you do any better than-"

---

308 Other contenders are "Prometheus, Zacharia, Euripides, Homer" as well as "Marcus Garvey Grafton" or "Booker T. Grafton" (SGT 49). As an aside, the name of *The Book of Negroes'* narrator, Aminata, is a name that Langston the Fifth, in *Any Known Blood,* might have used, adding to the cornucopia of (possible) names that partly echo throughout and between Hill's works; Langston the Fifth "would have tendered the name Aminata, which meant 'the peaceful one'" (AKB 210) for the baby his wife lost the very day he cheated on her.

309 Interestingly, Hill's *Black Berry, Sweet Juice* is not only based on a saying he remembers from childhood (and his father's "own sarcastic version" of it, which goes, "The blacker the berry / The sweeter the juice / But if you get too black / It ain't no use." BBSJ 21). It also plays on the title of a novel by Wallace Thurman, *The Blacker the Berry – A Novel of Negro Life* (1972; published 1929) which satirizes the Harlem Renaissance's signature "New Negro Movement" inspired by the 1925 publication of Alain Locke's *The New Negro* (1970).

310 Cf. on these autobiographical aspects *Black Berry, Sweet Juice*: "I find it interesting that I had already, at that young age, internalized the value that it wasn't good enough for black people to do something ordinary, predictable or shallow." (BBSJ 23) Whereas this part of Hill's education is reflected in Ben's notion that Mahatma should aspire to do "some great thing", the insistence on becoming a well-respected professional with a high-paying job is transferred from Hill's father onto Langston IV: "Indeed, since we were children, our father had hammered into our heads the obligation to move into this direction. We were all to become engineers, doctors, or lawyers – and we better damn well become the best and the most famous engineers, doctors, or lawyers in Canada." (BBSJ 79)

(AKB 22), at which point he breaks off his tirade. Being continuously subjected to such overt criticism, Langston the Fifth is of course fully aware of his being considered a family failure.[311] The responsibility to live up to his name weighs, as it does for Mahatma, too heavy on his shoulders, yet he cannot get rid of it. "They should have named him [Langston's brother Sean] Langston. But they didn't. They gave the name to me, the first born of the fifth generation."[312] (AKB 7) If anything, Langston the Fifth has learned to accept his status as a genealogical underachiever, and to take sarcastic comfort in the fact that he is actually able to deal with his role of being the family failure, wryly observing: "But it also takes something to fall from the treadmill of great accomplishments, to fail, even at the tasks of being a husband and a potential father[313] and a writer, to march to the gates of middle age and look ahead and accept that you will not change the world." (AKB 4f.) Aunt Millicent "Mill" Cane uses the same phrasing when she tells Langston the Fifth that "[y]ou're not a real Cane. You've fallen off the treadmill, or never gotten on it." (AKB 132) Donna Bailey Nurse observes that "Langston [the Fifth] feels like a loser – and his domineering father, the pompous Dr. Langston the Fourth, entirely agrees." (2003, 173; also cf. on this aspect Siemerling 2004, 34f.) Langston V decides to prove both of his relatives wrong by heading to Baltimore, where he plans to write a novel about his family's history.[314]

In this, however, Langston Cane the Fifth differs from Mahatma Grafton – or rather: their fathers, Ben and Langston the Fourth, differ. While Ben had always been into the preservation and writing up of the chronicles of family and community (he himself had begun a draft of a "history of our people", SGT 58), Langston the Fourth has no interest in anyone – least of all himself or his son – digging up the family history. "I know what you want to do there [in Baltimore]. Family roots. Forget that nonsense", Langston IV berates his son (AKB

---

311 While the blunt, explicit criticism dished out by Langston the Fourth could (however remotely) be interpreted as some sort of hapless attempt to motivate his son, it is a behind-the-back disparagement that leads to a final rupture in their relationship; eighteen months prior to Langston the Fourth's dropping by in his son's office, Langston the Fifth had overheard his father comment on the son's about-to-fail marriage, claiming "I don't know what Ellen [Langston the Fifth's former wife] sees in him", AKB 46.

312 Langston the Fifth is aware, however, of the fact that Sean, successful as he is in his job, would not make his father entirely happy, either, as his homosexuality would eventually prevent him from having a standard, run-of-the-mill family (cf. AKB 58).

313 While on a tour of Niger and Mali, Langston the Fifth had been unfaithful to his pregnant wife; dramatically, she lost their baby the very night he committed adultery. Langston V considers his infidelity the major reason for his failed marriage and thus holds himself responsible. He later learns that at least two of his ancestors had in fact not been the epitomes of integrity, for which they are revered in his family, either; Langston the First was charged with bigamy (which he denies while he simultaneously admits, in his memoirs, to have had extra-marital relationships), while Langston the Third was infidel when stationed in Europe during World War II (he somewhat idiosyncratically blames the war and racism in the military for his mishap; when he leaves the woman he slept with in Lyon, he mumbles, "Look what this war has done to me. If only they had sent me right home." AKB 181).

314 Siemerling 2004 equally attributes Langston the Fourth with the marker "domineering" (34).

57). The reason for Langston the Fourth's rejection is twofold. The first reason is a particular family secret which he does not want to be dragged into light, namely the fact that his sister Mill had once been a prostitute and that she from the beginning disapproves of her brother's interracial marriage.

The second reason is a general take on the vocation of a writer and/or historian. Langston the Fourth is a social activist, not an esthete. He has tried to instill in Langston the Fifth a sense of decisiveness (in his own words, "Didn't I teach you not to talk gobbledygook?", AKB 56) and considers activism the only road to achievement. Tellingly, his doctorate – and this is something that distinguishes him from his partial blueprint, Lawrence Hill's late father Daniel G. Hill[315] – is in medicine rather than in the social sciences or the arts and humanities. Although Langston the Fourth is a good story-teller himself, he does not consider writing – writing *fiction*, to boot – a desirable career. It is indicative of Langston the Fourth's character, of his disrespect regarding his son's choice to become an author, and his role in the recon-struction of the family history that Aberdeen "Ab" Williams, who accompanies the Cane fam-ily for three generations, does not hand documents concerning the first Langston Cane to Langston the Fourth but to his son, the aspiring author. Langston IV, Ab concludes, would not be interested in these documents nor would he know what to do with them, as he is "a man who *does* things" (AKB 339; my emphasis) – in contrast to his oldest son, who *writes* ('mere-ly' writes, Langston the Fourth would hasten to add). Langston the Fifth is fully aware of the unappreciated nature of the author both in general and – poignantly so – in his father's opin-ion. Focusing through Yoyo, who is reflecting on his own prospects of becoming a writer, Hill characterizes Langston the Fifth's being an author, employing Yoyo's usual semi-naïve, semi-wise tone:

> Langston [V] was up writing every night and every morning and he wasn't even a writer. He even admitted it. Had never published anything. Had never been paid for his writing, except for a few thousand speeches that an educated twelve-year-old could have written. Yet, never-theless, he said he was writing. Didn't expect to make any money from it, didn't know if he'd finish it, didn't even know if it was worthy of being called a novel, but he was at it, writing every day. So would Yoyo. But Yoyo had to be focused. He couldn't afford to waste time on hand-wringing, anxiety-laden memoirs that might never be finished or published. He had to do something marketable.[316] (AKB 256f.)

Langston is writing without any serious prospect of material compensation; he will likely not become famous; there is no security in writing and there is no end in sight; basically, he is not even convinced of the literary quality of his work – but he still goes on. In the end, he even

---

315 'G.' for 'Grafton', a name of course echoed in the name of Mahatma and Ben Grafton in *Some Great Thing*. Lawrence Hill has a general tendency to include names of family members in his novels, such as Aminata (BN), Savoie (a colleague of Mahatma's, SGT), May (Aminata's daugh-ter, BN), Evangeline (wife of Daddy Moses, BN).

316 "Not marketable" was the answer African-Canadian writer Marlene NourbeSe Philip routinely received from Canadian publishers; cf. Barbara Godard's discussion of Philip's experiences (1993, 156).

jeopardizes his relationship with Annette, who is unwilling to play second fiddle to Langston's research activities, which she, like his father, does not classify as a proper job in the
first place (*"Work.* Give it a break. You're investigating your family's history", she tells
Langston the Fifth, contrasting, like Ab before, working, i.e. *doing* something, with writing;
AKB 496; emphasis in the original). Langston the Fifth's sense of mission is thus a mostly
self-propelled notion, frowned upon by most of his friends and family at least initially.[317]
When asked by Yoyo early on about his job, Langston the Fifth gives an answer that reeks of
self-deprecation but also hints at his sense of vocation; he tells the African, "I have no job, but
I am doing something" (AKB 116), instinctively warding off the expected distinction between
actually doing something and being an author. Consequently, Langston the Fifth certainly
does not begin research for his novel expecting to shed his air of underachievement, as Nurse
suggests (qtd. above). Rather, he shares – more precisely: progressively discovers in himself –
Ben's near-obsessive interest in what he is researching and writing about. As George Elliott
Clarke observes: "It is not until Cane V begins to document it [his family's history] that he
can begin to sense that *writing* will be his own contribution to his family's greatness." (2002a,
312; emphasis in the original)

Like Mahatma Grafton in *Some Great Thing*, Langston Cane the Fifth had been writing mindlessly for years (cf. his belittling of speechwriting quoted above or Mahatma Grafton's disaffection with the minor events he is obliged to write articles on) before discovering
the issues that would make him push through the writing process no matter how little it paid,
how little it is valued or understood. Even more so than Mahatma Grafton, Langston the Fifth
also has to overcome the full force of the predilections, biases and expectations of his father,
who, in contrast to Ben Grafton, wholeheartedly disapproves of his son's newly-awakened
vocation.[318] In the end, however, it is Aberdeen "Ab" Williams who, as is characteristic of his
role in *Any Known Blood*, has some sound advice for the disenchanted speechwriter:

---

317 Yoyo in fact tells him to "publish this [book] and write another" (AKB 499), but considers writing an entirely leisurely activity ("It's easy, writing, isn't it? [...] Writing is a snap. You can do
it." ibid.); cf. Clarke 2002a, 311, who identifies a Laferrièrean streak in this comment. Mill,
though at first just as dismissive as her brother, in the end wholeheartedly embraces the project.
Sean supports the idea from the start even though mostly, it must be suspected, out of a reflex to
spite their father and close ranks with his brother.

318 Langston the Fifth's ambition is not a new but indeed a rekindled one, as he had harbored the
thought of researching and compiling a family history for years (cf. AKB 3). Langston the
Fourth's disapproval of course is irrespective of a certain degree of profiting, in fact, from his
son's activities; not only does Langston the Fifth's research confirm his father's own oral story-
telling, it also brings him back into contact with his estranged sister, intensifies contact with his
oldest son and enlivens his daily routine (in which he has taken to dropping in on unsuspecting
acquaintances he thinks are still morally indebted to him in some way or the other; cf. AKB 28f.).

I know you're interested in who your people were.[319] Why don't you write about them? You told me years ago you wanted to do it. Write, Langston. Go write. Go do the one thing that all the achievers in your family were too busy and too important to do. (AKB 12)

In terms of authorship, Mahatma Grafton in *Some Great Thing* eventually finds his calling in the act of writing (more specifically, in writing about something he actually cares about), thus finally also living up to his father's expectations. Aminata, in *The Book of Negroes*, both ensures her mental well-being and her sociopolitical, even historiographic, influence through writing – two rewarding aspects she is fully aware of. Langston the Fifth, however, turns to composing a novel against all odds; he lacks Aminata's early determination to be a *djeli*, a witness or chronicler. He cannot even give a rational reason for his urge to write; when Mill asks him why he wants to know the family history, he answers "I just need to know." Likewise, he rebuffs her comment to get a family and a job with a simple "Can't do that." (AKB 132) Ultimately, Langston the Fifth does of course succeed in the mission of writing his book and he does find fulfillment, yet he also knows that he will not be met with easy recognition by either his father or society at large. Evidently, there is a certain sense of self-deprecation in terms of financial and social recognition, but there is also an air of self-confidence, maybe even a slight trace of pride in this stance on authorship, particularly in the conception of a vocation that is followed through against the currents (which African-Canadian poet Marlene NourbeSe Philip has so wonderfully captured in the title of her 1983 poetry collection *Salmon Courage*). In any case, the role of the author – conflated here with the story's narrator and the novel's protagonist – underlines the difficulties and obstacles that must be overcome in an endeavor such as the fictional recreation of a family's and a community's history. If their memories have sunk into oblivion over time or have been buried on purpose, an author has to dig long and deep in order to drag them to the fore and into the light. The 'job' (if indeed this label fits) of an excavator of memories and a chronicler through fiction might thus not be immediately rewarding, as Langston Cane the Fifth in *Any Known Blood* demonstrates, but both his example and Hill's other writer-narrators underline the importance of their task in individual as well as collective terms.

---

319 Note the ambivalence of the term "people" here, which of course extends to Langston's immediate but also extended 'family'. It is an obvious aspect underlying the entire novel that Langston the Fifth in his research in fact uncovers actual family history but along with it unearths forgotten bits and pieces of a larger, more comprehensive Black North American presence. Donna Bailey Nurse is certainly right when she states "what this book is not. It is not a dramatized jeremiad of wrongs inflicted on the African peoples. And it is not the embodiment of their diasporic journey. Nor is this novel the story of a race." However, the novel is more than she, though in a laudatory way, grants it: "Rather, *Any Known Blood* follows one man's frequently hilarious, often romantic, sometimes poignant trek through family history along the road to self-discovery." (2003, 173) Located somewhere between "a race" and "one man", however, Hill deals with the history of a people indeed, namely those Black North Americans who can identify – or be identified – with (a link in) the *chain* of Canes presented in *Any Known Blood*. The very structure of the novel suggests that this is not a work limited to the act of individual "self-discovery."

6.2.2. Few holes to fill: Authenticity and assertiveness

What, then, does the role ascription of the author outlined above effect in *Any Known Blood*? I will argue that by portraying a narrator-cum-author who does not perform the task of writing for either riches or recognition but out of a sense of vocation, even mission, Hill underlines the fact that Langston the Fifth is not about to 'fool around' with the issues he is representing. Why would Langston take on the task of writing "hand-wringing, anxiety-laden memoirs that might never be finished or published" (AKB 257, focalized through Yoyo) and then undermine his own writing? His primary vocation, after all, is to excavate the family history, not to write just any novel; that is why Langston is not even sure about the literary quality of his work (cf. ibid.), while he is entirely sure that he is onto something in terms of discovering neglected parts of (Black) North American history. Thus, when he uncovers Robert Wilson's journal and finds mention of Langston the First in it, he – quite pompously, in fact – lets the narratee know: "I started scanning Wilson's diary entries for the month of June. Nothing. July. Nothing. But I hit gold in August. I found new information about the history of the United States and Canada." (AKB 380) Consequently, Langston the Fifth may not be confident about his writing skills (as he is quite self-conscious about a number of issues, including his environment's assessment of his success, or rather: failure), but he is both excited about and proud of the research he is conducting and the results he is producing in this regard.

While it would be imprudent, of course, to equate the character of Langston the Fifth with the author Lawrence Hill, there are some obvious parallels – a notion which does not come as a surprise considering the novel's overall autobiographical permeation. Additionally, Hill has on various occasions outlined his approach to writing, often with particular reference to his family; cf. for instance Hill 2001, 2003, 2006, or 2008, the interview found in the appendix of this thesis, and the bits Flagel quotes from a telephone interview (2005). The novel's overall impetus, I would claim, also reflects and reinforces Langston the Fifth's stance: while he might write in a breezy style (sometimes maybe even too breezy, as will be discussed later on), the issues themselves are not dealt with in an ironic, satirical or self-subversive way.[320] Neither the narrator-cum-author Langston the Fifth nor the author Lawrence Hill, then, exposes the historical claims they stake to challenges or to questioning inherent in their own stories. Both, however, are keenly aware of the constructedness of their work and the potential of willful and/or helpful usage of historiography: they let their respective readers know that their memory constructions are indeed constructions, but they underline their belief that their versions of a collective memory provide a maximum of faithfulness to their sense of historical truth and also provide a version which is *significant* and should therefore play a role in the construction of larger collective memories.

---

320 Donna Bailey Nurse correctly identifies a "witty, self-deprecating first person narrator" and the "novel's ironic tone" (2003, 174). This does not imply, however, that Hill pokes fun at the historical topics he covers. Where he has let the tone of his writing dominate the content, Hill has, with hindsight, expressed his doubts (cf. section 6.3.3., in which Hill's fictional rendition of a Ku Klux Klan raid in Oakville is discussed).

Though some of the modes and literary devices already discussed in sections 4.1. (p. 57), 4.2. (p. 63) and 5.1.2. (p. 81) indeed apply to *Any Known Blood* as well, Hill also deals in explicit and very specific ways with issues of 'faction' and/or the fictional authenticity of Langston the Fifth's story. By the term 'fictional authenticity' I intend to indicate that Hill of course makes no pretense as to the fictionality of his story. He does, for instance, not *in fact* claim that one 'Langston Cane the First' actually took part in John Brown's raid on Harpers Ferry. Yet he emphasizes – in this case, paratextually – that there is an historical model for Langston the First's narrative, namely Osborne Anderson's account of the attack.[321] Moreover, he authenticates, *within* the boundaries of his fiction, the fictional account given by Langston the Fifth. *Any Known Blood* faces the same choice which Neo-slave narratives face (after all, it even incorporates such an account within the novel's larger narrative structure): it can refer to the historical aspects it (necessarily) incorporates either in a questioning or in an assertive, affirmative way. It has been explicated in section 4.2., "Hill's Faction and Historiographic Metafiction", that historiographic metafiction is ultimately characterized by the former approach, i.e. by the exposure of what is considered the inaccessibility of the past in any reliable way.

In a heterogeneric literature such as the (Neo-) slave narrative, there is a vast array of possibilities to do so. One could, for instance, present contrasting accounts of the same event, pit oral reports against written documentation, have different time levels at odds with each other, focalize incoherently through different characters, and so on. Hill, however, in *Any Known Blood* takes a different approach; although it may at first seem as if he did indeed include metafictional doubts and ironies, we discover upon close reading that in fact, Hill incorporates numerous ways of providing fictional authentication, i.e. a narrative that is believable in itself and which *does not question* the very possibility of knowing the past; quite the contrary, it underlines the *importance* of getting to know the past in order to be able to 'tell it like it is'[322] and draw appropriate conclusions for the present and the future.

Thus, in *Any Known Blood*, it might be an arduous task for Langston the Fifth and the people assisting him in his quest to dig up the evidence they need, but digging it up is what they achieve in the end, thus being able to compile a believable (hi)story. Believable, it must be added, in the sense of fictional authenticity, that is in terms of an inherent internal cohesiveness, not necessarily in terms of a compulsive mirroring of existing historical accounts. It

---

321 Quite similarly, Lawrence Hill states in "A Word About History" appended to *The Book of Negroes* that there was no actual 'Aminata Diallo' (probably not even a hired ex-slave *such as* Aminata) working on the Book of Negroes; yet there *was* indeed such a ledger – of which several copies still exist – so that the historical context in which he situates his characters is a largely veracious one.

322 The expression "Tell it like it is" (the title of an essay by Ralph Ellison, 1965; also the title of a 1966 hit single by African-American singer Aaron Neville) is used in *Any Known Blood* by an Oakville parishioner who spurs Langston the Third on to tell a White church congregation that "[h]aving survived slavery, and Reconstruction, and lynching, some Negroes don't care to see themselves mocked in a minstrel show." (AKB 288f.) Knowledge of the past is thus a preeminent condition for appropriate action in the present.

has been detailed above that Hill subscribes to an approach that clearly underlines the fictionality of a story but navigates this story within a corridor of what Hill terms his "understanding of history" (Hill, Appendix 298). At the same time, Hill's fictional rendition, based on this understanding, might well be subversive in that it does not conform to mainstream conceptions of historical events, or rather: facts. His version might provide – and frequently does – a counter-hegemonic account that aims to rectify what is considered a misperception or a lack of recognition in the first place. It does so, however, by presenting, in an *assertive* manner, a version of its own that may thus be opposed to other versions. *Any Known Blood* does not challenge the conventions of the historical novel *per se*; instead, it uses them to create a forceful portrayal of previously neglected aspects of (Black) North American history and present/presence.

Donna Bailey Nurse claims that Langston the Fifth is "a narrator we cannot always trust" (2003, 173) – after all, he passes for a number of different nationalities and conceals his true identity even from his employer. In fact, however, there are two caveats to this view. First, Langston the Fifth is very particular in regard to whom he misleads on issues of his identity. The examples from the novel show that he would use a fake identity (rather: a fake racial and/or national identification) almost exclusively to subvert racial stereotyping or to reveal preposterous requirements; Langston uses his ability to pass for instance when countering the infamous Question ('Where are you from?'), when claiming a false nationality on a job application which illegitimately requires the candidate to identify his race (AKB 2), or when identifying as a Sikh if it is Sikhs who are verbally assaulted (cf. AKB 1f.). Acquainting people in more relaxed contexts however – meeting Yoyo for the first time is one example (cf. AKB 95ff.) –, Langston the Fifth would faithfully account for his roots and personal history. Thus, as *Any Known Blood*'s oft-cited introductory passage has it, Langston the Fifth may "float to great advantage" his ambiguous appearance, his "seeming like a contender for many" races (AKB 1). Yet, he does so only if provoked.

The second, and more profound, caveat is that we cannot single Langston the Fifth out as an unreliable narrator simply because he misguides other *characters*. Right away, Langston the Fifth tells his readers that he is both able and prone to engage in racial masquerade and willful self-identification. There is no reason to doubt that he indeed does so – in fact, we witness several occasions and examples, among them the amusing interplay between his boss at the provincial ministry (where he is considered Algerian) and Langston the Fourth on an unannounced call. Moreover, the level of confessional content in Langston the Fifth's account of his own life is high – and presented, as in *The Book of Negroes, sans* irony. He does, for instance, not hold back on the tragic and morally more than questionable events surrounding his wife's abortive pregnancy. Although casually withholding crucial information from the people who surround him, there is no solid evidence that Langston the Fifth should be as unreliable a narrator as he is towards other characters on occasion; after all, he follows a calling and could hardly afford to have his narration questioned or undermined (least of all by himself).[323]

---

323 The same applies to other characters who had (until Langston the Fifth's attempts at uncovering the family's history) lived with lies big and small, which are subsequently revealed; aunt Mill, for

From an early stage of his project, Langston the Fifth is aware of the fact that if he ever manages to research and write the family history, it would have to be in the form of a novel, not an historical account (cf. AKB 378). At first glance, then, his narrative may seem strictly fictional. As has been pointed out before, Langston the Fifth's story is overtly self-conscious in terms of its awareness of being fiction and thus prone to subjectivity and willfulness, but it is self-confident in terms of the *content* it presents. When aunt Mill asks Langston the Fifth why he wants to hear all about his ancestors, the following dialogue ensues:

> [Mill:] 'What are you going to do with it [the family story]?' [Langston the Fifth:] 'Write about it.' 'Write what?' Mill asked. 'A novel.' 'How are you going to do that? I don't have enough stuff to fill a whole book.' 'I'll use my imagination to fill in the holes.' 'You'll be using a lot of imagination, in that case. What's the point of filling most of a book with your imagination?' 'That's what writers do. That's what I want to do.' (AKB 133)

A superficial reading could thus corroborate the notion that *Any Known Blood* indeed tends toward historiographic metafiction as Hill underlines the idea that his own novel is likewise "using a lot of imagination" to make up for the lack or inaccessibility of foundational "stuff" on which to base his writing. Quite obviously, Hill in this metafictional dialogue echoes his comments in the acknowledgments appended to the novel (cf. AKB 507ff.), disclosing the high level of fictionality in spite of the novel's autobiographical saturation. We need to avoid, however, jumping to the conclusion that we are thus dealing with historiographic metafiction here, as Siemerling, for instance, does, *en passant* declaring that "Hill's text, an example of historiographic metafiction, delivers cross-cultural experiences through the writer Langston Cane V" (2004, 38).[324] First of all, there is (again) no questioning of the accessibility of the past *in general*. The composition of the book envisioned by Langston the Fifth complies to the concept of 'faction' outlined in section 4.1. ("Lawrence Hill's Explorations in Faction", p. 57ff.) in failing to undermine the ability of fiction to indeed incorporate historical facts, not just historical events. What we are dealing with, then, is – as in Hill's other novels – a mix of fact and fiction. In order to determine the ratio of ingredients in this mixture, however, we need to contextualize the quotation above. While the conversation between Mill and Langston the Fifth seems to suggest that there would be very little fact and an abundance of fiction in

---

instance, had been a prostitute, which she – understandably – does not share with anyone in the family except her brother; she had, though officially having broken ties with her family, also in fact secretly been at her father's funeral. These lies, however – petty and otherwise – are revealed as Mill progressively comes to trust her nephew and his project. These revelations thus further the process of truthfully reconstructing the family history.

324 In a comment on the embedded slave narrative, Siemerling to a certain degree contradicts his own assessment, claiming that Langston the First's "survival and escape allow for his tale to be told with the effect of the heightened authenticity that comes with a first person point of view." (2004, 40). If in fact *Any Known Blood* adhered to the characteristics of historiographic metafiction, the first person narrative mode would be used to achieve quite the opposite, viz. an emphasis on subjectivity, construction, errors, limits to knowledge and the like. Why the first-person point of view would lend authenticity to the embedded slave narrative but not to the remaining parts of the novel – written almost exclusively in the very same mode – is likewise not entirely clear.

Langston the Fifth's book,[325] the way this scene continues provides a counterbalance to the assumption of decidedly large holes to fill with imagination. It turns out that Mill indeed *has* "enough stuff to fill a whole book" (cf. above) – and the two Canes even set out to acquire more "stuff", viz. documentation relating to the family history.

In the very follow-up to Mill's skeptical comments concerning the holes to be filled by imagination, she grants Langston the Fifth access to her own archive for the first time, handing Langston one of a large number of boxes which are filled with family documentation she has accumulated over the years and which clutter her home: "The cardboard box had letters, high school photos, certificates, church documents, and transcripts of oral history interviews that Langston the Third and Rose had given." (AKB 133) Two notions become immediately evident: First, the holes that need to be filled by imagination might not be that big and numerous after all. Langston the Fifth's novel is, in fact, to an overwhelmingly large degree made up of, or based on, archival material, which is of course supplemented by Langston's own autobiography. None of the stories he relates about the four Langston Canes before him has actually been drawn from imagination alone: in regard to Langston the First, the latest Cane discovers the memoirs (which largely conforms to the characteristics of a slave narrative); Langston the Second has likewise left some notes, though to a far lesser extent (corresponding to his lesser significance in the novel); the material on Langston the Third, in contrast, is extensive and includes a variety of different materials (cf. above). For his representation of Langston the Fourth, his son can rely on three elements: written documentation, Langston the Fourth's own story-telling, and eyewitness accounts, including those of aunt Mill and the writer-narrator himself. Langston the Fourth's account thus clearly passes for what Jan Assmann would term communicative memory (cf. Welzer 2008, 13f.).

The second notion that is evident from the content of Mill's archives is the multiplicity of media conveying the collected memories of the Cane family.[326] Consisting of visual as well

---

325 It is crucial to remember that even though the author Lawrence Hill discusses, qua literature, different approaches to writing, it is not the actual level of fictionality in *his* novel that is negotiated by Mill and Langston the Fifth. We can draw indirect conclusions pertaining to Hill's own stance from their remarks, but primarily, they discuss an intraliterary fictional writing. Keeping the two levels strictly separated, one can thus only assume that Langston the Fifth might indeed reflects Hill's views on the writing process (and in fact, he does, as a comparison with Hill's own nonfictional statements shows), but the discussion remains fictional in that it pertains to *Langston's* novel and the conceptions put forward by the characters involved.

326 It is only through the process of ordering, composing, indeed "recreat[ing]" "reconstruct[ing]" (as Langston the Fifth himself announces; AKB 3, 116) his family history that the collect*ed* memories slumbering in Mill's archival boxes are revived – resurrected, in a way, from their cardboard coffins, if this metaphor may be invoked. Only then are they imbued with meaning and can thus exert their influence on identity-formation processes as collect*ive* memories. The effect on Langston the Fifth's self-identification is, on a personal level, quite immediately present, for instance when he feels connected to Langston the First because they are, according to Langston the Fifth, both social misfits; Mill agrees with this observation and comments that it seems Langston the First "had a loose chromosome that skipped a few generations and turned up in you [Langston V]." (497) On what grounds exactly Langston the Fifth should not "fit in", however, is doubtful. Siemerling's suggestion that Langston "lives with both a certain freedom and a paternal trap"

as legal documents and, importantly, the recording (though in writing) of oral testimonies by Langston the Third and his wife, the materials compiled by Mill represent the wealth of media through which memories can be transmitted and for which an equal degree of validity is claimed. Likewise, they underline the validity of 'unofficial' history *vis à vis* 'official' history. In this respect, there is a functional role differentiation in *Any Known Blood* that sets it apart from *The Book of Negroes* but strongly connects it to *Some Great Thing*: in Hill's first two novels, we encounter both an archivist and a story-telling writer who sifts through the existing raw materials (collected by Ben Grafton and Millicent Cane respectively) and gives the necessary form to the materials stowed away in folders and boxes, instilling meaning *qua* coherence in the process. Crucially, then, it is the work of the writer – Mahatma Grafton and Langston the Fifth – to delve into the storage memory of their people (double meaning intended) and bring to the fore a version of their past that is a *usable* one. Of course, it is these versions that we are presented with in the two novels by Hill, i.e. we are confronted with memories selected, structured and brought to the fore by two narrators – as well as, perforce so, by Hill himself.

  In *The Book of Negroes*, Hill employs a slightly different approach, in which his writer-narrator, due of course to her historical position, is unable to rely extensively on pre-existing archives but is part and parcel of *creating* the archives in the first place. Aminata's writing in a way is the prequel to Langston the Fifth's writing: not only is she instrumental in the drawing up of documents such as the ones used by Langston the Fifth (even though he does not employ the actual Book of Negroes, he incorporates similar documentation); with her life story, she provides an eyewitness account just like the slave narrative that is passed on by Langston the First and pasted in Langston the Fifth's novel. While Aminata thus records the history of her people in a collective, synchronic way as an eyewitness, Langston the Fifth uses accounts like these to add a diachronic level. By supplementing his own life story Langston the Fifth then adds another diachronic layer which in turn is eventually bound to become part of the archive.

(2004, 42) does not provide a satisfactory answer either, as this notion certainly does not make Langston a misfit as Siemerling claims. In contrast to Langston the First, a runaway slave who makes it to Canada and lives in an almost all-White environment, Langston the Fifth's sticking out seems rather limited (nor is Langston V by character a rebel; more often than not, he shies away from direct confrontation). It must be added, however, that the conception of a misfit is supplemented by Langston the Fifth's declaration that he "love[s Langston the First] for his mixture of weakness and dignity" (ibid.), a trait that indeed resurfaces in his great-great-grandson, who is otherwise not a particularly tough or renegade character. It is fitting that Langston the Fifth should be the only Cane who is not involved in serious violence or fighting: Langston the First escapes slavery (where he is not only subjected to physical punishment but also poisons an overseer with arsenic), while Langston the Third and Langston the Fourth serve in World War I and II respectively (about Langston the Second we get to know too little to tell with any reliability). Langston the Fifth, in contrast, is on the receiving end of physical attacks if at all (cf. the Baltimore drive-by shooting in which he is first accidentally shot at and then knocked down and mugged).

Like the slave narrative, *Any Known Blood* is in general a heterogeneric narrative, inter-spersed with multiple 'found pieces' both fictional and extratextually authentic.[327] In addition to fictional letters, documents, newspaper articles, and the like, Hill inserts bits and pieces he has plucked from other sources, such as the quotes by Brown and Douglass which he incorpo-rates. Furthermore, and characteristically for Hill's writing, he includes real-life, often histori-cal, events. He fictionalizes these events but, as has been argued above, never twists them out of proportion or shape. In the case of *Any Known Blood*, the autobiographical nature of the novel, read in conjunction with the non-fictional *Black Berry, Sweet Juice*, which extensively deals with family and identity issues as well, provides a multitude of opportunities to pinpoint these real-life inserts. A central example can be found in what is called the 'Norville Watson incident', which is based on a case that Lawrence Hill's father, Daniel Hill, took as far as the Supreme Court of Canada (cf. BBSJ 57ff.).[328] In *Any Known Blood*, Hill both recounts, clad in the world of Langston the Fourth, the story the way his father had told it to him (cf. AKB 33ff.) and refers to the court ruling itself (cf. AKB 237). Yet interestingly, Hill attributes to this embedded story – whose real-life model has not only been published non-fictionally but even officially been documented by a court ruling – the doubts and ambiguities of any memory construction:

> Over the years, I have heard many versions of the Norville Watson story, Round One. The following version is the one I choose to believe. It's one of my father's earliest versions – or, at least, one of the earliest versions that I remember hearing. (AKB 33)

While writing his novel, Langston the Fifth is thus acutely aware of his position as the person *choosing* the elements to be presented and the way in which they are recounted. This aware-ness of course highlights the nature of any memory representation; selectivity and its con-structive character are two of its most central defining features. What Langston the Fifth thus suggests is, essentially, that he is aware of the constructedness of the representation of his father's memory *but* that he has carefully chosen a version that he considers most authentic. In fact, the narratee will find that the version Langston the Fifth chooses to believe is corrobo-rated, within the novel, by a court ruling cited by the narrator. The oral account of Langston the Fourth is hence authenticated, which, as will be discussed later on, is a frequent feature throughout *Any Known Blood*. Providing an authentication for his embedded story, Langston the Fifth underlines the reliability of his selection even though it *is* in fact a selection.[329] The

---

327 I will concentrate on the elements that have a direct bearing on the issues at hand; of course, Hill also employs a variety of other generic ingredients, such as the classic 'whodunit' in regard to the abduction of Dr Norville Watson (and, later on, Langston the Fourth as well as Aberdeen "Ab" Williams). On the central influence of another genre, the family memoir, see Flagel 2005.

328 The bottom line in both accounts is that Langston the Fourth / Daniel G. Hill Jr. and his wife de-cide to rent an apartment but are turned down on a racial basis (in the novel, by a doctor named Norville Watson); the ensuing court ruling indeed confirms the practice of denying rent to interra-cial couples.

329 In the same vein, Langston the Fifth's brother Sean doubts their father's stories, which, however, turn out to be veracious in the end: very early on in his narrative, Langston states: "I grew up with

author thus illustrates his trustworthiness by being open enough to admit to a constructive, creative element in his story-telling but likewise authenticating it.

Now, on the level of Lawrence Hill writing *his* novel, we are dealing with a similar, almost parallel mechanism. The reader is – qua Langston the Fifth – made aware of the fictionality of the story he or she is indulging in, and advised of the selectivity and constructedness of the memories Hill incorporates in his work. Yet if the reader cares to check the version that is offered (and whose possibly arbitrary nature he or she is so explicitly made aware of), the story turns out to be corroborated by other accounts (e.g. BBSJ or Government of Ontario 2009).[330] Thus, the version *Hill* decides to tell is authenticated non-fictionally as much as the version Langston the Fifth chooses to tell is authenticated within the novel. While the constructedness and selectivity of memories is underlined, then, Hill makes equally clear that the version he opts for is a version that is the closest to "his understanding of history" (cf. above). Langston the Fifth's comment concerning the variety of versions available provokes a check of veracity; it then turns out that we are given a maximally veracious account, so why should we opt *not* to follow the narrator Langston the Fifth on his choice? Likewise, if we follow a version of the matters presented in *Any Known Blood*, why not stick to the choices made by Lawrence Hill? He makes us aware of the fact that they *are* choices yet he equally provides an authentication for them. Thus, rather than presenting an account that is question-ing itself (as would be the case with historiographic metafiction), we are dealing with an ac-count that *seems* to question but in fact corroborates and authenticates itself.

Bluntly, *Any Known Blood* is of course still fiction *pure laine*, but it is assertive in its claims of representing – not in way of a detailed mirroring, but in terms of general lines – authentic memories. Throughout *Any Known Blood*, it is repeatedly and explicitly stressed that Langston the Fifth is dedicated to a faithful representation and assisted in this regard by the people who are keeping archives: aunt Mill, for instance, tells him to "better get the facts right" if he wants to include her in his novel (AKB 179). Likewise, Langston the Fifth re-marks at one point that he can now engage in telling the story of Langston the Third because, as he says, "I had enough information to start putting it together." (AKB 234) The holes, it turns out, are really not very big and not very numerous. Lawrence Hill, when asked about his approach to fiction writing and his role as a preserver of memories, initially (modestly) denies having much of a refined role conception for himself in the first place, but then continues to

---

four family legends – one about each of my direct paternal ancestors. Every year, my father would add another tantalizing detail, but refuse to go any further. [...] Sean, my brother, would say, 'He's not telling us any more, because he doesn't know any more, and most of what he's told us probably isn't true anyway.'" (AKB 4)

330 It is positively ironic that the Government of Ontario should actually link their mentioning of the Bell vs. Ontario case to an excerpt from Lawrence Hill's *Black Berry, Sweet Juice* (cf. Govern-ment of Ontario 2009).

elaborate on his position, stressing both his ambition as a writer of *fiction* and as a writer who nonetheless aligns his writing along certain standards of historical veracity or truth:[331]

> I don't often step back and look at myself or at my work so lucidly. This could be a matter of self-delusion, but I think my primary identity is as a novelist and a story-teller. I do not feel that my primary identity is as a record-keeper or as a restorer of history. I think that this is secondary. The historian in me, the record-keeper, is a happy sub-employee. He is working away in the shadow of the novelist. If it were my primary preoccupation, I guess I would have become a historian. Although I do believe that historians and novelists can work very well together and can support each other. I could never have written the novels I have written without the work of historians. But I feel I can do something often which historians can't often do, which is to dramatize the past so that readers step naturally into it. [...] But yes, I do like to feel that I could contribute to a sort of resuscitation of Black history, particularly elements that are largely unknown in Canada. It is part of who I am. And it is part of who I have become as a writer. (Hill, Appendix 302)

The sub-employee to Hill's writer thus checks and supervises the work of his boss, the novelist, to make sure he keeps his bearings in terms of historical veracity (if not accuracy). There are only the rarest of instances when providing the requisite historical background information in Hill's fiction is done in a slightly artificial or forced way, for instance when he has Yoyo write a newspaper article on the Harpers Ferry raid (cf. AKB 406f.) so that he can get the necessary information across to the reader in a concise and coherent manner before providing the story from Langston the First's limited point of view (i.e. through the 'reproduced' ex-slave's memoirs), which is necessarily incomplete.[332] At times, the nesting of one story within another and the interlaced documents and accounts can get somewhat laborious as well.[333] The effect, however, is a pivotal one in terms of fictional authentication. Conven-

---

331 It hardly needs pointing out again that Hill evidently believes in something like 'historical truth'; cf. chapter 4.1.

332 Likewise, there are only very few occasions of Hill's not living up to the otherwise subtle self-authentication of Langston the Fifth's story, which is usually done through fluid transitions, reciprocal documentary validation or through dialogic means. Direct metanarrative comments like the following are hence the very exception: "...Yoyo sat at his kitchen table and brought his pen to paper. I know, because he told me about it." (AKB 256) As Langston the Fifth clearly was not present at the moment, he lets the narratee know, in an uncharacteristically heavy-handed way, how he acquired this information. Other instances of an equally limited point of view are more elegantly or more simply dealt with, e.g. when Langston the Fifth at one point reports, "... [Yoyo] dropped to the ground and slid back behind several legs and got behind the bakery truck and – I saw as I backed out into the street – started running" (AKB 229), or simply states, "Yoyo, after telling me that story, said he had to go to bed" (AKB 226). While the latter examples are more or less seamlessly integrated into the telling of events, the first one sticks out in narrative terms, though it still underlines the stringency of the limited point of view of the first-person narration, which is – as far as the frame narrative is concerned – never abandoned.

333 One of the actual quotes by Frederick Douglass (one of several which Hill implements in his novel; cf. in this case AKB 422 and Douglass 1999, 636) illustrates this shortcoming. This quote is inserted – and indented in terms of print – in the guise of notes taken by the abolitionist Nathan Shoemaker during a speech at Storer College, Virginia. Shoemaker's journal, in turn, is inset (and indented) in Langston V's account, which itself constitutes Lawrence Hill's *Any Known Blood*.

tionally, Hill uses different documents to reciprocally verify each other; the same applies to documents and oral accounts. What we are faced with, then, is not the "tension between orality and the scribal tradition" identified by Walcott (2003, 70), but rather their convergence and mutual authentication. Thus, when Langston the Fifth and his odd team of research assistants[334] consult an archivist at the Harpers Ferry museum, they are told: "Possibly, [John Brown's] raiders had included Langston Cane, of Canada. Because there was no independent verification of his claims, scholars have tended to leave him out." (AKB 426)[335] "His claims" refers to Langston the First's memoirs, which Langston the Second had given over to the museum along with a short account of how he got hold of it.[336] What Langston the Fifth can now provide is the "independent verification" of the authenticity of Langston the First's account which had so far been lacking: at Storer college, where Langston the Second had studied to become an A.M.E. minister,[337] Langston and his team had discovered Nathan Shoemaker's

---

Thus, the historical figure Douglass is used as a fictional character in *Any Known Blood*; he approaches Langston II because he knew Langston I; this meeting, as well as the speech by Douglass, is recorded by Shoemaker; Shoemaker's journal is found by Langston V, who uses it in his novel; finally, Lawrence Hill presents Langston V's account as *Any Known Blood*.

In Shoemaker's journal, Langston V also finds the decisive reference to Langston I's narrative, which is handed to Langston II by his father – who had reputedly been dead – on the night of Douglass's speech. Shoemaker quotes (in his journal, which is reprinted by Langston V, whose story is told in Lawrence Hill's novel) Langston II who, in turn, quotes Langston I on his slave narrative which he passes on to his son. Characters reciprocally authenticating their respective accounts thus are significant elements of Hill's story, yet once in a blue moon this process turns into a slightly tedious procedure.

334 Langston and his companions in fact span all shades that Black North Americans come in, as Langston's slightly tongue-in-cheek description illustrates: "There was Yoyo, who was as dark as dark got, and a good deal darker than Mill. There was Annette, who was of a medium complexion, and then there was me – Zebra Incorporated." (AKB 400) G. E. Clarke takes the narrator's self-portrayal as describing Langston the Fifth as "a bit of a chameleon, or a mask-wearing Negro." (2002a, 312; also cf. 220f.) Also cf. Siemerling (2004, 42f.), who expounds on the respective autobiographical aspects but fails to take note of Clarke's valuable essay "Canadian Biraciality and Its 'Zebra' Poetics."

335 The archivist, however, also admits that the official record is not necessarily comprehensive: even though he might not have come across Langston the First's participation in any official history books, "that doesn't mean he wasn't there." (428)

336 Although the fact that Langston II likewise wrote a short autobiographical piece (at six pages, it is very short indeed) underlines the increasingly dense documentary evidence assembled by Langston V, Langston II still remains a flat character in his/Hill's novel (cf. Forster 1988). Even his memoirs are hardly a profitable source of information or an embodiment of stringency, carrying the following notation: "A brief, personal recollection, for the purposes of historical clarity. NOT for publication." (AKB 398f.) Though the spirit of providing posterity with historical evidence is laudable (and, in fact, in accordance with the overall impetus of Langston the Fifth's writing), this task is hardly compatible with the simultaneous veto on making the document public. The document's title is thus as paradoxical as its author is merely an incidental character in the novel.

337 At one point, Lawrence Hill himself confuses two Langston Canes, writing that it was Mill's "great-grandfather", thus Langston the First, who studied at Storer (AKB 399), while in fact it was Langston the Second, *Langston the Fifth*'s great-grandfather, who went to Storer College.

journal, in which he recounts the passing on of the document from Langston the First to Langston the Second – a discovery George Elliott Clarke terms "the novel's *pièce de résistance*" (2002a, 311).

The Storer College episode itself is one of the most forceful underpinnings of the claim that history actually *is* accessible to us; the notion of the archive plays a pivotal role here. As the four-person team sifts through the documents stored in the basement of the college, they assemble, bit by bit, a clearer picture of the past and of Langston the Fifth's forebears. In this almost classic quest for truth, they uncover historical secrets which have lain dormant for generations – historical secrets, though, which *are* available and virtually *waiting* to be discovered. Mill declares the archive to be, in fact, an archetypal Black entity when she tells Langston the Fifth: "That's what colored people do, son. They shut down a building and leave all the papers alone, instead of throwing them out. That way, if some fool like you wants to come along once every hundred years and waste three good days digging through it, he's welcome to do so." (AKB 399) It is interesting to note that, in keeping with the overall image of buildings as metaphors of mnemonic processes, it seems that basements are the place where the lost, forgotten, neglected or suppressed memories are waiting to be recovered. Langston the Fifth finds Shoemaker's journal in the basement of the college; the same applies to the Oakville Historical Society, in whose basement he discovers the diary of Robert Wilson (cf. AKB 279f.). Hidden from plain sight, slightly underground, quietly stored away but available for retrieval if some effort is exerted, the memories kept in a basement are a perfect image for what is termed, not coincidentally, 'storage memory'.[338]

When forwarding his father's documents, Langston the Second in turn had enclosed a letter to the museum in which he admits he was not sure if the memoirs were truthful, but that their account did indeed "coincide with stories passed on to me by my mother. Some of these stories I have passed on to my own children." (427) Thus, there is a convergence of two writ-

---

338 It is illustrative of differential levels of accessibility of memories that in Mill's utterly cluttered house, Langston the Fifth faces a jumble of boxes and crates full of random documents onto which Langston the Fifth, in an effort to give his tale meaning, has to impose order to begin with, while Aberdeen "Ab" Williams's place is as thoroughly organized as his memory (cf. AKB 338). (Cf. Draaisma 2000, 13f. on mnemonic techniques which, dating as far back as antiquity's *ars memoriae*, use places and houses to metaphorically/imaginarily 'store' items in order to be able to retrieve them more quickly and more faithfully, e.g. for rhetorical purposes.)

In her short section on "Houses in slave narrative and family memoir novel" (sic; 2005, 246ff.), Flagel comments on the usage of homes and houses as markers of diverging status, but not on their metaphorical function in regard to memory. Cf. for instance Langston the Fifth's musing when he tours the Oakville neighborhood where he was raised: "I stopped on the sidewalk to admire the imposing, unpredictable shapes of the houses. They were like masked faces in the dark. Each one hinted of movement, personality, family history. There's nothing more humbling than family history." (AKB 46) The Canes' own house embodies, to a point of mnemonic archetype, the family legacy; formerly belonging to Captain Wilson (cf. AKB 48), who helped Langston the First escape slavery, it is the place where Langston the Fourth proposes to Dorothy (cf. AKB 89) before buying the house back (it had been sold in the 1940s, cf. AKB 335); it is also the home in which Langston the Fifth grows up.

ten documents and an oral account that underlines the reliability of the specific story in question; moreover, however, the given example is an instance of a general verification of oral history that can be found throughout the novel. Instead of presenting *contrasting* memory versions – as one would, for instance, expect from historiographic metafiction –, the oral and written accounts in *Any Known Blood* habitually confirm and corroborate one another. Not only does this mutual verification provide a fictional authenticity that lends an air of credibility to the claims superseding the fictional level, it also positions oral history as a credible source for memory constructions. If, the logic goes, oral accounts are unfailingly verified by written documents, then orature should be counted among the reliable modes and media of passing on memories. This is an important factor on the fictional level (as it lends believability to the story's rare oral narratives *not* corroborated in some way by written documents or other evidence, such as photographs) as well as on the level of Hill's actual writing process: after all, he strongly relies, as he freely admits, on the oral passing on of stories from his family in both his fictional and his non-fictional work (cf. AKB 507; BBSJ 241). The fictional authentication thus also spills over into authenticating a larger body of work.

The same mechanism of course applies to African-Canadian literature as a whole: if Black Canadian authors provided fiction which dominantly questioned and challenged its *own* propositions, then obviously it would lose a substantial part of its (sociopolitical, historiographic, memory-retaining) impact. In point of fact, then, the vast majority of African-Canadian literature adheres to the approach also chosen by Hill: to be counter-hegemonic and subversive in content but self-confident and assertive in tone and presentation. Langston the Second, in his letter to the Harpers Ferry museum, summarizes the position of overtly leaving the question of veracity to the reader but at the same time presenting strong evidence in favor of the views advanced as follows: "Not wishing to play God with history, however, I am forwarding the document. I leave questions of its veracity up to your judgment." (AKB 427) In terms of the document in question, Langston the Second certainly believes in its authenticity, as does Langston the Fifth; the novel's author, Lawrence Hill, does not provide evidence that would prompt a reader to contest their views either. In the same vein, African-Canadian literature, being a highly contemporary, largely post-1970s strand, overtly acknowledges its fictionalization of histories and collective memories without pretending to ignore the contested line between fact and fiction; it is a literature that is openly striving to sway its readership and promote the inclusion, for instance, of the Black presence in a larger collective memory. The best way to engage in this endeavor, it seems, is to be as faithful to the historical record as possible, thus being able to authenticate any claim by pointing to the 'facts' – and the purported twisting of these facts by whitewashed constructions.

To paraphrase Langston the Second's comment when he passes on his father's slave narrative, African-Canadian writers do not wish "to play God with history"; they are "forwarding the [counter-hegemonic memory construction]" and "leave questions of its veracity up to [our] judgment." (Ibid.) Just like Langston the First's narrative, however, the 'story' presented in and through Black Canadian literature is thoroughly authenticated, intriguing, and often written in a "masterful" way (George Elliott Clarke on *Any Known Blood*'s embedded slave narrative; 2002a, 312). Moreover, as Langston the Fifth remarks when he uncovers said account, we may well discover aspects that were formerly unknown to us: the claim to have "found new information about the history of the United States and Canada" actually suits Black Canadian writers of fiction better than it suits Langston V (AKB 380; also cf. the beginning of this section, p. 193). It is one of the preeminent goals of African-Canadian literature to harness this kind of 'forgotten' information for identity formation processes; in short: to retrieve these neglected aspects from the background of the collective memory and render them serviceable for current identification processes.

6.2.3. *Generational and transitional*

Not only is Langston the Fifth in *Any Known Blood* dedicated to getting "his facts right" (Millicent Cane; cf. above), he is also intrigued by the generational passing on of the family memories and the connection to his ancestors he successively establishes. The generational bridging that Langston the Fifth achieves by collecting the oral and written accounts of his ancestors is exemplified in a variety of ways, two of which are particularly noteworthy: first, the links are personified in a character who is genealogically not even a member of the Cane family but belongs to it nonetheless as a "surrogate uncle" (Flagel 2005, 248) to Langston the Fourth and Langston the Fifth. Aberdeen "Ab" Williams has accompanied three generations of Langston Canes, beginning with Langston the Third. He thus perfectly embodies the generational memory in which eyewitness memories are passed on orally (communicative memory in Jan Assmann's terminology). Second, the transitions between the different time layers, embedded stories, narrative perspectives, and various documents (such as letters or diary entries) serve to collapse the distinct Canes' experiences into a more or less unified family history that is – fragmented as it may originally be due to the different spatial and temporal settings – in fact one long genealogical line that provides a cumulative context for both Langston the Fifth's individual self-identification and a progressively fleshed-out memory construction regarding a variety of aspects of the Black presence in North America, which is equally weaving a number of loose ends into a more or less coherent strand.

Aberdeen "Ab" Williams serves as the embodiment of a generational memory that spans the three Cane generations from Langston the Third to Langston the Fifth. Indeed, his own genealogy runs parallel to the Cane family's, with Aberdeen's grandfather arriving in Oakville as a fugitive slave aided by Captain Wilson just like Langston Cane the First (cf. AKB 300). Coming to the Cane household of Langston the Third (in whose parish Ab's grandfather was the sexton), Ab himself serves as a handyman and a caretaker, also becoming a psychological parent for Langston the Fourth and especially for his sister Mill(icent). Langston the Fifth gets to know him as a grandfatherly figure with whom he meets – in stark contrast to his own father, whom he usually avoids – on a regular basis. Ab, who is, strictly speaking, an external eyewitness to the Cane family, is thus the bearer of a large amount of their family memories.

Yet his function goes beyond being a *keeper* of memories; he also acts as a judge over who gets access to certain family documents, and who does not (cf. the selective passing on of secret documents regarding Langston the First, which he hands not to Langston the Fourth but to his son; also cf. the following discussion as well as p. 190). Aberdeen's generation-spanning memory is underlined by his actual age as well as his appearance; during the Watson kidnapping, which Aberdeen ultimately resolves, a police officer remarks that Ab, who is 88 at the time, is "looking as if he's four hundred years old" (AKB 343); Langston the Fifth even tells him: "You're not normal, Ab. You're a thousand years old." (AKB 9) Like the *djeli* who, if he dies, takes the knowledge of one hundred men with him, as Aminata observes in *The Book of Negroes* (cf. BN 55), Ab unites within himself the memories of several genera-tions – to the point of seeming 'ancient'. Like Aminata at the time of her writing down her life story, however, Ab is anything but fragile or unreliable. Not only does he solve the 'who-dunit' surrounding the Watson abduction (in which both Langston the Fourth and he himself are eventually involuntarily implicated); he is in perfect health (cf. e.g. AKB 9, 11),[339] sup-plies the Cane household with healthy food and low-calorie cooking, still takes care of small repairs (a skill he was already renowned for at Langston the Third's parish in Oakville) and acts as an advisor to the whole family.

Most prominently, however, Hill underlines that Ab is a believable eyewitness. As with Aminata's memory, which is not at all hazy or distorted despite her old age, Aberdeen's memory is likewise presented as unfailing, superior even to the young Langston the Fifth's recollection. The first character to take the stage in *Any Known Blood* apart from the narrator himself, Ab refers to a meeting that the young man had forgotten but Aberdeen had remem-bered, claiming: "Maybe [I'm old], but I've got a better memory than you" (AKB 9).[340] It is an indication of Aberdeen's status and functional importance that he is included in such an early scene with Langston the Fifth in the first place; right from the beginning, it is made clear that Ab is in a position of power in terms of the memories he incorporates and selectively dis-tributes. Langston the Fifth, for instance, tells the narratee that he "had heard, from Aberdeen and from my father" about Langston the First; Aberdeen, in turn, tells Langston the Fifth that "[t]here are a lot of things you don't know about your family. [...] There are things your fa-ther doesn't even know." (AKB 11) In fact, it is Ab who withholds from Langston the Fourth the incriminating evidence of Langston the First's bigamy charges (cf. AKB 339) that he re-ceived from his own grandfather and eventually passes on to Langston the Fifth, who faithful-ly relies on Ab's stories, admitting for instance: "the little I do know [in this case, about Mill]

---

339 The very same police officer who claims Ab looks "four hundred years old" (cf. above) also states that "[h]e's the best-looking old man I ever saw." (344) Likewise, Langston the Fifth at one point tells Aberdeen that he "can see why they used to call [Ab] 'Dark Gable.'" (AKB 9)

340 This claim is in fact undisputable given that even when reminded by Aberdeen, Langston the Fifth needs a minute to call to memory that they were supposed to meet the week before. Some of the theories developed by Ab over the years, however, seem more disputable (for instance Ab's devo-tion to theories revolving around Africans discovering the North American continent in small boats around 500 AD, cf. e.g. AKB 8) but are clearly singled out by Hill as being disputable in-deed; while Ab's family-related memories are corroborated by other oral accounts as well as by documentation that is successively unearthed, some of his more controversial theories are imme-diately contradicted by other characters).

comes from him." (AKB 8) As with other memories of the Cane family, the things Langston the Fifth learns from Ab about his aunt turn out to be the truth; likewise, of course, the reader gradually comes to trust the stories Ab passes on and which he thus inserts, from a semi-outsider's position, into the genealogical story of the Cane family.

The issue of the papers incriminating Langston the First with charges of bigamy exemplifies, on the level of plot and character, the important position Ab holds as a 'broker' of memories. It also underlines, on the level of memories, the aspects of selectivity and constructedness. The papers that Ab received from his grandfather had been passed on to Langston the Third before coming into the Williams family. Langston III had read the charges and decided that they should be obscured in order to deflect damage from the Cane family – obscured, that is, only temporarily: "I'm not one for destroying historical documents, although I'm tempted", Langston the Third declares (AKB 301). He consequently seals the documents, hands them to Aberdeen's grandfather and asks him to make sure they are kept secret for at least fifty years (that would be 1974) so that none of the people directly implicated should still be alive. Hence, Langston III actively manipulates the family history and thus its self-conception; had it been known before Langston V's discovery that Langston I was a possible bigamist, the self-perception of Langston IV, for instance (who considers the Canes, up to and including Langston IV, i.e. himself, a long line of overachievers in moral, sociopolitical as well as professional terms), would have been altered dramatically – as would, of course, the relationship with his son and, as a direct result, Langston V's self-confidence and family standing.

Having said that, Langston the Third does not aim at permanently manipulating the family history; he also makes sure that one day it can be rectified and a faithful representation be restored. In other words, he cannot bring himself to establish a permanent misrepresentation of the family/intergenerational memory while at the same time wishing to protect those immediately involved; in all likelihood, he also wants to exempt himself from coming to terms with and reappraising the life of his own grandfather. Postponing a re-evaluation until at least 1974, Langston the Third manages to avoid an irreversible misrepresentation while still giving priority to his immediate needs of self-identification – after all, his own record of faithfulness is not unblemished, and the relationship with his wife's family is quite tense so that he could hardly afford to be seen as a link in a family chain of adulterers. He cannot bring himself to permanently erase the blemish, however, and leaves it to the following generations to dig up and deal with issues he has temporarily taken off the record and the agenda of self-identification, thus effectively halting a family discourse revolving around the failures of the Cane family in order to afford more space to their achievements. Of course, it is up to Langston the Fifth and his chronicling/writing to re-engage that discourse – in which he ultimately finds his own salvation as he recognizes that his family is not as picture-perfect as he had been made to believe. This affords him the breathing room to live his own life independently of the heightened expectations derived from a slightly misrepresented family history. It is, then, Langston the Fifth's task to recover the suppressed, but not permanently erased, family memories.

All of these processes of course comprehensively reflect the construction of collective memories; as Aleida Assmann states, "[i]t is far more difficult to incorporate into [a group's] memory moments of shame and guilt, as these cannot be integrated into a positive collective self-perception." (A. Assmann 2001, 309; my translation) It should be obvious that Aleida Assmann's conception of storage vs. functional memory finds an almost self-evident application here: Langston the Third has – for reasons of cleansing his (genealogical) self-definition – relegated the blemishing[341] memories to the background, i.e. the storage memory, where it is rendered unavailable for current (self-)definition processes. The negative memory of Langston the First's bigamy in *Any Known Blood* is thus temporarily neutralized and, quite literally, stored away for future retrieval; the sealing of the incriminating documents is a highly symbolic gesture in this regard. They are in fact retrieved from the 'stockroom' of memories by Langston the Fifth, whose job it becomes to sift through the storage memory of 'his people'[342] and bring as much evidence to the fore as he can in order to assemble a memory version that is as faithful as possible. Aberdeen tells Langston the Fifth early on to bring all of these memories to the functional memory by writing about them: "Go do the one thing that all the achievers in your family were too busy and too important to do." (AKB 12)

Aberdeen himself, in turn, appeals to Langston the Fifth to make sure that *he* will also be remembered and *his* story will be passed on as well; to Langston the Fifth, he says: "When that happens [i.e. when he dies], there won't be anybody putting me in any history book. But will you love me – or love my memory – any less because I never amounted to much?" (AKB 11) Of course, Langston the Fifth will include him in his novel-in-progress, irrespective of Ab's supposed (non-) achievements.[343] This unconditional inclusion is based on two aspects:

---

341 We have to keep in mind that both Langston the Second and Langston the Third are A.M.E. ministers for whom moral standards are an essential element both personally and professionally. Adultery, even bigamy – though 'merely' running in the family – must of course have been considered damaging not only to their self-conception but to their (professional) reputation as well.

342 The deliberate ambiguity of Aberdeen's phrase "your people" (AKB 12) has been noted before. Ben Grafton, the father of the protagonist, narrator and writer of *Some Great Thing*, Mahatma, revealingly uses the very same phrase when he teaches his son about Black North American history and its heroes: "As a boy, [Mahatma] had been told countless times about the life of Gandhi. And about famous blacks. Booker T. Washington. Marcus Garvey. Harriet Tubman. Langston Hughes. Ben had talked about them daily. But Louise, Mahatma's mother, always cut the sermons short. 'Stop filling the boy's head with nonsense,' she often said. 'It's not nonsense,' Ben would reply, 'It is the story of his people.'" (SGT 47)

343 In the same way, Mill insists – after initially resisting Langston the Fifth's project altogether – on not being erased from the story either: "You seem to think that only men are in your family story. But I was there, too. [...] I was there, I keep telling you, and I won't be left out of this story." Mill's perseverance underlines her personal stake in the family history, yet it also strengthens both the largely neglected female perspective of that history and the authenticity of her oral accounts on the basis of her being an actual eyewitness.

Regarding the female perspective in *Any Known Blood*, Cuder-Domínguez correctly identifies the novel as "male-oriented" (2003, 63); Clarke (cf. 2002a, 310) and Walcott (cf. 2003, 67) likewise comment on the novel's focus on male achievement, though Walcott, after noting his own considerable sense of inconsistency, also suggests that *Any Known Blood* "might be more profitably read

first, it illustrates that Langston indeed loves his surrogate grandfather and takes Ab's honorary family membership for granted; second, it highlights a feature that also characterizes the Neo-slave narrative, that is the bottom-up approach to history (cf. chapter 5.2., "Narrative, Memory, Authenticity I", of this thesis). The fact that Ab may not have "amounted to much", as he purports – well aware of the fact that this would not be a category according to which Langston the Fifth, himself an underachiever in his father's eyes, would judge him – does not preclude his being a part of history. Moreover, it even less precludes his being a part of what is largely a counter-history (or rather: a counter-model of collective memory constructions) in novelistic form, namely Langston the Fifth's (family) chronicle. Langston the Fifth accordingly takes historiography in his own hands, assuming control over matters of representation – including, among others, Aberdeen Williams's story, which is so closely linked to the Canes' own one.

Taking control of the (self-)representation of one's people of course has been a formidable goal of the original slave narrative; it has been a pointed, sometimes poignant and satirized, post-Civil Rights Movement impetus of the (US) Neo-slave narrative, and it is a foremost concern of African-Canadian literature in its struggle to correct a distorted hegemonic representation. In a word, then, African-Canadian achievements, much like Aberdeen Williams's life, will be cherished and remembered even though they may not make it into official history books. In fact, African-Canadian literature has been concerned with 'everyday heroes' and 'lesser celebrities' to a remarkable extent. Black Canadian literature, with its focus on historical concerns, of course always has had to content itself with a marginalized presence, telling the stories of ex-slaves, refugees, the disappointed and disillusioned – those who indeed rarely made or make it into history books.[344] Telling the stories of a community that has been kept, in disproportionately high levels, from gaining entry into official histories except as receivers of White Canada's benefactions, Black Canadian literature has often been concerned with the 'Aberdeen Williamses' of Canada in an effort to make up for an underrepresentation in official/dominant discourse. In *Any Known Blood*, Ab Williams makes clear that this representation is not aimed at a fulfillment of personal vanity, a fact he underlines by explicitly putting his own person on a par with his memory ("will you love me – or love my memory – any less"; cf. above). Ab thus personifies the communicative memory, which constitutes the span of the eyewitness's lifetime; he also personifies the bridging of the stories of several generations of Langston Canes and thus also the chain of their *people's* stories, which reaches from the (ex-slave's) past into the present (of the writer who keeps the ex-slave's memory alive).

---

as Milicent [sic] Cane's story" based on the notion that it is "through her that Cane V is able to complete his investigation." (2003, 69) Given the fact that Hill's narrative focuses on a patrilinear genealogical sequence whose youngest member is both the story's writer and its narrator does not leave a lot of breathing room for the contention that Mill, though an important hand in the research Langston the Fifth is conducting, might actually occupy a pivotal position.

344 The term "history books" here is evidently meant to indicate mainstream accounts, not the writings specializing in African-Canadian history in particular (cf. the respective section in Junne 2003 for an annotated bibliographical guide on the latter).

We find a similar effect on a wholly different level of *Any Known Blood:* While Ab Williams embodies the fluent transition from one generation of Canes to another one on the level of fictional characters, Hill also uses the transitions from one narrative layer to another to underline the connectedness of the respective generations, thus creating a sense of a stringent development and a diachronic coherence that underlines the (often disputed) African-Canadian community's cohesion in terms of its historical development.[345] *The Book of Negroes*, in comparison, is written from the perspective of Aminata Diallo, an author-cum-narrator who inserts several embedded narratives into a frame narrative that reflects the time level of writing. These embedded narratives are sequenced chronologically and consist of the narrator's experiences, beginning with her childhood and ending with a merging of the time level of the embedded narrative and the frame narrative. In *Any Known Blood*, Hill proceeds along similar lines, though the sequencing of the embedded narratives is roughly inverse, i.e. the narrator-cum-writer Langston the Fifth begins with uncovering and describing the least remote family history, slowly working his way backwards through the family genealogy, a process that strongly reflects archaeological excavation.[346] Moreover, in contrast to Aminata Diallo, Langston the Fifth also extensively includes in his account events he did not experience himself; he does so both through the unmediated reproduction of diaries, letters and other written documents, but also through narration which he bases on oral or written accounts but which he himself reconstructs and renders in prose, thus subordinating them to his own selection, his style and point of view.

It has been shown in the discussion of *The Book of Negroes* and its switching back and forth between different time levels that Aminata's recollections are often triggered by sensations such as a certain smell, sound or sight. In *Any Known Blood*, Hill needs to employ additional means for transitions, as Langston the Fifth does not exclusively describe his *own* recollections: consequently, the fluent 'slipping' into a certain memory cannot always be effected by a triggering sensation. Instead and/or additionally, Hill uses a variety of narrative tech-

---

345 Aberdeen Williams in fact adds a synchronic dimension to this diachronic parallelism between the separate generations of Canes; we thus discern similarities through the years as well as between different members of the African-Canadian community. There is, for instance, an underlying congruence of Aberdeen's experience of the 1930 outburst of racial hatred towards his interracial relationship and Langston the Fourth's experience of 'living under the gaze' when he walks the streets with his White wife in the 1960s (the epilogue, which chronicles a similar event, is devoid of time markers and thus stresses the endurance and sad timelessness of the phenomenon). It is no coincidence that both of these fictional episodes are based on actual events, modeled on the historical case of Ira Johnson and Lawrence Hill's own father, respectively (cf. sections 6.3.3. and 6.3.4.).

346 This is a general tendency only; Langston the Fifth's own and his father's stories (the level of communicative memory, that is) in particular are inserted at various points throughout the novel, not adhering to either forward or reverse sequencing.

Regarding the imagery of digging up the past, archival research such as conducted by Langston the Fifth would in fact not necessarily yield the most recent records first. Archaeological excavation, in contrast, is one of the few scientific historical procedures that indeed largely necessitate an inverse chronological process.

niques to achieve a unifying effect meant to join the stories of the distinct Cane generations, thus bridging the past and the present.

Any Known Blood's I-narrator Langston Cane the Fifth fades out time and time again, thus blurring the line between past and present, between history and fiction and between writing a history and a memoir. The instances of blurring are not meant, however, to mask the distinctiveness of the different levels and layers; Hill, for instance, does not suggest that fact and fiction *cannot* be separated. Rather, he takes the reader from one layer to the next in a fluent motion while clearly acknowledging the different levels *per se*; conveniently, frame narrative and embedded stories are sectioned off into separate chapters more often than not. Typically, Hill passes from the frame narrative through the discovery of a certain document into the respective document's time layer. When Langston the Fifth is allowed for the first time to sift through Mill's archives, for instance, he discovers an exchange of letters between Langston the Third and Rose (his future wife). The first letter is inserted into the text by the simple addition of quotation marks; there is no indention, no difference in font size, nothing to set it apart visually from the rest of Langston the Fifth's prior account (cf. AKB 133). The reply, however, which is reproduced directly beneath the text of the first letter, is indented, uses a smaller font and is generally typeset in a way as to resemble the layout of a letter. Hill thus has Langston the Fifth successively step back as a narrator from his own text in order to be able to move onto another time level.

Consequently, after the reproduction of Rose's reply, a new chapter begins in which a third-person omniscient narrator (who frequently but not exclusively focalizes through Langston the Third) tells the story of the third Langston's emerging romance with Rose Bridges and the obstacles involved therein. Hill consequently 'zooms out' from Langston the Fifth's words by employing a sequence that begins with his own words in a first-person perspective, followed by a letter reproduced in the *formatting* of Langston the Fifth's own (written) words. Gradually stepping further away from the conflation of writer and I-narrator, the second letter is reprinted in a formatting independent of Langston the Fifth's usual (written) story-telling. Finally, we end up with a third-person narration that is entirely void of Langston the Fifth as a narrator – though his function as the novel's *writer* is of course unimpaired. Hill thus step by step zooms away from Langston the Fifth and in again onto Langston the Third, using Mill's archive as a bridge between the two levels. Appropriately, then, the present is connected to the past through the archive – documents enable us to uncover past events and slip into their (hi)story. It is self-evident that this approach endows the archive with powers that are disputed by conceptions of historiographic metafiction, which in fact hold that we need to *question* the reliability of indeed gaining access to a past 'as it was'.

It is worthwhile to note that in the course of Langston the Third's story, the narrative perspective shifts once more; while the omniscient third-person narrator is maintained throughout, there is a short insert in which the narration shifts from the past tense into the present tense and back. The junction between the past- and the present-tense sections is almost imperceptible. There is no time lag or shift of locale, and the only advance indication of any shift at all is a lack of quotation marks that should have closed Langston's last dialogue

with his supervising Lieutenant before the shift of tenses (though the missing closing quotation marks could just as well be a typesetting error; cf. AKB 162). In any event, the reader of
course is drawn into the action more immediately by the use of the present tense. The shift
also implies a further zooming in on Langston the Third as the distance between reader and
story is further reduced, though Hill does not go as far as collapsing narrative and narrated
time. The present tense narrative is maintained only for a brief section, which is followed by
another zooming out (by changing back to the past tense) and eventually a new chapter which
begins, again, with Langston the Fifth contemplating the letters between Langston the Third
and Rose. Another letter is then fictionally reprinted (cf. AKB 169) so that the narrative perspective has come full circle.[347] Langston the Fifth's novel, represented in *Any Known Blood*,
thus mirrors the excavation technique used by Langston V in his research. Delving into a certain historical period and resurfacing to the present is the novel's constant motion pattern.

      While Hill at times uses the inconspicuous, or at least implicit, oscillation between
past and present that is effected by shifts of perspective or narrative tense, he also employs an
alternative technique, which is the explicit notification by the narrator. Reflecting,
metanarratively, his writing process, Langston the Fifth frequently announces the shift into
another strand of the story. This technique, while likewise stressing the connection between
past and present, is distinct from the implicit oscillation described above in its highlighting of
the constructedness of Langston's story. It does not undermine the overall ability to access the
past, either, yet it *discloses* the processes of shifting, narratively, between memory constructions that are inherently the story-teller's own on the one hand and pre-mediated constructions
that are *re*-remembered[348] on the other hand.[349] If the jargon of cinematic techniques – such as

---

347 In short: beginning with Langston the Fifth's first-person, past tense perspective, going through
    an interwoven, then a reprinted letter by Langston the Third, the gaze moves away from Langston
    the Fifth and onto Langston the Third from an omniscient, third-person, past tense perspective fol-
    lowed by a present tense passage; the past tense is then re-introduced, followed by a shift away
    from Langston the Third and back onto the past-tense I-narration of Langston the Fifth.

348 Re-remembering here indicates the sequential repetition of an encoding-decoding process, viz. the
    reconstruction of a reconstruction. Though premeditated, the re-remembering process is not nec-
    essarily less intense: "Re-memory, accompanied by grief and trauma, is not an easy experience.
    Often the trauma of the event and the trauma of re-remembering it blur as past becomes present
    and trauma is relived again and again." (Young 2005, 94) Mill, for instance, had kept her former
    life as a prostitute a secret; when Langston the Fifth uncovers (unbeknownst to Mill) this aspect of
    her past, he has second thoughts about his right to drag someone else's life into the open: "I won-
    dered if the whole family research project was a bad idea. I had forced my way into Mill's life and
    learned the one thing that she wanted to keep secret." (AKB 386) As would be expected, the hurt-
    ful re-remembering of the traumatic aspects of Mill's past in the end proves to heal some of the
    family wounds as it bridges the gap between Mill and her brother, yet the very process, as Lang-
    ston the Fifth's doubts demonstrate, is often a painful one.

    The usage of 're-remembering' here bears only a faint resemblance to Nobel laureate Toni Morri-
    son's well-known conception of "re[-]memory", which does not indicate a mere sequential repeti-
    tion of the processes of storage and retrieval. On Morrison's re[-]memory of course see her best-
    selling novel *Beloved*, in which the protagonist Sethe explains to her daughter Denver: "Some
    things go. Pass on. Some things just stay. I used to think it was my rememory. You know. Some
    things you forget. Other things you never do. But it's not. Places, places are still there. If a house

'zooming in/out' – was to be maintained, the explicit announcement of a juncture or transition is akin to subtitling a new scene to let the viewer know the time and whereabouts (while, in contrast, the implicit transition described above would abstain from the subtitle and let the viewer be carried into the new setting more or less unwittingly). In his dual function of author and narrator, Langston the Fifth, for instance, at one point announces: "I dove into writing again. I was ready to resume the story of my grandfather, Langston the Third. [Blank line.] In April 1923, two sharp blasts from the Marlatt and Armstrong tannery awakened the Cane family at six-thirty on their first morning in the new Oakville residence." (AKB 261) After switching over to the time layer of Langston the Third, the writer-narrator Langston the Fifth entirely disappears behind an omniscient third-person narrator and thus reduces his dual role to the single one of author (the reader of *Any Known Blood* of course remains fully aware of the fact that the third-person passages are still part of Langston the Fifth's novel and largely derive directly from his research). In this vein, Langston on occasion reminds the narratee that even though he might step back as a narrator, he is still fulfilling his role as an author – an author who bases his fictional writing on non-fictional documentation.[350] Leading over to the

---

burns down, it's gone, but the place – the picture of it – stays, and not just in my rememory, but out there, in the world." (1988, 38) Cf. Morrison's important essay "The Site of Memory" (2008) for an insightful discussion. For further analyses of Morrison's rememory conception cf. for instance the collections by Middleton (1997; particularly the essay by Rushdy) and Plasa/Ring (1994; Lidinsky deals with rememory and collectivity); also cf. Rushdy 1997, Holland 2000, 50ff. and King 2000 (who also employs Cathy Caruth's excellent ideas on re-representing and re-remembering; cf. 157ff.); Plasa 1998 focuses, as most other critics, on *Beloved*; for Morrison's own thoughts on traumatic memories cf. e.g. the interviews in Morrison/Taylor-Guthrie 1994 (particularly the one by Marsha Darling, 246ff.) and Morrison/Denard 2008.

Also cf. on re-remembering or "secondary remembering" Casey 2000, 50 ff., who, however, falsely claims that re-remembering is expressed by "one of the main German words for recollection, '*Wiedererinnerung*,' literally a remembering *again* or *re-remembering*." (ibid., 51) The coinage *Wieder(-)erinnerung* indeed means 're-remembering', but far from being "one of the main German words for recollection", it is not even part of the German lexicon (as, for instance, authoritatively canonized in the *Duden Wörterbuch*).

349   Both constructions of course adhere to modes of storytelling and are subject to processes of selection and reworking; yet, eyewitness accounts, compared to memory retrieval through documents, orature or other sources, of course eliminate one level of mediation and modulation. Langston the Fifth at one point also uses an explicit notification in order to lead over to a memory of his own, which is triggered by a current event and then immediately externalized into writing: Langston reads about the Watson abduction in the paper and begins to ponder his father's statements on the matter; "What exactly did my father think this was, if not a bona fide kidnapping? [Two blank lines] It was time for the continuation of the Norville Watson story. I got a refill of café au lait and started writing. [Two blank lines.] I met Norville Watson when I was ten years old." (AKB 237) Instead of moving from the frame narrative into an embedded story concerning his ancestors, Langston the Fifth inserts his own recollections, hence aligning *his* autobiographical memories with those he reconstructs of the Langston Canes before him. Narratively, he thus joins the ranks of Canes to be remembered in his novel.

350   Again, being fully aware of the difficulties of separating fictional from non-fictional writing in a genre such as autobiography (in which diaries, journals etc. are a distinct part), I maintain that the diaries incorporated in Langston the Fifth's novel are *meant to be read* as nonfictions (though of

post-Civil War story of Langston the Second, Langston the Fifth notes: "…I settled down to write my great-grandfather's story. [page break; "Chapter 20"] Langston the Second remembered it as the longest trip he'd taken in his life. It had seemed endless. Later, he wrote in a journal that he and his brothers had crossed Lake Ontario in a steam ship…" (AKB 410).

Langston the Fifth, however, is not the only one who initiates transitions between the different diachronic layers. In one scene, it is Langston the Fourth who triggers the changeover to an embedded story when he is about to tell his son the story of his searching out Mill in 1945 (the older Langston is in the army at the time): "'Here it comes. The story takes place in the States, during World War II, around 1945.' [Two blank lines.] Private Langston the Fourth lifted the handbag…" (AKB 362) We are facing several transitions here. Evidently, there is a movement from the 1995 frame narrative into the embedded narrative that takes place in 1945, so there is a change of time and setting as well as of narrative layer. Accordingly, we also have a shift from first-person to third-person perspective (which is not evident in the brief passage quoted above). Moreover, however, we also have a transition from oral to written account, which of course is indicative both of large parts of Langston the Fifth's project – a project that, after all, rests to a considerable degree on the orature that he gathers from people such as his parents, his aunt Mill or Aberdeen Williams – and of the original slave narrative's characteristic bridging of oral and written tradition (cf. the respective discussion in chapter 5.2. of this thesis). Additionally, Hill underlines the closeness between Langston the Fourth and the Fifth, who might not get along too well as individuals but share a large set of common memories; fluently, the narrative passes from Langston the Fourth's autobiographical story-telling, *retold* in the writings of his son, on to Langston the Fifth's own writing about his father. Indicated by a brief note (a 'subtitle' providing the place and time of the story to follow), Langston the Fourth morphs from being an embedded narrator – i.e. the narrator of a story *within* the story that Langston the Fifth narrates and writes – to a character whose story is told without a noticeable narrator. At the same time, Langston the Fifth's position changes from listener-author-narrator (who, according to his own recollection and externalization, listens to his father's oral story-telling) to being an author exclusively, as his roles of identifiable first-person narrator and devout listener to his father's stories fade into the background. Not even his role as an author is explicit anymore when the embedded story of Langston the Fourth commences, yet as the overall, encompassing work is supposedly Langston the Fifth's novel, this is the role that can hardly be shed or stepped back from.

A final example underlines the function of oscillating back and forth between frame narrative and embedded narratives as well as between the embedded narratives themselves, frequently accompanied by changes of perspective and/or the insertion of documentation such as diaries or letters. The boundaries separating the narrator-cum-author and his sources as

---

course we have to keep in mind that on the level of Hill's novel, they are fictitious to begin with). Within Langston the Fifth's novel, the reproduction of journals, letters and other autobiographical elements is supposed to authenticate his writing, which is why these elements are conceptualized in contrast to fiction (cf. Mill's juxtaposing "stuff", viz. 'fact', with "imagination", viz. 'fiction', AKB 133; also cf. above).

well as the different time layers of his story seem permeable, so that Langston the Fifth is able to pass back and forth between the past and the present, taking advantage of numerous oral and written accounts. Some of these accounts are easily available (his father's stories, for instance, which the older Cane liberally dishes out particularly if they make him appear in a favorable light), yet some are hard to come by (e.g. the archives at a closed-down college that Langston and his companions have to bribe their way into). It is not the case that past and present are indistinguishable; upon close reading, it is possible to tell which Langston is referred to at almost any given moment, even though the defining addition 'First' to 'Fifth' is habitually omitted to great effect. *Any Known Blood* is governed by a sensibly structured chronological undercurrent, even though at the surface level, the reader is often initially dazzled. A notable example is the transition from the novel's second to its third chapter, which broadly corresponds to a shift from the level of Langston the Fifth and the frame narrative to the embedded story at the level of Langston the Fourth's initial years in Canada. The complex shift begins with the frame narrative, in which Langston the Fifth learns that Langston the Fourth plans to visit his old-time nemesis Norville Watson. Chapter two closes with the phrase "Norville Watson had opened a medical practice there [on Bloor Street, Toronto] shortly after he had denied my parents rental accommodation in 1954" (AKB 27), thus foreshadowing the story of how Langston the Fourth and his wife were refused as tenants on racist grounds.

Instead of shifting right into this part of the Cane family history, however, Hill opens chapter three with a continuation of the first-person frame narrative by Langston the Fifth, though forwarding to a different spatial and temporal setting: Langston retreats, as is his habit, to a café to ponder his relatively bleak situation ("if one had to lose a job, childless and divorced was the best way to go", AKB 28). Langston recalls that his mother had told him about his father's newly developed routine of unexpectedly dropping in on people. This thought, triggered by a past comment from Langston the Fifth's mother, prompts him to recollect a story his *father* had told him about a de facto segregated night club in Toronto, in which an Africadian boxer named Winston Carruthers had severely beaten up a racist bouncer around 1970. Though the bouncer had started the fight, Carruthers had been sentenced to eighteen months in jail. Langston the Fifth narratively slips into the incident at the club (a situation in which he could not in fact have been present) without being detectable as a narrator, returning, however, to the first-person perspective when reflecting his family's reaction towards the case (which, of course, he would have experienced in person). Langston the Fifth at several points emphasizes his presence and direct witnessing of the incident's repercussions (claiming that "I sat by the television" when Carruthers dropped by to see his father, AKB 30, or recalling that "[o]ne time, I heard him mumble" about Carruthers, AKB 31, etc.). From the recollection of Carruthers visiting his father in 1964, Langston moves on to describe his father in turn calling on Carruthers in 1995.[351] The latter visit triggers a switching back to the point

---

351 To all appearances, there is a slight mishap involved in the sequencing on Hill's side: "Some twenty-five years ago" (AKB 28), as Langston the Fifth recalls, Carruthers got into the fight at the Toronto club, which would mean (given that the frame narrative is set in 1995) that the incident took place some time around 1970. Carruthers is sentenced to eighteen months in prison (cf. AKB

of departure, viz. his father's plan to see Norville Watson. Before in fact telling the story of
Watson denying rent to his parents, however, Langston inserts a caveat in which he admits
that there are many versions of this story and that the one he will retell is his choice alone (cf.
the discussion of reconstruction and assertiveness in this chapter; 199f.). Eventually, Langston
the Fifth engages in unfolding the story of the Watson incident. While doing so, however,
Langston uses a final complication that reflects the presence of the past, which seems to in-
trude upon him while he is sitting in the café and sharing his thoughts in what is almost a
stream-of-consciousness technique. Simultaneously, Langston in his own narrative indulges
in the past from his present position. Past and present thus seem to be mutually approaching
each other until they meet and conflate in a space of recollection. At this point, Langston the
Fourth's story, initially told by Langston the Fifth, seems to tell itself as the narrator steps
back (though leaving a lingering remnant of the author Langston the Fifth):

> Dad was in his last year of medical school, and my mother had finished her studies and taken
> a job with the Toronto Labor Committee for Human Rights, and it fell upon her to head out
> on her lunch hour to find a place for them to live. They both wanted to rent part of a house.
> After rejecting a few flats that had cockroaches or that demanded princely rents, Dorothy
> found the perfect flat on the second floor of a house on Palmerston Boulevard. Langston
> could walk to the university in twenty minutes. (AKB 33)

Moving almost imperceptibly from calling his parents 'dad' and 'mother' to calling them,
with a third-person (narrator's) distance, 'Langston' and 'Dorothy', Langston the Fifth employs a shift that reflects the novel's overall construction: switching back and forth between
first-hand eyewitness reports and the reconstruction of orature and written documentation,
Langston the Fifth bridges – not questions! – the borders between his experiences and the
experiences others have made and have either recorded or otherwise passed on. The amalgam
is a collect*ed*, but also collect*ive* (hi)story, a memory version that might be one out of many,
yet the one Langston the Fifth "choose[s] to believe." (Ibid.) The complex transitions between
the Cane generations, between different media, different carriers of recollection, and different
narrative modes thus underline the complexities that characterize the remembering, reconstructing and passing on of memories. In the same vein, they also illustrate the complexities
of writing. In the end, it is difficult for both a writer and a reader to make sense of the different voices, perspectives and events, but it is possible nonetheless – after all, the constructions
performed by Langston the Fifth are not arbitrary and do not come out of the blue; they are
based on evidence and incentives provided by orature and archival material which are amal-
gamated into the fictional account. In terms of memory constructions, Hill thus underlines
that we can indeed rely on external sources, that we can lay claim to collective memories over

---

29), of which he serves nine; this would add another three quarters of a year to Langston the
Fifth's estimate. Carruthers comes to Langston the Fourth looking for a job after being released
from prison, yet his visit (and subsequent employment) is set in the summer of *1964* (cf. AKB
31). There is no indication, however, that Hill included this temporal discrepancy to create ambivalence or to hint at failing memory as in historiographic metafiction; rather, the chronological
inconsistency is likely a mere error indeed.

generations and integrate into our own experiences and self-conception memories that were not originally ours but transmitted narratively. As Mill puts it, "I have heard so many stories about [Langston the Fourth's] wedding that I feel as if I attended it." (AKB 5).

Both Aberdeen Williams and the transitions between different layers of Langston the Fifth's account – the first one on the level of characters embodying/carrying memories and the latter one on the level of literary devices – serve to bridge the generations and join the different levels or stories included in Hill's novel. They reveal but supersede the seams between past and present; they blur boundaries, yet they do not blur them in the sense of masking but in the sense of bridging and taking the reader effortlessly and subtly from one (hi)story to another. Both also underline the actual *possibility* and the effect of indeed accessing the past and including collective memories that span generations. Yet *Any Known Blood* does not stop at abstractly indicating the possibility and processes involved in excavating and bringing to the functional memory those memories that have been buried. It also puts forward examples of these memories, thus discussing a (counter-)identity that is based on a faithful inclusion and representation of a set of key memories – as opposed to a (supposedly) white-washed, lopsidedly selective mainstream construction.

6.3. Movements II:
Back and Forth Across the 49th Parallel

> *Oakville, Mattie agreed, was a strange and lovely town. No-*
> *body beat up on you, or brought out a whip, or threatened to*
> *drag you back into slavery. But colored people were still made*
> *to feel like outsiders. 'The only talking that white people here*
> *want to do with me is about how wicked American slavery is,*
> *and how I must think I have died and gone to paradise, now*
> *that I'm in Oakville.' (AKB 461)*

6.3.1. Embedded slave narrative

North American slavery is one of the central key memories repeatedly expatiated upon in African-Canadian literature. As far as *Any Known Blood* is concerned, it is of course Langston the First who personifies the North American history of slavery by covering (like Aminata Diallo in *The Book of Negroes*) aspects ranging from plantation slavery in the southern US to the expectation of a Promised Land north of the 49th parallel. Hill comprehensively covers the topic of slavery by inserting a (Neo-) slave narrative into his novel.[352] This Neo-slave narra-

---

352 For a discussion of the (Neo-) slave narrative, cf. chapter 5.2., p. 83ff. I will use the terms Neo-slave narrative and slave narrative interchangeably in this section, though strictly speaking, we are clearly dealing with a *Neo*-slave narrative here, i.e. a fictional emulation of the original, autobiographical slave narratives written by ex-slaves. Yet Hill's narrative is written almost entirely in the mode of a classic slave narrative, so that both terms can be applied here liberally.

tive consists of the fictional memoirs of Langston the First and is 'reprinted' as a first-person narrative that takes the guise of a classic slave narrative. It is made clear earlier in the novel that the memoirs we are presented with here are the very same ones that Langston the First (who had been presumed dead) had handed to his son, who in turn at some point forwards it to the Harpers Ferry museum.[353] The embedded slave narrative comprises the entire second-to-last chapter of *Any Known Blood* (chapter 22) and is its most expansive subpart. Though not explicitly dealing with issues of appropriation and autonomous authentication, it is clear that the slave narrative in question shows relevant parallels to Aminata Diallo's account in *The Book of Negroes*. Both dispense with the modes of external authentication largely relied upon by the original slave narrative (e.g. in form of testimonies or documents by White amanuenses or patrons). It is not clear, however, if Langston the First's account was indeed meant for publication, whereas Aminata's story is overtly conceptualized as a written testimony targeting a wider readership.

Langston the First's slave narrative begins with the characteristic phrase "I was born" (AKB 429; also cf. the respective remarks on p. 123f. of this thesis), yet diverges from the standard opening by citing an exact date of birth instead of a rough estimate; while the classic slave narrative emphasizes the fact that the slaves were deprived of knowing for sure their own spatial and temporal origins, *Any Known Blood*'s embedded slave account emphasizes knowledge, authenticity and assertiveness instead of enforced ignorance.[354] Langston the First thus gives as his date of birth the year 1828, then goes on to sketch losing his freedom and being separated from his parents, who are successively sold south.[355] The description of plantation slavery matches both the classic mould and Aminata's narrative, encompassing cruel

---

353 Langston the Second considers the memoir of interest to the museum because of its description of John Brown's raid and the corresponding claim that Langston the First was part of the attack.

354 The introductory phrase "I was born" finds a mirror expression in the chapter's last lines, which read: "There's no point regretting what I've done. I had to live the way I was born. That ends my account." (AKB 494) Three aspects are included here: first, plainly, Hill uses the final expression as a narrative structural device to notify the reader of the fact that the embedded slave narrative has indeed come to an end. Second, Langston the First summarizes his life, which was in fact a life of both valor and misconduct (the latter pertaining to his repeated unfaithfulness in particular; cf. AKB 463, 465, 469f., 482f.). Third, the closing remarks relate back to the first lines of Langston the First's memoir and have to be read in connection with them: "I was born in Virginia in 1828. I will not say that I was born a slave, for I do not care for the word. I was born free, but a tobacco plantation owner named Jenkins took my freedom." (AKB 428) If, then, Langston "had to live the way [he] was born", it was a life preordained by his enslavement and subsequent re-liberation. His story thus had to unfold along the lines of trying to reverse the outrageous injustice that he suffered when he was objectified, i.e. when he was declared mere property by Jenkins.

355 Again, there are remarkable (though relatively unsurprising) parallels to Aminata's experiences, e.g. the fact that Langston is visited by his mother from time to time after she is sold to another plantation (cf. Chekura's visits to the Appleby plantation where Aminata is enslaved) or the emotional crippling caused by the passed-on trauma of enslavement, which frequently forestalls loving relationships. Langston the First admits: "It causes me great shame to say that, on the third visit, I told my mother I hated her." (AKB 42) Cf. Fanta's infanticide in the face of passing on her status of property; also cf. Aminata's admission of hardly being a cheerful mother.

whippings, rape, and humiliation (cf. AKB 429ff.). Langston the First experiences the power-lessness and associated shame at being unable to help his fellow slaves in the same way that Aminata repeatedly experiences the agonizing impotence in the face of slavery (just as in the Freetown incident described in *The Book of Negroes*, there is a swift and deadly stop to a rescue attempt by a daring individual; cf. AKB 433, BN 399f.). Similarly, the feeling of help-lessness and the witnessing of ruthless cruelty make Langston the First pose questions of the-odicy just as *The Book of Negroes*' Fanta, during the Middle passage, and Aminata repeatedly do: "I don't believe in such a thing as God, for I have seen too much to believe that He would condone the things Man has done to Man." (AKB 432)[356] In the end, Langston the First poi-sons an overseer to avenge the humiliation of a female slave and thus overcomes, albeit in a morally more than questionable way, his powerlessness. In 1850, having secretly learned to read and write (another characteristic element of the classic slave narrative and a trait he shares with Aminata, who is as avid a learner as Langston), he forges a pass with which he escapes from the Maryland plantation he had been sold to by his original owner.

Making his way north on his own and without any specific planning, Langston quite accidentally comes across an Underground Railroad station run by a Quaker. Another Quaker saves him in Canandaigua (southeast of Rochester on Lake Ontario) by hiding him in a crawl space. It is this very same crawl space – at least, as much is suggested – that Langston the Fifth finds at the very outset of his journey to Baltimore when he begins to research the fami-ly history (cf. AKB 61ff.). Clearly, thus, there is a generational bridging achieved by Lang-ston the Fifth's discovery, turning the safe house which harbored Langston the First in the 1850s into a literal site of memory. Like the very first Langston Cane in his life-saving crawl space, memories are buried slightly beyond sight, hid away underneath the surface. Yet there are pointers and sources that Langston the Fifth can rely on in his search, which turns into a veritable quest: his interest is piqued by a "historical plaque describing the building as a safe house on the Underground Railroad in the 1840s and 1850s." (AKB 60) The location indeed matches family lore: "According to a family legend," Langston the Fifth reports, "one of my ancestors – a fugitive slave – holed up for some time in this town." (AKB 61)[357] It turns out

---

356 Likewise, religion for Langston the First seems to be the 'opium of the slaves' (to modify the famous but often misquoted phrase by Karl Marx): Langston the First does not mind other peo-ple's adhering to the Christian faith, "[b]ut I think the Bible is just a scheme to keep Negroes from slitting their masters' throats." (447) Accordingly, when he joins John Brown's party in their fight against slavery, it is not because, as John Brown holds, slavery is a sin against God but a sin against man (cf. AKB 466). Ironically, Langston the First fathers two generations of church min-isters.

357 Langston had identified his father as the source of this information before (AKB 60). Note the ironic usage of the phrase "holed up" in this context; the crawl space indeed is "a hole about three feet wide, four feet deep, and five feet long", complete with a "coffin-sized tunnel" (AKB 61). The comparison with a coffin is repeated by Langston the First in his memoirs as well as by Ab-erdeen, who has gathered his information and adopted the comparison from his grandfather. The metaphorical uniformity of course points to the fact that even though we are facing different ac-counts or points of view, the memory in question *per se* is still the factual basis of these accounts – a basis, that is, that all of them try to faithfully describe.

that the family orature conforms to the written record left by Langston the First so that the chain of evidence becomes fairly unquestionable. In extension, of course, this mutual verification spills over into other realms so that, for instance, Langston the Fourth's story-telling – which is shown to be unequivocally dependable in the case of Langston the First's hideout – gains a general air of reliability. In an extended reciprocal verification of Langston the First's story and the orature surrounding it, Hill also uses the authority of Aberdeen Williams (which, in turn, is itself confirmed by the additional verification), whose grandfather had been a contemporary and a friend of the first Langston Cane. Aberdeen fills in Langston the Fifth with "more details. [...] A fugitive slave, [Langston the First] had apparently spent some nights hiding in damp, coffin-like conditions near Canandaigua in upper New York State." (AKB 341) Thus, the memory of Langston the First's hiding out is corroborated once more.

Ultimately, there is thus a fourfold, reciprocal authentication of different modes of memory transmission: there is the communicative memory embodied by Aberdeen Williams, who has gained his information directly from a (semi-external) eyewitness. Then there is the intra-family lore that is exemplified by Langston the Fourth's story-telling. This orature represents generational memory just as Aberdeen Williams's recollection, yet it is four times removed instead of twice, thus not being derived directly from an eyewitness. Both kinds of oral transmission are corroborated by the written documentation that Langston the Fifth uncovers and which is independent of the existing orature (as the memoirs had been unheard of before Langston the Fifth stumbles upon them). The two kinds of orature as well as the written memoirs then point to the fourth element in this equation, which is the 'real-life' evidence: literally a *site* of memory, the crawling space at the safe house illustrates the important notion of place as containing, embodying and symbolizing memory (cf. p. 203 of this thesis). As for the content of the substantiated memory, which is collectivized through the use of a number of different carriers and even media, it is of course the dangerous and demanding exodus of slaves from the (southern) United States northwards that is narratively remembered. As in *The Book of Negroes*, the passage from the United States into Canada(-to-be) is of central importance in Hill's second novel for two reasons: first, this passage (which incidentally for both involves a water crossing) is structured as an Exodus and is supposed to take the respective protagonists to a Land of Milk and Honey. Second, the aftermath of this passage is central to and indicative of the novels' approaches to the history of Blacks in *Canada*. As for *The Book of Negroes*, the depiction of a Canaan not secured (as discussed in section 5.3.4. of this thesis, cf. p. 170ff.) heavily relies on Aminata's first experiences in Canada and on both the explicit and implicit comparison between Canada and the United States. For *Any Known Blood*, the constant migrations and remigrations of the successive generations of Langston Canes manifest this point *in extenso*.

6.3.2. Canada and the US: Langston the First

> *Here [in Canada], I had nothing and knew no one to ask for as-*
> *sistance. But I had chosen freedom, with all its insecurities, and*
> *nothing in the world would make me turn away from it.*
> *(Aminata, BN 313)*

> *I was bone tired. And I was hungry. But I was in Canada, and I*
> *was free, so bone tired and hungry didn't matter. (Langston*
> *Cane the First, AKB 448)*

While African-Canadian literature mirrors a number of aspects characterizing Canadian literature *in general*, the tendency to define (African-)Canadian identity in relation – most often, in
contrast – to the United States is a particularly distinctive similarity. Association with or, considerably more frequently so, dissociation from the US has been a staple ingredient of Canadian self-identification,[358] and it is also noteworthy in terms of the Black Canadian community: "English Canadians – whether black, white, yellow, or brown – only agree that they are
not Americans. [...] What both English and French Canadians know is that they are better
than Americans." (Clarke 1998, 100) *Any Known Blood* in particular is concerned with the
migration back and forth across the 49th parallel, as has been repeatedly pointed out.[359] Scholarly discussion of *Any Known Blood* – limited as it is – falls roughly into two prevailing lines
of argument.

One approach, personified by Rinaldo Walcott, backed up by Pilar Cuder-Domínguez
and, particularly so, Moreen Moynagh, holds that Hill emphasizes, by having the Cane family
variously cross the US/Canada border, the permeability of that boundary and the diasporic
nature of the Black North American community.[360] The differences, it is implied in this view,
between the United States and Canada are not as decisive as occasionally suggested by schol-

---

358 Virtually every history of Canadian literature will deal extensively with this issue; also cf. for
    instance Wilkins 1998, the essays in LaBossière 1994 or the recent study on Canadian and Ameri-
    can Studies provided by MacLean 2010.

359 Cf. Clarke 2002a, 310ff.; Cuder-Domínguez 2003; Flagel 2005; Moynagh 2005b; Nurse 2003,
    173f.; Siemerling 2004; Walcott 2003, particularly 67ff.

360 Siemerling agrees with Walcott here to a certain extent, yet largely retracts this position towards
    the end of his essay, conceding that the inclusion of the US in African-Canadian narratives "does
    not mean, however, that they are not Canadian stories, or imitate a 'model blackness'." (2004,
    44f.; the term 'model blackness' is borrowed from Clarke, cf. 2002, 27.) Siemerling further pro-
    vides evidence from Hill's non-fiction writing (such as the *Globe and Mail* article "Black Like
    Us." [2000]) to underline the point that Hill in fact emphasizes a distinctly *Canadian* approach.
    Cuder-Domínguez equally qualifies her approach when concluding that African-American and
    African-Canadian literatures in fact reflect communities which are more disparate than suggested
    by a conception of a North American African diaspora (cf. 2003, 72), though also arguing that
    "African Americanness [provides] a more appropriate example for the modeling of African Cana-
    dian citizenship" than the White European backdrop employed in *Some Great Thing* (2003, 61).

ars such as Gorge Elliott Clarke (see particularly his "Contesting a Model Blackness" and "Must All Blackness Be American?", 2002a, 27ff. and 71ff.). Walcott, however, *over*emphasizes the similarities and *under*states the differences between the two North American nations and cultures. A considerable share of the reception of *Any Known Blood* explicitly reverses the false claim that the US and Canada are principally antonyms in terms of their racial history and their present attitude. What they do, however, is to throw out the baby with the bath water. Hill, who must be considered a specialist in the field – himself being the son of migrants between the two North American nations and having repeatedly lived both north and south of the border – is far from blurring the differences between Canada and the US in *Any Known Blood*.[361] Neither, it must be added immediately, is he reverting to the stereotypical conception of Canada as a Canaan for Blacks. Yet there is, as there generally tends to be, a golden mean,[362] an in-between way that acknowledges both the crucial differences between the United States and Canada – say, between a slave society and a society with slaves – and the similarities that have so frequently been ignored as well, such as the fact that Canada actually *has* a slavery past in the first place. As the exemplifications already indicate, this section is about nuance in part, but it is also simple in its claim that *Any Known Blood* is indeed concerned with representing, as African-Canadian literature in general is wont to, the past and present Black Canadian situation *faithfully*. As such, it resists both the depiction of a Canadian 'paradise' while at the same time stressing the distinctiveness of the *Canadian* experience.

In a nutshell, then, the claim that *Any Known Blood* makes in unison with the majority of African-Canadian literature is that Canadian racism, both past and present, might be a more subtle variant than its US counterpart, but that it has existed and continues to exist nevertheless. This is hardly a revolutionary insight, as Black Canadian cultural writing has propounded this notion for decades; George Borden, for instance, distinguishes in his 1988 poem "Fashions of Slavery" between European, British, American and Canadian style 'slavery', contrasting American plantation slavery with the Black Canadian experience: "False 'freedom' land - / strained welcome - / subtle hatred - / covert discrimination - / Slavery... Canadian style." (Borden 1988) Yet in dealing with African-Canadian literature, it seems that this understanding has regularly been disregarded. Two almost opposing misconceptions must thus be rectified: the first is the whitewashed representation of collective memories that depicts Canada as a safe haven for Blacks in the past and present. The other, however, is a lopsided view purporting that US-American and Canadian Blacks essentially share a common collective memory exhaustively based on shared diasporic experiences. Succinctly, the collective memory advanced by African-Canadian literature is a *distinct* construction, yet it is not a version that is content with reflecting a contrasting moral and sociopolitical superiority.

---

361 When coming to Canada for the first time, Langston the Fourth remarks that "it wasn't really another country at all – it was just Canada" (AKB 67), which, if taken as a straight-faced remark, would support the view put forth by the proponents of the notion of blurred boundaries. The subsequent comparisons, however (frequent and elaborate as they are; cf. the discussion below), clarify the tongue-in-cheek, at least semi-ironic nature of Langston the Fourth's observation.

362 This is both a commonplace and one of Western philosophies founding ideas, cf. Aristotle's *Nichomachean Ethics* (1998).

In the discussion of *The Book of Negroes* it has been pointed out that Aminata exposes in her account – which, like Langston's, spans both North American nations – the *de jure* freedom she enjoys in Canada on the one hand, yet the discrimination and disappointments she endures on the other. Likewise, the genealogical line of Langston Canes, moving back and forth across the 49th parallel, represents a version of Canada that incorporates both the advanced degree of freedom and equality that the Canes indeed enjoy in Canada, yet also the difficulties they face in a country that contrasts itself with the United States in blindingly favorable terms. Though the issue of border crossings in *Any Known Blood* has been dealt with to a considerable degree (at least in relation to the limited overall scholarly attention dedicated to the novel in the first place), the prevailing mode is one of a general assessment regarding the mere fact that several generations of Langston Canes *do* cross the border back and forth. A closer look at the way in which the respective Langston Canes juxtapose their different experiences, however, yields insights beyond and even contrary to the assumption that Hill aimed at a presentation of a unified North American diasporic region and/or the monodirectional influence of African-American on African-Canadian life and culture (the reverse mode is in fact almost never discussed for obvious reasons).

The zigzagging of Langston Canes in *Any Known Blood* might at first sight appear arbitrary, yet it adheres to a certain pattern of migration: with the exception of Langston the Second, all Langston Canes cross the border *twice*, so that they can relate their experiences bidirectionally, noting on the differences between the two North American nations from both points of view. Langston the Fifth is the only Cane whose migration is a) a distinctly temporary, even short-term one, and b) a move in which the 'pull' is far greater than the 'push', even though he decides to elope after being divorced and fired. Langston the Fifth does not intend to settle down in Baltimore, which is an important distinction in an evaluation of the different levels of attractiveness attributed to either one of the two North American nations. Langston the Fifth is in search of his roots, yet he intends to claim them only metaphorically/fictionally, not in practical terms of permanent relocation. Langston the First, in contrast, who establishes the family tradition of migration, bases his decision to leave the United States on a push factor that could hardly be more convincing; it is the urge to escape slavery which drives him from the US. The fact that he chooses Canada as his destination (the alternative would have been to escape southwards, which is an option often not taken into account; cf. Switala 2001, 14f.; Shadd/Cooper/Frost 2005, 17) is based on the mythical conception of a Canaanesque refuge in the North. This notion of a paradisiacal Canada, however, materializes only on the basis of the slavery south of the 49th parallel and thus would not exist without the Peculiar Institution in the United States.

In fact, the very first thing Langston learns about Canada is a mistake in name – and in condition – that underlies the entire conception of Canada for the fugitive slave. While he is enslaved in Maryland, Langston is allowed to run a certain amount of errands for his master, thus briefly coming into contact with other Blacks, who tell him of a mythical place devoid of slavery: "I learned which way was north. Passing through Petersville and talking quick to Negroes – free and captive – I learned that to the north, in a land called Canaan, all men are free." (AKB 436) Langston is thus in fact mistaken – his mix-up is not a pun or a nickname he gives to Canada: he actually believes Canada *is* 'Canaan'. The mere fact that Langston is indeed *mistaking* Canada for Canaan suggests that there is no actual convergence of the two terms. Langston soon discovers that Canada is not in fact called Canaan and that it is sociopolitically no Promised Land either. Langston's confusion clearly reflects the mistaken notion which, according to Black Canadian authors, still dominates collective memory discourse. The two terms, though often taken to be synonyms in regard to Black North Americans, are in fact distinct entities: Canada is *no(t)* Canaan.

Obviously, however, the fate awaiting Langston the First after his ride on the Underground Railroad is an outstanding improvement over his status in the United States. When Langston asks Matilda, the cook aboard Captain Wilson's ship and Langston's future wife, what Oakville, which they are headed for, is like, she answers: "'I call it Nicefolksville,' she said. 'They'll nice you to death.'" (AKB 445) Plainly, the prospect of being 'niced to death' is in no way comparable to the atrocities Langston had experienced in bondage. There is, however, already a certain allusion to a possible downside of Oakville, even though it is not yet fully discernible from Matilda's literal answer. Two readings of Matilda's oracle are possible: first, that Oakville is so friendly as to be dull; second, that there is an actual malignancy underneath the nicety – after all, death is implied here as well. Langston later on also learns about the latter aspect, yet when he first reaches the Canadian shore of Lake Ontario, gratitude is his dominant emotion: "I was bone tired. And I was hungry. But I was in Canada, and I was free, so bone tired and hungry didn't matter." (AKB 448) The very same feeling is reflected in *The Book of Negroes* when Aminata comments upon coming to Canada: "Here [in Canada], I had nothing and knew no one to ask for assistance. But I had chosen freedom, with all its insecurities, and nothing in the world would make me turn away from it." (BN 313) Hill thus underlines, in both novels, that the material insecurity his protagonists face are more than offset by the essential, even existential, notion of their freedom. In isolation, these comments would indeed support the view that Canada contrasts more than favorably with the United States. The expectation of a literal Canaan, however, is refuted even in these very flattering comparisons; the biblical Promised Land, after all, clearly incorporates the promise of a material wealth that neither Langston nor Aminata immediately find in Canada.[363]

Moreover, the larger contexts of the respective stories undermine the assumption of a Canaanesque Canada. In *The Book of Negroes*, for instance, it becomes abundantly clear be-

---

[363] The biblical Canaan is characterized as "a good and spacious land, a land flowing with milk and honey" (Exodus 3:8). In fact, the first thing that the Israelites' scouts report is that the land is, in a literal sense, as fruitful as promised (cf. Numbers 13:26-27 on the scouts returning with fruit from the Promised Land). In terms of the importance of economic well-being and opportunity for the newly-arrived Blacks, it suffices to point, once more, to the fact that out of economic desperation, a number of legally free Blacks indentured themselves for life, a danger documented in both *Any Known Blood* and *The Book of Negroes*. In this regard, the 'Canadian Dream' of Black North Americans is comparable to the American Dream's *promise* (which, in fact, is a misconception) of material success as a reward for hard work (cf. Hochschild 1995, particularly Part One and Part Three dealing with the historical context and the African-American experience respectively).

fore Aminata even leaves for Nova Scotia that the promises of the British are not to be trust-ed; Aminata herself had entered into the Book of Negroes various names of slaves who were expected to remain enslaved in Canada as well. In *Any Known Blood*, the 1930 Ku Klux Klan raid in Oakville, for instance, precedes the embedded slave narrative by several chapters so that the reader is clearly aware of the persistence of racism in spite of the *de jure* freedom celebrated by Langston the First in 1850. Nonetheless, the first comparison between the Unit-ed States and Canada made by any Langston Cane is predominantly favorable. It does point, however, to the overall aspiration of presenting Canada as the historically more accommo-dating nation and still disclosing its shortcomings.

Throughout *Any Known Blood*'s embedded slave narrative, a limbo between compet-ing experiences is the most decisive feature of Langston the First's life as a Black Canadian in the mid-19th century. Langston is caught between the vastly greater freedom he enjoys on the one hand and the limits to his autonomy, which are based on racial stereotyping but remain unacknowledged, on the other hand (in fact, the limits and prejudices imposed on him are not only ignored but bluntly denied by pointing south of the border). Langston is put up temporar-ily by the abolitionist Captain Wilson, for whom he catches rats. Going into an Oakville store for the first time in order to buy arsenic for poisoning rats, Langston faces the subtle racism that characterizes his new home. In a highly revealing way, he is made to wait for all White customers to be served first,[364] then he is asked what "a Negro [was] going to do with arsenic" (AKB 455), as if a Black person would do something different with arsenic than a White one.[365] The shopkeeper continues to treat Langston as if he were a child, which Langston counters, in the manner of Aminata, with mock naïvety: "Do you actually think I am your son?" (ibid.) While the remaining customers mutter about Langston as if he were absent, the shopkeeper tells Langston, who charges his purchase to Wilson's account, that he should have told him "in the first place that you were here on [Wilson's] behalf", to which Langston re-plies: "I'm here on my behalf. But it's going on his account." (Ibid.) Wittily, Langston thus establishes his subjectivity and autonomy, making clear that due to his newly achieved status, he will govern his own affairs and not be directed by others.

On top of demonstrating his emancipation, he even seems to reverse stereotypical as-sumptions about role distribution by suggesting that while *he* is in fact in possession of agen-cy in this case, it is Wilson who is somehow obliged to pay for his expenses. The shopkeeper, however, continues to subject Langston to stereotypical conjectures, showing utter surprise at his request to sign for the goods he has bought: "You can write, can you?" (ibid.) Like

---

364 This is one of the quintessential African-Canadian experiences; cf. for instance Daddy Moses in *The Book of Negroes*, who tells Aminata that she should "[g]et good and comfortable at the back of the line" (BN 316; cf. section 5.3.4. of this thesis).

365 The shopkeeper of course is unaware of the irony involved here: while Langston is indeed fetch-ing arsenic to poison rats, he *had* killed an overseer with rat poison before. The toxin thus sym-bolizes Langston's skills (as a masterful rat catcher, the ex-slave eventually even comes to a cer-tain level of economic security, if not prosperity) but also his vengeance. The very substance he used to kill a slave-driver with is now employed to render a service to Captain Wilson, who had rescued Langston the First from slavery.

Aminata in *The Book of Negroes*,[366] Langston displays the skill essential to deconstruct stereo-typical assumptions about Black inferiority and assert his humanity: he is literate. The former slave is thus able to fend off and revert the subtle racism directed at him in Canada, yet it is made explicit that there *is* a certain degree of – albeit restrained – discrimination in the True North as well, exemplified by the shopkeeper's behavior and pejorative comments ("Well, that takes the cake. A nigger who needs arsenic and knows how to write." ibid.). Langston the First continues to make experiences of this kind so that his oscillating between gratefulness for the absence of institutionalized slavery (and, for the most part, of overt violence) and the suffering from institutionalized as well as individual racism becomes his – as well as the Black community's – defining condition in Oakville.

> Oakville, Mattie agreed, was a strange and lovely town. Nobody beat up on you, or brought out a whip, or threatened to drag you back into slavery. But colored people were still made to feel like outsiders. 'The only talking that white people here want to do with me is about how wicked American slavery is, and how I must think I have died and gone to paradise, now that I'm in Oakville.' (AKB 461)

In the early 1800s, i.e. only four or five decades prior to this remark, Mattie's observation that in Canada, no one "threatened to drag you back into slavery" would simply have been coun-terfactual, as Hill also points out in *The Book of Negroes* (where he expansively comments on the fear of re-enslavement that gripped the Black community).[367] As of 1850/51, Mattie cata-logues the three most defining issues facing the (recent) African-Canadians: the absence of slavery and its concomitant cruelty; the subtle racism and racial othering prevailing in Cana-da; the denial of racism accompanied by and based on a favorable comparison with the United States that positions Canada as an alleged paradise for Blacks. Insisting on a Canadian pre-eminence in racial matters is one of the distinctive reactions of White Canadian characters in *Any Known Blood* whenever there is even a hint of disparagement regarding their achieve-ments and moral integrity. When John Brown, the US-American abolitionist whose raid Langston the First joins later on, and Captain Wilson, the Canadian abolitionist who assisted, at great personal risk, the first Langston to escape slavery, meet for the first time, a telltale dialogue unfolds:

> 'The bondage of men. It is a blight to our great nation.' [Brown said.] '*Your* great nation,' Captain Wilson said. 'We are on *British* soil, here.' 'Correct,' Brown said, 'but surely we are not insensitive to the outrages of slavery. Canada West, after all, is only a quarter century

---

366 Aminata is likewise faced with incredulity when she confronts Whites with her literacy (the very phrasing of a surprised White person in Nova Scotia bears a strong similarity to the shopkeeper's remark in *Any Known Blood*: "You kin read, kin ya?" BN 450). Cf. for a thorough discussion of the emancipatory effects of literacy and its importance for the (Neo-) slave narrative chapter 5.2., "Narrative, Memory, Authenticity I".

367 The dwindling of legal slavery in Canada prior to its official abolishment in 1834 of course spurred nose-snubbing and augmented the feeling of moral superiority. Langston the First re-marks that, while in the US the Fugitive Slave Act took effect, "[i]n Canada West, there was a lot of talk about the abolition of *American* slavery." (AKB 466, my emphasis)

removed from slavery.' 'Mr. Brown,' Captain Wilson said, 'I beg you not to patronize me in
my own country and in my own home. [...]'   (AKB 471, my emphasis)

Dismissing a specifically *Canadian* history of slavery, Wilson, in a reaction characteristic
both individually and collectively, refuses to be lectured on the shortcomings of the True
North. Still, John Brown, whose moral integrity – in contrast to his sanity[368] – is undoubted in
Any Known Blood, confronts the Canadian with the historical truth of Canada's involvement
in North American slavery. Evidently, John Brown's position in this dispute corresponds to
Hill's position as a writer of counter-hegemonic historical fiction: running the risk of outright
dismissal of his undertaking and of being accused of belittling the Canadian achievements in
terms of racial equality, he still propounds a collective memory version that explicitly comprises and assimilates the darker spots in Canadian history. It must be added here that reactions toward Hill's continued efforts to present a faithful version of Black Canadian history
have in fact not corresponded to the reaction displayed by Wilson here; at worst, Hill's exer-
tions have been ignored, while at best (and this is the prevailing response by far), they have
been critically and popularly embraced, a fact vividly underlined by his latest novel being
longlisted for the Giller Prize and awarded the Commonwealth Writers Prize. Yet recent suc-
cesses notwithstanding, African-Canadian literature still is in a position where it might be
accused of ungratefully fouling its own nest: why, in fact, must they exhibit Canadian slavery
and Canadian racism while in comparison, the United States have done and continue to do so
much worse? The answer is, as has been expounded in this thesis repeatedly, that African-
Canadian literature is involved in creating a *faithful* version of collective memory constructions in order to arrive at a more balanced and fair national self-perception[369] (from which, of
course, sociopolitical claims may be derived).

6.3.3. *Canada and the US: Langston the Second and the Third*

> *What is the Klan doing here? You never told me they were in
> Canada. (Hazel, AKB 315)*

Langston Cane the Second is the only Cane who does not cross the border twice. When, shortly after the Civil War, he moves from Canada to Baltimore with his mother, Matilda Cane,
and his two brothers, Langston Junior and Langston Senior, he "remember[s] it as the longest

---

368 Historians disagree about the degree of Brown's fanaticism. For a critical stance, cf. particularly
   Oates 1984. DuBois 1997 takes a far more appreciative view, while Reynolds 2005 sets out to
   demonstrate Brown's history-changing impact.

369 It should be fairly obvious in this context that there is a strongly *national* focus involved here;
   indeed, it is the very pitting of the United States against Canada that is attacked in its current form
   but established on a different level. Consequently, there is no smelting of the two nations in a
   diasporic crucible as is assumed every so often. Instead, the Canadian distinctiveness as a Promised Land is undermined but *replaced* by a more differentiated, nuanced picture which nonetheless claims a pronounced distinctiveness.

trip he'd taken in his life." (AKB 410) From the very beginning of Langston the Second's journey, distance and contrast is thus stressed rather than closeness and similarity. The Canes' relocation is haunted by bad omens – Langston's puppy dies in the Pittsburgh heat and when they arrive in Baltimore, his mother is coughing blood – foreshadowing a bleak period in the life of Langston II. While he had noticed the change in temperature before (and found the heat in the US oppressing), he notices further differences between his Canadian home and his future domicile:[370]

> Langston [II] noticed the noise. The commotion. The stink. The heat. But, more than anything else, he gaped at the masses of Negroes. [...] they squeezed into neighborhoods festering with screams and smoke and excrement. (AKB 411)[371]

Having run out of work in Canada, Matilda had decided to go back to Baltimore in search for a better life. What the Canes find is a place where they are part of a much larger Black community than they had been up north, yet it is – as Langston's observations vividly underline – a community that is crammed, run-down, dirty and desperate.[372] When Matilda realizes she may have made a mistake, it is too late for the Canes to turn back. "You oughta git on back up north", she is told (AKB 410), but the advanced stage of her illness will not permit her to undertake another journey of more than 700 kilometers to go back to Oakville, Ontario. In comparison, then, Oakville seems to have been the better alternative for the Canes, who are, however, stuck in a city whose atmosphere becomes increasingly repressive. The fact that Langston is not used to the warm temperatures is indicative of the socialization which has not pre-

---

370 The change in temperature, though considerably stereotypical, is a common indicator of the border crossing and the perceived differences between Canada and the United States. Aminata, in *The Book of Negroes*, equally notices the climatic differences when travelling between Canada and the US for the first time (cf. BN 312). Hill also uses the clichéd difference in temperature in tongue-in-cheek ways in *Any Known Blood*, for instance in a dialogue between Millicent Cane and Yoyo, in which Yoyo explains that he used to live in Winnipeg for some time. "'I don't know where *that* is.' [Millicent responds; ironically, she *had* known where Cameroon is when they spoke about Yoyo's roots before.] 'North of Minneapolis. That's what I always tell Americans.' 'That must have been halfway to the North Pole. You must have froze [sic] your backside out there.'" (AKB 223)

371 The description of Baltimore's Black neighborhood is strongly reminiscent of the portrayal of Canvas Town (New York) and Birchtown (Nova Scotia) in *The Book of Negroes*. One thing is made clear, however: "'It's not their fault,' Nathan Shoemaker [a Quaker, grandson of a well-known abolitionist and later on foster parent of Langston the Second] said. 'They've been squeezed in here like animals. What else could you expect?'" (AKB 417) The entire atmosphere is even evocative of a slave ship or pen such as variously described by Aminata, relying heavily on the olfactory element ("'My God, the stench,' said a man", ibid.). For an example of a similarly underdeveloped community in which the horrid sanitary conditions were condoned – possibly even consciously brought about – by city officials, cf. the history of Africville (see p. 52 of this thesis).

372 In fact, the Black community is so overcrowded that serious problems ensue, as one community member explains to Matilda: "The problem with Baltimore is there's too many culluds. There's gettin' to be so many of us that the white peoples are starting to hate us." (AKB 411)

pared him or his family for conditions south of the border. In terms of racism, they have come to Baltimore overly naïve, unwary and unprepared.

In the Freedmen's Bureau, where Matilda is looking for support (but is sexually harassed instead), the Canes are told to watch out for "snatchers" who take boys as "apprentices" (AKB 412). In fact, the kidnapping of Black boys has grown into a profitable business: "Children were being stolen away and made to work. The papers said it was like slavery all over again." (AKB 416) The recurrence of a slavery-like institution of course starkly comments on the situation of Blacks in Baltimore.[373] The Canes, however, are blithely unaware of such dangers, having grown up in an environment which did not pose dangers of this magnitude to the African-Canadians. While Matilda admits that she does not know what a 'snatcher' is, Langston the Second applies his 'Canadian' standards to the living conditions of Blacks in the US: he believes he knows the nature of the 'apprenticeship' the boys are forced into – after all, it was quite common for boys to take up an apprenticeship with one of the local craftsmen in Oakville (cf. AKB 412). Matilda finds employment in Nathan Shoemaker's house but soon dies of her lung ailment. Shortly after her death (and predictably so in terms of narrative logic), Langston's brothers are in fact captured by snatchers, while Langston the Second manages to escape the kidnappers and is subsequently adopted by Shoemaker.

Langston II's misunderstanding of 'apprenticeship' in regard to the kidnappers provides the inverted parallel to Langston I's mix-up of 'Canada' and 'Canaan' (cf. above). While the latter experiences the hell of slavery in the US, looking for ways to escape north, the former has come to the US after the Civil War, unprepared for the less-than-subtle racism that still dominates race relations in the US at the time. Thus, Canada contrasts favorably with the United States in the case of Langston II, who is the first Langston Cane to permanently cross the Canada-US border southwards. Nonetheless, he does not remigrate but moves on to become a church minister at Bethel A.M.E., a vocation in which he is succeeded by his son, Langston the Third, who is born in Annapolis, Maryland, in 1896.

While Langston the Second is only a minor character in the novel, Langston the Third receives ample space. He joins a segregated regiment in World War I, though only half-heartedly expecting that upon returning from Europe, the African-American soldiers would be welcomed back with open arms. His regiment is indeed among the last to be pulled from Europe (cf. AKB 175), an experience which mirrors the treatment of *Canadian* Blacks in both *Any Known Blood* and *The Book of Negroes*.[374] When he finally returns home, he has not only

---

373 The post-slavery danger of being recaptured finds its parallel in *The Book of Negroes*' description of the constant danger of re-enslavement Aminata and her fellow Blacks face even in Canada (cf. BN 208, 321). Neo-slavery thus looms over both North American nations – again, however, in smaller scale north of the 49th parallel (which is underlined not only by the Canes' ignorance of the problem but also by the fact that in *The Book of Negroes*, the danger in Canada is described but does not affect the protagonist directly, while in *Any Known Blood*, the snatchers actually kidnap Langston II's two brothers in Baltimore).

374 Cf. Langston I, who is kept waiting in the store where he wants to buy arsenic (discussed above) as well as once more Aminata's disillusionment when she learns that the newly arrived

been unfaithful to his wife – which he blames on the overlong deployment in France – but also realizes that his skepticism concerning White America's attitude towards its Black soldiers was in fact justified. In a letter to Rose, Langston had written in February 1919:

> The colored boys over here can't wait to get home. They think everything will be different, now that they've fought for their country. I'm not so sure. The way I see it, white people in America haven't seen – and won't necessarily care to know – what we have gone through in the trenches. (AKB 175)

Just like his son, Langston Cane IV, Langston III is disenchanted with the United States when he returns from war. When he is offered a parish in Oakville in 1923, he thus gladly accepts, also hoping that a relocation would improve his ailing marriage to Rose (cf. AKB 190). Arriving in Toronto by train, Langston soon develops a very nuanced understanding of Canadian race relations. On their first night in Canada, they sit, "to their amazement, next to white folks in an Italian restaurant." (AKB 192) Adding ambivalence to this rather flattering depiction, however, Hill hastens to pour some water into the wine of racial equality in Canada: "They were assured, however, that not every restaurant and not every hotel would admit black people. You just had to know where to go." (ibid.) Thus, the initial experiences made by Langston in Canada reflect, as is the novel's general pattern concerning the assessment of matters of race in Canada *vis à vis* the United States, a stock taking *en miniature*: in the early 1920s, segregation in Canada is far less severe than in the United States, where the color code reigns supreme. Yet segregation, at least on an informal and inconsistent level, does in fact exist.

Langston the Third once more experiences the often submerged limits of African-Canadian equality a short time after he, Rose, and Mill(icent) have settled in at their new home (Langston the Fourth is not yet born, but he has been conceived on their first night in Oakville). Having been called to pray for a Black boy dying from dehydration, Langston manages to get the boy into a 'politely segregated' hospital, as the only doctor who used to treat Black patients had moved away. The boy's sickness itself is based on the bad living conditions that most of Oakville's Black residents endure (cf. AKB 277f.), signifying again the structural racism that pervades their lives. Barely having been able to stop a driver willing to take the boy to a hospital in the first place, Langston has to go over the nurse's head to actually see a doctor: in contrast to an old woman who is "white as a starched shirt" (AKB 276) and comes to the hospital after Langston's emergency to be given an appointment for her "swollen legs" immediately (ibid.), there are no doctors and no appointments available for a dying Black boy. In the end, however, the minister is able to convince a doctor to treat the boy – who thus survives in spite of his obvious status as a second-class citizen and human being.

This episode vividly underscores the experiences made by Langston III in other instances, such as the minstrel play performed by Blacks and Whites alike, which he eventually manages to call off. More importantly, however, the experiences made by Langston III are mirrored by the ones his son and grandson make. Langston IV is denied rent on racial grounds

---

Africadians are at the end of the line when it comes to land distribution in Nova Scotia (cf. discussion in section 5.3.4.).

in Canada, and Langston V saves a Black boy in a drive-by shooting in Baltimore when no-body else sees fit to help the wounded adolescent.[375] The underlying common ground between these examples, both Canadian and US-American, is the existence of a type of racism which (in Canada earlier than in the US) is non-institutional, not legally anchored but a *de facto* living condition. Given the fact that Hill links the restrained racism experienced by Langston III to the one his offspring faces, it must be argued that what is exposed here is an ongoing process of racial discrimination. Collective memories (such as the injustices remembered by Black communities all over Canada, personified for instance by Edith Clayton in Nova Scotia) mingle with communicative memories of contemporary injustices to form a mutually reinforcing key memory of subtle discrimination which – in contrast to racism in the United States – remains largely unacknowledged.

One of the pivotal – and maybe most controversial – scenes depicting the differences between the US and Canada in terms of racism is the portrayal of a Ku Klux Klan (KKK) raid in Oakville in 1930. It is also a scene which is indicative of Hill's approach to 'faction'.

Langston the Third shelters an interracial couple (Aberdeen "Ab" Williams and his girlfriend Evelyn, whose mother is violently opposed to Evelyn's involvement with a Black man and had hence called the KKK) in his house when five cars with Klansmen drive up to his home and demand that he turn over the couple. While Langston's mother-in-law is struck with panic and incredulity ("What is the Klan doing here? You never told me they were in Canada." AKB 315),[376] Langston is quickly able to recover from the shock and leaves the house to confront the Klan members. Setting up two crosses in Langston's front yard and lighting one of them, the Klansmen are temporarily held up by Langston, who produces a gun. When all the window panes have been shattered and Langston's house is about to be set on fire, Oakville's police chief Phillips appears with the mayor and another church minister as

---

375 In fact, Langston the Fifth is taken for a White man when assisting the boy; a bystander angrily lets him know: "No matter, Mr. White Man, he's gonna die, we all die around here, what you doin' here watchin' us all die?" (AKB 217)

376 Hazel's disbelief is mirrored by Roberta Small's, who is the wife of the Presbyterian Church minister. When Langston hides his kids in her basement, she cannot believe that the KKK has actually come to Oakville ("The Klan? In Oakville? You're kidding!" AKB 314). In fact, the attitude revealed by Langston's mother-in-law and Roberta Small is significant on two levels: first, it is comparable to the naïve approach taken by Langston II towards the term "apprenticeship", whose distorted and threatening implication of being taken into neo-slavery never crosses his mind. Hazel and Roberta quite simply are not used to connecting the Klan with Canada. Their socialization does not include KKK members in the True North. Likewise, Langston's children, when seeing the hooded Klansmen for the first time, assume they have dressed up as ghosts for a costume party (cf. AKB 313; the scene is written somewhat awkwardly as the lead-up to the children's assumption, their having been to a costume party, is inserted a little artificially). Yet there is a second aspect to the ignorance that is exhibited: at least for the adults involved, there is certainly the relatively sheltered situation in Canada which contributes to their incredulity. Also, however, there is a certain degree of finger-pointing and an air of superiority involved; after all, blunt racism as the one exhibited by the KKK could only exist in the rabidly racist United States, the logic suggests, while in Canada, such overt racism is unheard of.

his deputies and the Klansmen are arrested on a series of minor offences such as arson and "[u]sing a mask unlawfully" (AKB 322).

Hill models this incident on a like event in Oakville on February 28, 1930, when seventy-five Klansmen drove from Hamilton to Oakville to prevent the marriage of an interracial couple, Ira Johnson and Isabella Jones (whose mother had notified the Klan of her daughter's plans). Hill describes the incident in detail in his non-fictional *Black Berry, Sweet Juice*, devoting the chapter "I Was Here Before the Klan" to the historical event and his own fictional rendition of it. He also describes the doubts and worries he has developed in retrospect regarding this scene:

> All the research I did on the arbitrariness of race and the importance of self-definition brought to mind an incident I fictionalized in my novel *Any Known Blood*. I now have some misgivings about the scene, and they stem from an encounter I had in 1997, while on a cross-country tour to promote the book. After a reading, I was approached by a white bookstore manager, who clasped my hand, took a minute to wax enthusiastic about the novel, and then said, 'You know what I really love about this novel? And do you know one of the reasons why it's going to sell? When I read your book, I didn't have to feel guilty for being white.' [...]
>
> Had I given the bookstore manager too much room to wander? Had I let her get into mischief? Had I allowed her to think that she didn't have to consider her own life in a society that still oppresses black people? [...] Was this scene sufficiently candy-coated to allow the bookstore manager to feel that the Klan's raid was an entertaining but insignificant part of Oakville's history? I'm afraid it was. (BBSJ, 213-215)

The 'candy-coating' Hill refers to pertains to the way in which the description of the KKK raid is written and which he describes as "a light, breezy writing style" (Hill, Appendix 296). A major factor in this almost inappropriately jovial style is the involvement of the character Renata Williams, the older sister of Aberdeen Williams and a committed member of Langston's church. When she enters the scene, "all two hundred and twenty pounds of her" (AKB 318), the effect is one of comic relief. Renata immediately starts cussing the Klansmen and tries to keep them from erecting their crosses on Langston's lawn – up to the point where she falls on the ringleader and the Klansmen "couldn't budge her" (ibid.).[377]

> So that's an example where I felt that if I could do one scene again, I would not have written it quite so lightly. I would have written it 'more ugly', so to speak. In the novel, the Klans-

---

377 There is one aspect, however, which justifies Renata Williams's inclusion in this scene: she is also opposed to the interracial relationship of her brother, repeatedly calling his girlfriend "white trash" (AKB 317, 323) and telling her brother that his relationship is a "provocation" (AKB 317) which only discomforts and troubles the community (cf. AKB 323). She does, however, bravely stand up to the Klansmen to defend the couple, irrespective of her misgivings. In *Black Berry, Sweet Juice*, Hill deals at length with some of the ambivalent reactions towards interracial relationships from within the Black community itself (cf. the book's chapter "But for the Interference with His Arrangement"). Again, what is incorporated into Hill's fiction is a nuanced, balanced account of sensitive issues; cf. for instance the inclusion of the touchy issue of African assistance in the transatlantic slave trade in *The Book of Negroes* (discussed in section 5.3.2.).

men coming to Oakville are shown as buffoons. They are idiots, and they are made light of in a way, and easily defused. I had some reservations about that afterwards, and that's why I wrote about it again in *Black Berry, Sweet Juice*. (Hill, Appendix 296)

Yet it is not simply the writing style or the comic elements that make this scene troublesome. Nor is it the fact that Hill does, as he concedes in *Black Berry, Sweet Juice*, downplay the threat actually exerted by the Klansmen, who in fact numbered more than seventy, not the mere twenty that are included in the fictionalized rendition. Hill, moreover, decisively under-rates the racist potential of the Oakville residents, portraying the Klansmen as a mere aberra-tion – a depiction that could have led the bookstore manager to feel 'off the hook' as much as the writing style itself. Renata Williams proclaims the ringleader a "wooden-headed fool" (AKB 318) – and entirely misses the point. The Klansmen's actions are not the result of fool-ishness, but of racial paranoia and hatred. There is a crucial difference here, as the mutual actions of twenty 'fools' are an unfortunate concurrence, while the mutual actions of twenty racists may express something more than individual discomposure and might hence reveal social deficiencies. Police chief Phillips contributes to the distorted understanding pronounced by Renata Williams when he cites the reason why the Klansmen are bringing shame onto the community:

> I never seen such a bunch of plain fools in all my life. [...] You're gonna make a laughing-stock out of Oakville. People are gonna talk about us across the country. *Oakville? Isn't that where the Ku Klux Klan burned a cross?* Ain't you men got a drop a sense in your heads? (AKB 321; italics in the original)

Phillips, though being an upright person and a brave police officer (after all, he stands up to a mob of agitated Klansmen with the support of the mayor and another priest only),[378] suggests that the main problem consists of the fact that some imbeciles blemish Oakville's good repu-tation. The issue seems to be that Oakville runs the danger of becoming a "laughing-stock", *not* that Oakville might be considered a place where blatant racism is allowed to thrive. In order to underline that there is nothing wrong with the community itself, Phillip goes on to assure Langston that he "happen[s] to know that ninety-nine people outa a hundred in Oak-ville would agree" with the statement that "[y]ou're good folks, Reverend Cane" (AKB 323; note the ambiguity of "folks" here – does Phillip mean the Cane family or Black people?). The fact that – contrary to the historical model – the Klansmen are not from out of town but members of the Oakville community itself is a rough indicator for the factual falseness of this claim, yet the key aspect is that Hill lets White Oakville 'off the hook' too easily here. Not only is the *tone* of the scene too gentle, the implication that Canada in fact is a nation where the Ku Klux Klan is but a bizarre aberration while its righteous citizens are strictly opposed to such foolishness is left to stand undisputed. In this scene, Canada is indeed presented as a Canaan as opposed to the United States (where Klansmen are not just a group of fools in silly

---

378 The fact that the police, politicians and the church stand up against the racists already suggest an all-encompassing social alliance against racial discrimination, which might lead to the easy con-clusion that the Klansmen have no support at all in a community like Oakville.

hoods). Hazel makes this assumption explicit when she summarizes the incident after Langston had to relocate to her native Baltimore due to a dwindling congregation in Oakville:

> 'Down here, the KKK wouldn't even give you time to open your mouth,' Hazel warned them. 'In Oakville, we met their nice northern cousins. But in the States, they'd swing you from a branch and there'd be no talking before or after.' (AKB 326)[379]

Having critically considered the way in which the KKK raid is presented in *Any Known Blood*, Hill's own retraction needs to be reemphasized. First of all, he has doubted the tone employed in the scene ("candy-coated", BBSJ 215). Furthermore, however, he states that he let the reader have too much room for interpretation on the import of the KKK raid, allowing for a reading which suggests "that the Klan's raid was an entertaining but insignificant part of Oakville's history" (ibid.). Consequently, if considering the raid "insignificant" and "entertaining" is a misinterpretation (aided by the structural weaknesses discussed above), what Hill originally wanted to show then must have been the *significance* and the *seriousness* of the raid. Furthermore, Hill grants that he "was writing against the grain of [his] historical understanding of the incident, working on a dramatic level that seemed appropriate to the novel." (Hill, Appendix 297) What we are dealing with, then, is an example of form overriding content; in this case, the light tone overriding the author's understanding of historical events. If this in fact is an issue that Hill in retrospect sees as a flaw, it can safely be assumed that what is striven for in general is historical accuracy. This of course strongly underscores the claim that Hill in his fiction aims at a faithful representation of the Black presence in Canada, as does the bulk of African-Canadian literature. Before a collective memory has been established which firmly places the existence of past and present racial discrimination and the African-Canadian tile in the overall Canadian mosaic, fiction actually questioning, underplaying or undermining these aspects will thus remain the exception. Rather, Black Canadian authors like Lawrence Hill will likely continue to write assertively, basing their 'factions' on what they perceive as the historical truth that needs to be more thoroughly acknowledged and incorporated into processes of collective self-definition.

What can be concluded, then, in terms of the fictional rendering of the Oakville KKK raid in *Any Known Blood* is that given a number of other factors shaping the narrative (such as the context of the episode in question, the fear that emanates from the description of Lang-

---

379 Notice the way in which the Oakville Klansmen are a (stereo-) typically Canadian 'other', being the "nice northern cousins." Regarding Hazel's favorable comparison and her choice of words ("they'd swing you from a branch"), see the poem "Blackman Dead" by Marlene NourbeSe Philip, who takes up the symbolic tree which stands for the lynching of a Black person. Philip concedes that overt violence like this is not typical of Canadian racism, yet she adds a bleaker tone to her poem, suggesting that instead, there is a considerable amount of covert racism:

> Toronto has no silk cotton trees
> strong enough to bear
> one black man's neck
> the only crosses that burn
> are those upon our souls
> (Philip 1980, ll. 49-53)

ston's and Hazel's initial panic, the inclusion of *numerous* further instances of racism in Canada, and the tone-setting opening sequence of the novel), it should be obvious that no serious reader could possibly presume that Hill in fact wants to dismiss Canadian racism as trivial. Nonetheless, the description of the said scene has – based on comic elements, a tone that is too breezy, the failure to fully appreciate the danger posed by the Klansmen, and an extensive vindication of Oakville's citizens – a significant potential to be misread as overly appeasing or conciliatory. The way the scene was *intended* to be read, and *can* be read because of other factors outlined above (and including the retrospective critical assessment by Lawrence Hill), it underscores the existence of serious racial hatred in Canada in the 1930s, even though this racial hatred is in fact somewhat dulled in comparison to the racism that was virulent in parts of the United States at the time.

Langston Cane the Third thus embodies the experience of a level of racial discrimination in Canada that is less severe than what he experienced in the United States. Nevertheless, the conditions in Canada are anything but paradisiacal for the African-Canadian community either – a fact which is commonly neglected or plainly disregarded. The KKK might not have gained as much terrifying prominence in Canada as it did in the US, yet it did exist, though the knowledge of its existence might not be part of mainstream collective memory (Roberta: "The Klan? [...] You're kidding!" AKB 314).[380] Moreover, Langston III also carries the burden of a collective memory which connects his contemporary experiences to the memory of outright slavery and thus contextualizes his experience with the KKK; this memory, comparable to Aminata's partly traumatic recollection being triggered by a current situation or sight (cf. for instance her fears when "surrounded by big white men with a purpose", BN 6) is elicited when he and Rose are looking for a house they could buy: "Simple, square pillars supported a verandah. That was good. Langston loved porches, but he'd never go for rounded pillars. Too evocative of plantation history." (AKB 292) Though removed from the actual experience of plantation slavery by two generations, it is still a memory that haunts and influences Langston III.[381] The effect of course is the bridging of past and present: the (faithful) representation of an ongoing process of diminishing, though not vanishing, racism.

---

380 G. E. Clarke likewise argues that, far more so than aggravations caused by a small-scale KKK in Canada, it is the nation's subtle racism which has shaped race relations: "Thus, blacks endured discrimination, but not thousands of lynchings and suffered segregated schools, but not – in numbers and force – the Ku Klux Klan." (2003b, 33f.)

381 The conjuring up of memories triggered by sensory impressions is an important device in *Any Known Blood* as well (cf. the discussion of memory-triggering in the context of *The Book of Negroes*, p. 145ff. of this thesis). For Aberdeen Williams, for instance, the smell of strawberries reminds him of the first night he spent with Evelyn (they form the interracial couple that prompts the KKK raid): "It's a light, sweet smell. [...] Her name was Evelyn Morris. And the first time we lay side by side was in a strawberry field. [...] And I've always remembered the softness of her skin. I can feel it now, on the tips of my fingers." (AKB 344) Olfactory impressions elicit the recollection of tactile impressions, thus creating a multisensory memory image. For Langston the First, strawberries trigger a very different memory – traumatic rather than romantic: "Colored people had been bending over and picking things off farmers' fields for hundreds of years in the United States, and I sure as hell wasn't going to do it in Canada." (AKB 459) The same memory

6.3.4. Canada and the US: Langston the Fourth

> *This wasn't the United States. Nobody would swear at him, or*
> *wave a gun. Langston waited for the refusal, Canadian-style.*
> *(AKB 35)*

When Langston Cane the Fourth comes to Canada after having served in the US Army in World War II, it is because of push- rather than pull-factors. The treatment of African-Americans in the army "was enough to make any black soldier hate America, [so he] left the United States and came to study at the University of Toronto." (AKB 62) There had been no delusions concerning a possible Land of Milk and Honey, simply the expectation that the situation up north could not have been any more repressive than in the United States. This is why Langston is pleasantly surprised when he realizes on his trip northwards that Canadians appear to react differently towards Black people than their US counterparts: on the bus trip, he is addressed as "Mister" – a matter of considerable surprise to Langston – and identified as an American, not an *African*-American (AKB 63), classified not based on his skin color but on his friendliness and talkativeness. The lady characterizing him this way even offers Langston to put him up in her boarding house, which even more dazzles Langston: "Where I come from, colored bus passengers don't often get offered accommodation by white strangers. Matter of fact, they don't sit together on buses." (AKB 64) The trip to Canada hence mirrors the experiences of his father, who marveled at sitting in a desegregated restaurant in Toronto. Furthermore, it is the inversion of Langston the Second's southbound trip from Canada to the United States, a trip overshadowed by sickness and death and ending in disillusionment. Hill thus offers a mutual rather than an individual occurrence, stressing that the Canes' experiences are not mere coincidences – rather, Hill characterizes, by means of diachronic, genealogical repetition, the general contrast between the two North American nations which he perceives.

The idea that underlying distinctive structure rather than mere twists of fate is portrayed here is underscored by the fact that Langston the Fourth's experience is a recurring one: right after arriving in Toronto, he asks a hot dog vendor for directions. The teenager immediately identifies Langston as an American; he, too, does not base his assumption on the fact that Langston is Black, but on his accent and his friendliness (cf. AKB 65). This prompts Langston, having arrived in Canada mere minutes ago, to compliment Canadians: "So, by my

---

is evoked at another point, when Langston the First visits the Black community at Chatham. For Langston, the town's extensive farming also triggers the traumatic memory of bondage: "I didn't like the idea of bending down over growing plants and breaking my back to pick them. The whole thing made me think of the Virginia plantation where I was born." (AKB 463) Langston is, on the whole, unable to forget his past; he cannot let go of the thought that his life is threatened even in Canada. Mattie, who later on marries Langston, believes his fears border on paranoia and – in vain – attempts to dissuade him from his fears: "'You're still thinking like a slave,' she said. '[...] We made it out of slavery, Langston. We have come this far, and nobody will crack our heads in Oakville.'" (AKB 462) Cf. on the persistence of memories to the point of paranoia Langston the Fourth's fears when he is caught in the women's washrooms at a Toronto restaurant (cf. AKB 80; the incident is discussed below).

reckoning, Canadians underestimate themselves. They'll help out a colored stranger, and that's already going some distance." (ibid.) In contrast to Langston III's arrival in Canada, however, this remark is not immediately qualified, at least not in an obvious way. Yet when Langston asks the hot dog vendor for the address where he has arranged board, there is a sub-tle caveat hidden beneath the young Canadian's answer: "'This Pembroke Street [where Langston is headed]. Is it in a colored neighborhood?' [Langston asks.] 'What do you mean by that?'" (AKB 66) The teenager's reply on the one hand indicates that he is, in a positive way, not race-conscious, which is a trait that Langston had encountered before when meeting the Canadian lady on the bus. This seeming unimportance of skin color is of course something Langston considers uplifting – after all, he is used to being classified according to race (dou-ble meaning intended here; Langston's remark on being used to sitting on segregated busses clearly shows that theoretical conceptions of a professed separate-but-equal approach have led to sociopolitical action as well). On the other hand, however, there is a dilemma embedded in the teenager's answer: there is no *conscious* blindness concerning race in Canada, but rather an unawareness or even ignorance of the proportions that Langston II, having been socialized in Canada, also expresses in regard to the Black community in Baltimore when leaving Cana-da for the US more than fifty years prior to Langston IV.[382]

While the adolescent Langston II is shocked by the sheer "masses of Negroes" in Bal-timore (AKB 411), his grandson is faced with an absence – whether an absence of a distinct community *per se* or an absence of an awareness of such a community's existence is not yet clear at this point; it turns out, however, that both factors play a decisive role. In Canada, Langston the Fourth realizes, he cannot count on there being a cohesive, vocal Black commu-nity,[383] nor can he count on this disparate community's presence being realized by White Ca-nadians. While this absence of race consciousness can be a blessing, it also implies two dis-tinct disadvantages: first, African-Canadians simply do not feature as a major factor in the construction of a Canadian self-identity. Second, in those cases in which race consciousness does indeed exist within the White community, it is primarily a negative one – which is then

---

382 Hill nicely phrases this point when writing about his youth in Don Mills, Ontario, in *Black Berry, Sweet Juice*: "Don Mills had a way of squishing the black out of you, by dint of sheer neglect." (BBSJ 52)

383 When he reaches Pembroke street, Langston finds that there was indeed an absence of a Black community in terms of racially based urban distribution; the lack of a predominantly Black neigh-borhood is something he is unaccustomed to and can at first not comprehend (just as the lack of an obvious race consciousness of the people he encounters takes him by surprise): "Langston con-cluded that in Baltimore or D.C. Pembroke Street would have been a black ghetto. But here in To-ronto, Pembroke Street was predominantly white. There were a few blacks, but they didn't seem any more beaten up than others. So where did black people live, anyway?" (AKB 66) The search for a real-life Black community is something that has occupied Hill himself for a long time ("Connecting with black people in a land with few clustered black communities has been a life-long journey for me." BBSJ 3). For Clarke, this is also an actual concern (which, of course, finds its reflection in African-Canadian literature): "This point [the lack of a *full-scale* 'black ghetto' anywhere in Canada] is one more example of 'the Canadian way' of polite racism: no ghettoes for blacks but *much* invisibility, poverty, overpolicing, and disrespect." (2003, 79)

not offset by an appreciation of African-Canadian achievements and a sense of belonging, by their being considered part of a Canadian whole. Hill uses a number of examples to underline this point; subtle racism does prevail in Canada, yet the discourse on race is muted to an extent that allows this submerged racism to continue in almost unimpeded ways.

The task Lawrence Hill, and indeed, the vast majority of African-Canadian authors, thus (have to) tackle is a twofold one: first, the establishing of a collective memory that positions the Black Canadian community both as a somewhat unified community in order to provide a sense of coherence and, second, to implement this collective memory into the larger Canadian one in order to achieve a more faithful basis for current processes of identity construction. African-Canadian literature hence strives to remedy both deficiencies encountered by Langston the Fourth, albeit, of course, on a more intellectual or abstract level than the distribution of people into distinct urban neighborhoods: by providing a counter-memory, Black Canadian writers strive to reverse the lack of a sense of African-Canadian community as well as the lack of that community's inclusion in mainstream self-perception. The fact that this counter-memory also includes problematic instances of the Canadian approach to race matters should be obvious. Hill underlines these examples by portraying numerous events which can be considered an embodiment of a more general conception of 'the' African-Canadian experience.

When Langston the Fourth moves into his first apartment, for instance, people suspect he is stealing from them; at least Langston perceives his fellow tenants' suspicion as being based on his race, though nobody confronts him on the issue (cf. AKB 69).[384] In fact, Langston IV has money stolen, too, and sets out to catch the thief. When indeed, Langston manages to snatch the young culprit by hitting him with a frying pan, he asks the boy: "Do you know where I come from, Johnny?" (AKB 70) Based on his initial, positive, experiences in Canada (which have been slightly blemished by the supposed suspicion held by Langston's neighbors),[385] Langston fully expects the young thief to realize that Langston is a US-American – meaning that "[d]own there", the thief could "get shot breaking into somebody's home" (ibid.) instead of merely being hit with a pan.[386] The boy, however, does not conform to the pattern Langston believes to have detected in Canada; instead, he bases his reply on Langston's race, immediately following his erroneous classification with a racist stereotype: "Africa? You're not a cannibal, are you?" (ibid.) Langston, in the course of the incident, is

---

384 The incident bears some resemblance to a recent incident in the United States; cf. the detention of eminent African-American scholar Henry Louis Gates, Jr. when 'breaking into' his own house (cf. Goodnough 2009, Thompson 2009).

385 After the incident, Langston's fellow tenants in fact come to trust him profoundly, asking him for medical advice, requesting assistance in writing letters and questioning him on matters of racial prejudice (cf. AKB 72f.).

386 Again, Hill uses a slightly tongue-in-cheek comparison between the US and Canada which plays on a further (stereo-) typical distinction: while in the US, robbers are shot, they are caught with the help of frying pans in Canada. What is suggested here, of course, is the lesser degree of Canadian vs. US-American gun-craziness generally assumed (and fostered by pop culture items such as the hugely successful movies by Michael Moore).

thus faced with two deep-seated prejudices, at least one of them based on blatant ignorance: one, that as a Black person, he should be prone to stealing; two, that he should actually be from Africa – and thus possibly be a cannibal. Hill does, however, include in this scene a counterbalance as well, again underlining his preference for a nuanced depiction. When Langston meets his fellow tenant Dorothy Perkins for the first time – Dorothy will later on become Langston's wife – she tells him not to call her "Ma'am", as it "shows a deference that [she finds] socially offensive" (AKB 69). Hence, there *is* a certain degree of informed race consciousness reflected in Langston's microcosm, even though it is limited to one person, as opposed to several people (ostensibly?) considering Langston either as not Black at all or negatively stereotyping Langston as a thief (or an African cannibal).

A further instance highlights the fact that Langston IV, having been socialized in the United States mainly, has a perception of race relations which slightly diverges from the one predominant in Canada. It also calls to mind again that racism in Canada does indeed exist by conjuring up the KKK raid in Oakville. When Langston takes out Dorothy to dinner (in order to introduce her to "Black folks' food", AKB 80), Dorothy is violently sick. Langston makes sure his date is alright, entering the restaurant's ladies' room to do so. Another client comes into the washrooms, sees Langston, screams and flees. Langston's thoughts reflect his experiences, yet in a Canadian contexts, they also seem to entail a certain amount of what might be considered fear bordering on paranoia: "Wonderful, he thought. Here come the cops. Here comes the Klan. Here come the forces of good. Here come the headlines: *Negro Arrested in Women's Toilet.*" (AKB 80) Who actually comes is the maître d', who is quickly convinced that Langston was simply assisting his sick girlfriend.

The double consciousness applied by Langston (cf. DuBois 2003, 9f.), the act of seeing himself in the given situation not only from his own perspective, but also from and through the viewpoint of a White person, indeed appears inappropriate in the given context. It is interesting to note, however, that Langston assumes that an interracial couple would not be taken for the normal, voluntary relationship it actually represents. The interracial relationship carries, for Langston, the burden of being the 'other'; he expects that his liaison is under scrutiny, even treated with disdain (Langston does in fact face these very same problems even in Canada later on).[387] His linking of the police, the KKK, and the media – combined, Langston sarcastically terms them "the forces of good" (AKB 80) – may appear excessive in this context, as they suggest an alliance of officials, public opinion and extreme racists; an alliance which of course does not materialize in even a remote way. The maître d's reaction does not indicate any racism at all. Yet Langston the Fourth had indeed been present when the KKK

---

387 Whenever he and Dorothy are in a public place, they have to live under the gaze of others: "On every street they walked, people turned their heads. Langston liked to catch them red-handed. He would turn and wave at the very moment another had pivoted to stare." (AKB 76) The feeling of being scrutinized has been described in a number of books; cf. for instance in a Canadian context Jennifer Kelly's 1998 *Under the Gaze. Learning to be Black in a White Society* or Himani Bannerji's 1993 *Returning the Gaze: Essays on Racism, Feminism and Politics*. Despite the reassuring welcome Langston receives in Canada, he soon finds that as part of an interracial couple, he has to cope with being considered an anomaly.

raided his father's home in Oakville.[388] The idea of the Klan's reacting on Langston's interracial relationship thus does not remain on a symbolic level – the Klan's embodying violently racist sentiments – but finds its foundation in Langston's past.

The conjuring up of the KKK incident, contrasted with the absence of racist sentiments in the given situation might thus, at this early point in the novel, suggest that racism in Canada has indeed dwindled into near non-existence. Langston's fears seem not to have materialized. It must be added that, moreover, Langston and Dorothy at that time would not have been allowed to sit together in a US-American restaurant in the first place. Racism in Canada is thus portrayed in this incident to be a mere shadow, a memory – one which actually, however, still haunts Langston (and, of course, a memory which is narratively invigorated in this scene). The Klan obviously does not come to raid the restaurant's washroom either for a Black man harassing a White woman or to threaten an interracial couple. It *does* however come for the latter reason even in Canada both factually and fictionally. Successively, thus, Hill provides the context of the given episode in order to provide a more fully fleshed-out portrayal of Canadian racism, progressively filling the reader in both on the absences of racism and the existence of diverse forms of discrimination north of the border.

One of these forms is the non-institutionalized segregation of public facilities such as restaurants. In a direct analogy to his father (cf. AKB 192), Langston the Fourth makes the experience that Canadian restaurants have varying policies concerning segregated seating. While Langston III is restricted to a only a certain number of restaurants offering integrated seating, the situation after World War II is inverted: only a number of restaurants still will not admit both Black and White customers. Thus, a change of scope or frequency has occurred, though not a reversal of the overall policy: segregation is still a matter of the proprietor's attitude. The improvement in terms of quantity has not (yet) effected a truly altered quality in racial discrimination. Langston himself is not even fazed by the ongoing existence of segregated facilities; rather, it is Dorothy who is intent on exposing and scandalizing segregated restaurants.[389] Wanting to enlist Langston's help to do so, she is squarely refused by Langston, who claims to have left the United States exactly because of segregation – and he is not about to consciously seek it out in Canada: "If I were so desperate to experience segregation, I would have stayed in Baltimore. [...] I left that and I'm not going back." (AKB 82) It takes Dorothy some nagging to actually bring Langston to abandon his escapist stance.

Literally and metaphorically, what Langston is thus agreeing to is to 'go back' indeed, which does not mean remigrating to the US but revisiting his past and facing, in his new

---

388 In terms of the novel's narrative sequence, the KKK raid is of course *foreshadowed* here, as this scene precedes the description of the Klan raid by several hundred pages. The effect is thus an *a posteriori* supplementation of an incident which the reader might consider unlikely at this early point of the story. The invocation of the Klan may seem far-fetched in the given situation, yet we later on learn that it is not as far-fetched as one might think, even given the general description of a more 'benevolent' Canadian racism as perceived by Langston IV when coming to Toronto.

389 Cf. the futile, but inspired attempts at exposing segregated restaurants undertaken by Hill's own mother (cf. BBSJ 43f.).

home, the discrimination he was originally escaping from when he left the United States in the first place and to which he then closed his eyes in Canada. The reduced level of exposure to discrimination in Canada hence seems to be acceptable for Langston IV. The contrast he invokes with the United States lets Canada appear in a sufficiently agreeable light that no further action on his part seems necessary. Consequently, if it can be evaded, racism is not one of Langston's major concerns, and in Canada, as opposed to the US, it *can* in fact be evaded. If a mixed-raced couple picks the right spots, which for Langston the Fourth are more frequently available than for his father when *he* came to Canada, and if the couple can put up with the stares they will inevitably receive, north of the border is a place where a Black man and a White woman can live in a relatively unperturbed way – which Langston is clearly unwilling to jeopardize by voluntarily getting involved in any trouble.

The actual situation at a segregated restaurant, however, quickly makes Langston realize that his tactics of cocooning himself in and closing his eyes to the existent racism is no option. Once agreeing to play along with Dorothy's plan to scandalize the 'politely segregated' restaurant, Langston finds the racism exhibited unbearable. Wittily, Langston and his company expose the owner's stance, which is made progressively plain, beginning with casually inattentive staff and food that the kitchen has suddenly run out of, and culminating in the owner's proclamation that they "don't serve colored" (AKB 84).[390] Langston's reply ("I want to reassure you that I didn't order colored. Actually, I don't eat colored people"; ibid.) is followed up by the sarcastic admission that "[y]our canned soup would have civilized me substantially" and would have kept him from "digging into crocodiles and the like." (AKB 85) Reversing the stereotypical assumptions – the 'uncivilized, dumb African' – causes Langston IV, who has always considered himself smarter than most people, immense pleasure. In the end, however, the party has to admit that their effort has been in vain for the most part: though they take pictures and distribute those, along with a complete description of the incident, to newspapers and the Ontario minster of labor, the reaction is disappointing, to say the least. The papers, if they run the story at all, offer only a few lines on their back pages. Officials react in predictably evasive ways: "The minister of labor mailed Langston a letter insisting that the Ontario government was opposed to racial discrimination, but that it couldn't prevent such an incident." (AKB 85) Neither the press nor politicians are particularly intent on initiating a discourse on Canadian race relations. In the end, Langston is even more discouraged from getting involved in exposing racial discrimination in Ontario, concentrating instead on his medical studies at the University of Toronto.

Langston IV becomes re-involved, however, when he and Dorothy try to rent an apartment, an episode Langston V refers to as 'the Norville Watson' incident. The episode is based, as has been pointed out before, on an actual case which Lawrence Hill's father took as far as the Supreme Court of Canada – and lost – in 1971 (cf. BBSJ 57ff.). In *Any Known*

---

390 Cf. Aminata, in *The Book of Negroes*, who is refused service in Nova Scotia with an almost identical phrase, though a more derogatory term is used ("We don't serve niggers", BN 313). More than a hundred years of racial discrimination in Canada are thus (intertextually) reflected in this statement.

Blood, Langston the Fourth and Dorothy, married by then, try to rent an apartment from Dr. Norville Watson, a local doctor, but are refused based on Langston's race. In fact, Watson takes pains not to verbalize his racist reasons in front of the couple, turning them down while inventing subterfuges in Janus-faced ways. Watson is plainer toward a White couple the Canes send over to his house to test their assumption that in fact, Watson is denying them rent based on racial prejudices:

> Some Italians and Portuguese live around here. But they're the nicest neighbors you could ask for. [...] And I can assure you that I know of no neighbors who are Negroes. I would draw the line there. As a matter of fact, a Negro posing as a medical student tried to rent this apartment today, and I would have nothing to do with it. (Norville Watson, AKB 39)

While Watson's discriminatory attitude is bluntly apparent, two underlying assumptions can be traced in this statement: first, that Watson's attitude is a *racist* one indeed. He is not generally xenophobic; there is, in his opinion, nothing wrong with immigrants from southern Europe, for instance. His revulsion is directed against Black people exclusively – that is where he "would draw the line" (ibid.). Second, Watson in fact assumes that Langston only *posed* as a medical student. This assumption not only illustrates Watson's deep-seated resentment; he actually *believes* that no Black person could possibly study medicine, which of course matches the stereotype Langston had revealed and piercingly countered in the segregated restaurant: the absurd conjecture that Black people are intellectually inferior (cf. p. 85ff. of this thesis). The Watson incident demonstrates that the racism existing in Canada is not necessarily a shallow, surface phenomenon; where it occurs, it may well be founded on longstanding assumptions of racial inferiority. Watson, when actually facing the Canes, does his best to mask his racism, just like the restaurant's owner at first tries to subtly 'discourage' Langston from dining there. Canadian racism is thus portrayed as an undercurrent which only surfaces every so often. Most of the time, it is so subtle as to being invisible. Having lived in Toronto for some time and having made his experiences with the trajectory of Canadian racism, this is what Langston had in fact expected before facing Watson: "This wasn't the United States. Nobody would swear at him, or wave a gun. Langston waited for the refusal, Canadian-style." (AKB 35)

Chronologically, Langston the Fourth thus progressively uncovers the current of Canadian racism – decidedly more subtle than in the United States, but not as evitable as he had assumed at first. While his initial encounters had been almost entirely positive, the limits of racial tolerance in the True North are successively unveiled. In terms of narrative sequence, however, Hill makes sure that by largely reversing the chronological order of events, the reader of *Any Known Blood* is presented with the most severe instances (Watson) before going through the less severe ones (the segregated restaurant; the assumption that Langston is a thief), and eventually ending up with the superficially encouraging ones (Langston's arrival in Toronto). This sequence enables the reader to properly contextualize the ostensibly positive, innocuous, or avoidable encounters. When the readers are presented with Langston's arrival in Canada, for instance, they learn that there seems to be no closely-knit cluster of predominantly Black residents, which of course at first sight does not immediately suggest that Black people are discriminated against in terms of housing conditions. The readers by then know, however, that renting in supposedly integrated neighborhoods is *not* as unproblematic as it may appear to be (Watson). The readers also know that, even in integrated housing conditions – which, for the most part, are easily available – Blacks have to deal with racial stereotypes and negative suppositions (Langston's fellow tenants).[391]

The readers are thus equipped with an *a priori* knowledge which Langston the Fourth is, often painfully, only acquiring step by step, enabling them to put Langston's experiences into perspective. As a result, the readers can question and qualify Langston's initial assumptions. His allegations, for instance, that "Canadians underestimate themselves" (AKB 65) or that he "left [segregation behind] and [is] not going back" (AKB 82) are thwarted to some extent. What is furthermore demonstrated by the inverted chronological sequence is the influence of memories upon current processes of recognition and assessment. Having Langston the Fourth's memories of his later experiences at hand when facing his earlier experiences, which means having hindsight in terms of Langston's development, the reader is able to judge the proceedings in a very different way. Thus, the accessibility of memories is used as a foil against which (narratively) subsequent events are measured. It is possible, then, to exploit the collective memory in order to differently assess past or present situations, with literature in general being able to provide said collective memory. Hill, in *Any Known Blood*, for instance provides the reader with the memory of subtle, non-institutionalized segregation, which can then be used to assess more faithfully the construction of a mainstream collective memory which holds Canadian history as the positive counterpart to the United States' approach to race. In terms of the given examples, the simple contrast of official segregation as opposed to *no* segregation is questioned. Instead, a more nuanced assessment is suggested: while in the United States, both the scope and the legal status of racial segregation made it the more relentless variant by far, Canada also has a history of segregation, albeit a more subtle one – "Canadian-style" (AKB 35).[392]

---

391 Flagel furthermore points to the mechanism of presenting the harshest incidents before presenting ostensibly milder ones as a method also providing the necessary pre-knowledge to properly contextualize the embedded slave narrative: "In other words, the Canada=free and US=slave dichotomy is interrupted through Hill's complicated repetitions and revisitings of border crossings. [...] The reverse chronological order of the family history manages to strongly contextualize the escape to freedom in Canada; a fugitive slave narrative that might otherwise be grist for the mill of hegemonic and whitewashed Canadian history is cleverly preceded in the novel by acts of racism perpetrated by the Oakville branch of the Klan and followed by Cane I's own experience of segregation and second-class treatment in Canada." (2005, 271)

392 This assessment is underscored by various examples supplementing the ones discussed above; cf. for instance the illegitimately segregated Toronto night club "Venus", which, in the 1970s, uses a process of racial screening to preclude Black clients. Langston the Fourth eventually becomes involved here as well (cf. AKB 28ff.).

6.3.5. *Canada and the US: Langston the Fifth*

The last Langston in the generational chain of Canes, Langston the Fifth, is the only Cane not crossing the 49th parallel in search of permanent relocation. He is not looking for a new home but for his roots, intending to research the family history in Baltimore, where each of his name-sake paternal forbears had lived at some point. Thus, in 1995, after semi-deliberately losing his job, Langston V buys a car and drives southwards. The first thing Langston notices, like each of his predecessors, is the comparatively milder weather: "I left the remnants of winter in Toronto and arrived in spring in Baltimore." (AKB 92) Yet, while spring promises newness, freshness, and novel experiences, there is also a sense of urgency or pressure – the heat Langston II found so oppressing (cf. AKB 411) is impending: "The air seemed pregnant with things to come. It seemed to be saying, I'm in your face, sucker, so breathe me in before I get too hot." (AKB 92) The promise of spring is furthermore diluted by the fact that, Langston IV's habitual complaints about *Toronto's* lack of trees notwithstanding, Baltimore is characterized at first sight by a distinct "absence of vegetation." (AKB 93)

The first person Langston the Fifth notices in Baltimore is a Black youngster who barely avoids being hit by Langston's car. This experience of course conjures up Langston the Second's initial impression, who was taken aback by meeting, at first sight, other Black people. There clearly is a general closeness between the first impressions gathered by Langston the Second and his great-grandson: apart from the different climate and the apparent divergence in the number of Black people, both remark on the disagreeable living conditions in the US in their comparisons: oppressive tightness and appalling sanitary conditions for Langston II, ramshackle houses, dilapidated infrastructure and drug dealers for Langston V. Both deplore Baltimore's quicker pace and the city's rush, which lends an air of precipitance to their arrival in the United States. [393]

Langston V expressly contrasts Baltimore with Canada in general, underlining the fact that the differences he perceives can be traced back to broader tendencies than the mere dissimilarity between a midsized Ontario community and a city in Maryland four times the size of Oakville. Stopping at a red light on a street full of potholes in Baltimore, for instance, and seeing other cars simply pass through, Langston expresses his bewilderment: "I came to a red light. I stopped. We tend to do that in Canada." (AKB 93) This comment sets the tone for numerous subsequent ones: Langston the Fifth's comparisons, in contrast to the observations by his predecessors, are frequently more or less humorous or ironic ones, though not ironic to the extent of reversing the observation itself. What unites the different Canes' assessment, however, is the slightly clichéd description of Canada and the United States. Canada is por-

---

393 The only Langston Cane not to initially consider Canada comparatively 'slow' is Langston the First. When he escapes slavery and comes to Oakville, he finds the town bustling with activity (cf. AKB 459f.), proceeding to contrast the "strange and lovely town" (AKB 461) with the "country of man-stealers" (AKB 459) he had fled from (regarding the term "man-stealers", cf. *The Book of Negroes*, where Aminata uses the same word to describe the Africans assisting in the transatlantic slave trade; BN 56).

trayed, by comparison, as colder, wealthier, Whiter, cleaner, greener, more law-abiding, and slower.[394]

This characterization is variously taken up, for instance by Langston's landlady, who tells him not to bring large amounts of cash because it is unsafe: "This is Baltimore. This is not Canada." (AKB 106; likewise, he is warned by an A.M.E. church member: "Somebody could shoot you. This *is* Baltimore." AKB 118; original emphasis.) In another instance, a Nation of Islam (NOI) member can tell that Langston, though mastering the Arabic *Salaam Alaikham* (sic; AKB 120) greeting used by the organization, could not possibly be an NOI member himself – because Langston dresses sloppily and because he is "from Canada. It's too cold up there for Muslims." (AKB 121) Though the remark again harks back to the stereotypical distinction based on climate and therefore is employed here half-humorously[395] (particularly given the second indicator, viz. "wearing brown socks with blue trousers", ibid.), it is also indicative of a more profound distinction: while in the US, the Nation of Islam has thrived and found vocal and popular representatives such as Elijah Muhammad, Malcolm X, and Louis Farrakhan, it has remained relatively undeveloped in Canada (the NOI has, for instance, opened its first mosque in Toronto as late as 1998 – one out of a total of around two hundred in the remaining Americas and the Caribbean; cf. Ben-Moshe 2004, 154 and Lemelle 2001). While it is certainly not due to Canada's climate, the NOI has indeed never gained considerable ground north of the border, which of course conforms, as has been pointed out before, to the characteristic absence of grand-scale revolutionary movements from African-Canadian as well as general Canadian history.[396]

More importantly, however, the (stereo-)typical contrast between Canada and the US is supplemented in terms of the respective countries' general race consciousness. Langston

---

394 Revealing the historical connection between the myth of Canada's nordicity and its stereotypical Whiteness/whiteness, Clarke states: "Voltaire notoriously dismissed the country [Canada] as 'nothing more than thirty acres of snow,' and it's certainly true that the bleak topography of winter – polar bears and permafrost, tuques and tundra – has fired the imagination of Canadian whiteness." (1998, 107)

395 The same approach, viz. to present unpleasant truths under the cover of humor, is also taken in a scene which involves Langston the Fifth and Annette Morton, whom Langston falls in love with in Baltimore. When Annette introduces herself, she says, "I haven't been shot or turned into anyone's prostitute or been beaten up on Pennsylvania Avenue, and I do have steady employment, so you can surmise that I'm a survivor, for a black Baltimorean." (AKB 393) Ironically, all of these things *have* happened, most of them to Langston himself: he has been involved in a drive-by shooting in Baltimore; it is revealed that his aunt Mill had been a prostitute; Langston has been beaten up on Pennsylvania Avenue following the shooting, and he is in fact jobless. The issues mentioned by Annette are thus in fact prevalent ones, which eliminates a considerable amount of irony from her statement and emphasizes the last part of her comment: she is indeed "a survivor, for a black Baltimorean." (Ibid.)

396 As Dieter Meindl (too) succinctly, and certainly a bit disparagingly, explained more than a quarter century ago: "The fact is that Canadian history suffers from another thing that makes it dull – [in] comparison with American history. As you probably all know, Canada had no revolutions, few Indian wars, an extremely quiet and orderly frontier..." (Meindl 1984, 42).

the Second had noticed the larger Black population in the US; his grandson, Langston the Fourth, had added to the same observation the notion that in Canada, there seemed to be almost no race consciousness to speak of – at least no obvious or immediately visible one, as he later realizes. Langston the Fifth, taking his father's trip the other way around (a "mirror in reverse", as Siemerling phrases it; 2004, 37), reinforces this notion. When trying to rent an apartment in Baltimore, Langston V faces what might be considered the inversion of the Norville Watson incident:

> [The White landlord] looked me up and down again and mumbled something half under his breath that was so outrageous I couldn't believe he had said it. What I thought I heard was 'Octoroon, I presume.' Where I come from, not very many people know the word meant someone who was one-eighth black. But Baltimore was obviously not Oakville. He asked me if I was clean and had clean habits. While I tried to ingest the question and figure out what answer to spit back, he offered 'reduced rent in exchange for certain nocturnal services, to be specified at your request.' 'No, thank you,' I said. 'Octoroons don't go in for such things.' [...] 'We must not know the same octoroons,' he said, still speaking barely above a whisper [...]. (AKB 94)

On the one hand, the landlord, while using a term which Langston rightly finds offensive, does in fact display a high level of race consciousness; as Langston the Fourth's arrival in Toronto underlines, it is this awareness of race which is largely absent from the construction of a Canadian collective memory. Langston the Fifth's remark that in Canada, the term "octoroon" itself would be unknown to most people of course reveals as much. On the other hand, however, the owner's attitude is – though informed – clearly a racist one nonetheless, as it categorizes Langston in terms of "a human body as being one-half or one-quarter or one-eighth or one-sixteenth black", in which case Hill, in *Black Berry, Sweet Juice*, suggests to "sign up for a high school biology class" (200). The outspoken way in which the landlord confronts and classifies Langston in terms of his race provides a last line of disparity from Norville Watson; while the Canadian takes pains not to articulate his racist assumptions in front of the people concerned (i.e. Langston IV and his wife Dorothy), the US-American landlord is very blunt in expressing them, even offering a stereotypical sexual insinuation about "octoroons" to Langston's face.[397]

The comparison between Canada and the US suggested by Langston the Fourth is thus corroborated by his son: the lack of an explicit race consciousness, along with a tendency of hushing up existent racism makes race/racism in Canada a matter largely absent from, or invisible in, public discourse. In the US, in contrast, race matters are consciously, openly dealt with. There is, however, a decided lack of subtlety pertaining to the issue of race south of the border; in the words of Hazel, Langston the Third's mother-in-law, Canadians are, in this respect, indeed the "nice [or at least the nicer] northern cousins" (AKB 326). Yet, as the Norville Watson incident and other experiences made by the successive Langston Canes

---

397 Hill indeed makes it appear at first as if the landlord was *not* as blunt, suggesting that he had "mumbled something half under his breath" – it turns out, however, that this seems to be his general mode of articulation (cf. "still speaking barely above a whisper", AKB 94).

demonstrate, the absence of an extensive public discourse on race does not make racism *per se* disappear in Canada. In fact, by concealing issues of race, stereotypical assumptions such as displayed by the owner of the segregated restaurant in Toronto or by Langston the Fourth's neighbors are allowed to fester without recognition, while there is no major awareness or appreciation of African-Canadians' achievements or historical significance to offset these stereotypes. These aspects are key concerns of Hill's writing: to provide a larger historical context for the Black presence in Canada; to undermine common racial stereotypes; to reveal the lack of a race consciousness in Canada; eventually, to contrast the United States and Canada in a *faithful* and nuanced way so that in the True North, simplified distinctions can no longer be used to banish race from public discourse and its externalization, viz. collective memory.

6.3.6. *Homecoming?*

Just as the Watson incident is finally resolved on a conciliatory note,[398] *Any Known Blood*'s ending eventually wraps up the loose strands of the novel's various plots in a lighthearted ending.[399] Millicent Cane, who is reconciled with her brother, Langston the Fourth, decides to move back to Oakville when Langston the Fifth is leaving Baltimore, telling her nephew: "I'm at the end of my life, Langston, and I want to go home." (AKB 388)[400] Her house, which has served as part of Langston's archive in his family research, is cleared out and sold. The memories held in Mill's jumble of documents are transferred into Langston's narrative to be preserved and passed on; they have thus served their purpose. On their car trip north, Langston V and Millicent are joined by Yoyo, who wants to live with his former sweetheart Hélène Savoie in Winnipeg,[401] and Annette Morton, who has forgiven Langston's preoccupation

---

398 When Watson is kidnapped by a group which calls itself "Africa First" but whose members turn out to be Neo-Nazis instead, Langston IV investigates the case, eventually being kidnapped himself. Both are freed with the help of Langston V and Aberdeen Williams, subsequently deciding to bury the hatchet (cf. AKB 357).

399 The ending of *Any Known Blood* is thus comparable to *The Book of Negroes*' conclusion in its slightly overwrought positive outlook. The latter's narrative turn of having Aminata's daughter May eventually reappear after years of abduction to provide closure for Aminata and to publish her memoirs might be assessed critically; it does indeed reveal a certain slightly artificial predetermination in terms of providing a hopeful, even happy ending.

400 Compare on this wish Aminata's desire, in *The Book of Negroes*, to go home to her native village of Bayo (cf. BN 412ff.). Aminata's hope, however, is frustrated by the ongoing existence of slavery. Having come to terms with the inaccessibility of her original home, Aminata resolves to content herself with the fact that at least she will not have to sail across the sea any more before she dies (cf. BN 448, 470).

401 Like Yoyo and Mahatma Grafton, Hélène Savoie is a character from Hill's debut novel *Some Great Thing*, incorporated "incestuously" (Clarke 2002a, 311) as a minor character in his second novel, *Any Known Blood* (note that in *Some Great Thing*, her name is spelled "Helen", as she 'passes' for an Anglophone; cf. SGT 238 for her name change). Grafton and Savoie only have miniscule appearances, while Yoyo in fact accompanies Langston the Fifth throughout his stay in Baltimore. Yet Hill very explicitly links the novels' two protagonists: "Funny name, Mahatma Grafton [Langston remarks]. Just about as onerous as Langston Cane the Fifth." (AKB 334)

with his writing, hence replenishing the research team which had accompanied Langston on his trip to Storer College. Thus, coming from the earliest family memories (as represented by Langston the First's memoirs, discovered by the motley troupe), they complete the cycle by jointly going back to Canada.[402] The novel's last border crossing hence offers closure not only in terms of the story's plots; it also symbolizes the return of the family's memories, gathered by Langston the Fifth, to Canada.

Mill, acting as a 'conductor' at the border checkpoint (cf. Siemerling 2004, 44, who links the journey northwards to the Underground Railroad),[403] identifies her entourage as family and the car is waved through; she thus makes good on a promise to continue the family history: "She [Mill] said our family had been moving back and forth across the border for five generations and that she would know how to handle this crossing." (AKB 504) The officer does indeed ask for identification, at which point a number of conclusions seem possible in terms of narrative logic; the solution Hill opts for is to have both Langston and Mill produce IDs while the others are exempt from providing proof of their family affiliation. Langston has been singled out because his skin color has rendered him the least likely family member ("'This one is your nephew?' The officer studied me." AKB 504), a final act of racial screening and a final hint at the fact that skin color does in fact play a decisive role in racial classification and assignation even though race is of course also a social construct (cf. Appiah 1998, 80ff. on the notion that race, though no 'essence', is more than a mere construct because it is *causal*).

The IDs produced by the two Canes are *Canadian* ones. This is important insofar as it underlines the national aspect as opposed to a transnational one – the Canes may live in Canada and the US alternately, yet the notion of distinct nations is not refuted.[404] The novel's last border crossing does indeed show a certain permeability of the 49th parallel, yet it also emphasizes the fact that what unites Mill and Langston (their closeness is indeed the reason their car is eventually waved through) is not the tone of their skin color, but their last name as well as

---

402 For Annette, the trip is not, as Millicent phrases it, a "homecoming" (AKB 501); she is on a "trial visit" (AKB 504) to test where the relationship with Langston will take them. Yet the fact that Langston is accompanied by a new partner of course implies the notion that the line of Langston Canes might continue in spite of Langston the Fifth's recent divorce – even though Langston's record in terms of relationships is, like Langston the First's and the Third's, not entirely unblemished.

403 Her new position seems to reinvigorate Mill; while having proclaimed before that she is "at the end of [her] life" (AKB 388), she now tells the officer that she might be old, but "a long way from dead." (AKB 505) This revitalization of course parallels the family history, which is reinvigorated and prolonged by Langston the Fifth. Metaphorically, reviving the memory of his family through narration thus corresponds to memories being brought from the storage layer to the functional layer of collective memory, where memories are re-inhabited.

404 Contrary to Rinaldo Walcott's assessment, who, promoting one of his favorite subjects, proclaims: "Hill's text is different from both Foster's and Alexis's because it refuses the idea of a stable nation that one might join." (2003, 68) On Walcott's notion that the nation does not hold explanative potential for (diasporic) identifications and the ensuing feud with G. E. Clarke, cf. the introduction to the second edition of *Black Like Who?*.

their Canadian citizenship. Skin color, however, supplies the reason why the officer does not question the other passengers' status as members of the family, which once more propounds an ambiguous notion of 'family' (Hill uses the word 'folks' here twice) as referring to either the immediate – consanguineous – or the extended family of the Black community.

Consequently, unity is achieved on the three different levels of race, actual family affiliation and Canadian nationality. The emphasis on being Canadian ties into *Any Known Blood*'s general approach towards transnationalism and the conception of a North American African diaspora as opposed to – or, as is argued here, in addition to – a distinctive African-Canadian experience. As has repeatedly been pointed out, Hill's fiction does not subscribe to notions of collapsing the two North American nations. Thus, Walcott's claim that in *Any Known Blood*, Hill "refuses a discreet US history, a discreet Canadian national history, as well as discreet histories of race, and its making an impact in contemporary life" (2003, 69) cannot be sustained by a close reading of the novel. Hill presents a genealogical line of border-crossers, yet each member of the Cane family *contrasts* rather than collapses Canada and the US. The family memories Langston the Fifth collects (by abstraction, they turn from *collected* memories to part of the *collective* memory) provide examples of a "discreet US history, [and] a discreet Canadian history" (ibid.); in fact they delineate particular branches of these histories, *Black* Canadian and *Black* US-American history, over the course of more than 150 years. The differences between Canada and the US portrayed in *Any Known Blood* are supplemented by diachronic differences, yet they are synchronic in scope as well. The racism faced by the successive Langston Canes successively dwindles (it does *not* disappear) in the course of the story both north and south of the border, yet major shifts occur when actually crossing it. This fact could not be more obvious than in the case of Langston the First, who crosses from slavery into freedom. Hill does not, however, fall into the trap posed by these contrasts and abstains from reverting to simplistic antipodes *à la* 'hell' vs. 'Canaan'.

Flagel rightly notices that "the Canada=free and US=slave dichotomy is interrupted through Hill's complicated repetitions and revisitings of border crossings" (2005, 271); more precisely, Hill refutes the depiction of Canada as a safe haven not through but in spite of the repeated border crossings (though Flagel is of course right in claiming that without the Canes' oscillation, the implicit contrasting would have been vastly more prone to an undifferentiated dichotomy as outlined above). Thus, Langston the Fourth indeed escapes legal, institutionalized segregation in the US; yet he successively discovers that Canada is no Land of Milk and Honey either: he can find integrated restaurants and housing easily enough, yet there are obvious examples of unofficial segregation. Most strikingly, however, the contrast between the United States and Canada in Hill's novel unveils vastly different attitudes, which complement sociopolitical action. While in Canada, there is in fact a sizably smaller Black community to begin with, the absence of a race consciousness or an awareness of Black Canadian history is striking; part of this inattentiveness is based on the notion that – again, particularly in comparison to the US – Canada does not have a problem with racial discrimination in the first

place.[405] As Hill states in *Black Berry, Sweet Juice* (commenting on a contemporary issue involving the custody case of a mixed-race boy): "And Canadians, being Canadians, have once
more proven our mastery of the art of burying our heads in the sand – insisting that race
doesn't matter in this country." (BBSJ 151)[406] The US, in contrast, are depicted in *Any Known
Blood* as being steeped in an attentiveness to matters of race, yet often perforce so, as the kind
of racism exhibited south of the border is often the significantly more overt one.

With his second novel, Hill consequently offers a portrayal of (Black) Canadian history which goes through segregation, the Ku Klux Klan, racial stereotypes, racial screening,
Neo-Nazis, refusal to rent to African-Canadians, the infamous Question,[407] head-turning, and

---

405 This notion is often based on three factors, or faulty assumptions: 1) There is no Black Canadian
community to speak of. 2) Canada has always been benevolent towards its racial minorities, especially Blacks (cf. the Underground Railroad). 3) Contemporary multicultural policies see to it that
racial discrimination cannot gain a foothold in Canada. Clarke discusses these aspects in his article "White Like Canada", where he grants that "one can travel huge tracts of the largest country in
the world [sic] and never lay eyes on another person of color." (1998, 98) The main problem he
identifies, however, is the lack of self-critical assessment underlying factors two and three:
"White Canada imagines itself to be congenial, hospitable, tolerant. There are plenty of white lib-
erals in Canada, but little white liberal guilt: Canadians do not believe that they have committed
any racial sins for which they should atone." (ibid., 101f.)

406 Cf. a very similar statement by G. E. Clarke, who notes in regard to the 1993 murder of Somalis
by Canadian soldiers: "As happens so often in the Great White North, racism was made to disappear." (1998, 109) Also cf. on this incident Clarke, Appendix 317f.

407 The Question, "Where are you from?" is one of the most-cited forms of subtle discrimination in
Canada. "Where are you from?", also used in the follow-up variant "Where are you *really* from?"
presupposes and insinuates that the person who is being asked does not belong to Canada, cannot
in fact be from Canada due to the color of his or her skin. As G. E. Clarke states: "That kind of forensic, trying to search out your genealogy, is done in Canada, specifically to in a sense root out
and uproot you from any kind of *Canadianité*. [...] it's part of the quiet way in which Canadian
racism gets executed." (Clarke, Appendix 308) In *Black Berry, Sweet Juice*, Hill includes a chapter on "The Question" (BBSJ 173ff.); also cf. Hazelle Palmer's *... But Where Are You Really
From?* (1997) as well as Adrienne Shadd's article "Where Are You Really From?" (Shadd 2001)
in the important anthology *Talking About Identity* (James/Shadd 2001), which also includes Hill's
essay "Zebra: Growing Up Black and White in Canada" (ibid., 44ff.; cf. 48f. on the Question).

In *Any Known Blood*, Hill uses multiple instances of the Question to underline its quintessential
'Canadianness', the subtle, even ostensibly friendly way in which it is used to express an essentialist and racist notion; in fact, a variation of the Question is used at the very beginning of the
novel (cf. AKB 1). Hill does, however, employ the Question in various contexts and emphasizes
the fact that it does indeed matter *who* is asking it (cf. AKB 100, 123, 138, 219, 223). The Question is also frequently used in Hill's first novel, *Some Great Thing* (cf. SGT 10, 50, 60, 62f., 183,
209).

A number of African-Canadian poets have used the Question to expose mainstream assumptions
of their being 'out of place' in Canada (many of these poems of course are collected in Palmer's
anthology). To cite but just one example of the implementation of the obnoxious Question in African-Canadian poetry:

[...] what did we know that our pan-colonial
flights would end up among people who ask stupid questions

subtle prejudices. What he does not go through in *Any Known Blood*, however, is the issue of *Canadian* slavery itself.

> Reading *Any Known Blood*, whose plot chronologically starts in 1850 [i.e. sixteen years after the official abolition of slavery in Canada], one could safely believe that slavery never existed in Canada and that the country was always a haven for runaway slaves. This is precisely the misunderstanding that George Elliott Clarke sets out to correct in *Beatrice Chancy*.'
> (Cuder-Domínguez 2003, 62)

Four years after the publication of Cuder-Domínguez' article, one does not need to turn to *Beatrice Chancy* alone to mitigate this lack – which takes us back to *The Book of Negroes* (published in 2007):[408] read in conjunction with *Any Known Blood*, the two novels in fact present a well-rounded, comprehensive and encompassing fictional (rather: 'factional') account of African-Canadian history, an attempt to provide a revivification of numerous memories which have so far been delegated to the back pages of history books – if at all. Hill thus enables and fosters the forwarding of these memories from the storage memory to the functional memory so that they may contribute to the way Canada perceives itself today.

---

like, where are you from … and now here we are on their road,
in their snow, faced with their childishness.
(Brand, "XIII", 1997, p. 75, ll. 7-10)
408 Cuder-Domínguez argues regarding Hill's *Any Known Blood*, Clarke's *Beatrice Chancy*, and Brand's *At the Full and Change of the Moon:* "All three attempt to address the cultural memory of black people through a historical retelling of slavery that is focalized through Canadian characters, concerns, and/or locations." (2003, 57) While for *Any Known Blood*, only two aspects of focalization hold true (hence the quotation's "and/or" qualifier), *The Book of Negroes* indeed incorporates all three aspects.

7. Conclusion

If Uncle Tom came to Canada, could conditions need improving? *(Winks 1997, 193)*

The construction of a national memory in particular is concerned with those points of reference that strengthen a positive self-perception and which are consistent with certain objectives of action. Victories are more easily memorized than defeats. [...] It is far more difficult to incorporate into [a group's] memory moments of shame and guilt, as these cannot be integrated into a positive collective self-perception. This applies to the persecution and eradication of Native peoples on different continents, to the deportation of African slaves, to the victims of genocide in the shades of World War One and Two. (A. Assmann 2001, 309; my translation)

I have been arguing in this study that Lawrence Hill's fiction, along with a significant share of African-Canadian literature, embarks on the difficult endeavor of integrating "moments of shame and guilt" – particularly "the deportation of African slaves" (cf. above) and the ensuing discrimination and maltreatment of enslaved, indentured or free Blacks – into a Canadian collective memory which has been constructed to reflect a (distorted) self-perception of Canada as a 'Canaan' for Blacks in both the past and the present. *Any Known Blood* and *The Book of Negroes* thus constitute part of a counter-memory whose goal is a restructuring of the prevalent, 'whitewashed' national memory of Canada. It undermines common stereotypes and notions of Canadian moral superiority and acknowledges memories that have been virtually purged from mainstream discourse for centuries. Rinaldo Walcott, in a reading of André Alexis's *Childhood*, Cecil Foster's *Slammin' Tar*, and Hill's *Any Known Blood*, states that "the moment of what Sylvia Wynter calls the counter-novel has arrived for black literature in Canada. [...] These counter-novels are reshaping both the literary landscape of Canada and simultaneously helping to rewrite Canadian historiography." (2003, 58)

Rewriting Canadian historiography, or, in terms of the theoretical framework employed in this study, rewriting the Canadian collective memory, is not a matter of solely rectifying an incorrect representation of matters of the past. Through remembrance, i.e. through 'inhabiting' memories, these issues become issues of the present as well. As George Elliott Clarke remarks in an interview: "And so the reason why I think many of us want to keep the discourse of slavery, specifically Canadian slavery, on the table, is to attempt, or to force, White Canadians to deal with racism today." Describing a prevalent goal of African-Canadian writers, he goes on: "I think that for a lot of us, it is trying to force racism onto the Canadian agenda, and remind people that we are not pristine." (Clarke, Appendix 317) While *The Book of Negroes* deals specifically with the issue of Canadian slavery and its more subtle cousin, indentured servitude, *Any Known Blood* traces a genealogical heritage from the days of slavery up to the multicultural Canada of the present. Both novels aim at an insertion of neglected parts of the (Black) Canadian history into mainstream constructions in order to both correct a lopsided view of the past and to undermine notions of superiority (mainly *vis à vis* the United States) in the present.

'Faction'

Putting the missing Black tiles of the Canadian mosaic in place requires assertiveness. Hill hence refrains – contrary to some scholars' opinion – from the literary mode of historiographic metafiction. More closely, his fiction resembles what Foley has termed the documentary novel, yet her conception focuses too narrowly on the economic aspects of slavery to serve as a model for Black Canadian literature's treatment of an issue which George Elliott Clarke rightly deems a "miniscule economic activity in comparison" (1999, 7). Borrowing from Hill's own usage, then, his writing has been classified here as 'faction', which implies historical writing which might be subversive in content but not in its assessment of historical 'truth'. More precisely, Hill's faction steers clear of the self-reflexive doubts characterizing historiographic metafiction. History *can* be accessed, in fact it must be accessed to bring to the fore those aspects currently neglected in processes of (self-)definition. The modes and interdependencies of historiography and fiction are exposed, yet they are not simply deconstructed; borrowing from strategic essentialism, Hill's faction acknowledges the existence of uncertainties but offers a self-confident reading of history in spite of these uncertainties. The archive, for instance, is not regarded as an inaccessible vault or as prone to unreliable constructions; some 'truth' can be unearthed if carefully checked against other versions supplied by other sources such as orature. Consequently, Hill does not provide contradictory memory versions or clashes between oral and written accounts, thus providing a reliable narrative which authenticates itself both fictionally and extra-fictionally. In terms of content, however, Hill's fictions are questioning, challenging, even subversive indeed, both undermining past and present hegemonic constructions and offering, assertively, alternative versions.

The Book of Negroes

The assertive nature of Hill's fiction is highlighted by a thorough comparison between the (Neo-) slave narrative and *The Book of Negroes*. Hill indeed provides what can be categorized as a Neo-slave narrative not only based on broad definitions but on his adherence to a large number of characteristics typical of the classic slave narrative. The first-person perspective of the fugitive narrator-cum-author, the basic teleological adherence to the triad of slavery–escape–freedom (conceived of as an analogy to the biblical Exodus), an emphasis on the acquisition of literacy as a means to establish the writer's subjectivity, the surmounting of voicelessness and the resulting disproval of an alleged inferiority and even inhumanity, the importance of authenticity, and the collectivization of the narrator's perspective as well as a number of additional criteria link Hill's novel to the classic slave narrative and its goals.

Not blindly emulating the slave narrative, however, *The Book of Negroes* diverges from its historical model in crucial points. While the classic slave narrative relied heavily on authentication by White amanuenses, abolitionists and other testimonials by Whites, *The Book of Negroes'* narrator explicitly rejects any interference with her story. Emancipation from White dominance in the telling of the Black Canadian (hi-)story lies at the core of this stance. The story thus offered implements a further decisive deviation: although the triad of slavery–escape–freedom is employed in analogy to the slave narrative's biblical motif of Israelites in Egypt–Exodus–Promised Land, the very essence of this Exodus is questioned. In a manner of speaking, Aminata adds inverted commas to the 'Promised Land' of Canada, which for her and her fellow Black Loyalists turns out *not* to be the land of racial equality and plenty they had been led to expect.

While the original slave narrative could not, for the sake of its sociopolitical ambition, critically assess the 'Canaan' the fugitive had reached, Hill is free to do so. In fact, it is a central ambition of *The Book of Negroes* to do so. After all, the image of the heavenly True North as opposed to the hellish United States is one of the key misrepresentations he sets out to expose and revert. Canada, it is claimed, neither was nor is the Canaan for Blacks as which it has been constructed by a mainstream version of Canadian collective memory. Instead of relying on the flawed key memory of the successful exodus north into freedom and equality, Hill offers his own version, which indeed goes through Canadian slavery, indenture and servitude; through segregation, discrimination and broken promises; through lynchings, racial violence and notions of Black inferiority. The horrors experienced by Aminata, the novel's protagonist, during the Middle Passage and plantation slavery in South Carolina are not mirrored on the same scale in (what was to become) Canada. Neither, however, has the True North turned out to be what she had been led to believe – incidentally, not what we as a contemporary readership have been led to believe by either the slave narrative or current hegemonic memory constructions. Though slavery was in fact less frequent and racism less violent north of the 49th parallel – which is reflected faithfully in Hill's novel –, slavery and racism remain slavery and racism. Hill's usage of the historical ledger called the Book of Negroes is an embodiment of this perspective as it reflects the ambiguity of the historical Black Canadian experience by recording both slaves and freed Blacks. It also reflects the current Canadian 'forgetfulness' surrounding the Black presence, as Hill notes: "Sadly, however, the *Book of Negroes* has been largely forgotten in Canada. And that is a shame." (2007a, 18) Consequently, it also reflects what Hill sets out to correct by tackling this very 'forgetfulness'.

In spite of the prolongation of oppression on a smaller scale and in spite of the disillusionment that is so characteristic for the Black experience as presented in *The Book of Negroes*, its protagonist Aminata emerges as a heroic figure not only for her mere survival, or the retention of her capacity to love. She becomes a *djeli*, a witness and a bearer of memories. She saves her own life by the act of remembering, yet far beyond her individual survival, she saves the memories of her fellow slaves and fugitives from being lost, subsequently publishing her and their story on her own terms. As such, she serves as a personification of Hill's (and many other African-Canadian writers') basic impetus: to remedy the perceived silence surrounding the Black Canadian experience and to correct prevailing whitewashed constructions.

Any Known Blood

The same impetus underlies Hill's second novel, *Any Known Blood*. Langston the Fifth, the novel's narrator-cum-author, finally finds – like his counterpart in Hill's first novel, *Some Great Thing* – issues worth writing about. For Langston, it is his family history, which reflects almost 170 years of the Black experience in North America. As in *The Book of Negroes*, Hill draws on the legacy of the slave narrative by including Langston the First's memoirs, an ex-slave's account of his life. Crucially, however, Aminata's journey north takes place at a time when slavery still existed in Canada, while Langston the First's exodus takes him, via the Underground Railroad, to a country devoid of institutionalized bondage. What both (Neo-) slave narratives depict, however, is the version of the 'Promised Land' they experience – an experience which does not necessarily comply with the supposed land of milk and honey (cf. Langston the First's telling initial confusion of the terms 'Canaan' and 'Canada'). As all Langston Canes except one cross the 49th parallel twice, Hill employs their perspectives to contrast the two North American nations. This idea runs counter to a number of scholars claiming that Hill largely collapses the US and Canada by portraying a highly porous boundary in order to counter the stereotypical dichotomy of the US as racist and Canada as benevolent. In fact, Hill does both: he explodes the myth of the safe haven both past and present, yet he also delineates crucial difficulties.

For Langston the First, coming to Canada means on a very essential level the escape from slavery, thus the gaining of his personal freedom and subjectivity. He encounters, however, partly malignant racism, racial segregation and early forms of denial that slavery had existed in Canada in the first place. His grandson, Langston the Third, is amazed at the level of desegregation when migrating north. However, he also makes the experience that many Blacks suffer under bad living conditions and 'polite' segregation even of public facilities such as hospitals, thus relegating African-Canadians to the rank of second-class citizens. The depiction of a Ku Klux Klan raid for an interracial couple sheltered in Langston the Third's house illustrates the existence even of overt, blatant racism in Canada in the 1930s (although Hill admits to having proceeded too recklessly with the raid's historical prototype, hence underlining his overall ambition to present historical matters as faithfully as possible). Langston the Fourth, when coming to Canada, is surprised at the friendliness he encounters; it seems as if Canadians did not even notice his race. It turns out that he is faced with both an absence of a distinct Black community and a general absence of any major race consciousness. The latter is fed by a muted discourse on race matters, which allows both for a blanking out of the Black Canadian presence and for the glossing over of existent racism. Langston the Fifth joins his paternal forbear in concluding that Canada, in comparison to the United States, is indeed the slower, wealthier, colder, less obviously racist, but also Whiter nation – the latter both in quantity and conceptual quality.

Any Known Blood thus goes through a number of issues relevant for the creation of a Black Canadian collective memory – and thus for the amelioration of a mainstream Canadian one: segregation, the Klan, racial stereotypes, racial screening, and the infamous Question are examples of memories which are brought from the storage to the functional memory in order to inform current processes of identity formation. The literal retrieval of memories by Langston the Fifth from archives in jumbled households or from storage basements serves as a metaphorical reference to the modes of memory retrieval; combined with orature passed down from generation to generation, they build the foundation of collected as well as collective memory. In *Any Known Blood*, there are few doubts pertaining to the accessibility of history such as found in historiographic metafiction. The different narratives, whether oral reports, official documents, or written memoirs, mutually authenticate one another to form an assertive, self-confident construction. Which, however, runs counter to some of the notions currently prevailing in hegemonic memory constructions – cf. Hazel's shock when seeing the hooded Klansmen on her son-in-law's lawn ("What is the Klan doing here? You never told me they were in Canada." AKB 315).

We are what we think we were

> *People act according to the history they* believe *has happened. [...] History as it is understood enters a political discourse, it becomes a participant in a power dialectic and it influences power relationships. [...] This applies to African-Canadian history* as it is understood *by both black people and white people. Approaching African-Canadian history is a political act, deliberate or not. How you approach it will determine the lessons you derive from it. You can even shape the future. (Walker 2007, 8; emphases in the original)*

In 1855, Benjamin Drew published *The Refugee: Narratives of Fugitive Slaves in Canada*, a collection of brief testimonies by former slaves who had fled the United States and come to Canada to find freedom and equality in the Dominion of the British Crown. Accordingly, the collection's original title supplement, *A North-Side View of Slavery*, a counter-manifesto to Adam Nehemiah's slavery apologetic *A South-Side View of Slavery* (1854), illustrated the distinctly abolitionist perspective. Drew's collection of more than a hundred short testimonies by the newly minted African-Canadians was uncompromisingly *engagé* in its objective. The statements amassed by Drew by and large convey but one message: slavery in the United States was hell, so that the interviewees fled to Canada – which, in contrast, was perceived as heavenly. In fact, the former African-Americans do not even devote much energy to describing their *new* home; Drew's ambition and the slaves' preoccupation staunchly centered around the Peculiar Institution to their south. Canada, however, is habitually *implied* in the slaves' testimonies as a *contrast* to the slave-ridden United States – if the slaves escaped hell, then the True North must be heaven indeed. It has become one of the major grievances and likely the most frequent criticism among contemporary African-Canadian writers that the lesson so thoroughly learned from the juxtaposition of the United States and Canada still reverberates today: basing mainstream self-perception on the idea of Canadian benevolence towards Blacks historically (being the terminus of the Underground Railroad, the safe haven for refugees), current Canadian majoritarian constructions still identify Canada as the benign nation. Canada's own slavery past as well as continuing racism is erased from the record – or, as I have argued, the collective memory of Canadian slavery and segregation is deselected in order to construct a diachronically stable, coherently positive image of Canada's dealings with 'its' Black minority.

In his introduction to Drew's collection, George Elliott Clarke outlines the connection between past and present which still dominates much of the discourse in and about Black Canada.

> Proudly, we Canadians blame the practice of African slavery in North America on two-faced Americans: those who preached hatred for monarchy and love of freedom, but only for citizens touting white skin, male genitals, and a Bible. We believe our schooling that our settler ancestors, because they did not rebel against the British Crown, evolved a superior social order and liberty to that of the violence-prone, if revolutionary, United States. These half-truths still compel our allegiance, thus inspiring a hint of Anti-Americanism in our public dialogues and justifying, painlessly, our ignorance about slavery in colonial Canada and about the persistence of racism in our 'post-modern, multicultural' nation. (Clarke 2008a, 10)

Even though the astounding denseness of this paragraph is not revealed stylistically, Clarke manages to squeeze into a few lines the summary of a discourse which has dominated Black Canadian historical, cultural and literary discourse for decades – a discourse prototypically represented in Hill's historical fiction. Clarke sets out by proclaiming, "[p]roudly, we Canadians" (all quotes in the subsequent paragraphs refer to the excerpt above), thus firmly establishing himself as a Canadian, with every right to make claims about Canada. The introductory emphasis on emotion is indicative of the trajectory of hegemonic constructions of collective memory: it instills pride in Canada's (historical as well as current) achievements, the nation's allegedly clean record. The usable past which is assembled by mainstream Canada, Clarke argues here, is emotionally charged. The affective impact is then used to promote *un*truthful renditions; this much is obvious from Clarke's usage of the phrase "half-truths", which, however, also implies that there *is* such a thing as the *full* truth – a stance shared by Lawrence Hill and his approach to 'faction'.

The full truth is simply not the version which underlies current Canadian self-identifications. Instead, half-truths largely inform the opposition between the United States and Canada, the "hint of Anti-Americanism" which Clarke discerns in what he, avoiding the term 'public discourse', calls "public dialogues".[409] Thus, the fact that Canada has largely ignored its own record of ill-treatment of Blacks has been covered up by consistently pointing to the United States as the nation adhering to racist, sexist, and religiously bigoted principles – freedom, it has been held in Canada, has *south* of the border only been extended only to those "touting white skin, male genitals, and a Bible." Aminata Diallo, in *The Book of Negroes*, does not tout any of the aforementioned, yet her experiences south of the 49th parallel are mirrored by her experiences in Canada, albeit on a distinctly smaller scale.[410]

The "'post-modern, multicultural' nation" – revealingly set in inverted commas – is based, Clarke argues, on the "ignorance" of both the past and the present, both "slavery in colonial Canada" *and* "the persistence of racism". The past is thus present not only in terms of being remembered, retold and reconstructed in African-Canadian literature; it is also present in its *de facto* continuation and in the continuing nescience revolving around past and present discrimination. Importantly, Clarke does not blame this ignorance on mere neglect. The suppression of memories of the Black presence in Canada is purposive and actively sought after: discursively, the "half-truths" of Canadian benevolence and US-American viciousness serve to *justify* and thus perpetuate the ongoing ignorance as well as self-perceptions as a positively post-modern[411] and multicultural society. The creation of a collective identity free of blemishes and fissures possibly created by "moments of shame and guilt [which] cannot be integrated into a positive collective self-perception" (A. Assmann 2001, 309; my translation) is thus enabled by the lopsided representation of the past. The collective memories selected and recreated in Hill's fiction, such as the key memories of slavery and segregation, but also the gaining of agency through literacy or the spirit of community pervading early Black settlements in Canada, are a way of narratively correcting these lopsided representations.

Whoever can tell what a (hypothetical?) national Canadian collective memory consists of has solved the riddle of Canadian identity – and thus antiquated large sections of Canadian literature. Quite obviously, I am not claiming to have solved this riddle. What I have dealt

---

409 The socio-political and historiographic discourse Clarke deals with here is clearly connected to literature; while it is not explicitly stated in the paragraph cited here, the mere fact that Clarke introduces a collection of (miniature) 'slave narratives' which he terms "(African-)Canadian Literature" in the title of his essay illustrates as much.

410 As has been pointed out throughout this study, various African-Canadian literary works supplement this approach; a prime example of incorporating Canadian slavery, for instance, is G. E. Clarke's *Beatrice Chancy*. Also cf. a number of poems dealing with slavery and/or disillusionment with Canadian race relations past and present: Allen 1993a-b; Bernard 1992a-b; Booker 2001a-b; G. Borden 1988a-g, 1991a-b; W. Borden 1992; Brand 1975, 1995, 1998a-d; Cambridge 1975; Carew 2000; Clarke 1983a-c, 1994, 2001a-d; Compton 2001; Cooper 1983, 1992a-f; Coopsammy 1985; Dabydeen 1987; Darbasie 1988; Dawes 1995, 1998, 2001a-b; Gaskin 1976; Goodison 2001; Harris 1986, 1989, 1996; Miguna 1995; Mordecai 1989; Philip 1980, 1983a-b, 1994; Senior 1998; Stewart 2001; Thompson 1999; Tynes 1987, 1993; Ward 1983; Wesley-Desmond 1992 (these poems are listed in a separate bibliographical section in the appendix).

411 Note Clarke's usage of the hyphenated version, which indicates not so much literary postmodernism *per se* but socio-political post-modernity.

with in this study is one specific instance of a perceived blank and a subsequent distortion in hegemonic constructions of Canadian collective memory. Hill's historical fiction engages in a rewriting of this particular absence by providing a reading of Canadian history which goes through a number of neglected issues of the African-Canadian experience. By re-inhabiting these memories fictionally, Hill brings them to the fore, shifting them to the functional memory and thus making them available for current processes of identity construction. One writer alone could of course never achieve such a feat. But Hill is not alone in this.

8. Bibliography

Adams, Bella. "Identity Politics." *Encyclopedia of Postcolonial Studies*. Ed. John Charles Hawley. Westport, Conn.: Greenwood, 2001. 239-242.

Adams, Rachel. "Blackness Goes South: Race and Mestizaje in Our America." *Imagining Our Americas: Toward a Transnational Frame*. Ed. Sandhya Shukla and Heidi Tinsman. Durham, NC: Duke University Press, 2007. 214-248.

Alexander, Ken, and Avis Glaze. *Towards Freedom: The African-Canadian Experience*. Toronto: Umbrella Press, 1996.

Alexis, André. *Childhood*. London: Bloomsbury, 1998.

Allen, Graham. *Intertextuality*. New York: Routledge, 2000.

Andrews, William L., and Henry Louis Gates, Jr., eds. *Slave Narratives*. New York: Library of America, 2000.

Appiah, Kwame Anthony. "Race, Culture, Identity: Misunderstood Connections." *Color Conscious: The Political Morality of Race*. Ed. Kwame Anthony Appiah and Amy Gutmann. Princeton, NJ: Princeton University Press, 1998. 30-105.

Aristotle. *The Nicomachean Ethics*. Oxford: Oxford University Press, 1998.

Arndt, Susan. African Women's Literature, Orature and Intertextuality: Igbo Oral Narratives as Nigerian Women Writers' Models and Objects of Writing Back. Bayreuth African studies series. Bayreuth: Eckhard Breitinger, 1998.

Assmann, Aleida. "Funktionsgedächtnis und Speichergedächtnis – Zwei Modi der Erinnerung." *Generation und Gedächtnis. Erinnerungen und kollektive Identitäten*. Ed. Kristin Platt and Mihran Dabag. Opladen: Leske + Budrich, 1995. 169-185.

Assmann, Aleida. Erinnerungsräume. Formen und Wandlungen des kulturellen Gedächtnisses. München: C.H. Beck, 1999.

Assmann, Aleida. "Kollektives Gedächtnis." *Gedächtnis und Erinnerung. Ein interdisziplinäres Lexikon.* Ed. Nicolas Pethes and Jens Ruchatz. Reinbek: Rowohlt, 2001. 308-310.

Assmann, Aleida. Der lange Schatten der Vergangenheit: Erinnerungskultur und Geschichtspolitik. München: Beck, 2006.

Assmann, Jan. "Kollektives Gedächtnis und kulturelle Identität." *Kultur und Gedächtnis.* Ed. Jan Assmann and Tonio Hölscher. Frankfurt a. M.: Suhrkamp, 1988. 9-19.

Assmann, Jan. Das kulturelle Gedächtnis. Schrift, Erinnerung und politische Identität in frühen Hochkulturen. München: C.H. Beck, 1992.

Assmann, Jan. "Das kollektive Gedächtnis zwischen Körper und Schrift. Zur Gedächtnistheorie von Maurice Halbwachs." *Erinnerung und Gesellschaft: Hommage à Maurice Halbwachs (1877 - 1945).* Ed. Hermann Krapoth and Denis Laborde. Jahrbuch für Soziologiegeschichte. Wiesbaden: VS Verl. für Sozialwiss., 2005. 65-80.

Assmann, Jan. *Religion and Cultural Memory: Ten Studies.* Cultural Memory in the Present. Stanford, Calif: Stanford University Press, 2006.

Atwood, Margaret. Survival: A Thematic Guide to Canadian Literature. Toronto: Anansi, 1972.

Baker, Houston A., and Patricia Redmond, eds. *Afro-American Literary Study in the 1990s.* Black Literature and Culture Series. Chicago: University of Chicago Press, 1989.

Bakhtin, Mikhail Mikhailovich. *Speech Genres and Other Late Essays.* Austin, Tex.: University of Texas Press, 1986.

Baldwin, James. *Nobody Knows My Name: More Notes of a Native Son.* [1961] New York: Vintage International, 1993.

Banita, Georgiana. "Canons of Diversity in Contemporary English-Canadian Literature." *History of Literature in Canada: English-Canadian and French-Canadian.* Ed. Reingard M. Nischik. Rochester, NY: Camden House, 2008. 387-412.

Bannerji, Himani, ed. *Returning the Gaze: Essays on Racism, Feminism and Politics.* Toronto: Sister Vision Press, 1993.

Barker, Chris. The Sage Dictionary of Cultural Studies. London: SAGE, 2004.

Barker, Chris. *Cultural Studies: Theory and Practice.* 3rd ed. Los Angeles: Sage, 2008.

Barker, Chris, and Dariusz Galasiński. Cultural Studies and Discourse Analysis: A Dialogue on Language and Identity. London: SAGE, 2001.

Barrett, Deirdre, ed. *Trauma and Dreams.* Cambridge, Mass.: Harvard University Press, 2001.

Barthes, Roland. "Der Tod des Autors." *Texte zur Theorie der Autorschaft.* Ed. Fotis Jannidis et al. Stuttgart: Reclam, 2000. 185-198.

Bast, Heike. "The Ghosts of Africville, Acadia and the African Continuum. (Re)claiming Ethnic Identity in Africadian Literature." *Zeitschrift für Kanada-Studien* 43 (2003): 129-142.

Beaulieu, Elizabeth Ann. *Black Women Writers and the American Neo-slave Narrative: Femininity Unfettered.* Contributions in Afro-American and African studies 192. Westport, Conn.: Greenwood Press, 1999.

Beaulieu, Elizabeth. "Neo-slave Narrative." *The Companion to Southern Literature: Themes, Genres, Places, People, Movements, and Motifs.* Ed. Joseph M. Flora, Lucinda Hardwick MacKethan and Todd W. Taylor. Baton Rouge: Louisiana State University Press, 2002. 535-536.

Belcher, Stephen Paterson. *Epic Traditions of Africa.* Bloomington: Indiana University Press, 1999.

Bell, Bernard W. *The Afro-American Novel and its Tradition.* Amherst: University of Massachusetts Press, 1989.

Ben-Moshe, Danny. "The State of Holocaust Negation." *Contemporary Responses to the Holocaust.* Ed. Konrad Kwiet and Jürgen Matthäus. Praeger Series on Jewish and Israeli Studies. Westport, Conn.: Praeger, 2004. 139-176.

Bernard, Delvina E. "U.I. Line." *Fire on the Water. An Anthology of Black Nova Scotian Writing.* Volume 2. Ed. George Elliott Clarke. Lawrencetown Beach, NS: Pottersfield Press, 1992. 130-131.

Bhabha, Homi K. *The Location of Culture.* Reprinted. Routledge classics. London: Routledge, 2007.

Bibb, Henry. "Narrative of the Life and Adventures of Henry Bibb, an American Slave, Written by Himself. With an Introduction by Lucius C. Matlack." 1849. *Slave Narratives.* Ed. William L. Andrews and Henry Louis Gates, Jr. New York: Library of America, 2000. 425-566.

Bielefeldt, Christian. "Musik." *Gedächtnis und Erinnerung. Ein interdisziplinäres Lexikon.* Ed. Nicolas Pethes and Jens Ruchatz. Reinbek: Rowohlt, 2001. 389-391.

Black, Ayanna. Interview. *Why We Write. Conversations With African Canadian Poets and Novelists.* Ed. H. Nigel Thomas. Toronto: TSAR, 2006. 1-13.

Blassingame, John W. "Using the Testimony of Ex-Slaves: Approaches and Problems." *The Slave's Narrative.* Ed. Charles T. Davis and Henry Louis Gates, Jr. Oxford: Oxford University Press, 1985. 78-97.

Blight, David W. *Beyond the Battlefield: Race, Memory, and the American Civil War.* Amherst, Mass.: University of Massachusetts Press, 2002.

Bloom, Harold. *The Anxiety of Influence: A Theory of Poetry*. 2nd ed. New York: Oxford University Press, 1997.

Borden, George A. "Fashions of Slavery." *Canaan Odyssey. A Poetic Account of the Black Experience in North America*. Dartmouth, NS: Black Cultural Centre for Nova Scotia, 1988. 6-7.

Borden, Walter. Tightrope Time. Ain't Nuthin' More Than Some Itty Bitty Madness Between Twilight and Dawn. Toronto: Playwrights Canada Press, 1987.

Borden, Walter. "The Hebrew Children." *Fire on the Water. An Anthology of Black Nova Scotian Writing*. Volume 2. Ed. George Elliott Clarke. Lawrencetown Beach, NS: Pottersfield Press, 1992. 40-42.

Boyko, John. *Last Steps to Freedom. The Evolution of Canadian Racism*. 2nd rev. ed. N/A: J. Gordon Shillingford, 1998.

Brainerd, Charles J., and Valerie F. Reyna. *The Science of False Memory*. Oxford: Oxford University Press, 2005.

Brand, Dionne. "Eurocentric." *Borderline. Contemporary Poems in English*. Ed. Clarke Wainwright, Li Grogan and Wallace Ross. Toronto: Copp Clark, 1995. 193.

Brand, Dionne, "XIII." *Land to Light on*. Toronto: McClelland & Stewart, 1997. 73-80.

Brand, Dionne. Bread out of Stone: Recollections, Sex, Recognitions, Race, Dreaming, Politics. Toronto: Coach House Press, 1994.

Brand, Dionne. *At the Full and Change of the Moon*. New York: Grove Press, 2000.

Brand, Dionne. A Map to the Door of No Return: Notes to Belonging. Toronto: Vintage Canada, 2002.

Brand, Dionne, and Krisantha Sri Bhaggiyadatta, eds. *Rivers Have Sources, Trees Have Roots: Speaking of Racism*. Toronto: Cross-Cultural Communication Centre, 1986.

Brathwaite, Wendy [Motion]. *Motion in Poetry*. Toronto: Women's Press, 2002.

Breyer, Thiemo. On the Topology of Cultural Memory: Different Modalities of Inscription and Transmission. Würzburg: Königshausen und Neumann, 2007.

Bristow, Peggy. "We're Rooted Here and they Can't Pull us up": Essays in African Canadian Women's History. Toronto: University of Toronto Press, 1994.

Brodzki, Bella. *Can these Bones Live? Translation, Survival, and Cultural Memory*. Cultural memory in the present. Stanford: Stanford University Press, 2007.

Brow, Robert. "The Curse of Ham: Capsule of Ancient History." *Christianity Today*. October 26, 1973. 8-10. Reprinted: 15 January 2009 <http://www.brow.on.ca/Articles/ CurseHam.html>.

Brown, William Wells. "Narrative of William W. Brown, a Fugitive Slave. Written by Himself." 1847. *Slave Narratives*. Ed. William L. Andrews and Henry Louis Gates, Jr. New York: Library of America, 2000. 369-424.

Brydon, Diana. "Detour Canada: Rerouting the Black Atlantic, Reconfiguring the Postcolonial." *Reconfigurations: Canadian Literatures and Postcolonial Identities; Littératures canadiennes et identités postcoloniales*. Ed. Marc Maufort and Franca Bellarsi. Bruxelles: P.I.E. Lang, 2002. 109-122.

Brydon, Diana. "Metamorphoses of a Discipline: Rethinking Canadian Literature within Institutional Contexts.". *Trans.Can.Lit: Resituating the Study of Canadian Literature*. Ed. Smaro Kamboureli and Roy Miki. Waterloo, Ont.: Wilfried Laurier University Press, 2007. 1-16.

Butler, Christopher. "The 'Idea' in Philosophy and in Literature." *Literature and Philosophy*. Ed. Herbert Grabes. Tübingen: Narr, 1997. 37-49.

Byerman, Keith Eldon. *Remembering the Past in Contemporary African American Fiction*. Chapel Hill: University of North Carolina Press, 2005.

Callahan, John F., ed. *Ralph Ellison's Invisible Man: A Casebook*. Casebooks in Criticism. Oxford: Oxford University Press, 2004.

Canadian Oral History Association. *Oral History Forum*. Double issue 21-22 (2001-2002).

Carew, Jan. "The Caribbean Writer and Exile." *Journal of Black Studies* 8.4 (1978): 435-475. Reprinted: 15 April 2009 <http://jancarew.googlepages.com/TheCaribbeanWriterand Exile.doc>.

Carretta, Vincent. *Equiano, the African. Biography of a Self-made Man*. Athens, Ga.: University of Georgia Press, 2005.

Carretta, Vincent. "Olaudah Equiano: African British Abolitionist and Founder of the African American Slave Narrative." *The Cambridge Companion to the African American Slave Narrative*. Ed. Audrey A. Fisch. Cambridge: Cambridge University Press, 2007. 44-60.

Casey, Edward S. *Remembering: A Phenomenological Study*. 2nd ed. Bloomington: Indiana University Press, 2000.

Cash, Adam. *Posttraumatic Stress Disorder*. Hoboken, NJ: Wiley, 2006.

Cashmore, Ernest. *Mike Tyson: Nurture of the Beast*. Oxford: Polity, 2005.

Casmier-Paz, Lynn A. "Footprints of the Fugitive: Slave Narrative Discourse and the Trace of Autobiography." *Biography* 24.1 (2001): 215-225.

Chaney, Michael A. Fugitive Vision: Slave Image and Black Identity in Antebellum Narrative. Bloomington: Indiana University Press, 2008.

Clairmont, Donald H., and Dennis William Magill. *Africville. The Life and Death of a Canadian Black Community.* 3rd ed. Toronto: Canadian Scholars' Press, 1999.

Clarke, Austin. *The Polished Hoe.* Toronto: Thomas Allen Publishers, 2002.

Clarke, George Elliott, ed. *Fire on the Water: An Anthology of Black Nova Scotian Writing.* Volume 1. Lawrencetown Beach, NS: Pottersfield Press, 1991.

Clarke, George Elliott, ed. *Fire on the Water: An Anthology of Black Nova Scotian Writing.* Volume 2. Lawrencetown Beach, NS: Pottersfield Press, 1992. [=1992a]

Clarke, George Elliott. "Hammonds Plains African Baptist Church." *Fire on the Water: An Anthology of Black Nova Scotian Writing.* Volume 2. Lawrencetown Beach, NS: Pottersfield Press, 1992. 147. [=1992b]

Clarke, George Elliott. *Lush Dreams, Blue Exile: Fugitive Poems, 1978-1993.* Lawrencetown Beach NS: Pottersfield Press, 1994.

Clarke, George Elliott, ed. *Eyeing the North Star. Directions in African-Canadian Literature.* Toronto: McClelland & Stewart, 1997.

Clarke, George Elliott. "White Like Canada." *Transition* ["The White Issue", ed. Kwame Anthony Appiah and Henry Louis Gates, Jr.] 73 (1998): 98-109.

Clarke, George Elliott. *Beatrice Chancy.* Victoria, BC: Polestar, 1999.

Clarke, George Elliott. "Milk." *Blue.* Vancouver: Polestar Book, 2001. 45.

Clarke, George Elliott. *Odysseys Home. Mapping African-Canadian Literature.* Toronto: University of Toronto Press, 2002. [=2002a]

Clarke, George Elliott. Foreword. *Motion in Poetry.* Motion (Wendy Brathwaite). Toronto: Women's Press, 2002. 6-7. [=2002b]

Clarke, George Elliott. "Inking BC in Black and Blue." *Essays On Canadian Writing* 79 (2003): 76-82.

Clarke, George Elliott. "Raising Raced and Erased Executions in African-Canadian Literature. Or, Unearthing Angélique." *Racism, Eh?: A Critical Inter-disciplinary Anthology of Race and Racism in Canada.* Ed. Camille A. Nelson and Charmaine A. Nelson. Concord, ON: Captus Press, 2004. 65-84.

Clarke, George Elliott. *George & Rue.* Toronto: HarperCollins, 2005.

Clarke, George Elliott. "Author's Note to the U.S. Edition." *George and Rue.* New York: Carroll & Graf, 2006. 5-6. [=2006a]

Clarke, George Elliott. Interview. *Why We Write. Conversations With African Canadian Poets and Novelists.* Ed. H. Nigel Thomas. Toronto: TSAR, 2006. 36-58. [=2006b]

Clarke, George Elliott. Interview. "'We Have to Recover Their Bodies': George Elliott Clarke." *Speaking in the Past Tense: Canadian Novelists on Writing Historical Fiction*. Ed. Herb Wyile. Waterloo: Laurier University Press, 2007. 133-164.

Clarke, George Elliott. "Introduction: Let Us Now Consider 'African-American' Narratives as (African-)Canadian Literature." *The Refugee: Narratives of Fugitive Slaves in Canada*. Ed. Benjamin Drew. Toronto: Dundurn Press, 2008. 10-24. [=2008a]

Clarke, George Elliott. *Blues & Bliss: The Poetry of George Elliott Clarke*. Sel. , and Jon Paul Fiorentino. Lancaster: Wilfrid Laurier University Press, 2008. [= 2008b]

Clarke, John Henrik, ed. *William Styron's* Nat Turner: *Ten Black Writers Respond*. [1968] Westport, Conn.: Greenwood Press, 1987.

Clifford, Mary Louise. From Slavery to Freetown: Black Loyalists After the American Revolution. Jefferson, NC: McFarland, 2006.

Cohen, Mark. *Censorship in Canadian Literature*. Montreal: McGill-Queen's University Press. 2001.

Collison, Gary Lee. *Shadrach Minkins: From Fugitive Slave to Citizen*. Cambridge, Mass.: Harvard University Press, 1998.

Compton, Wayde, ed. *Bluesprint: Black British Columbian Literature and Orature*. Vancouver: Arsenal Pulp Press, 2001.

Cooper, Afua. "Roots and Branches." *Memories Have Tongue*. Toronto: Sister Vision, 1992. 23.

Cooper, Afua. Foreword. *T-Dot Griots: An Anthology of Toronto's Black Storytellers*. Ed. Steven Green and Karen Richardson. Victoria, BC: Trafford, 2004. i-iii.

Cooper, Afua. The Hanging of Angélique. The Untold Story of Canadian Slavery and the Burning of Old Montréal. Athens: The University of Georgia Press, 2006.

Cooper, Afua. "Unsilencing the Past: Memorializing Four Hundred Years of African-Canadian History." *Multiple Lenses: Voices from the Diaspora Located in Canada*. Ed. David Divine. Newcastle-upon-Tyne: Cambridge Scholars, 2007. 11-22.

Couser, G. Thomas. *Altered Egos: Authority in American Autobiography*. New York: Oxford University Press, 1989.

Cross, Wilbur. *Gullah Culture in America*. Westport, Conn.: Praeger, 2008.

Cuddon, John Anthony. The Penguin Dictionary of Literary Terms and Literary Theory. 3rd ed. Oxford: Blackwell, 1992.

Cuder-Domínguez, Pilar. "African Canadian Writing and the Narration(s) of Slavery." *Essays on Canadian Writing* 79 (2003): 55-75.

Davey, Frank. Post-national Arguments: The Politics of the Anglophone-Canadian Novel since 1967. Toronto: University of Toronto Press, 1993.

Davis, Charles T., and Henry Louis Gates, Jr., eds. *The Slave's Narrative*. Oxford: Oxford University Press, 1985. [=1985a]

Davis, Charles T., and Henry Louis Gates, Jr. "Introduction: The Language of Slavery." *The Slave's Narrative*. Oxford: Oxford University Press, 1985. xi- xxxiv. [=1985b]

Davis, Felecia. "Uncovering Places of Memory". *Sites of Memory. Perspectives on Architecture and Race*. Ed. Craig Evan Barton. New York: Princeton Architectural Press. 2001. 27-37.

Davis, Paul. A. "Scott's Histories and Fiction in Waverley and the 'Fictional Essays.'" *REAL* (Yearbook of Research in English and American Literature). Vol. 9. Ed. Herbert Grabes, Winfried Fluck and Jürgen Schlaeger. Tübingen: Gunter Narr, 1993. 1-33.

Derrida, Jacques. *Acts of Literature*. Ed. Derek Attridge. New York: Routledge, 1992.

Dickson-Carr, Darryl. *The Columbia Guide to Contemporary African American Fiction*. New York: Columbia University Press, 2005.

Diedrich, Maria. Ausbruch aus der Knechtschaft. Das amerikanische Slave Narrative zwischen Unabhängigkeitserklärung und Bürgerkrieg. Stuttgart: Franz Steiner, 1986.

Diedrich, Maria. "Afro-amerikanische Literatur." *Amerikanische Literaturgeschichte*. Ed. Hubert Zapf. Stuttgart: J.B. Metzler, 1997. 402-425.

Diedrich, Maria, Henry Louis Gates, Jr., and Carl Pedersen. "The Middle Passage Between History and Fiction. Introductory Remarks." *Black Imagination and the Middle Passage*. New York: Oxford University Press, 1999. 5-20.

Divine, David, ed. *Multiple Lenses: Voices from the Diaspora Located in Canada*. Newcastle-upon-Tyne: Cambridge Scholars, 2007.

Dixon, Melvin. "Singing Swords: The Literary Legacy of Slavery." *The Slave's Narrative*. Ed. Charles T. Davis and Henry Louis Gates, Jr. Oxford: Oxford University Press, 1985. 298-317.

Douglass, Frederick. "My Bondage and My Freedom." [1855] *Autobiographies*. Ed. Henry Louis Gates, Jr. New York, NY: Library of America, 1994. 103-452.

Douglass, Frederick. "John Brown. Speech Delivered at Storer College, West Virginia, May 30, 1881." *Frederick Douglass: Selected Speeches and Writings*. Ed. Philip S. Foner. Chicago: Lawrence Hill Books, 1999. 633-647.

Douglass, Frederick. "Narrative of the Life of Frederick Douglass, An American Slave. Written by Himself." [1845] *Slave Narratives*. Ed. William L. Andrews and Henry Louis Gates, Jr. New York: Library of America, 2000. 267-368.

Draaisma, Douwe. *Metaphors of Memory: A History of Ideas about the Mind.* Cambridge: Cambridge University Press, 2000.

DuBois, W. E. B. Dusk of Dawn: An Essay Toward an Autobiography of a Race Concept. New Brunswick, US: Transaction Books, 1984.

DuBois, W. E. B. *John Brown.* Ed. John David Smith. Armonk, NY: Sharpe, 1997.

DuBois, W. E. B. *The Souls of Black Folk.* [1903] New York: Fine Communications, 2003.

Echterhoff, Gerald, and Martin Saar. "Einleitung: Das Paradigma des kollektiven Gedächtnisses. Maurice Halbwachs und die Folgen." *Kontexte und Kulturen des Erinnerns. Maurice Halbwachs und das Paradigma des kollektiven Gedächtnisses.* Konstanz: UVK, 2002. 13-35.

Echterhoff, Gerald. "Die Rahmen von Erinnerungen: Das gedächtnistheoretische Werk von Maurice Halbwachs aus kognitions- und sozialpsychologischer Perspektive." *Erinnerung und Gesellschaft: Hommage à Maurice Halbwachs (1877 - 1945).* Ed. Hermann Krapoth and Denis Laborde. Jahrbuch für Soziologiegeschichte. Wiesbaden: VS Verl. für Sozialwiss., 2005. 247-270.

Eckstein, Lars: Re-Membering the Black Atlantic. On the Poetics and Politics of Literary Memory. Cross Cultures 84. Amsterdam: Rodopi, 2006.

Egan, Susanna, and Gabriele Helms. "Life Writing." *The Cambridge Companion to Canadian Literature.* Ed. Eva-Marie Kröller. Cambridge: Cambridge University Press, 2004. 216-240.

Eggers, Michael. "Trauma." *Gedächtnis und Erinnerung. Ein interdisziplinäres Lexikon.* Ed. Nicolas Pethes and Jens Ruchatz. Reinbek: Rowohlt, 2001. 602-604.

Elgersman, Maureen G. Unyielding Spirits: Black Women and Slavery in Early Canada and Jamaica. New York: Garland, 1999.

Ellis, R. J. Harriet Wilson's "Our Nig": A Cultural Biography of a "Two-Story" African American Novel. Costerus New Series 149. Amsterdam: Rodopi, 2003.

Ellison, Ralph. "Tell It Like It Is, Baby." *The Nation* 201 (1965): 129-136.

Ellison, Ralph. Interview. "The Essential Ellison: Ishmael Reed, Quincy Troupe, and Steve Cannon." *Conversations with Ralph Ellison.* Ed. Maryemma Graham. Jackson: University Press of Mississippi, 1995. 342-377. [=1995a]

Ellison, Ralph. *Invisible Man.* [1952] New York: Vintage International, 1995. [=1995b]

Engler, Bernd, and Kurt Müller. *Historiographic Metafiction in Modern American and Canadian Literature.* Beiträge zur englischen und amerikanischen Literatur Bd. 13. Paderborn: F. Schöningh, 1994.

Equiano, Olaudah. *The Interesting Narrative and Other Writings.* Ed. Vincent Carretta. New York: Penguin, 1995.

Bibliography 269

Erdfelder, Edgar. "Gedächtnistäuschungen." *Gedächtnis und Erinnerung. Ein interdisziplinäres Lexikon.* Ed. Nicolas Pethes and Jens Ruchatz. Reinbek: Rowohlt, 2001. 207-208.

Erll, Astrid. "'Mit Dickens spazieren gehen'. Kollektives Gedächtnis und Fiktion." Kontexte und Kulturen des Erinnerns: Maurice Halbwachs und das Paradigma des kollektiven Gedächtnisses. Ed. Gerald Echterhoff, Martin Saar and Jan Assmann. Theorie und Methode Sozialwissenschaften. Konstanz: UVK, 2002. 253-266.

Erll, Astrid. "Kollektives Gedächtnis und Erinnerungskulturen." Konzepte der Kulturwissenschaften. Theoretische Grundlagen - Ansätze - Perspektiven. Ed. Ansgar Nünning and Vera Nünning. Stuttgart: J. B. Metzler Verlag, 2003. 156-186.

Erll, Astrid. "Medium des kollektiven Gedächtnisses: Ein (erinnerungs-) kulturwissenschaftlicher Kompaktbegriff." Medien des kollektiven Gedächtnisses. Konstruktivität – Historizität – Kulturspezifität. Ed. Astrid Erll and Ansgar Nünning. Berlin: Walter de Gruyter, 2004. 3-23.

Erll, Astrid. "Literatur als Medium des kollektiven Gedächtnisses." Gedächtniskonzepte der Literaturwissenschaft: Theoretische Grundlegung und Anwendungsperspektiven. Ed. Astrid Erll and Ansgar Nünning. Media and Cultural Memory 2. Berlin: de Gruyter, 2005. 249-276.

Erll, Astrid, ed. Mediation, Remediation, and the Dynamics of Cultural Memory. Media and Cultural Memory = Medien und kulturelle Erinnerung 10. Berlin: de Gruyter, 2009.

Este, David C. "Black Canadian Historical Writing." *Journal of Black Studies* 38.3 (2008): 388-406.

Falconbridge, Anna Maria, and Alexander Falconbridge. *Narrative of Two Voyages to the River Sierra Leone During the Years 1791-1792-1793.* Ed. Christopher Fyfe. Liverpool: Liverpool University Press, 2000.

Falola, Toyin, and Warnock, Amanda. *Encyclopedia of the Middle Passage.* Westport, Conn.: Greenwood Press, 2007.

Fanon, Frantz. *Black Skin, White Masks.* New York, NY: Grove Press, 2008. [=2008a]

Fanon, Frantz. *The Wretched of the Earth.* New York, NY: Grove Press, 2008. [=2008b]

Federman, Raymond. *Surfiction: Fiction Now and Tomorrow.* Chicago: Swallow Press, 1975.

Flagel, Nadine. "Resonant Genres and Intertexts in the Neo-Slave Narratives of Caryl Phillips, Octavia Butler, and Lawrence Hill." Diss. Dalhousie University, 2005.

Foley, Barbara. Telling the Truth: The Theory and Practice of Documentary Fiction. Ithaca, NY: Cornell University Press, 1986.

Forster, E. M. "Flat and Round Characters." *Essentials of the Theory of Fiction.* Ed. Michael J. Hoffman and Patrick D. Murphy. Durham: Duke University Press, 1988. 40-47.

Foster, Cecil. A Place Called Heaven: The Meaning of Being Black in Canada. Toronto: HarperCollins, 1996.

Foster, Cecil. Where Race doesn't Matter: The New Spirit of Modernity. Toronto: Penguin Canada, 2005.

Foster, Cecil. Blackness and Modernity: The Colour of Humanity and the Quest for Freedom. Montreal: McGill-Queen's University Press, 2007.

Foucault, Michel. *Power/knowledge: Selected Interviews and Other Writings, 1972-1977.* Ed. Colin Gordon. New York: Pantheon Books, 1980.

Foucault, Michel. *The Archaeology of Knowledge.* Trans. A. M. Sheridan Smith. London: Routledge, 2002.

Frost, Karolyn Smardz. "The Underground Railroad and the Creation of Public Memory." *Multiple Lenses: Voices from the Diaspora Located in Canada.* Ed. David Divine. Newcastle-upon-Tyne: Cambridge Scholars, 2007. 177-194.

Frye, Northrop. "Conclusion to the First Edition of *Literary History of Canada.*" [1965] *Northrop Frye on Canada.* Collected Works of Northrop Frye, Vol. 12. Ed. Jean O'Grady and David Staines. Toronto: University of Toronto Press, 2003. 339-372. [=2003a]

Frye, Northrop. "Conclusion to the Second Edition of *Literary History of Canada.*" [1976] *Northrop Frye on Canada.* Collected Works of Northrop Frye, Vol. 12. Ed. Jean O'Grady and David Staines. Toronto: University of Toronto Press, 2003. 448-465. [=2003b]

Frye, Northrop. "Canada: New World Without Revolution." [1975] *Northrop Frye on Canada.* Collected Works of Northrop Frye, Vol. 12. Ed. Jean O'Grady and David Staines. Toronto: University of Toronto Press, 2003. 435-447. [=2003c]

Gaines, Ernest J. *The Autobiography of Miss Jane Pittman.* [1971] New York: Bantam Dell, 2009.

Galtung, Johan. Peace by Peaceful Means: Peace and Conflict, Development and Civilization. London: Sage, 1996.

Gates, Henry Louis, Jr. *"Race", Writing, and Difference.* Chicago: University of Chicago Press, 1986.

Gates, Henry Louis, Jr. *Figures in Black: Words, Signs, and the "Racial" Self.* Oxford: Oxford University Press, 1989.

Gates, Henry Louis, Jr. *Loose Canons: Notes on the Culture Wars.* New York: Oxford University Press, 1993.

Gates, Henry Louis, Jr. Introduction. *The Classic Slave Narratives.* 1987. New York: Signet Classics, 2002.

Gates, Henry Louis, Jr., and Hollis Robbins. *In Search of Hannah Crafts: Critical Essays on The Bondwoman's Narrative.* New York: Basic Civitas Books, 2004.

Genetsch, Martin. *The Texture of Identity: The Fiction of MG Vassanji, Neil Bissoondath and Rohinton Mistry.* Toronto: TSAR, 2007.

Genette, Gérard. *Palimpsests: Literature in the Second Degree.* Stages vol. 8. Lincoln: University of Nebraska Press, 1997.

George, Rosemary Marangoly. *The Politics of Home: Postcolonial Relocations and Twentieth-century Fiction.* Cambridge: Cambridge University Press, 1996.

Gerlach, Andrea. "Africville. Die Zerstörung des Bewusstseins einer 'Ethnic Community.'" *Zeitschrift für Kanada-Studien* 17.2 (1997): 153-165.

Gingell, Susan. "Teaching the Talk that Walks on Paper: Oral Traditions and Textualized Orature in the Canadian Literature Classroom." *Home-work: Postcolonialism, Pedagogy, and Canadian Literature.* Ed. Cynthia Conchita Sugars. Ottawa, ON: University of Ottawa Press, 2004. 285-300.

Godard, Barbara. "Marlene Nourbese Philip's Hyphenated Tongue, or Writing the Caribbean Demotic Between Africa and Arctic." *Major Minorities: English Literatures in Transit.* Ed. Raoul Granqvist. Amsterdam: Rodopi, 1993. 151-176.

Godard, Barbara. "Notes from the Cultural Field: Canadian Literature from Identity to Hybridity." *Essays on Canadian Writing* 72 (2000): 209-247.

Goldenberg, David. The Curse of Ham: Race and Slavery in Early Judaism, Christianity, and Islam. Princeton: Princeton University Press, 2003.

Goodnough, Abby. "Harvard Professor Jailed; Officer Is Accused of Bias." *New York Times Online.* July 20 2009 <http://www.nytimes.com/ 2009/07/21/us/21gates.html>.

Gordon, Dexter B. *Black Identity: Rhetoric, Ideology, and Nineteenth-century Black Nationalism.* Carbondale, Ill.: Southern Illinois University Press, 2006.

Government of Ontario. "Work at the Ontario Human Rights Commission." June 30 2009 <http://www.archives.gov.on.ca/english/on-line-exhibits/dan-hill/human-rights.aspx# life_cover>.

Greene, J Lee. *Blacks in Eden: The African American Novel's First Century.* Charlottesville: University Press of Virginia, 1996.

Griese, Hartmut M., and Jürgen Mansel. "Sozialwissenschaftliche Jugendforschung. Jugend, Jugendforschung und Jugenddiskurse: Ein Problemaufriss." *Soziologische Forschung. Stand und Perspektiven: Ein Handbuch.* Ed. Barbara Orth, Thomas Schwietring and Johannes Weiss. Opladen: Leske + Budrich, 2003. 169-195.

Groß, Konrad. "Zum Problem der kanadischen Identität." *Kanada: Eine interdisziplinäre Einführung.* Ed. Hans Braun and Wolfgang Klooß. Trier: WVT, 1994. 194-206.

Groß, Konrad. "Identity - Identities: Infamous Canadian Pastime, Venerable Quest, or Trivial Pursuit?" *O Canada: Essays on Canadian Literature and Culture.* Ed. Jørn Carlsen. Aarhus: Aarhus University Press, 1995. 26-37.

Gutiérrez-Jones, Carl Scott. *Critical Race Narratives: A Study of Race, Rhetoric, and Injury.* New York: New York University Press, 2001.

Hadaller, David. *Gynicide: Women in the Novels of William Styron.* Madison, N.J.: Fairleigh Dickinson University Press, 1996.

Haehnel, Birgit, and Melanie Ulz, eds. Slavery in Art and Literature: Approaches to Trauma, Memory and Visuality. Berlin: Frank & Timme, 2010.

Halbwachs, Maurice. *Das Gedächtnis und seine sozialen Bedingungen.* Berlin: Luchterhand, 1966.

Halbwachs, Maurice. *Das kollektive Gedächtnis.* Stuttgart: Enke, 1967.

Halbwachs, Maurice. *The Collective Memory.* New York: Harper & Row, 1980.

Halbwachs, Maurice. *On Collective Memory.* Ed., transl. and with an introduction by Lewis A. Coser. Chicago: The University of Chicago Press, 1992.

Halbwachs, Maurice. Stätten der Verkündigung im Heiligen Land: Eine Studie zum kollektiven Gedächtnis. Ed. Stephan Egger. Edition discours 21. Konstanz: UVK, 2003.

Hale, Thomas A. *Griots and Griottes: Masters of Words and Music.* Bloomington: Indiana University Press, 1998.

Hall, Stuart. "Minimal Selves." *Black British Cultural Studies: A Reader.* Ed. Houston A. Baker, Jr., Manthia Diawara and Ruth H. Lindeborg. Black Literature and Culture. Chicago: The University of Chicago Press, 1996. 114-119. [=1996a]

Hall, Stuart. "New Ethnicities." *Black British Cultural Studies: A Reader.* Ed. Houston A. Baker, Jr., Manthia Diawara and Ruth H. Lindeborg. Chicago: University of Chicago Press, 1996. 163-172. [=1996b]

Hamilton, Sylvia. "Naming Names, Naming Ourselves: A Survey of Early Black Women in Nova Scotia." *'We're Rooted Here and they Can't Pull us up': Essays in African Canadian Women's History.* Ed. Peggy Bristow. Toronto: University of Toronto Press, 1994. 13-40.

Hammill, Faye. *Canadian Literature.* Edinburgh: Edinburgh University Press, 2007.

Handley, George B. *Postslavery Literatures in the Americas: Family Portraits in Black and White.* Charlottesville, Va.: University Press of Virginia, 2000.

Hanke, Michael. Kommunikation und Erzählung: Zur narrativen Vergemeinschaftungspraxis am Beispiel konversationellen Traumerzählens. Würzburg: Königshausen & Neumann, 2001.

Hansberry, Lorraine. *A Raisin in the Sun*. London: Methuen, 2001.

Harris, Jennifer. "Ain't No Border Wide Enough: Writing Black Canada in Lawrence Hill's *Any Known Blood*." *The Journal of American Culture* 27.4 (2004): 367-374.

Hartmann, Andreas. "Geschmack." *Gedächtnis und Erinnerung. Ein interdisziplinäres Lexikon*. Ed. Nicolas Pethes and Jens Ruchatz. Reinbek: Rowohlt, 2001. 230-232.

Hartmann, Ernest. "Who Develops PTSD Nightmares and Who Doesn't." *Trauma and Dreams*. Ed. Deirdre Barrett. Cambridge: Harvard University Press, 2001. 100-113.

Heath, Tom. "Documentary." *Encyclopedia of Literature in Canada*. Ed. William H. New. Toronto: University of Toronto Press, 2002. 297-301.

Hedin, Raymond. "The Structuring of Emotion in Black American Fiction." *Novel. A Forum on Fiction* 16.1 (1982): 35-54.

Heffernan, James Anthony Walsh. *Museum of Words: The Poetics of Ekphrasis from Homer to Ashbery*. Chicago: The University of Chicago Press, 2004.

Heglar, Charles J. Rethinking the Slave Narrative: Slave Marriage and the Narratives of Henry Bibb and William and Ellen Craft. Westport, Conn.: Greenwood Press, 2001.

Henderson, Carol E. Scarring the Black Body: Race and Representation in African American Literature. Columbia, Mo.: University of Missouri Press, 2002.

Hill, Daniel G. *The Freedom-Seekers: Blacks in Early Canada*. Agincourt: Book Society of Canada, 1981.

Hill, Lawrence. *Some Great Thing*. Winnipeg: Turnstone Press, 1992. [=SGT]

Hill, Lawrence. Trials and Triumphs: The Story of African-Canadians. Umbrella Press, Toronto, 1993.

Hill, Lawrence. Women of Vision: The Story of the Canadian Negro Women's Association. Umbrella Press, Toronto, 1996.

Hill, Lawrence. *Any Known Blood*. Toronto: HarperCollins, 1997. [=AKB]

Hill, Lawrence. Introduction. *Underground to Canada*. Barbara Smucker. Toronto: Puffin Canada, 1999. 5-8.

Hill, Lawrence. "Black Like Us: Canada is Not Nearly as Integrated as We Like to Think." *The Globe and Mail* 9 February 2000.

Hill, Lawrence. Black Berry, Sweet Juice. On Being Black and White in Canada. Toronto: HarperCollins, 2001. [=BBSJ]

Hill, Lawrence. "Dad Will Always 'Live Within Us.'" *Toronto Star* 6 July 2003: A8.

Hill, Lawrence. *Seeking Salvation: A History of the Black Church in Canada.* Film documentary. Travesty Productions, Toronto, 2004.

Hill, Lawrence. Interview. *Why We Write. Conversations With African Canadian Poets and Novelists.* Ed. H. Nigel Thomas. Toronto: TSAR, 2006. 131-147.

Hill, Lawrence. "Freedom Bound." *The Beaver* February/March 2007. 16-23. [=2007a]

Hill, Lawrence. *Someone Knows My Name.* New York: W.W. Norton & Co., 2007. [=2007b]

Hill, Lawrence. The Deserter's Tale: The Story of an Ordinary Soldier Who Walked Away from the War in Iraq. Toronto: House of Anansi Press, 2007. [=2007c]

Hill, Lawrence. *The Book of Negroes.* Toronto: HarperCollins, 2007. [=BN]

Hill, Lawrence. Interview. "Projecting History Honestly: An Interview with Lawrence Hill." Jessie Sagawa. *Studies in Canadian Literature/Etudes en Littérature Canadienne* 33.1 (2008): 307-322.

Hill, Lawrence. "Is Africa's Pain Black America's Burden?" [2005] *The Walrus* February 2005. Reprinted: June 15 2009 <http://www.walrusmagazine.com/ articles/2005.02-essay-african-american-culture-history/>.

Hobi, Viktor. "Kurze Einführung in die Grundlagen der Gedächtnispsychologie." *Vergangenheit in mündlicher Überlieferung.* Ed. Jürgen von Ungern-Sternberg and Hansjörg Reinau. Colloquium Rauricum 1. Stuttgart: Teubner, 1988. 9-33.

Hochschild, Adam. Bury the Chains. Prophets and Rebels in the Fight to Free an Empire's Slaves. Boston: Houghton Mifflin, 2005.

Hochschild, Jennifer L. *Facing up to the American Dream: Race, Class and the Soul of the Nation.* Princeton, NJ: Princeton University Press, 1995.

Hoffman, Barbara G. *Griots at War: Conflict, Conciliation, and Caste in Mande.* Bloomington: Indiana University Press, 2000.

Holland, Sharon Patricia. *Raising the Dead: Readings of Death and (Black) Subjectivity.* Durham, NC: Duke University Press, 2000.

hooks, bell. "Aesthetic Inheritances: History Worked by Hands." *Yearning.* Boston: South End Press, 1990. 115-122.

Horton, James Oliver. *Landmarks of African American History.* American landmarks. New York: Oxford University Press, 2005.

Hudson, Peter. "Editor's Note: In the Country of the Snow Blind." *West Coast Line* [North: New African-Canadian Writing] 21 (1997): 5-6.

Hughes, Langston. *The First Book of Negroes.* New York: Franklin Watts, 1952.

Hughes, Langston. "Harlem." The Langston Hughes Reader: The Selected Writings of Langston Hughes. New York: George Braziller, 1958. 123.

Hughes, Langston. "I, Too." *The Collected Works of Langston Hughes. Volume 1: The Poems 1921-1940.* Ed. Arnold Rampersad. Columbia: University of Missouri Press, 2001. 61-62.

Hutcheon, Linda. "History and/as Intertext." *Future Indicative: Literary Theory and Canadian Literature.* Ed. John Moss. Ottawa: University of Ottawa Press, 1987. 169-184.

Hutcheon, Linda. A Poetics of Postmodernism: History, Theory, Fiction. New York: Routledge, 1988.

Hutcheon, Linda. The Canadian Postmodern: A Study of Contemporary English-Canadian Fiction. Toronto: Oxford University Press, 1993.

Imperato, Pascal James. *Historical Dictionary of Mali.* 2nd ed. Metuchen, N.J.: Scarecrow, 1986.

Ingham, E. G. *Sierra Leone After a Hundred Years.* London: Frank Cass, 1968.

Jack, Allen. "The Loyalists and Slavery in New Brunswick." *Transactions* [Royal Society of Canada] 4 (1898): 137-185.

Jacobs, Harriet Ann. "Incidents in the Life of a Slave Girl. Written by Herself. Edited by L. Maria Child." 1861. *Slave Narratives.* Ed. William L. Andrews and Henry Louis Gates, Jr. New York: Library of America, 2000. 743-948.

James, Carl E, and Adrienne Lynn Shadd, eds. *Talking About Identity: Encounters in Race, Ethnicity, and Language.* Toronto: Between the Lines, 2001.

Jameson, Fredric. "Postmodernism, Or the Cultural Logic of Late Capitalism." *New Left Review* 146 (1984): 53-92.

Junne, George H. The History of Blacks in Canada: A Selectively Annotated Bibliography. Westport, Conn.: Greenwood Press, 2003.

Kamboureli, Smaro. *Scandalous Bodies: Diasporic Literature in English Canada.* Don Mills: Oxford University Press, 2000.

Kassin, Saul M., Steven Fein, and Hazel Markus. *Social Psychology.* 8th ed. Belmont, CA: Cengage Wadsworth, 2011.

Kawash, Samira. Dislocating the Color Line: Identity, Hybridity, and Singularity in African-American Narrative. Stanford: Stanford University Press, 1997.

Keizer, Arlene R. Black Subjects: Identity Formation in the Contemporary Narrative of Slavery. Ithaca: Cornell University Press, 2004.

Keller, Barbara. "Konstruktion." *Gedächtnis und Erinnerung. Ein interdisziplinäres Lexikon.* Ed. Nicolas Pethes and Jens Ruchatz. Reinbek: Rowohlt, 2001. 315-318.

Kelly, Jennifer. Under the Gaze. Learning to be Black in a White Society. Halifax: Fernwood Publishing, 1998.

Kilian, Crawford. *Go Do Some Great Thing: The Black Pioneers of British Columbia.* [1978] 2nd ed. Burnaby, BC: Commodore Books, 2008.

King, Martin Luther, Jr. "Reverend Martin Luther King, Jr., Ennobles the Civil Rights Movement at the Lincoln Memorial." *Lend Me Your Ears. Great Speeches in History.* Ed. William Safire. New York: W. W. Norton, 1997. 531-536.

King, Nicola. *Memory, Narrative, Identity: Remembering the Self.* Edinburgh: Edinburgh University Press, 2000.

Kipling, Rudyard. "The White Man's Burden." *Imperialism and Orientalism: A Documentary Sourcebook.* Ed. Barbara Harlow and Mia Carter. Oxford: Blackwell, 1999. 362-363.

Klooß, Wolfgang. "Canadian Multiculturalism and Some Recent Trends in Anglophone Writing." *Us/them: Translation, Transcription and Identity in Post-colonial Literary Cultures.* Ed. Gordon Collier. Cross/cultures 6. Amsterdam: Rodopi, 1992. 65-75.

Klooß, Wolfgang. "Die englischsprachige Literatur." *Kanada: Eine interdisziplinäre Einführung.* Ed. Hans Braun and Wolfgang Klooß. Trier: WVT, 1994. 170-193.

Knutson, Susan. "'I Am Become Aaron': George Elliott Clarke's *Execution Poems* and William Shakespeare's *Titus Andronicus.*" *Canadian Cultural Exchange: Translation and Transculturation = Échanges Culturels au Canada.* Ed. Norman Cheadle and Lucien Pelletier. Waterloo, ON: Wilfrid Laurier University Press, 2007. 29-56. [=2007a]

Knutson, Susan. "The Mask of Aaron. 'Tall Screams Reared out of Three Mile Plains': Shakespeare's *Titus Andronicus* and George Elliott Clarke's Black Acadian Tragedy, *Execution Poems.*" *Readings of the Particular: The Postcolonial in the Postnational.* Ed. Anne Holden Rønning and Lene Johannessen. Cross-cultures 89. Amsterdam: Rodopi, 2007. 157-170. [=2007b]

Kogawa, Joy. *Obasan.* New York: Anchor Books, 1994.

Kölbl, Carlos. "Olfaktorisches Gedächtnis." *Gedächtnis und Erinnerung. Ein interdisziplinäres Lexikon.* Ed. Nicolas Pethes and Jens Ruchatz. Reinbek: Rowohlt, 2001. 425.

Krampe, Christian J. "Inserting Trauma into the Canadian Collective Memory: Lawrence Hill's *The Book of Negroes* and Selected African-Canadian Poetry." *Zeitschrift für Kanada-Studien* 29.1 (2009): 62-83.

Krampe, Christian J. "Visualizing Invisibility, Reversing Anonymity: A Case Study in African-Canadian Literature." *Slavery in Art and Literature: Approaches to Trauma, Memory and Visuality.* Ed. Birgit Haehnel and Melanie Ulz. Berlin: Frank & Timme, 2010. 301-340

Kristeva, Julia. "Wort, Dialog und Roman bei Bachtin." *Literaturwissenschaft und Linguistik – Ergebnisse und Perspektiven.* Ed. Jens Ihwe. Frankfurt a.M.: Athenäum, 1972. 345-375.

Kristeva, Julia. *The Kristeva Reader.* Ed. Toril Moi. New York, NY: Columbia University Press, 1986.

Kristeva, Julia. *The Portable Kristeva.* Ed. Kelly Oliver. European Perspectives. New York: Columbia University Press, 2002.

Kröller, Eva-Marie. *The Cambridge Companion to Canadian Literature.* Cambridge: Cambridge University Press, 2004.

Kuba, Richard. "Die Entschleierung des 'dunklen Kontinets': Zur kartographischen Entdeckung Westafrikas." *Wir und das Fremde. Nell-Breuning-Symposium Rödermark Oktober 2002.* Ed. Philipp Wolf and Stefanie Rück. Münster: Lit, 2004. 341-362.

Kuester, Maertin. "The English-Canadian Novel from Modernism to Postmodernism." *History of Literature in Canada: English-Canadian and French-Canadian.* Ed. Reingard M. Nischik. Rochester, NY: Camden House, 2008. 310-329.

LaBossière, Camille R., ed. *Context North America: Canadian US Literary Relations.* Ottawa: University of Ottawa Press, 1994.

Lavie, Peretz, and Hanna Kaminer. "Sleep, Dreaming, and Coping Style in Holocaust Survivors." *Trauma and Dreams.* Ed. Deirdre Barrett. Cambridge, Mass.: Harvard University Press, 2001. 114-124.

Lejeune, Philippe. *Der autobiographische Pakt.* Frankfurt am Main: Suhrkamp, 2005.

Lemelle, Anthony J., Jr. "Nation of Islam". *Organizing Black America: An Encyclopedia of African American Associations.* Ed. Nina Mjagkij. New York, NY: Garland, 2001. 356-359.

Lenger, Friedrich. "Geschichte und Erinnerung im Zeichen der Nation. Einige Beobachtungen zur jüngsten Entwicklung." *Erinnerung, Gedächtnis, Wissen: Studien zur kulturwissenschaftlichen Gedächtnisforschung.* Ed. Günter Oesterle. Göttingen: Vandenhoeck & Ruprecht, 2005. 521-536.

LeVert, Suzanne. *Sierra Leone.* Cultures of the world. New York: Marshall Cavendish Benchmark, 2007.

Library and Archives Canada. "Black Loyalists Digital Collections Site." *Electronic Collection: A Virtual Collection of Monographs and Periodicals.* 7 May 2009 <http://epe.lac-bac.gc.ca/100/200/301/ic/can_digital_collections/blackloyalists/index. htm>.

Link, Franz. "The Slave Narrative Novel." Literaturwissenschaftliches Jahrbuch im Auftrage der Görres-Gesellschaft 34 (1993): 277-304.

Locke, Alain. *The New Negro.* New York: Atheneum, 1970.

Löffler Arno. "The Rebel Muse." Studien zu Swifts kritischer Dichtung. Tübingen: Niemeyer, 1982.

Loftus, Elizabeth F., and Katherine Ketcham. *The Myth of Repressed Memory: False Memories and Allegations of Sexual Abuse.* New York: St. Martin's Press, 1994.

Luban-Plozza, Boris, Mario DelliPonti, and Hans H. Dickhaut. *Musik und Psyche. Hören mit der Seele.* Basel: Birkhäuser, 1988.

Lukács, Georg. *The Historical Novel.* Lincoln, Neb.: University of Nebraska Press, 1983.

Lutz, Hartmut. "Multikulturalität als Stärke der zeitgenössischen kanadischen Literatur." *Kanadische Literaturgeschichte.* Ed. Konrad Groß, Wolfgang Klooß and Reingard Nischik. Stuttgart: J. B. Metzler, 2005. 310-335.

Mackenthun, Gesa. Fictions of the Black Atlantic in American Foundational Literature. London: Routledge, 2004.

MacLean, Alyssa. "Canadian Studies and American Studies." *A Concise Companion to American Studies.* Ed. John Carlos Rowe. Malden, MA: Wiley-Blackwell, 2010. 387-406.

Mama, Amina. Beyond the Masks. Race, Gender and Subjectivity. London: Routledge, 1995.

Mann, Gregory. Native Sons: West African Veterans and France in the Twentieth Century. Durham, NC: Duke University Press, 2006.

Marcus, Laura. *Auto/biographical Discourses: Theory, Criticism, Practice.* Manchester: Manchester University Press, 1994.

Markowitsch, Hans J., and Harald Welzer. Das autobiographische Gedächtnis: Hirnorganische Grundlagen und biosoziale Entwicklung. 2nd ed. Stuttgart: Klett-Cotta, 2006.

McCallum, Sarah. "Remaking the Wor(l)d: a Poetics of Resistance and Transformation in Marlene Nourbese Philip's *she tries her tongue: her silence softly breaks.*" [minuscules *sic*] *Postcolonial Perspectives on Women Writers from Africa, the Caribbean, and the U.S.* Ed. Martin Japtok. Trenton, NJ: Africa World Press, 2003. 151-172.

McKeon, Michael. *Theory of the Novel: A Historical Approach.* Baltimore, Md.: Johns Hopkins University Press, 2000.

McNally, Richard J. *Remembering Trauma.* Cambridge, Mass.: Harvard University Press, 2003.

Meindl, Dieter. Zur Literatur und Kultur Kanadas: Eine Erlanger Ringvorlesung. Erlangen: Palm & Enke, 1984.

Mellard, James M. *Beyond Lacan.* Albany: State University of New York Press, 2006.

Metcalf, John. *What Is A Canadian Literature?* Guelph: Red Kite Press, 1988.

Middleton, David L., ed. *Toni Morrison's Fiction: Contemporary Criticism.* New York: Garland, 1997.

Mills, C[harles] W. *The Racial Contract.* Ithaca: Cornell University Press, 1997.

Minter, David. "Conceptions of the Self in Black Slave Narratives." *American Transcendental Quarterly: A Journal of New England Writers* 24 (1974): 62-68.

Misztal, Barbara A. *Theories of Social Remembering. Theorizing Society.* Buckingham: Open University Press, 2003.

Mitchell, Angelyn. The Freedom to Remember: Narrative, Slavery, and Gender in Contemporary Black Women's Fiction. New Brunswick, N.J.: Rutgers University Press, 2002.

Mitchell, William J. Thomas. *Picture Theory: Essays on Verbal and Visual Representation.* Chicago: University of Chicago Press, 1995.

Mordecai, Philip. Interview. *Why We Write. Conversations With African Canadian Poets and Novelists.* Ed. H. Nigel Thomas. Toronto: TSAR, 2006. 178-197.

Morris, Paul. "From 'Stalewart Peasant' to Canadian Citizen: Immigrant Identity in Early Twentieth-Century Canadian Fiction." *The Canadian Alternative.* Saarbrücker Beiträge zur vergleichenden Literatur- und Kulturwissenschaft 28. Würzburg: Königshausen & Neumann, 2004. 52-64.

Morrison, Toni. *Beloved.* New York: Vintage International, 2004.

Morrison, Toni. "The Site of Memory." *What Moves at the Margin. Selected Nonfiction.* Ed. Carolyn C. Jackson. Denard, Miss.: University Press of Mississippi, 2008. 64-80.

Morrison, Toni, and Carolyn C. Denard. *What Moves at the Margin: Selected Nonfiction.* Jackson, Miss.: University Press of Mississippi, 2008.

Morrison, Toni, and Danille Taylor-Guthrie, eds. *Conversations with Toni Morrison.* Jackson, Miss.: University Press of Mississippi, 1998.

Morton, Stephen. *Gayatri Chakravorty Spivak*. Routledge Critical Thinkers. London: Routledge, 2003.

Moss, Laura, ed. *Is Canada Postcolonial? Unsettling Canadian Literature*. Waterloo, ON: Wilfrid Laurier University Press, 2003. [=2003a]

Moss, Laura. "Is Canada Postcolonial? Introducing the Question." *Is Canada Postcolonial?* Waterloo: Wilfrid Laurier University Press, 2003. 1-26. [=2003b]

Moynagh, Maureen. "Africville, an Imagined Community." *Canadian Literature* 157 (1998): 14-34.

Moynagh, Maureen. "Uses of Cultural Memory." *Canadian Literature* 170-171 (2001): 193-195.

Moynagh, Maureen. "National Countermemories: 'This History's Only Good for Anger': Gender and Cultural Memory in *Beatrice Chancy*." *Signs: Journal of Women in Culture and Society* 28.1 (2002): 97-124.

Moynagh, Maureen. *African-Canadian Theatre*. Toronto: Playwrights Canada Press, 2005. [=2005a]

Moynagh, Maureen. "Eyeing the North Star? Figuring Canada in Postslavery Fiction and Drama." *Comparative American Studies: An International Journal* 3.1 (2005): 15-27. [=2005b]

Myrdal, Gunnar. *An American Dilemma: The Negro Problem and Modern Democracy*. [1944] New Brunswick, NJ: Transaction Publishers, 1996.

Nelson, Camille A., and Charmaine A. Nelson. Racism, Eh?: A Critical Inter-disciplinary Anthology of Race and Racism in Canada. Concord, ON: Captus Press, 2004.

Nelson, Jennifer J. "The Space of Africville. Creating, Regulating, and Remembering the Urban 'Slum.'" *Race, Space, and the Law: Unmapping a White Settler Society*. Ed. Sherene Razack. Toronto: Between the Lines, 2002. 211-232.

Nelson, Jennifer J. *Razing Africville: A Geography of Racism*. Toronto: University of Toronto Press, 2008.

Nelson, Katherine. "Memory and Belief in Development." *Memory, Brain, and Belief*. Ed. Daniel L. Schacter and Elaine Scarry. Cambridge, Mass.: Harvard University Press, 2001. 259-289.

Neumann, Birgit. Erinnerung – Identität – Narration: Gattungstypologie und Funktionen kanadischer "Fictions of Memory." Berlin and New York: Walter de Gruyter, 2005.

Ngũgĩ wa Thiong'o. Decolonising the Mind: The Politics of Language in African Literature. London: Currey, 1986.

Nichols, Charles H. "The Slave Narrators and the Picaresque Mode: Archetypes for Modern Black Personae." *The Slave's Narrative*. Ed. Charles T. Davis and Henry Louis Gates, Jr. Oxford: Oxford University Press, 1985. 283-297.

Nießeler, Andreas. "Erinnerung als Teilhabe. Aspekte sozial- und kulturanthropologischer Gedächtnistheorien." *Ich bin mein Erinnern: Über autobiographisches und kollektives Gedächtnis*. Ed. Günther Bittner. Würzburg: Königshausen & Neumann, 2006. 143-159.

Niethammer, Lutz. "Diesseits des 'Floating Gaps': Das kollektive Gedächtnis und die Konstruktion von Identitäten im wissenschaftlichen Diskurs." *Generation und Gedächtnis: Erinnerungen und kollektive Identitäten*. Ed. Kristin Platt and Mihrand Dabag. Opladen: Leske + Budrich, 1995. 25-50.

Nolan, Faith. "Africville." *Fire on the Water. An Anthology of Black Nova Scotian Writing. Volume 2*. Ed. George Elliott Clarke. Lawrencetown Beach, NS: Pottersfield Press, 1992. 118.

Nora, Pierre. "General Introduction: Between Memory and History." *Realms of Memory: Rethinking the French Past*. 3 vols. Ed. Pierre Nora and Lawrence D. Kritzman. New York: Columbia University Press, 1996. 1-20.

Northup, Solomon. *Twelve Years a Slave*. Mineola NY: Dover Publications, 2000.

Nova Scotia Archives & Records Management. "John Clarkson's Account of the Story of Lydia Jackson." *African Nova Scotians in the Age of Slavery and Abolition*. May 4 2009 <http://www.gov.ns.ca/nsarm/virtual/africanns/ transcript.asp?ID=57>.

Nünning, Ansgar. Von historischer Fiktion zu historiographischer Metafiktion. Band 1:Theorie, Typologie und Poetik des historischen Romans. Trier: WVT Wiss. Verl. Trier, 1995.

Nünning, Ansgar. Von historischer Fiktion zu historiographischer Metafiktion. Band 2: Erscheinungsformen und Entwicklungstendenzen des historischen Romans in England seit 1950. Trier: WVT Wiss. Verl. Trier, 1995.

Nünning, Ansgar. "Von der fiktionalisierten Historie zur metahistoriographischen Fiktion: Bausteine für eine narratologische und funktionsgeschichtliche Theorie, Typologie und Geschichte des postmodernen historischen Romans." *Literatur und Geschichte: Ein Kompendium zu ihrem Verhältnis von der Aufklärung bis zur Gegenwart*. Ed. Daniel Fulda and Silvia Serena Tschopp. Berlin: de Gruyter, 2002. 541-570.

Nünning, Ansgar. "Historiographie und Literatur." *Metzler Lexikon Literatur- und Kulturtheorie*. 3rd rev. ed. Stuttgart: Metzler, 2004. 259-260. [=2004a]

Nünning, Ansgar. "Historiographische Metafiktion." *Metzler Lexikon Literatur- und Kulturtheorie*. 3rd rev. ed. Stuttgart: Metzler, 2004. 260-261. [=2004b]

Nurse, Donna Bailey. What's a Black Critic to Do? Interviews, Profiles and Reviews of Black Writers. Toronto: Insomniac Press, 2003.

Nurse, Donna Bailey. Introduction. *Revival. An Anthology of Black Canadian Writing.* Toronto: McClelland & Stewart, 2006. XI-XXII. [=2006a]

Nurse, Donna Bailey, ed. *Revival. An Anthology of Black Canadian Writing.* Toronto: McClelland & Stewart, 2006. [=2006b]

O'Keeffe, Tadhg. "Landscape and Memory: Historiography, Theory, Methodology." *Heritage, Memory and the Politics of Identity: New Perspectives on the Cultural Landscape.* Ed. Niamh Moore and Yvonne Whelan. Aldershot: Ashgate, 2007. 3-18.

O'Meally, Robert G., ed. *New Essays on Invisible Man.* Cambridge: Cambridge University Press, 1988.

Oates, Stephen B. *To Purge This Land With Blood: A Biography of John Brown.* 2nd ed. Amherst: University of Mass. Press, 1984.

Okpewho, Isidore. *African Oral Literature: Backgrounds, Character, and Continuity.* Bloomington: Indiana University Press, 1992.

Olick, Jeffrey Keith. "Collective Memory: The Two Cultures." *Sociological Theory* 17.3 (1999): 333-348.

Olick, Jeffrey Keith. The Politics of Regret: On Collective Memory and Historical Responsibility. New York: Routledge, 2007.

Olney, James. "'I Was Born': Slave Narratives, Their Status as Autobiography and as Literature." *The Slave's Narrative.* Ed. Charles Twitchell Davis and Henry Louis Gates, Jr. Oxford: Oxford University Press, 1985. 148-174.

Pachai, Bridglal. *Peoples of the Maritimes: Blacks.* Halifax: Nimbus, 1997.

Pachai, Bridglal, and Henry Bishop. *Images of our Past: Historic Black Nova Scotia.* Halifax: Nimbus, 2006.

Palmer, Hazelle, ed. *"...but where are you really from?".* Toronto: Sister Vision, 1997.

Paolini, Albert J. *Navigating Modernity. Postcolonialism, Identity, and International Relations.* Ed. Anthony Elliott and Anthony Moran. Boulder: Rienner, 1999.

Parker, Theodore. *The American Scholar.* Ed. George W. Cooke. Boston: American Unitarian Association, 1907.

Pateman, Carole. *The Sexual Contract.* Stanford.: Stanford University Press, 1988.

Paternoster, Raymond, and Leeann Iovanni. "The Labeling Perspective and Delinquency: An Elaboration of the Theory and an Assessment of the Evidence." *Readings in Contemporary Criminological Theory.* Ed. Peter Cordella and Larry J. Siegel. Boston: Northeastern University Press, 1996. 171-188.

Patterson, Orlando. *Slavery and Social Death: A Comparative Study.* Cambridge: Harvard University Press, 1982.

Patterson, Orlando. "Authority, Alienation, and Social Death." *African American Religious Thought: An Anthology.* Ed. Cornel West and Eddie S. Glaude, Jr. Louisville: Westminster John Knox Press, 2003. 99-155.

Perkyns, Dorothy. *Last Days in Africville.* Toronto: Dundurn Press, 2003.

Peterson, Merrill D. *John Brown: The Legend Revisited.* Charlottesville: University of Virginia Press, 2002.

Petty, Sheila. Contact Zones: Memory, Origin, and Discourses in Black Diasporic Cinema. Detroit: Wayne State University Press, 2008.

Philip, Marlene NourbeSe, "Blackman Dead." *Thorns.* Toronto: Williams-Wallace, 1980. 36-37.

Philip, Marlene NourbeSe. *Salmon Courage.* Toronto: Williams-Wallace, 1983.

Philip, Marlene NourbeSe. *Harriet's Daughter.* Oxford: Heinemann, 1988.

Philip, Marlene NourbeSe. Frontiers: Selected Essays and Writings on Racism and Culture, 1984-1992. Stratford, ON: Mercury Press, 1992.

Philip, Marlene NourbeSe. *Showing Grit: Showboating North of the 44th Parallel.* 2nd ed. Toronto: Poui, 1993.

Philip, Marlene NourbeSe. "What's in a Name?" *Grammar of Dissent: Poetry and Prose by Claire Harris, Marlene Nourbese Philip, Dionne Brand.* Ed. Carol Morrell. Fredericton, NB: Goose Lane, 1994. 123.

Philip, Marlene NourbeSe. *A Genealogy of Resistance and other Essays.* Toronto: Mercury Press, 1997.

Phillips, Caryl. *Cambridge.* London: Bloomsbury, 1991.

Píccinato, Stefanie. "The Slave Narrative and the Picaresque Novel." *The Black Columbiad: Defining Moments in African American Literature and Culture.* Ed. Werner Sollors and Maria Diedrich. Harvard English studies 19. Cambridge, Mass.: Harvard University Press, 1994. 88-98.

Pierce, Yolanda. "Redeeming Bondage: The Captivity Narrative and the Spiritual Autobiography in the African American Slave Narrative Tradition." *The Cambridge Companion to the African American Slave Narrative.* Ed. Audrey A. Fisch. Cambridge: Cambridge University Press, 2007. 83-98.

Plasa, Carl. *Toni Morrison: Beloved.* Columbia critical guides. New York: Columbia University Press, 1998.

Plasa, Carl, and Betty J. Ring. *The Discourse of Slavery: Aphra Behn to Toni Morrison.* London: Routledge, 1994.

Pollard, Cherise A. "Self Evident Truths. Love, Complicity, and Critique in Barbara Chase-Riboud's *Sally Hemings* and *The President's Daughter*." *Monuments of the Black Atlantic: Slavery and Memory*. Ed. Joanne M. Braxton and Maria Diedrich. Münster: Lit, 2004. 117-130.

Pope, Rob. The English Studies Book: An Introduction to Language, Literature and Culture. 2nd ed. London: Routledge, 2007.

Posnock, Ross, ed. *The Cambridge Companion to Ralph Ellison*. Cambridge: Cambridge University Press, 2005.

Prince, Althea. *Being Black: Essays by Althea Prince*. Toronto: Insomniac Press, 2001.

Quashie, Kevin Everod: *Black Women, Identity, and Cultural Theory. (Un)becoming the Subject*. New Brunswick: Rutgers University Press, 2004.

Rak, Julie. *Auto/biography in Canada: Critical Directions*. Waterloo, Ont.: Wilfrid Laurier University Press, 2005.

Raymond, W. O. "The Negro in New Brunswick," *Neith* 1 (1903): n.p.

Reed, Ishmael. *Flight to Canada*. [1976] New York, NY: Scribner Paperback Fiction, 1998.

Reid-Pharr, Robert F. "The Slave Narrative and Early Black American Literature." *The Cambridge Companion to the African American Slave Narrative*. Ed. Audrey A. Fisch. Cambridge: Cambridge University Press, 2007. 137-149.

Reinhart, Werner. Pikareske Romane der 80er Jahre: Ronald Reagan und die Renaissance des politischen Erzählens in den USA (Acker, Auster, Boyle, Irving, Kennedy, Pynchon). Mannheimer Beiträge zur Sprach- und Literaturwissenschaft Bd. 52. Tübingen: Gunter Narr, 2001.

Revonsuo, Antti. "Did Ancestral Humans Dream for Their Lives?" *Sleep and Dreaming: Scientific Advances and Reconsiderations*. Ed. Edward F. Pace-Schott et al. Cambridge: Cambridge University Press, 2002. 275-294.

Reynolds, David S. John Brown, Abolitionist. The Man Who Killed Slavery, Sparked the Civil War, and Seeded Civil Rights. New York: Vintag Books, 2005.

Ricard, Alain, and Flora Veit-Wild, eds. Interfaces Between the Oral and the Written = Interfaces entre l'écrit et l'oral. Amsterdam: Rodopi, 2005.

Richards, David: Masks of Difference. Cultural Representations in Literature, Anthropology, and Art. Cultural Margins 2. Cambridge: Cambridge University Press, 1994.

Richardson, Karen, and Steven Green, eds. *T-Dot Griots: An Anthology of Toronto's Black Storytellers*. Victoria, BC: Trafford Publishing, 2004.

Richler, Mordecai. *Barney's Version*. Toronto: Knopf, 1997.

Rider, Janine. The writer's Book of Memory: An Interdisciplinary Study for Writing
    Teachers. Mahwah, N.J.: L. Erlbaum Associates, 1995.

Ring, Betty J. "'Painting by Numbers:' Figuring Frederick Douglass." *The Discourse of
    Slavery: Aphra Behn to Toni Morrison.* Ed. Carl Plasa and Betty J. Ring. London:
    Routledge, 1994. 118-143.

Robart-Johnson, Sharon. *Africa's Children: A History of Blacks in Yarmouth, Nova Scotia.*
    Toronto: Natural Heritage Books, 2009.

Roberts, Richard L. Warriors, Merchants, and Slaves: The State and the Economy in the
    Middle Niger Valley, 1700-1914. Stanford: Stanford University Press, 1987.

Robertson, R. T. "Another Preface to an Uncollected Anthology: Canadian Crisitcism in a
    Commonwealth Context." *ARIEL* 4.3 (1973): 70-81.

Rodgers, Lawrence Richard. *Canaan Bound: The African-American Great Migration Novel.*
    Urbana, Ill.: University of Illinois Press, 1997.

Roth, Philip. *Exist Ghost.* Boston: Houghton Mifflin, 2007.

Roy, Beth. 41 Shots - and Counting: What Amadou Diallo's Story Teaches us about Policing,
    Race, and Justice. Syracuse, N.Y.: Syracuse University Press, 2009.

Rushdy, Ashraf H. A. "'Rememory': Primal Scenes and Constructions in Toni Morrison's
    Novels." *Toni Morrison's Fiction: Contemporary Criticism.* Ed. David L. Middleton.
    New York, London: Garland, 1997. 135-164.

Rushdy, Ashraf H. A. *Neo-Slave Narratives: Studies in the Social Logic of a Literary Form.*
    Race and American Culture. New York, NY: Oxford University Press, 1999.

Rushdy, Ashraf H. A. "The Neo-Slave Narrative." *The Cambridge Companion to the African-
    American Novel.* Ed. Maryemma Graham. 2004. 87-105.

Ryan, Tim A. *Calls and Responses: The American Novel of Slavery since Gone with the
    Wind.* Southern literary studies. Baton Rouge: Louisiana State University Press, 2008.

Saar, Martin. "Mahnmal." *Gedächtnis und Erinnerung. Ein interdisziplinäres Lexikon.* Ed.
    Nicolas Pethes and Jens Ruchatz. Reinbek: Rowohlt, 2001. 359-361.

Saikia, Dipli. "Writing From the Border, Doing Away With Margins: Carl Muller's Sri
    Lankan Burgher Narrative." *Embracing the Other: Addressing Xenophobia in the New
    Literatures in English.* Ed. Dunja M. Mohr. Amsterdam: Rodopi, 2008. 97-112.

Samuel, Raphael, and Paul Richard Thompson. Introduction. *The Myths We Live By.* London:
    Routledge, 1990. 1-22.

Saunders, Charles. "Standing Tall, Walking Proud: Black Arts in Nova Scotia." *The
    International Review of African American Art* [Special issue "Celebrating the African
    Canadian Identity"] 10.1 (1992): 12-16.

Schacter, Daniel L., ed. *Searching for Memory: The Brain, the Mind, and the Past*. New York, NY: BasicBooks, 1996.

Schacter, Daniel L., ed. *Memory Distortion: How Minds, Brains, and Societies Reconstruct the Past*. Cambridge, Mass.: Harvard University Press, 1997.

Schacter, Daniel L., and Elaine Scarry, eds. *Memory, Brain, and Belief*. Cambridge, Mass.: Harvard University Press, 2001.

Schama, Simon. Rough Crossings: Britain, the Slaves, and the American Revolution. London: BBC Books 2005.

Schmidt, Patrick. "Zwischen Medien und Topoi: Die Lieux de mémoire und die Medialität des kulturellen Gedächtnisses." *Medien des kollektiven Gedächtnisses. Konstruktivität – Historizität – Kulturspezifität*. Ed. Astrid Erll and Ansgar Nünning. Berlin: Walter de Gruyter, 2004. 25-43.

Schmidt, Siegfried J. "Gedächtnis und Gedächtnistheorien." *Metzler Lexikon Literatur- und Kulturtheorie*. Ed. Ansgar Nünning. 3rd rev. ed. Stuttgart: Metzler, 2004. 216-218.

Scholes, Robert E. *Fabulation and Metafiction*. Urbana: University of Illinois Pr., 1979.

Schulz, Dorothea E. "Griot." *Gedächtnis und Erinnerung. Ein interdisziplinäres Lexikon*. Ed. Nicolas Pethes and Jens Ruchatz. Reinbek: Rowohlt, 2001. 240-242.

Sears, Djanet, ed. *Testifyin': Contemporary African Canadian Drama*. 2 Vols. Toronto: Playwrights Canada Press, 2000/2003.

Sekora, John. "Red, White, and Black: Indian Captivities, Colonial Printers, and the Early African-American Narrative." *A Mixed Race: Ethnicity in Early America*. Ed. Frank Shuffelton. New York: Oxford University Press, 1993. 92-104.

Senior, Olive. "Ancestral Poem." *Jamaica Woman: An Anthology of Fifteen Jamaican Women Poets*. Ed. Pamela Mordecai and Morris Mervyn. Kingston, Jamaica: Heinemann Educational Books, 1980. 77-78.

Shackleton, Mark. "Canada." *The Routledge Companion to Postcolonial Studies*. Ed. John McLeod. London: Routledge, 2007. 83-94.

Shadd, Adrienne Lynn. "'Where Are You Really From?' Notes of an 'Immigrant' from North Buxton, Ontario." *Talking About Identity: Encounters in Race, Ethnicity, and Language*. Ed. Carl E. James and Adrienne Lynn Shadd. Toronto: Between the Lines, 2001. 10-16.

Shadd, Adrienne Lynn, Afua Cooper, and Karolyn Smardz Frost. *The Underground Railroad: Next Stop, Toronto!* 2nd ed. Toronto: Natural Heritage Books, 2005.

Shaw, Rosalind. Memories of the Slave Trade: Ritual and the Historical Imagination in Sierra Leone. Chicago: University of Chicago Press, 2002.

Siemerling, Winfried. "'May I See Some Identification?': Race, Borders, and Identities in *Any Known Blood.*" *Canadian Literature* 182 (2004): 30-50.

Sinanan, Kerry. "The Slave Narrative and the Literature of Abolition." *The Cambridge Companion to the African American Slave Narrative.* Ed. Audrey A. Fisch. Cambridge: Cambridge University Press, 2007. 61-81.

Smith, Stephanie A. "Harriet Jacobs: A Case History of Authentication." *The Cambridge Companion to the African American Slave Narrative.* Ed. Audrey A. Fisch. Cambridge: Cambridge University Press, 2007. 189-200.

Smith, T. Watson. "The Slave in Canada." Collections of the Nova Scotia Historical Society for the Years 1896-98 10 (1899): n.p.

Smith, Valerie. "Neo-Slave Narratives." *The Cambridge Companion to the African American Slave Narrative.* Ed. Audrey A. Fisch. Cambridge: Cambridge University Press, 2007. 168-185.

Smucker, Barbara. *Underground to Canada.* [1977] Toronto: Penguin, 1999.

Spaulding, A Timothy. Re-forming the Past: History, the Fantastic, and the Postmodern Slave Narrative. Columbus: Ohio State University Press, 2005.

Spillers, Hortense J. Black, White, and in Color: Essays on American Literature and Culture. Chicago: University of Chicago Press, 2003.

Spivak, Gayatri Chakravorty. "Subaltern Studies: Deconstructing Historiography." 1985. *The Spivak Reader: Selected Works of Gayatri Chakravorty Spivak.* Ed. Donna Landry and Gerald M. MacLean. New York, NY: Routledge, 1996. 203-236.

Spray, W. A. "The Blacks in New Brunswick." *Canadian Culture. An Introductory Reader.* Ed. Elspeth Cameron. Toronto: Canadian Scholars' Press, 1997. 339-349.

Staines, David. "The State of Contemporary Canadian Literature." *Canada and the Nordic Countries in Times of Reorientation: Literature and Criticism.* Ed. Jørn Carlsen. Aarhus: Nordic Association for Canadian Studies, 1998. 21-30.

Stanzel, Franz K. "Historie, historischer Roman, historiographische Metafiktion." *Sprachkunst. Beiträge zur Literaturwissenschaft* 26.1 (1995): 113-124.

Straub, Jürgen: "Personale und kollektive Identität: Zur Analyse eines theoretischen Begriffs." *Identitäten.* Ed. Aleida Assmann and Heidrun Friese. Frankfurt a.M.: Suhrkamp, 1998. 73-104.

Styron, William. *The Confessions of Nat Turner.* Vintage International. New York: Vintage Books, 1993.

Sugars, Cynthia Conchita, ed. *Unhomely States: Theorizing English-Canadian Postcolonialism.* Peterborough, Ont.: Broadview press, 2004.

Switala, William J. *Underground Railroad in Pennsylvania.* Mechanicsburg, Pa.: Stackpole Books, 2001.

Taylor, Mark L. The Executed God: The Way of the Cross in Lockdown America. Minneapolis, Minn.: Fortress Press, 2001.

Tettey, Wisdom J., and Korbla P. Puplampu. "Continental Africans in Canada: Exploring a Neglected Dimension of the *African-Canadian* Experience." *The African Diaspora in Canada. Negotiating Identity and Belonging.* Calgary: University of Calgary Press, 2005. 3-23.

Thomas, H. Nigel, ed. Why We Write. Conversations With African Canadian Poets and Novelists. Toronto: TSAR Publications, 2006.

Thompson, Krissah. "Harvard Professor Arrested At Home." *Washington Post online.* July 21 2009 <http://www.washingtonpost.com/wp-dyn/content/article/2009/07/20/AR2009 072001358.html>.

Thomson, Colin A. *Blacks in Deep Snow. Black Pioneers in Canada.* Don Mills: J.M. Dent & Sons, 1979.

Thurman, Wallace. *The Blacker the Berry: A Novel of Negro Life.* [1929] New York: AMS Press, 1972.

Toomer, Jean. *Cane.* New York: Liveright, 1993.

Truth, Sojourner. "Narrative of Sojourner Truth, a Northern Slave, Emancipated from Bodily Service by the State of New York, in 1828. With a Portrait." 1850. *Slave Narratives.* Ed. William L. Andrews and Henry Louis Gates, Jr. New York: Library of America, 2000. 567-676.

Tynes, Maxine. "Africville." *Woman Talking Woman.* Porters Lake, NS: Pottersfield, 1990. 62.

Van der Kolk, Bessel A., and Onno van der Hart. "The Intrusive Past: The Flexibility of Memory and the Engraving of Trauma." *Trauma: Explorations in Memory.* Ed. Cathy Caruth. Baltimore: The Johns Hopkins University Press, 1995. 158-182.

Wagner-Egelhaaf, Martina. *Autobiographie.* Stuttgart: Metzler, 2000.

Walcott, Rinaldo. "The Desire to Belong: The Politics of Texts and Their Politics of Nation." *Floating the Borders: New Contexts in Canadian Criticism.* Ed. Nurjehan Aziz. Toronto: TSAR, 1999. 61-79.

Walcott, Rinaldo. Rude: Contemporary Black Canadian Cultural Criticism. Toronto: Insomniac Press, 2000.

Walcott, Rinaldo. *Black Like Who? Writing Black Canada.* 2nd rev. ed. Toronto: Insomniac Press, 2003.

Walker, James W. St. G. *A History of Blacks in Canada*. Hull: Canadian Government Publication Center, 1982.

Walker, James W. St. G. The Black Loyalists. The Search for a Promised Land in Nova Scotia and Sierra Leone 1783-1870. Toronto: University of Toronto Press, 1992.

Walker, James W. St. G. "African Canadians." *Encyclopedia of Canada's Peoples*. Ed. Paul Robert Magocsi. Toronto: University of Toronto Press, 1999. 139-176.

Walker, James W. St. G. "Approaching African-Canadian History." *Multiple Lenses: Voices from the Diaspora Located in Canada*. Ed. David Divine. Newcastle-upon-Tyne: Cambridge Scholars, 2007. 2-10.

Walker, Margaret. *Jubilee*. [1966] London: Houghton Mifflin, 1999.

Wandhoff, Haiko. Ekphrasis: Kunstbeschreibungen und virtuelle Räume in der Literatur des Mittelalters. Berlin: de Gruyter, 2003.

Wang, Lu-in. *Discrimination by Default: How Racism Becomes Routine*. Critical America. New York: New York University Press, 2006.

Waugh, Patricia. Metafiction: The Theory and Practice of Self-conscious Fiction. London: Methuen, 1984.

Weber, Angelika. "Autobiographisches Gedächtnis." *Gedächtnis und Erinnerung. Ein interdisziplinäres Lexikon*. Ed. Nicolas Pethes and Jens Ruchatz. Reinbek: Rowohlt, 2001. 67-70.

Weinstein, Cindy. "The Slave Narrative and Sentimental Literature." *The Cambridge Companion to the African American Slave Narrative*. Ed. Audrey A. Fisch. Cambridge: Cambridge University Press, 2007. 115-134.

Welzer, Harald. Das soziale Gedächtnis: Geschichte, Erinnerung, Tradierung. Hamburg: Hamburger Ed., 2001.

Welzer, Harald. Das kommunikative Gedächtnis: Eine Theorie der Erinnerung. 2nd ed. München: Beck, 2008.

Wertsch, James V. *Voices of Collective Remembering*. Cambridge: Cambridge University Press, 2002.

White, Hayden. "The Question of Narrative in Contemporary Historical Theory." *History and Theory* 23 (1984): 1-33.

White, Hayden. *Figural Realism: Studies in the Mimesis Effect*. Baltimore, Ma.: Johns Hopkins University Press, 2000.

Whitfield, Harvey Amani. Blacks on the Border: The Black Refugees in British North America, 1815-1860. Burlington, Vt: University of Vermont Press, 2006.

Wilkins, Peter. "Defense of the Realm: Canada's Relationship to The United States in Margaret Atwood's *Surfacing*." *Literature and the Nation*. REAL (Yearbook of Research in English and American Literature) 14. Ed. Brook Thomas. Tübingen: Narr, 1998. 205-222.

Wilson, Ann. "Beatrice Chancy: Slavery, Martyrdom and the Female Body." *Siting the Other: Re-Visions of Marginality in Australian and English-Canadian Drama*. Ed. Franca Bellarsi. Brussles: Peter Lang, 2001. 267-278.

Wilson, Ellen G. *The Loyal Blacks*. New York: Capricorn Books, 1976.

Winks, Robin W. *The Blacks in Canada: A History*. 2nd ed. Montreal: McGill-Queen's University Press, 1997.

Woods, Tim. *Beginning Postmodernism*. Manchester: Manchester University Press, 1999.

Woodward, C. Vann, "History From Slave Sources." *The Slave's Narrative*. Ed. Charles T. Davis and Henry Louis Gates, Jr. Oxford: Oxford University Press, 1985. 48-58.

Young, Hershini Bhana. *Haunting Capital: Memory, Text and the Black Diasporic Body*. Hanover, NH: Dartmouth College Press, 2006.

Zamora, Lois Parkinson. The Usable Past: The Imagination of History in Recent Fiction of the Americas. Cambridge: Cambridge University Press, 1997.

Zander, Horst. Fact - Fiction - "Faction": A Study of Black South African Literature in English. Tübingen: Narr, 1999.

Zimmermann, Jutta. Metafiktion im anglokanadischen Roman der Gegenwart. Trier: WVT Wiss. Verl., 1996.

9. Appendix

African-Canadian 'Faction':
A Conversation with Lawrence Hill

CHRISTIAN KRAMPE: Throughout your fictional work, the concept of story-telling, of collecting and passing on stories is a vital issue. Whether the narrator relates her own life story, as in The Book of Negroes, *assembles the family story, as in* Any Known Blood, *or embarks on a quest for a story that is actually worth telling, as in* Some Great Thing[412] – *your protagonists are, like your father, story-tellers.[413] Always, there is history conveyed alongside and through this story-telling. Do you think your narrators and your narrations acquire additional importance from the fact that these (hi-)stories have never, or rarely, been told before?*

LAWRENCE HILL: Yes, part of my work is to excavate and dramatize aspects of Canadian history that are little known, undervalued, misunderstood or forgotten. That does not guarantee that I am writing well. But it adds to the moral heft of the work, and to its historical significance. So whether it has to do with Canadians participating in John Brown's raid in Harpers Ferry, Virginia, or the role of railroad porters in the early 1900s in Winnipeg, Manitoba, or the largely forgotten British military ledger called the "Book of Negroes", I'm interested in exciting readers about history. Many Canadians feel that Canadian history is – as I used to say in my school years – colossally boring. And actually, it's not boring if one breathes life back into it, including all of its drama and color – and I use 'color' in the widest sense of the word. Often, in schools in Canada, we don't get much interesting history, and some of our most significant moments are swept under the rug. So yes, I feel that celebrating neglected narratives is part of my role.

In terms of being a story-teller, do you see yourself as a sort of djeli, *or* griot?[414]

---

412 Hill, Lawrence. *Any Known Blood.* Toronto: HarperCollins, 1997. *Some Great Thing.* Winnipeg: Turnstone Press, 1992. *The Book of Negroes.* Toronto: HarperCollins, 2007.

413 Hill regularly credits his father with instilling in him a passion for story-telling, cf. *Black Berry, Sweet Juice* (esp. the first chapters) and "Dad will always 'live within us.'" (Hill, Lawrence. *Black Berry, Sweet Juice. On Being Black and White in Canada.* Toronto: HarperCollins, 2001. "Dad will always 'live within us.'" *Toronto Star* 6 July 2003: A8.)

414 A *djeli* (or *griot* in French) is a West-African story-teller. As a rule, this position is hereditary and limited to men. However, Aminata, the female protagonist of Hill's 2007 novel *The Book of Negroes,* is able to survive the Middle Passage psychologically and emotionally because she imagines herself to be a *djeli,* a position she later temporarily holds in an African village. Later on in

That would be taking it too far. I see myself as a writer who is interested in mining specific aspects of the Black experience that will translate into drama of universal appeal. I don't feel that I am writing for a Black – or for any particular – readership, and I hope that even if the stories are rooted in specific cultural or historical zones, that people from a variety of backgrounds will identify with it. I find it interesting to note that stories arising from specific socio-geographic locations often hold the most universal appeal for readers.

There has been a Black presence in Canada, as you told your audience today,[415] dating back to Mathieu da Costa, and there have, since the beginning of the Black presence in Canada, been two assumptions in mainstream Canadian self-perception, as I understand it: that a) Blacks have never played an important role in Canadian history – that's the notion of invisibility – and b) if there was indeed a Black presence, that Canada has always behaved benevolently towards its Black population, particularly of course in comparison to the slave-ridden and immoral United States. This view also suggests that during slavery, Canada was the Canaan for fugitive slaves and today, Canada's multiculturalism is proof positive that Canada's Blacks live in a modern Canaan, right? The idea of the Promised Land which, considering all its broken promises, turns out to be everything but a paradise crops up in The Book of Negroes *time and time again. Do you, in general, feel a need to undermine some of the White mainstream constructions of Canadian history and Canadian identity, particularly as pertaining to race?*

Yes. We have a self-serving, self-congratulatory and myopic way of seeing our past that is predicated on a celebration of our perceived moral victories, while neglecting parts of our past that are more embarrassing or problematic. We glorify ourselves as morally superior to the Americans to our south. Canada is an interesting and rich country, but we do ourselves a disservice if we can't look honestly at our past and at our present. For example, we received Blacks into Canada through the Underground Railroad and allowed fugitive slaves their freedom here – but only if they were escaping American slavery. If you happened to be born a slave in Canada, tough luck. And although we have a pluralistic society, we still face problems of social injustice and have a spotty history. Right up until the mid-1960s, our governments strove to keep racial minorities out of Canada. We put head taxes on Chinese people who wanted to immigrate to Canada, forcing them to pay outlandish amounts of money if they wanted to come here and denying them the vote. We interned Japanese Canadians in the Second World War, simply because they were of Japanese origin. Even though they were Canadians, we treated them as enemies of the state. We had an immigration policy in Canada that specifically excluded people of color in the most explicit of ways. British subjects were welcome to come to Canada in the early 20th century. But for the purposes of immigration,

---

the novel, she becomes a *djeli*-like figure in England as well, telling her (life) story in schools and other venues.

415 Hill had given a presentation at the University of Trier, Germany, prior to the interview.

those in Jamaica and Barbados were not considered to be British subjects, even though they *were* British subjects; it turns out that in terms of immigration policy, they were excluded from the definition of being British. I feel that Canada is a good country with great promise, but we don't encourage self-understanding and public dialogue by burying our heads in the sand. We should recognize our historical warts and learn from them.

In The Book of Negroes, *the narrator Aminata tells us: "The dead infant [whose funeral Aminata joins] was the child I had once been; it was my own lost [son] Mamadu; it was every person who had been tossed into the unforgiving sea on the endless journeys across the big river." Do I understand the text correctly when I claim that Aminata, though her story in all its details and richness is of course unique, embodies a certain set of shared experiences, that she stands for an entire community which has been through the same – or at least a similar – sort of suffering?*

Absolutely. Aminata moves from Mali to South Carolina, to Manhattan, to Nova Scotia, to Sierra Leone and eventually to England. But she is not the only one. Other people had similar migrations. So yes: Her personal story, her loves, her losses and her victories are unique, but they reflect the experiences of thousands of other Blacks in the same time and places.

You said in your presentation earlier today that you consider these people going to Sierra Leone[416] to be abolitionists in their own right. But there's also a kind of a darker side to this medal, because that was a total brain drain to the Black community. Isn't there a certain desertion aspect to this move to Sierra Leone as well, because only the top of the crop was allowed to go, obviously, and it was devastating to the Black community that remained behind?

Devastating to the White community as well! The Whites of Nova Scotia worked hard to prevent Blacks from going. On the one hand, they abused them when they were there, but on the other hand, they didn't want to let them leave. The Nova Scotian Blacks could not sail to Sierra Leone if they were indebted, indentured or enslaved. Apparently, some people cooked up false debts to prevent Blacks from leaving. In the papers, some commentators derided Blacks as naïve and unloyal for wanting to sail to Africa. Blacks offered a cheap source of labor! The exodus was a slap in the face to White Nova Scotians, because it suggested to observers – including the people of England – that not all was well in Nova Scotia. It raised the ire of some White Nova Scotians to see these Blacks preparing to leave. Blacks who had economic opportunities tended to be the ones who left. But other Black Loyalists remained behind, and they are the ancestors of some Blacks living in Nova Scotia today. So they did survive and

---

416 In 1792, around 1,200 disenchanted Black Loyalists sailed from Nova Scotia to the new colony of Sierra Leone.

persevere in their communities, which are the oldest Black communities in Canada. In the short term, I imagine that the departure of 1,200 Black Loyalists for Sierra Leone impaired the prospects of the remaining community. The Black Loyalists who chose to stay, or had to stay, were thereafter less numerous, and to a certain degree, in numbers there is strength and opportunity.

By the way, White people from Nova Scotia – from my readings – seemed to agree that the exodus hurt the local economy. Take Shelburne, which was the main town on the South shore, where more than half of the Nova Scotian Blacks settled. It had become a boom town and the fourth biggest North American port during the early Loyalist years in the mid 1780s, but it withered later and the exodus of the Blacks surely contributed to its downfall.

Tying in with the job and economic issue here: In The Book of Negroes, *you portray a White mob's raid on Birchtown. They claim that the Blacks are taking their jobs. The same holds true for the Neo-Nazi group in* Any Known Blood *that abducts Dr Watson, Dr Cane and Ab Williams. They have the same racist logic. They even argue, and I quote: "We [i.e. Whites] are being crowded out in our own country." Their country? How would it be their country? And why should these be 'White jobs'? Do you think, though, that every reader will realize the implicit racial hatred and feelings of White supremacy behind these kinds of anger? If I read that on a superficial level, I could imagine that some people do not realize the implicit racism in that statement and that they would just agree, 'Yeah, the Blacks were taking their jobs.'*

I don't think that a serious reader would reach that conclusion. It would be absurd to suggest that *The Book of Negroes* and *Any Known Blood* condone attacks on Black Canadians. I observe in both novels that racial hatred can arise in the context of economic insecurity, but the latter does not justify the former. Often, groups that feel most threatened economically are the ones who rise up against their perceived competitors. In Loyalist Nova Scotia, black settlers faced the violent anger of unemployed or underemployed White former soldiers who believed that Blacks were undercutting their salaries. In the Reconstruction Era, after the Civil War, the very moment that Blacks win their formal emancipation from slavery becomes the time when they are most likely to be lynched in the United States. If I write about such moments, does that mean that I am justifying oppression? Not in my mind. And North America is not the only place in the world where these issues have arisen. Issues of economic insecurity seem to justify, for people in many countries and eras, racist outbreaks of the most hideous sort.

I know I'm taking the role of the devil's advocate here, but one might argue that in Any Known Blood, *your portrayal of race relations in Canada is rather conciliatory. You do talk about Canadian racism and limited upward social mobility, and there is the Klan in Oakville, but Canadian racism is presented as a more subtle variant. Furthermore, Canada is the terminus of the Underground Railroad in that novel, and of course that is a historical fact.*

Mattie exposes the air of Canadian moral superiority, but admits that in Oakville, "nobody beat up on you, or brought out a whip, or threatened to drag you back to slavery." In The Book of Negroes, *you grapple to a greater extent with the uglier sides of Canadian racism: The fact that slavery did exist in Canada as well, the fact that many African-Canadians were bitterly disappointed when their Promised Land turned out to be no Canaan at all, the fact that many African-Canadians decided to leave this land of broken promises. After writing* Any Known Blood, *did you feel you needed to rectify or add to the picture presented there?*

Yes. Whether it has to do with the Klan coming to Oakville, or various acts of segregation or racism in Canada, such as the difficulty Langston Cane IV and his wife have renting an apartment in Toronto as an interracial couple – something my parents experienced as well – there are plenty of instances of racism in Canadian society. *Any Known Blood* opens with a love scene between a Black man and a White woman interrupted by a rock being thrown through the window, protesting against their interracial love. So I would say that issues of racism are present in the novel. However, it relies on a light, breezy writing style. It's an easy read, in a way. And it has plenty of humor, which sweetens what might otherwise be bitter pills for the reader. So it's a different style, which might lead a reader to conclude that the novel is not critical of Canadian society, although I feel that it is. But having defended it a little: absolutely, I felt some concern after the fact about whether I had gone a little too lightly in certain areas, and indeed, in the book *Black Berry, Sweet Juice. On Being Black and White in Canada*, I have a chapter in which I go back to the Ku Klux Klan raid in Oakville and say what impression I was given by some readers after the book came out. One reader told me that she could feel good about this book because it didn't make her feel guilty about Canadian society. Part of me would like to be a bit more brash and not to worry at all if a reader wants to take such a crazy approach [viz. rely on a single scene and ignore the overall impetus of the novel]. Why should I care? On the other hand, it made me wonder if I had gone too lightly on the Ku Klux Klan raid in Oakville in 1930. In retrospect, I did go lightly on it in the novel, so I returned to revisit it in a harsher light in *Black Berry, Sweet Juice,* documenting how ugly and oppressive the Klan's visit to Oakville was in 1930. So that's an example where I felt that if I could do one scene again, I would not have written it quite so lightly. I would have written it 'more ugly', so to speak. In the novel, the Klansmen coming to Oakville are shown as buffoons. They are idiots, and they are made light of in a way, and easily defused. I had some reservations about that afterwards, and that's why I wrote about it again in *Black Berry, Sweet Juice.*

And this – your coming back to it and your comment [in Black Berry, Sweet Juice*] on the reader, a librarian, who felt she was off the hook – is actually the reason why I'm asking. As for me, it just never crossed my mind to take even this scene lightly. I reread the scene, and especially the first part of that scene is so intense and so fear-inspiring...*

Yes, when the KKK comes looking for him in Oakville, Aberdeen doesn't want to come out of the house. It was appropriate to the novel. I was writing against the grain of my historical understanding of the incident, working on a dramatic level that seemed appropriate to the novel. On the one hand, I have ambivalent feelings about this, which is why I wrote about it again in a non-fiction genre. On the other hand, if a reader chooses to take a radical interpretation of something I've written, it's out of my hands. I'm not responsible. The librarian who thanked me for not making her feel guilty did not *want* to feel guilt, or to think about some of the nastier aspects of Black history in Canada, or to have her nose rubbed in it. She was looking for a light read, and my novel suited her purposes. On the whole, it's not healthy for me as a novelist to worry about this. If I had to go around second guessing readers' reactions, it would be paralyzing. I would never write. And with that kind of anxiety, I would never have named a novel *The Book of Negroes*. I feel it's best to give readers the benefit of the doubt, to assume that they're smarter than I am, and to accept that they're free to do what they will with my words.

Speaking of the impact of an audience's responses: Last year, Ibrahima Thioub from the University of Dakar was in Trier for a conference on trauma and slavery in contemporary art. He gave a paper that caused quite a stir. One of his points was that Africans themselves had confronted neither their own history of intra-African slavery nor their complicity in the Atlantic slave trade. He said that 'the slaves that the Europeans bought did not fall from the sky onto the beaches to be picked up by the slave-traders', which is an almost verbatim quote. People reacted intensely, almost aggressively to that. In The Book of Negroes, *you of course deal with both these aspects: There's the woloso[417] named Fomba...*

Whether it offends you or not, it's a fact that Africans were involved in capturing Blacks and moving them forcibly from the interior of Africa to the coast, for the purposes of the transatlantic slave trade. At the time when my characters were abducted, around 1756, Europeans were not in any number traveling deep into the heart of West Africa. They had explored and mapped the coast in detail, but they did not know what the interior looked like. Their maps betray an ignorance of the interior of Africa. One of the first Europeans to travel far into the interior of West Africa is the Scottish doctor Mungo Park in 1799, which is after my characters were abducted. He becomes the first European to say that these old maps of Africa show the Niger River flowing in the wrong direction. Europeans were not established in the interior of West Africa in the mid 1700s. African captives were brought to them – sometimes from far inland, as Mungo Park observed – by other Africans who traded them for goods. Hearing about this upsets some people.

Recently, I was talking about it in a high school in Toronto and one student got angry at me for saying this. Slavery has existed for a long time in human history. Slaves were kept

---

417 *Woloso* is a term for an intra-African domestic slave.

in the Roman Empire, and in Africa prior to the transatlantic slave trade. In my view, the transatlantic slave trade is one of the most monstrous inequities of humanity and can't be compared with the African slavery prior to it in terms of the scale of the atrocities. But it doesn't serve honest debate to pretend that these things did not happen. If I have to show Aminata being moved from the interior of Africa to the coast, to be faithful to my understanding of history, I must have Africans involved in her capture and forced migration overland. I should add that prior to her capture, Aminata grows up with a slave in her own village in the country we now know as Mali. She doesn't truly see Fomba for who he is until he, too, is abducted and sent with her in chains to the Americas.

And you also have Aminata say, "For whom do you think they're stealing each other?" And then she adds, "We had an expression in my village. 'Beware the clever man who makes wrong look right.'" So I think it is clear where the text is headed in that regard. The question is simply: did you catch heat for that?

Not a lot. A little bit. A student here and there. But I have not caught a lot of heat. I think that Aminata's struggle and her difficulties in her own enslavement are all the more pointed if one realizes that in her own village, a slave is kept. In a way, she is discovering something about herself as she is discovering that she did not even really think about this man and his position until she comes into a similar position herself. I just think that makes her story more interesting.

Plus, there is a tragic element, because Aminata feels responsible for Fomba [in South Carolina, where they both work for the same slave holder] and vows to protect him, and then she can't.

She is first a bit embarrassed by him, but she does feel responsible for him in America. His situation is so traumatic that he loses the faculty of speech. I was so interested in the resilience of childhood. I set out to imagine: How much pain do you have to go through before you might lose your mind and never get it back? Surely some Africans taken on this horrible journey lost their minds and never regained their senses. And then of course there are variations: Fomba can function physically, but he can't or won't speak after his enslavement in South Carolina, which to me is interesting. But Aminata is younger and somehow more resilient. She is also a bit more fortunate. She is spared some of the worst elements of the Middle Passage because of her age and her situation. She's protected a little bit…

…by the ship's doctor; and then she becomes more literate and can improve her situation. But as you mentioned the Middle Passage as, say, the 'great silencer', this great trauma-inducer,

it's interesting how you treat the subject of trauma breeding trauma. Take Fanta,[418] for example: She is a mother to a newborn child and from the very first moment of the infant's life, she can't feel love for her. All the love has drained out of her. In the end, she kills her baby and the baby of another woman, then she attempts to kill herself. And Aminata has the same sort of passing on of her trauma, but on a distinctly smaller scale. She says something like 'there was not a lot of joy in me to pass on to my child.' So trauma breeds trauma. How long do you think the passing on of this trauma has been going on? Is it still going on? Does it still reverberate?

Think of inter-generational hostilities among warring families or clans. Your great grandfather might have been slighted and you still carry on as the mortal enemy of your perceived enemy. I was interested in the different ways that people respond to this pressure. We react in different ways. Aminata becomes an astounding survivor. She survives physically and emotionally. She does not become engulfed in hatred – which is a miracle. She might easily become engulfed in hatred and bitterness and become murderously vengeful, but she does not. Fanta is another kettle of fish, reacting in different ways to similar pressures. Fanta is so overcome by the horrors visited upon her that she has to lash out. She doesn't want anybody else to go through this, and so she takes down other people, including babies, rather than have them endure slavery. And also, I think it is common that when we are terribly abused, we often lash out against our own people. It is hard to lash out successfully against those who oppress us. So it is easier for Fanta to kill Black babies than it is to kill White adults who are armed and fight back.

You just raised the issue of powerlessness, that Fanta is powerless to rise up against her abusers. There are a couple of scenes that are, I think, vital to Aminata's coming to understand her own powerlessness and grappling with this. As a child, in a slave coffle, she was shocked when she understood that other people were not going to try to free her, to help her. Decades later, there is a slave coffle is passed right through Freetown. And Aminata sees this child who is in a way her alter ego. *And she can't help her. And then afterwards, of course, at the slave castle, she is looking down at the exact same pit where she was kept and dehumanized, and again, she can't do a thing for the slaves right there, right then.[419] Is writing this powerlessness, this obscene sense of impotence, as difficult as writing some of the gory things?*

---

418 Fanta is one of the wives of the chief of Bayo, Aminata's home village. She is abducted alongside Aminata and Fomba, the chief's *woloso*.

419 When Aminata returns to Africa, she lives in Freetown, Sierra Leone for a while. Slave trade is still common in this part of Africa, so one day, she witnesses a slave coffle resembling the one she was in as a child. Later on, she visits the slave castle on Bance Island where she was held captive before being shipped to America. Aminata, being a free and respected woman by then, is shown around the facility and from a window spots the place where she used to be kept in a pen-like construction, awaiting the Middle Passage.

It was hard. And sad. But I try to be real. I try to listen to my intuitions. Let's be honest: what is Aminata going to do? She's in Freetown, she's an older woman, this slave coffle is coming through. She knows that two Nova Scotian Blacks have already died in the process of trying to prevent this slave coffle from passing through Freetown. What can she really do? As a child, she believed that somebody would protect her. She believed in a code of honor and that some big person out there would take care of her, given her belief that her own parents – were they alive – would have intervened to save her and others from being led in chains for months overland. She just couldn't get her head around the reality that of all these Black people, all these villagers, nobody came out to save her from the slave coffle. It was heartbreaking, for her as a child. As a much older woman in Freetown, when she herself witnesses a child slave being led to the coast, she cannot stop what she sees. But she is not entirely powerless. She can't save this girl who is passing through Freetown, but she goes to fight for the abolition of slavery. She writes her story. She loves and helps the people around her. A powerless victim is an uninteresting character. A character does not become interesting by dint of being stomped on, but by asserting her humanity, even in the smallest ways. Aminata can't snap her fingers and save someone from a terrible fate, but she tries to make a better world, and she succeeds.

Wherever she goes, she spreads literacy. And she educates. So that might mean saving, or at least improving, a few lives wherever she goes.

She spreads literacy. She cares for others. She tries to make a better world, as corny as that sounds. And she leaves her story, which she hopes others will find. Ultimately, she feels that if she can tell her story, then her life has some meaning. If somebody can find her writings and be uplifted by it, life is not all for naught. She is not a superhero, but she is courageous.

Just the mere fact of surviving the Middle Passage, slavery, her migrations back and forth over this great body of water, which she loathes, is very courageous…

… yes, but she does more than survive. She loves. She has the courage to love. How easy it is to shut down love if one has endured horrors. But still she risks love. I feel that she is heroic in her own way.

Aminata's story is based on your reading of the Black experience in North America, so it is fiction rooted in history. Likewise, you allude to what you called in your talk today the con-cept of 'faction' [fact + fiction] very early on in Any Known Blood. *In that text, Langston V says that "years have passed since I've had the courage to write – or, more properly, to rec-reate – my family history," emphasizing this constructive aspect. This of course does not only apply to any kind of fiction, it is also true for any kind of memory that we have: we recreate, reconstruct by selecting memories and by adding to them where we feel it is necessary to do so in order to arrive at a 'harmonized' or 'unified' version. Langston's technique, like yours, I suppose, is to "use [his] imagination to fill in the holes," as he says. Do you feel that as a writer, you have to make readers aware of the fictional, constructivist elements of remembering and story-telling?*

No, I don't feel that that is my guiding principle. I don't feel the need to warn readers that they are reading fiction. I am playing with the motivation of a narrator to step into the process of writing, to justify oneself or navigate through trouble, and to find meaning in life. But I don't think what I am doing is remind the reader 'In case you didn't get it, this is fiction, and you shouldn't forget that.' I like to draw the reader into a fictional bubble. My chief impulse is to tell a story that makes sense of life. Having said that, at the end of *Any Known Blood* and *The Book of Negroes*, I did insert an afterword that acknowledged places where the novels had coincided with history, and other places where they had not. As they exit a novel, I think some readers appreciate a chance to view the work in an historical context.

Ben, in Some Great Thing, *is taking the role of a record-keeper, of an archivist, just as Aunt Mill is in* Any Known Blood. *Record-keeping, the passing on of oral history as well as documents such as photographs, letters or journals are one of the most salient and recurring aspects of your work. The protagonists in all of your novels are of course writers who explicitly set out to write the histories of either their family and/or 'their people', and you occasionally play with the ambivalence of 'ancestry' and 'my people' in your novels, so the reader doesn't quite know, 'Is this referring to family or is this an extended kind of relationship?' Obviously, by relating these documents, these histories and stories, you yourself act as a preserver of history because you are a person who passes on his stories to the next generations lest the memories be lost. Is that a role description you can identify with?*

In a way. On a personal level, I have played this role in my own family. Growing up, I was the middle child, and always the one to be digging out nuggets of family history and dragging them to the attention of my siblings and parents. I don't often step back and look at myself or at my work so lucidly. This could be a matter of self-delusion, but I think my primary identity is as a novelist and a story-teller. I do not feel that my primary identity is as a record-keeper or as a restorer of history. I think that this is secondary. The historian in me, the record-keeper, is a happy sub-employee. He is working away in the shadow of the novelist. If it were my primary preoccupation, I guess I would have become a historian. Although I do believe that historians and novelists can work very well together and can support each other. I could never have written the novels I have written without the work of historians. But I feel I can do something often which historians can't often do, which is to dramatize the past so that readers step naturally into it. This is often but not always important to me. *Some Great Thing* has many aspects that are contemporary; only a small part is historical. And *Any Known Blood* has many aspects which are contemporary too, so it is not an exclusively historical novel. Now I am working on a novel that is entirely contemporary. But yes, I do like to feel that I could contribute to a sort of resuscitation of Black history, particularly elements that are largely unknown in Canada. It is part of who I am. And it is part of who I have become as a writer. I don't know how long this will continue. Stepping from book to book, I'll have to find out each time what makes me passionate and what draws me in.

Thinking of your role as an author and of your influences, this just crossed my mind: Ben in Some Great Thing *is mainly influenced by African-American writers and thinkers. They're the usual suspects, and you were influenced by them, you say in* Black Berry, Sweet Juice. *Names like Washington, Garvey, Hughes, Wright etc. crop up...*

... Garvey's not American!

*You're right of course, he's Jamaican, but his appeal was to African-Americans. Is this rely-ing on African-*American *thought and literature a perpetual situation for African-*Canadians, *or will there be a time when African-Canadians will be able to draw from a specifically Afri-can-Canadian strand of literary and cultural thought? And does it make a difference?*

As a teenager, when I began to read adult literature, I couldn't have named an African-Canadian writer. As a young man, I could have named Austin Clarke, but he was the only Black Canadian writer on my radar screen in the mid-late 1970s. And now, there are many talented and successful African-Canadian writers, men and women, so I have the hope that there is a tradition being built up and that these names will be celebrated and known and will sort of allow for a greater sense of Canadianness in the understanding of Black experiences in the world. So yes, I am hopeful. There really is a renaissance of Black Canadian writing going on right now. It is not only felt at the level of Canadian writers, who are engaged with the computer or with the pen. But publishers are also showing an unusually intense interest in Black Canadian writing and are publishing these writers and are trumpeting them with energy. That is promising. I hope that things will continue to open up and that over time, it will be easier to refer to Canadian writers and to Canadian writing having to do with Black experi-ences, and not just rely on American or other international models. My two teenaged daugh-ters keep getting handed *To Kill a Mockingbird* by their Canadian teachers, and this – and perhaps *Huckleberry Finn* – is the only Black-themed literature that they are asked to read in school. It's important for young readers to discover Harper Lee and Mark Twain, but Canadi-an students really must be exposed to a wider range of literature about the Black experience, including writing by Black Canadians.

Is there a danger in this renaissance of the same kind of showcasing that happened during the Harlem Renaissance? You said that publishers are taking a huge interest in African-Canadian literature – which they do, that's obvious…

… the danger of a fad that will burn out in the end? Yes. I fear a situation where a publisher might say, 'Well, Black writers? We already got a Black writer, I don't see why we'd need another one.' You would never say that about a White writer. It could be that in a few years, books about the Black experience will no longer be fashionable, marketable, or interesting to Canadian publishers. For the time being, Canadian publishers are snapping up books by and about Blacks in Canada. For the time being, some of these books are selling like hotcakes. As for what will happen next, who knows? But I'm optimistic that we will never turn entirely back to the past, now that Canadian writing and publishing has become so thoroughly diversified.

Thank you very much.

Racism Not Allowed, this is Canada:
An Interview with George Elliott Clarke

CHRISTIAN KRAMPE: *I have to admit that after reading 'Milk' in your collection* Blue, *I actually found myself rethinking my whole project. After all, I might just be doing the sort of lifeless, in every aspect anemic criticism you're scolding. So, I was wondering if today you'd be in the mood of* Blue, *or rather in the mood of* Lush Dreams, Blue Exile, *where I also encountered a lot of love and beauty. Dr Clarke, how angry are you today? In what kind of mood are you?*

GEORGE ELLIOTT CLARKE: [Dr Clarke gives a brief outline of his works so far, as well as of his experiences in Durham, North Carolina, where he taught. This part of Clarke's answer is inaudible on tape.] I began to feel more and more comfortable there [in Durham], in terms of an attitude of freedom. As I was going to say: This is clichéd stuff, and I cannot define it very well, except to say that I began to understand for myself personally that I was free to say things in ways I had never felt really free to say in Canada. You know, Durham was a place I didn't feel I had to comb my hair. And actually, I would go out sometimes forgetting to comb my hair, and I would be mortified and had to run back to the apartment and do something with my very bad afro. But I realized that nobody really cared, so I could actually go and teach a class with my hair looking like Don King. It was okay, because it was America, and it was like freedom – I could do that. And in a poetic sense, I started to feel the same kind of thing. And as for writing *Beatrice Chancy*, and dealing with the kind of subject matters I'm dealing with there, I just really felt free to do it. Really. And that mood carried on, even after I left the United States and came back to Canada and started writing *Blue*. Most of the poems in *Blue* ought to have been written in the United States. In *Blue*, I deliberately set out to write in a way that was for me as unfettered as I felt I could be. And also, I have got to give Irving Layton some credit, because I really liked his sensibility and his sense of liberty and freedom and saying whatever he wanted to say in poetry. And I decided, 'Okay, this is the same kind of thing, same kind of idea I want to pursue, I want to try and do this.'

So, a long answer to your very good question. But that mood I hope is still there. In fact, I have got a collection coming out later this year, called *Black*. When I wrote *Blue*, I knew *Black* would be the follow-up. And *Black* goes further than *Blue*. Which got the kind of reaction I hoped it would get in Canada. Maybe it would have gotten no reaction at all in the United States. You know, this is not a high school, puerile, sophomoric kind of thing, trying to get attention. What I was trying to do in *Blue* was to write beautiful poetry about ugly things – from time to time, ugly things. But *Black* is going to go further. It is going to be even nastier. Even though most of the poems were written after leaving the US, I still have it; the mood I'm in is still to try to push whatever boundaries might exist. I want to push them, a little at least. And then redeem myself, in case the critical reaction is, 'Oh my God, this is really bad poetry. We're not even sure we like this guy anymore.' What I plan to do is an epic poem – yes, I am saying it here for the first time: an epic poem based on Black Nova Scotian history, and influenced – I admit – very much by Pound, but then, also by the Bible and by a lot of other works, but particularly by an out-of-the-way text put together by a Canadian poetry collective called Pain Not Bread.

But the final part of the answer to your question is: I have just published another book of dramatic verse – I don't even want to call it a verse play, because it's the extended version of a libretto – called *Québecité*. And it rhymes. It is full of rhymes. It's very un-postmodern. Not only is it full of rhyme, it is also full of direct topical references, which I have almost always made a fetish of avoiding, but in this book, I talk about designers of clothing, people riding Vespa scooters, cell phones are in there – just to give it a kind of early 21st century sensibility, even though I have to confess that the book itself is going to sound very 1960ish, and early 1960ish, which is actually the time period I had in mind in the beginning, in putting it together, and I think the sentiments are falling into that territory of time as well. But the bottom line is: it was commissioned work, yet I had a lot of fun writing it. The actual opera has beautiful music. And I hope that people who might pick up *Québecité* will enjoy the fun, or the spirit of fun with which I approached the story – and especially the use of rhyme. Which is also something: as a contemporary, postmodern 21st century poet this is a device I've used sparingly in other books, but basically like most of us have avoided it, because it sounds so childish sometimes, and so simplistic. But what I discovered in writing for myself, and writing *Québecité,* was: it is a lot of fun! Rhyme is fun! Just the idea of yoking together two very disparate ideas, or entities, or subjects, just for the sake of the chiming of syllables and vowels is amazing! It is an amazing idea – who would have thought of it!

See, it's the hip-hop experience!

It is hip-hop, absolutely! That's right, it is rap! And I had so much fun reading it aloud for people, and hoping that they would laugh at the moments I think they should laugh at! I have to confess I don't consider it to be very, very serious poetry at all, it's light, it was written for an opera, but at the same time, the publisher said, 'Hey, we're going to publish it, we like it!' And I said, 'Okay, great!' And that helped me to polish it a bit more and fill it out a bit more and try to say a few more things. Long answer to your first question about mood, but to sum up: the mood has been one of aggressiveness and trying to push boundaries, with the deviation of *Québecité* into something lighter and just for fun. But with *Black*, I am going to be back into some deliberately very serious territory. And then I will feel free to move on into what, if I am able to write it, is going to be an epic collection of hymns. That is how I perceive it. And so I imagine there is not going to be anything really salacious and nasty in it, but rather an attempt to tell an inspiring story of the formation of the African Baptist Association in Nova Scotia which I see as being the central Africadian achievement, no matter what other people may want to say about it. It is not the Taj Mahal, you know, it is not the Cathédrale de Notre Dame, and it is not a Picasso or anything like that – but it's ours. And the fact that a bunch of poor people, who were largely illiterate, built twenty-four churches on their own with nobody's help, using their own architectural style – unique, really –, I think deserves a commentary, deserves a kind of deliberately triumphalist clearing of territory around that achievement. And I do think it was an achievement. And as a child of that church, it's my way of giving something back to a church that I hope will let me join [laughter] before I die.

The questions will be a little out of context now after each answer, but: which poets aside from the 'usual suspects' like Dionne Brand, Claire Harris, and Marlene NourbeSe Philip, would a researcher have to include in his or her analysis? What are your favorites? I know you're into the Maritime writers: Maxine Tynes, Gloria Wesley-Daye (or Wesley-Desmond).

It's true that these writers are very, very important in terms of tracing a genealogy of Africadian literature and texts and so forth. But in terms of African-Canadian literature as a whole, and I would imagine that we're here thinking about English mainly, then of course: Pamela Mordecai, Olive Senior, both of them Jamaican-born writers, are very important. Also the spoken-word poets, like Motion - or Wendy Brathwaite, if one prefers –, Andrea Thompson and of course Suzette Mayr's chapbook *Zebra Talk*; she has also published another book of poems independent of that, which in my mind are very, very strong, very powerful pieces. And if I try to move to some other traditions, there are also some more: Saptel Bonaventure is from Montreal. There's also an up-and-coming young poet who goes by the name Nah-ee-lah, also Montreal-based, but working in English. And I think that these poets are also pushing a lot of boundaries. If you think about a playwright too, like Walter Borden, whose play is in poetry; I think it is hard to ignore.

And then, Lorena Gale, whose most recent play, *Je me souviens*, is written in poetry as well, and a very compelling piece of drama, setting her claim to be considered Québécoise – despite the fact that she is also First Nations, African, and South-Asian all together, and bilingual. And living in Vancouver currently.[420] But she's someone who was born and raised in Montréal, so why shouldn't you be considered Québécoise? So we are moving a little bit away from direct poetry into people working in other genres. Wayde Compton, from the west coast – *49ᵗʰ Parallel Psalm,* also, I think, is unignorable. David Woods, Maxine Tynes from the east coast: also very crucial as poets. Let me see… I've got a whole bunch of names that could probably be up here, but I am most excited about some of the younger people, who are basically coming out of a performance poet circle like Jason Selman in Montreal, and some of his cohorts. It's funny, I should have total recall – everybody's names! Who else could I men-

---

420   Gale died on June 21, 2009.

tion? Especially people who have not really received their due. I will mention Pamela Morde-cai, and I think her last book *Certifiable* was really incredible, and it should have gotten a whole lot more attention. And Olive Senior, who's just brought out the *Encyclopedia of Jamaican Culture*, a massive achievement!

She has written Gardening in the Tropics...

That's right, that is her Canadian-published book of poetry. And of course – it's embarrassing not to have mentioned her right away – also someone who comes from a more oral side of poetry, and specifically Jamaican poetry: Louise Bennett, who we are very lucky to be able to now claim as Canadian.[421] There's also, of course, Lorna Goodison, who's tendentially Canadian, married to a Canadian, and who's taught on and off at the University of Toronto, and has international reputation. So there's a number of people, I think, that we can afford to think about in terms of what they have to say about their own experiences in terms of their delight in poetry and their own analyses of what it means to be Black in Canada or simply of African heritage in the New World.

You yourself seem, in your poetry, to have an ambivalent attitude towards Canada: we find a sort of estrangement, a feeling of exile, and the experience of hostility of course towards African-Canadians on the one hand, but also a deep love and admiration for certain people and places on the other – Nova Scotia would of course come to mind immediately. How complex is your attitude towards the land you live in? I know it's a question that you'd probably have to write a book about to answer.

That's a book-length question. It is a question that has several parts. Let me begin first of all with the experience of estrangement and alienation: it's real. It's real. I am a Canadian who loves Canada, but who is not loved by Canada, and who is not accepted by Canada, and who is driven away from Canada. And my experience is not unusual for many other Black and visible minority and Aboriginal Canadians. This is our pain – unless, of course, we adopt the attitude, 'We really couldn't care less whether Canada accepts us or not, we prefer to be someplace else.' And I will say frankly that I think that some of the immigrant Canadian writers do have that great escape of being elsewhere: 'we can go home'. I mean, Austin Clarke has written about this: you can go home to Barbados. Although I don't really think he can go home again, you can't get stuck in the same place twice. And I mean, he has changed a lot. He's actually more Canadian than Barbadian now, although I would never say that in front of him. But in any event, to get to the point here again: I think those of us who either were born and raised in Canada or who have truly adopted Canada as our major domain of residence – I don't say we have to write about it, but it's the place where we are at home more or less,

---

421 Bennett died on July 26, 2006.

where we have our real estate, whatever that is, whether it is a house or apartment, our homestead or whatever.

There *is* a sense of alienation, because we are not accepted as Canadians. And the question that comes up, that illustrates this point again and again and again is the infamous, notorious question that every Canadian of color knows, that he or she is going to be asked: 'Where are you from?' And the reason why most of us react so negatively to that question is that our interpretation of it is: 'You don't belong here. You have to have come from some place else. Okay, we're nice enough to welcome you and accept you into our country, but you must be from someplace else.' Now, there are immigrant Blacks who are offended by that question. So imagine how someone who has roots going back seven generations feels when asked that question. Not only that, but my accent places me outside of Canada. Even though it is a very good Nova Scotian, or specifically Black Nova Scotian accent, I'm someone who has to explain where I'm from and why I speak the way I do everywhere I go in the country. And even in Ontario, even in Toronto, where I live. And that also contributes to a sense of alienation.

In other words: In every way that I can think of that counts, my fellow and sister Canadians' first reaction to me is as an outsider. Even though I know this culture so intimately, even though I know their history better than they do, and their culture better than they do, I am outside of it, and I am not going to be considered as somebody who has any authority to speak about it, because I don't come from the right race and the right ethnicity – or ethnicities – that are prepared to be accepted as Canadian. It is a galling fact that a White immigrant to Canada will be accepted more as Canadian than any Black person, including any Black person who's been in Canada for generations. And when people turn around to me and say, 'Oh, your roots go back even further than my family's', that doesn't cut any ice with me, because I don't believe it's about residency. I believe it's about color. If I was White no one would even bother asking me or trying to fair it out. If I said 'Yeah, I just arrived from England two days ago', or if I said, 'My family background is British', they would still say, 'What about your grandparents, your great-grandparents?'

Where are you really *from?*

Yes, 'Where are you *really* from?' That kind of forensic, trying to search out your genealogy, is done in Canada, specifically to in a sense root out and uproot you from any kind of *Canadianité*. So I resist it, I resist the question, and I oppose it, and I usually play with it and try to change the person's consciousness, who is asking it. I do understand that there is, you know, a human interest in understanding where someone is from. At the same time, there is a lot of political baggage attached to that question in Canada that is not attached to it in the United States, for instance – where I've also had the advantage of living for five years. If somebody asked me in the United States, 'Where are you from?', I would not take it as an assault on my identity, or as an attack at all; but rather, it's just simple curiosity, because of my unusual (for America, my unusual) accent. And I would feel, 'Okay, fine, I can accept that'.

But in Canada, it's part of the quiet way in which Canadian racism gets executed. And Austin Clarke has a wonderful analysis of this, I believe: in his non-fiction, in his essays, he talks about Canadians having an attitude of 'pre-possessiveness'. And I feel that this word – no matter how unwieldy it may be on the tongue, or at least on some of our tongues –, I feel that he's absolutely dead-on, he's right, that Canadian racism is based on an attitude of, 'We were here first. And you, by virtue of your color and land of origin, and sometimes religion, have no right to claim anything that we don't choose to just give you out of charity'. And that attitude, I think, runs through everything, in terms of public policy, resource sharing, economic opportunity, and so on. 'Now, we were here first, we will benefit ourselves first, and those of you who are not Canadian – and we know who you are, because we can see you visibly, you are visible minorities – you are not *really* part of us, you are immigrants first of all, and so you're just here by the grace of our charity, and you should just be happy about that, because: aren't we the best country on earth? And *shut up* with your complaints. There is no racism here. Nor was there slavery, nor was there segregation.'

So there's the whole thing that an immigrant writer – objection: an immigrant writer of color – is up against in this country, and you can't blame anyone for saying, 'It's a shame I have got to live here. Because I'm not accepted, and damn, the climate is awful, and I could be in Barbados, or in Trinidad, where most people look like me, where I'm not challenged about my identity, and I can make a decent living with a nice climate', and so on. Or at least a very livable climate, an enjoyable climate. And while Black immigrant writers may have these kinds of attitudes, so can indigenous, so to speak, indigenous Black Canadian writers, have the very same attitude of rejection. But I will also say: I believe it even cuts deeper, and it's more bitter. Because we do have a claim on an historical presence in the country, and therefore have rights to say that this country is as much ours as it's anybody else's, and we should be treated with respect without constantly having to explain our presence. Which is essentially what happens: 'Explain yourself! Why are you here? What's going on?' So I'm agreeing with you about the alienation.

That was your 'on the one hand', and on the other hand, there is this love for certain people, certain things and certain places, like Nova Scotia, the Maritime orature and literature, and how that affects your love for the country as a whole, or love for the nation as a whole. Do you separate the two of those, as in, 'I love this region, but the country approaches me with a different attitude?'

A great question, once again, and let me say that when I left Nova Scotia to go to university in 1979 in Ontario, my first time to really go away from home for a long time, I was very much schooled in a kind of Afro-centric, Black nationalist thought when I was a teenager – eighteen, nineteen – from people like Rocky Jones, Walter Borden, the Halifax, Afro-centric-thinking crew. And I hung out with them for a solid year, and I read all the books, listened to the music, got all the arguments, and I left feeling that I was involved in a kind of Black enterprise. And I went to Waterloo, Ontario, and I went there first, originally, to study Black Canadian history, that was exactly why I went to Waterloo. And I ended up not taking a single course there in history – Black Canadian history – because they were never offered when I was on campus. So when I'm leaving Nova Scotia, I'm thinking in very Afro-centric ways, and then I get to Ontario, southern Ontario. And I end up in a well-to-do, German-Canadian setting, very prosperous, and with very obvious wealth, in ways I had never really quite experienced or seen in Nova Scotia.

On the one hand, people reacted to me as to someone who was from the Caribbean, someone expected to speak with a Caribbean accent, and I did not. But that was the first point of identification, that people thought, 'You must be from the Caribbean'. And it was the first time I actually had that thrown at me, you know, 'What island are you from?' And I would start saying 'Cape Breton' eventually, but in any event, if I wanted any sense of community or solidarity, obviously, it was with the only Black people, my classmates and friends who were from the Caribbean. And it was great, but there was one problem with that, and that was the erasure of my Nova Scotianess, because one of the problems I had was that people would say to me, 'Well, we have this, that, and the other thing that marks, that distinguishes, our culture as being Jamaican, Barbadian, or Trinidadian, or what have you.' And my friends at Waterloo would say, 'What do you have?' And I was scratching my head, saying, 'Well, you know, we got bagpipes,' and they looked at me and they said, 'Uuh, that looks like White culture. What do you have that's Black?' And I would say, 'Well, my family is Black, and the church I went to is Black, and I'm Black.' But I found myself stumbling to answer these questions.

What exactly can I lay claim to that is distinctly mine, and also distinctly Black? And that forced me into reading a lot of East Coast history, and geography, trying to understand this place that I was from, so I would have better answers. And it is from that kind of investigation that I wrote my first book of poetry, *Saltwater Spirituals and Deeper Blues*. It came out of this trying to think through what it meant to be Black Nova Scotian, all the while thinking in very abstract terms – I believe – in writing that book. I mean, there is a lot of fairly abstract stuff, based on the history, but also influenced too much by T. S. Eliot, John Milton, but still trying to think, 'What is this identity? What does it mean?' The book is a mish-mash of different things. Nonetheless, the most coherent parts, dealing with the church history, and so on, and the life of Richard Preston, which I tried to give an epic form to, stealing from Nat Turner's life, was, again, an effort to try to delineate a vibrant Black culture and history that could stand equal in certain ways to Jamaica, Barbados, and Trinidad. To answer that question, 'What do you have?', which I'm finding myself sometimes to still be trying to answer, because it is still one of the first attacks. And it all goes back right to the 70s; for some Caribbean-Canadian, Afro-Caribbean-Canadian intellectuals I was looking at, historically speaking, this goes back to the 60s and 70s.

When I first began to look at Black Nova Scotia, the reaction was, 'There is nothing there!' We have Henry Frances's *Forgotten Canadians – The Blacks of Nova Scotia* as proof of this attitude, 'Oh my God, you people created nothing! There is no Black culture in Nova Scotia, there is nothing!' They would all just see the poverty, they would see the illiteracy, and say, you know, 'Hell, we come from families and homelands where everybody is well-educated, and people even have money. And here we are, looking at you: poor, dispirited, lost, stranded in the midst of the Whiteness, you lost African-Americans, and what did you ever do? Why should anybody pay any attention to you?' Part of my whole project as a writer and a scholar is to try to answer that question, 'Why should anybody pay attention to us? What *did* we do that is of any consequence? What *is* our Black culture anyway? What kind of history do we have to bring to the rest of diaspora to make anybody care?' So I was reading all of the East Coast history and sociology – especially Black Nova Scotian history and sociology – texts about Africville, even about the street that I lived on.

It was really bizarre to be sitting in Waterloo, Ontario, reading a sociological study done in the late 1960s about the street I lived on, and Black people on it, how much they made, who lived where; no names were given, but I went, 'That's my house they're talking about!' And I felt immensely homesick. Immensely. It is hard for me to describe, so I don't think any of the poems really capture it; except maybe in a bad way, a very superficial way, "Crying the Beloved Country", which is in my first book. It was a very real attempt on my part to try to articulate what Nova Scotia, or parts of Nova Scotia, meant for me in a visceral, heart-felt, soulful fashion. And why being in southern Ontario seemed to me almost a kind of exile. Away from that. And again, this is all stuff that is hard to articulate. It was the way people spoke, the kind of parties people would have in their homes. The fact that we would all watch an African American boxing match and feel very bonded as a community, even though these were people fighting who had never heard of us. Or to watch a show with Dionne Warwick or the Supremes' singer, Diana Ross, and in a sense identify and comment on their singing abilities. And particularly, and especially, in the church. And on top of that, the geography. Yes, the Atlantic Ocean at Halifax, or off Halifax, means something to me! The beautiful floral, abundant, fruitful vegetation of the Annapolis Valley means something to me. That may not mean anything to anybody else, but for me, it was beautiful and lovely and lush and attractive and *not* the bush country and *not* the survival ethos of Margaret Atwood. It was actually something that was livable and enjoyable and pleasurable, and the young women looked delectable, and they *were* delectable, and so on. So it was a place of love and passion and sensuality and sensuousness, and as someone who obviously has romantic depths, this fed my poetic. I guess the work that best captures that sense of love – in some sense alienation, but it's more a sense of love – is *Whylah Falls,* because I wrote that out of my experience as a social worker in Halifax and in the Annapolis Valley.

And on the one hand, the people I was working with as a social worker were low-income and did have difficulties in their lives, social and familial difficulties – that, frankly, I was no good at solving. On the other hand, to me, as a Haligonian who grew up in the city and then coming back to the countryside (even though my mother's family is from the country, from the same part of Nova Scotia, from the Annapolis Valley), living in the Annapolis Valley, and visiting these people, staying in their homes, partying with them, drinking with them, falling in love with them, I found that their lives were beautiful. Maybe in a very super-ficial city-slicker, urbanized way, and I am willing to confess that: I am willing to confess to a degree of romanticism. Although I also recognize that people were alcoholic, were violent in their relationships, people were unlucky and unsatisfied and dissatisfied, and people had low incomes, and people lived in homes that were not up to snuff. But having gone through all the sociological realities of pain and hardship and suffering, nevertheless, at the end of the day, they were beautiful people. They had beautiful expressions, ways of speech, and so on. Food and delight. And life and passion and love, which again, might sound like a very superficial anthropological kind of gaze, but I was there, I experienced the people. There was hospitality, generosity, I eavesdropped on people's stories of pain and hardship, and all of this was articu-lated in the most beautiful, Shakespearian English, and especially the song and music was just ingenious, just great. And I felt a very strong connection to that community, to these commu-nities rather, in the Annapolis Valley. And *Whylah Falls*, as much as it might be about 'love' (in quotation marks), is really about love for that community, and region, the geography and even the history. The way people made lives for themselves out of all the misery that they faced.

In effect, if I go back to *Saltwater Spirituals*, there's a poem called "Love Poem Re-garding Weymouth Falls. For Shelley". And that is really the first time I tried to write about this love for the landscape. In fact, it is an embarrassing poem, because it wasn't so much a love poem for Shelley, it is a love poem for Weymouth Falls. Shelley is in there, too, but it is somehow about Weymouth Falls; the title even says so, right? When I went to Weymouth Falls for the first time in '78, I was immediately struck by it, because here it is, this rural Black community. This is a powerful thing. And in fact, this is something that my immigrant, or Caribbean-born writers don't understand: the vitality or the importance of this concept of the rural Black community in a place like Canada. Because they are not supposed to exist. They are not supposed to exist. How could such a collection of basically African American little communities survive for two hundred years in the face of all the racism, economic dislo-cation, poverty, illiteracy? How did they manage to survive but maintain a sense of pride, dignity, fun, pleasure, poetry, music, art, religion, all of that? And I am not being naïve, but I will argue that the poetry, the art, the music, the food made people's lives rich. Despite the poverty, despite the oppression: rich! And that was in fact the resistance. They said, 'Okay, you've given me nothing, but we'll make something marvelous out of it'. I saw that in the quilts the people made, I saw it in the way people did language, I saw it in the way people made music for themselves. They would listen to records, but somebody would have a guitar, and somebody would play, somebody would sing, so there is this home-made music, too – not just bought, industrialized music. Their own music. Folkish, yes. Folkish and country-western. Along with the spirituals, and so on. That kind of vibrancy for me was intoxicating. That's why I have that ambivalence.

Might the focus on blues that I'm going to take as far as music is concerned[422], *might the focus on blues be the wrong direction to take in dealing with African-Canadian poetry? Of your youth in Halifax, you write, and I quote: "gospel and country music were, at times, preferred over blues, jazz, soul, and funk." That's from* Odysseys Home, *obviously. Is blues more of an influence on African American rather than on African-Canadian poetry?*

Yes, I would say. This is always very difficult to quantify, and I don't think that your approach is off at all, I have got to remember to say this too. But Frederick Ward – I should have mentioned him right away, Frederick Ward is a major figure – definitely should be read. Now, Frederick Ward is an African American; he's someone, as an African American, obviously steeped in blues and jazz, and it is redolent in his work, it is pervasive in his work. And there are a few West Coast writers who – also again coming from an African American background, like Fred Booker – I think would be a good example. I mean, he is also an acoustic guitarist, so he has the blues in his stuff, it is just there. And Wayde Compton: blues are there via Jimmy Hendrix in his work, because he is more of a Jimmy Hendrix-generation type than a strictly blues type. But for others of us – and I would include people like Austin Clarke in that regard, and certainly myself, and probably Dionne [Brand], and NourbeSe [Philip], and Claire Harris –, if there are blues, and certainly there are blues in our works at different points, it's more abstracted. That is to say that we come to it with the academic knowledge of the importance of blues in African American culture, also with the personal, lived enjoyment of the music for ourselves, but we are engaged, as I would argue, more intellectually. That is not to say that it isn't as good or as legitimate as the organic kind of blues experience that someone who is coming out of African-America would have, but that we are using it, first of all, in a connection to a larger, pan-African discourse involving the blues. And at the same time, we are utilizing it as a distinctive Black poetic form – Black American poetic form, but still Black poetic form – that we can use in the same way that we can say, 'Okay, I'm going to use Haikù', a form taken from Japanese, or some form of Chinese verse, knowing that that's what we're doing: we're borrowing it from them, or Ghazals from Persian, or Indian poetry, or the Indian classical tradition. Or, for that matter, sonnets, from the Italian and the English tradition, so that the idea of blues becomes yet another poetic form. That's why I say it is more of an abstraction for those of us who do not have the blues as an essential background.

At the same time I see that I have a good friend in Nova Scotia, his name is Gilly [Gilbert] Daye, and he is nothing but blues. He is pure blues. And he would argue here with me in front of you and say, 'No, there is a blues tradition in Nova Scotia, there really is.' And I think he is right about that. But I would tussle with him about exactly what that constitutes. Is that one family, two families, or actually twenty families involved in making music on a gen-

---

422 At the time of the interview, I was pursuing an analysis of blues and jazz influences on African-Canadian poetry, which in the end turned out to be unsatisfactory mainly because the blues influences were indeed too 'intellectualized,' 'pre-mediated,' so that their origins and models lay in an African American context rather than in a Black Canadian one – a line which is interesting in itself but was not what I wanted to elaborate on at the time.

erational basis – handed on? Which still doesn't disqualify – it makes it very real. But it doesn't make it broad-based, either, in a sense. Unfortunately, we don't have records. We don't have records to go back and say, 'Oh yeah, there was this, and there was that and the other thing'. So I would only go by my own experience growing up in the province, which was basically: people would play the records in the pub, the music of the day, so in that sense, blues were around, because when the blues were popular in Black America, they were most likely popular in Nova Scotia. At the same time, they weren't continued as a kind of heritage, so that we must always play the blues. In the same way, they weren't really continued in African America either. You know, the blues had their day, and then it passed on, and soul came in, and other things came in, so people said, 'Okay, we don't sing blues any more'. Unless you are like Robert Cray and you do it almost as a specific kind of hobby. It is somewhat like saying, 'I'm going to reclaim blues for African Americans'. And I think Africadians, or Black Nova Scotians, may have listened to the blues, danced the blues, when blues was a popular kind of music. And when it ceased being popular, became art music, it was like, 'It's over, we don't do blues any more'.

So, for me, and, again, I think for a number of contemporary Black Canadian artists, you may talk about the blues, you may use the blues, [but] it is an art form, as opposed to a form that is coming out of a living artery. I came to the blues – this is embarrassing, or actually, it isn't embarrassing to mention it, I will say it – I came to the blues through Bob Dylan. Right, it was listening to Dylan and reading about Dylan and learning about his absorption of African American blues, that I actually went out and listened to Muddy Waters, and everybody else. And then Gilly Daye. I spent a year sharing an apartment with Gilly Daye, and he had the best blues records around, so I did get a blast of blues. But again, it all came through searching for it, and deliberately imbibing it, as opposed to just everyday lived experience.

On the other hand, the church music was an everyday lived experience. That was our music. That is what we had all the time. That was always there. Everybody knew the songs. And spirituals are what we spontaneously sang. So, to me, that was like, 'That's our music. That's a natural thing right there, that everybody knows.' Blues to me is a very specific, special thing that some people would know. So, I think pursuing the blues as a way of understanding African-Canadian poetry, or even just Africadian poetry, is legitimate. Absolutely legitimate, and soul music, for that matter, they are all legit. But I would say that blues and jazz are intellectualized music for us, which again, does not take away from the legitimacy, no no. Because those of us who choose to write out of the spirit of John Coltrane, or Charles Mingus, or Miles Davis, *do* feel the music, *are* taking it seriously, and do feel connected with the transnational, pan-African experience. Well, it is transnational, because a lot of these musicians are African American, or are inspired by calypso from Trinidad, or jump-up music from Nigeria, or carnival music from Barbados, or reggae of course from Jamaica. It is still in a sense informing our writing, our world view, and even if these forms are all ultimately intellectualized by writers, by their usage we're signaling our connection to a larger African world. I think that is really fundamentally the most powerful aspect of the work. Just speaking for myself personally, it is that that gives us community with other Black writers. The fact that we can signal these same musicians and same songs, or same songbooks. This is the one way that we can have discourse across our various ethnicities, national boundaries, and specific historical experiences, which are sometimes very different.

'Transcultural' – the topic of the Grainau meeting, 'Twenty-five Years of the GKS' – there we go... [423]

Absolutely! Absolutely, it's all music in the end. It's all about the music, which allows the connection. You know, when I think of Marlene NourbeSe Philip's beautiful poem, "Meditation on the Declension of Beauty by the Girl With the Flying Cheekbones". Of which the title itself is already musical. But if you read that poem aloud, and I've reprinted it in my *Eyeing the North Star* anthology, if you read that poem aloud, it's a jazz/blues poem like no nobody's business, serious! Or if you look at Frederick Ward's "Blind Man's Blues", an epic poem in just a very short, compact piece of time, a brilliant poem, absolutely brilliant poem. Brand's "Blues Spiritual for Mammy Prater", as well. Or the blues motifs that show up in Djanet Sears's *Harlem Duet,* which is not poetry but drama, of course, or for that matter the drama of George Boyd, another major dramatist out of Nova Scotia. And then again, I keep coming back to Frederick Ward, who personally, I think, does Black English better than anybody else I've ever read – and that includes Toni Morrison. I think he's a brilliant, brilliant, user of the tongue, of the language. And Claire Harris, if you think about her poem "Policeman Cleared in Jaywalking Case". If you read that poem aloud – and I mean, reading aloud is crucial – even though it looks like prose on the page, you can really feel this accumulation of musical energy, that by the time I've read this poem out aloud, has sent chills down everybody's spines – mine, everybody's. Because it's a very powerful ending for that poem – "Look, you girl, I signify". Or if you look at the writing of David Odhiambo, especially *Diss/ed Banded Nation*, or his play *Afrocentric*, or the pieces that are included in *Eyeing the North Star*, that are called simply "Lip", are very musically-based prose. I think *Afrocentric* is actually written in poetry, it's a play, but written in poetry. Or, for that matter, Lorena Gale and her play, *Angélique*, where music is a very crucial motif throughout. So it is basically, again, the music that creates that pan-African community better than anything else. Because it can't be language, and it can't be culture. It's the music – which still comes out of the culture – that allows that connection.

One thing that's really important to me, is that metaphorically, you sometimes connect the concept of slavery to the state of African-Canadians today, for example when you speak of the "whip / and lash of joblessness" ("Responsive Reading"). To me, it suggests that slavery lives on in a sort of capitalist power structure that keeps up white domination or supremacy,

---

423 The interview took place at the 25th Annual meeting of the Association for Canadian Studies in the German-Speaking Countries in Grainau, Germany.

whatever. Other examples would include "Blackman Dead" by Claire Harris, in which she links the shooting of an African-Canadian in Toronto to past lynchings. It seems that the ways and means have changed, but the basic principle remains in place. Do you think that this is a common, or a wide-spread, feeling among African-Canadians or African-Canadian poets?

Oh, that is a great question, too. Look, see, you have got to write this as a dissertation, that's worth a million dollars: if you can answer this question, that is your dissertation. Look, again, it's extremely difficult, because slavery in terms of Canada itself, forget about the Caribbean, forget about African-America for a second, slavery in Canada is a blank space in the Canadian memory, [something] that most Canadians aren't even aware of that they are suffering from. Those of us who choose to refer to it, those of us who choose to bring it up, sometimes constantly, do so – and I mean, for myself, it's an effort – not to embarrass White Canadians. So obviously, you're not personally responsible, you were not around, and neither were my ancestors around to deal with it. But what I am trying to do by raising the issue of slavery is to contest the willful White Canadian blindness around their/our racism as a people, as a nation. And unless we are willing to face up to it, we are going to continue to treat our minority peoples badly in our country – while we are still thinking we are treating them well. Which is the great Canadian bizarre irony. Which is that Canadians are constantly patting themselves on the back, saying, 'We're doing a great job about race, aren't we?'

'Look at the Americans – they are the bad guys. We up here have always been the safe haven for African Americans, and we're the Black-friendly country, no racism here.'

'No racism here. Racism not allowed, this is Canada. It's a great place.' And yes, I confess it is a great place. I came back from the United States, just to speak for me personally. But the problem is that the racism that *does* exist in Canada, which is very pervasive and very real, and very effective in limiting people's opportunities, and shutting them out of public debate – and consensus about who even *is* essentially a Canadian – is such that we have to have a discussion about the history of segregation, of slavery, of Aboriginal clearances, etc., before we can really turn the page and say, 'Okay, *now* we're going to start trying to be good people and nice people'. But right now it is really being a huge hypocrisy that Canada is perpetrating on Canadians themselves and on the rest of the world. And it is a dangerous hypocrisy. And I don't think that Canadians of color are going to be saying, 'Okay, everybody here is so nice, we're just going to accept the racism', I don't think so. I think that people will – in fact, the present generation most likely will – begin to say, 'Enough is enough. You have to face facts and deal with this, so you can create real equality of opportunity for everybody'. And so the reason why I think many of us want to keep the discourse of slavery, specifically Canadian slavery, on the table, is to attempt, or to force, White Canadians to deal with racism today.

I think that generally, as you are just saying, and as I said too, there is this whole thing about the United States as the great Satan: 'Oh my God, they're so racist down there.' I have to make jokes about this: this is one of the things that happened to me when I went down to the South to live in the Upper South, North Carolina; when I came back to Canada, people would ask me, 'Wow, how can you deal with the racism down there?' And my answer, my standard answer, was, 'Oh, you know, it was pretty easy, I grew up in Halifax.' *[Laughter]* Now, *they* wouldn't laugh. They wouldn't see the humor in that, right? But I would just think to myself, 'How dare you suggest to me that the South is so rottenly racist, when actually, the South is really nowadays pretty good.' Pretty good, because, for one thing, there are a lot of African Americans there; the Whites who tend to be racist tend now to be more Canadian about it, polite and 'don't-say-anything'. And there's no need to, really; they just go about their business, and mind their own business, no-one is running around in hoods and burning crosses any more. Happily that day is gone. So actually, in terms of racism in the South, it's pretty healthy, pretty healthy these days. And lots of African Americans in fact are moving from the North, where they have been for generations, back to the South. Because it is – frankly – friendlier, funkier, more down-to-earth. The cuisine is better, although it definitely gives you more heart attacks. And the climate is nicer.

The Great Re-Migration...

Exactly! The Great Re-Migration. So, but to come back to those things: I think that for a lot of us, it is about trying to force racism onto the Canadian agenda, and remind people that we are not pristine. And that is, again, a very important point, to keep reminding everyone because otherwise, we will do what we did in 1993, and I use 'we' here deliberately. In early 1993, the Canadian government quite rightly intervened in Somalia, like the Americans, by sending a small peace-keeping force to help disarm the militias and get food out to starving Somalis and so on. A humanitarian mission, generally speaking. But: we sent our elite military squad, the top of the top, the best of the best, the crème de la crème of the Canadian Forces. And guess what: The Canadian Airborne Regiment, as it was called, consisted of Nazis and Ku Klux Klansmen basically. Tax-payer supported. The higher brass knew that the whole unit had been infiltrated by these extreme right-wingers and racists (and sexists, it may as well be said, too), and they sent that body, that group of guys, down to Somalia, where they tortured two Somali youths and lynched one. A fact that was hushed up by the military and by the Ministry of Defense, and the Minister of Defense later became Prime Minister – Kim Campbell, our first female prime minister – and everybody said things like, 'Well, we didn't know anything was going to happen, we didn't think anything really was wrong'.

There was a Royal Commission on it, and basically, the Royal Commission said, 'Well, mistakes were made, and they shouldn't have been sent, but the brass didn't think there was anything wrong...' But the real issue was: how on earth did the Ku Klux Klan and the Nazis infiltrate our elite military unit? At taxpayers' expense! That should have been the number one issue on the agenda regarding that, as well as providing compensation and a big apology to the Somalis, about what we did – we did collectively – to two juveniles. That is unbelievable! We violated their human rights, for crying out loud! And did so under the Canadian flag, with Canadian tax dollars. And that means I am personally implicated in what they did in my name to Somalis. But the Canadian government did not look at it that way. They said, 'Racism isn't an issue here.' And race was the absolute issue! Which is why these kids were tortured and lynched in the first place – it was because of their race. I am sorry for getting so keyed up about this, but to me, it is one prime example of how our refusal to deal with racism perpetuates the most horrific and most vile kinds of racism. In a quiet, polite way. Which still has very damaging consequences for people it impacts.

But then again, if you are coming from the Caribbean, you have Caribbean slavery to deal with and to remember, and to talk about. And again, I am referring to Brand's "Blues Spiritual for Mammy Prater". The photograph of a woman who survived slavery and lived to talk about it. Who then becomes, in Brand's eyes, a heroine. You know, she has been able to bear us witness of 'I survived massa, and his whips and everything'. And the same thing for Marlene NorbeSe Philip and her writing and reclaiming the real history of the European conquest of Africa, and the colonization of the Caribbean, and so forth. Austin Clarke refers to it more in terms of an African American motif, except for *The Polished Hoe*, which is about slavery in Barbados, for crying out loud. The aftermath of the slavery in Barbados. Okay, but that is the first work where he has actually confronted that question head-on. Usually, it is a meditation on African American slavery, and then, what does that really mean to him? When you see some of the writings of the 1970s and so on. So, slavery, and of course Paul Gilroy and Toni Morrison have written a lot about this, in terms of an African American and African-Caribbean context. And in terms of Gilroy, slavery remains living memory for us. Living memory because the outcome, the results of slavery have not been ameliorated yet. We do not live in racism-free societies yet. And the racism that we still endure goes all the way back to slavery.

James Walker, in writing his history of the Black Loyalists, makes the point in the 1970s that the reason why Black Nova Scotians were so badly treated is because their forebears had been slaves. In Nova Scotia. And people, in a sense, remembered that. In terms of collective memory, 'Oh yeah, you Black people are just like slaves. You *are* slaves. You *were* slaves. And so we're going to treat you like you're slaves even though it's 1935. You're still slaves to us'. So in a sense, this refusal to talk about the slave past, particularly in Canada, allows again for this perpetuation of racist attitudes. I am not even going to touch the issue of reparations. I am not going to go there, because for me, and this is only a very personal point of view, I just don't know… On one hand, other peoples, other groups have demanded reparations and have succeeded in getting them in a sense that there is a great model there for African-Canadians, and African Americans, and African-Caribbeans to demand payback for all that unpaid labor of the past, and all the horrible living conditions that ensued afterwards. Yes. I have got to say I would not deny if somebody sent me a reparations check, especially if it was in several figures; that would be okay. But: in reality, I think it is far more important that societies who inherited slavery, or that developed as a result of slavery, attend to the consequences of contemporary racism in a very committed and serious fashion. That, to me, would do a hell of a lot more to ameliorate the injustice than sending someone a check. Although I do not think very many of us would send it back, because, as they say, 'Money in the bank is always nice to have'. But, again, in a very real way, I do think it is a question of morality and social transformation more than it is about literally paying someone money for whatever trouble you could compute. In fact, no money could be paid, because the bill is too large.

So, although I am not going to try to frustrate those people who want reparations – I wish them well, because I would probably benefit, too – I think what we are really trying to promote is the social and moral transformation and the political transformation. I go back to Brand again: for her, the drive to face slavery has been most successful in two societies: Cuba and Grenada, when Grenada had a socialist government. That is when, in these two societies, socialism was in play; the people had free health care, education, and I say *did* have in the case of Grenada, and a real opportunity to… not maybe to become rich, certainly not rich, but an opportunity to have good lives, with decent living conditions. That slavery, the legacy of slavery, was finally counteracted. And so, the failure of the Grenadian revolution – or rather the crushing of it in a coup, and then later by US troops, backed by a smattering of other Caribbean troops falling in – meant a kind of reinstatement of slavery in Grenada, so that Cuba remains the one last place where a stand was effectively made against slavery – against the legacy of slavery – in the Caribbean. And so therefore a place to be celebrated, and protected, and defended, and Fidel live forever, please! Right? And Claire Harris is very interesting in this regard, because I think she is someone who writes about the indentured servitude of Indians in Trinidad, and the impact of that servitude on that community and the relations with Blacks. But it also shows up, again, in Marlene NorbeSe Philip with her play, *Coups and Calypsos*.

So where I am going with all this stuff is, again: slavery remains an issue for us, because justice has not been achieved. And so slavery has to be continuously – no matter if we talk about the Caribbean, or Canada, or America – has to constantly be put forward, first of all to explain to ourselves who *we* are, why we are here, or there, rather, in the New World. And that is another point too, which I could have said in the talk today,[424] you know: very simply and directly, Africans are in the New World because of slavery and colonialism, absolutely. I am not saying we would not have gotten there eventually anyway, and not saying we were not there first, as some scholars in fact argue we were, through Mali sailors and others, making their way to South America eons ago, well before Columbus. But all of that to one side – it does not matter to me, really. The point is that our understanding of who we are is, in terms of diaspora, absolutely tied up with the whole process of colonization and slavery. And so we can never easily be Canadian, or Jamaican, or Trinidadian, or American, or even African-Canadian, or African American, until we deal with slavery, and what it meant, and how our forebears dealt with it, and what its legacy is for us personally today. And so it can never go away, it can never disappear, until, again, there is real justice in a society. Then we can say,

---

424 Dr Clarke gave a talk titled "Reading Europe in Contemporary African-Canadian Texts" on the day of the interview.

'Okay, we turned the corner'. Now, people can say, 'Please stop talking about it, it was five hundred years ago, three hundred years, two hundred years ago – please, when are we going to stop talking about it?' We will stop talking about it when we feel there is no need to remind everybody that this happened, and that happened…

Walter Benn Michaels, American critic, Jewish-American literary critic, has an article, in *Transition* from 1995, where he talks about the need for Jews to remember the Holocaust, and for Blacks – and he really means Black Americans – to remember slavery. It is a very nuanced article, I am not going to do it justice, and I should not even bring him up; I am just bringing him up because I think you might want to have a look at it. Walter Benn Michaels does a brilliant job of developing the nuances around why these two communities are constantly needing to remember these injustices. And basically – again, this is a very nuanced article –, part of his argument, if I am not misreading him – and I might be, I confess that – seems to suggest that neither of these communities could exist without the memory of this trauma, and that recovering this memory is a means of continuing the bonds of this community. I think there is some truth to this, at least in terms of African American, also Afro-Caribbean, African-Canadian communities. In Canada, there are so many things that divide us that we do have to lay claim to some kind of common history in order to have some grounds for unity. And so that common history does go through slavery, does go through colonialism, and of course the experience of racism today in Canada. So, partly, too, remembering of this trauma is, again, a way of building some intellectual unity among our very disparately originated communities.

You know what? These are going to be the closing words of my thesis. That's just perfect and exactly what I was aiming at. Well, thank you very much!

Representation of African-Canadian writers in three Canadian literary prizes

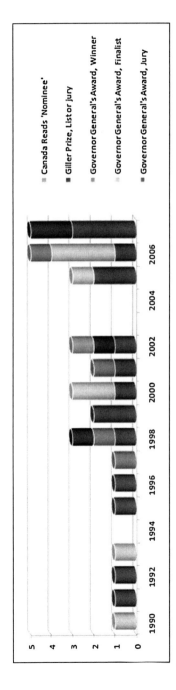

Illustration 4

Sources: Prizes' respective websites

- Governor General's Award: http://www.canadacouncil.ca/prizes/ggla/

- The Giller Prize: http://www.scotiabankgillerprize.ca/

- CBC's Canada Reads: http://www.cbc.ca/books/canadareads/

Select Thematic Bibliography of African-Canadian Poetry (1975-2001)

Selected poems dealing with slavery

and/or disillusionment with Canadian race relations past and present

Allen, Lillian. "Nothing But a Hero." *Women Do This Every Day. Selected Poems.* Toronto: Women's Press, 1993. 50-51. [=1993a]

Allen, Lillian. "With Criminal Intent." *Women Do This Every Day. Selected Poems.* Toronto: Women's Press, 1993. 62-63. [=1993b]

Bernard, Delvina E. "Lullaby for Cole Harbour." *Fire on the Water. An Anthology of Black Nova Scotian Writing. Volume 2.* Ed. George Elliott Clarke. Lawrencetown Beach, NS: Pottersfield Press, 1992. 129-130. [=1992a]

Bernard, Delvina E. "We Women." *Fire on the Water. An Anthology of Black Nova Scotian Writing. Volume 2.* Ed. George Elliott Clarke. Lawrencetown Beach, NS: Pottersfield Press, 1992. 127-128. [=1992b]

Booker, Fred. "On Burnaby Mountain: Summer 1978." *Bluesprint: Black British Columbian Literature and Orature.* Ed. Wayde Compton. Vancouver: Arsenal Pulp Press, 2001. 140-146. [=2001a]

Booker, Fred. "One Road to the Sea." *Bluesprint: Black British Columbian Literature and Orature.* Ed. Wayde Compton. Vancouver: Arsenal Pulp Press, 2001. 138-139. [=2001b]

Borden, George A. "… For no Good Reason." *Canaan Odyssey. A Poetic Account of the Black Experience in North America.* Dartmouth, NS: Black Cultural Centre for Nova Scotia, 1988. 16-17. [=1988a]

Borden, George A. "A Race Defaced." *Canaan Odyssey. A Poetic Account of the Black Experience in North America.* Dartmouth, NS: Black Cultural Centre for Nova Scotia, 1988. 3-4. [=1988b]

Borden, George A. "Accusation." *Canaan Odyssey. A Poetic Account of the Black Experience in North America.* Dartmouth, NS: Black Cultural Centre for Nova Scotia, 1988. 2. [=1988c]

Borden, George A. "Fashions of Slavery." *Canaan Odyssey. A Poetic Account of the Black Experience in North America.* Dartmouth, NS: Black Cultural Centre for Nova Scotia, 1988. 6-7. [=1988d]

Borden, George A. "I Died B'fore it Ended." *Canaan Odyssey. A Poetic Account of the Black Experience in North America.* Dartmouth, NS: Black Cultural Centre for Nova Scotia, 1988. 14-15. [=1988e]

Borden, George A. "I Never Heard Their Cry." *Canaan Odyssey. A Poetic Account of the Black Experience in North America.* Dartmouth, NS: Black Cultural Centre for Nova Scotia, 1988. 12-13. [=1988f]

Borden, George A. "Plantation North." *Canaan Odyssey. A Poetic Account of the Black Experience in North America.* Dartmouth, NS: Black Cultural Centre for Nova Scotia, 1988. 19-21. [=1988g]

Borden, George A. "Forgotten Holocaust." *Fire on the Water. An Anthology of Black Nova Scotian Writing. Volume 1.* Ed. George Elliott Clarke. Lawrencetown Beach, NS: Pottersfield Press, 1991. 163-164. [=1991a]

Borden, George A. "To my Children I Bequeath." *Fire on the Water. An Anthology of Black Nova Scotian Writing. Volume 1.* Ed. George Elliott Clarke. Lawrencetown Beach, NS: Pottersfield Press, 1991. 166-167. [=1991b]

Borden, Walter. "The Hebrew Children." *Fire on the Water. An Anthology of Black Nova Scotian Writing. Volume 2.* Ed. George Elliott Clarke. Lawrencetown Beach, NS: Pottersfield Press, 1992. 40-42.

Brand, Dionne. "Requiem." *One out of Many. A Collection of Writings by 21 Black Women in Ontario.* Ed. Liz Cromwell. Toronto: Wacacro, 1975. 18.

Brand, Dionne. "Eurocentric." *Border Lines: Contemporary Poems in English.* Ed. A[ndy] J. Wainwright et al. Toronto: Copp Clark, 1995. 193.

Brand, Dionne. "Blues Spiritual for Mammy Prater." *No Language is Neutral.* Toronto: Coach House, 1998. 14. [=1998a]

Brand, Dionne. "return (I)." *No Language is Neutral.* Toronto: Coach House, 1998. 7. [=1998b]

Brand, Dionne. "return (II)." *No Language is Neutral.* Toronto: Coach House, 1998. 12. [=1998c]

Brand, Dionne. Untitled (1st poem in chapter "No Language is Neutral"). *No Language is Neutral.* Toronto: Coach House, 1998. 19-31. [=1998d]

Cambridge, Vibert C. "The West Indian." *Excuse Me! ... May I Offer Some Interpretations?* Toronto: Wacacro, 1975. n.p.

Carew, Jan. "Africa – Guyana!" *Fiery Spirits & Voices. Canadian Writers of African Descent.* Ed. Ayanna Black. Toronto: HarperPerennial, 2000. 57.

Clarke, George Elliott. "Beech Hill African Baptist Church." *Saltwater Spirituals and Deeper Blues*. Porter's Lake, NS: Pottersfield Press, 1983. 16. [=1983a]

Clarke, George Elliott. "II – Genealogy." *Saltwater Spirituals and Deeper Blues*. Porter's Lake, NS: Pottersfield Press, 1983. 66. [=1983b]

Clarke, George Elliott. "VIII – Exodus." *Saltwater Spirituals and Deeper Blues*. Porter's Lake, NS: Pottersfield Press, 1983. 72. [=1983c]

Clarke, George Elliott. "Hammonds Plain African Baptist Church." *Lush Dreams, Blue Exile. Fugitive Poems, 1978-1993*. Lawrencetown Beach, NS: Pottersfield Press, 1994. 72.

Clarke, George Elliott. "Exile." *Blue*. Vancouver: Raincoast/Polestar, 2001. 25. [=2001a]

Clarke, George Elliott. "Identity II." *Execution Poems*. Wolfville, NS: Gaspereau Press, 2001. 21. [=2001b]

Clarke, George Elliott. "Prosecution." *Execution Poems*. Wolfville, NS: Gaspereau Press, 2001. 39. [=2001c]

Clarke, George Elliott. "The Killing." *Execution Poems*. Wolfville, NS: Gaspereau Press, 2001. 35. [=2001d]

Compton, Wayde. "JD." *Bluesprint: Black British Columbian Literature and Orature*. Vancouver: Arsenal Pulp Press, 2001. 272-273.

Cooper, Afua. "Breakin' Chains." *Breakin' Chains*. Toronto: Weelahs Publications, 1983. 46-47.

Cooper, Afua. "Fleeing Girl of Fifteen in Male Attire." *Memories Have Tongue*. Toronto: Sister Vision, 1992. 42. [=1992a]

Cooper, Afua. "Harriet Shepherd." *Memories Have Tongue*. Toronto: Sister Vision, 1992. 40. [=1992b]

Cooper, Afua. "Marie Joseph Angélique." *Memories Have Tongue*. Toronto: Sister Vision, 1992. 39. [=1992c]

Cooper, Afua. "My Piece." *Memories Have Tongue*. Toronto: Sister Vision, 1992. 79-82. [=1992d]

Cooper, Afua. "Seven Children." *Memories Have Tongue*. Toronto: Sister Vision, 1992. 41. [=1992e]

Cooper, Afua. "Roots and Branches". *Memories Have Tongue*. Toronto: Sister Vision, 1992. 23. [=1992f]

Coopsammy, Madeline. "Immigrant." *Other Voices: Writings by Blacks in Canada*. Ed. Lorris Elliott. Toronto: Williams-Wallace, 1985. 23-24.

Dabydeen, Cyril. "My Country, North America, and the World." *A Shapely Fire. Changing the Literary Landscape*. Oakville, ON: Mosaic, 1987. 106.

Darbasie, Nigel. "After Image." *Last Crossing: Poems*. Edmonton: Nidar Communications, 1988. 49.

Dawes, Kwame. "Some Tentative Definitions XI." *Wheel and Come Again: An Anthology of Raggae Poetry*. Fredericton, NB: Goose Lane, 1998. 77.

Dawes, Kwame. "Sabbath." *Midland*. Fredericton, NB: Goose Lane, 2001. 74. [=2001a]

Dawes, Kwame. "Ska Memory." *Midland*. Fredericton, NB: Goose Lane, 2001. 15. [=2001b]

Dawes, Kwame. "Soul Captives." *Resisting the Anomie*. Fredericton, NB: Goose Lane, 1995. 122-124.

Gaskin, Ron. "Chains and Shackles." *Canada in Us Now: The First Anthology of Black Poetry and Prose in Canada*. Ed Harold Head. Toronto: NC Press, 1976. 78.

Goodison, Lorna. "About the Tamarind." *Travelling Mercies*. Toronto: MacClelland and Stewart, 2001. 14-16.

Harris, Claire. "Travelling to Find a Remedy." *Travelling to Find a Remedy*. Fredericton, NB: Fiddlehead Poetry Books and Goose Lane, 1986. 21-26.

Harris, Claire. "A Dream of Valor and Rebirth." *The Conception of Winter*. Harris, Claire. Stratford, ON: Williams-Wallace, 1989. 28-31.

Harris, Claire. "Sister (y)our Manchild at the Close of the Century." *Dripped in Shadows*. Fredericton, NB: Goose Lane, 1996. 51-62.

Miguna, Miguna. "Volcanic Song." *Afrika's Volcanic Song*. Toronto: AV Publications, 1995. 7-31.

Mordecai, Pamela. "Protest Poem." *Journey Poem*. Kingston, JA: Sandberry Press, 1989. 51-52.

Philip, Marlene NourbeSe. "Oliver Twist." *Thorns*. Toronto: Williams-Wallace, 1980. 5-6.

Philip, Marlene NourbeSe. "The Voice of the Lost Ones." *Salmon Courage*. Toronto: Williams-Wallace, 1983. 38. [=1983b]

Philip, Marlene NourbeSe. "Black Fruit (II) (For Bruce)." *Salmon Courage*. Toronto: Williams-Wallace, 1983. 16-17. [=1983a]

Philip, Marlene NourbeSe. "Blackman Dead." *Grammar of Dissent: Poetry and Prose by Claire Harris, Marlene Nourbese Philip, Dionne Brand*. Ed. Carol Morrell. Fredericton, NB: Goose Lane, 1994. 109-110.

Senior, Olive. "Meditation on Yellow." *Wheel and Come Again: An Anthology of Raggae Poetry*. Fredericton, NB: Goose Lane, 1998. 174-180.

Stewart, Priscilla. "A Voice From the Oppressed to the Friends of Humanity." *Bluesprint: Black British Columbian Literature and Orature*. Ed. Wayde Compton. Vancouver: Arsenal Pulp Press, 2001. 49.

Thompson, Andrea. "Fire Belly." *Eating the Seed*. Victoria, BC: Ekstasis Editions, 1999. 13-19.

Tynes, Maxine. "Baobab Journey." *Borrowed Beauty*. Porters Lake, NS: Pottersfield Press, 1987. 40.

Tynes, Maxine. "This Dartmouth at Alderney Gate, 1990." *The Door of My Heart*. Lawrencetown Beach, NS: Pottersfield Press, 1993. 52-53.

Ward, Frederick. "Escape Patterns." *The Curing Berry*. Toronto: Williams-Wallace, 1983. 11.

Wesley-Desmond, Gloria. "Defeat." *Fire on the Water. An Anthology of Black Nova Scotian Writing. Volume 2*. Ed. George Elliott Clarke. Lawrencetown Beach, NS: Pottersfield Press, 1992. 69.

Canadiana
Literaturen / Kulturen, Literatures / Cultures, Littératures / Cultures

Herausgegeben von: Klaus-Dieter Ertler und Wolfgang Klooß

www.peterlang.de

Christina Schäffer

The Brownies' Book: Inspiring Racial Pride in African-American Children

Frankfurt am Main, Berlin, Bern, Bruxelles, New York, Oxford, Wien, 2012.
536 pp., 26 fig.
Mainzer Studien zur Amerikanistik. Vol. 60
Edited by Renate von Bardeleben und Winfried Herget
ISBN 978-3-631-63690-9 · hb. € 85,95*

The Brownies' Book: Inspiring Racial Pride in African-American Children offers a descriptive analysis and interpretation of America's first magazine for young African-Americans. Published by W.E.B. Du Bois in cooperation with Jessie Fauset and Augustus Granville Dill, the monthly hoped to foster a new African-American identity by (re)connecting "the children of the sun" with Africa, by turning them into proud Americans, and by educating them to be global citizens. The editors turned the crow into a positive symbol of blackness and provided photographs which proved that "black is beautiful" to increase the self-esteem of black youths. The magazine was a harbinger of the Harlem Renaissance and served as a creative outlet for many African-American writers and artists, among them many women.

Content: Genesis of the magazine · Components · The Construction of Positive Images · In Search of a Usable Past (Africa, Slavery, Lynching and Racism, the South, Euro-American Traditions, Black Culture Heroes) · The Three Dimensions (Africa, America, the Global Community) · Demise and Legacy (Effie Lee Newsome, Harlem Renaissance)

*The e-price includes German tax rate. Prices are subject to change without notice

Frankfurt am Main · Berlin · Bern · Bruxelles · New York · Oxford · Wien
Distribution: Verlag Peter Lang AG
Moosstr. 1, CH-2542 Pieterlen
Telefax 0041 (0)32/376 17 27
E-Mail info@peterlang.com

40 Years of Academic Publishing
Homepage http://www.peterlang.com